# Promoting Socio-Economic Development through Business Integration

Shalini Kalia
*IMT Ghaziabad, India*

Bhavna Bhalla
*IMT Ghaziabad, India*

Lipi Das
*IMT Ghaziabad, India*

Neeraj Awasthy
*IMT Ghaziabad, India*

A volume in the Advances in Finance, Accounting, and Economics (AFAE) Book Series

BUSINESS SCIENCE Reference
An Imprint of IGI Global

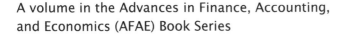

Managing Director: Lindsay Johnston
Managing Editor: Austin DeMarco
Director of Intellectual Property & Contracts: Jan Travers
Acquisitions Editor: Kayla Wolfe
Production Editor: Christina Henning
Development Editor: Brandon Carbaugh
Cover Design: Jason Mull

Published in the United States of America by
Business Science Reference (an imprint of IGI Global)
701 E. Chocolate Avenue
Hershey PA, USA 17033
Tel: 717-533-8845
Fax: 717-533-8661
E-mail: cust@igi-global.com
Web site: http://www.igi-global.com



Library of Congress Cataloging-in-Publication Data

Library of Congress Cataloging-in-Publication Data

Promoting socio-economic development through business integration / Shalini Kalia, Bhavna Bhalla, Lipi Das, and Neeraj Awasthy, editors.
pages cm
Includes bibliographical references and index.
Summary: "This book builds on available literature in the field of socio-economic development in developing countries, providing further research opportunities in this field"-- Provided by publisher.
ISBN 978-1-4666-8259-7 (hardcover : alk. paper) -- ISBN 978-1-4666-8260-3 (ebook : alk. paper) 1. Industries--India. 2. Business enterprises--India. 3. Economic development--India. I. Kalia, Shalini, 1974-

HC435.3.P774 2015
338.0954--dc23

2015003984

This book is published in the IGI Global book series Advances in Finance, Accounting, and Economics (AFAE) (ISSN: 2327-5677; eISSN: 2327-5685)

British Cataloguing in Publication Data
A Cataloguing in Publication record for this book is available from the British Library.

# Advances in Finance, Accounting, and Economics (AFAE) Book Series

Ahmed Driouchi
*Al Akhawayn University, Morocco*

ISSN: 2327-5677
EISSN: 2327-5685

Mission

In our changing economic and business environment, it is important to consider the financial changes occurring internationally as well as within individual organizations and business environments. Understanding these changes as well as the factors that influence them is crucial in preparing for our financial future and ensuring economic sustainability and growth.

The **Advances in Finance, Accounting, and Economics (AFAE)** book series aims to publish comprehensive and informative titles in all areas of economics and economic theory, finance, and accounting to assist in advancing the available knowledge and providing for further research development in these dynamic fields.

Coverage

- Health Economics
- Interest Rates and Annuities
- Economics of Innovation and Knowledge
- Corporate Finance
- Bankruptcy
- Wages and Employment
- Macroeconomics
- Economics of Intellectual Property Rights
- Microeconomics
- Applied Accounting

IGI Global is currently accepting manuscripts for publication within this series. To submit a proposal for a volume in this series, please contact our Acquisition Editors at Acquisitions@igi-global.com or visit: http://www.igi-global.com/publish/.

The Advances in Finance, Accounting, and Economics (AFAE) Book Series (ISSN 2327-5677) is published by IGI Global, 701 E. Chocolate Avenue, Hershey, PA 17033-1240, USA, www.igi-global.com. This series is composed of titles available for purchase individually; each title is edited to be contextually exclusive from any other title within the series. For pricing and ordering information please visit http://www.igi-global.com/book-series/advances-finance-accounting-economics/73685. Postmaster: Send all address changes to above address. 

## Titles in this Series

*For a list of additional titles in this series, please visit: www.igi-global.com*

*Standardization of Financial Reporting and Accounting in Latin American Countries*
Isabel Lourenço (University Institute of Lisbon, Portugal) and Maria Major (University Institute of Lisbon, Portugal)
Business Science Reference • copyright 2015 • 314pp • H/C (ISBN: 9781466684539) • US $200.00 (our price)

*Handbook of Research on Globalization, Investment, and Growth-Implications of Confidence and Governance*
Ramesh Chandra Das (Katwa College, University of Burdwan, India)
Information Science Reference • copyright 2015 • 526pp • H/C (ISBN: 9781466682740) • US $345.00 (our price)

*Handbook of Research on Sustainable Development and Economics*
Ken D. Thomas (Auburn University, USA)
Business Science Reference • copyright 2015 • 462pp • H/C (ISBN: 9781466684331) • US $325.00 (our price)

*Green Economic Structures in Modern Business and Society*
Andrei Jean-Vasile (Petroleum-Gas University of Ploiesti, Romania) Ion Raluca Andreea (Bucharest Academy of Economic Studies, Romania) and Turek Rahoveanu Adrian (University of Agronomic Sciences and Veterinary Medicine, Bucharest, Romania)
Business Science Reference • copyright 2015 • 325pp • H/C (ISBN: 9781466682191) • US $195.00 (our price)

*Handbook of Research on Behavioral Finance and Investment Strategies Decision Making in the Financial Industry*
Zeynep Copur (Hacettepe University, Turkey)
Business Science Reference • copyright 2015 • 525pp • H/C (ISBN: 9781466674844) • US $245.00 (our price)

*Agricultural Management Strategies in a Changing Economy*
Gabriel Popescu (Bucharest Academy of Economic Studies, Romania) and Andrei Jean-Vasile (Petroleum - Gas University of Ploiesti, Romania)
Business Science Reference • copyright 2015 • 439pp • H/C (ISBN: 9781466675216) • US $225.00 (our price)

*Handbook of Research on In-Country Determinants and Implications of Foreign Land Acquisitions*
Evans Osabuohien (Covenant University, Nigeria & German Development Institute, Germany)
Business Science Reference • copyright 2015 • 430pp • H/C (ISBN: 9781466674059) • US $265.00 (our price)

*Handbook of Research on Strategic Developments and Regulatory Practice in Global Finance*
Özlem Olgu (Koç University, Turkey) Hasan Dinçer (Istanbul Medipol University, Turkey) and Ümit Hacıoğlu (Istanbul Medipol University, Turkey)
Business Science Reference • copyright 2015 • 433pp • H/C (ISBN: 9781466672888) • US $235.00 (our price)

IGI GLOBAL
DISSEMINATOR OF KNOWLEDGE
www.igi-global.com

701 E. Chocolate Ave., Hershey, PA 17033
Order online at www.igi-global.com or call 717-533-8845 x100
To place a standing order for titles released in this series, contact: cust@igi-global.com
Mon-Fri 8:00 am - 5:00 pm (est) or fax 24 hours a day 717-533-8661

# Table of Contents

**Foreword** ............................................................ xix

**Preface** ............................................................ xxi

**Acknowledgment** ............................................................ xxv

**Chapter 1**
Regional Economic Imbalances: Business and Foreign Direct Investment in India ............................................................ 1
*Jitender Bhandari, Ansal University, India*
*Manmohan Rahul, Ansal University, India*
*Shalini Rahul Tiwari, IMT Ghaziabad, India*

**Chapter 2**
Role of Knowledge Workers in Business Process and Innovation ............................................................ 17
*Appasaheb Naikal, S P Jain School of Global Management, Singapore*
*Mayank Bapna, PT Prizer Primindo 19G, Indonesia*

**Chapter 3**
Technological Innovations in Management Education ............................................................ 30
*Shalini Kalia, IMT Ghaziabad, India*
*Nishant Puri, IMT Ghaziabad, India*
*Indrani Chakraverty, IMT Ghaziabad, India*

**Chapter 4**
Emergent Trends in Sustainable Technologies in Thailand: Developing OTOP-Based Manufacturing Capabilities in Rural India ............................................................ 48
*Samarth Gupta, Institute of Management Technology Ghaziabad, India*
*Garima Yadav, Institute of Management Technology Ghaziabad, India*
*Amit Choudhary, Institute of Management Technology Ghaziabad, India*
*Amanpreet Kaur, Institute of Management Technology Ghaziabad, India*

**Chapter 12**
Solar Micro Grids: Impact and Future in Rural Uttar Pradesh – Case Study on MGP ...................... 164
*Rahul Singh, IMT Ghaziabad, India*
*Anirban Sharma, IMT Ghaziabad, India*
*Amanpreet Kaur, IMT Ghaziabad, India*
*Mansi Gupta, IMT Ghaziabad, India*
*Kannan TS, IMT Ghaziabad, India*

**Chapter 13**
Study of Carbon Footprint in Organizations ........................................................................................ 176
*Kapil Mendiratta, IMT Ghaziabad, India*
*Subhadeep Bhattacharyya, IMT Ghaziabad, India*
*Grandhi Venkata Abhinav, IMT Ghaziabad, India*

**Chapter 14**
NGO Sudhaar: Empowering the Livestock Dependents .................................................................... 192
*Pragun Aggarwal, IMT Ghaziabad, India*
*Ronit Anand, IMT Ghaziabad, India*

**Chapter 15**
Mapping the Rural Retail of India ....................................................................................................... 205
*Aditya Vashisth, Institute of Management Technology Ghaziabad, India*
*Aparajita, Institute of Management Technology Ghaziabad, India*
*Parul Gupta, Institute of Management Technology Ghaziabad, India*
*Pravin Patil, Institute of Management Technology Ghaziabad, India*
*Rohit Agarwal, Institute of Management Technology Ghaziabad, India*

**Chapter 16**
Revitalizing ICDS: India's Flagship Child Care Program ................................................................. 217
*Jeremiah Jacob, Institute of Management Technology Ghaziabad, India*

**Chapter 17**
Feasibility of Implementation of Solar Bottle Bulb in Urban Slums of India ................................... 236
*Akshay Maggu, Institute of Management Technology Ghaziabad, India*
*Jaideep Garg, Institute of Management Technology Ghaziabad, India*

**Chapter 18**
Business, Government, and Society Synergy for Sustainable Livelihood: A Case Study of Sabars from Jharkhand ......................................................................................................................... 252
*Ranjana Agarwal, IMT Ghaziabad, India*
*Parag Agarwal, IMT Ghaziabad, India*

**Chapter 19**
An Empirical Investigation into the Key Characteristics of Socio-Technical Societies: Social Identity, Social Exchange, and Social Vicinity .................................................................................... 263
*Shailja Agarwal, IMT Ghaziabad, India*

**Chapter 20**
Rural Innovations: Text and Cases ........ 275
*Roopesh Rao, Shri Ramdeobaba College of Engineering and Management, India*

**Chapter 21**
Organic Farming: Growth and Issues ........ 292
*Aditya Vikram Agrawal, Institute of Management Technology Ghaziabad, India*
*Charu Sharma, Institute of Management Technology Ghaziabad, India*
*Neha Joshi, Institute of Management Technology Ghaziabad, India*
*Siddharth Jindal, Institute of Management Technology Ghaziabad, India*
*V. Raghavendra, Institute of Management Technology Ghaziabad, India*
*Vaibhav Kango, Institute of Management Technology Ghaziabad, India*

**Chapter 22**
Jugaad Inc: Evolution of Frugal Entrepreneurship and Lean Start Ups ........ 310
*Neelendra Nath, IMT Ghaziabad, India*
*Somtirth Chaudhuri, IMT Ghaziabad, India*
*Parikshit Sarkar, IMT Ghaziabad, India*
*Sayantan Saha, IMT Ghaziabad, India*
*Bineydeep Singh, IMT Ghaziabad, India*
*Neha Bhardwaj, IMT Ghaziabad, India*

**Chapter 23**
Tackling Energy Issues in Rural India ........ 324
*Riju Antony George, IMT Ghaziabad, India*
*Vijayshree M., IMT Ghaziabad, India*
*Pavan Dev Singh Charak, IMT Ghaziabad, India*
*Kaustubh Singh Rana, IMT Ghaziabad, India*
*Shagun Agarwal, IMT Ghaziabad, India*
*Ambadipudi Venkata Sai Dhiraj, IMT Ghaziabad, India*

**Chapter 24**
Waste Management Initiatives in Rural India ........ 338
*Rishi Kumar, Institute of Management Technology Ghaziabad, India*

**Chapter 25**
Capacity Building through Knowledge Management: How Vedic Concepts Can Interpret the Occurrences at Maruti Suzuki India, Manesar ........ 355
*Shampa Chakraberty, NSHM Knowledge Campus, India*

**Compilation of References** ........ 378

**About the Contributors** ........ 395

**Index** ........ 411

# Detailed Table of Contents

**Foreword** .......... xix

**Preface** .......... xxi

**Acknowledgment** .......... xxv

**Chapter 1**
Regional Economic Imbalances: Business and Foreign Direct Investment in India .......... 1
*Jitender Bhandari, Ansal University, India*
*Manmohan Rahul, Ansal University, India*
*Shalini Rahul Tiwari, IMT Ghaziabad, India*

The importance of inflow of Foreign Direct Investment (FDI) in economic development of India is widely known, analyzed and well accepted in the post-liberalization era. But such inflows have created regional disparities within India owing to their concentration in select geographical locations (states) only. This should be brought into socio-economic discourses and policy formulation and as such, this chapter is an attempt to understand the linkage between FDI and regional economic growth of India. The chapter is divided into three parts.Part-1presents phases of evolution of FDI policies that made an impact on the business condition in India post independence,Part-2presents economic condition of various states and also discusses the FDI inflows to these states since 1991.In Part-3, some policy measures has been suggested to remove this anomaly in our development process so as to make economic development with FDI more stable and inclusive.

**Chapter 2**
Role of Knowledge Workers in Business Process and Innovation .......... 17
*Appasaheb Naikal, S P Jain School of Global Management, Singapore*
*Mayank Bapna, PT Prizer Primindo 19G, Indonesia*

Highly skilled knowledge workers are the main driving force for innovation; however, their innovation may not always ensure the achievement of business goals. Only the alignment of the innovation with business goals can transform their innovation into individual performance. Similarly variation in individual capabilities of knowledge workers may not lead to final business goals. This paper focuses on knowledge workers, their performance, the business processes followed and effectiveness of the business processes to enhance productivity of the organizations.

Technological innovations significantly enhance the effectiveness of the teaching learning process at all phases of academic pursuit. An array of evolved application software, middleware, and hardware help orchestrate an enriching learning environment. Technology enabled devices such as multimedia projectors, interactive e-boards and collaborative e-learning are now interwoven into the fabric of academic life alongside traditional methods. Moreover, the current generation, having grown up in an immersive ICT-driven environment, is completely at ease with online collaborative techniques. It is imperative that their skills be harnessed maximally by providing them with a learning platform that is optimally boosted by hi-tech accoutrements. This paper puts into perspective recent developments in modern tools and techniques involved in management education. It also examines the effectiveness of technological tools currently deployed in leading B-schools of India and Mexico. As these two emerging economies bear many similarities, it presents an interesting case for comparison. Through survey responses across disciplines in institutions in both countries, the study analyses the accessibility, usability, relevance, effectiveness, and challenges involved in using these technologies. Our study aims to analyse the technological tools and techniques which are beneficial to education system.



OVOP concept has been one of the keenly studied rural marketing and social innovation concepts in the world. While many countries have successfully implemented this model under various names, forms, strategies and areas; there is still a lot of scope for analysing and carefully implementing this unique business model for the development of Rural Innovation and Social Entrepreneurship. Studies have shown that while the Asian countries like Thailand, Japan, Malawi and even Nepal have successfully implemented this concept and reaped its benefits, some of the nations like India, South Africa and others are yet to follow a methodical approach towards the implementation of this interesting social business proposition. The Kasetsart Journal of Social Sciences has been focussing on developing such capabilities for enhancing social business proposition and understanding the contribution of community involvement in social re-engineering. While lot of emphasis has been paid on developing innovative social ventures for Rural India, a concept like OVOP/OTOP is certainly the need of the hour. In this chapter we intend to investigate the various aspects of an OVOP/OTOP implementation and propose solutions for social business development in Rural India based on the foundations of the OVOP/OTOP concept that has been a pioneer for development of social entrepreneurship across the world.

**Chapter 5**


*Somansh Kumar, Institute of Management Technology Ghaziabad, India*
*Mayank Rawat, Institute of Management Technology Ghaziabad, India*
*Priyangshu Mahanta, Institute of Management Technology Ghaziabad, India*
*Ashish Bhadauria, Institute of Management Technology Ghaziabad, India*
*Manjusha Subramanian, Institute of Management Technology Ghaziabad, India*
*Sarthak Awasthi, Institute of Management Technology Ghaziabad, India*

In this chapter the authors have tried to identify the feasibility of setting up a community radio station in agriculture hubs in India to create awareness about various agriculture credit schemes, government sponsored schemes, best farming practices and weather information amongst farmers. The authors are of the opinion that a more informed farmer will lead to better planning and stave off farmer suicides. While the community radio program could be an effective medium for disseminating information, its penetration and acceptance in a rural community depends upon some key factors such as proximity of the place to an urban location where visual media enjoys a wider audience. The chapter attempts to bring forth the challenges faced in establishing a CR program in Raghunathpur in the state of Uttar Pradesh and sheds light on why the initiative may not be viable. Finally the authors conclude the study by suggesting other alternatives of empowering the Indian farmer in such locations.

**Chapter 6**


*Kartik Chachra, Institute of Management Technology Ghaziabad, India*
*Gowtham Seelam, Institute of Management Technology Ghaziabad, India*
*Harshit Singh, Institute of Management Technology Ghaziabad, India*
*Mayukh Sarkar, Institute of Management Technology Ghaziabad, India*
*Anshul Jain, Institute of Management Technology Ghaziabad, India*

The Indian Agriculture has been an area with varied challenges. This sector is responsible for the growth rate and generating a per capita income. This sector generates a whopping 28% of the total GDP of India and over 15% of the total exports. The usage of Internet and phone technology can fill these gaps to a large extent. A continuous two way interaction among the farmers and agricultural scientists will ensure agricultural extension. A landmark step was taken on January 21, 2004 when the Department of Agriculture & Cooperation, launched Kisan Call Centers (KCC) with the help of the extensive telecom industry to deliver extension services to the farming community. The main purpose of these call centers is to answer the queries raised by the farmers in their local language, on continuous basis. At present the Kisan Call Centers are running from 14 locations all over India. In this chapter, we are trying to analyze how this strategy to help the farming community was introduced and how it is being implemented.

The chapter highlights the innovation of two entrepreneurs. The significance of the innovation on our society regarding the health issues has been focused. Two entrepreneurs and their innovation have been studied very closely. They were interviewed as well as their websites were studied thoroughly. The result of the study shows a close bonding between innovation and creativity.



In this chapter, the impact of rising cost of fuel and inability of government to supply electricity round the clock leading to spurt in frugal innovations utilizing alternative sources of energy has been analyzed. Rice is one of the prime crops of India, Rice husk, perceived as waste by many, being abundant and available at low cost can be major contributor in alternate energy. Due to lack of awareness of the potential of rice husk it is discarded as waste and results in waste disposal problem and methane emission. The use of rice husk for electricity generation in efficient manner has potential to transform agricultural waste into a valuable fuel and could help in boosting farm economy. This study explores the usage of rice husk and its untapped potential as a major fuel source. The target markets are villages in India with 400-500 households having ample biomass feedstock.



Changing of the world scenario, blurring boundaries in international and national markets and shifts in demographic profile of people have opened a new chapter of management thinking on 'strategies for retention of talent'. Skill unavailability, employee poaching, high costs of training and development, absolute necessity of international exposure are the alarming signals for organizations to shrug off their complacency-nap and get going for talent management. Talent Management is a wide function encompassing strategic planning, talent staffing, development-focus, performance management, compensation management etc. to manage retaining talent in the organization. This review paper is an attempt to throw some light on this vista.

The intention of this chapter was to explore the reasons as to why the poor in Indian cities shun banking services. On the basis of a survey of 25 low-income daily wage earners, it was noted that although there is awareness about banks, strict ID card requirements and corruption are the major explanations of this sociological happening. Further, in this chapter, the authors have tried to document the steps taken by the Serva UP Gramin Bank to address this issue. Finally, based on the results of a research survey and field visits to the Serva UP Gramin Bank, recommendations of encouraging private banks to compete in the rural market and increasing the reach of the bank branches have been enumerated.



Dairy farming is one of the growing industries. It offers multiple opportunities to people and leave a sustainable impact on society, environment and economy. In this chapter we discuss about its reach and establishment in rural areas and how this industry can play an instrumental role in rural development. The present case captures and reviews the functioning of a dairy farm situated in Ghaziabad, Uttar Pradesh, a state in India. The chapter narrates the role of various heads working at this farm and elaborates the steps involved from procuring the dairy products to its treatment and finally to its catering to the consumer, this case is developed through a rigorous literature review. To assess and establish the role of dairy farming in rural development, this chapter discusses the three tier AMUL model of Gujarat, India is also reviewed. This model by now is the most structured one and lays the foundation for dairy farming in the country. It also demonstrates that dairy farming can become instrumental in rural development.



Like most of the developing countries, India also has a large number of off-the-grid villages. In spite of government's efforts at rural electrification, many villages cannot hope for grid power in the near future because the cost of setting up the distribution infrastructure. But when these villages come on grid, they place an additional demand on the distribution network and most states are already facing several hours of power cuts because conventional electricity is scarce. Thus these villages remain un-electrified for the simple reason that electricity is not available. This case study deals with the innovative business model

**Chapter 16**
Revitalizing ICDS: India's Flagship Child Care Program ..... 217
*Jeremiah Jacob, Institute of Management Technology Ghaziabad, India*

ICDS-Integrated Child Development Services is India's only government program for combating the rampant malnutrition prevalent in young children. In this chapter, the authors aim to examine the need and scope of ICDS scheme, its services and countrywide reach; considering that every fifth child in the world lives in India, this scheme is critical to ensuring that today's children who are our citizens of tomorrow are well nurtured and nourished, thus securing the country's future. Also its efficacy in achieving stated objectives is assessed through analysis of vital parameters such as nutritional status, mortality rates etc. Further, the bottlenecks facing the scheme such as lack of adequate sanitation facilities and supervisory staff etc. are studied and the initiatives taken by the government to revitalize it are also examined. The transformation into Mission Mode has ushered in programmatic, institutional and management reforms and renewed thrust on creating awareness through an Information, Education and Communication (IEC) campaign.

**Chapter 17**
Feasibility of Implementation of Solar Bottle Bulb in Urban Slums of India ..... 236
*Akshay Maggu, Institute of Management Technology Ghaziabad, India*
*Jaideep Garg, Institute of Management Technology Ghaziabad, India*

Reach of undisrupted electricity is a perennial problem that is faced by urban slums in India. Through this chapter, the authors aim to study the feasibility of implementation of a ground breaking idea that will help in fighting this problem in a cost effective way and that has already been implemented in Philippines on a large scale. Further, given the present scenario of development in India, this chapter also tries to focus on the ways in which this product can be introduced on a commercial level covering one slum at a time. Also, this chapter revolves around the usability and identification of the most suitable and cost effective way to implement this idea in the desired target group. The chapter ultimately hopes to drive its readers to find the best solution to the proposed problem.

**Chapter 18**
Business, Government, and Society Synergy for Sustainable Livelihood: A Case Study of Sabars from Jharkhand ..... 252
*Ranjana Agarwal, IMT Ghaziabad, India*
*Parag Agarwal, IMT Ghaziabad, India*

In the post globalization era, synergy of Business, Government, and Society (BGS) forces is paving the way for development. This chapter gives an example of a case where BGS forces work together for development. The chapter discusses livelihood issues of Sabars, a tribal group from Jharkhand, located in Eastern India. A local NGO was working for upliftment of tribal people.. The Sabars were given training in making handicrafts under a project under Government of India. The focus of the training programme was on creating marketable handicrafts based on tribal's inherent art and culture. Problems were faced in marketing the products. Students from MBA College were roped in to provide solutions for marketing. The chapter discussed how social issues can be tackled collaboratively by all sectors of society. This chapter is based on primary data and is primarily qualitative in nature.

**Chapter 19**
An Empirical Investigation into the Key Characteristics of Socio-Technical Societies: Social Identity, Social Exchange, and Social Vicinity ........ 263
*Shailja Agarwal, IMT Ghaziabad, India*

The Internet has moved human interaction to a virtual dimension where users connect with each other through social networks. A social network comprises users and relations between these users (Wasserman & Faust, 1994), wherein relations connote "the collection of connections between members of a group" (Wasserman & Faust, 1994). This chapter looked to explain the reasons behind using social networking sites. Analysis of the collected data used a factor analysis to study the characteristics of the emerging socio-technical society amongst the students. The chapter identifies social identity, social exchange and social vicinity as the key characteristics of the emerging socio-technical societies. A gradual but paradigm shift from traditional societies to knowledge based societies was observed. While on one hand, a high dependency and usage of social networking websites (SNWs) was observed, on the other hand, the level of trust and dependency between the community members was found to be diminishing. The chapter reveals the emergence of a socio-technical community amongst students which is characterized by the need to create a social identity, a change in the style of social exchange and expansion of social vicinity. The findings suggest directions for future research.

**Chapter 20**
Rural Innovations: Text and Cases ........ 275
*Roopesh Rao, Shri Ramdeobaba College of Engineering and Management, India*

In a country like India innovations are more referred as "jugaad". Though the dictionary does not explain such kind of words, but every person in India understands the importance of jugaad. India has one of the largest systems for agricultural research in the world. However this system has focused predominantly on strengthening of cereal production under irrigated conditions. It would be essential that they participate in all decision making which cater to overall development of rural india. India also needs to increase its efforts to tap into the rapidly growing stock of global knowledge through channels such as FDI, technology licensing, importation of capital merchandise that embody knowledge, as well as advanced products, components, and services. This chapter analyses and focuses on various innovative practices done with the help of Government, Public Private Partnership, private Players, Individuals, NGOS, etc

**Chapter 21**
Organic Farming: Growth and Issues ........ 292
*Aditya Vikram Agrawal, Institute of Management Technology Ghaziabad, India*
*Charu Sharma, Institute of Management Technology Ghaziabad, India*
*Neha Joshi, Institute of Management Technology Ghaziabad, India*
*Siddharth Jindal, Institute of Management Technology Ghaziabad, India*
*V. Raghavendra, Institute of Management Technology Ghaziabad, India*
*Vaibhav Kango, Institute of Management Technology Ghaziabad, India*

India practised organic farming in early centuries but Green revolution lead to shift of farming to fertilizer based farming. So, in this chapter the focus is to elucidate the idea of organic farming and its growth over the years across the countries with focus on India. Organic farming is a type of farming method where the crops are sowed and raised by using organic wastes instead of the regular use of pesticides

and insecticides. This method has been quickly accepted and adopted by most of the countries across the world with the number being 144 in the year 2010 with major percentage being practised in developing nations. Out of this, India has just about 0.03 percent of the total land under organic farming across the world. India has witnessed a significant growth in organic farming since the last few years, keeping in sync with the world market.

**Chapter 22**
Jugaad Inc: Evolution of Frugal Entrepreneurship and Lean Start Ups ........................................ 310
*Neelendra Nath, IMT Ghaziabad, India*
*Somtirth Chaudhuri, IMT Ghaziabad, India*
*Parikshit Sarkar, IMT Ghaziabad, India*
*Sayantan Saha, IMT Ghaziabad, India*
*Bineydeep Singh, IMT Ghaziabad, India*
*Neha Bhardwaj, IMT Ghaziabad, India*

The essence of an entrepreneur's effort lie in finding solutions to challenges. Monetary profit is a byproduct of entrepreneur's success and not the main agenda or measure of it. This bare nature makes entrepreneurship a risky business. In spite of all the rigor and challenges, entrepreneurs never cease to exist; in fact now we are seeing an unprecedented surge in their numbers. This surge has changed the whole dynamics of the entrepreneurial environment. A study of changing norms, style and sentiment of entrepreneurs is in order. In this chapter we study changing times and style of entrepreneurship; the evolution of new age entrepreneurs and their approach. Is this trend lasting or will burst like a bubble? Is it increasing uncertainty at conventional jobs or people have developed a deep lust for entrepreneurship? With so many startups coming up these days, how to evaluate them? These are the few questions which have risen and await adequate response.

**Chapter 23**
Tackling Energy Issues in Rural India ........................................................................................ 324
*Riju Antony George, IMT Ghaziabad, India*
*Vijayshree M., IMT Ghaziabad, India*
*Pavan Dev Singh Charak, IMT Ghaziabad, India*
*Kaustubh Singh Rana, IMT Ghaziabad, India*
*Shagun Agarwal, IMT Ghaziabad, India*
*Ambadipudi Venkata Sai Dhiraj, IMT Ghaziabad, India*

India is an energy deficient country and this deficiency is more felt in the rural villages of India. More than half of the villages are not electrified. Villages have many renewable resources and if these resources are put into effective use, the energy crunch can be mitigated. Such a renewable resource is rice husk which is perceived as a waste product. In this chapter, the authors have studied the potential of rice husk as a source of electricity for the rice producing villages of India. A particular village in the state of Uttar Pradesh was chosen to conduct the research to analyze the viability of a rice husk power plant. Various methods of converting biomass into energy have been discussed and based on research the biomass gasification method has been suggested as the most appropriate. The various advantages and challenges of using this technology, uses for by-products are discussed in this chapter. A workable business model has also been outlined along with future strategies and implications.

**Chapter 24**
Waste Management Initiatives in Rural India .......................................................................................... 338
*Rishi Kumar, Institute of Management Technology Ghaziabad, India*

In this chapter, the author aims to present an overall view of the Waste Management practices employed in rural parts of India and their overall sustainability in terms of present scenario. It would discuss the successful models employed in some parts of the country and the reason, that why they are not prevalent or expand to the rest of the nation inspite of them being successful in their own territory. It would also discuss the various Initiatives taken by the government in this regard such as the Total Sanitary Campaign which aimed at bringing an improvement in the general quality of life by creating awareness on improving the sanitation facilities and providing health education in rural parts of the country. This chapter also suggests about the further improvements that can be done in the overall model by including other stakeholders like Local Gram Panchayats, NGOs and community people.

**Chapter 25**
Capacity Building through Knowledge Management: How Vedic Concepts Can Interpret the Occurrences at Maruti Suzuki India, Manesar .......................................................................................... 355
*Shampa Chakraberty, NSHM Knowledge Campus, India*

This chapter talks about the history of Maruti which is marked by exploitation of workers through extraordinary work pressure, harassment by arbitrary issuing of show-cause notices and charge-sheets, transfers, suspensions, criminal intimidation, terminations without inquiry, reducing the labour costs by contractualisation of work-force, devising mechanisms to extract maximum work effort from workers, getting rid of the relatively older workers or those with disabilities or medical condition etc. are methods that act against the interest of workers. In this chapter one of the Vedic philosophy's systems namely Karma- Mimamsa is explained by the author who thinks that karma alone awards fruits to the performer of Vedic ritual and the reward is consistent with the karma of the performer of the ritual. Where there is good karma, there is good fruit and vice versa. Dharma comes from the Lord, karma comes from the Lord, but the fruit comes from karma itself.

**Compilation of References** .......................................................................................... 378

**About the Contributors** .......................................................................................... 395

**Index** .......................................................................................... 411

# Foreword

India is in the transition phase from a developing to a developed economy. There is a need for more case studies and research papers reflecting the new age rural milieu of India. I am delighted to present to you the book titled "Promoting Socio-Economic Development through Business Integration" which deals with issues related to rural innovation, capacity building, knowledge management, rural entrepreneurship and technology. This compendium is an outcome of intense research undertaken by faculty members of Business Communication area and students at IMT-Ghaziabad as part of the Centre for Rural Innovation & Capacity Building through Knowledge Management, Entrepreneurship and Technology (CRICKET); and faculty members from other business schools in India. The compendium is an effort to enable the globalized audience to have an insider's perspective on innovative growth strategies in rural India.

This comprehensive publication aims to be an essential reference source and builds on the available literature in the field of socio economic development in developing countries. It also provides scope for further research opportunities in this dynamic field. It is expected that this book will provide the necessary resources for policy makers (Government and Private), Research Scholars, Academicians, Practitioners, NGOs and Self Help groups in developing nations across the globe. I am confident, this text will be a useful contribution to the business world.

I must compliment the publisher, IGI Global, and the editorial team of IMT-Ghaziabad comprising Dr Shalini Kalia, Dr Bhavna Bhalla, Ms. Lipi Das, and Dr Neeraj Awasthy for adhering to the strict standards of reviewing process and ensuring that only quality India specific case studies and research papers broadly relating to the domains of Socio- Economic Development are incorporated in this compendium. I hope that the compendium would ignite new thoughts and direction for research in an emerging market like India.

Happy Reading!

*N. L. Ahuja*
*Institute of Management Technology Ghaziabad, India*

**Narender Lal Ahuja**, *Dean-Academics and Professor at the Institute of Management Technology Ghaziabad, is a Fellow/PhD from the Indian Institute of Management Calcutta. Recently, he participated in Harvard Business School's Glo-Coll program in 2014-15. Dr Ahuja has over 35 years' experience of teaching finance and accounting courses to MBA/PGDM participants at high ranking institutions including IMT Ghaziabad, IIM Calcutta, XLRI Jamshedpur and Faculty of Management Studies (University of Delhi) besides foreign assignments. He has served as a Commonwealth (CFTC) Expert in Finance, University of Buea, Cameroon for four years (2000-2004) and also taught at business schools in Tanzania and the Seychelles. Dr Ahuja has extensive experience in executive training, case writing, research and publications. He has presented research papers at several international conferences including Harvard University (USA), Oxford University (UK), Greece, Israel and other places. He has won Case-writing competitions organized by London Business School (2007, 2008) and CEEMAN-Emerald, Europe (2012). Two of his cases are registered with European Case Clearance House (ECCH). He has been a consultant/trainer to several public and private sector organizations.*

# Preface

Welcome to the World of Business Integration in India!

Developed economies have been characterised by having goals of poverty elimination and productive employment firmly rooted in their social structures, government policies and social contracts. In contrast, a developing economy like India is always challenged in terms of attaining goals of gainful employment and inclusion due to the varied nature of its social and societal structures, political ideologies and levels of development in each state. Thus, despite knowing that business integration could be a panacea for socio-economic development; it becomes an arduous task for any single government or an organization to undertake it. On the other hand, India has experienced improved performance levels in pockets (such as communities, organizations, areas) wherever such integration has happened. This book aims to explore and study those 'pockets' wherever improvements have been observed; so as to make meaningful conclusion for other areas/communities/organizations to adopt and implement. Each initiative undertaken for improving socio-economic performance can then be woven together in the fabric of business integration to bring about a large scale transformation in our society. India, will then, be believed to have become '*developed*'.

The book *Promoting Socio-Economic Development through Business Integration* is an attempt to create world-class intellectual capital by harnessing potential of India-centric research projects and builds on available literature in the field of socio-economic development in developing countries, providing further research opportunities in this field. Research scholars, academics, policymakers, government officials, and more will find this book to be a crucial source of knowledge to their respective disciplines

## ORGANIZATION OF THE BOOK

The book is organized into 25 chapters. A brief description of each of the chapters follows:

Chapter 1 gives a perspective on Regional Economic Imbalances; Business and Foreign Direct Investment (FDI) in India. In this chapter, an attempt has been made to understand the linkage between FDI and regional economic growth of India.

Chapter 2 focuses on knowledge workers, their performance, the business processes followed and effectiveness of the business processes to enhance productivity of the organizations.

Chapter 3 endeavors to focus on technological Innovations in management education. This chapter puts into perspective recent developments in modern tools and techniques involved in management education; and examines the effectiveness of technological tools currently deployed in leading B-schools of India and Mexico. The study analyses the accessibility, usability, relevance, effectiveness, and challenges involved in using these technologies.

Chapter 4 highlights the emergent trends in sustainable technologies like 'One village one Product (OVOP)' concept (especially in the context of Thailand) which has been one of the keenly studied rural marketing and social innovation concepts in the world and how this could be modelled to develop OTOP based manufacturing capabilities in rural India.

Chapter 5 identifies the initial challenges of setting up a radio community program in a particular rural community and weighs the benefits and limitations of undertaking such a venture. The study tabulates the areas of communication gap across three stakeholders- the market place, rural community and/or government.

Chapter 6 gives a perspective on the impact of Kisan Call Centers on the farming sector. Currently, the Kisan Call Centers are running from 14 locations all over India with an objective to answer the queries raised by the farmers in their local language, on continuous basis. The chapter tries to analyze how this strategy to help the farming community was introduced and how it is being implemented.

Chapter 7 highlights the innovation of two entrepreneurs. The significance of the innovation on our society regarding the health issues has been focused. The result of the study shows a close bonding between innovation and creativity.

Chapter 8 studies the rice husk power systems and explores it as alternate source of energy. The rising cost of fuel and inability of government to supply electricity round the clock to every part of country motivated the industry to search for alternative sources of energy. This study explores the usage of rice husk and its untapped potential as a major fuel source.

Chapter 9 is dedicated to studying 'Talent Management' as an area of growing concern in the field of human resource management. Retention of good employees and the role that various factors have in an employee's decision to stay or leave an organization are much sought-after themes of contemporary management research. This chapter emphasizes that a talent-management strategy needs to link to business strategy to make sense.

Chapter 10 endeavours to decode the rural outreach for banks in India, the challenges and possible solutions including use of banking services like remittance services to transfer the money home. The objective of this study was to explore this occurrence by investigating the reasons as to why the rural people in cities shun such banking services. Further, this study analyses the perspective of the banks by documenting the steps taken by the Serva UP Gramin Bank to address this issue.

Chapter 11 is dedicated to the role of dairy farming in rural development as it offers multiple opportunities to people and leaves a sustainable impact on society, environment and economy. The present case captures and reviews the functioning of a dairy farm situated in Ghaziabad, Uttar Pradesh, a state in India.

Chapter 12 deals with the innovative business model of the company "Mera Gao Power" which addresses the need for electricity in rural India by setting up "Solar Micro Grids". The chapter analyses the impact of Solar Power on the socio-economic parameters of the villages in which this project has been implemented based on data collected from some villages where the micro grids have been setup. The chapter also discusses various challenges faced by this company in sustaining and expanding this business model.

Chapter 13 aims to study how socially/ environmentally conscious today's firms are, and what course of actions are being taken towards a greener and carbon neutral society in terms of saving basic equivalents of resources such as paper, water, electricity etc. This study aims to present an analysis of how Indian corporate houses and their employees currently are and how they could be engaged in contributing to a greener environment.

Chapter 14 talks about the NGO Sudhaar and how to empower the Livestock Dependents. This case details Sudhaar's dilemma on how to convince the rural households regarding feasibility of the business and successfully launching the same thereafter.

Chapter 15 gives a perspective on mapping the rural retail scenario of India. The rural retail in India operates under the realms of mom and pop stores, which are, relatively, yet to adopt the accounting and operating standards of the developed world, yet, are selling the flagship products of global FMCG giants like Unilever and Procter & Gamble. The case here tries to sensitize its readers towards what is one of the largest privatized and yet highly unorganized retail store formats in the world. The case in question also talks about how the backward integration and adoption of set standards by the small time retailers can in turn benefit the end consumer tangibly as well as intangibly. Overall, the chapter tries to communicate to its readers, the importance of understanding the dynamics of doing business in rural retail sector of India, whether relatively organized or unorganized.

Chapter 16 talks about revitalizing Integrated Child Development Services (ICDS) -India's Flagship Child Care Program. ICDS is India's only government program for combating the rampant malnutrition prevalent in young children. This chapter aims to examine the need and scope of ICDS scheme while assessing its efficacy in achieving stated objectives.

Chapter 17 underlines the feasibility of implementation of solar bottle bulb in urban slums of India. Through this case study, the authors aim to study the feasibility of implementation of a ground breaking idea that will help in fighting this problem in a cost effective way and that has already been implemented in Philippines on a large scale.

Chapter 18 highlights an example of overall interaction of BGS forces which is aiming at Sustainable development. In the post globalization era, synergy of Business, Government and Society, (BGS) forces is paving the way for development. The chapter illustrates how forces of BGS are working together for upliftment of Sabars, a primitive tribal group in Jharkhand.

Chapter 19 entails an empirical investigation into the key characteristics of socio-technical societies. The study in the chapter identifies social identity, social exchange and social vicinity as the key characteristics of the emerging socio-technical societies.

Chapter 20 on rural innovations analyses and focuses on various innovative practices adopted in India with the help of Government, Public Private Partnership, private Players, Individuals, NGOS, etc. The innovation system in any country consists of institutions, rules, and procedures that affect how it acquires, creates, disseminates, and uses knowledge.

Chapter 21 talks about growth and issues related to organic farming. India practiced organic farming in early centuries but green revolution led to shift of farming to fertilizer based farming. The chapter enumerates how organic farming has various advantages over the traditional farming methods, which can be an over-shadow to its higher cost.

Chapter 22 encourages spirit of entrepreneurship through Jugaad Inc. – a study of changing times and style in domain of entrepreneurship, the evolution of new age entrepreneurs and their approach. Is this trend going to stand the test of time or will burst like a bubble? Is it just increasing uncertainty at conventional job spaces or people have developed a deep lust for entrepreneurial environment? With so many start-ups coming up these days, how do people evaluate them? These are the few questions which have arisen in recent times and are discussed in this chapter.

Chapter 23 seeks to highlight the measures relating to energy issues in rural India. India is an energy deficient country and this deficiency is observed more in the rural villages of India. Villages have many renewable resources and if these resources are put into effective use, the energy crunch can be mitigated. Such a renewable resource is rice husk which is perceived as a waste product. This chapter looks into the energy issues in rural India, the feasibility of rice husk power generation in rural India, the technology used and the advantages and concerns of implementing rice husk generators.

Chapter 24 presents an overall view of the waste management practices employed in rural parts of India and their overall sustainability in terms of present scenario. It discusses the successful models employed in some parts of the country and the reasons for not being prevalent in the rest of the nation despite being successful in their own territory. It also discusses the initiatives taken by the government in this regard and how further improvements can be done in the overall model by including other stakeholders like Local Gram Panchayats, NGOs and community people.

Chapter 25 focuses on capacity building through knowledge management especially how vedic concepts can interpret the occurrences at Maruti Suzuki India, Manesar, Delhi National Capital Region.

*Shalini Kalia*
*Institute of Management Technology Ghaziabad, India*

*Bhavna Bhalla*
*Institute of Management Technology Ghaziabad, India*

*Lipi Das*
*Institute of Management Technology Ghaziabad, India*

*Neeraj Awasthy*
*Institute of Management Technology Ghaziabad, India*

# Acknowledgment

At the outset we would like to thank Dr Bibek Banerjee, the Director & Academic Mentor, Institute of Management Technology, for extending his continued guidance and support throughout the project. Further, we would like to thank each one of the authors who contributed their time and expertise to this book.

We wish to acknowledge the valuable contributions of the reviewers regarding the improvement of quality and content presentation of chapters. Most of the authors also served as reviewers; we highly appreciate their dual contribution.

The rich inputs of IGI Global editorial and production team have significantly helped us in smooth sailing of this project, sincere thanks to all of them for always being available to guide us.

*Shalini Kalia*
*IMT Ghaziabad, India*

*Bhavna Bhalla*
*IMT Ghaziabad, India*

*Lipi Das*
*IMT Ghaziabad, India*

*Neeraj Awasthy*
*IMT Ghaziabad, India*

# Chapter 1
# Regional Economic Imbalances:
## Business and Foreign Direct Investment in India

**Jitender Bhandari**
*Ansal University, India*

**Manmohan Rahul**
*Ansal University, India*

**Shalini Rahul Tiwari**
*IMT Ghaziabad, India*

## ABSTRACT

*The importance of inflow of Foreign Direct Investment (FDI) in economic development of India is widely known, analyzed and well accepted in the post-liberalization era. But such inflows have created regional disparities within India owing to their concentration in select geographical locations (states) only. This should be brought into socio-economic discourses and policy formulation and as such, this chapter is an attempt to understand the linkage between FDI and regional economic growth of India. The chapter is divided into three parts.* ***Part-1*** *presents phases of evolution of FDI policies that made an impact on the business condition in India post independence,* ***Part-2*** *presents economic condition of various states and also discusses the FDI inflows to these states since 1991.* ***In Part-3****, some policy measures has been suggested to remove this anomaly in our development process so as to make economic development with FDI more stable and inclusive.*

## 1.0 INTRODUCTION

In economic theory and academic discussion, FDI has a positive relationship with economic growth has been validated. Post 1950, MNC and international trade increased dramatically in all continents and India being no exception invited foreign capital in various forms and sizes. Post 1991, India witnessed significant amount of FDI inflows in few of its States and Union Territories and consequently showed better growth prospects. It also raised issues like regional disparity and economic imbalance among the

DOI: 10.4018/978-1-4666-8259-7.ch001

states because of FDI accumulation in few states. An attempt has been made in the present chapter to understand this relationship. The chapter is divided in three parts where Part 1 is an overview of FDI policies post, Part II, discusses the economic condition of various States and then an attempt has been made to understand the relationship between FDI and regional economic development. The policy measures have been discussed in Part-3 of the paper.

## 1.1 Evolution of FDI Policies in India since Independence

After independence, the FDI policy of India can broadly be classified in four phases where each phase characterized with changing attitude of respective governments towards foreign capital and its role in economic development. The first Phase or Phase I can be back tracked from 1948 to 1966. Under this period India adopted the policy of welcoming foreign capital but with caution. The second phase was the period 1966-1979 where in this period the policy stance of India towards FDI was hardened. The period 1980-1990 was the beginning of the adoption of the policy of liberalization of the economy albeit partially. Post 1991, government of India completely changes its policy towards FDI, recognizes the role of FDI in the overall growth of the economy and consequently making the policies more liberal and welcoming.

**(Phase-I): The Period of "Cautious welcome policy" [1](1948-66)** -After independence India adopted a cautious approach towards foreign capital. This approach was based on the experience India had with the foreign companies before independence. The sizeable presence of British capital in pre-independence India had done little to promote development, its large presence in extractive industries, plantations, shipping, banking and insurance were geared to promoting colonial interests. The Industrial Policy Resolution (IPR) 1948 recognized that participation of foreign capital and enterprise particularly as regard to the industrial techniques and technical know-how would be helpful in achieving the objective of rapid industrialization. However it was also emphasized that foreign capital should be properly regulated. But in IPR1956, import substitution policy followed with a view to build local capabilities was adopted and in order to promote technological development, technology imports and foreign investment in high technology areas were allowed. In 1963-64, the Government of India decided to give the 'letter of intent' to foreign companies to proceed with their capital projects, instead of making the company finds an Indian partner. In 1965 certain tax concession was made for Non-Resident Account.

**(Phase II): The Period of "Selective and restrictive policy" (1967-79)** - After having shown openness and receptivity towards foreign capital, policy regime became further selective and restrictive during the period of 1968-79. Under the IPR 1970, the large industrial houses and foreign enterprises were permitted to enter in the 'core and 'heavy investment' sectors except industries reserved for the public sector. But in 1973 the Foreign Exchange Regulation Act was amended and branches of foreign companies in India and Indian Joint Stock Companies in which non-resident interest was more than 40% were expected to bring down their non –resident share holding to 40% within a period of 2 years. However, basic and core industries and export oriented industry engaged in manufacturing activities needing sophisticated technology were allowed to carry on business with non-resident interest with permission from RBI. As a result many multinationals such as IBM and Coca Cola closed down their operations in India whereas other companies followed statutory requirement and likes of Unilever diversified their production base in order to fulfill export obligations as required under FERA in return for retaining majority equity ownership. During the period 1967-79, the total number of collaboration agreements reached an all-time low of just 242 (Kumar 1994). There were further relaxations in the rules pertaining to encourage non-resident investment. But in a major policy shift by the government in 1977, foreign investment and acquisition of technology necessary for India's industrial development could be allowed where they were in national interest and on terms determined by the government. As a rule, majority interest in ownership and effective control could be in Indian hands except in highly export oriented and sophisticated technology areas. This policy shift led to huge foreign capital exodus from the Indian soil.

**(Phase III): The Period of Partial liberalization Policy (1980-90) -** If the second phase was restrictive in nature, the third phase was the beginning of liberalization era in the foreign capital policy matters. The government revised the foreign investment policy in 1980 by adding portfolio FDI and new bank deposits policies. The RBI also simplified the exchange control procedures. In 1983-84 the government also took many initiatives in the form of tax benefit on investment, exemption in long term capital gains arising from exchange of any foreign exchange assets etc, relaxations granted to NRI investment, abolition of estate duty and permission to NRIs to subscribe to the MoA of a new company. The government also decided to remove the ceiling of Rs. 40 lacs for making investment in India by NRIs in private limited companies. The total number of collaboration agreement approved per year increased from 242 during the period 1967-79 to 744 during the period 1980-88. All the measures adopted during the phase –III were in fact precursor to the next set of policies which were announced in 1990s. In fact the process of economic reforms has really begins in 1980s.

**(Phase IV): The Period of "Liberalization and Open door policy" -**After the balance of payment crisis in 1990-91, India adopted a series of policy reforms under the Structural Adjustment Programme (SAP) as suggested by the IMF. Under this SAP framework, India adopted open door policy towards FDI. These reform policies ushered a new era in Indian economic system. Following are some of the major highlights of New Economic Policy (NEP):

- Abolition of industrial licensing except for 18 industries
- Introduction of the dual approval system for FDI proposal viz., (i) through an automatic approval channel for FDI in 35 priority sectors by RBI and (ii) through Foreign Investment and Promotion Board (FIPB)/ Secretariat for Industrial Assistance (SIA)
- Existing companies were allowed to hike their foreign equity up to 51% in priority sector.
- Removal of restrictions of FDI in low technology sectors.
- Removal of condition for FDI with necessary technology agreements.
- Permission for Non-Residents Indians (NRIs) and Overseas Corporate bodies (OCBs) under automatic route with repatriation of capital income to invest up to 100% equity in high priority industries.
- India becomes a signatory to the Convention of the Multilateral Investment Guarantee Agency (MIGA) for protection of foreign investments.

All the above measures lead to major shift in the FDI policies post 199. More modified features of the new policy are:

(1) Manufacturing sectors are open up to 100 per cent FDI under the automatic route except defense production where it is capped at 26 per cent. FDI is not allowed in a few services including retail trading (except single brand), lottery business and gambling. In the permitted services, foreign equity is allowed below 50 per cent.

(2) FDI is currently allowed only up to 49 per cent in scheduled air transport services or domestic passenger airlines.

(3) Broadcasting services also have similar rules. Up linking of non-news television channels is the only broadcasting service permitted to have 100 per cent FDI after clearance by the Foreign Investment Promotion Board (FIPB). Majority foreign equity is not allowed in cable television networks and direct-to-home (DTH) operations.
(4) FDI is allowed only up to 26 per cent in print media.
(5) FDI is allowed up to 74 per cent in financial services such as private banks. Insurance however, can get FDI only up to 26 per cent.
(6) Minority foreign equity up to 49 per cent is permitted in asset reconstruction companies (ARCs), stock exchanges, depositories, clearing corporations and commodity. Except for ARCs, the FDI space is capped at 26 per cent for these sectors.
(7) In telecommunication services—both basic and cellular—although FDI up to 74 per cent is allowed, only 49 per cent is allowed under automatic route with the rest requiring approval from FIPB.

## 2.0 TRENDS IN FDI INFLOWS IN INDIA

Foreign Investments were always present in Indian economy since independence but the real importance has been given to FDI after 1991 economic reforms. Initially the volume of FDI flow was not large but gradually the magnitude of FDI increases rapidly (Figure 1). The total amount of FDI flow was meager $167 million in 1991 which quickly increases to $1374 million in the year 1994-95. But the real surge of flows comes after year 2000. Prior to 2002, RBI used to define FDI in its own way. But the definition used by the RBI was not as per the international benchmark definition adopted by the majority of the countries. In year 2002, RBI setup an expert committee to look into the matter of definition of FDI. The committee which was headed by Mr. I. Srinivas from DIPP recommended that India should also follow the international benchmark definition for the better reflection and comparison of FDI flows to Indian economy. It is only after the recommendation of Srinavas committee, RBI adopted the definition given in the Balance of Payment Manual (BoPM) (5th Edition), published by the IMF[2]. As soon as India adopted this definition, the quantum of FDI flows suddenly increased. But real big FDI proposals stated coming in the latter half of this decade. In the year 2007-08 the total FDI inflows touched US$ 24581 million. In the following year it has touched US$ 27331 million (Figure 1). But in the year 2009-10 it fell marginally due to the Global Economic crisis. On in all one can say that FDI inflows to Indian economy are significant and robust and the flow will only grow as the Government is further liberalizing the policies related to FDI.

The overall trend of FDI inflow in India since 1991 has gone up considerably. Now India has been ranked as one of most attractive destination of investment in the world[3].

### 2.1 Sector Wise Analysis of FDI in India

In recent years most of the FDI has come in the Service sector (22%), IT sector (9%) and in Telecommunication Sector (9%). Housing and Real sector also able to attract sizeable amount of FDI since 2000. On the other hand Construction activities got around 7% of the FDI money whereas Automobile sector and Metallurgical sector got 4% each of FDI. Also the Chemical and Petroleum sector got 2% each of the FDI amount (Figure 2). May be the government should try to attract investment in infrastructure and manufacturing industries for rapid economic growth.

*Figure 1. FDI inflows in India since 1991 (US$ Million)*
*Source: Based on the data available on the website of Ministry of Commerce, Government of India (Department of Industrial Policy and Promotion, Government of India, n.d.).*

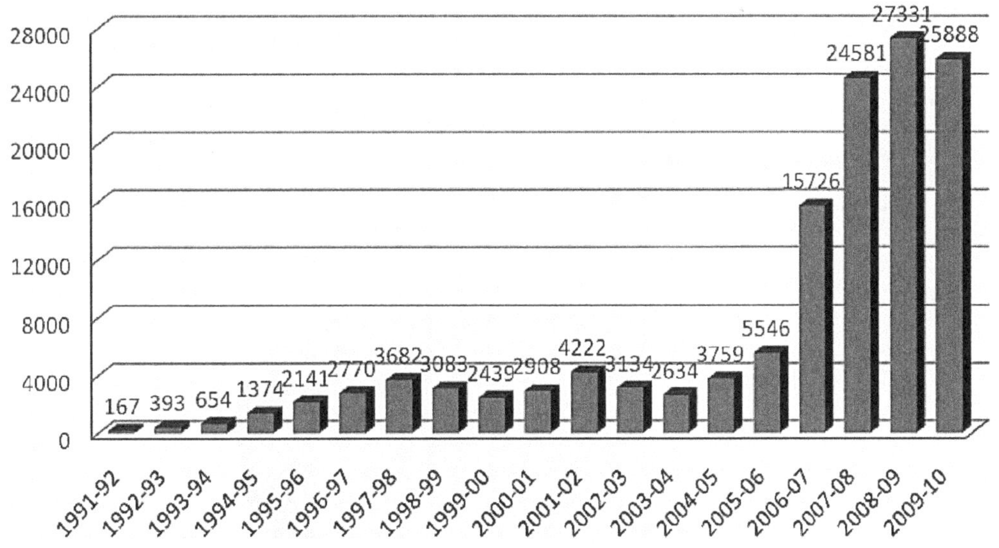


## 2.2 Country Wise Analysis of FDI

In India, about 43.5% of total inflow of FDI comes from Mauritius[4] whereas the share of Singapore and US is about 9% and 8% respectively in the period of 2000-09. Other important source of FDI inflows are UK, Netherlands, Cyprus, Japan, Germany, UAE and France (Table 1).

## 2.3 Regional Imbalances in India

In India huge variation can be found across states and territories in regard to physical geography, culture, and economic conditions. Some states have achieved rapid economic growth in recent years, while others are lagging behind. On the one hand there are states like Gujarat which recorded 11.79% growth for the period 2003-07 whereas state like Madhya Pradesh has grown by just 3% in last 8 years. Some smaller states has also shown robust growth in last eight years but one reason could be the relatively smaller size of their economy e.g. the growth rate of Maharashtra was 5.98% in the period 2000-08 that includes Mumbai, is not bad considering the size of the state domestic product of Maharashtra (Table 2). In 1960s and 70s, Punjab and Haryana made rapid economic progress as Green Revolution basically confined to these two states and some other pockets of India. This led to uneven growth in various parts of country. Then in recent years Southern India and Western part of India has made rapid stride in economic development. The famous IT revolution started in Bangalore and then later spread to other neighboring states like Tamil Nadu and Andhra Pradesh. Later, it does spread to other parts of India like Delhi NCR, Kolkata and Mumbai. But it does not spread to other regions of India. Similarly, industrial development is basically confined in Gujarat, Maharashtra and some southern states like Tamil Nadu and Karnataka. At the time when Indian economy in move some states lagged behind especially states from North and Central India and also the eastern part of India.

*Figure 2. Sector wise FDI inflows in percentage (April 2000- December 2009)*
*Source: Based on FDI fact sheet, December 2009 (Department of Industrial Policy and Promotion, Government of India, n.d.).*

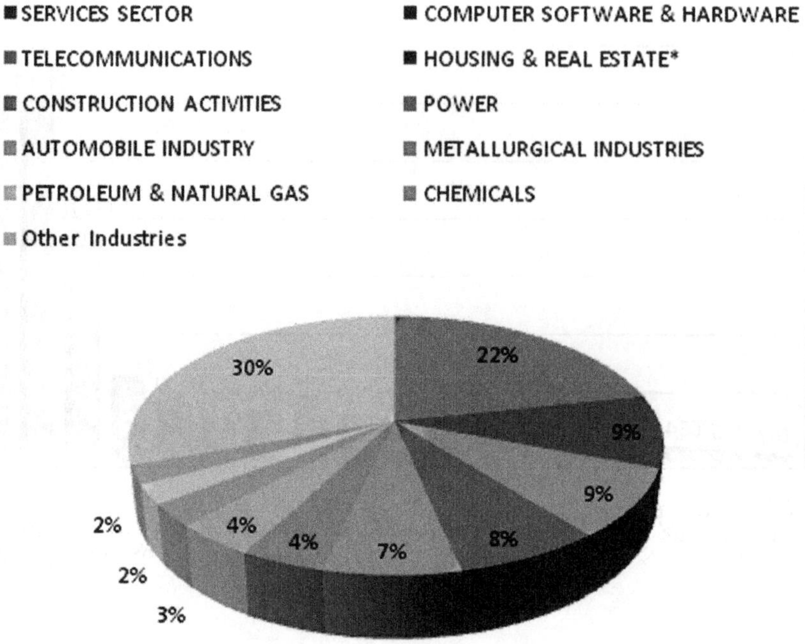


*Table 1. Major Source Countries of FDI in India (2000-09)*

| S.No. | Country | (In Rs) | (In US$) | %age to total FDI Inflows |
|---|---|---|---|---|
| 1 | Mauritius | 2,041,964.02 | 45,777.80 | 43.5 |
| 2 | Singapore | 420,400.38 | 9,517.84 | 8.96 |
| 3 | U.S.A. | 355,362.90 | 7,918.67 | 7.57 |
| 4 | U.K. | 247,455.61 | 5,610.67 | 5.27 |
| 5 | The Netherlands | 195,387.90 | 4,359.15 | 4.16 |
| 6 | Cyprus | 164,682.91 | 3,612.57 | 3.51 |
| 7 | Japan | 164,213.69 | 3,611.29 | 3.5 |
| 8 | Germany | 120,690.40 | 2,711.89 | 2.57 |
| 9 | U.A.E. | 68,296.94 | 1,507.18 | 1.46 |
| 10 | France | 66,393.89 | 1,469.31 | 1.41 |

Source:FDI fact sheet, December 2009 (Department of Industrial Policy and Promotion, Government of India, n.d.).

*Table 2. Growth rate of GSDP % (constant prices) as per the State/UT from 1997-98 to 2008-09 (as on 12-11-09)*

| Sl. No. | States | 1997-98 | 1998-99 | 1999-00 | 2000-01 | 2001-02 | 2002-03 | 2003-04 | 2004-05 | 2005-06 | 2006-07 | 2007-08 | Average Growth Rate 2003-04 to 2007-08 |
|---|---|---|---|---|---|---|---|---|---|---|---|---|---|
| 1 | Andhra Pradesh | -1.37 | 12.16 | 4.58 | 8.16 | 4.22 | 2.73 | 9.35 | 8.15 | 10.24 | 11.16 | 10.62 | 9.9 |
| 2 | Arunachal Pradesh | 3.12 | 3.13 | 4.01 | 7.07 | 15.7 | -4.31 | 10.94 | 16.46 | -4.86 | 12.69 | 3.74 | 7.79 |
| 3 | Assam | 0.99 | -0.22 | 3.18 | 2.53 | 2.6 | 7.07 | 7.07 | 3.74 | 4.94 | 6.97 | 6.06 | 5.55 |
| 4 | Bihar | -3.85 | 7.59 | 3.68 | 16.04 | -4.73 | 11.82 | -5.15 | 12.17 | 1.49 | 22 | 8.04 | 7.71 |
| 5 | Chhattisgarh | 3.11 | 5.34 | 0.24 | -5.17 | 13.2 | -0.06 | 16.55 | 5.49 | 6.94 | 7.99 | 8.63 | 9.12 |
| 6 | Goa | 2.82 | 22.61 | 2.11 | -3.74 | 4.5 | 7.08 | 7.49 | 10.19 | 11.33 | 10.37 | 11.14 | 10.1 |
| 7 | Gujarat | 2.11 | 7.18 | 1.02 | -4.89 | 8.41 | 8.14 | 14.77 | 8.88 | 13.44 | 9.09 | 12.79 | 11.79 |
| 8 | Haryana | 1.43 | 5.56 | 7.65 | 8.06 | 7.73 | 6.59 | 10.13 | 8.64 | 9.37 | 14.2 | 9.35 | 10.34 |
| 9 | Himachal Pradesh | 6.38 | 7.21 | 6.61 | 6.32 | 5.21 | 5.06 | 8.08 | 7.56 | 8.54 | 9.2 | 8.59 | 8.39 |
| 10 | Jammu & Kashmir | 5.66 | 5.19 | 4.48 | 3.53 | 1.96 | 5.13 | 5.17 | 5.23 | 6.17 | 6.25 | 6.28 | 5.82 |
| 11 | Jharkhand | 26.3 | 5.71 | -2.75 | -9.85 | 6.79 | 2.54 | 8.03 | 15.21 | 2.79 | 12.53 | 6.18 | 8.95 |
| 12 | Karnataka | 6.91 | 12.72 | 5.33 | 1.42 | 2.8 | 4.55 | 3.46 | 9.85 | 13.53 | 7.33 | 12.92 | 9.42 |
| 13 | Kerala | 2.89 | 7.06 | 7.54 | 3.53 | 5.17 | 7.3 | 6.25 | 9.97 | 9.17 | 11.1 | 10.42 | 9.38 |
| 14 | Madhya Pradesh | 5 | 6.56 | 10.5 | -6.93 | 7.12 | -3.91 | 11.42 | 3.08 | 6.48 | 4.75 | 5.25 | 6.2 |
| 15 | Maharashtra | 5.56 | 3.36 | 9.74 | -2.1 | 4.05 | 6.81 | 8 | 8.71 | 9.67 | 9.82 | 9.18 | 9.08 |
| 16 | Manipur | 8.77 | 2.16 | 12 | -6.35 | 6.81 | -0.46 | 10.84 | 9.7 | 3.95 | 5.24 | 3.38 | 6.62 |
| 17 | Meghalaya | 6.13 | 9.87 | 7.79 | 5.45 | 6.89 | 3.79 | 6.78 | 7.11 | 6.08 | 5.34 | 5.2 | 6.1 |
| 18 | Mizoram | NA | NA | NA | 4.97 | 6.52 | 10.39 | 3.19 | 4.15 | 2.38 | 5.51 | 5.54 | 4.15 |
| 19 | Nagaland | 7.82 | -4.01 | 0.8 | 18.46 | 9.98 | 8.22 | 10.16 | 6.65 | 5.22 | NA | NA | 7.34 |
| 20 | Orissa | 13.14 | 2.45 | 5.17 | -1.14 | 6.25 | -0.06 | 14.71 | 12.61 | 6.37 | 12.12 | 5.85 | 10.33 |
| 21 | Punjab | 3 | 5.59 | 5.63 | 3.93 | 1.92 | 2.85 | 6.07 | 4.95 | 4.5 | 7.32 | 6.54 | 5.88 |
| 22 | Rajasthan | 11.32 | 4.02 | 2.11 | -2.01 | 10.87 | -9.9 | 28.67 | -1.85 | 6.89 | 11.81 | 7.33 | 10.57 |
| 23 | Sikkim | 7.14 | 7.06 | 3.48 | 7.59 | 7.88 | 7.31 | 7.89 | 7.72 | 8.94 | 7.15 | 7.4 | 7.82 |
| 24 | Tamil Nadu | 8.2 | 4.73 | 6.11 | 5.87 | -1.56 | 1.75 | 5.99 | 11.45 | 11.89 | 11.29 | 4.41 | 9.01 |
| 25 | Tripura | 10.27 | 9.91 | 7.11 | 5.88 | 14.07 | 6.41 | 5.88 | 8.14 | 9.09 | 8.43 | NA | 7.89 |
| 26 | Uttar Pradesh | -0.09 | 2.75 | 5.49 | 2.19 | 2.17 | 3.72 | 5.27 | 5.4 | 5.25 | 7.18 | 7.16 | 6.05 |
| 27 | Uttarakhand | 1.8 | 1.66 | 0.82 | 12.04 | 5.53 | 9.92 | 7.61 | 12.99 | 6.42 | 10.4 | NA | 9.36 |
| 28 | West Bengal | 8.25 | 6.36 | 6.88 | 3.84 | 7.32 | 3.78 | 6.2 | 6.89 | 5.72 | 8.77 | 7.74 | 7.06 |
| 29 | All India | NA | NA | NA | 4.35 | 5.81 | 3.84 | 8.52 | 7.47 | 9.52 | 9.75 | 9.01 | 8.85 |

Source: Central Statistical Organization (CSO), 2009

## 2.4 FDI Inflows and Regional Imbalances

Though it is true that there are many factors responsible for the economic growth but investment is one of the most important determinants for growth. Now the states that have been able to attract maximum FDI are the one those who are showing good economic growth rate since last few years. There seems to be a correlation between economic growth and inflow of FDI in that region[5]. If we analyze the total amount of inflow of FDI we will find that maximum amount of FDI has gone to Mumbai region that includes Maharashtra and some other smaller Union Territories. The total inflow of FDI is about US$ 35000 million (3-5% of total inflow) share since January 2000 till August 2009. Similarly the other region where the FDI inflows are large compare to other region is Delhi region that includes part of Haryana and Uttar Pradesh. This region is also known as Delhi-NCR region. The total inflow was around US$ 18000 million (19% of total inflow). The third region that able to attract about 6% of total inflow of FDI since the year 2000, are Karnataka and Gujarat region respectively. Likewise, Tamil Nadu, Andhra Pradesh and West Bengal region attracted about 5%, 4% and 1% of the total inflow of FDI since the year 2000 till 2009. Rest of the regions has less than 1% share in the total inflow of FDI (Table 3, page 17). Regions like Uttar Pradesh, Uttaranchal, Bihar, Jharkhand, Madhya Pradesh, Assam and other North Eastern states have got negligible share in the FDI inflows. Consequently most of them have shown less economic growth compare to the states that got more share of FDI inflows[6]. Therefore we can deduce that there is positive relation between FDI inflow and economic growth of the states. These FDI flows have fuelled the economic growth of these states further and thereby increases the gap between rich and poor states. The states that are relatively poor were not been able to attract sufficient FDI.

## 2.5 FDI and Foreign Technology Cases (FTC) Approved (1991-2007)

The other set of information which also indicate to the FDI flow and regional imbalances is the information about approved proposal of FDI and Foreign Technology Cases (FTC) in India since 1991. Naturally if a state is getting more technology transfer based investment, it will help in industrialization and ultimately increases the economic growth of the state. The bulk of it has gone to Maharashtra (20%), Delhi (12%), Tamil Nadu and Karnataka (9%) respectively, whereas states like Andhra Pradesh and Gujarat were able to attract around 5% and 4% respectively. Similarly, states like Madhya Pradesh, Orissa and West Bengal has 3% of the total share of FDI and FTC approved (Figure 3). This data also indicates that FDI has flown to the states who were relatively progressive and become more progressive with the help of FDI they received subsequently (Table 3). This statistics is important because it establishes the data about the FDI linked technological transfer and that eventually helps these states became more prosperous with time.

## 2.6 Plant Location and FDI

A study was conducted by National Council of Applied Economic Research (NCAER) in 2009 on FDI and its growth linkages[7]. One of the objectives of this study was to take stock of the spatial spread of the FDI-enabled production facilities in India during the past five years (2001 to 2006). The production facilities to be studied include manufacturing plants as well as service providing facilities, located in cities other than metros and Class- 1 cities[8], and in rural areas, in particular. Under this study 401 FDI-enabled manufacturing firms with total 1273 plants was studied. These plants were spread over

*Table 3. Regionwise FDI inflows (2000-09)*

| Sl. No. | Regional Offices of RBI | States Covered | 2000-2005 (Jan-Dec) | 2006 (Jan-Dec) | 2007 (Jan-Dec) | 2008 (Jan-Dec) | 2009 (Jan-Aug.) | Cumulative Total (from Jan. 2000 to August 2009) | | |
|---|---|---|---|---|---|---|---|---|---|---|
| | | | Rs | Rs | Rs | Rs | Rs | Rs | US$ | % Share)* |
| 1 | Mumbai | Maharashtra, Dadra & Nagar Haveli, Daman & Diu | 179,787.56 | 159,073.24 | 185,171.54 | 628,425.75 | 420,724.18 | 1,573,182.27 | 35,450.31 | 35.85 |
| 2 | New Delhi | Delhi, Part of UP and Haryana | 220,760.85 | 97,848.07 | 138,569.78 | 93,542.60 | 266,959.53 | 817,680.85 | 18,185.55 | 18.39 |
| 3 | Bangalore | Karnataka | 64,561.25 | 28,192.09 | 49,632.24 | 96,529.63 | 37,176.95 | 276,092.15 | 6,273.18 | 6.34 |
| 4 | Ahmedabad | Gujarat | 27,932.33 | 16,387.57 | 11,833.93 | 173,302.78 | 35,550.31 | 265,006.92 | 6,033.75 | 6.10 |
| 5 | Chennai | Tamil Nadu, Pondicherry | 52,030.97 | 51,925.27 | 28,918.82 | 58,155.86 | 37,753.49 | 228,784.41 | 5,103.03 | 5.16 |
| 6 | Hyderabad | Andhra Pradesh | 27,373.26 | 25,174.72 | 31,846.67 | 62,029.81 | 33,950.89 | 180,375.34 | 4,103.35 | 4.15 |
| 7 | Kolkata | West Bengal, Sikkim, Andaman & Nicobar Islands | 12,438.81 | 2,882.89 | 16,192.16 | 21,508.30 | 1,823.61 | 54,845.77 | 1,293.38 | 1.31 |
| 8 | Jaipur | Rajasthan | 177.92 | 2,308.53 | 776.76 | 16,808.76 | 1,748.74 | 21,820.71 | 461.24 | 0.47 |
| 9 | Panaji | Goa | 4,843.72 | 3,508.82 | 363.8 | 2,497.31 | 6,769.38 | 17,983.03 | 389.84 | 0.39 |
| 10 | Chandigarh` | Chandigarh, Punjab, Haryana, Himachal Pradesh | 14,775.90 | 848.63 | 1,922.65 | 0 | 0 | 17,547.18 | 384.22 | 0.39 |
| 11 | Kochi | Kerala, Lakshadweep | 2,989.94 | 944.49 | 1,027.81 | 3,516.57 | 3,319.00 | 11,797.81 | 264.69 | 0.27 |
| 12 | Bhopal | Madhya Pradesh, Chattisgarh | 1,633.68 | 749.42 | 2,045.52 | 1,226.11 | 1,666.49 | 7,321.21 | 163.11 | 0.16 |
| 13 | Bhubaneshwar | Orissa | 2,616.64 | 1,035.94 | 302.63 | 0 | 2,130.53 | 6,085.74 | 132.57 | 0.13 |
| 14 | Guwahati | Assam, Arunachal Pradesh, Manipur, Meghalaya, Mizoram, Nagaland, Tripura | 417.43 | 0 | 110 | 1,764.66 | 87.96 | 2,380.05 | 55.11 | 0.06 |
| 15 | Kanpur | Uttar Pradesh, Uttranchal | 0.3 | 556.15 | 160.17 | 0 | 1,294.96 | 2,011.58 | 43.45 | 0.04 |
| 16 | Patna | Bihar, Jharkhand | 27.35 | 6 | 0 | 0 | 0 | 33.35 | 0.75 | 0.00 |
| 17 | Region not indicated | Region not indicated | 244,368.63 | 112,130.85 | 186,075.38 | 237,946.61 | 124,595.15 | 905,116.62 | 20,543.68 | 20.78 |
| Sub. Total | 856,736.55 | 503,572.68 | 654,949.86 | 1,397,254.74 | 975,551.16 | 4,388,068.96 | 98,881.31 | 4,388,064.99 | 98,881.21 | 100 |

**Source: SIA Newsletters and RBI data base**

*Figure 3. State wise FDI and Foreign Technology Cases (FTC) Approved (1991- 2007)*
*Source: Based on Secretariat for Industrial Assistance (SIA) Newsletters (various editions), Ministry of Commerce & Industry, Government of India*

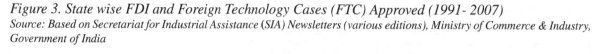

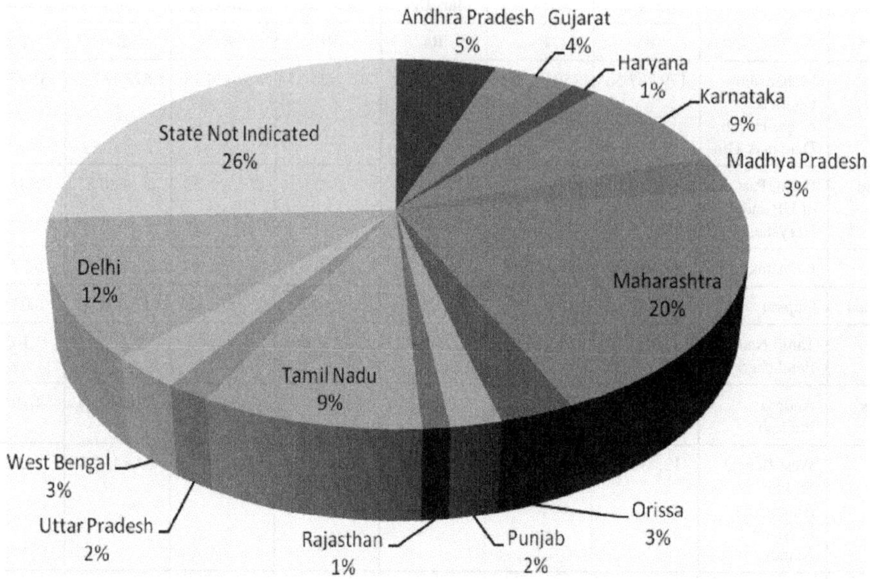


294 cities in India. 84% of these 294 cities comes under the Class-3 category. Other than FDI enabled - manufacturing firms, 100 FDI-enabled service firms are also analyzed. These 100 service firms has 1257 service facilities spread over 369 cities and 84% of these cities were Class-3. Major findings[9] of the study are as follows (Map-2):

- 54% of 1,273 plants located in Class-3 cities
- 20% manufacturing plants in Maharashtra; 11% in Gujarat; 10% in Tamil Nadu; 9% in Karnataka; and 7% in West Bengal
- The state-wise share of Class-3 cities in all cities having FDI-enabled manufacturing plants: 90% in Gujarat; 87%in Andhra Pradesh; 85% in Tamil Nadu; 82% in Karnataka; 67% in Maharashtra
- 35% of 1,257 FDI- enabled service firms' facilities are located in Class-3 cities
- 20% service facilities in Andhra Pradesh; 18% in Karnataka; 17% in Maharashtra; 12% in Tamil Nadu
- The state-wise share of FDI-enabled service facilities located in Class-3 cities: 61% in Andhra Pradesh; 43% in Karnataka; 18% in Tamil Nadu; and 3% in Maharashtra

On the basis of the above findings of the study, we can conclude that FDI-enabled plants are spread across various states with relatively high concentration in Maharashtra, Gujarat, Tamil Nadu, Karnataka and West Bengal. A significant proportion (54%) of manufacturing plants is located in Class-3 cities. FDI-enabled service facilities have relatively high concentration in Andhra Pradesh, Karnataka, Maharashtra, and Tamil Nadu (Map-1, page 20). It means that this survey also supports our assumption that FDI may be one of the reasons that led to regional imbalances. As we can observe from the findings, majority of FDI enabled industries in manufacturing and services are located in states that had the better economic performance in comparison to other states.

*Table 4. State-wise Number of Approvals and Amount Approved of Foreign Direct Investment (FDI) and Foreign Technical Collaboration (FCI) in India(August 1991 to December 2007) (Amount in Rs. Million and US$)*

| States/UTs | No. of Approvals | | | Amount of Foreign Direct Investment Approved | | %age to Total FDI Approved |
|---|---|---|---|---|---|---|
| | Total | Technical | Financial | (In Rs.) | (In US$) | |
| Andhra Pradesh | 1360 | 280 | 1080 | 160677.42 | 4105.73 | 5.33 |
| Assam | 28 | 21 | 7 | 374.03 | 9.27 | 0.01 |
| Bihar | 50 | 23 | 27 | 7397.05 | 180.18 | 0.25 |
| Gujarat | 1304 | 608 | 696 | 130334.46 | 3408.53 | 4.33 |
| Haryana | 940 | 356 | 584 | 40941.3 | 1072.86 | 1.36 |
| Himachal Pradesh | 108 | 64 | 44 | 12356.45 | 311.5 | 0.41 |
| Jammu & Kashmir | 6 | 3 | 3 | 84.1 | 2.42 | 0 |
| Karnataka | 2741 | 516 | 2225 | 249339.92 | 6139.71 | 8.28 |
| Kerala | 350 | 75 | 275 | 18590.04 | 464.25 | 0.62 |
| Madhya Pradesh | 252 | 78 | 174 | 92774.05 | 2522.28 | 3.08 |
| Maharashtra | 5388 | 1371 | 4017 | 581528.5 | 14457.69 | 19.3 |
| Manipur | 2 | 0 | 2 | 31.85 | 0.89 | 0 |
| Meghalaya | 5 | 0 | 5 | 529.6 | 13.66 | 0.02 |
| Nagaland | 2 | 1 | 1 | 36.8 | 1.03 | 0 |
| Orissa | 161 | 67 | 94 | 84283 | 2399.01 | 2.8 |
| Punjab | 225 | 74 | 151 | 57405.04 | 1426.4 | 1.91 |
| Rajasthan | 357 | 109 | 248 | 31297.81 | 837.7 | 1.04 |
| Tamil Nadu | 2826 | 660 | 2166 | 252140.26 | 6496.68 | 8.37 |
| Tripura | 4 | 1 | 3 | 30.88 | 0.74 | 0 |
| Uttar Pradesh | 842 | 288 | 554 | 49353.16 | 1330.39 | 1.64 |
| West Bengal | 723 | 211 | 512 | 81546.72 | 2248.63 | 2.71 |
| Chhattisgarh | 51 | 31 | 20 | 24829.33 | 597.79 | 0.82 |
| Jharkhand | 84 | 57 | 27 | 1465.15 | 42.67 | 0.05 |
| Uttaranchal | 57 | 26 | 31 | 1542.75 | 45.15 | 0.05 |
| Andaman & Nicobar | 8 | 0 | 8 | 137.87 | 3.56 | 0 |
| Arunachal Pradesh | 2 | 0 | 2 | 110.6 | 3.52 | 0 |
| Chandigarh | 86 | 12 | 74 | 3241.7 | 80.34 | 0.11 |
| Dadra & Nagar Haveli | 72 | 48 | 24 | 1239.8 | 35.93 | 0.04 |
| Delhi | 2999 | 315 | 2684 | 352804.55 | 9505.5 | 11.71 |
| Goa | 293 | 70 | 223 | 10388.41 | 260.99 | 0.34 |
| Lakshadweep | 1 | 0 | 1 | 5 | 0.19 | 0 |
| Mizoram | 1 | 0 | 1 | 15.22 | 0.35 | 0 |
| Pondicherry | 132 | 42 | 90 | 12912.03 | 314.86 | 0.43 |
| Daman & Diu | 45 | 15 | 30 | 608.94 | 15.15 | 0.02 |
| State Not Indicated | 6206 | 2519 | 3687 | 751984.78 | 20613.05 | 24.96 |
| India | 27711 | 7941 | 19770 | 3012338.56 | 78948.6 | 100 |

Source: SIA Newsletters Various Editions, Ministry of Commerce and Industry, Government of India

## 3. CONCLUSION

In the present chapter an attempt has been made to establish the relationship between FDI inflows to various states and their economic progress. The underlying assumption is that FDI inflows lead to economic growth but at the same time it also increases the regional imbalances. After 1991 economic reforms policies, Indian economy has witnessed a surge in FDI inflows. But the majority of this flow is confined to select few states and regions. As we compare the regions in India that has shown relatively better performance and then match the same with places where the FDI flow is more, we realized by and large that they are the same states or regions. This biasedness is created because of the FDI flow that has increased the gap of industrial production between the different states and regions of India. In between 1960s to 1970s, it was Green revolution that created the regional imbalances even though the overall food production went up in India. Now perhaps it seems that FDI can also be accused of repeating the same error as it is increasing the overall economic growth of the country but also increasing the gap between different regions because of the difference in their economic prosperity.

*Figure 4. Spatial Spread of FDI-enabled Manufacturing Plants*
*Source: NCAER study on FDI and its linkages, 2009*

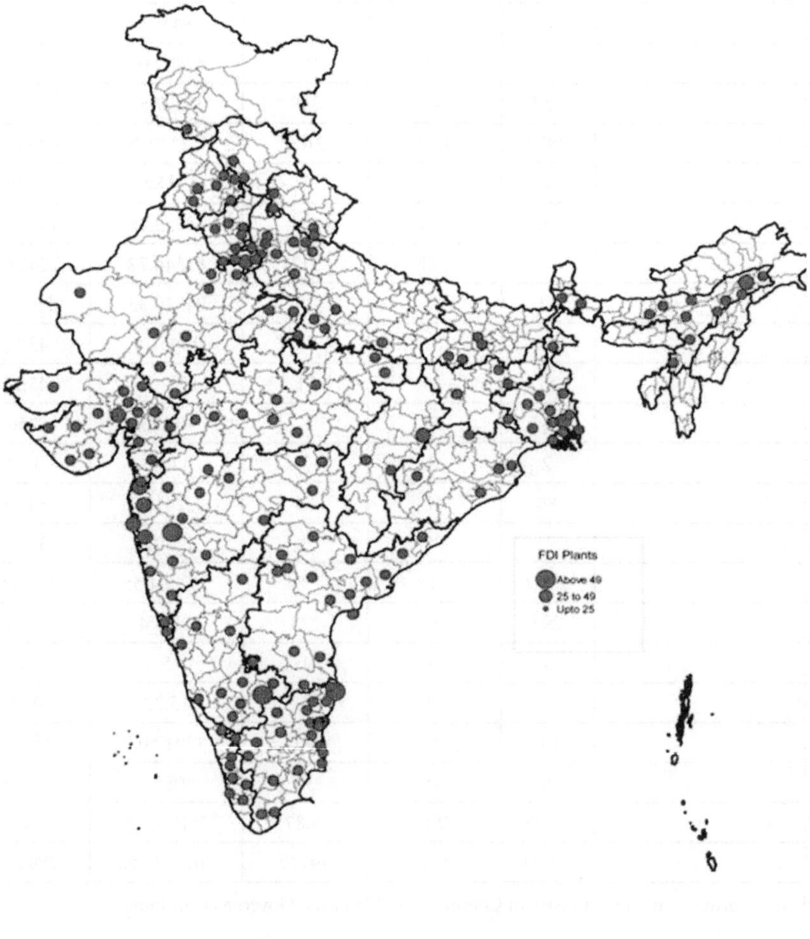

*Figure 5. Spatial Spread of FDI-enabled Service Facilities in India*
*Source: NCAER study on FDI and its linkages, 2009*

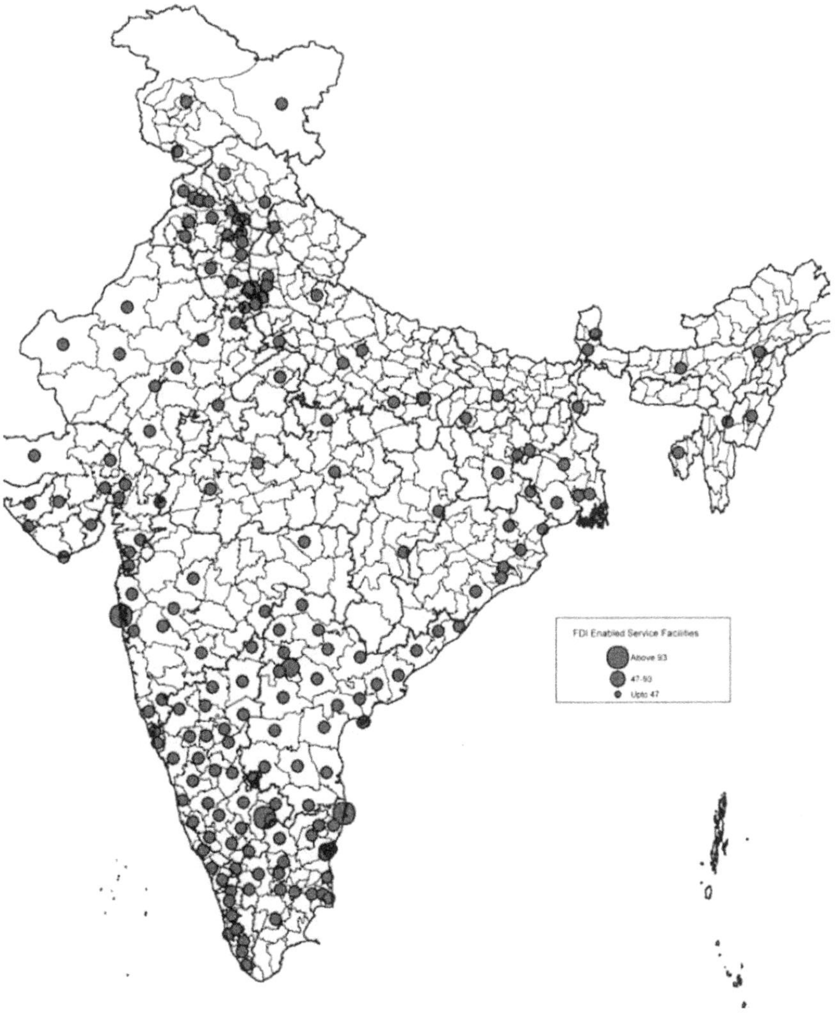


Accordingly, the Centre as well as various State governments needs to take step to correct the present situation. The Central government through its policies can motivate the institutional foreign investors for the FDI to those states which are relatively backwards. This could be done by giving tax incentives, subsidies and by providing them better infrastructure facilities etc. But the onus is more on the respective state governments as they need to understand the importance of FDI in the overall growth process. They can set-up special cell to promote their state to the prospect investors. Here one could take the example of states like Gujarat and Karnataka. They, on annual basis call the investor meet at a grand level and inform the probable investor about their state and the various advantage which their states offer in comparison to other states in India. The states need to identify the areas in which they have comparative advantage. They need to highlight those sectors to the foreign investors. The other important step could be to understand the factors that brings FDI in a particular location e.g. law and order situation in the state, the quality of infrastructure, availability of raw material, the quality of workforce, tax laws etc.

It is high time that the Centre and the respective State government take note of this growing disparity and try to reduce the gap between the states.

If we take the case of China, they have enjoyed unprecedented high economic growth for last three decades. There are many studies that suggest that regional growth in China has however been unbalanced and has led to some serious consequences which Chinese policy makers are now trying to rectify. There are issues of stability of the Chinese society and also the sustainability of current high economic growth in the country.

The above argument also opens doors for researchers and academicians whether the states in India are really ready to offer the host advantages to the investing organizations by remaining sustainable and also at the same time be on the path of moderate economic growth. This also means that there should be politically stable government whose commitment to the development of state can be transmitted to the investors over a period of time. States like Haryana in last 10 years was successful in bringing FDI because it saw political stability. States like Jharkhand, Chhattisgarh and West Bengal have abundant resources and there is a necessity for the inflow of FDI to develop and to prosper. The state governments have also reflected their commitment but somehow they were not very successful in attracting FDI because of poor infrastructure, tribal unrest and other movements.

We have a very stable and democratic central government in India for the last 15 years, thanks to the mandate given by the people of India through their electoral process. It seems that the policy makers want to create a difference in the way things were conducted and will be conducted. Many historic agreements, be it nuclear proliferation treaty with US or progress in WTO round of talks safeguarding the interest of Asia at large, issue of security council permanent membership, new trade negotiations with China, Russia and US were by and large successful. The inflow of FDI in last 10 years have tripled and with time a lot more FDI will be seen in Indian states with decreased regional disparity.

## REFERENCES

Adelman, I., & Chenery, H. (1966). Foreign Aid & Economic Development: The Case of Greece. *The Review of Economics and Statistics*, *48*(1), 1–19. doi:10.2307/1924853

Balasubramanyam, V. N. (2003). *Foreign Direct Investment in India*. Lancaster University Management School, Working Paper, 2003/001

Central Statistical Organization (CSO). (n.d.). *Database*. Retrieved from http://www.cso.ie/en/databases/index.html

*Centre for Monitoring Indian Economy*. (n.d.). Retrieved from www.cmie.com

*Department of Industrial Policy and Promotion, Government of India*. (n.d.). Retrieved June 28, 2010, from www.dipp.ac.in

Kumar, N. (1994). *Multinational Enterprises & Industrial Organization: The Case of India*. New Delhi, India: Sage Publications.

Ministry of Commerce & Industry, Government of India. (n.d.). *SIA Newsletters*. Retrieved from http://www.sia-web.org/publications/sia-newsletter/

National Council of Applied Economic Research (NCAER). (2009). *FDI in India & its Growth linkages. Sponsored by Department of Industrial Policy & Promotion, Ministry of Commerce & Industry.* Government of India.

Neuhaus, M. (2006). The Impact of FDI on Economic Growth- An Analysis for the Transition Countries of Central & Eastern Europe. Physica-Verlag, Springer Co ltd.

## KEY TERMS AND DEFINITIONS

**DIPP:** Department of Industrial Policy & Promotion responsible for formulation of FDI Policy and promotion, approval and facilitation of FDI.

**Economic growth:** Economic growth refers to the increase in GDP over a period of time.

**FDI Inflows:** FDI inflows refer inward FDI which a country receives in a financial year.

**Post liberalization:** It refers to the post 1991 time period when India adopted the policy of economic reforms.

**Regional Imbalances:** Regional imbalances here refers to the region wise unequal growth in India.

## ENDNOTES

1. When a group of businessmen in New York asked Prime Minister Nehru about the Indian Government's policy towards foreign investment, he is reported to have looked out of the window and commented on the weather. This shows his disregard towards the foreign capital (Balasubramanyam and Mahambare 2002).
2. There are three main components of FDI as per the BoPM, 5th edition. They are namely (1) Equity capital, (2) Reinvested earnings and (3) Other capital. But in India, prior to 2002, FDI includes only the Equity Capital component out of the above three elements.
3. According to a survey done by A.T. Kearney Incorporationin 2009.
4. Probably it is because India has double tax avoidance treaty with Mauritius. Therefore if a foreign investor wants to invest in India, he can get it routed through Mauritius to take advantage of Tax benefit.
5. State wise data for FDI inflow is not available easily and even if it s available it is not up to date. That is why the FDI data provided by RBI on its regional office basis is used as Proxy for States as this data is comprehensive and up to date.
6. States like Uttrakhand may have shown good economic growth rate but one must remember that it could be because it is relatively small state and the base size of the economy is also small and these small states also gets special economic package from the Central Government.
7. This study titled "FDI in India and its Growth Linkages" commissioned by the Department of Industrial Policy and Promotion (DIPP), Ministry ofCommerce and Industry, Government of India to NCAER.

[8] Cities across various states classified into three classes of cities based on their population size, viz., Class-1, Class-2 and Class-3 cities. Class-1 cities are towns with a population of 1,000,000 (one million) and above, Class-2 cities are towns with apopulation between 5,00,000 and 1,000,000, and Class-3 cities are towns with a population of less than 5,00,000. The purpose of this classification is to locate the movement and final plant location of FDI firms.

[9] Only those findings that are relevant for the present paper has been discussed here.

# Chapter 2
# Role of Knowledge Workers in Business Process and Innovation

**Appasaheb Naikal**
*S P Jain School of Global Management, Singapore*

**Mayank Bapna**
*PT Prizer Primindo 19G, Indonesia*

## ABSTRACT

*Highly skilled knowledge workers are the main driving force for innovation; however, their innovation may not always ensure the achievement of business goals. Only the alignment of the innovation with business goals can transform their innovation into individual performance. Similarly variation in individual capabilities of knowledge workers may not lead to final business goals. This paper focuses on knowledge workers, their performance, the business processes followed and effectiveness of the business processes to enhance productivity of the organizations.*

## 1. INTRODUCTION

Today's economy is defined as the knowledge-based economy. Peter Drucker has aptly said that "To make knowledge work productive would be the greatest work of the century, just to make the manual task productive was the great management task of the last century (Peter Drucker, 1969).

Even during the primordial stage of the 'industrial age, the corporate managements had clear goals "work must be carried out with due care and accuracy to achieve high quality of product". In order to safeguard the reputation of a company it is necessary to consistently produce high quality of products within the time-to market constraints. Consequently, to achieve this, the day-to-day goals of the employees must be streamlined with the business goals and employees are expected to deliver allocated work within the deadlines.

DOI: 10.4018/978-1-4666-8259-7.ch002

With the ever increasing complexity of the products, managements started following a set of processes to be carried out in the organizations. But the processes carried out at the beginning of the industrial age and those carried out in the late 20th century changed dimensions of business world. The companies are rooted in the same values even today, though the working conditions have changed. As the economy all over the world became knowledge centric, the complexity of tasks started growing. Thus tapping the ideas and innovations in employees and employing it to productive use such that they are aligned with the business goals became a very tedious task for organizations.

To carry out this knowledge work effectively, an expert or skilled staff is necessary. People possessing these qualities, which help them to make better decisions, and thus help the businesses to prosper, are called knowledge workers. Knowledge workers have thus gained a significant importance in helping the organizations to achieve high levels of productivity and hence attain a distinguished status in the world-markets. The businesses cannot become successful only by employing knowledge workers. There has to be a set of processes that would help govern the organization effectively. Business processes are incorporated in the organizations to determine the business goals, derive the individual goals for everyone in the company, and achieve them (Davenport, 2005). A knowledge worker is anyone who works for a living at the tasks of developing or using knowledge. For example, a knowledge worker might be someone who works at any of the tasks of planning, acquiring, searching, analyzing, organizing, storing, programming, distributing, marketing, or otherwise contributing to the transformation and commerce of information and those who work at using the knowledge so produced. A term first used by Peter Drucker in his 1959 book, Landmarks of Tomorrow.

A knowledge worker is a person that adds value to an organization by processing existing information to create new information that could be used to define and solve problems. Some examples of knowledge workers include

- Lawyers
- Doctors
- Diplomats
- Law-makers
- Software developers
- Managers
- Bankers
- Chief Information Officers
- Knowledge Managers
- Librarians
- Content Managers
- Information Officers
- Knowledge Analysts

Knowledge workers are often the core of the organization. It can be their ideas, experiences, interpretations, and judgments that keep the company business and the economy and society – moving forward. They invent new products, develop new strategies, lead negotiations, and help keep the company ahead of the competitors.

Business Processes also demand aligning business goals with individuals and giving the knowledge workers a conducive environment, which will assist in enhancing their imagination and innovation, and in turn ensure high productivity and performance. The business processes designed should not depend on a single individual's performance. They should be designed such that irrespective of low performance from individual workers, the business goals are still met.

## 1.1 Research Question

What is the role of knowledge workers in business process and innovation?

To answer this research question, we draw on the business process and innovation perspective literature and integrate it with knowledge workers theory and practices in various industries. We propose a model for process adopted by companies supported by brief literature review.

## 1.2 Research Motivation

The Primary Research involves the collection of data that is not documented. Primary research will be conducted to:

- Understand the role of knowledge workers in business process and innovation.
- Identify various processes that are followed by companies in business process management.
- Make recommendations for designing a business process that helps to achieve business goals irrespective of individual performance of the knowledge workers.

# 2. WHAT IS A BUSINESS PROCESS?

Davenport & Short (1990) defined *business process* as "a set of logically related tasks performed to achieve a defined business outcome."

A process is "a structured, measured set of activities designed to produce a specified output for a particular customer or market. It implies a strong emphasis on how work is done within an organization, in contrast to products focus on what. A process is thus a specific ordering of work activities across time and place, with a beginning, an end, and clearly identified inputs and output: a structure for action." (Davenport 1993).

Born (1994) defines a process as: "A process consists of a sequence of steps which transforms information from initial state (input) to a final state (output). A key characteristic of a process is that it can be broken down into less complicated processes.

Various processes are followed by companies, depending on the nature of the work carried out. The general structure of Business Processes carried out by various companies is depicted below.

## 2.1 Literature Review

All organizations have business processes that produce and deliver end products to meet their customer's needs. These processes transform inputs into outputs by means of capital and labor resources (Anupindi, et al 2004). The business processes include several tasks of a company or organization as part of its workflow. Workflows, also known as process models, comprise individual tasks that assembled together and account for various aspects of an overall business process (Kim, et al. 2010). In today's highly competitive environment it's not possible to meet customers ever growing needs by individual departments; hence companies are forced to put forward collective efforts across interdependent departments. As a result, organizations have become a collection of business processes that must be modelled, managed and improved (McCormack & Johnson, 2001). To have effective processes in place clear understanding among interconnected departments is essential. Customer relationship management, enterprise resource planning, Six Sigma, and more recently business process management (BPM), for example, all utilize the concept of 'processes. In addition to transcending these initiatives 'process' can also be found in multiple sectors, and as key elements of performance improvement frameworks (e.g. European Foundation for Quality Management, EFQM)" (Smart & Maddern & Maull 2009). These literature reviews give us a clear indication that this BPM is customer and people centric. People play a key role in formulating and executing the processes in any business. Hence, Melao and Pidd (2000) said Business Process Management (BPM) refers to activities performed by organizations to design, implement, operate, manage, and improve their business processes by using a combination of models, methods, techniques, and tools. But nowadays most of the BPM is automated, thanks to advancement in information and communication technology (ICT). BPM uses information technology (IT) application to support or automate business processes fully or partially by providing computer-based systems support. These technology-based systems support and streamline business transactions, reduce operational costs, and promote real-time visibility in business performance. There is an enormous amount of academic literature available on how IT is playing a key role in streamlining BPM. But we found very little research on the role of knowledge workers in BPM (see Table 1). Hence in this paper, we attempt to briefly evaluate and explain the role of knowledge workers play in business process management. Based on the above literature review we present the BPM model adopted by most of the companies.

*Figure 1. Processes adopted by companies*

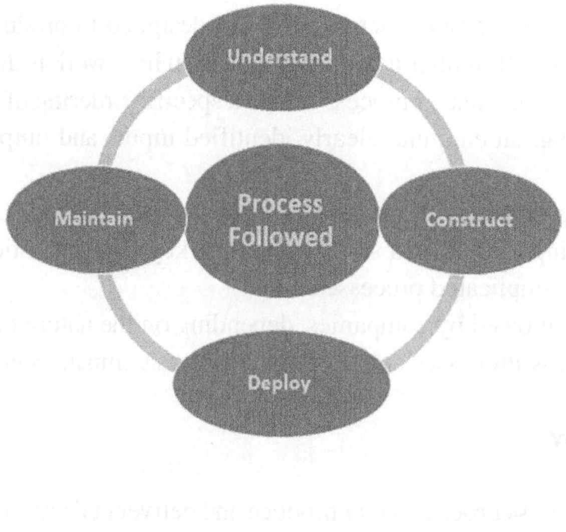

## 2.2 Business Process Model

### Understand

a) Develop Business Case by interacting with the client
b) Define the Project Scope
c) Assess the Risks
d) Provide Solution
e) Identify resources and skill sets required
f) Define a schedule plan with goals and deadlines
g) Identify the infrastructure requirements. For example, infrastructure requirements for IT companies would refer to hardware, software, communications link, LAN/WAN and security.

### Construct

a) Project Plan
b) Architecture and Design
c) Development
d) Regular Product Building
e) Regular automated product testing
f) Test results fix the bugs
g) Accept change requests and provide the respective changes in the delivery schedules

### Deploy

a) Set up 'user acceptance test' environment
b) Ask clients to carry out 'user acceptance tests '
c) Set up the deployment infrastructure with the required software
d) Run test cases in the deployment server to ensure integrity and performance of the final product
e) Deliver the required manuals
f) Train the clients and administrators on the product

### Maintain

a) Accept bugs and minor changes and provide the delivery date
b) Provide a 24-by-7 support for priority issues

Business Processes are highly complex, hence business process management is employed to check the correctness of these business processes.

BPM not only encompasses the discovery, design and deployment of business processes but also executive, administrative and supervisory control over them to ensure that they remain compliant with business objectives for the delight of customers (Smith and Fingar, 2002).

According to Steve Towers: "Business Process Management (BPM) is a natural and holistic management approach to operating business that produces a highly efficient, agile, innovative, and adaptive organization that far exceeds that achievable through traditional management approaches".

Business Process management comprises three major activities:

(1) Process Design
(2) Process Execution
(3) Process Monitoring

(1) **Process Design:** This process encompasses the design of new processes to be implemented, or capture of existing processes. The existing processes can be remodeled to enhance productivity. A large amount of emphasis is given on designing the processes correctly because it would eventually lead to better results, as the design stage logically affects a large number of parts in an integrated system. In this step the design is tested for its correctness of functionality.

(2) **Process Execution:** This process involves execution of complete business processes. Because of the complexity of business processes, they are fragmented into modules and then executed. With the help of patchwork, the modules can again be integrated.

(3) **Process Monitoring:** This process encompasses tracking of individual processes and hence the performance of each process can be monitored.

Initially business process management focused on business processes alone. Business Processes involves human interaction. Knowledge workers in the organizations carry out the business processes in conjunction with their personal goals and help the organizations to come up with innovative products, which help organizations to achieve new heights of success.

## 3. WHO ARE KNOWLEDGE WORKERS?

With the emerging knowledge economy, the management guru Peter Drucker coined the phrase knowledge workers. He said knowledge workers are those who know how to allocate knowledge to productive use.

Thomas has further said that: A knowledge worker is one who gathers data/information from any source; adds value to the information; and distributes value-added products to others. (Thomas and Kappes, 1993).

Although workers are involved in the work they carried out, knowledge workers are characterized by a higher degree of commitment, understanding, and responsibility for work. Thus knowledge workers are an asset for an organization (Drucker, 2007).

For example, an airplane mechanic is also a knowledge worker. The mechanic is the burdened with the task to ensure whether a plane is flight-worthy. He carries out testing and evaluation before the flight so that the necessary fixing can be done. Information about the history of the plane, what work has been done, what regular maintenance is due, what modifications need to be made are collected together in an integrated data system. All the necessary parts are made available and fixed before the plane comes to the hanger. Thus here the knowledge of the mechanic is of utmost importance. His judgments are based on his knowledge. It is the knowledge of the mechanic and collaborating with a team of people that makes this mechanic a knowledge worker (Megill, 2004).

To be a knowledge worker it is not sufficient to possess knowledge and use it on the job or simply mean working with data and information. A knowledge worker must be highly educated and possess expertise and skills in the particular domain of his work.

All the technical, managerial and professional workers are knowledge workers. They are information handlers or processors rather than people who genuinely add value to information to create new knowledge. Also, knowledge workers are not necessarily concentrated to the knowledge-based industry, but any job that involves decision making based on the knowledge and expertise in the best interest of their enterprise are knowledge workers (Allee, 1997).

A knowledge worker is a knowledge generator, who brings in inductive and deductive reasoning to look into complex problems. To comprehend, knowledge workers embody experience, innovation, creativity, and transformation of experience into knowledge for leveraging products and services (Davenport, 2005).

## 3.1 Knowledge Workers and Business Processes

With the shift of focus of the new age towards 'knowledge' and 'innovation' managers must consider better and efficient working methods. The work carried out today is called the knowledge work and the people who carry it out are called knowledge workers. Knowledge work requires an integrated environment that facilitates knowledge sharing rather than hoarding it (Andersen Consultant, 1998).

*Table 1. Key Research using the concept of "business process and knowledge workers"*

| Author | Methodology/Sample | Results Findings |
|---|---|---|
| Chandra & Thooyamani (2010) | Doctoral research work, the questionnaire and interview techniques were adopted for conducting the research | Research and analysis shows that technical knowledge in the field of working has been given the maximum importance and transcendental meditation has been given the minimum importance. |
| Bolis, Brunoro, & Sznelwar (2012) | Exploratory research | This paper clearly identifies the knowledge workers' contributions to success and suitability |
| Tempest (2009) | Qualitative research based on 32 interviews with managers and relevant third parties concerned with television production. | This paper highlights the learning implications, both positive and negative, arising from the understanding of the role of temporary workers in learning for innovation in network contexts. |
| Poell, Van, & Krogt (2003) | Critical examination of Nonaka and Takeuchi's theory about knowledge-creating companies through literature review and case study research | Authors partially disagree with Nonaka and Takeuchi's theory about knowledge-creating companies |
| David & Ann (2008) | Theoretical paper with literature review | This paper talks about how boosting the cognitive capability of individual knowledge workers can creates an atmosphere where individuals become knowledge creators and innovators. |
| Drucker (1999) | Theoretical paper. | This paper evaluates the role and responsibilities of knowledge workers in the 21st century. |

It is an accepted fact that creativity and productivity would lead an organization to the top of the success ladder. To achieve this acme employing a bunch of knowledge workers is not sufficient. Wisdom possessed by knowledge workers will be of no significant use if the organizations do not follow a definite set of rules to achieve productivity. Since knowledge workers are spread unevenly across the organizations, due to the complexity of their work they would need to collaborate effectively, with others in – different time zones, functions, physical locations, and even organizations (Cervera, 2012).

The 'Collaborative working' approach is proving to be a more efficient way of organizing industrial production (Allee, 1997).

## 3.2 Measurement of Performance of Knowledge Workers

Since most of the tasks carried out by knowledge workers are intangible, the tasks become immeasurable. Their performance evaluation becomes a tedious task. Since knowledge workers always feel the need to contribute more to the projects they are involved in, their managers must assign them projects that they personally feel interesting and are aligned with the organizations goals (Lewis, 2005).

Knowledge workers usually being told, the work that they should carry out and the steps, or the approach, or the process that they must follow during the accomplishment of the particular task. Typically in organizations that carry out highly complex jobs, the work is distributed among employees. Following this approach the knowledge work processes can be easily followed and measured. This process can also eliminate the redundant steps. But usually knowledge workers resist being told to follow the instructions. So their performance evaluation becomes very tedious (Davenport, 2005).

Performance management in the industrial age was a very simple task because the performance could easily be measured by evaluating the productivity of the workers. But in this knowledge centric industry, the work carried out by knowledge workers is intangible, so it is a complicated task to measure it. Knowledge could also be evaluated by the number of work hours. But the movement of work from offices to homes has eliminated this criterion for measurement as well. Measurement of knowledge work varies on the basis of industry, process and job. Knowledge workers can be evaluated on the following basis:

1) Measuring the volume knowledge produced.
2) Evaluating the quality of decision and the impact of the decision or the action taken on the basis of knowledge.
3) Evaluation can also be done by looking at the fact whether the given goal is achieved within the given time frame or deadline (Davenport, 2005).

Process orientation is one aspect that can be considered to improve knowledge workers' performance. Knowledge workers might benefit from the type of discipline and structure, while they can also remain free and their creativity won't be improvised (Davenport, 2005).

# 4. DISCUSSION

Highly competitive markets constantly demand new ideas and innovative products. Thus with the accelerated pace of innovations taking place over the past few years, the information in this sector of technology has proliferated. If this information is not percolated in a systematic way in knowledge workers' hierarchy, it can result in unclear goals and low gains.

Knowledge is embedded in knowledge workers and work teams. This knowledge is a source of value for organizations. Leveraging this knowledge is especially critical in organizations that rely on knowledge worker teams to deliver products and services, but the value of this knowledge often goes unrealized. Teams do not make full use of members' knowledge if members fail to integrate the unique expertise each member possesses (Nonaka and Takeuchi 1995).

Every team is a blend of workers having various capabilities. Autonomy in the work environment can lead knowledge workers with potential to innovate products and ideas that may not result in company gains. There is a need to consistently direct such employees so that their innovations can be productized. This innovation that helped the company to achieve its goals has increased individuals' performance. At the same time knowledge workers may seem to underperform. This may happen because of unclear goals, lack of pertinent information to carry out a job, and mismatch of the skill sets.

Creating a proper channel of information to knowledge workers to carry out a job is an important aspect. Hence business processes assist in channelizing such information and optimize the human resource capabilities.

Businesses strive to attain success in today's challenging business environment. The backbone that helps organizations to achieve success in this competitive world is the business processes. These business processes assume one more forms through business process reengineering, employment empowerment, total quality management and customer focus (Dutta S. and Manzoni J., 1999).

Business processes encompass two parts: business process improvement and business process design.

Business Process Design: This is the elementary step and the foundation for any organization to become successful. A business process is a description of tasks and outcomes associated with a business activity. The business process is often drawn, depicting tasks, roles, resources and actions to be taken according to the business needs.

Since business processes and knowledge work hand-in-hand, business processes can be segmented on the basis of knowledge activity involved in it. The knowledge work would differ on the basis of knowledge created, distributed, and applied.

## 4.1 Knowledge Creation

Knowledge creation is the most crucial task of process management. Knowledge creation can be completely unstructured, unmeasured, and repeatable. One common approach of knowledge creation processes is to break them up into pieces or stages. Then concentrating on each stage, knowledge creation process can be carried out with greater accuracy (Dutta and Manzoni, 1999).

### Definition Knowledge Creation

Knowledge creation is nothing but formation of new ideas through interactions between explicit and tacit knowledge holders. As defined by Ikujiro Nonaka, it consists of socialization (tacit to tacit), externalization (tacit to explicit), combination (explicit to explicit), and internalization (explicit to tacit). Nonaka developed a knowledge creation model and called it as SECI model.

Knowledge creation, according to Nonaka's SECI model (Figure 2), is about continuous transfer, combination, and conversion of different types of knowledge, as users practice, interact, and learn. Knowledge creation is a result of the interplay among multiple people who involved in discussions or conversations. Actions, interactions, brainstorming sessions and debates are the driving force in creating new knowledge. It is also proven that unstructured work environments produce creativity and innovation.

*Figure 2. Spiral of knowledge creation by Nonaka & Takeuchi (1995)*

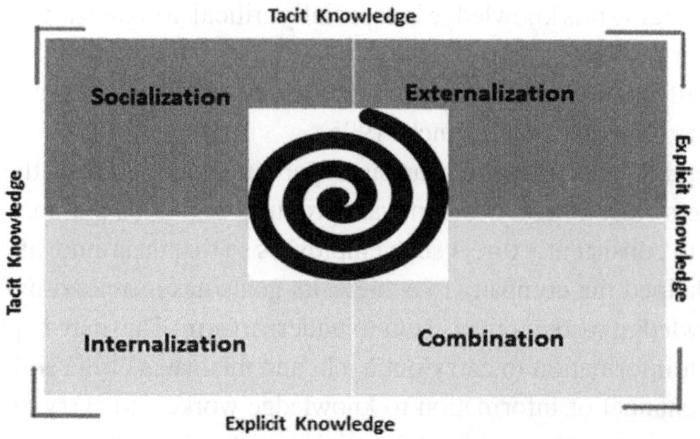


To enable and encourage knowledge sharing the organizations must identify where and in what forms knowledge exists. They must provide the appropriate mediums for knowledge sharing. Informal communications are the driving force in capturing tacit knowledge and Information technology (IT) is critical in facilitating explicit knowledge.

## 4.2 Knowledge Distribution

Sharing and transfer of knowledge is called knowledge distribution. Eg. Journalism and library services are knowledge distribution channels. The sharing of knowledge is difficult to enforce, since it is very difficult to guess how much a person knows or how diligently he has worked to search the knowledge. Knowledge worker groups that share knowledge perform better (Dutta and Manzoni, 1999).

Hence knowledge distribution can be easily achieved through formal and structured training programs. Still organizations loose lot of important knowledge due to the high turnover of employees. Much of an organization's strength is its know-how and institutional experience. So knowledge cannot be rehired.

So it's not easy to capitalize on-the-shelf knowledge that resides at various layers of the organization and converts it into actionable knowledge that can be used by employees for business process and innovation. To harness this organizational knowledge companies can adopt the following two systems of knowledge distribution: knowledge push and knowledge pull.

The push system involves emails, blogs, information sharing sessions, orientation program, group discussions, training, and RSS feeds, which provides an opportunity to exchange quality information and knowledge.

The pull system involves content management systems, web portals and search engines. But people must be willing to go and search for required knowledge. It involves lots of efforts and stress to identify suitable knowledge in this system.

## 4.3 Knowledge Application

Applying knowledge to jobs which is filtered through human brain is termed as knowledge application. The primary objective of organizations is to make the knowledge workers to apply the knowledge that is present rather than develop new one. Knowledge creation is an essential process and is part of most of the knowledge work. In some cases reuse of knowledge is of utmost importance (Dutta and Manzoni, 1999).

From the above segmentation, it is clear that companies should look into the various aspects of business processes, i.e., knowledge creation, distribution and application with intricacy. If these processes are incorrectly carried out or designed, then even if the knowledge workers perform well, the business cannot succeed.

It is a necessity for organizations to evaluate the effectiveness of these business processes. This can help to find the loopholes in the processes and guarantee performance of the business processes. Thus business process improvement strategies can be employed.

Business process improvement is usually known as Business Process Reengineering (BPR). BPR helps businesses to improve existing processes and model them so that they can help organizations to develop newer and better products.

"Reengineering is the fundamental rethinking and radical re-design of business processes to achieve dramatic improvements in critical, contemporary measure of performance, such as cost, quality, service and speed" (Hammer, Shanton, 1995).

If the business processes takes care of all the above mentioned aspects, then the business ought to become successful irrespective of individual performances.

## 5. FUTURE RESEARCH DIRECTIONS

Knowledge workers play vital role in business process and innovation. But till the date a limited research has been done on this topic. So it would be interesting to explore and study knowledge workers in a specific area or industry like manufacturing, automobile or aviation industry.

## 6. CONCLUSION

Knowledge workers work as part of highly interdependent groups comprising of experts from various fields, backgrounds and skills. In order to carry out the given job successfully teamwork and individual contributions are very important to achieve the undertaken project objectives. (Davenport, 2005). Knowledge workers perform highly complex tasks, and they prefer to operate in autonomy. Their autonomy inevitably leads to a divergence of both team and organizational goals. However, knowledge workers must be motivated by their autonomy associated with some degree of empowerment (Kessler, 1998).

Productivity of knowledge workers depends on the following six factors:

1) The task assigned to knowledge workers
2) Whether they are given enough autonomy to do their job
3) Continuous innovation has to be part of knowledge workers task
4) Knowledge workers require continuous learning through their tasks
5) Tasks carried out by knowledge workers demans quality
6) They should be treated as an asset for the organization. (Drucker, 2007)

Quality in knowledge work and knowledge-worker's productivity largely depends on the quality of processes. Similarly, efficiency in carrying out the tasks should not be individualistic in nature; rather, it should be sustained by designing and improving the business processes.

The ultimate goal of designing a business process is to evaluate the type of work that has to be carried out by knowledge workers, aligning this work with the business goals, embedding it in the business processes and reengineer it for better results. The business process designed should incorporate the aforementioned six factors to enhance the productivity of knowledge workers. These are the important aspects that would help organizations to sustain the consistent growth in innovation.

Designing a business process based on the guidelines mentioned in this paper would ensure that business goals are always achieved irrespective of individual performance of the knowledge workers.

## REFERENCES

Allee, V. (1997). *The Knowledge Evolution, Expanding Organizational Intelligence*. Boston: Butterworth Heinemenn Publication.

Anupindi, R., Chopra, S., Deshmikh, S., Mieghem, J., & Zemel, E. (2004). *Managing business process flows*. New Delhi: Pearson Education.

Awad, E., & Ghaziri, H. (2004). *Knowledge Management*. Singapore: Pearson Education International.

Bolis, I., Brunoro, C., & Sznelwar, L. (2012). The workers role in knowledge management and sustainability policies. *Work (Reading, Mass.)*, *41*(1), 2713–2720. PMID:22317131

Bradley, A., & McDonald, M. (2011). *The social organization: How to use social media to tap the collective genius of your customers and employees*. Boston: Harvard Business Press.

Cervera, R. (n.d.). *Knowledge Process Management*. Retrieved March 10, 2013, from http://hosteddocs.ittoolbox.com/LC071805.pdf

Darnton, G., & Darnton, M. (1997). *Business Process Analysis*. Boston: International Thompson Business Press.

Davenport, T. (2005). *Thinking for a Living: How to get better Performance and Results from Knowledge Workers*. Boston: Harvard Business Press.

David, H., & Ann, M. (2008). Making knowledge workers more creative. *Research Technology Management*, *51*(2), 40–46.

Drucker, P. (2007). *Management Challenges for the 21st century*. Oxford: Butterworth-Heinemenn Publication.

Dutta, S., & Manzoni, J. (1999). *Process Re-engineering, Organizational Change and Performance Improvement*. London: McGraw-Hill Publishing Company.

Kessler, D. (1998). *Knowledge workers revealed: New challenges for Asia*. Hong Kong: Economic Intelligence Unit.

Kim, J., Gil, Y., & Spraragen, M. (2012). Principles for interactive acquisition and validation of workflows. *Journal of Experimental and Theoretical Artificial Intelligence, 22*(2), 103–134-103–134.

Lewis, K. (2004). Knowledge and Performance in Knowledge-Worker Teams: A Longitudinal Study of Transactive Memory Systems. *Management Science*, *50*(11), 1519–1533. doi:10.1287/mnsc.1040.0257

McCormack, K., & Johnson, W. (2001). *Business process orientation: Gaining the e-business competitive advantage.* St. Lucie Press. doi:10.1201/9781420025569

Megill, K. (2012). *Thinking for a living: The coming age of Knowledge Work.* Walter de Gruyter & Co. doi:10.1515/9783110289671

Naikal, A., & Paloti, R. (2005). Knowledge Sharing: A Key For KM Success. In *Proceedings of 7th MANLIBNET Convention*. Kozhikode: IIM Kozhikode.

Poell, R., Van, F., & Krogt, V. (2003). Learning strategies of workers in the knowledge-creating company. *Human Resource Development International*, *6*(3), 387–403. doi:10.1080/13678860210136080

Smart, P., Maddern, H., & Maull, R. (2009). Understanding Business Process Management: Implications for Theory and Practice. *Ritish Journal of Management*, *20*(4), 491–507.

Smith, H., & Fingar, P. (2002). *Business Process Management: The Third Wave*. Meghan-Kiffer.

Tempest, S. (2009). Learning from the alien: Knowledge relationships with temporary workers in network contexts. *The International Journal of Human Resource Management, 20*(4), 912–927-912–927.

## KEY TERMS AND DEFINITIONS

**Business Innovation:** Business innovation is an organization's process for introducing new ideas, workflows, methodologies, services or products.

**Business Process:** A structured, measured set of activities designed to produce a specified output for a particular customer or market.

**Explicit Knowledge:** Any thought or experience which is documented or coded and is filed or archived is explicit knowledge. For Example books, periodicals, standards, patents, manuals, etc.

**Knowledge Management:** Process of capturing, developing, sharing, and effectively using organisational knowledge.

**Knowledge Sharing:** is an activity through which knowledge is exchanged among people, friends, families, communities or organizations.

**Knowledge Workers:** knowledge worker is one who gathers data/information from any source; adds value to the information; and distributes value-added products to others.

**Tacit Knowledge:** This resides in the minds of individuals, skills, experiences, value judgments, context sensitivity, etc. are examples of tacit knowledge.

# Chapter 3
# Technological Innovations in Management Education

**Shalini Kalia**
*IMT Ghaziabad, India*

**Nishant Puri**
*IMT Ghaziabad, India*

**Indrani Chakraverty**
*IMT Ghaziabad, India*

## ABSTRACT

*Technological innovations significantly enhance the effectiveness of the teaching learning process at all phases of academic pursuit. An array of evolved application software, middleware, and hardware help orchestrate an enriching learning environment. Technology enabled devices such as multimedia projectors, interactive e-boards and collaborative e-learning are now interwoven into the fabric of academic life alongside traditional methods. Moreover, the current generation, having grown up in an immersive ICT-driven environment, is completely at ease with online collaborative techniques. It is imperative that their skills be harnessed maximally by providing them with a learning platform that is optimally boosted by hi-tech accoutrements. This paper puts into perspective recent developments in modern tools and techniques involved in management education. It also examines the effectiveness of technological tools currently deployed in leading B-schools of India and Mexico. As these two emerging economies bear many similarities, it presents an interesting case for comparison. Through survey responses across disciplines in institutions in both countries, the study analyses the accessibility, usability, relevance, effectiveness, and challenges involved in using these technologies. Our study aims to analyse the technological tools and techniques which are beneficial to education system.*

DOI: 10.4018/978-1-4666-8259-7.ch003

## INTRODUCTION

The change in nature of business and industry within the newly created borderless market environment, increasing demand for management education, and the revolution in information technology provide an opportunity to change the curricula and delivery system of management education. The use of technology in course instruction is a favourable transition in higher education. Educational researchers have estimated that more than 40 billion dollars have been spent in the US on educational technology infrastructure and training in the past ten years (Amiel & Reeves, 2008). The developed countries education system has been extensively advancing due to integration of IT and education. Although developing countries have gradually embraced these innovative pedagogical tools, the scenario is not that encouraging. For example in India, premier institutions have access to all facilities in terms of educational technology but still a large number of business schools depend only on conventional lecture method in imparting knowledge. Therefore, the technology gap in developing countries provides an opportunity to use IT supported education technologies for better delivery of education, easier access to a number of knowledge sources, sharing through networks and quality distance learning in management education. (Sharma, 2013)

This study is focussed on impact of IT on management education in developing countries and analyses the scope and efficiency of technological innovations. The major objectives of this study are to:

- Identify the technological tools that can be effectively used for management education
- Analyze extent of usage of these tools; their efficiency; and challenges for technology adoption in developing countries
- Outline future scope of technological innovations in management education

## REVIEW OF LITERATURE

Information technology has brought about a revolution in learning and classroom productivity through economies of scale, mass customization, teaching convenience, and alternative means of assessment (Massy & Zemsky, 2005). With the help of IT enabled technological innovations, educators are exploring new instructional approaches enabling them to deliver educational programs to a larger and more diverse student population. These new instructional approaches permit an expanding market for their educational services which increase the impact of their educational institution as well as their potential revenue base.

Classroom technology investments are also being driven by evidence that technology enhances student learning (Krentler & Willis-Flurry, 2005). Some of the benefits that technology provides to diverse learning styles are (Parker & Burnie, 2009):

- Variety of learning styles through multi-media software
- Better engagements with students
- Less time spent writing on the board and less note taking allows time for discussion.
- Increased student/teacher interactions.

Use of the internet to support learning and teaching is growing significantly as more and more educational organisations are recognising the potential that it offers (Jefferries & Hussain, 1998; Norzaidi et al., 2007a, b). More than 50 percent of students' assignments are based on information from the internet (Norzaidi & Intan Salwani, 2008a, b). Thus, today, it is difficult to imagine the academic life without access to the internet (Spennemann et al., 2007).

It is crucial to understand the impact of technology on education and learning processes as technology can aid as well as hinder student learning. Whenever new technology is introduced, there is a process of change that comes with its implementation (Fahmy, 2004).

In addition, the trainers' attitudes towards technology also influence the impact of technology on students' learning. Trainers with positive attitudes towards using technology in class may not only encourage students' using technology but also try to make the most of new technology in class. However, negative attitudes towards technology use in class may prevent the trainers from making the best use of technology (Harris, 1997). A number of studies reported their lack of knowledge and confidence in using technology to incorporate it into the class they teach. This is one of the common barriers in incorporating technology by trainers into the curriculum (Topp et al., 1995; Ali, 2003; Marx, 2005; Zelin & Baird, 2007).

Research indicates that despite increasing commitment by educational institutes to infuse IT into the instruction and learning process, faculty have generally been slow to integrate this technology in to the instruction and learning process. Peluchette and Rust (2005) reported that 77% of management professors believed that instructional technologies enhanced their teaching effectiveness, but time constraints related to learning and using the technology were important factors. Allocation of time for faculty to learn new technology techniques was also a concern cited by business school chairs (Gatlin-Watts et al., 1999).

Diffusion theory states that when an innovation is introduced to a social group not all individuals of the social group adopt the innovation at the same rate. Abrahams (2010) identified the following barriers to technology adoption:

- Perception
- Resistance to change
- Technological support
- Financial support
- Infrastructure
- Knowledge/information
- Technophobia

An innovation is more likely to be adopted if (Abrahams, 2010):

- Potential adopters perceive the innovation to be something they can try out before adopting.
- It is compatible with their personal and professional goals.
- It is not too complex.
- It is better than another innovation (or the status quo).
- It has some observable benefits (Surry et al., 2005).

For this study, based on secondary research and the discussions with management students and faculty, the following teaching-learning tools have been identified that can be effectively utilized in management education (Classroom Technology Reference Guide; Sharma, 2013; Leidner & Jarvenpaa,1995; Salas et al.,2009):

1. LCD Projectors (type of video projector for displaying video, images or computer data on a screen or other flat surface. It is a modern equivalent of the slide projector or overhead projector)
2. 3D screens, with all supporting technology and equipment like 3D glasses (AKA stereo display – a display device capable of conveying depth perception to the viewer)
3. Over-Head Projectors (is a variant of slide projector that is used to display images to audience using transparency sheets)
4. Computer Lab equipped with latest softwares for activities like data analysis, simulation games, ERP systems etc.
5. Language Lab (state of the art equipment for learning nuances of languages.)
6. Simultaneous Translation equipment (useful for foreign students or students not familiar with primary medium of instruction)
7. Drop Box / Sharepoint (Platforms for cloud storage, file synchronization, document management, sharing, and collaboration)
8. Google Documents/ Google Drive (for collaborative creation and less complex editing of documents, file sharing etc.)
9. WEB OPAC (Online database/catalogue of available books and magazines to locate them in the physical library)
10. E-Library (Database of books / journals / publications / magazines stored in electronic format with direct online access)
11. Online Simulation Games (Example: Informatist and Markstrat; The games put groups of students against each other by forming them into companies who all operate in the same market in same conditions, to see who can maximize net worth, stock price, market share, and net profit)
12. Offline Simulation Games (Example- A stock market environment is created in a real physical place where students physically act as stock brokers or customers and trade in this simulated stock market)
13. Black Board (Internet-based education software providing various platforms. Ex: classroom and community learning platforms, online collaborating tools, data analysis tools, and a platform for administering quizzes, putting up exam results, attendance etc. It also offers platform for integration of access to campus facilities through one card. For more details refer http://www.blackboard.com)
14. SMART Board (Interactive White Board which can be used like a touch screen and supports open files, display and move images, and dynamic use of fingers or tools to write, draw, move, or erase on the board)
15. Career Preparation related software/Technology (Example: Vmock.com, porot.com, with full access to the website resources. This tool prepares participants for writing resume, handling interviews etc)
16. Interactive and Dynamic Digital Newspaper Boards (where various news studies are displayed like newspaper cuttings, but it is in digital format, with more comprehensive news coverage, on an interactive screen acting like the pin board)

17. Video/Audio Conferencing System or Multiple Location Classrooms connected to a single video/ audio conference or webinar.
18. Internet enabled classrooms in which the students are allowed to use the internet on their PCs or mobile phones (With or without restrictions on accessible websites)
19. Intranet Network for sharing of classroom material, faculty presentations documents etc.
20. OLT or On Line Teaching System (An enterprise wide resource planning system to fully integrate the activities like academic assignments, administering quizzes, access to exam results and grades, electives, and other administrative activities like fees at one place with no redundancy of data.)

## NEED OF THE STUDY

Research shows that technological advancements across the globe have hugely impacted instructional design at all levels of education. Management professionals in today's context need to be technologically adept. Thus, the importance of adopting more effective pedagogies and technological tools in management education cannot be ignored. Technology in education has not caught up to its full potential in countries like India and Mexico, which have huge population with a large percentage of youth. Technological tools already implemented may or may not be having the impact on learning outcomes, that they should as per research.

Thus, there is a need to express in measurable terms, the current scenario in the implementation and adoption of technological tools in management education. Only then can we know the extent to which the potential of such tools is currently being tapped. This measurement will serve as a first step towards charting the optimal path towards utilizing technology to its full potential. This study attempts to create that base specifically for management Institutes in India and Mexico.

## METHODOLOGY

The study was conducted in two phases. In the first phase, based on the secondary research and discussion with management students and faculty, 20 teaching learning tools were identified as listed in the previous section. In the second stage, the primary research was done through questionnaire survey on a sample of students from premier B-Schools in India and Mexico.

The questionnaire comprised nine questions to obtain data on what technological tools are used (out of the twenty tools listed in the literature survey) in their respective B-schools. The following parts of the survey captured the students' perception on how effective the tools are and what tools they would like to see in the future. The survey also captured the challenges faced by students in learning from the use of technology tools in the educational environment. There were three further questions which aimed at collecting qualitative information from respondents regarding other tools being used or desired to be used apart from the listed ones and their general observations on the access and/or use of technological tools in teaching pedagogy in their institute.

*Figure 1. Usage of technological tools in management education in India and Mexico*

| India | Technology Used Regularly | Mexico |
|---|---|---|
| 66.7 | LCD Projectors | 61.7 |
| | 3D Screens | |
| 42.9 | Over-Head Projector (using transparency sheets) | |
| | Computer Lab equipped with latest relevant softwares | |
| | Language Lab | |
| | Simultaneous Translation Equipment | |
| | Drop Box/ Sharepoint | 48.9 |
| 73 | Google Documents/ Google Drive | |
| 63.5 | WEB OPAC (Library with Online Public Address Catalogue) | |
| 61.9 | E-Library | |
| | Online Simulation Games | |
| | Offline Simulation Games | |
| | Black Board | |
| | SMART Board (Touch Screen Dynamic Board) | |
| | Career Preparation related software/Technology | |
| | Interactive and Dynamic Digital Newspaper Boards | |
| | Video/ Audio Conferencing System or Multiple Location Classrooms | |
| 55.6 | Internet enabled classrooms | 68.1 |
| 79.4 | Intranet Network for sharing of study material | 61.7 |
| 85.7 | OLT or Online Teaching System | |

## FINDINGS AND DISCUSSIONS

### Extent of Usage of Technology in Education in India and Mexico

In developing countries like India and Mexico, the penetration of highly sophisticated technologies in B Schools is still taking roots. In context of the B-Schools surveyed, the technologies highlighted in Figure 1 are most regularly used in both the Indian and Mexican B-Schools. (Figure 1 highlights only those technologies for which majority of the respondents marked ‘Used Regularly’.)

A snapshot of current usage scenario of the 20 Listed Technologies is given in Table 1. The complete usage statistics is given in Table 3 (Appendix).

Table 1 highlights only that level of usage for each technology, which was indicated by the majority of the respondents. The technologies highlighted in bold showed very similar usage in both countries. The three technologies (Item no. 6, 7 and 20) showed opposite extent of usage in the two countries. Figure 1 and Table 1 clearly show LCD Projectors, Internet Enabled Classrooms, and Intranet network for sharing of study material as the technologies most regularly used in B-schools of both countries.

*Table 1. Snapshot of current usage scenario of the 20 technological tools*

| | Technology | India | | | | Mexico | | | |
|---|---|---|---|---|---|---|---|---|---|
| | | **Used Regularly** | **Not Much Used** | **Not Available** | **Not Aware** | **Used Regularly** | **Not Much Used** | **Not Available** | **Not Aware** |
| **1** | LCD Projectors | 66.7% | | | | 61.7% | | | |
| **2** | 3D Screens | | | 85.7% | | | | 70.2% | |
| 3 | Over-Head Projector (using transparency sheets) | 42.9% | | | | | 51.1% | | |
| **4** | Computer Lab equipped with latest relevant softwares | | 60.3% | | | | 44.7% | | |
| **5** | Language Lab | | | 49.2% | | | | 53.2% | |
| 6 | Simultaneous Translation Equipment | | | | 44.4% | | 44.7% | | |
| 7 | Drop Box/ Sharepoint | | | 33.3% | | 48.9% | | | |
| 8 | Google Documents/ Google Drive | 73.0% | | | | | 46.8% | | |
| 9 | WEB OPAC (Library with Online Public Address Catalogue) | 63.5% | | | | | 55.3% | | |
| 10 | E-Library | 61.9% | | | | | 53.2% | | |
| **11** | Online Simulation Games | | 49.2% | | | | 46.8% | | |
| **12** | Offline Simulation Games | | 41.3% | | | | 48.9% | | |
| **13** | Black Board | | | 39.7% | | | | 51.1% | |
| **14** | SMART Board (Touch Screen Dynamic Board) | | | 74.6% | | | | 80.9% | |
| 15 | Career Preparation related software/ Technology | | 41.3% | | | | | | |
| **16** | Interactive and Dynamic Digital Newspaper Boards | | | 68.3% | | | | 44.7% | |
| 17 | Video/ Audio Conferencing System or Multiple Location Classrooms | | | 55.6% | | | 55.3% | | |
| **18** | Internet enabled classrooms | 55.6% | | | | 68.1% | | | |
| **19** | Intranet Network for sharing of study material | 79.4% | | | | 61.7% | | | |
| 20 | OLT or Online Teaching System | 85.7% | | | | | | 55.3% | |

For Indian B-Schools alone, the top five technologies used regularly are:

1. OLT or OnLine Teaching System (85.7%)
2. Intranet Network for sharing of study material (79.4%)
3. Google Documents/ Google Drive: (73%)
4. LCD Projectors (66.7%)
5. WEB OPAC (Library with Online Public Access Catalogue) (63.5%)

Similarly for Mexican B-schools alone, the top five technologies used regularly are:

1. Internet enabled classrooms (68.1%)
2. Intranet Network for sharing of study material (61.7%)
3. LCD Projectors (61.7%)
4. Drop Box / SharePoint (48.9%)
5. Over-Head Projectors (using transparency sheets) (42.9%) (refer Appendix)

A crucial resource utilization issue brought to light in Figure 1 and Table 1 is the fact that computer labs equipped with latest relevant softwares are 'Not Much Used' in both countries. About 60% respondents from Indian B-Schools and nearly 45% respondents in Mexican B-Schools said that Computer Lab equipped with latest relevant softwares was 'Used but not much'. This shows that while computer labs are there, the students do not use them regularly. Some of the reasons for this could be that systems in the labs are not equipped with latest relevant softwares which students would like to use more often to support their learning needs. Lack of training in utilizing available tools and technologies may also be leading to this situation. This study takes a deeper look at some of the commonly faced challenges in utilizing technological tools in later sections.

The use of simulation games, both online and offline, are extremely common in top B-schools across the world. As a pedagogical technique, it is proven to be of high effectiveness in making the right impact on the learning outcome. However, in both India and Mexico, the usage of these games is 'not much'. Almost 50% the respondents in both countries said that both online and offline simulation games were being 'Used but not Much'.

Certain technologies were found to be used heavily in one country but not available in the other. For example, we find that nearly 50% of the respondents from Mexican B-schools say that Dropbox/ Sharepoint as cloud storage and sharing tools is "Used Regularly'. However, in Indian B-Schools usage of such tools is non-existent shown by the fact that 33% of the student respondents said this particular technology is 'Not Available'. In both countries though, Intranet Network seems to be used heavily for sharing files; 79% & 62% respondents from India and Mexico respectively report that this resource is 'Used Regularly'.

Similarly, we find that OnLine Teaching System (OLT) is a technology widely used in Indian B-Schools (86% respondents say it is used regularly) and is also perceived by more than 50% of the students as effective (refer Figure 3). However, this technology is not available in Mexican B-Schools (55% respondents say 'Not Available'). However, Mexican respondents seem to be aware of OLT or a similar technology, as 51% also perceive it as 'effective' (refer Figure 3). This may be an indicator for appropriate authorities in participating Mexican B-Schools to consider implementation of this technology sometime in the near future.

*Figure 2. Technological tools not available in Indian and Mexican B-Schools*

| INDIA | Technology Not Available | MEXICO |
|---|---|---|
| | LCD Projectors | |
| 85.7 | 3D Screens | 70.2 |
| | Over-Head Projector (using transparency sheets) | |
| | Computer Lab equipped with latest relevant softwares | |
| 49.2 | Language Lab | 53.2 |
| | Simultaneous Translation Equipment | |
| | Drop Box/ Sharepoint | |
| | Google Documents/ Google Drive | |
| | WEB OPAC (Library with Online Public Address Catalogue) | |
| | E-Library | |
| | Online Simulation Games | |
| | Offline Simulation Games | |
| | Black Board | 51.1 |
| 74.6 | SMART Board (Touch Screen Dynamic Board) | 80.9 |
| | Career Preparation related software/Technology | |
| 68.3 | Interactive and Dynamic Digital Newspaper Boards | 44.7 |
| 55.6 | Video/ Audio Conferencing System or Multiple Location Classrooms | |
| | Internet enabled classrooms | |
| | Intranet Network for sharing of study material | |
| | OLT or Online Teaching System | 55.3 |

Some technologies, like translation equipment, are context driven. This means that in cases where there is no language barrier, such technology is not implemented. For example in India, 44% students responded by saying that they were 'not aware' of such a technological tool. B-Schools in India are host to foreign exchange students from France, Germany and many European countries every year. But, since the medium of instruction is always English, there is no need for such a technology. However, in Mexico since medium of instruction is traditionally Spanish, translation equipment is necessary for full-time foreign students and international exchange students who have no training in Spanish. Thus, in Mexico, nearly a third of the respondents (all respondents were natives and can be safely assumed to be proficient in Spanish) say it is used regularly (refer Appendix). However, a majority respondents (44.7%) (All respondents were natives) also say that translation equipment is used though not much. This anomaly may be because lack of proper awareness of native students about how often such equipment is used. It may also be indicative of other factors at play like increase in usage of English as language of instruction in some leading B-Schools in Mexico. However, going deeper into such factors was outside the scope of this study.

The technologies which are not available in institutions of both countries are (refer Figure 2):

1. 3D screens
2. Language Lab
3. SMART Board (Touch Screen Dynamic Board)
4. Interactive and Dynamic Digital Newspaper Boards

*Figure 3. Technological tools perceived as highly effective in Indian and Mexican B-Schools*

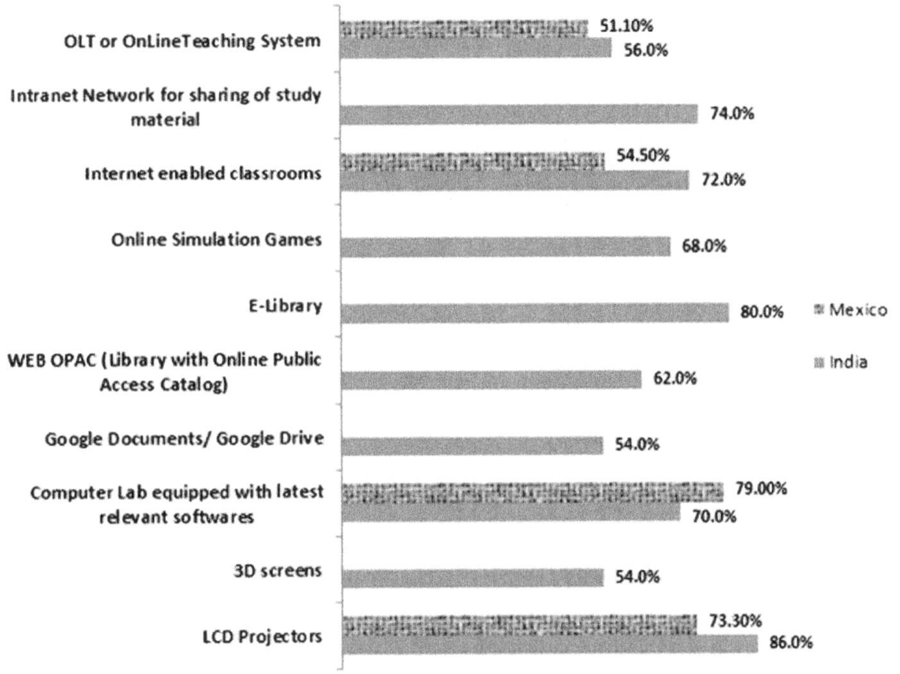


The same technologies were also among those mentioned by more than 50% of the respondents in either one / both the countries as 'want to see implemented in future' (Refer Figure 5). Around 60-70% respondents said they would like to see these technologies implemented in their institution in future. Figure 2 shows those technologies for which majority of the respondents marked 'Not Available'.

## Effectiveness of Technological Education Tools

To measure effectiveness of existing and/or perceived effectiveness of potential technologies, respondents were asked as to how effective they thought the listed technologies were in terms of helping them achieve learning objectives and student engagement in class.

Figure 3 summarizes the result for B-schools from both the countries. It shows only those technologies only which more than 50% of the respondents perceived as highly effective (i.e. gave a rating of either '1' or '2' on a scale of 5, '1' being the highest). If we look at the effectiveness perceptions for both schools together, four technologies come out in common: Computer Labs with Latest relevant softwares, LCD projectors, Internet Enabled Classrooms, and OLT. However, if we look at the absolute percentages, they are very low. For example, more than 1/3rd of the student respondents in India feel computer labs are not highly effective. Similarly 1/3rd of the student respondents in Mexico feel that LCD projectors are not highly effective. This indicated that the overall effectiveness of existing technologies can be improved much more.

In fact the utilization of some of these resources may be much lower than optimal. For example, in the case of Computer Labs, about 60% respondents from Indian B-Schools and nearly 45% respondents in Mexican B-Schools said that Computer Lab equipped with latest relevant softwares was 'Used but not much' (refer Table 1). This, as pointed out earlier, is a resource utilization issue that may need attention of the appropriate authority.

*Figure 4. Challenges in effective implementation of technological tools (Combined %age of total respondents)*

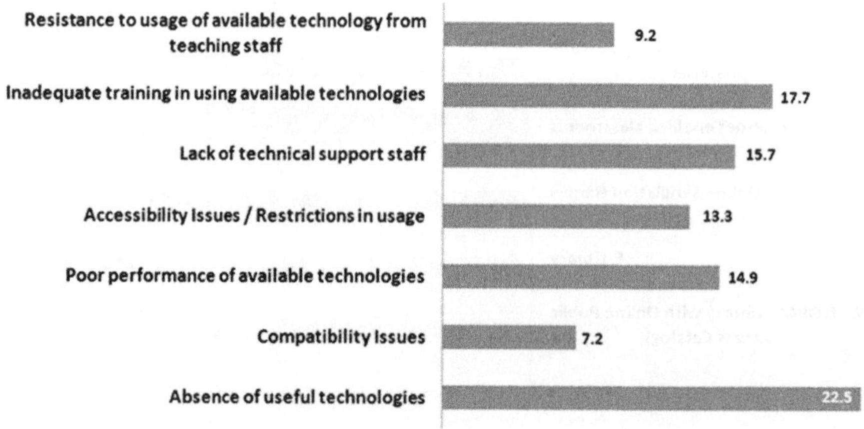


## Challenges in Effective Implementation of Technological Tools

The survey captured data on the major roadblocks faced by the students in utilizing technological tools to enhance learning and maximise impact of the pedagogy. Seven most common issues/problems were identified and Figure 4 summarises the responses of respondents from both the countries, with regard to each of those 7 items. (Note: the percentages have been rounded off to single decimal place.)

The major problems students usually face are *Absence of useful technologies; Inadequate training in using available technologies*; *Lack of technical support staff; Poor performance of available technologies; and Accessibility Issues.*

*Figure 5. Top technological tools that students want to be implemented in future*

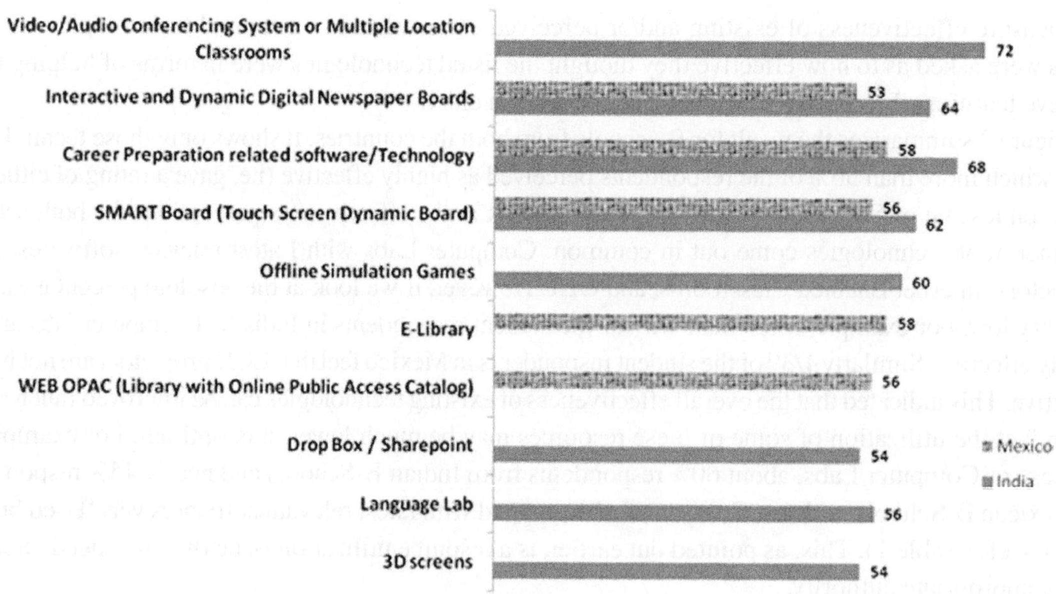

## Future Scope of Implementation/Utilization of Technologies

An inference can be drawn from the survey results on the future scope of implementation of new technologies. In the survey, for each listed technology the students were asked if it should be implemented in their school in future or it should not be implemented in future or it is already in use or they didn't know about the technology (and hence cannot comment). On the basis of the responses, an analysis was done to understand what kind of demand is there for these technologies in the future. Figure 5 shows those technologies for which more than 50% respondents said they would like to see it implemented in future. It corresponds to the highlighted figures in the 'Yes' Columns in Table 2.

As can be seen in Figure 5, technologies that come out in common are Career Preparation related software/Technology, SMART Board, and Interactive and Dynamic Digital Newspaper Boards. Language Lab was another technology that follows closely as 47% respondents from Mexico, with 56% from India, wanted to see it implemented in future (Refer Table 2). These technological tools are either not available or not much used (Refer Table1) in institutions in both the countries and students see value in the implementation and use of these technologies in future.

3D Screens is another technology which is currently not available in either institution, but students, especially in Mexico, didn't really see it as one that they would definitely like to see it implemented in the near future. This may be because students are still not sure as to how much value can be added to the teaching-learning outcomes through its implementation.

This particular section about future implementation also threw up certain other interesting observations. The same are articulated in the following paragraphs and draw reference from Table 2.

Table 2 shows only those values in the 'Yes' column that were above 50%. In the table, 'Computer Labs' and 'Online Simulation Games' come out as the only two technologies where the students' responses seem 'mixed'. In B-Schools of both countries, students were divided on whether 'Computer Labs with Latest Relevant Softwares' were already in use or needed to be implemented in future. In India, 46% voted for future implementation while another 46% said it was already in use. Similarly in Mexico, while 38% respondents wanted to see it implemented in future, another 44% said it was already in use.

A similar 'division of opinion' can be seen in the case of Online Simulation Games as has been highlighted in Table 2. These observations confirm the findings from the earlier section of Current Usage Scenario, wherein the same technologies were found to be 'used but not much' (Refer Table 1 and Figure 1). This anomaly reinforces the earlier stated problem that these tools are currently not being utilized to their most optimal level. Students' responses indicate scope for further improvement in utilization of the benefits these technologies can provide to the fullest possible extent.

Students were also asked if they wanted certain 'other' technologies that they know about apart from the ones listed to be implemented in the near future. Majority of the students in India have responded as 'no' (40%) or 'not aware' (34%). In Mexico, majority of the students responded as 'no' (33%) or 'not aware' (42%). Thus, students were either not aware of other further technologies that can be implemented in this context or did not think any other technologies need to be implemented in the near future.

*Table 2. Future scope of implementation of technological tools*

| Technology | India | | | | Mexico | | | |
|---|---|---|---|---|---|---|---|---|
| | Yes | Not Needed | Already in Use | Not Aware | Yes | Not Needed | Already in Use | Not Aware |
| LCD Projectors | | | | | | | | |
| 3D Screens | 54.00% | | | | | | | |
| Over-Head Projector (using transparency sheets) | | | | | | | | |
| Computer Lab equipped with latest relevant softwares | 46.00% | 4.00% | 46.00% | 4.00% | 38.00% | 11.00% | 44.00% | 7.00% |
| Language Lab | 56.00% | | | | 47.00% | | | |
| Simultaneous Translation Equipment | | | | | | | | |
| Drop Box/ Sharepoint | 54.00% | | | | | | | |
| Google Documents/ Google Drive | | | | | | | | |
| WEB OPAC (Library with Online Public Address Catalogue) | | | | | 56.00% | | | |
| E-Library | | | | | 58.00% | | | |
| Online Simulation Games | 42.00% | 2.00% | 56.00% | | 42.00% | 7.00% | 49.00% | 2.00% |
| Offline Simulation Games | 60.00% | | | | | | | |
| Black Board | | | | | | | | |
| SMART Board (Touch Screen Dynamic Board) | 62.00% | | | | 56.00% | | | |
| Career Preparation related software/ Technology | 68.00% | | | | 58.00% | | | |
| Interactive and Dynamic Digital Newspaper Boards | 64.00% | | | | 53.00% | | | |
| Video/ Audio Conferencing System or Multiple Location Classrooms | 72.00% | | | | | | | |
| Internet enabled classrooms | | | | | | | | |
| Intranet Network for sharing of study material | | | | | | | | |
| OLT or Online Teaching System | | | | | | | | |
| Any Other | 10.0% | 40.0% | 16.0% | 34.0% | 24.0% | 33.0% | | 42.0% |

## CONCLUSION AND RECOMMENDATIONS

**Future Path:** The technologies that must be implemented in the near future are:

a. SMART Board
b. Career Preparation related software/Technology
c. Interactive and Dynamic Digital Newspaper Boards
d. Language Lab

In addition, existing technologies and infrastructure needs to be improved so that cases like underutilization and wastage of resources like computer labs equipped with sophisticated research tools, journal subscriptions, software subscriptions etc. does not happen. Latest software and hardware must be there to support effective usage. Similarly Online simulations games need to be used more often in B-Schools of both countries to optimize the learning outcome intended through these tools.

**Effective Implementation of Tools:** It doesn't suffice to simply have technologies. The problems associated with utilizing them must be addressed. The stakeholders must be trained to be able to use them and extract value out of these technologies. In addition there needs to be adequate trained support staff to ensure smooth operation of these technologies. In cases of complex tools like Online Teaching system, research tools, data analysis tools etc, students should be trained in the beginning of the course so that they can become proficient in the technologies and even be able to adapt to new technologies later in their professional lives.

**Faculty Involvement:** The faculty must be actively involved in introducing students to use of various technologies from the start till the end of their management course. This will help students to get immersed in a technologically driven world of work. Teachers who have the knowledge of relevant technologies and tools must take lead to ensure students learn to use new technologies and adapt to them. For ex: Using online collaboration tools, cloud based sharing tools, analysis softwares, simulations etc.

**Drive Technological Growth:** The results of the survey show that these schools have many useful and relevant technologies in place. Not only are they in place, at least 60% of them are also effective in achieving their purpose and are being used to a good extent (refer Table 1 and Figure 3). Thus, we can say that B-Schools in developing economies of India and Mexico are already on that path. The growth in this area must be driven continuously towards upgrading technology to meet benchmarks and keep abreast of changing times.

## FUTURE SCOPE OF STUDY

The study needs to be extended to faculty which will enable a student-faculty responses comparison to validate the gaps identified in this study.

The study can also be extended to do a comparison of technologies used in B-School classroom of developed Countries and those in developing countries. There are many technological tools in existence, but it is important to filter out and apply those that are found to have a positive impact on the learning outcome. Since many such technologies have been tried and tested in developed countries like the US and Canada, it could act as a genuine indicator of a direction for technological implementations for B-Schools in developing countries. However, in that perspective it must be borne in mind that blind application of what has worked in the developed countries may not be successful in our context.

The major limitation of the study is small sample size. Due to resource constraints 50 students each from Indian and Mexican B-Schools were surveyed. The sample size taken from similar B-Schools from India and Mexico remains too small to safely generalize for the two developing economies. As a future scope of study, the research could be conducted with bigger number of student respondents.

Some other questions to further ponder upon in this context are what combination of technologies is optimal for a B-School to use? Is it the faculty's responsibility to actively involve technology in their pedagogy? Should having cutting edge technologies be a central goal for educational institutes of India and Mexico? These questions are context-specific and demand deep study to justify the use of specific technologies in a B-School classroom.

## REFERENCES

Abrahams. (2010). Technology adoption in higher education: a framework for identifying and prioritising issues and barriers to adoption of instructional technology. *Journal of Applied Research in Higher Education, 2*(2), 34 – 49.

Ali, A. (2003). Faculty adoption of technology: Training comes first. *Educational Technology, 43*(2), 51–53.

Amiel, T., & Reeves, T. C. (2008). Design-based research and educational technology: Rethinking technology and the research agenda. *Journal of Educational Technology & Society, 11*(4), 29–40.

*Classroom Technology Reference Guide. EdTech Magazine by CDW-G.* (2013). Retrieved December 20, 2013 from http://www.edtechmagazine.com/higher/sites/edtechmagazine.com.higher/files/041713_rg_g_classroomtech_121833.pdf

Fahmy, M. (2004). Thinking about technology effects on higher education. *The Journal of Technology Studies, 33*(1), 53–58.

Gatlin-Watts, R., Arn, J., & Kordsmeier, W. (1999). Multimedia as an instructional tool: Perceptions of college department chairs. *Education, 120*(1), 190.

Harris, R. (1997). Teaching, learning and information technology: Attitudes towards computers among Hong Kong's faculty. *Journal of Computing in Higher Education, 9*(2), 89–114. doi:10.1007/BF02948780

Jefferies, P., & Hussain, F. (1998). Using the internet as teaching resource. *Education + Training, 40*(8), 359–365. doi:10.1108/00400919810239400

Krentler, K. A., & Willis-Flurry, L. A. (2005). Does technology enhance actual student learning? The case of online discussion boards. *Journal of Education for Business, 80*(6), 316–321. doi:10.3200/JOEB.80.6.316-321

Leidner, D. E. & Jarvenpaa, S. L. (1995). The Use of Information Technology to Enhance Management School Education: A Theoretical View. *MIS Quarterly, 19*(3), 265-291.

Marx, S. (2005). Improving faculty use of technology in a small campus community. *T.H.E. Journal, 32*(6), 21–43.

Massy, W., & Zemsky, R. (2005, June). *Using information technology to enhance academic productivity*. Paper presented at the Enhancing Academic Productivity Conference, Wingspread, WI. Retrieved November 16, 2013, from http://www.educause.edu/LibraryDetailPage/666&ID=NLI0004

Melerdiercks, K. (2005). The dark side of Norzaidi, M.D., Chong, S.C. and Intan Salwani, M. (2008a). Perceived resistance, user resistance and managers' performance in the Malaysian port industry. *Aslib Proceedings: New Information Perspectives*, *60*(3), 242–264.

Norzaidi, M. D., Chong, S. C., Azizah, A., Intan Salwani, M., Rafidah, K., & Rohana, Z. (2007a). The effect of students' backgrounds and attitudes on computer skills in Malaysia. *International Journal of Management in Education*, *1*(4), 371–389. doi:10.1504/IJMIE.2007.015198

Norzaidi, M. D., Chong, S. C., Intan Salwani, M., & Rafidah, K. (2008b). A study of intranet usage and resistance in Malaysia's port industry. *Journal of Computer Information Systems*, *49*(1), 37–47.

Norzaidi, M. D., Chong, S. C., Murali, R., & Intan Salwani, M. (2007b). Intranet usage and managers' performance in the port industry. *Industrial Management & Data Systems*, *107*(8), 1227–1250. doi:10.1108/02635570710822831

Parker, B., & Burnie, D. (2009). Classroom Technology in Business Schools. *AACE Journal*, *17*(1), 45–60.

Peluchette, J. V., & Rust, K. (2005). Technology use in the classroom: Preferences of management faculty. *Journal of Education for Business*, *80*(4), 200–205. doi:10.3200/JOEB.80.4.200-205

Salas, E., Wildman, J. L., & Piccolo, R. F. (2009). Using Simulation-Based Training to Enhance Management Education. *Academy of Management Learning & Education. University of Central Florida*, *8*(4), 559–573.

Sharma, K. D. (2013). *Impact Of Information Technology On Management Education Through Distance Mode*. Academic Press.

Spennemann, D. H. R., Artkinson, J., & Cornworth, D. (2007). Sessional, weekly and diurual patterns of computer lab usage by students attending a regional university in Australia. *Computers & Education*, *49*(3), 726–739. doi:10.1016/j.compedu.2005.11.006

Surry, D. W., Ensminger, D. C., & Haab, M. (2005). A model for integrating instructional technology into higher education. *British Journal of Educational Technology*, *36*(2), 327–329. doi:10.1111/j.1467-8535.2005.00461.x

Topp, N., Mortenson, R., & Grandgenett, N. (1995). Building a technology-using faculty to facilitate technology-using teachers. *Journal of Computing in Teacher Education*, *11*(3), 11–14.

Zelin, R., & Baird, J. (2007). Training faculty to use technology in the classroom. *College Teaching Methods & Styles Journal*, *3*(3), 41–48.

## KEY TERMS AND DEFINITIONS

**Black Board:** Internet-based education software providing various platforms.

**Digital Newspaper Boards:** Online platform where various news studies (newspaper cuttings) are displayed in digital format.

**Drop Box/Sharepoint:** Platforms for cloud storage, file synchronization, document management, sharing, and collaboration.

**E-Library:** Database of books / journals / publications / magazines stored in electronic format with direct online access.

**Language Lab:** Audio-visual installation used as an aid in language teaching.

**OLT or On Line Teaching System:** An enterprise wide resource planning system to fully integrate the activities at one place with no redundancy of data.

**Pedagogical Tools:** Tools that are used for teaching and learning purpose.

**Simulation Games:** Activities intended to engage participants in real life situations for the purpose of training, analysis, or prediction.

**Translation Equipment:** Equipment used for translation of language and is useful for people not familiar with primary medium of instruction.

## APPENDIX

*Table 3. Complete usage statistics: Indian and Mexican B-Schools*

| | Technology | India | | | | Mexico | | | |
|---|---|---|---|---|---|---|---|---|---|
| | | Used Regularly | Not Much Used | Not Available | Not Aware | Used Regularly | Not Much Used | Not Available | Not Aware |
| 1 | LCD Projectors | 66.7% | 9.5% | 22.2% | 1.6% | 61.7% | 23.4% | 8.5% | 6.4% |
| 2 | 3D Screens | 1.6% | 3.2% | 85.7% | 9.5% | 2.1% | 4.3% | 70.2% | 23.4% |
| 3 | Over-Head Projector (using transparency sheets) | 42.9% | 14.3% | 38.1% | 4.7% | 42.6% | 51.1% | 4.2% | 2.1% |
| 4 | Computer Lab equipped with latest relevant softwares | 31.7% | 60.3% | 4.8% | 3.2% | 34.0% | 44.7% | 14.9% | 6.4% |
| 5 | Language Lab | 3.2% | 25.4% | 49.2% | 22.2% | 0.0% | 21.3% | 53.2% | 25.5% |
| 6 | Simultaneous Translation Equipment | 3.2% | 12.7% | 39.7% | 44.4% | 29.8% | 44.7% | 10.6% | 14.9% |
| 7 | Drop Box/ Sharepoint | 14.3% | 28.6% | 33.3% | 23.8% | 48.9% | 36.2% | 6.4% | 8.5% |
| 8 | Google Documents/ Google Drive | 73% | 23.8% | 3.2% | 0.0% | 25.5% | 46.8% | 17.1% | 10.6% |
| 9 | WEB OPAC (Library with Online Public Address Catalogue) | 63.5% | 28.6% | 4.8% | 3.1% | 8.5% | 55.3% | 25.5% | 10.7% |
| 10 | E-Library | 61.9% | 31.7% | 4.8% | 1.6% | 2.1% | 53.2% | 23.4% | 21.3% |
| 11 | Online Simulation Games | 39.7% | 49.2% | 7.9% | 3.2% | 29.8% | 46.8% | 12.8% | 10.6% |
| 12 | Offline Simulation Games | 17.5% | 41.3% | 23.8% | 17.4% | 17.1% | 48.9% | 19.1%% | 14.9% |
| 13 | Black Board | 23.8% | 12.7% | 39.7% | 23.8% | 23.4% | 10.6% | 51.1% | 14.9% |
| 14 | SMART Board (Touch Screen Dynamic Board) | 4.8% | 3.1% | 74.6% | 17.5% | 0.0% | 6.4% | 80.9% | 12.8% |
| 15 | Career Preparation related software/ Technology | 12.7% | 41.3% | 20.6% | 25.4% | 27.7% | 29.8% | 21.3% | 21.3% |
| 16 | Interactive and Dynamic Digital Newspaper Boards | 3.1% | 11.1% | 68.3% | 17.5% | 4.2% | 27.7% | 44.7% | 23.4% |
| 17 | Video/ Audio Conferencing System or Multiple Location Classrooms | 4.7% | 27% | 55.6% | 12.7% | 21.3% | 55.3% | 19.1% | 4.3% |
| 18 | Internet enabled classrooms | 55.6% | 30.2% | 11.1% | 3.1% | 68.1% | 19.1% | 12.8% | 0.0% |
| 19 | Intranet Network for sharing of study material | 79.4% | 14.3% | 4.8% | 1.5% | 61.7% | 31.9% | 6.4% | 0.0% |
| 20 | OLT or Online Teaching System | 85.7% | 9.5% | 3.2% | 1.6% | 2.2% | 19.1% | 55.3% | 23.4% |

# Chapter 4
# Emergent Trends in Sustainable Technologies in Thailand:
## Developing OTOP-Based Manufacturing Capabilities in Rural India

**Samarth Gupta**
*Institute of Management Technology Ghaziabad, India*

**Amit Choudhary**
*Institute of Management Technology Ghaziabad, India*

**Garima Yadav**
*Institute of Management Technology Ghaziabad, India*

**Amanpreet Kaur**
*Institute of Management Technology Ghaziabad, India*

## ABSTRACT

*OVOP concept has been one of the keenly studied rural marketing and social innovation concepts in the world. While many countries have successfully implemented this model under various names, forms, strategies and areas; there is still a lot of scope for analysing and carefully implementing this unique business model for the development of Rural Innovation and Social Entrepreneurship. Studies have shown that while the Asian countries like Thailand, Japan, Malawi and even Nepal have successfully implemented this concept and reaped its benefits, some of the nations like India, South Africa and others are yet to follow a methodical approach towards the implementation of this interesting social business proposition. The Kasetsart Journal of Social Sciences has been focussing on developing such capabilities for enhancing social business proposition and understanding thè contribution of community involvement in social re-engineering. While lot of emphasis has been paid on developing innovative social ventures for Rural India, a concept like OVOP/OTOP is certainly the need of the hour. In this chapter we intend to investigate the various aspects of an OVOP/OTOP implementation and propose solutions for social business development in Rural India based on the foundations of the OVOP/OTOP concept that has been a pioneer for development of social entrepreneurship across the world.*

DOI: 10.4018/978-1-4666-8259-7.ch004

## INTRODUCTION

Unequal growth in different areas is one of the major problems faced by many developing countries. While the cities and towns tend to develop and grow rapidly with business activity increasing day-by-day in these areas, the rural areas seem to be left untouched by this development. The private business sector does not have any incentive to get into the rural areas and do business there. So the Government has to come up with various methods to increase business activity in rural areas so as to achieve its socialist objectives. One such effort to build capacity and make the rural areas thrive with economic activity is the Thailand Government's 'One Tambon One Product' project also known as the OTOP Project. Under this project, Government has tried to make the rural areas self-sufficient by empowering them to produce and sell certain products that are indigenous in nature and are made through the skill and expertise of the local people. The Government gives these products branding and marketing support and helps in creating a unique identity of the product as being produced by the local communities (Phonsuwan, & Kachitvichyanukul, 2010). The idea is to involve the entire community to come together and develop a product based on their creativity and Thai wisdom and improve the product on aspects such as quality, capital, and technology, markets etc. so that these products are able to create jobs and generate incomes for the local people producing them. This aims at reducing the migration of people from rural areas to urban areas in search of employment opportunities. The long-term goal is capacity building in rural areas to generate income and sustain the population (Denpaiboon & Amatasawatdee, 2012).

## OTOP BUSINESS MODEL IN THAILAND

The OTOP Project was started in Thailand by its former Prime Minister Thaksin Shinawatra drawing its inspiration from a similar model in Japan known as the One Village One Product (OVOP) program. Under this program, the Government aims to promote the products manufactured by the locals in the rural areas (Savitri, 2008). The Government reviews the products manufactured by rural people and gives them an OTOP rating which is based on the product quality, manufacturing technology and income and employment generating capability of the product. The rating is given on a scale of 5 and the product which receives a 5 star rating is branded by the Government as a 5star OTOP product. This gives assurance about the quality of the product and makes it capable of competing in the global market. Through this program, the Government aims to increase the competitiveness of such indigenous products so that these could become a long term source of income for the people living in the rural areas (Jaiborisudhi, 2011). As of 2004, 573 products are recognized as OTOP 5 star products. These products are divided into six categories which are Food, Beverage, Textile and Garments, Household and Decorations, Handicrafts and Souvenirs and Herbal Products. The Governments helps the manufacturers of these products by marketing and promoting these products. It helps in creating a global market for these products by increasing their visibility and reach. The products are also promoted through an OTOP exhibition which is held annually called the 'OTOP mid-year'. It also aims at improving the skills, knowledge and expertise of the producers of these products which in turn will help in improving the standard of the product. The main aim is to make the rural communities self-dependent by creating a steady stream of income and employment generation for them. This will prevent the migration of people from rural to urban areas in search of employment opportunities and help in the balanced development of the country. Also the Thai culture and wisdom is promoted through these products and people learn to appreciate the creativity and way of life of Thai people. This project aims at building a stable income stream for the people which will serve the future generations as well and help in creating a strong economy.

The OTOP project since 2001 has been formally established to create jobs and strengthen local communities. The basic principles of human development, self-reliance and g-localization have guided the whole OTOP movement. This has led to the development of employment and increase in rural business revenues. While the onus for developing OTOP based market lies with the government of any country, its implementation may be supported by non-profit and non-governmental organizations (Claymone & Jaiborisudhi, 2011). These organizations have time and again given extensive support to social entrepreneurship models in various emerging countries including India, Thailand, China, etc. However, some countries have fared well on these factors while others are still lagging behind. It is believed that 21$^{st}$ century is the century for Asian Development; however, it is important to understand the complex nature of local businesses in various Asian Countries.

It is important to understand that the OTOP benefits may not be measured in economic terms only. The benefits of the movement have been instrumental in preserving the local heritage and products of Thailand. The various programmes of the government which were not able to reach the far-flung rural areas, now caught the imagination of the rural farmers. Local and governmental integrations is inherent in the implementation of OTOP marketing and manufacturing products. This includes 76 provinces, 876 districts, 7255 sub-districts and 79830 villages of Thailand which are now connected by the OTOP Movement at the sub-district (Tambon) level (Murayama, 2011).

One-town-one-product (OTOP) concept has been known since the late 1970s in many names. For some, the term OTOP is previously referred as the One-village-one-product (OVOP) movement in Japan. The movement initially aimed to add high value to a set of selective local products. The value added was needed to ensure local and regional development in terms of product development and brand recognition. Historically, the OVOP movement began in Ōita Prefecture in the late 1970s under then-governor Morihiko Hiramatsu. For this movement, the prefecture's communities selected specific products and searched for ways to add high value to these products. This concept was essential for local economic and social development. This effort resulted in individual villages had unique, competitive, and high quality products to sell in the markets. There are many examples of OTOP around the world today. They initially include Thailand and Taiwan. Other countries have also adapted the concept, including Cambodia, Brunei, Ethiopia, Ecuador, Indonesia, Kenya, Malawi, Sri Lanka, etc.

The OVOP movement (as well as the OTOP concept) is considered to be community-centric approach. Preserving local knowledge, strengthening local products, and injecting a sense of ownership to community affairs and well-being were the key driver for the success (e.g., expansion and sustainability). Specifically, from the Japanese perspective, the OVOP helped prevent further loss of local population (as economic development tends to force migration out from local villages), focus and nurture local products that reflect community's image and public recognition, promote self-reliance within a local community. The success of the OVOP depends on its three major components (Kaoru et. al., 2011):

1. **Local:** A local community needs to create nationally- and internationally-accepted products which reflect uniqueness and authenticity that cannot be found in other locations.

2. **Self-reliance and creativity:** A local community needs to be creative in adding high value to selected products. This creativity should come from the local knowledge that has been accumulated over the generations.
3. **Human development:** A local community needs to recognize the potential of human capital within. Building local spirits and fostering strong families through the incomes from the sales of local products are essential in retaining local population and preventing citizen migration to other locations.

From the Thailand's viewpoint on the OTOP concept, the attempts to promote local economic and social development have begun with His Majesty King Bhumibol Adulyadej (also known as King Rama IX of Chakri Dynasty) royally-initiated projects which were initiated in the 1960s. During this period (i.e., Vietnam War) and subsequently the Cold War, Thailand was faced with the threats from communist insurgency which aimed to recruit people from the rural areas where economic and social development was far behind the cities and urban areas. The royally-initiated projects, more than 3,000 initiatives today, aimed at raising the standards of rural life and helping rural population to be self-reliant. The primary aim was derived from the premise that the jobs needed to be created locally for strong communities. These jobs needed to provide sufficient incomes (either primary or secondary) to local populations. During the height of the Cold War, the royally-initiated projects were considered as strategic importance for national security.

For instance, several the royally-initiated projects were part of an initiative resulted in the development of the highlands in northern Thailand which was faced with the problems relating to communist recruitment, rural migrations to the urban areas, destruction of the forests through slash-and-burn, and drugs, especially opium. The efforts had gained global recognition for the success in eradicating poppy cultivation for opium and heroin, and improving the wealth of local people. Instead, the projects helped promoted a wide variety of cash crops, especially temperate plants, which would be demanded by city dwellers such as teas, fruits, and vegetables. Other local products (e.g., hand-woven products such as apparels, accessories, and home décor, hand-woven/tufted carpets, ceramics, mulberry paper and products) were promoted continuously. Due to unique climate, after careful research and experimentation, these cash crops became successful with additional value added such as fresh strawberries to jams and dried products. It is estimated that more than 100,000 people have been directly benefited from the projects with a great deal of impacts on the development of other drug prevention programs in many countries.

Many royally-initiated projects have also received international recognition. For instance, one proejct was awarded the Ramon Magsaysay Award for International Understanding in 1988. In the same year, it also received the Thai Export Award 1988 for its outstanding activities to promote Thai exports of fresh vegetables and fruit and canned fruit. The project also won an award from the Drug Advisory Program of the Colombo Plan in Sri Lanka in December 2003 on the occasion of the 30th anniversary of the Drug Advisory Program. Nowadays, the local farmers grow more than 300 crops. The cultivation success is based on continuous training in new crop-growing methods. Local communities feel that people there could earn sufficient incomes with local crops while their ways of life has been preserved. Interestingly, three volunteers in each small village began to grow cash crops and fruit trees to replace opium. These volunteers proved that they could earn a lot of money from their crops, with the Royal Project assistance in harvesting and marketing of their products. Realizing the new opportunity without having to migrate to other places, the farmers decided to follow suit. It is important to recognize that the unwavering support by His Majesty King Rama IX has served as the inspiration and has resulted in OTOP development and extension.

The success of Thailand's OTOP stems from many factors. To achieve the desirable level of family income, the local communities need to be able to highlight what would represent their products that were perceived to be unique and attractive nationally, and could further be extended. The use of local knowledge, materials, ingredients, and culture would form the basis for product selection. This is essential for self-sufficient and would be able to attract more affluent urban population. The roles of higher education as well as local governments are essentially in the value-added areas. Various factors which play an important role in a successful implementation of OTOP program are (Chandoevwit, 2003):

1. Basic research and design For instance, the food and eatery products require expiration date and product nutrition information. The local herbal supplements need content and ingredient information as well as testing results. The knowledge on creative design for non-food items should be created. Value-added techniques for food and fresh product are constant needed- fruits to dried and canned fruits, and eventually to food supplements.
2. Marketing and pricing For instance, the handicraft and garment product need better knowledge and understanding on customer preference on colors, shapes, and styles. It is important to note that, in many countries, OTOP products are unique and local so their prices should reflect this special authenticity. OTOP should not be perceived as inexpensive items. In these countries, people from the urban areas often drive to the local communities to purchase and also to learn more about the products.
3. Engineering and production For instance, the knowledge on planning, ingredient and raw material management, warehousing, record keeping and databases, and quality assurance is needed to ensure continuous (all-year-round) production.
4. Sales and Distribution For instance, the webpage development can be an alternative to promote OTOP products. The distribution and delivery of products should be developed for better handling methods and channels to reach customers.
5. Promotion and knowledge to the general public For instance, product knowledge should be constantly made to urban population. Campaign and promotion through local non-governmental organizations and governmental agencies should be planned in conjunction with new or improved OTOP products- exhibitions, conferences, seminars, workshops, and road shows.
6. Continuous OTOP improvement For instance, continuous research and development or R&D for OTOP improvement need to be made for product characteristics, functionality, tastes, appearance, packaging, etc. In addition, R&D should include the further use of local materials and production efficiency. Product rating should also be part of the improvement efforts.

For Thailand, OTOP has made a long journey towards more and more public recognition. From the specific efforts by His Majesty King Rama IX to eradicate the poverty in the rural areas and to strengthen national security, successive governments have recognized the OTOP potentials in many ways, especially economic and social development. The 1997 economic crisis helps reinforce to need to become more self-reliant as the reliance on foreign direct investment did not prevent the nation's economic collapse. The following governments, especially former Prime Minister Chuan Leekpai, have focused more efforts on solving social problems such as migration and environment (due to the use of non-local products- the children from many rural communities consume soft drink and snacks that are not healthy and the consumption lead to more waste and pollutions.) by focusing on local economic development (Kuhonta, 2004). The philosophy, advocated by His Majesty King Rama IX, has been widely adapted and practiced today.

At the present, no longer limited to products, Thailand's OTOP has now moved into the area of local services such as home stay for local cooking or making local handicrafts as well as eco-tourism. In other words, the OTOP movement continues to evolve and should be constant studied by both practitioners and researchers. In conclusion, the OTOP's economic and social benefits cannot be measured by higher income, more family security, and less migration alone. The OTOP efforts have led to more appreciation and understanding of local knowledge which will be preserved for future generations. As shown by the royally-initiated projects during the Cold War, stronger local communities mean a strong and stable nation for the future.

## KEY SUCCESS FACTORS FOR SUCCESSFUL IMPLEMENTATION

In order to successfully implement and execute the OVOP concept in India, it is imperative to understand and analyse the key success factors that make OVOP a huge success in some of the existing markets (Kurokawa et.al., 2010). This will help to develop a pre-market strategy for a successful pilot implementation in Indian markets. (Table 1 shows a list of existing OVOP equivalent movements across the world). By performing a cost-benefit analysis on these existing equivalents, the Indian entrepreneurs can get an estimate about the potential of OVOP implementation in Indian rural markets.

The idea behind this model is to create a local product gaining visibility in the market worldwide (Routray, 2007). For this purpose various factors will pay a major role in this such as:

- **Support from government**: India is a developing nation where government still plays a major role in the business. Due to lack of opportunities in India it is required too. The implementation of this model requires the front end support by the government or its agency. The government support is also required for product quality authorization. Also, it requires the infrastructural and technical aid to make this initiative successful in India. The aid can be in the form of subsidies as well.
- **Manufacturing needs**: This model is based on developing a product in local areas. Due to the lack of expertise in local areas this practice is difficult to execute in India. To make it successful what is required is the opportunity as well as the equipment to produce the products which caters to the demand of people worldwide.
- **Selecting best products**: To benchmark a product it is required to select the best products which are produced locally and also meeting international standards. These products should be able to create a brand of their own in market and sell by name.
- **Human resource:** Producing and developing quality product requires expertise. Also, to extend this model to services also, human resource will be a major factor to be emphasised upon. The training of local people is a much needed requirement for this as one major objective of this is to make local people self-reliant in order to reduce migration.
- **Exhibition and selling opportunities:** It requires the platform for recognition of product to create a known brand and develop market for itself. For ex- Trade Fare provides the opportunity to different states to showcase their best products to gain visibility in the market.
- **Development of quality product:** Quality is not only a buzz word but a necessary demand of today's era. To establish a successful brand image on international front it is required to develop quality product which is above the normal category to gain competitiveness and unique standing in the market. This will generate a positive demand and make the model successful.

*Table 1. Examples of OVOP equivalents (adapted from Oita OVOP, 2010)*

| S. No. | OVOP Equivalent | Location |
|---|---|---|
| 1 | One Factory One Product | Shanghai, China |
| 2 | One City One Product | Shanghai, China |
| 3 | One district One Product | Shanghai, China |
| 4 | One Village One Treasure | Wuhan, China |
| 5 | One Town One Product | Jiangsu, China |
| 6 | One capital One Product | Jiangsu, China |
| 7 | One Village one Product | Shanxi, China |
| 8 | One Village One product | Jiangxi, China |
| 9 | One Barangay, One Product | The Phillippines |
| 10 | One Region One Vision | The Phillippines |
| 11 | Satu Kampung Satu Produk Movement | Malaysia |
| 12 | Back to Village | East Java, Indonesia |
| 13 | One Tambon One Product Movement | Thailand |
| 14 | One Village One Product Movement | Cambodia |
| 15 | Neuang Muang Neuang Phalittaphan Movement | Laos |
| 16 | Neg Bag Neg Shildeg Buteedekhhn | Mongolia |
| 17 | One Village One Product Day | Los Angeles, USA |
| 18 | One Parish One Product Movement | Louisiana, USA |
| 19 | One Village One product | Nepal |
| 20 | One Village One (or more) product | Oita, Japan |

- **Information technology and communication:** The model requires the updated knowledge of accurate business news and business laws. It also requires the knowledge of business rivals and business networks. So, IT is the supporting aid to this model which will play major role in making this model efficient.
- **Continuous research and development**: For the continuous OTOP improvement it is required that R&D activities are taken up timely to gain early advantage of business opportunities. R&D is also required for further product quality development and knowledge of updated technology.

## 3. Market for OTOP in India

One town one product concept has been successfully implemented in China, Thailand and Philippines' as well. The backbone of this business model is proper support from Government to SME's and rural market. India over the years has been talking about tapping the untapped market and targeting the bottom of the pyramid (Torri, 2009). But this proposition has not taken any substantial effect. The OTOP concept can give a huge boost to many small industry scattered all over India (Torri, 2010). Few of the markets where this model can be applied are:

- **Jute Products:** India being world's largest producer of Jute, gives a great opportunity to market jute products. West Bengal is largest producer of Jute products such as Jute shopping bags, jute wine bags. Such products are very famous in urban cities and town. These products have long life and are sold under no brand by local manufacturers. There is no distinct difference between the product qualities.
- **Kullu shawls:** Himachal Pradesh, a land full of surprises from best of Shawls to unique tea. The shawls made here are also exported to other countries. The local weavers have been doing this job from ages and it runs in their genes.
- **Lucknow Embroidery:** Chikan, a traditional style of embroidery from Lucknow is very famous all around for their fine art form. This embroidery is done all types of clothes and needs precision and technique.
- **Madhubani painting:** or Mithila painting practised in Mithila region of Bihar, India. This form of art has a huge potential and can be pushed to a larger scale. The painting is done with fingers, twigs, brushes nib pens and matchsticks using natural dyes and colours. It has been attracting many local players and tourist as well. People visiting Bodh Gaya and other tourist attraction spot in and around Bihar have been mesmerised by this art form. These painting can be made into wallpapers and printed on Sarees etc.

One of the models existing currently is the SWADESHI Online. It's a platform where products made locally are sold through its members. The working model from "Swadeshi" is totally different, but the products have given visibility to many small industries. There are multiple products and manufacturers with some distinct feature but lack proper funding or support. Once proper channel or platform is provided, it can turn out to be profitable as well as support these talents from being extinct (Sharma et. al., 2011).

## THE ROAD AHEAD

One of the primary steps towards development of OTOP movement in India is to develop a suitable administrative structure which can handle and manage this huge implementation across India. The complexity of OTOP implementation in India arises from the federal structure of Indian Government. This needs a thorough analysis of the "best-of-both-the-worlds". While the OTOP implementation in Japan can guide on the localization of the OTOP movement, in Thailand the central government has played a more important role. (Figure 1 demonstrates three-layer architecture of OTOP Administration). This model displays how at the National Level, the Prime Minister's Office can play a critical role in the overall guidance and development of the OTOP movement. This would be sub-ordinated by Provincial and District OTOP offices which may be headed by State Governments and District Magistrates respectively. The primary role of the provincial and district OTOP offices would be to select the products for OTOP development, integrate various implementation results and prepare the budgets for OTOP development and quality improvement in these areas. The OTOP plan after being developed is finally executed at the Tambon (Village) level. In context of India, the Tambon may also refer to Taluka or Tehsil.

The Planning Process for implementation of OVOP/OTOP may be conceived as a top-down approach. Especially if the implementation is a relatively new one, this procedure may be adopted. The procedure may be developed using a PPP- Public Private Partnership model and its implementation may be divided into two segments- production (responsibility of the Public Sector) and marketing (responsibility of the

*Figure 1. Three-layer architecture of OTOP Administration (adapted from Kazuhiro, 2009)*

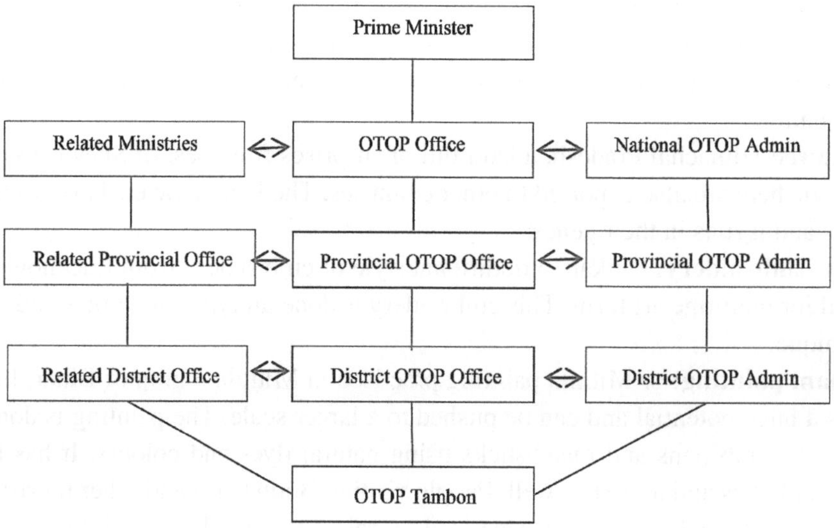


Private Sector). This means that the products that have to be implemented and brought under OTOP/OVOP regime may be selected by the Government and later when adequate information about local and market factors is available, they may be customized on expert technical advice. In other words, the implementation of a fresh OTOP/OVOP programme may be based on a top-down approach, but as the programme gains experience, it is advisable to iteratively modify it to suit the needs of local manufacturers and marketers making it a bottom-up approach.

In his discussion on Local Handmade Paper industry in Nepal, Shakya (2011) has displayed how the annual implementation programme for OVOP products may be developed by the District OVOP Committee in consultation with the local producers, local enterprises and other stakeholders. (Figure 2 OVOP Planning Process).This programme is then presented to the OVOP Secretariat for review which examines the proposal, places a ceiling on the budget and plans the activities to be performed in the upcoming OVOP implementation cycle. This process may be iteratively improved with the proposals being returned back to the District Committee for further improvements and comprehensive suggestions. After the deliberations have taken place and a proper proposal is in order, it may be presented to the Central Committee for rectification and final approval from the Planning Division. In case of India, the Planning Commission headed by the Prime Minister approves and budgets the five-year plans for the country's economic future. It may be advisable to develop a similar OVOP committee under the aegis of the Planning Commission for performing OVOP related planning and implementation activities.

In order to ensure proper implementation of the OVOP programme, we have suggested various techniques that may be adapted from various OVOP implementations across the world and combine them to follow a best-of-all-worlds approach. However, it may also help to identify certain roadblocks that may hit the OVOP programme implementation in its due course of development. In order to learn from other's mistakes, we may summarize certain key limitations that the Government of India may have to consider before implementing the OVOP programme in India (Karki, 2012):

*Figure 2. OVOP Planning Process (adapted from Shakya, 2011)*

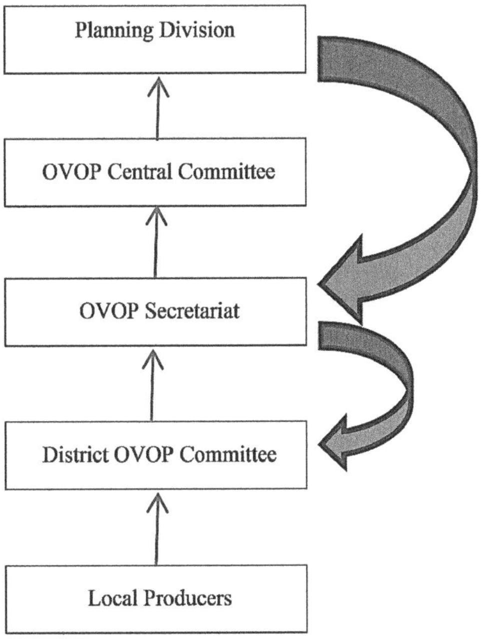


- OVOP programme is not about national aspirations but also about local pride. Hence any government that intends to develop OVOP programme must focus on utilizing local resources, understanding climatic conditions and engaging local skills and leadership while bringing uniformity into the OVOP production and implementation process. The Japanese philosophy of OVOP implementation may prove to be the best possible case study available in this regard.
- Since production phase of OVOP may be dependent on Government funding, adequate endorsement by the government in policy and development documents may be required for removing any such barriers at the ground level. The Planning Commission of India may play a pivotal role in this regard by suggesting proper ground level studies and preparing adequate budget for OVOP implementation in India.
- Since OVOP programme can be a powerful tool in alleviation of poverty and inclusive growth of far fletched areas, removal of corruption in payment of benefits and delays in Budget release may play the spoilsport in successful implementation of such an indigenous programme.
- Adequate number of subject matter specialists may be involved to speed up the decision making process and to ensure complete reach to the maximum number of primary and secondary beneficiaries.
- With the PPP model in place, it becomes extremely important that the government ensures that not only production is completed on its part, but also to ensure proper market promotion and brand equity for the Private marketers.

## CONCLUSION

Through this paper we have tried to understand the key emergent trends in rural development through OTOP manufacturing trends. These products not only serve to create an identity for a rural product but also help the local manufacturer get the right price and value for his products. Though India has seen such products being developed in certain regions of the country, we still lack a formal structure for developing sustainable capabilities for their usage in a formal mechanism. In order to ensure social entrepreneurship and rural inclusion, OTOP based manufacturing and engineering may prove to be the most useful in ensuring a brighter future for our manufacturers by making them aware of the emerging trends in engineering and technology and building TQM capabilities in their production system so as to be able to compete with the global products.

## REFERENCES

Chandoevwit, W. (2003). Thailand's Grass Roots Policies, *TDRI. The Quarterly Review*, *18*(2), 3–8.

Claymone, Y., & Jaiborisudhi, W. (2011). A study on one village one product project (OVOP) in Japan and Thailand as an alternative of community development in Indonesia. *The International Journal of East Asian Studies*, *16*(1), 51–60.

Denpaiboon, C., & Amatasawatdee, C. (2012). Similarity and difference of one village one product (OVOP) for rural development strategy in Japan and Thailand. *Japanese Studies Journal*.

Jaiborisudhi, W. (2011). OVOP Network toward in East Asia and a Case study in Thailand: The authority between the government and the general public. *The International Journal of East Asian Studies*, *16*(1), 14–18.

Kaoru, N., Kunio, I., Aree, W., Aree, C., Sombat, S., & John, T. (2011). One Village One Product - Rural Development Strategy In Asia: The Case Of OTOP In Thailand. *RCAPS Working Paper (11)*.

Karki, B. B. (2012). Doing business and role of government for entrepreneurship development. *Journal of Nepalese Business Studies*, *7*(1), 53–62.

Kazuhiro, T. (2009). *Keizai Kaihatsu Seisaku Ron*. Tokyo, Japan: Kyoto University Press.

Kuhonta, E. M. (2004). The political economy of equitable development in Thailand. *The American Asian Review*, *21*(4), 69–108.

Kurokawa, K., Tembo, F., & Velde, D. W. T. (2010). Challenges for the OVOP movement in Sub-Saharan Africa-Insights from Malawi, Japan and Thailand. *JICA-RI Working Paper (18)*.

Murayama, H. (2011). OVOP Network toward in East Asia and a Case study in Thailand: The authority between the government and the general public. *The International Journal of East Asian Studies*, *16*(1), 63–65.

Oita OVOP International Exchange Promotion Committee. (2010). *OVOP Movement: Fruits of OVOP*. Retrieved from http://www.ovop.jp/en/index.html

Phonsuwan, S., & Kachitvichyanukul, V. (2010). *Management System Models to Support Decision-making for Micro and Small Business of Rural Enterprise in Thailand*. Paper presented at 2nd International Science, Social Science, Engineering and Energy Conference.

Routray, J. K. (2007). One village one product: strategy for sustainable rural development in Thailand. *CAB (College of agricultural banking) Calling, 3*(1), 30-34.

Savitri, D. (2008). An approach of Sustainable development: Rural Revitalization as the Pioneer of OVOP movement. *Journal of OVOP Policy, 1*(7), 21–30.

Shakya, G. (2011). Understanding One Village One Product in Japan, Thailand and Nepal. Agro Enterprise Centre/Japan International Cooperation Agency (JICA) Nepal Office.

Sharma, A., Gupta, S., & Yadav, S. (2011). *Identifying various Factors that Affect Quality of Agribusiness Management Software*. Paper presented at International Conference on Issues and Challenges in Networking, Intelligence and Computing Technologies.

Torri, M. C. (2009). Community entrepreneurship among lower castes in India: A grassroots contribution towards poverty alleviation and rural development under conditions of adversity and environmental uncertainty. *Journal of Developmental Entrepreneurship, 14*(04), 413–432. doi:10.1142/S1084946709001338

Torri, M. C. (2010). Community-based enterprises: A promising basis towards an alternative entrepreneurial model for sustainability enhancing livelihoods and promoting socio-economic development in rural India. *Journal of Small Business and Entrepreneurship, 23*(2), 237–248. doi:10.1080/08276331.2010.10593484

## KEY TERMS AND DEFINITIONS

**OTOP:** One Tambon One Product: the movement similar to OVOP introduced by Thanksin Shinawatra, former Prime Minister of Thailand.

**OVOP:** One Village One Product; the movement for encouraging a village to selectively produce goods with high added value.

**Rural Innovation:** Ideas, concepts and creativity that play an instrumental role in development of shared benefit for the rural areas.

**Rural Marketing:** The two-way process of understanding the needs of Rural areas for flow of goods from urban areas to rural areas and vice versa.

**Social Entrepreneurship:** Developing business techniques and business models that attempt to solve social problems in an entrepreneurial manner.

**Social Innovation:** Ideas, concepts and creativity that play an instrumental role in development of shared benefit for the larger society.

**Social Reengineering:** Identifying potential problem areas, deriving solutions based on innovative solutions that fundamentally change the way work gets done.

**Social Venture:** A business established by a social entrepreneur for providing systemic solutions to larger problems of the society while maintaining profitability of the business.

# Chapter 5
# Feasibility Study for Setting up a Community Radio


**Somansh Kumar**
*Institute of Management Technology Ghaziabad, India*

**Ashish Bhadauria**
*Institute of Management Technology Ghaziabad, India*

**Mayank Rawat**
*Institute of Management Technology Ghaziabad, India*

**Manjusha Subramanian**
*Institute of Management Technology Ghaziabad, India*

**Priyangshu Mahanta**
*Institute of Management Technology Ghaziabad, India*

**Sarthak Awasthi**
*Institute of Management Technology Ghaziabad, India*



## ABSTRACT

*In this chapter the authors have tried to identify the feasibility of setting up a community radio station in agriculture hubs in India to create awareness about various agriculture credit schemes, government sponsored schemes, best farming practices and weather information amongst farmers. The authors are of the opinion that a more informed farmer will lead to better planning and stave off farmer suicides. While the community radio program could be an effective medium for disseminating information, its penetration and acceptance in a rural community depends upon some key factors such as proximity of the place to an urban location where visual media enjoys a wider audience. The chapter attempts to bring forth the challenges faced in establishing a CR program in Raghunathpur in the state of Uttar Pradesh and sheds light on why the initiative may not be viable. Finally the authors conclude the study by suggesting other alternatives of empowering the Indian farmer in such locations.*


## INTRODUCTION

"Agriculture is still the world's most widespread occupation. Half of humankind tills the soil, over three-quarters of them by hand. Agriculture is like a tradition handed down from generation to generation in sweat, graft and toil, because for humanity it is a prerequisite of survival."

DOI: 10.4018/978-1-4666-8259-7.ch005

With more than 1.2 billion mouths to feed in the country alone, leaving aside the ones outside the country, and still maintain healthy food reserves, the task of the agriculture sector in India is awe-inspiring. The sector's contribution to the Indian economy **may have** declined, and rightly so, in the years gone-by, but the importance of the sector is not lost on us Indians.

India is principally an agricultural country. The Indian agriculture department, with its allied sectors, is unquestionably the largest livelihood provider in India. Most of the industries also depend upon the sector for their raw material requirements. Steady investments in technology upgrade, irrigation channels, accentuation on modern agricultural practices and provision of agricultural credit and subsidies are the major factors contributed to agriculture magnification.

Ministry of Agriculture's Department of Agriculture and Cooperation acts as the nodal institution responsible for agricultural development in India. The body has under its purview the formulation and implementation of national policies and other programmes which help the country to lead on the path of rapid agricultural growth, with the help of proper utilization of the country's resources like land, water, soil and flora.

But, despite the Indian agriculture sector being renowned over the world as a powerhouse, there still exist many a challenge. Some of these arise due to the booming and uncontrolled population growth of India. This calls for efforts to raise the productivity per unit of the land. The water resources available are limited. And the ones that are available need to be utilized properly. The agricultural growth has to fulfil the food security needs of the nation on one hand and help in reducing the rural poverty.

Underlying all this lays the importance of the farmers of India. It would not be unjust to say that close to 70% of the country's population comprises farmers. It is needless to say that they form the backbone of India, in more ways than one. They produce the cash-crops enabling our country's exports and feed the mouths of India. Also, they are responsible for raw materials that our industries desperately need. To perform all these duties, what does a farmer need? He needs arable land, water, seeds, etc. But most importantly, a farmer needs information. Relevant and timely information. This could include any information on some of the best farming practices applied throughout the world, information on weather trends, and information on how to reach the desired markets without the interference of the "middlemen". All this allows a farmer to make correct decisions regarding the choice of crops to plant, where to buy his inputs and finally where to sell his produce with profitable margins. (The World Bank, 2012)

Bachhav (2002) in his study on the "Information Needs of the Rural Farmers: A Study from Maharashtra, India: A Survey" has brought out some astonishing facts to the light. According to him, the needs of the farmer "are different according to the state of developments of the concerned rural areas". These needs could very well vary from village to village, in the same district itself. In his study, he indicates that farmers involved in wheat production may be more concerned about market rates and available transportation facilities, whereas the farmers in Arunachal Pradesh need information on pest and disease management. His study rightly shows that majority of farmers did not have easy or any access to information related to their main activities. Babu et al. (2011) in their study on information needs of Tamil Nadu's farmers, found out that there were a lot of constraints in accessing the right information for the farmers. Some of these included "poor availability, poor reliability, lack of awareness of information sources available among farmers and untimely provision of information". (Babu, 2011)

One way to cater to such informational needs in a regular and timely manner is the conceptualization called Community Radio, hereby referred to as CR in the rest of the document. These are not your traditional broadcasts of radio, and are very much different from the commercial and public broadcasting methodologies. CR stations set up for such broadcasts are responsible for serving interests of communities segregated on the basis of geography, ethnicity, etc. The content transmitted is usually in the local dialect, prepared for a specific audience. Such a content may or may not be provided by commercial radio stations. And if provided, the concerned community may not be able to access the same. Most of such setups are non-profit and operated by people or communities they serve. They do however need business models to cover the operating expenses.

The major objectives of the study are:

- To study the effectiveness of regional community radio centers for rural development
- To study and analyze the feasibility of setting up a community radio service in the area of study

## BACKGROUND

Back in the days, the wisdom of the elders comprised the tried and tested, prime source of knowledge. This was collective knowledge passed on from generation to generation. When there was a generation gap, the same knowledge resided within the family and relatives. But the method had its own share of disadvantages. The most evident being that such knowledge was not documented anywhere, and was confined to a specific geographical location.

For some past years, meaningful, though ineffective efforts have been tried out by the Indian government to bring about agricultural development. But these efforts have been in vain, and shown only a meagre fraction of results that were expected. Most of the failures are a direct result of introduction of a wide variety of large scale farming and processing technologies. It is however a good sign for coming days, to note that there is now a slip in emphasis from the big musical scale of measurement transformation approach to the small scale melioration strategy approach which is attuned to Indian farm practices.

But a bigger reason for these failures can also be the treatment of information delivery, or the lack thereof, to the concerned farmers. As often transpires, agricultural information is not integrated with other development programs to address the numerous related problems that are faced by these same farmers. Information is an essential ingredient in agricultural development programs but Indian farmers hardly ever feel the impact of agricultural innovations either because they have no access to such vital information or because it is poorly disseminated. The information provided, however beneficial it maybe, is exclusively fixated on policy makers, investigators, and those who manage policy decisions with scant attention paid to the information needs of the targeted benefactors of such policy decisions. The non-provision of such useful agricultural information is a key factor that has greatly limited agricultural up gradation in developing countries like ours. If the afore mentioned approaches to agricultural development programs are to work, present and future Indian governments need to take incipient approaches to information dissemination and management that grow out from a clear understanding of what farmers information needs are.

One major factor responsible for the lack of awareness in the farming community is high level of illiteracy. Irrespective of the number of information dissemination programs that the government or any other body may start, it would be ineffective since the recipients would not be able to understand and absorb this information. For this problem, there needs to be an orthodox approach of assigning knowledge workers who could disseminate this information to the farmers.

It is hard to categorically pin point the exact information needs of farmers, especially when there's so much changing round the clock in this field. It would be wise to assume that some of these needs are related to resolution of problems like pest control, weed control, insufficiency of moisture, and fertility of soil, credit schemes available to farmers, and many more of them.

Therefore, we can categorize the needs of the farmers mainly into agricultural inputs, agricultural credit, technology changes, and marketing needs. Farms operated using modern techniques need to help out the smaller farms' productivity by contributing to the above listed needs. They could also help out by giving out timely information about fertilizers, variety of seeds, plant protection methods and chemicals, machinery involved, and water. If even some of these factors are paid attention to, there can be a vast difference to the productivity of the small scale and underdeveloped farms in question.

Information regarding agricultural credit schemes available to farmers in the form of loans and advances granted, to finance and service production activities related to agriculture, needs to be conveyed to the farmers in a timely manner. India has seen a huge number of farmer suicides because of unavailability of timely loans. Because of low levels of literacy, farmers are unaware of the already available credit schemes, and this fall prey to loan sharks, and this further creates problems for them when they are unable to repay the huge interests levied. To reap the benefit of credit, farmers need information relating to sources of loan such as names of lenders, location and types of existing credit sources. They need information on the terms of loans such as the interest rates, loanable amount and mode of repayment. Information regarding agricultural credit gets to small scale farmers usually through channels such as relations, friends, neighbors, government officials, commercial and credit banks. Grass root organs such as village heads and local government officials are used to diffuse such information because of their personal touch with small scale farmers. Knowledge workers need to intensify their efforts in educating farmers to increase their level of awareness.

When it comes to marketing their produce, farmers needs information which enables him to make rational and relevant decisions. He needs information like variety of crops to be grown in a particular season, the current market prices, the future market trends to enable a farmer to plan his produce, etc.

This information requirement by farmers is not always fixed, and differs between categories of farmers. Thus, the solutions need to be targeted to specific groups, based on criterion like land holding size or region's climatic conditions. For example, the needs of farmers who operate under rain-fed conditions will differ from those operating in irrigated areas.

## Experiments in the Past

India tried to address such problems by launching a television program called Krishi Darshan. The aim was to provide agricultural information to the farming communities of India. It is a highly accurate source of information, and caters to most of the geographical locations of the country. The information transmitted is updated regularly. (Manisha & Deb, 2009). But despite being one of the longest running program on Indian television, it has had some problems associated with it, right from the beginning. It was and still is inaccessible in most parts of the country due to unavailability of television sets in every household, especially in the villages (and the irony being in the fact, that it was aimed to cater to the rural audience!). Also is the issue of language due to which most of the valuable information is "lost in translation".

## Emergence of Community Radio/CR as an Alternative

"According to the World Association of Community Radio Broadcasters (AMARC 1998), the philosophy of community radio is to use the medium as a voice of the voiceless, the mouthpiece of the oppressed people (be it on racial, gender or class grounds) and generally as a tool for development."

The vitality of group media for group strengthening and democratization is well known. Furthermore voice based media are particularly important in the Indian connection, given the poor reading proficiency levels in rustic regions. Nonetheless, notwithstanding radio being an effective channel for voice-based group media, groups and free associations were prohibited to set up their own radio stations.

Group radio, despite the fact that new to India, has been known to be an engaging medium since a long time. Radio Sagarmatha in Nepal assumed a fundamental part in restoring vote based system. Dialogs on CR between the Hutu and Tutsi tribes in Rwanda helped compromise deliberations after the genocide. All over the world, in Brazil, Bolivia, Poland, Thailand, group radio has given voice to the individuals to air their contemplations and assumption.

## Criticisms/Constraints

A group radio station might be harshly characterized as a short go radio station that indulges the data needs of groups living in encompassing ranges. CR stations regularly include nearby group parts in project handling, revolved around points including discourses on urban luxuries in the zone, wellbeing and cleanliness, counsel on basic financial exercises, for example, horticulture, and even neighborhood people melodies and social occasions.

This thought of group radio is sort of prohibitive on the grounds that it particularly characterizes groups along geographic limits. A group can however be geologically scattered and Internet radio could be utilized to associate group parts not gathered with one another. Anyhow we will run with this basic definition for the present. Despite the fact that actually a CR station is much the same as an ordinary AM or FM radio station, its concentration on provincially applicable substance which is regularly socially spurred, differentiates it from private and business radio stations, a large portion of which, for the most part show tunes and excitement related substance.

India has been truly a latecomer to this guaranteeing channel of individuals strengthening through group media. Until late 2006, just instructive establishments were permitted to set up grounds radio stations having a transmission extent of 10-15km. This was later stretched to incorporate non-benefit offices, agrarian exploration organizations, and schools, to set up group radio stations that might include nearby groups in the substance processing process.

Before going further, it would best to list such similar initiatives undertaken by various organizations/institutions, and observe their successes or shortcomings. SRM University launched a Community Radio called the SRM Muthucharam CR, which covered the aspects of education, health, agriculture and occupation which play a vital role in the development of a community. Muthucharam CR extends its service from 10 to 15 kilo-meters in and around Kattankulathur block. The radio service has created a prompt knowledge and interest about the service of the community radio to its community. (SRM Muthucharam, 2013)

Another such project was implemented by the Mudra Institute of Communications, Ahmedabad (MICA). The institute launched its community radio service on the 14th of November 2005, with a mission towards education and use of communication to help in the betterment of neighboring communities. The latest season of Micavaani was launched in four villages near MICA - Ghuma, Telav, Shela and Kaneti. (MICA, 2010)

*Table 1. Attributes of Raghunathpur*

| Attributes | Values |
|---|---|
| State | Uttar Pradesh |
| District | Panchsheel Nagar |
| Area | 3 $km^2$ |
| Population | 4300 |
| Population Density | 1400/$km^2$ |
| No. of households | 662 |
| Males | 2289 |
| Females | 2011 |
| Official Language | Hindi |
| Time Zone | IST (UTC +5:30) |
| Coordinates | 28.696714°N 77.723817°E |
| PIN | 245101 |
| Vidhan Sabha Constituency | Dhaulana |

The models described above targeted a particular locality and strived towards the progress of the community through dissemination of information. A feasibility study was first initiated before implementation of the programs. It is quintessential to determine whether the benefits projected can outrun the costs incurred in launching a community radio program. Also the targeted population should be receptive of the idea. Hence an extensive study on the feasibility of the program in the selected community should be conducted before introducing a community radio program.

## AREA OF STUDY

For the study undertaken, it was necessary for the demographics of the area to match the requirements closely. There was a need to target nearby areas which have predominantly been hubs of agricultural activities. Upon due diligence, it was observed that the village of Raghunathpur fit the criterion perfectly for the study as per information in Table 1.

Raghunathpur village, is a part of Hapur Mandal Tehsil, Meerut Division in Ghaziabad District and is located 6.3 km distance from its Mandal Main Town Hapur.

Anwarpur (1km), Girdharpur Tumrail (2km), Nizampur (2km), Nan (3km), Kamalpur (3km) are the nearby villages to Raghunathpur. Raghunathpur is surrounded by Dhaulana Tehsil towards west, Gulaothi Tehsil towards South, Rajpura Tehsil towards north, Bhojpur Tehsil towards east.

Hapur, Pilkhuwa, Modinagar, Muradnagar are the nearby cities to Raghunathpur.

This place is in the border of the Ghaziabad District and Meerut District. Hindi is the Local Language here.

Kastla Kasambad railway station, Pilkhua railway station are the very nearby railway stations to Raghunathpur. However, Ghaziabad railway Station is major railway station 32Km near to Raghunathpur.

## THEORETICAL FRAMEWORK

A framework had to be carefully devised to assess whether the methodology that worked to an extent in MICA and SRM University could be implemented in rural communities near Ghaziabad, that exhibit the same demographic characteristics. This would require careful research on the existing models to determine the changes that need to be incorporated while targeting a specific community. The goals had to be specific. The research would primarily focus on agricultural households with the primary intention of organizing program schedules concerning information related to agriculture commodities. Raghunathpur village near Dasna, Uttar Pradesh met all the necessary criteria for study and hence it was taken up for primary research.

Certain key parameters were intentionally kept common to evaluate the compatibility of the existing models. For instance similar to Ghuma; a village where Micavaani was launched, Hindi was the local language. In addition, the climatic conditions were similar in both the locations. Also farming was considered as the most practiced occupation in both the villages. High illiteracy levels, non-penetration of the visual and audio media, unreliable information, and lack of round the clock electricity were some of the other parameters which were identified for drawing a comparison. The paper would at a later stage highlight the research parameters and significant differences observed in both the communities despite exhibiting similar characteristics. Considering the demographic and geographic divide of India, one size fits all cannot be the strategy. (Unnithan, 2013)

A CR is a dedicated initiative towards the welfare of a community. In doing so, it must also adhere to policy guidelines approved by the Government of India. As such transmitter power and range (10-15 km), maximum height of antenna (30 meters), number of permissible radio stations, were taken in account. The equipment setup time, average time taken for license approval and involvement of permissible parties were some of the additional factors considered in determining the viability of the model. One important parameter was the regional dialect. The surveys conducted had to be in the same dialect as spoken by the majority of the community.

The framework would focus on key parameters to be researched upon; such as relevance of information for the farming community, their exposure to audio media, rules and guidelines to be adhered while serving the community and the medium of survey. While the foundation would be the same as the existing models, unique layers would be added based on observations made from primary research. This would help identify research objective, appropriate design and methodology which are discussed in later sections.

### Research Design

The research objective of studying the effectiveness of community radio centers for rural development was taken by primary research. On the other hand, research objective of setting up a community radio center was done through secondary research. The primary research was conducted through surveys administered to the residents of the local village Raghunathpur.

The procedure involved in setting up a radio station was found out through secondary research.

## Research Methodology

A survey is being done to evaluate the existing issues both quantitatively and qualitatively. Care was also taken to make sure that the intended meaning of the message was clearly conveyed to the respondents. The survey was translated in the local language and if the need arose the questions were read out to the participants and the responses were gathered.

The survey comprised of questions that quizzed them to check their awareness about the latest measures taken by the government. It was administered to around 20 villagers and their responses were audio recorded.

Secondary data sources included media organs such as The Economic times, The Hindu and other periodicals.

The single-most major secondary resource that provided rural data is the CENSUS of INDIA 2011 which is the largest compilation of rural demographic data.

The village was sampled as per 3 major parameters:

- Age group (25-50)
- Occupation (Agriculture)
- Gender (Predominantly men and few women)

The time schedule available was less (about 3 months), therefore the sample size chosen was small. The population was also homogeneous since it was taken from only one village.

The fact that the population was homogeneous is not significant to our discussion because the community radio would be designed for one village/community at a time, exclusively.

The program schedule that would be prepared, shall keep into account the responses collected. The responses indicated that villagers were interested in 3 major aspects of news:

- Weather reports/forecast
- News on subsidiaries (Market rates of the products as well)
- News on new technology (its availability, cost, etc.)

## DATA ANALYSIS

Figure 1 shows that the all villagers know Hindi because it is the native language while 5.00% know Basic English whereas no one knows Punjabi. Also to mention, the dialect of Hindi is different from the one spoken in the urban parts of India. The highest percentage (60.00%) belongs to the age group 25-35 years followed by the age group of 35-45 (25.00%). Under educational status, maximum numbers of persons surveyed i.e. (70.00%) are either illiterate of have basic education up to Class 5, 25.00% dropped out after Class 8, while 5.00% studied till Class 10. This clearly indicates the level of education in this area. The schools which provide senior secondary or matric education are missing in the area.

*Figure 1. Characteristics of the population*

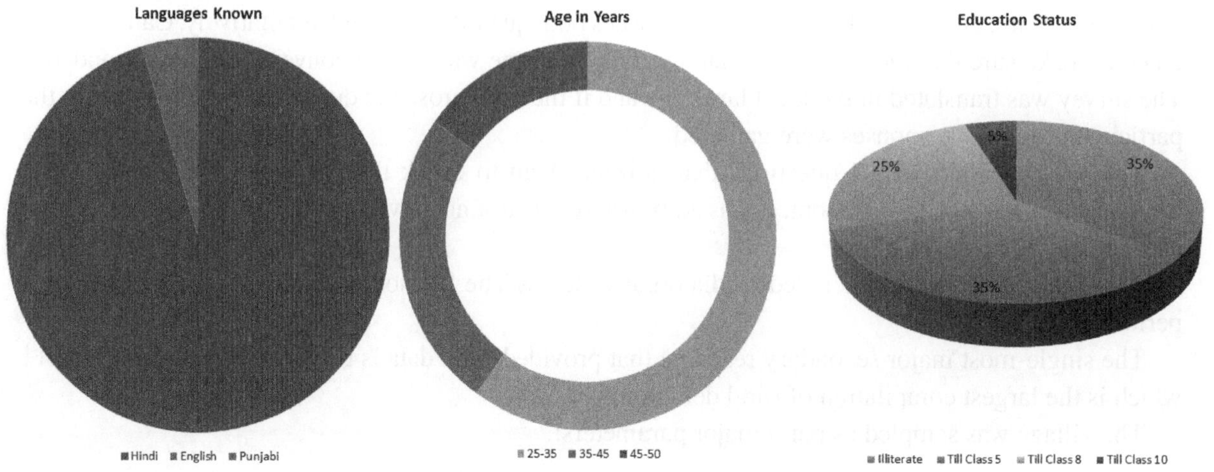


## Radio Listeners

As shown in Figure 2, the majority of farmers in the area listen to radio, thereby confirming that the farmers are aware of the radio, have access to it and can use it. It is a good sign for the CR project as familiarity with radio is of utmost important for the project.

## Work Schedule: Start

The purpose of taking the information from Figure 3 was to identify the time when the farmers will be available to use the information provided by the CR. And we can see that majority of the farmers leave for work very early in the morning before day breaks, "tadke tadke" (as we call it in Hindi in the northern parts of India).

*Figure 2. Percentage of radio listeners*

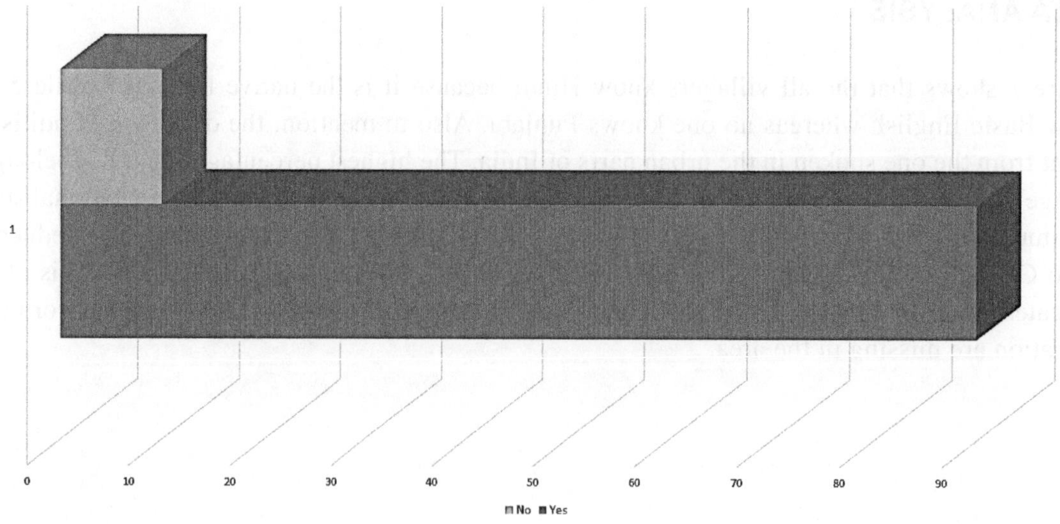

*Figure 3. Time for start of work*

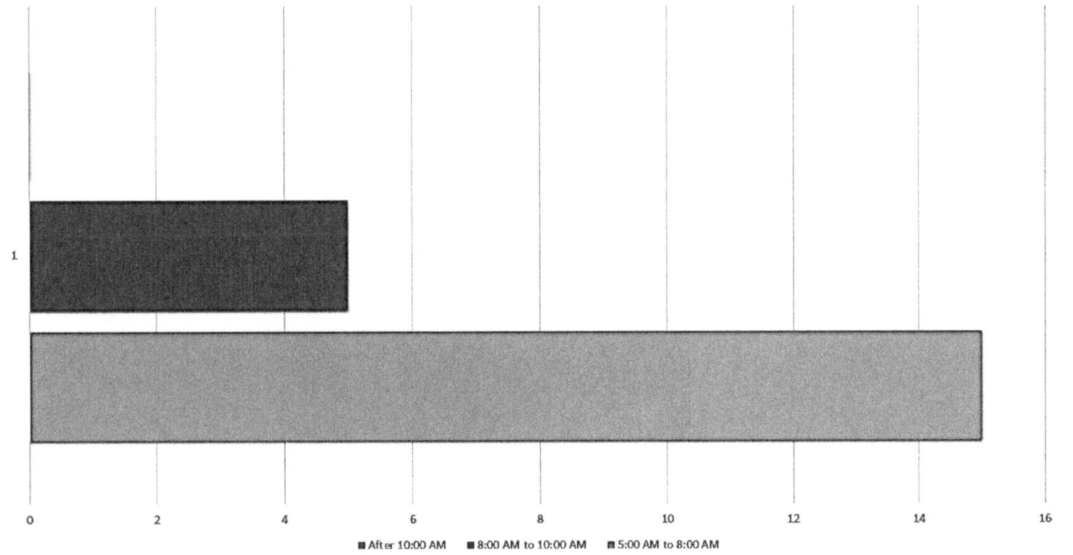


## Work Schedule: End

With Figure 4, we are able to identify the daily working schedule of the farmers. From the responses we can see that the farmers are available in the evening after work but not in the morning before starting the work.

*Figure 4. Time for end of work*

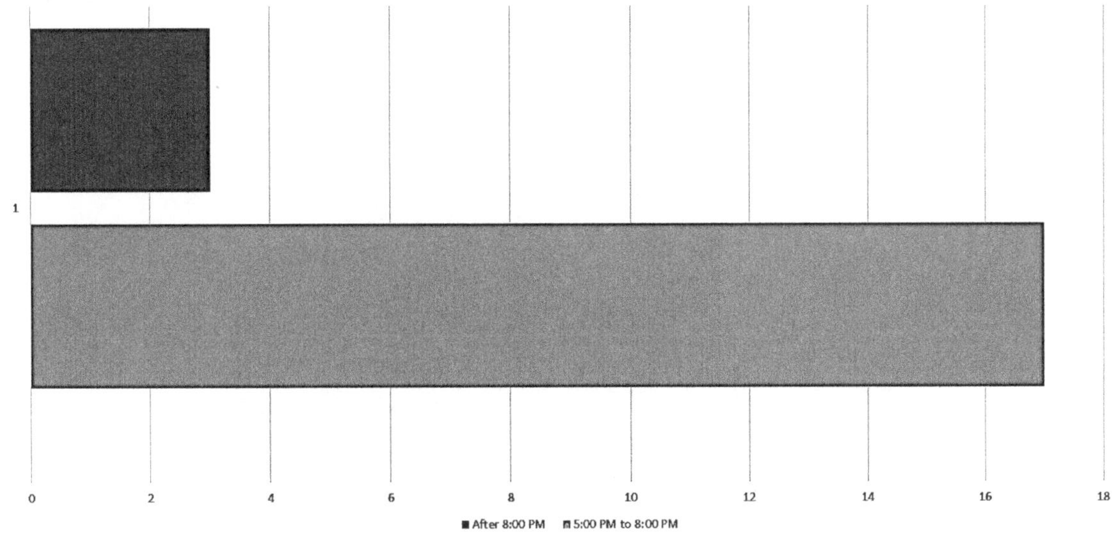

*Figure 5. Awareness of government schemes*

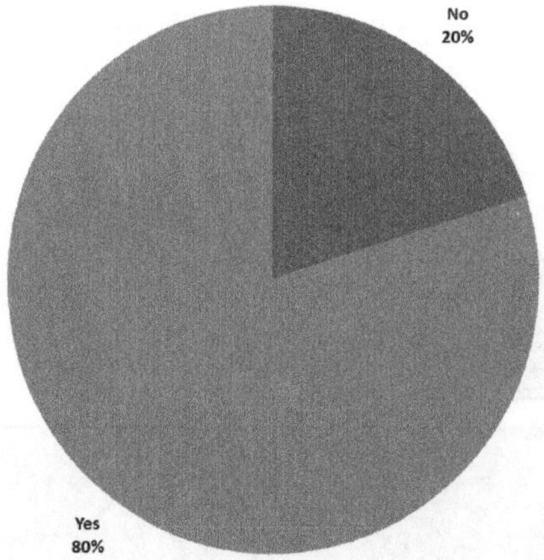


## Awareness about the Various Schemes and Plans by the Government

As per Figure 5, majority of the people in this area are aware about the schemes and plans provided by the Government. We can attribute this finding to the presence of Television in this area.

## Is Information Needed?

We can see from the Figure 6 that these farmers require the information to be able to successfully plan for their plantations, irrigations and reaping processes.

## Irrigation Problems

As per Figure 7, the season shifts in this area, being a little irregular, and the facilities for irrigation can be the reason for this kind of mixed response regarding the irrigation problems.

*Figure 6. Need for information*

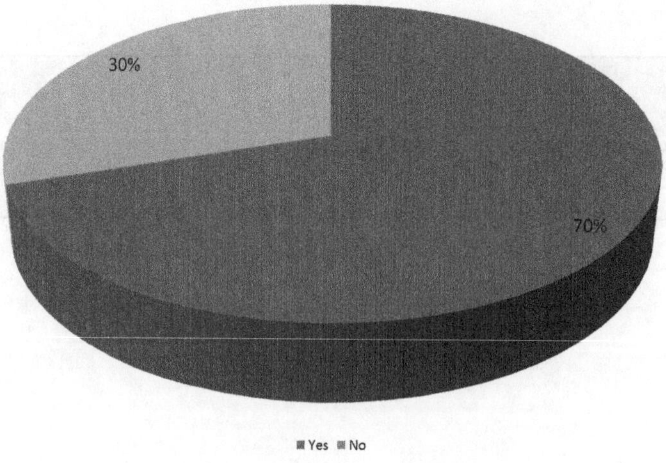

*Figure 7. Irrigation problems*

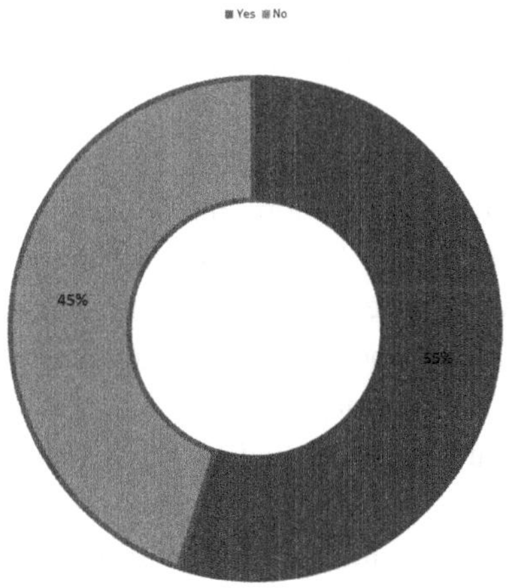


*Figure 8. Time of year when problems arise*

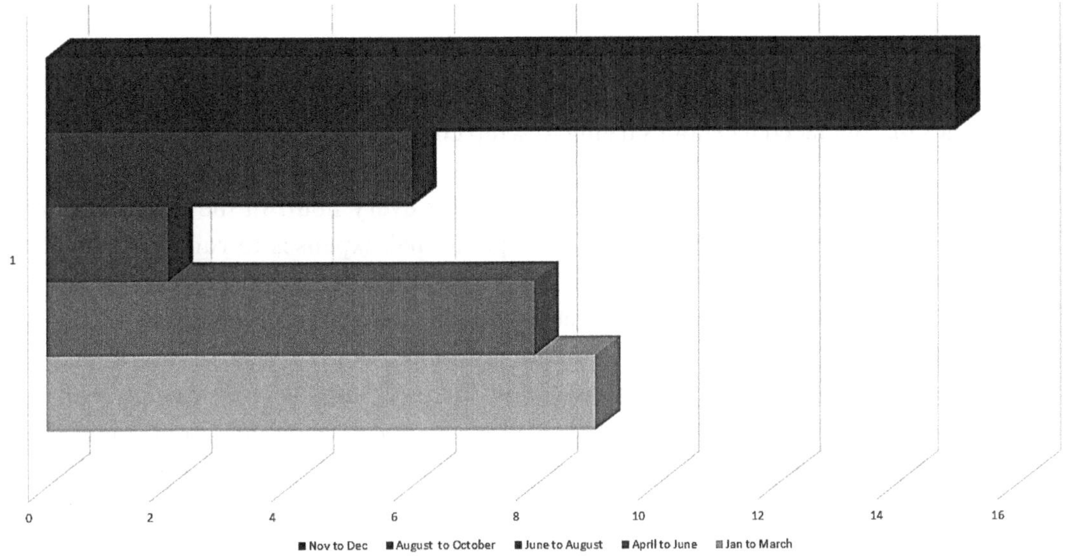


## When is the Problem Faced?

Except for the monsoon season, when there is abundance of rain, and the retreating monsoon season, the farmers face problems with the irrigation, especially the winter season, as per Figure 8.

## RESULTS AND FINDINGS

The survey was done with a sample of 20 people. The age group of the sample was from 25 to 50 years. People and the income groups chosen were just above poverty line. This was done to keep in mind the relevance of the Community Radio.

Given the fact that the area of Raghunathpur is only at a small distance from Ghaziabad, which is a developing city as it is an integral part of NCR, the presence of Television media is prominent. This is one of the primary reason why there was a mixed response for the acceptability and usability of community radio.

From the survey we can see that the people are not averse to listening to radio but they would rather prefer to have an Audio & Visual communication channel for information like TV than a just audio channel like Community radio. The people have their beliefs and trust the knowledge shared by the elders and the experienced members of the society when it comes to their profession. Although they are facing problems regarding irrigation, they are able to manage and mitigate the damages caused by the lack of irrigation. As far as the Government schemes and plans for the farming community of the country are concerned, the people are aware of that by the TV media and the other members of their society, i.e. word of mouth.

Hence, Community Radio cannot be a feasible medium for knowledge sharing for this locale, and thus cannot be a huge success like that of Micavaani and SRM Muthucharam Community Radio due to the presence of television media.

## CHALLENGES FOR COMMUNITY RADIO STATIONS

Some challenges that are faced by entities trying to setup community radio stations are:

- CR stations are allowed 5 minutes of promoting for every hour. In the event that generally showcased, this could help take care of the operational expenses to run the CR station and pay compensations to the staff. However it is for all intents and purpose infeasible for asset-crunched CR station administrators to get business aptitudes and search for publicists while they additionally prepare great quality radio substance. We feel that having a focal organization like Gram Vaani search for publicizing for their sake will be exceptionally useful. Anyhow it is additionally critical to make other income streams for group radio. We have various fascinating thoughts focused around coupling radio with telephony benefits, which we will diagram in a consequent post.
- The setup utilized by most stations is truly fundamental — simply a machine and microphone, joined with the FM transmitter by means of a blender. Despite the fact that straightforwardness is great, the absence of intuitive frameworks, for example, phones, field reporting instruments, and substance offering, makes it harder to maintain engagement from the group. Indeed programming used to run the radio station can have a noteworthy effect on its prosperity. Most CR stations presently utilize Winamp to play out radio projects, and need to depend on hacks to do live telecast, or interleave ads between projects. An expert radio mechanization framework is exceptionally important to scale exercises, however at present there is no free and open-source framework that gives a one-stop answer for play-out, show, telephony, SMS, and Internet content imparting.

As examined prior, India has been late to determine the possibilities of group radio. In a matter of seconds, there have been activities from the legislature yet there are issues which need to be determined for group radios to work adequately. As indicated by the approach rules surrounded by Government of

India the authorizing technique is dreary and the invested individuals need to go through a methodology of screening and leeway from Home service, Defense and so on. This could be a deterrent to the street ahead for group radios on the grounds that the time it now, tedious and not empowering enough for non-government organizations.

In the present worldwide framework keeping out the private part from an activity which proposes to achieve the length and width of the nation might be doubtful. Reserving in eager private associations for setting up group radio stations can take the procedure forward at a speedier pace. Be that as it may, the private area could be permitted to work just under solid administrative components from the legislature, generally the motivation behind the stations to achieve the minimized will be lost and the group radio stations can wind up getting to be market driven cash making machines.

Group radio could be the main impetus behind introducing changes in the living state of the populace of the nation. It can positively help India in getting created by giving open doors for advancement. A splendid future sits tight for the group radio stations in the nation gave the material and human assets are channelized legitimately.

## SUGGESTIONS AND FUTURE IMPLICATIONS

The study has provided insights into agricultural sector's information needs. The importance associated with timely information has been growing among the farming communities. The Community Radio Station concept was suggested to address such demands after having observed the success of similar such initiatives taken up by MICA and SRM University. However, based on our primary research, the popularity of such a program is higher in remotely located villages, like the ones served by CR stations of MICA and SRM. This is due to the low penetration of visual media in the form of television in such villages. Rural communities like Raghunathpur, which are closer to developing or developed cities like Ghaziabad have shown mixed response on acceptability and usability of the radio medium, because of the impact of the visual media. Households, where television is still a luxury commodity, prefer radio sets as a means of information and entertainment, and thus would be ready to accept programs broadcasted by a dedicated CR station.

The study implicates that either a CR station should target a rural community which has minimal exposure to television media; or new initiatives for investment in dedicated government promoted television programs be encouraged. But as mentioned earlier, there already exists a dedicated program called Krishi Darshan, which has been running for a long time on Doordarshan, but has not been able to reach isolated areas of the country, because of low penetration of televisions in such areas. This formed the basic reason for undertaking the study.

## MOBILE PHONES: AN EMERGING ALTERNATIVE?

With the technology boom fairly visible throughout India, chance of availability of a mobile phone in a household, even in a village, is more than that of a television set or a radio set. Mobile phone can be used as a potent medium for benefitting the local communities. When utilized properly in a centralized infrastructure, it can act as a medium for bottom-up knowledge sharing, as a tool for behavior change communication, and an open forum to bring accountability and transparency in the work of local service providers. Some of the benefits can be detailed as follows:

- **Knowledge Sharing:** In the domain of agriculture, questions can be conveyed to a pool of resource experts. The experts can answer the questions, and these question-answer snippets can be posted on a forum for the benefit of other community members. This can help in building a unique combination of bottom-up needs identification based on questions asked by people, and add to it corresponding relevant top-down authoritative content developed by experts. This way, the community consequently bamboozles both planets, amazing educative substance, essential parts of which are contextualized for utilization by the group.
- **Accountability:** The medium can act as a data generation tool for social audits. Public pressure imposed through criticism in mass media thus made the service providers more responsive.
- **Business Impact:** The success of this low cost medium of transmitting information can result in opening up of venues for ancillary businesses and related meta-markets in the field of agriculture. Equipment and technologies not utilized till date will be up for grabs, since the market would get expanded. The resulting marketing opportunities will shape up the future of agriculture in the country.

## REFERENCES

Babu, S. C. (2011). *Farmers' information needs and search behaviours: Case study in Tamil Nadu, India.* International Food Policy Research Institute. Retrieved October 7, 2013, from http://www.ifpri.org/sites/default/files/publications/ifpridp01165.pdf

Bachhav, N. B. (2012). Information Needs of the Rural Farmers: A Study from Maharashtra, India: A Survey. *Library Philosophy and Practice (e-journal).* Paper 866. Retrieved October 7, 2013 from http://digitalcommons.unl.edu/libphilprac/866

Besson, L., & Carot, D. (Producers), Bertrand, Y.A. (Director). (2009). *Home* [Motion picture]. United States: Elzevir Films Sub-District Details. (n.d.). Retrieved December 24, 2013, from http://censusindia.gov.in/PopulationFinder/Sub_Districts_Master.aspx?state_code=09&district_code=07

Dutta, S. (2010). Community Radio: Revenue Structure and Possibilities in India. *Global Media Journal,* 1-1. Retrieved December 25, 2013, from http://www.caluniv.ac.in/Global mdia journal/Commentaries-june-2010/soumya datta.pdf

*India: Issues and Priorities for Agriculture.* (2012). Retrieved October 7, 2013, from http://www.worldbank.org/en/news/feature/2012/05/17/india-agriculture-issues-priorities

Manisha, M., & Deb, S. M. (2009). *Indian Democracy: Problems and Prospects.* Anthem Press.

MICAVAANI. (2010). *Transmitting on 90.4 MHz.* Retrieved October 7, 2013, from http://www.mica.ac.in/home/introducing-mica/life-at-mica/student-committees/micavaani

Ministry of Information Broadcasting, Govt. Of India (2011). *Community radio awareness.* Author.

Ozowa, V. (n.d.). *Information Needs of Small Scale Farmers in Africa: The Nigerian Example.* Retrieved December 24, 2013, from http://www.worldbank.org/html/cgiar/newsletter/june97/9nigeria.html

Seth, A. (n.d.). *The community radio movement in India*. Retrieved December 23, 2013, from http://www.gramvaani.org/wp-content/uploads/2013/05/community-radio-indian-history.pdf

*SRM Community Radio | Home*. (n.d.). Retrieved October 7, 2013, from http://www.srmuniv.ac.in/muthucharam/

Unnithan, C. (2013, August 10). MICA students launch new season of community radio. *The Times of India*. Retrieved October 7, 2013, from http://articles.timesofindia.indiatimes.com/2013-08-10/news/41265647_1_community-radio-listeners-mudra-institute

Vaani, M. (n.d.). *A voice-based communication platform for the BoP*. Retrieved December 23, 2013, from http://www.gramvaani.org/wp-content/uploads/2014/04/mobile-vaani-mar-2014.pdf

*Village, R., Tehsil, H., & District, G.* (n.d.). Retrieved December 24, 2013, from http://www.onefivenine.com/india/villages/Ghaziabad/Hapur/Raghunathpur

## KEY TERMS AND DEFINITIONS

**Conceptualization:** The act of coming up with a solution after due interpretation of facts and thoughts.

**Doordarshan:** An Indian public service broadcaster, which provides television, radio, online and mobile services.

**Ethnicity:** A person's grouping based on their culture, religion, language or the like. Community: A social entity of people which shares common values and practices.

**Krishi Darshan:** An Indian television program broadcasted on Doordarshan, which caters to agricultural needs of farming audiences.

**Micavaani:** A community radio station dedicated to social relevance, operated independently by the students of Mudra Institute of Communications, Ahmedabad.

**Transmitter:** An electronic device used to amplify, modulate and radiate signals from an antenna.

# Chapter 6
# The Impact of Kisan Call Centers on the Farming Sector

**Kartik Chachra**
*Institute of Management Technology Ghaziabad, India*

**Harshit Singh**
*Institute of Management Technology Ghaziabad, India*

**Gowtham Seelam**
*Institute of Management Technology Ghaziabad, India*

**Mayukh Sarkar**
*Institute of Management Technology Ghaziabad, India*

**Anshul Jain**
*Institute of Management Technology Ghaziabad, India*

## ABSTRACT

*The Indian Agriculture has been an area with varied challenges. This sector is responsible for the growth rate and generating a per capita income. This sector generates a whopping 28% of the total GDP of India and over 15% of the total exports. The usage of Internet and phone technology can fill these gaps to a large extent. A continuous two way interaction among the farmers and agricultural scientists will ensure agricultural extension. A landmark step was taken on January 21, 2004 when the Department of Agriculture & Cooperation, launched Kisan Call Centers (KCC) with the help of the extensive telecom industry to deliver extension services to the farming community. The main purpose of these call centers is to answer the queries raised by the farmers in their local language, on continuous basis. At present the Kisan Call Centers are running from 14 locations all over India. In this chapter, we are trying to analyze how this strategy to help the farming community was introduced and how it is being implemented.*

## INTRODUCTION

The role of agriculture in India's socio-economic development is inherent since ancient times. Even today agriculture forms a significant part of the GDP and overall growth and sustainability of India. This sector provides employment to 51% of the total workforce, being the largest economic sector amongst others such as mining, tourism, retail, textile, industry and services. That being mentioned, the challenges before the agricultural practices in India are immense. It will not only benefit the overall economic progress of the country, but is also essential for the workforce of the nation, two thirds of which, directly or in-

DOI: 10.4018/978-1-4666-8259-7.ch006

directly depends on the same. It contributes to around 27% of the GDP of India and somewhere around 13-16% of the exports. Still, the yields are not only lesser than expected, they are highly unstable and the gaps in technology transfer are much more intense as compared to those in areas that are irrigated.

Kisan call center is a Government of India initiative under the department of Agriculture and Co-operation. This initiative is primarily aimed towards assisting the farmer community for any issues or queries that they may have and also in training them to face the immense inevitable challenges. These knowledge centers are active throughout India providing services to farmers in terms of assistance and guidance in solving their problems in their regional local languages. Providing a structure to this entire operation of query handling involves effective use of technology, networking, a strong knowledge base, technically educated and informed staff. These call centers make use of an extensive telecommunication network, having a strong back end Management Information System to address the queries of farmers across the country, regarding agriculture practices and latest farming techniques. The scheme's objective is to serve the farming community spread over 5 lakh villages across the nation.

The need of the hour is to pay greater and more focused attention to information by extensively using the appropriate tools and technologies that help farmers cope up with the diverse challenges and learn new opportunities on a continuous basis. To capitalize on future export opportunities of agriculture products, the country needs to match global standards in terms of quality, stability and hygiene. Hence, the farmer should be aware and informed of the latest efficient agricultural practices.

The Kisan Call Center aims to fulfill the following:

- Fast and effective spreading of information
- Minimizing the gap between Farmer and Research Labs, agriculture universities, market, corporates
- On demand specific individual knowledge transfer and adequate facilitation
- Efficient use of the huge and complex telecom infrastructure

While the state of Kentucky, US is following GAP (Good Agricultural Practices) to ensure safety from post production deceases in the crops, and the GAP in Rome (Italy) are focused on setting up protocols and appropriate processes, the services provided by KCC are rather educational and informative in nature. They aim to educate the farmer with innovative and new technologies and techniques that should be implemented in order to yield better results.

Recently, to facilitate the queries of the farming community in an easier way, the Department of Agriculture and Cooperation has come up with an idea of Kisan SMS (Short Messaging Service) Portal. The users have to register and enroll themselves via a mobile number. Once registered, the user will receive regular updates about weather and agricultural alerts, absolutely free of cost. In this case, a farmer will be getting an SMS messages providing expert information and delivering services on his mobile from agriculture scientists at various levels. The services cover diverse areas such as crop production and protection, animal husbandry, fisheries as well as dairying.

New types of information and services are expected to be included as the system progresses based on the different requirements of farmers. Some of these include:

1. Weather information including forecast
2. Alerts for farming related facts
3. Timely Information regarding disease/pests outbreaks
4. Technology related support for crop cultivation according to local conditions
5. Awareness of new crop variety
6. Market know how
7. Soil fertility reports

## THEORETICAL FRAMEWORK

Here we describe the concept and structure of the implemented knowledge based service, also the infrastructure and technology involved in connecting the farmers with the personnel who address their individual queries in their local language. The steps for a typical calling procedure can be seen in Figure 1, below. Each call follows a pre-defined protocol and queries are addressed according to their nature by various levels of representatives, from agriculture graduates, postgraduates equipped with computer systems, Subject Matter Specialists (SMSs) or Subject Matter Experts (SMEs) having sound technical knowledge, and various other but related scientists to promptly assist the farmers with their respective questions and doubts. This way these call centers provide extension services to the farmer community according to the nature of the problem. This is an opportunity for businesses with the existing extension services to grow their network further to help farmers in remote areas of the country adopt better practices.

*Figure 1. Steps involved in a typical calling procedure*
*Source: National Institute of Agricultural Extension Management*

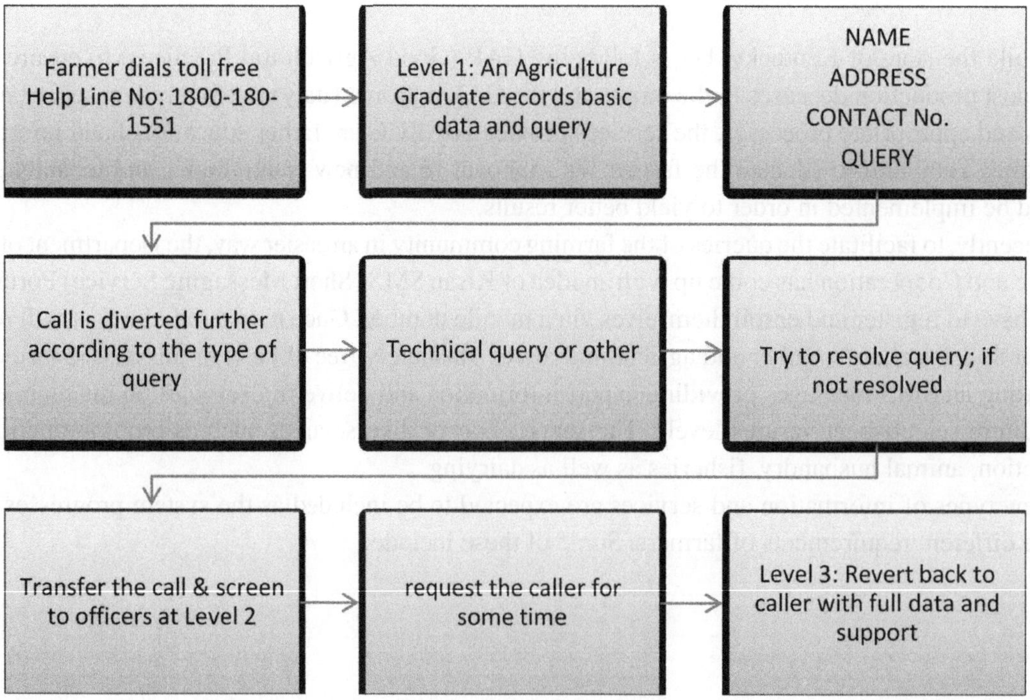

When a KCC (Kisan Call Center) representative receives a call, he or she addresses the query based on their own knowledge and understanding. Also, the representative has access to a knowledge database containing FAQs, which is updated continuously with every incoming and outgoing call. The different type of calls can be identified as—

Technical Query:

- Crop Production
- Crop Protection
- Horticulture
- Agriculture
- Animal Husbandry
- Marketing

Others include:

- Admin related query
- Regarding Government Schemes
- Subsidy
- Seeds Positioning
- Gypsum, Fertilizers, Pesticides
- Credit and insurance

Farmers can provide feedback on the agriculture services provided by the government and the private sector; this helps in regular monitoring and improvement in services.

These call centers are generally a part of an organization like Research Stations, ATICs, Agriculture Colleges or are outsourced, as per the specific requirements. The objectives of such ATICs are the provision of a single and streamlines delivery system for the services and products to the kisans (farmers) and other FIGs as a continuous process of technology dissemination innovation. They also encourage the callers/users and facilitate them to provide their valuable feedback. The services offered by the call centers usually include customer support, multi-lingual direct assistance and other services. The senior agriculture scientists and experts in the government system are Nodal Officers.

The infrastructure of Kisan Call Centers is divided into three levels:

- **Level I:** A Call Center that is professionally managed including all the basic requirements for a stable network and smooth communication. The call center management dedicated for the KKC services maintains Local Area Network (LAN), Air Conditioning, equipment such as computers, headphones and an Uninterrupted Power Supply. Qualification representative: M.Sc. in Agriculture
  - The major functions carried out by a Level I representative are being a first point of contact to the farmers, he attends the call with a welcoming message and takes the question down and feeds that into the computer by himself. The operator will be fluent in the local language and in most of the cases he is equipped to answer the question himself.

- **Level II:** A response center handling the services of Subject Matter Specialists for individual problem based query resolution. This contains upgraded and more robust technology setup as compared to Level I. Qualification of representative: PhD. In Agriculture, with 10-15 years of experience in relevant sector.
    - The Level II representative holds certain responsibilities like answering the questions if the Level I representative couldn't answer the questions posed by the farmer. The Level II representatives comprises of the Subject Matter Specialists who stays at their respective places like educational institutions or the Govt. Offices. Depending on the expertise they hold the specific question will be forwarded to those persons. The expertise basically will be classified depending upon the crop or certain other parameters. In any case if the person is unavailable then there is a callback option where the question poser will be called back in mostly less than 72 hours.
- **Level III:** the Nodal Cell comprising of the Nodal Institutions is also fully equipped with the appropriate logistic support. The senior officers resolve queries and problems using software analysis tools. Qualification of manager: Masters in Agriculture, having 5-10 years of experience

For Level II and Level III support, agriculture agents are nominated from various institutions and organizations all over India. Proper training and induction is provided to the nominated graduates.

An important part of this organization is the Human Resource. The personnel attending calls need to possess basic skills to attend to farmers' calls effectively. Few skills identified are

- **Soft Skills**
    - Greeting and facilitation
    - Ability to speak using farmer's language
    - Usage of simple sentences and words
    - Patient listening
    - Probation of the details
    - Diagnosis of the query/problem raised by the farmer
    - Answering at the level of the farmer
- **Communication Skills**
    - Empathizing with the caller
    - Active listening
    - Commitment to assist the caller
    - Assertive responses
    - Relating with local or personal experiences, as need be
    - Polite replies
    - Subtle modulations or transitions in voice
    - Closing the calls with greetings as well
- **Computer Operating Skills**
    - Basic know how of the mouse and the keyboard
    - Basic know how of the internet
    - Receiving and sending electronic mails

For successful implementation of any system there is always a need to monitor and review the regular performance using methods such as feedback from inside and outside the organization. Storing the data by Nodal Offices on a regular basis lays the foundation of such an extensive knowledge base. Analysis of the collected data takes place at these Nodal Institutions by specialist suitable for the job. The same Nodal Institutions are also responsible for documentation and reporting that help in creating consolidated courses of action for individual farmer's query.

## OBJECTIVE

- Study of the concept and mechanism of operation.
- Understanding the ground level function of Kisan Call Centers.
- Analyzing the structure of the scheme.

## RESEARCH DESIGN

Based on the learning and research, the elements of survey and data collection were inferred, by focusing on the planning, implementation and management of Kisan Call Centers. Certain Measurement indicators were identified to assess their performance and recommend opportunities for improvement. Parameters that were chosen include

- Number of daily calls received
- Agent quality
- Network sustainability
- Infrastructure
- Utility of software and technology
- Training

The expectations of the government and other stakeholders in the scheme were used to form an understanding about the size of the scheme. Some of the expectations from this scheme:

- Over 500 calls per day
- Technically sound personnel with good communication skills to resolve problems efficiently
- Smooth network quality and reliable connections
- Building regular Database
- Adequate infrastructure matching all technical requirements
- Simple User Interface of software
- Technical training to be continuously provided to representatives

A strong software tool that has been developed by Telecommunications Consultants India Ltd. (TCIL) supports Kisan Call Centers and ensures instant and continuous connectivity across the entire network. The Management Information System enables technical assistance to farmers and recording of queries to build a database, which is accessible all times to the KCC.

The database mainly consists of questions asked by farmers along with their answers. Report generation software is bought in use by the agriculture graduates having a user interface to generate reports based on specific parameters entered by the agents, according to the requirements of the concerned farmer. The filters used for scanning through database for generation of report are date, location, crop, problem etc. This data is made available over the Internet once the report is generated.

## RESEARCH METHODOLOGY

Secondary data was gathered from various sources such as articles, journals and case studies from the Ministry of agriculture. This data was the basis of obtaining an in depth knowledge of the concept leading to a structure for the research.

Primary research was conducted involving site visit of KCC's nodal office in Ghaziabad. Information was gathered on the implementation and response of farmers towards the scheme. The objective of the primary research was to conduct analysis of data collected and inferring the grass root level implementation implications of the scheme. Further, identifying loopholes, if any and providing recommendations based on the learning and findings.

## LITERATURE REVIEW

Maximizing the crop productivity is one of the major problems in a country like India where agriculture is the primary occupation. The crop productivity poses a huge problem pertaining to the amount spend on raising the crop and the amount a farmer can earn selling the crop in the market. One among the many reasons for not achieving the desired output is that the expert advice is not reaching the farmers on time. There is a lot of information gap between the research and actual practice. To bridge this gap, the research paper (P. Krishna Reddy and R. Ankaiah, 2005) mentions about a framework. According to the framework mentioned, each farmer will be equipped with Agricultural information dissemination system (AgrIDS) which is cost effective. This helps the farmers to cultivate with the help of both the crops related, location related experts.

The proposed framework mentions the integration of IT services, which grew rapidly over the last few decades, with agriculture. As it was mentioned that all the farmers will be made available, the AgrIDS system, so that the farmers can get the timely advise from the experts. It involves the pictures taken from the fields and then they will be transferred to the experts. They will have a look at those pictures and then will provide the advice analyzing them. The advice definitely will not be based on the received pictures alone but there are lot many details the experts, in their own area of expertise, will suggest the farmers which crops to elect and raise depending upon some of the major factors influencing the agriculture like rainfall, soil type, weather etc. Also financial experts suggest the farmers about the crops which possibly will have high demand in the international or the domestic market which will help the farmers to earn profits. Also production of certain crops in the country is rather scarce when the consumption is taken into consideration so government can take steps into providing certain schemes that can motivate the farmers to raise that crop.

The research paper (P. Krishna Reddy and R. Ankaiah, 2005) also mentions about the drawbacks of the traditional system. At present the insights given to the farmers are in a generic and not specific to the certain farmers so for some the advice helps but a lot people might get affected either by not getting the desired productivity nor the profits. It does not cover all the farmers but only a few. There are numerous reasons some being the literacy levels, lack of awareness etc. The traditional process is just a one way process and if the farmers need more information on what they have been farming they couldn't get the information on time. The major drawback being unaccountability – number of advices given and the number of advices that are turned out to be useful. The proposed AgrIDS overcomes these drawbacks to a major extent.

The AgrIDS system will be using the data ware housing technologies, data mining techniques. Saving large amounts of data has become an easy task in the recent years. So all the queries that the system will receive in the form of either text or photos will be recorded along with the answers. This data being saved can be used in the future if the advice is requested for similar kind of problem by a farmer. In the present world extensive information is available online and there are many companies whose business model runs only on the data. With all of this enormous amount of data available it can be analysed and then refined so that the patterns can be drawn using the data mining techniques. Extrapolating the data available simulation models can be developed so that the future possibilities can be drawn from them. For all of this to happen the internet should be made available to all class of people where they can make use of the system proposed.

The system consists of various parts including farmers, coordinators, AEs and Agricultural information system where all of them are integrated using internet. The amount a farmer would invest in receiving the advices is substantially less by using this system. Amount of pesticides and fertilizers to be used for a crop can be moderated based on the actual requirement for high output. Because of lack of experience of the farmers they might not be using the adequate amounts of pesticides or the manure. So making this AgrIDS system available to the farmer, the money a person spends on the fertilizers will be saved substantially.

A research was taken up by a group of researchers from MSSRF (M.S Swaminathan Research Foundation) about the technical advancements in the field of crop husbandry that took place in the country pre – post independence periods and their implications. The research paper (R. Rukmani) mentions about the ICAR system which developed around 3000 hybrids and high yielding varieties related to various crops which promises more productivity and less prone to diseases. Some of these varieties were used in the country to witness a huge increase in the crop productivity. The statistics backs the fact that the growth rate in the 1990$^{s}$ was less compared to 1980$^{s}$ possible reason mentioned was because of the lack of the proactive decisions by the country in that time frame. Also the challenges faced by the government are the Intellectual property rights adoption and the assessment of advances in the biotechnology fields. The policies during the early decades after independence will have to see a significant change to meet the present changes in the field of the crop husbandry.

Considering both the research papers, (R. Rukmani) mentions about how the scientific technology totally shifted the face of agriculture to meet the growing demand and also mentions that some amends to the present policies are required to withstand the changes in this present world. This research paper (P. Krishna Reddy and R. Ankaiah, 2005) mentions about a framework consisting of AgrIDS that will help the farmers. While during the early decades when there was only a limited connectivity among the people, the state had taken steps to help farmers use the ICAR developed crop varieties (like Rice, Wheat and some Cereals) and it took decades for the crop productivity to reach to the current state. While taking into account the connectivity among people and the reach of any information in the present day, with advancements in the scientific development and integrating those with the IT models such as AgrIDS will definitely help the increase in the crop productivity.

Kisan call center have been one of the most pioneering initiatives by the Government of India. According to a report published in Asia Pulse, the Kisan call centers in India received 318,106 calls in total. These calls were from farmers who belonged to remote and tribal areas who sought solutions for their problems that varied from agriculture to animal husbandry. The Indian Society of Agricultural Professionals (ISAP) released this data. The ISAP is the organization that sponsors the functioning of the call centers. The article further stated that most of the queries originated from Shivouri and Shajapur districts in Madhya Pradesh. Also, the tribal areas over there also called up these centers to clear their doubts. The number of calls relating to agriculture crops were 173,274, while those about horticulture summed up to 93,299 and 12,802 were from the field of animal husbandry. Currently, the service has been made available from 6 AM to 10 PM, except for Sundays and gazetted holidays. The service is provided beyond these hours by an IVRS system.

There are fifteen subject specialists that are employed and available at the call centers in Madhya Pradesh who work in two shifts to ensure maximum time is available to cater to the queries of farmers. The Kisan call center here is managed and run by National Agricultural Development Project through a private public partnership. The Kisan call centers are equally effective when it comes to solving the problems of farmers in the hilly regions of Himachal Pradesh. A study conducted by Sharma and Singh in 2011 concentrated on two cash crops that are grown in the region, apple and tomato. These crops are grown in the high and medium hills of the state respectively. According to the study, the farmers who used the services of the calls center were more informed about their crops and benefitted from it. The productivity of crops of these farmers was much higher than those who did not used the services. It suggested that the farmers should be educated by the media and government about the call center so that farmers can grow their crops more effectively and scientifically.

Recently, the Government has collaborated with IFFCO Sanchar Limited for the restructuring of the KCC's. The new call centers would be state of the art and shall provide professional assistance as well as well technical innovations to the existing service network. These include call barging that will be handled by experts and officers of the government, video conferencing, dynamic monitoring of the working of the call centers. The books and reference material provided to the employees will also be upgraded to the latest editions of modern agricultural practices. The IKSL (IFFCO Kisan Sanchar Ltd.) has attempted to provide many innovation, interactive and engaging services for the farmers that subscribe to the KCCs. These services and its subscription is absolutely free of charge and includes benefits and activities like free voice messages on a daily basis to every subscriber, on his area of interest, call back facilities, mobile quizzes, common forums and focus groups. Their prime mission is to empower the rural section of the society and the farmers with high quality and germane services and information, through proper telecommunication and other communication channels.

84% of farmers were satisfied with the advice that they received from the call center personnel, as stated by the study conducted by Administrative Stall College of India in 2012. The study further revealed that the advice helped the farmers in efficiently managing their fertilizer and pesticide usage, which reduced the weeds, pests and diseases in crops. Moreover, this initiative is built and structured in a manner to accommodate continuous evaluations and monitoring, that would help the same to grow in a more effective manner. After the research, it was also found that TNAU (Tamil-Nadu Agricultural University) formed Farmer's Associations – FIG (Farmer Interest Group) which is essentially an independent and self-managed group of farmers with common goals and interests. The members of this group pool in their resources, so that by uniting their resources, they can work towards the fulfilment of their common goals and objectives and share the consequential benefits.

## DATA ANALYSIS

Nodal officers in Delhi and Ghaziabad aided in collection of data, to assess the performance and grass root level implementation of KKCs. The Scheme was launched at the time when BJP government was in power in India and the KKCs received recognition, showing good results and positive response from farmers.

The services provided through KCCs are monitored and reported by these Nodal offices. Although, the offices were equipped with all the facilities claimed by the government, a lackadaisical attitude was observed on our visits to the offices in New Delhi and Ghaziabad. All over the scheme has a total outreach to over 1500 villages and around 30 districts in 17 states of the country. This scheme has also provided employment to over 1800 BPL (Below Poverty Line) youth, living in rural India, by conducting training programs.

The knowledge base has grown immensely since the inception of these call centers. KCCs have enabled spread of knowledge amongst farmers and access to information easy by providing a proper channel supported by the government and private parties. States where the scheme has been most successful, like, Bhopal, Madhya Pradesh have KCCs running in Public Private Partnerships (PPP). A list of call centers across major states can be seen in Table 1.

## RESULTS AND FINDINGS

The important findings from the project research are that Kisan Call Centers have:

- Transformed and impacted the lives of more than 1.25 lakh farmer families.
- Provided Specialized Training and job opportunities to over 1800 BPL youth.
- Promoted Entrepreneurial developments to bring in greater avenues for private ventures to agriculture graduates.
- The Bhopal KCC alone has answered up to 5 lakh queries during 2008-11.
- Made effective use of technology. A robust MIS system helps in advisory services and building knowledge base.
- Over 250 graduates, those have been certified as Crop Certified Advisor (CCA).
- Highest calls recorded for the vegetable growers, closely followed by food grain growers and fruit growers. 23.5 percent of the calls were recorded for the information about various diseases in the crops and 6.9 percent of the calls were related to animal husbandry.

*Table 1. Call centers across major states*

| S.no | State/ UT | KCC Location | Language | Telephone Lines (Outgoing- incoming) |
|---|---|---|---|---|
| 1. | Andhra Pradesh | Hyderabad | Telugu | 2-3 |
| 2. | Bihar | Patna | Hindi | 1-2 |
| 3. | Jharkhand | Ranchi | Hindi | 2-3 |
| 4. | Chhattisgarh | Raipur | Hindi | 3-4 |
| 5. | Delhi | New Delhi | Hindi | 2-4 |
| 6. | Dadra, Nagar Haveli | Ahmedabad | Gujarati | 1-2 |
| 7. | Gujarat | Ahmedabad | Gujarati | 3-4 |
| 8. | Punjab | Chandigarh | Punjabi | 2-3 |
| 9. | Haryana | Chandigarh | Hindi/Haryanvi | 3-4 |
| 10. | Himachal Pradesh | Shimla | Hindi | 2-3 |
| 11. | Jammu & Kashmir | Jammu | Dogri, Kashmiri, Ladhaki | 2-3 |
| 12. | Karnataka | Bangalore | Kannada | 2-3 |
| 13. | Kerala | Trichur | Malayalam | 1-2 |
| 14. | Maharashtra | Nagpur | Marathi | 2-4 |
| 15. | Uttar Pradesh | Kanpur | Hindi | 3-4 |
| 16. | Rajasthan | Jaipur | Hindi | 2-3 |
| 17. | Tamil Nadu | Coimbatore | Tamil | 2-4 |
| 18. | Uttarakhand | Dehradun | Hindi | NA |
| 19. | Arunachal Pradesh | Itanagar | Adi | NA |
| 20. | Assam | Guwahati | Assamese | NA |

*NA—Not Available

Source: Directorate of Extension - KCC

## SUGGESTIONS AND FUTURE IMPLICATIONS

The use of technology is critical to bridge the economic gap prevailing in the country, to stimulate growth by building individual capacity to generate value through learning the immense opportunities in agriculture and allied services. A shortcoming in the TOT (Transfer of Technology) model is a prominent challenge for the current private and public extension systems, however, the effective and efficient use of telecommunication channels, relevant technologies and internet, this gap can be bridged by a considerable extent.

After studying and analyzing the concept implemented by the government with the emergence of KCCs, we suggest that more private organizations should show participation in such initiatives, by forming alliances with the government and NGOs. In states where the scheme is to be launched, the mobile carrier partner companies can come up with initial promotional offers for farmers, such as distribution of registered sim cards to them. This would encourage the farmers, make life easier for them and spread greater awareness amongst them regarding KCCs.

Also, more importance should be given to courses like CCA (Crop Certified Advisor) and the youth, especially in the rural parts of the country, should be encouraged to pursue this as a career option.

Contemporary technology should be leveraged more effectively to facilitate growth. Promotional campaigns using mobile wagons and kiosks should effectively spread the scheme to untouched remote areas of the country.

## REFERENCES

Chouhan, R. S., Kumar, Dushyant, & Sharma, H O (2011). Performance of Kisan Call Center: A Case Study of Kisan Call Center of Indian Society of Agribusiness Professionals Bhopal (Madhya Pradesh). *Indian Journal of Agricultural Economics*. Retrieved October 9, 2013, from http://search.proquest.com/docview/912670940?accountid=50136

Dhyani, S. (n.d.). *BPO Caretel announced the achievements of their "Kisan Call Center" project As Kisan Call Center completes its successful 5th Year*. Retrieved October 10, 2013 from http://www.indiaprwire.com/pressrelease/agriculture/2009011718157.pdf

*IFFCO Kisan Sanchar Ltd*. (n.d.). Retrieved February 12, 2014, from http://www.iksl.in/

*KCC: Features, Directorate of Extension*. (n.d.). Retrieved October 10, 2013, from http://vistar.nic.in/training/locations.asp

*Kisan Call Center*. (n.d.). Retrieved May 5, 2013, from http://agricoop.nic.in/policyincentives/kisancalldetail.htm

Krishna Reddy, P., & Ankaiah, R. (n.d.). *A framework of information technology-based agriculture information dissemination system to improve crop productivity*. Ministry of Communications and Information Technology, Department of Information Technology, New Delhi, India. Retrieved May 17, 2014, from http://www.currentscience.ac.in/php/toc.php?vol=088&issue=12

Mukherjee, A. (2007). Fodder on the Line. *Business Today, 16*(9), 62. Retrieved October 8, 2013, from http://web.ebscohost.com/bsi/detail?sid=62b7dd32-2b33-47ea-9c6f-f67a8b588225%40sessionmgr14&vid=1&hid=19&bdata=JnNpdGU9YnNpLWxpdmU%3d#db=bth&AN=24844647

*Over 300,000 MP Farmers Indian used Kisan Call Center: Report, Asia Pulse Pty Ltd*. (2010). Retrieved October 10, 2013, from http://search.proquest.com/docview/759359583?accountid=50136

Rahul, A. (2011). *Kisan Call Center: Bridging the information gap*. Retrieved October 10, 2013, from http://www.thebetterindia.com/2304/kisan-call-center-bridging-information-gap/

Rao, S., & Sharma, V.P. (n.d.). *Tele-Agri-Advisory Services for Farmers: a Case Study of Kisan Call Center in Andhra Pradesh*. Academic Press.

Rukmani, R. (n.d.). *Measures of Impact of Science and Technology in India: agriculture and rural development*. Retrieved May 21, 2014, from http://www.currentscience.ac.in/Downloads/download_pdf.php?titleid=id_095_12_1694_1698_0

Sharma, B. R., Singh, P., & Sharma, A. (2011). *Role of Kisan Call Centers in Hill Agriculture*. Indian Society of Agricultural Economics. Retrieved October 11, 2013, from http://search.proquest.com/docview/912670948?accountid=50136

Tiwari, R. (2012). Government ropes in IFFCO Kisan Sanchar Limited to improve Kisan Call Centers [Agriculture]. *The Economic Times* (Online). Retrieved October 7, 2013, from http://search.proquest.com/docview/1011117854?accountid=50136

*User Manual Version 1.0 for Kisaan SMS Portal*. (n.d.). Retrieved September 8, 2013 from http://farmer.gov.in/advs/User%20Manual%20for%20Kisaan%20SMS%20Portal_Ver1%200.pdf

## KEY TERMS AND DEFINITIONS

**AgrIDS:** Agricultural information dissemination system, an online system proposed where the entire process of examining the crop and suggesting the productive steps by the specialists can be done online.

**ATIC:** Agricultural technology information Centre, a place where the information regarding the agriculture can be available.

**GAP:** Good Agricultural Practices, the best practices that can be adopted to attain the best possible output.

**KCC:** Kisan Call Center, a call center where farmers can get their queries regarding the agriculture can be answered.

**PPP:** Public Private Partnerships, a type of partnership where the public, private together is involved to raise the capital and be a part and owner of certain project.

**SME:** Subject Matter Experts, a part of the KCC where they would be answering the questions addressed to them to their best in order to resolve the farmer's queries.

**TOT:** Transfer of technology, where the use of technology among the stake holders.

# Chapter 7
# Tale of Two Entrepreneurs

**Roma Mitra Debnath**
*Indian Institute of Public Administration, India*

**Shyamli Singh**
*Indian Institute of Public Administration, India*

**Astha Gupta**
*IMT Ghaziabad, India*

## ABSTRACT

*The chapter highlights the innovation of two entrepreneurs. The significance of the innovation on our society regarding the health issues has been focused. Two entrepreneurs and their innovation have been studied very closely. They were interviewed as well as their websites were studied thoroughly. The result of the study shows a close bonding between innovation and creativity.*

## INTRODUCTION

Innovation is a continuous process associated with evolution of life. Population explosion necessitates acceleration of more and more innovations. India is a developing country. Hence, it is facing challenges in every field, from education to environment. This brings up the need of innovation ecosystem consisting of institutions, technological up gradations, and hassle free environment. Here, it should also be noticed that innovation is different from invention. (Fagerberg, 2006), "Invention is the first occurrence of an idea for a new product or process; while innovation is the first attempt to carry it out into practice."

Entrepreneurs, on the other hand, are the risk takers. They are decision makers as well as good managers. They are capitalists and have a bend to explore the market opportunities. They have the ability to combine various products creatively.

According to R. David Lankes' Atlas of New Librarianship, innovation is further defined by entrepreneurial activities. In the text his example centers around the capital or resources needed by an entrepreneur to successfully implement an innovative idea. Thus entrepreneurship demonstrates the innovation by putting the idea or concept into practical use with the infusion of resources, be it capital or support of institutional leadership.

DOI: 10.4018/978-1-4666-8259-7.ch007

In one of the research papers "Entrepreneurship and Open Innovation in an Emerging Economy" the authors stated that entrepreneurship is a creative process in which individuals engage in some form of generative and open learning. This activity permits the acquisition of new knowledge (Miller & Friesen, 1983; Popper & Lipshitz, 1998). New knowledge when linked with individual's existing understanding and business experience results in the generation of new ideas (Oguz, 2001). The importance of individuals and organizations being engaged in innovative learning can be enhanced through generation of new ideas.

Kirton (1976) suggested that individuals approach to solving problems is located on a continuum ranging from adaption to innovation. Western firms are giving more and more importance to creativity, innovation, and shared knowledge for individual and organizational development. Leading companies such as AT&T, American Express and United Airlines have recognized the importance of employees learning from each other and from customers to develop innovative solutions to organizational problems.

Eric von Hippel in his classic book, Sources of Innovation, identifies end-user innovation as the driving force for ideas and solutions that can bring a change to processes, products and services. Innovation takes different directions as it impacts products and processes. This includes changing the method that a process takes in how it is delivered to the end-user, changing what services are offered and this might include discontinuing outdated services or support. These types of innovations are observed in businesses as they change to meet customer demands, with modifications in offerings as per vendors' interest, or methods that improve the efficiency of the individuals involved (Crumpton, 2012).

Innovation is not a new phenomenon in the evolution of society, but it is a process inherent to human development. Ancient societies searched those elements that not only increase those means of subsistence obtained from natural resources, but also reduce the effort necessary to carry out their work and to facilitate the transport of individuals and products. According to Sternberg & Lubart (1999), creativity is related to entrepreneurship since they define entrepreneurship as a form of creativity that can be labeled as business or entrepreneurial creativity because often new businesses are original and useful. Studies have found that entrepreneurship and innovation are positively related to each other and interact to help an organization to flourish (Zhao, 2005; Flynn et al., 2003). More over, a significant line of research argues that cities and regions function as incubators of creativity and innovation (Lee et al., 2002, 2004; Thomson, 1965; Park et al., 1925).

With the introduction of more sophisticated innovations, the benefits of these innovations were considered as well as the negative effects on society, on employment and on human behaviour (Miguel-A´ngel Galindo & Marı´a-Teresa Me´ndez-Picazo, 2013).

Over the years, many government and private agencies have started up with various innovation schemes that have encouraged the budding entrepreneurs to materialise innovations, convert ideas into sustainable products and pave the way for entrepreneurial culture in the country. It is also important to consider the entrepreneur along with the innovative technology. He is that person who was ready to take risk, and come up with better technologies for the betterment of the society. Two of such marvellous innovations and promising entrepreneurs' journey has been discussed in the chapter.

## TALE OF BRAINCHILD INNOVATION: MOZZIQUIT

### Background

Sitting back at his office, and looking outside the window, Ignatius Orwin Noronha remembers the days when his product "MozziQuit" (MQ) Mosquito Trap" was just in the ideation phase. He had exchanged several mails with government officials and Angel Investors to conceptualize his product and set up his own company and was anxiously waiting for their response. 52 years old, Ignatius Orwin is the sole inventor of MQ and the Managing Director of Leowin Solutions Pvt. Ltd., registered under Companies Act on 18th June, 2008 to innovate, manufacture and market eco-friendly products. He is a self-trained innovator with thorough knowledge of product innovation lifecycle. He has worked in the Middle East for ten years. Back in India, he manufactured waterproofing chemicals and executed works in and around Mangalore city. Thereon, he also started manufacturing products of polymer in 2001-02 to repair deteriorated structures of containers found above the sea at Jawaharlal Nehru Port Trust, Mumbai.

Mr. Noronha has another feather of innovation in his cap. He proposed 2" thick modified concrete-mix design to Indian Oil Corporation Limited (IOCL) in December 1999 instead of conventional 12" thick concrete mix. It would be used for roads and driveways with specific claim on allowing the concreted roads for movement of vehicles after 24 hours of concreting without waiting for 28 days of stated period, saving time and costs. IOCL tested the sample on 6th December, 1999 after 24 hours of concreting, and awarded the first project of Concreting Driveway at Goregaon Petrol Pump in 2000. This technology is testimonial even after 10 years of its use because of its performance and quality. It would save five times of concrete cost and time, as India has got huge requirement of road infrastructure.

Concrete mixture releases greenhouse gases like carbon dioxide and other by-products like fly ash and sulphur, which when in contact would lead to problems like skin burns, rashes, irritation in the eyes, nose, and throat, and other respiratory diseases like asthma. So MQ is not only reducing the usage of concrete, but also benefitting the environment indirectly.

## Mosquito Apparatus: "MozziQuit"

Mr. Orwin, the brain child behind the innovation of the famous mosquito trap "MozziQuit" has carried out R&D on the product since 2001. His Eureka! Moment was after observing an American Product Mosquito Magnet at Shri Shakthi Gas & Energy the exclusive distributor of American Bio-Physics Inc. at Hyderabad, priced at 1.1 million per unit with operating cost of five thousand per month for three LPG cylinders and for a hazardous chemical called Octenol. Octenol is used along with carbon dioxide in mosquito repellants and traps to attract mosquitoes and other biting insects. However, it mimics human breath, leading to problems like asthma, skin rashes, irritation in the eyes, and ingestion.

Raw materials combined, this electronic device works on the unique heat and light generating technology within the device to attract mosquitoes. Mosquitoes are attracted by unique vacuum system integrated within the device, and are killed instantly. Dead mosquitoes can then be disposed of through the removable collection container in the device (Figure 5). The apparatus uses less than three Watts of power consumption which is only five paise per day. Even if the electricity cost is increased, it would not cross three digits for five years (Table 1). The product so designed works without the use of any chemicals and combat mosquito menace.

Available in two sizes "MQ Max®" (Figure 1) and "MQ Mini®" (Figure 2), the device involves a one-time investment of Rs. Two Thousand Nine Hundred and Ninety and Rs. One Thousand Five Hundred respectively. It does not involve any hidden charges and daily consumables as in the case of other mosquito repellants available in the market, making it as the lowest acquisition cost of killing mosquitoes in India. It provides efficacy to the system, i.e. the waste can be checked personally from catch net container. The product is effective up to ten thousand square feet area without barriers. It even sucks invisible and minute dust particles, as tested by Raman Research Institute Bangalore and certified by National Institute of Malaria Research, India.

## Assessment of "MozziQuit"

Existing mosquito repellent mats, coils, and traps do not kill mosquitoes. In fact these machines keep them away from a designated area by releasing harmful radiations and chemicals which not only have side-effects on skin, and also leads to continuous headaches in some people but also leads to mosquito multiplication (Table 2). Regular maintenance is also required to purchase and refill the repellents leading to high costs.

MQ, on the other hand, attracts and kills mosquitoes, stops multiplication, and prevents diseases. It is easy to use and is environmental friendly viz, it neither uses any chemical nor release any kind of harmful fumes having side-effects on human bodies. The performance can be checked at regular intervals. It is value for money as it involves one time acquisition cost with zero maintenance. It saves up to 37% of cost and energy in two years, 74% in five years, and 86% in ten years. It is sustainable in long run and can be used anywhere from big houses to flats, schools to colleges, hospitals to big corporations. It is highly effective within half hour of its operation and hence is required to be switched only for one to two hours during the evening.

"MozziQuit" was displayed on the vision summit of ISA Technovation 2010, organized by the Indian Semiconductor Association and was recognized as ISA's Best Electronics Product of the Year – 2010 in Healthcare sector (Figure 6). For this master invention, Mr. Noronha was awarded gold medal from Mr. Rakesh Singh, Additional Secretary of Information and Technology at the Taj West End, Bangalore (Figure 3). National Institute of Malaria Research has certified the product, *as reported by daijiworld.com/news, 2010.*

Further, Mr. Noronha has already been granted patent for MQ and received some ten design registration certificates (Figure 9) from Indian Patent and Designs Office.

## Quality Assurance and Industrial Tie-Ups

MQ has been acknowledged by various institutes and government agencies. The sample has been tried, tested and approved for use by National Institute of Malaria Research, Bangalore and Indian Council of Medical Research, Bangalore (Figure 8). Mr. Noronha has also been also offered Research and Development facilities by Delhi branch of these institutes on contract basis. Further, IC$^2$ Institute, University of Texas at Austin, USA has recommended commercialization of MQ in India (Figure 7) as well as globally during the Analysis Report presentation at DST-Lockheed Martin India Innovation Programme in 2010 (Figure 4).

Defense Research & Development Establishment (DRDE) of Defense Research & Development Organization (DRDO), Ministry of Defense, has signed Engagement Agreement with Orwin on 6th September, 2010 after assuring the quality of the product. Last but not the least, Raman Research Institute Bangalore has also tested the product and named it as the only product with Zero emission of UV radiation.

## Environment-Socio-Economic Impact

The objective of this master innovation was to create mosquito free environment, and reduce the number of people being affected by mosquito borne diseases. Emergence and resurgence of mosquito-borne diseases, namely malaria, dengue, filarial, typhoid, jaundice, encephalitis, and chikungunya are well known in tropical and subtropical regions. Such diseases impose socio-economic burden on humanity, some of which, still do not have any cure.

According to World Health Organization (WHO) fact sheet 2011-2012, India has the highest malaria burden with an estimated figure of 24 million registered cases per year. During 2010-2011, 219 million patients were registered being affected by malaria, out of which 1.1 million deaths were averted globally. Other diseases are also painful and are increasing in prevalence. It is said that these diseases have killed people more than those killed so far in all the wars combined. More than $5 billion are spent on patients infected with malaria alone. But, in spite of so much spending, the diseases continue to explode from time to time because the mosquitoes develop resistance towards medicines and chemicals.

Climatic changes have taken place to a great extent in developing countries like India, Africa, and China. There is storm surges, coastal flooding, sea-level rise, weather changes, erratic electricity and water supply, reduced agricultural productivity, and droughts in some areas which leads to ill-health and disrupted livelihoods in both rural and urban populations. These changes in bio-diversity have further lead to multiplication of mosquito and mosquito-borne diseases resulting in risk of mortality rate.

These diseases are also one of the causes of poverty and a major hindrance to economic development. Poverty increases the risk of mosquito-borne diseases as people below poverty line do not have the financial capacities to prevent or treat the disease.

The economic impact of mosquito borne diseases is worse. From loss of money involved in healthcare to time in terms of number of working days. It might also lead to brain damage from cerebral malaria and decreased productivity. This would further be liable for some 40% hospital admissions, 50% out-patient visits. Overall resulting in 40% loss of public health spending, investments, and tourism *as per malariaconsortium.org*.

## Way Ahead

In the Fifth Assessment Report released by Intergovernmental Panel on Climate Change (IPCC) has stressed upon the impact of emission of greenhouse gases, and climatic changes, causing skin diseases, and respiratory problems. Further, multiplication of mosquitoes result in mosquito-borne diseases like malaria, typhoid, chikungunya, etc.

The targets and objectives of the government will be attained only when progress is made towards a healthy and disease free society. There is a strong need for the government and the innovators to work in tandem, as a team, and innovate in the field of healthcare, in terms of anti-disease drugs, medicines, creams, ointments, healthcare schemes and programs, mosquito repellants, that mark the history of inventions. Innovative products like “MozziQuit” should be strongly supported, promoted, and funded by various government agencies in order to improve upon the society and bring it at par with international standards.

The sudden telephone ring brings Mr. Noronha out of his reverie. It was his secretary with the reminder for his meeting with government officials in fifteen minutes. He thanks her and gathers all his thoughts for the meeting regarding his invention’s funding.

## GROWING GREEN IS THE NEW COOL: SNOWBREEZE

### Background

Experts have cited age as one of the factors affecting creativity. Creative output relates to how an individual questions the status quo. According to Bob Kelleher, from 99EmployeeEngagement.com, creative thinking will be the way we define leadership in the future as questioning the status quo of existing services and ideas. However, one of our creative designers and innovator, Shri M B Lal, has questioned this with his mind boggling innovation.

Retired Bureau Chief and Assistant Editor of The Statesman and 85 years old innovator got the idea of innovation during a hot afternoon in the summer of 2007. There was a power cut for seven hours and to curb the heat his wife placed a large tub full of ice under the fan, which gave the family some respite and an idea to build an innovative air conditioner. One of the economic and environmental friendly innovations works on the basic principle of ice energy. The product was created for the elderly and sick people facing difficulties due to extreme weather conditions and power cuts. Different models are available in the market depending on the usage, suffering in similar circumstances. The same are available in the market and online at greenairconditioner.org and indiamart.com.

Power shortages everywhere is hampering the economy, specially industrialization and electrification of rural areas where networks of poles and wires stand without power. Since most of the high demand for power during summer is caused by air conditioning on a massive scale, the power shortage witnessed can be substantially reduced if conventional air conditioning systems are replaced with ice-based air conditioning systems, which are already in vogue in parts of Europe and America, as reported by the author in Outlook Magazine, 29 August, 2010.

The retired journalist invested some 1.5 Lakhs on testing the product and building eight trial models. He promoted his special device through newspapers, books, magazines, and website snowbreeze.org and has applied for patent too. The walking stick does not deter him to stand and walk. He himself uses iPad much faster than a 12 year old kid. Chinese electronics company, Zhejiang More, is already manufacturing and selling the equipment in China.

### Snowbreeze: World's Most Economic Air Conditioner

Snowbreeze, world's most economic AC works on the basic principle of ice energy. It is 100% green. The 12 inch electronic device uses ice, water, electric pump, and as much electricity as a cooler. It has many added advantages. It brings comfort to millions of people from heat at a low cost; serves as a lifesaver for the sick and elderly of all classes during power breakdowns; requires less energy as compared to other ACs; reduces pollution; and the most important saves electric power for the country, besides rendering numerous other minor benefits. Further, it runs easily on power backup and the cooling effect does not make the room humid. The Snowbreeze project has established beyond a shadow of doubt that it is possible and easy to air-condition rooms, offices and halls of all types with ice and chilled water.

The Green Gandhian AC is a cooler with a drawer at the bottom. There is a metal drum inside it consisting of handful of coils and mesh of PVC pipes, along with two pumps fitted at the bottom of. Half the drum has to be filled with water. Blocks of ice are loaded on top of the mesh of pipes, resting on the water. It functions on the simple process of evaporation and condensation found in the Himalayas.

River and seawater evaporate and rise up to form clouds. When clouds hit mountains, water turns into snow and flows back down into the rivers. The fan then gives a cooling effect. Complete working of the model can be seen on the website.

Snowbreeze can bring down the temperature by seven degrees centigrade in an hour in a closed room. It is energy efficient, i.e. compared to an average 1.5 ton AC guzzling 2,000 watts it draws only 100 watts. There are different models of the contraption made out of plastic drums, metal boxes and desert coolers, designed differently for different purposes. The desert cooler is the most effective, costing about Rs 15,000. The plastic drum model costs about Rs 5,500. The box type would cost anywhere between Rs 5,000 and Rs 6,000 depending on the amount of copper used. The latest model "makes its own ice".

Snowbreeze comes in variety of designs and models to comply with the need of different users. While it can fit the needs of every section, those requirements have to be classified in groups and standard designs have to be developed for each group. Thus an enlarged redesigned European concept would be ideally suited for air conditioning large rooms, offices and halls. The Bucket or Desk-top model would be the best choice for a small room. At the same time for automated cooling the Water Cooler model may be considered. The same are enlisted below.

## Snowbreeze 1: Match for Wall AC

Designed in several shapes and sizes Snowbreeze 1 runs on a stream of compressed air for 100 to 150 feet through aluminium grooves fitted in a separate casing around an aluminium drum packed with ice. This energy saving air conditioner is that innovation in the field of air conditioner which protects us from heat and cold at the least cost. It is cheap, 90% energy saving, and 100% 'green' gadget that a carpenter can fabricate in three to four days. This unique cooling device has never been invented before.

This AC is converted into room heater also by removing the lid of the ice-drum. Suspend a 300 to 500 watt halogen bulb from a bar resting on its rim, with its frame tilted inward, in the upper half of the drum, filling the lower 40% of it with water and leaving a gap of half to one inch between the water and the bulb-frame. Then switch on the system. Warm air will start blowing into the room within 10 minutes. The warming up period could be reduced to five minutes or less if, to start with, you put pre-heated water in the drum. It keeps the room cooled and dehumidified for about 8 hours when it has to be refilled with ice after draining out condensed water. (Figure 10)

## Snowbreeze 2: Unique Self Cooling AC

Snowbreeze 2 is a unique cooling device which harnesses the self-cooling energy of water in conjunction with ice. It is based on the centuries old self-cooling 'matka' (pitcher) principle, which sets in motion an automatic convection current in a water body. (Figure 11)

## Automated Snowbreeze: Multipurpose AC

The latest 90% energy saving, 100% green, fully automated model of Snowbreeze is designed to match a wall air conditioner. Their chief advantage is that it costs practically nothing and keeps the room cool and comfortable during the summer and monsoon seasons. (Figure 12)

## Mini Snowbreeze: Boon for old and sick

Mini Snowbreeze is a boon for elderly people with limited means. It helps the sick to cope up with the weather and power breakdowns. Mini-Snowbreeze is a cheap but effective air conditioner which can run on an inverter and keep a small room cool and dehumidified for eight hours with "free" ice from the family fridge (Cost Rs.2,500-$50). (Figure 13).

## Snowbreeze Room Heater

Converting Snowbreeze 1 into a power saving room heater is a simple process. Remove the lid of the ice drum. Suspend a 300 to 500 watt halogen bulb from a bar resting on its rim, with its frame tilted inward, in the upper half of the drum, filling the lower 40% of it with water and leaving a gap of half to one inch between the water and the bulb-frame. Then switch on the system. Warm air will start blowing into the room within 10 minutes. The warming up period could be reduced to five minutes or less if pre-heated water is poured in the drum. (Figure 14)

## Battery Powered Rural Unit

It is a special model suited for rural areas where power is available for just a few hours a day or not at all. It can run for eight hours at a time on a specially designed power unit equipped with an automatically recharging 15-ampere dry battery and a 6" DC fan. (Figure 15)

## Worldwide News

Ice-powered air-conditioning is catching up worldwide and products like Snowbreeze are popular in parts of the world. They have been deeply acknowledged by economists all over the world.

## China

China is already manufacturing and exporting electronic devices on the same concept, ice energy. Chinese electronics company, Zhejiang More, has started the process of manufacturing and selling the equipment in China. Details can be viewed at zjmore.manufacturer.com.

## Europe

The energy crunch and climate change have forced intelligent leadership in Europe to invest resources and scientific talent in alternative ways of air-conditioning which is one of the biggest power guzzlers. In this race for options ice has clearly emerged the front runner, source greenairconditioner.org.

## USA

America woke in September 2010 when consortium of municipal utilities in California began retrofitting government offices and commercial properties with systems that use ice made at night to replace air-conditioning during the day. It is part of a pilot program for the devices, which are built by Windsor, CO-based Ice Energy. If widely deployed, they could reduce fuel consumption by utilities by up to 30% and put off the need for new power plants.

Over the next two years, these eleven participating utilities will install 6,000 devices at 1,500 locations, providing 53 megawatts of energy storage to relieve strain on the region's electrical grid. The project is the first large-scale implementation of Ice Energy's technology. Brian Parsonnet, Ice Energy's chief technology officer, says the technology can cut a building's power consumption by 95 percent during peak hours on the hottest days. Cutting demand for electricity during peak hours reduces the need to build new power plants, as reported by ice-energy.com on 19 May, 2010.

## London

According to Economist Magazine, London, 17 July, 2010, five percent of all offices in southern Europe have switched over to ice as the cooling agent for air-conditioning their premises should serve as a shot in the arm to the enthusiasts of green cooling as a means to combat climate change. This means that millions of square meters of office space in Mediterranean Europe (which includes Portugal, Spain, southern France, Italy and the nine Balkan countries) are being cooled with ice.

This shows that the launch of the European concept model and the Water Cooler model, the three-year old Snowbreeze project has arrived at a definitive stage. Further, use of ice for cooling rooms as an alternative to conventional air conditioning is fairly wide spread in southern Europe. "In countries where electricity is cheaper at night some air-conditioning machines now take a different approach. As the evening beckons, they start making ice. During the day fans blow air over the ice. In southern Europe roughly one in 20 air-conditioned offices is now cooled with ice, cutting electricity bills by about 10%."

Snowbreeze has proved that the saving in electricity bills would be much higher if the European offices made their ice in ordinary ice plants and were not obliged to use their power guzzling air conditioning systems to make ice. Air conditioning is one of the highest power consumers in the world. IBM reckons that in some centres about half of all the electricity consumed is spent cooling equipment.

## Other Countries

Canada, Brazil, and other parts of the world are also manufacturing ice-based air-conditioning systems. Ice run cooling is also becoming popular on ships worldwide, as reported by news.cnet.com.

Also, western technology has paid more attention to heating buildings than to cooling them. Huge effort has gone into warming up buildings as efficiently as possible; less into cooling them down. New developments would make cooling systems greener still because they would use less power. Hence, there is need of electronic devices like Snowbreeze.

In Western countries, ice energy could be used to rationalize the power load distribution between day and night; take advantage of the low night temperatures when water can be frozen with 20% less power; and derive the benefit of differential day and night power rates; with a total power saving ranging between 10% to 30%.

In poor countries like India, ice-run air conditioning, when practiced on a large scale, would cut power consumption by 50 to 70%. This is so because it offers the scope for regulating the quantity of ice used, according to the intensity of heat which varies vastly with location, season and hour of the day. Thus ice could be produced more cheaply and with less power with ordinary ice plants than with air-conditioning units. Developing nations should also import western techniques of designing ice-run units and channeling the air flow.

## Inventor's Take on the Impact of Innovation

"The capital city roughly consumes about one thousand Megawatt additional electric power for heating and cooling during peak summer and winter months. This extra burden on the power starved metropolis could be reduced by more than 50% by overhauling and simplifying the cooling and heating systems. The whole world is searching frantically for cleaner, cheaper, alternative sources of power", says Shri M.B.Lal. "Generating more power beyond certain limits is not only prohibitively expensive, but also brings in more pollution, global warming, disease and deprivation", he adds.

Further, the inventor reported, "According to the BSES chart of power consumption in electrical appliance issued with every bill, a refrigerator consumes about 100 watts of power in one hour while a 1.5-ton room air conditioner consumes 2 kilowatts of power in one hour, which is sufficient to produce 30 kilograms of ice in an ice factory or 20 kg in a refrigerator. With that much ice, Snowbreeze can keep a room almost equally cool and dehumidified for eight hours. One might say there are distribution losses in ice deliveries. But, under Indian conditions electricity transmission losses are no less, for which there are a variety of reasons including technical deficiencies and massive "thefts", committed in the open, and the biggest problem in India, mainly by the richer power guzzling sections of society such as big factories and large bungalows and flats.

Add to that the colossal investments in the shape of electrical energy and finance to create the giant-sized infrastructure of power houses and transmission lines for every additional megawatt of power. If you take all this into account you will arrive at the sobering conclusion that a gadget which consumes one unit of energy per hour is in fact using two, the other half being invisible."

According to the 85 year old inventor, "Example of over a dozen European countries is a visible demonstration of my belief that ice provides the only practical "green" option to the present power intensive and highly polluting mode of air-conditioning. There are several alternative for sources of energy such as solar power, thermal heating systems and evaporative techniques as possible options, but ice-cooling is the most widely used among them all. These examples induce more confidence in ice-based air-conditioning in the minds of Indian scientists and technologists holding high positions who can carry this movement forward. It will also help to convince the media while publicizing the idea."

"What The Economist leaves unsaid is equally important. While it reports on big offices resorting to ice for cooling rooms it is silent on the involvement of private house-holds in this new movement. Presumably their number would not be so large. After dabbling in this field for four summers I too have arrived at the conclusion that recourse to ice for cooling space will be most economic and efficient in bulk-using applications and not immediately as practical in piecemeal usage in the hands of individuals, unless they use a made-to-order water cooler model unit.

To reach out to individual homes we need standardized ready-made models of Snowbreeze and an automated supply chain of ice from ice-factories to the home in replaceable containers available at wholesale rates to each user. Taking a cue from the success of the European experience builders and designers of big buildings and towers should include ice-plants in their designs in place of elaborate conventional air-conditioning systems", he added.

The fantastic innovator also says that making of Snowbreeze is very easy. Until standardized small units enter the market, enterprising individuals can make their own model with the help of a mechanic, after studying the material on the website, greenairconditioner.org.

### Fan Following

Undoubtedly Shri Lal has a huge fan following. He has received more than 500 mails and thousands of hits on his website, greenairconditioner.org. There has been mention if Snowbreeze in various newspapers, TV reports and Google displays on over a 20,000 websites (Table 3). All this suggests that consumers are waiting for a standard model to come in the market which can be bought off the shelf. This is not the case only in India, but worldwide (Table 4).

### Way Forward

Snowbreeze, undoubtedly, is the need of hour. The energy consumed by Snowbreeze, including energy used in making ice, is only 10% to 20% of the wall AC's consumption of power. However, the handling costs of market ice on a small scale, plus the manual labour involved in operating in individual homes are yet to be addressed.

The Water Cooler model offers a viable solution to many such problems and situations. But it has to be operated at a high intensity, of say chilling 15 to 20 litres of water per hour per 100 sq ft. if, besides cooling the room, it has to control humidity as well.

While making a comparative analysis of conventional and ice-based cooling, energy and resources spent (per unit) on creating the huge power infrastructure at public cost should also be considered. When we use one unit of power, we are in fact consuming two. The other invisible unit being the power we use to create and operate the infra-structure of power houses, transmission lines and coal mines.

## CONCLUSION

The innovators face many challenges during the process of innovation. Bureaucratic system, financial crunch, administration hassles, too much of paper work, designing B-plans, prototyping, R&D, market research, surveys, commercialization, and many more. But inspite of so many challenges, India has grown rapidly with the help of its people, who are inherently innovative and entrepreneurial. It ranks 66 in the Global Innovation Index, 2013. Like India, many developing and developed nations have much to offer to the world in terms of their innovation models of growth. Collective efforts of all would turn the world into one dynamic and sustainable nation.

Innovative spirit is required to carry out the changes and build a sustainable future for the generations to come. And those who are able to demonstrate those innovations with tangible products and services that impact and change the existing processes, become the future entrepreneurs of. Innovation takes leaders who are willing to invest in an open and creative culture that will foster new ideas and break standard or conventional thinking in carrying out professional responsibilities. These leaders need to incorporate innovation strategies into the strategic planning process in order to make innovation real and sustainable (Michael A. Crumpton, Innovation and Entrepreneurship, 5 July, 2012)

Apart from the above mentioned challenges, some factors should also be considered in building the culture of innovation in the economy. One of them is public and private institutions. These institutions play a very important role in lifting up the entrepreneurs, facilitating them in obtaining the resources needed to develop their creative product or service. Another important factor to be stressed upon is social climate. Relieving the entrepreneurs from stress of financial crunch, administration hassles would only stimulate them to carry out their activities.

As we have seen, there are numerous examples in every field of how innovative and creative ideas have impacted the end-user. Creativity and entrepreneurism is encouraging for a new vision of future. Last but not the least, according to Schumpeterian approach innovation plays a central role in the economic growth process and the entrepreneur is the vehicle to introduce the new technologies to improve the firms' activity and to obtain higher profits.

## REFERENCES

Crumpton, M. A. (2012). Innovation and entrepreneurship. *The Bottom Line: Managing Library Finances*, *25*(3), 98 - 101.

Fagerberg. (2006). *Innovation, technology and the global knowledge economy: Challenges for future growth*. Paper presented at the "Green roads to growth" conference, Environmental Assessment Institute, Copenhagen, Denmark.

Flynn, M., Doodley, L., & Cormican, K. (2003). Idea management for organizational innovation. *International Journal of Innovation Management*, *7*(4), 417–442. doi:10.1142/S1363919603000878

Kirton, M. (1976). Adaptors and innovators: A description and measure. *The Journal of Applied Psychology*, *61*(5), 622–629. doi:10.1037/0021-9010.61.5.622

Lee, S. Y., Florida, R., & Acs, Z. J. (2004). Creativity and entrepreneurship: A regional analysis of new firm formation. *Regional Studies*, *38*(8), 879–891. doi:10.1080/0034340042000280910

Lee, S. Y., Florida, R., & Gates, G. (2002). *Innovation, human capital, and creativity*. Working paper, Software Industry Centre, Carnegie Mellon University, Pittsburgh, PA.

Miguel-Ángel Galindo, María-Teresa & Méndez-Picazo, (2013). Innovation, entrepreneurship and economic growth. *Management Decision*, *51*(3), 501 – 514.

Miller, D., & Friesen, P. H. (1983). Strategy-making and environment: The third link. *Strategic Management Journal*, *4*(3), 221–235. doi:10.1002/smj.4250040304

Oguz, F. (2001). How entrepreneurs learn? A practical interpretation. *METU Studies in Development*, *28*(1/2), 183–202.

Park, R., Burgess, E., & McKenzie, R. (1925). *The City*. Chicago, IL: University of Chicago Press.

Popper, M., & Lipshitz, R. (1998). Organizational learning mechanisms: A structural and cultural approach to organizational learning. *The Journal of Applied Behavioral Science*, *34*(2), 161–179. doi:10.1177/0021886398342003

Sternberg, R. J., & Lubart, T. I. (1999). The concept of creativity: prospects and paradigms, 3. In R. J. Sternberg (Ed.), *Handbook of Creativity*. New York, NY: Cambridge University Press.

Thomson, W. (1965). *A Preface to Urban Economics*. Baltimore, MD: John Hopkins Press.

Zhao, F. (2005). Exploring the synergy between entrepreneurship and innovation. *InternationalJournal of Entrepreneurial Behaviour and Research*, *11*(1), 25–41. doi:10.1108/13552550510580825

## KEY TERMS AND DEFINITIONS

**Emerging Economies:** A rapid growth in the global economy that has a huge potential for development but also poses various risks like political, social and financial. The BRICS countries are such.

**Entrepreneurship:** It is the willingness to develop, to organize and to manage a business entity in order to make a profit.

**Innovation:** It is the process of translating an idea into a service or a product that adds values for which the consumers are willing to pay. It refers to creating an effective processes for services or products that increases the probability of a business and provides a competitive edge over others.

**Technology:** A deliberate application of information in various stages like designing, production and consumption of the product or services in the society.

## APPENDIX

*Figure 1. Sample MQ Max*

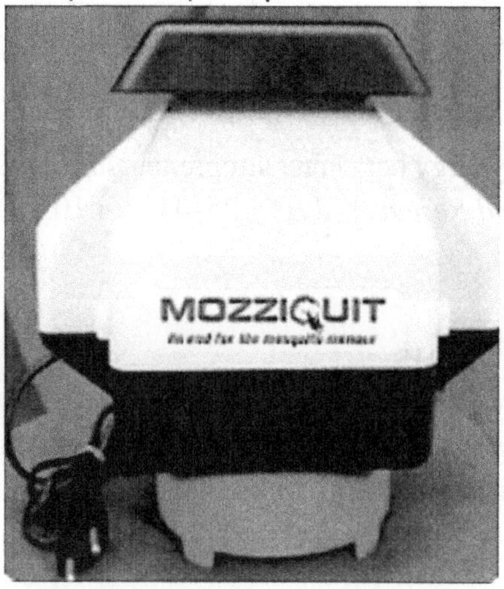


*Figure 2. Sample MQ Mini*

*Figure 3. Mr. Noronha receiving award by Rakesh Singh, additional secretary at the vision summit of ISA Technovation 2010*

*Figure 4. Receiving Gold Medal from Shri Prithvi Raj Chavan, Minister for Commerce and Industry in DST-Lockheed Martin India Innovation Programme on 20th May, 2010, Delhi*

*Figure 5. Collection of mosquitoes in bottle in 30 days*

*Figure 6. ISA Best Electronic Product of the Year 2010*

*Figure 7. Recommendation from IC² Institute, USA, 2010*

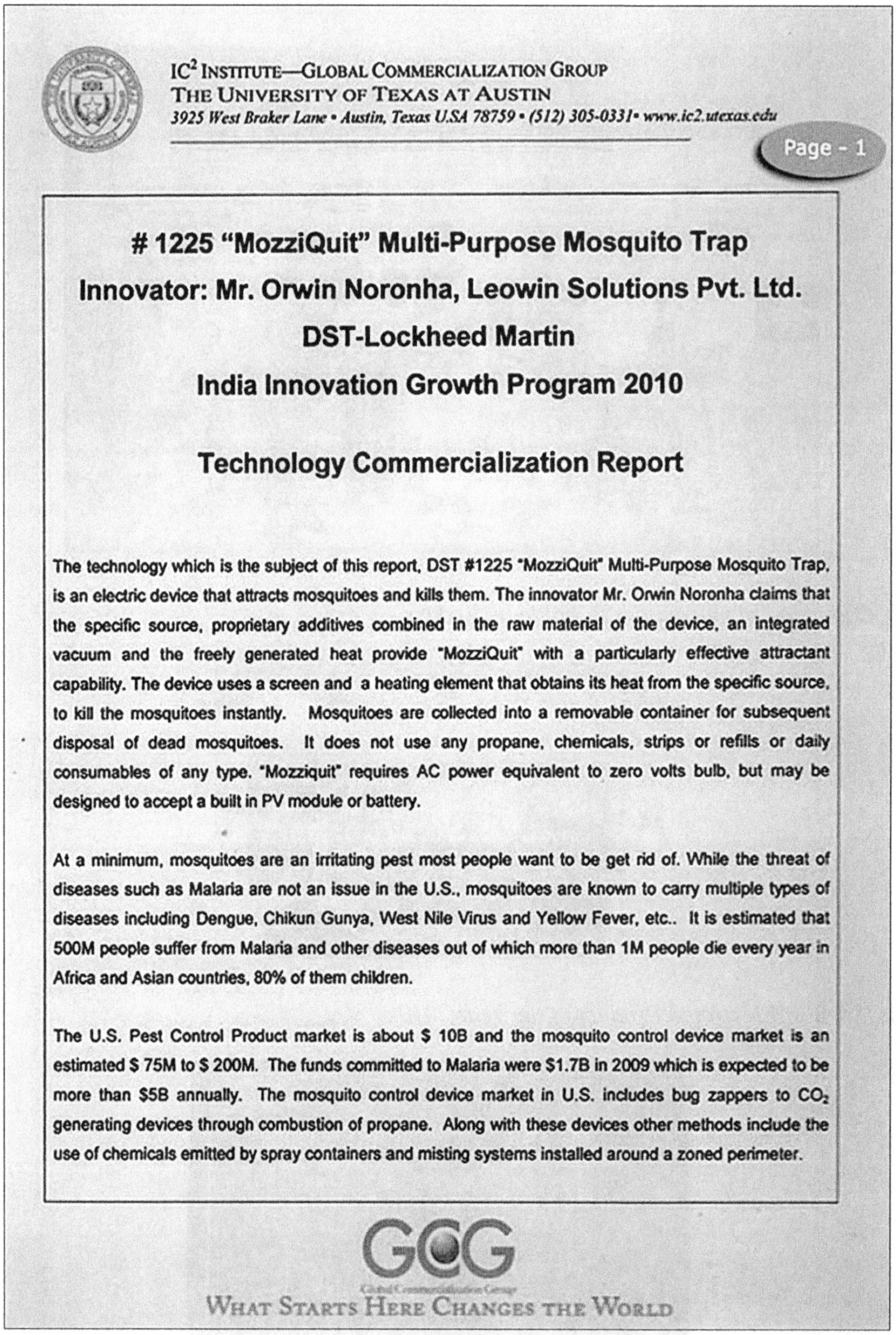

IC² INSTITUTE—GLOBAL COMMERCIALIZATION GROUP
THE UNIVERSITY OF TEXAS AT AUSTIN
*3925 West Braker Lane • Austin, Texas USA 78759 • (512) 305-0331• www.ic2.utexas.edu*

Page - 1

**# 1225 "MozziQuit" Multi-Purpose Mosquito Trap**

**Innovator: Mr. Orwin Noronha, Leowin Solutions Pvt. Ltd.**

**DST-Lockheed Martin**

**India Innovation Growth Program 2010**

**Technology Commercialization Report**

The technology which is the subject of this report, DST #1225 "MozziQuit" Multi-Purpose Mosquito Trap, is an electric device that attracts mosquitoes and kills them. The innovator Mr. Orwin Noronha claims that the specific source, proprietary additives combined in the raw material of the device, an integrated vacuum and the freely generated heat provide "MozziQuit" with a particularly effective attractant capability. The device uses a screen and a heating element that obtains its heat from the specific source, to kill the mosquitoes instantly. Mosquitoes are collected into a removable container for subsequent disposal of dead mosquitoes. It does not use any propane, chemicals, strips or refills or daily consumables of any type. "Mozziquit" requires AC power equivalent to zero volts bulb, but may be designed to accept a built in PV module or battery.

At a minimum, mosquitoes are an irritating pest most people want to be get rid of. While the threat of diseases such as Malaria are not an issue in the U.S., mosquitoes are known to carry multiple types of diseases including Dengue, Chikun Gunya, West Nile Virus and Yellow Fever, etc.. It is estimated that 500M people suffer from Malaria and other diseases out of which more than 1M people die every year in Africa and Asian countries, 80% of them children.

The U.S. Pest Control Product market is about $ 10B and the mosquito control device market is an estimated $ 75M to $ 200M. The funds committed to Malaria were $1.7B in 2009 which is expected to be more than $5B annually. The mosquito control device market in U.S. includes bug zappers to $CO_2$ generating devices through combustion of propane. Along with these devices other methods include the use of chemicals emitted by spray containers and misting systems installed around a zoned perimeter.

GCG

WHAT STARTS HERE CHANGES THE WORLD

*Figure 8. Approval from NIMR/ICMR*

**Integrated Disease Vector Control Project**
Under the Administrative Control of
NATIONAL INSTITUTE OF MALARIA RESEARCH
(Indian Council of Medical Research)
**Ministry of Health and Family Welfare**
ICMR Complex, Poojanahalli, Kannamangla Post
Off. NH-7, Near BIAL Trumpet Bus Stop, Devanahalli, Bangalore-562 110

Ref: NIMR/BNG/ Mosq. Trap /2008-301 Date: 02.02.2009

M/s. Leowin Solutions Pvt. Ltd.
"El-Shaddai", # 13/2, 2nd Cross,
Beside Assisi Church, St. Thomas Town,
International Airport (Link) Road, Bangalore – 560084

**Kind Attn: Mr. Ignatius Orwin Noronha,**

**Sub: Performance Certificate**

**Ref: Request to Test Performance of your "MozziQuit" Mosquito Trap**

Dear Mr. Noronha

We refer to your request made to us in June 2008 to conduct the Performance Test on "MozziQuit" Mosquito Trap device.

As per the data of tests conducted at indoor as well as outdoor locations, we inform you that mosquitoes (mainly *Culex* spp.) are attracted by the "MozziQuit" Mosquito Trap device, get trapped inside the device and dead mosquitoes are collected in the removable collected container located at the bottom of the device.

"MozziQuit" Mosquito Trap is useful to kill the adult mosquitoes which will reduce the total mosquito population. This will help reduce the adult mosquito population and the disease transmitted by them.

*Figure 9. Patent and design registration certificates*

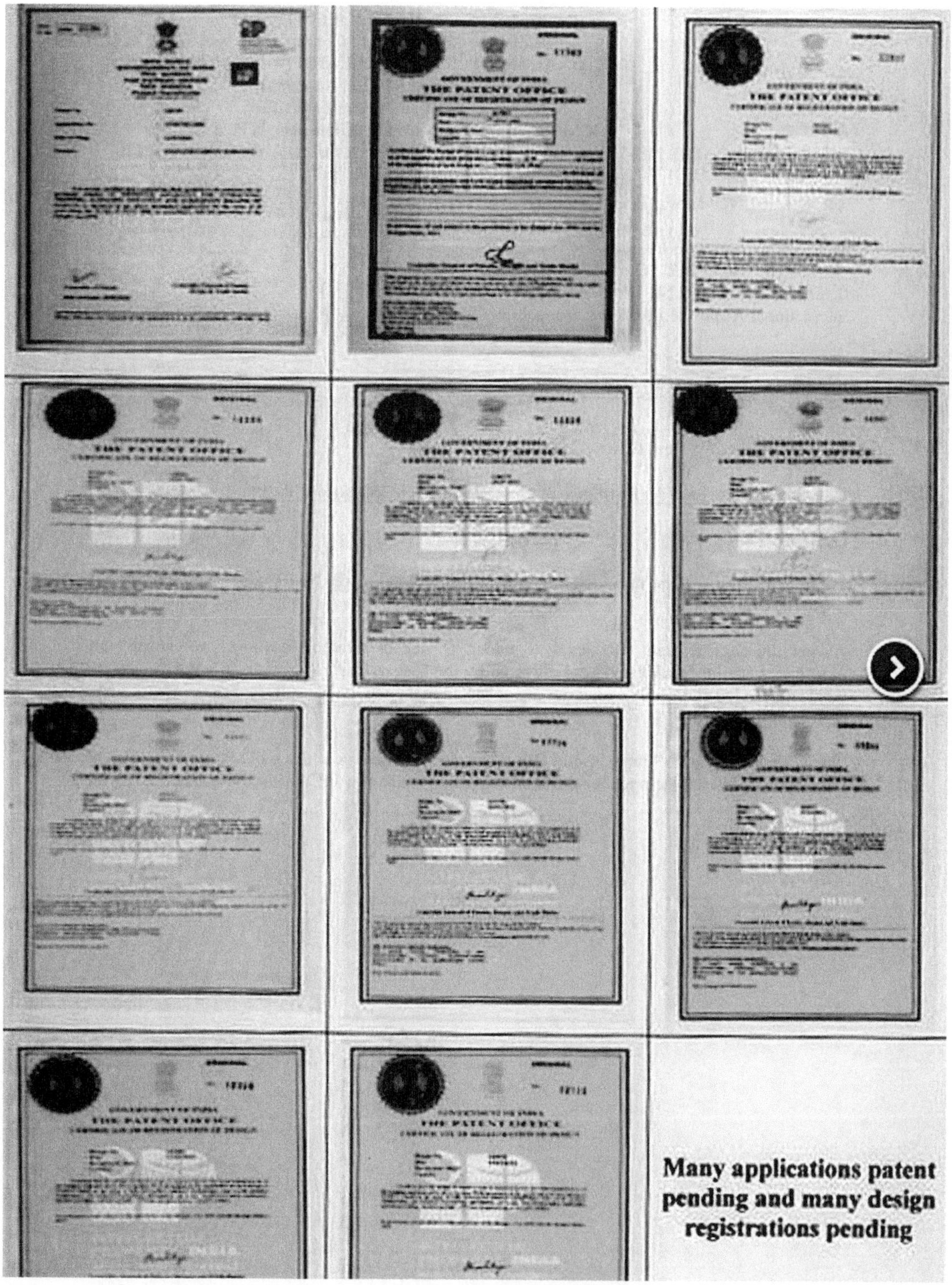

*Figure 10. Snowbreeze 1: Match for wall AC*

*Figure 11. Snowbreeze 2 (unique self cooling AC)*

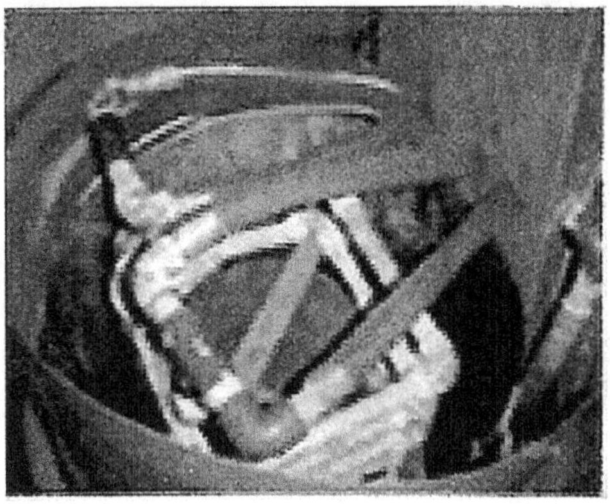

*Figure 12. Automated Snowbreeze: multipurpose AC*

*Figure 13. Mini Snowbreeze: Boon for old and sick*

*Figure 14. Snowbreeze room heater*

*Figure 15. Battery powered rural unit*

*Table 1. Cost comparison between MQ and other repellents*

| | All Mosquitoes Repellents | "Mozziquit" Mosquitoes TRAP MQ-MINI | Savings to Users per Unit | % Savings to Customer |
|---|---|---|---|---|
| Cost of device | Rs. 27 | Rs. 1,500 | | |
| Cost of retail per year priced at Rs. 1 Per day whereas in actual use it is at Rs. 3 per day | Rs. 1,095 | | | |
| Cost of electricity charges Rs. 0.25 per day for mosquito repellents and 0.05 per for "Mozziquit" | Rs. 91 | Rs. 18 | | |
| Total cost per year to the user | Rs. 1,213 | Rs. 1,518 | | |
| Cost of 2 years | Rs. 2,246 | Rs. 1,536 | Rs. 890 | 37% |
| Cost of 5 years | Rs. 6,065 | Rs. 1,590 | Rs. 4,475 | 74% |
| Cost of 10 years | Rs. 12,130 | Rs. 1,680 | Rs. 10,450 | 86% |
| Demand in India, African and global market per month | >10,000,000 units | | | |

*Table 2. Multiplication rate of mosquitoes which could be eliminated by the use of "MozziQuit"*

| Mosquitoes Day 1 | No. of Female Mosquitoes on Day 100 Assuming 50% Female out of 300 Eggs | No. of Female Mosquitoes on Day 200 Assuming 50% Female out of 300 Eggs | No. of Female Mosquitoes on Day 300 Assuming 50% Female out of 300 Eggs |
|---|---|---|---|
| 1 | 150 | 22500 | 3375000 |
| 10 | 1500 | 225000 | 33750000 |
| 100 | 15000 | 2250000 | 337500000 |
| 1000 | 150000 | 22500000 | 3375000000 |

*Table 3. Number of hits on the website (Intra country comparison)*

| Day | Number of Visits | Pages | Hits | Bandwidth |
|---|---|---|---|---|
| 01 March 2010 | 17 | 19 | 280 | 6.34 MB |
| 02 March 2010 | 14 | 25 | 267 | 11.67 MB |
| 03 March 2010 | 28 | 48 | 458 | 24.87 MB |
| 04 March 2010 | 22 | 25 | 298 | 7.09 MB |
| 05 March 2010 | 399 | 958 | 8308 | 633.79 MB |
| 06 March 2010 | 9648 | 17988 | 191995 | 11.86 GB |
| 07 March 2010 | 110 | 189 | 1794 | 100.06 MB |
| 08 March 2010 | 1607 | 3592 | 32733 | 2.16 GB |
| 09 March 2010 | 712 | 1323 | 12470 | 833.05 MB |
| 10 March 2010 | 403 | 763 | 7659 | 481.25 MB |
| 11 March 2010 | 311 | 603 | 5685 | 364.34 MB |
| 12 March 2010 | 216 | 420 | 3807 | 259.46 MB |
| 13 March 2010 | 216 | 400 | 4144 | 243.98 MB |
| 14 March 2010 | 193 | 354 | 3459 | 231.46 MB |
| 15 March 2010 | 211 | 335 | 3715 | 198.68 MB |
| 16 March 2010 | 176 | 288 | 2985 | 176.71 MB |
| 17 March 2010 | 215 | 402 | 3740 | 263.90 MB |
| 18 March 2010 | 164 | 289 | 3208 | 162.29 MB |
| 19 March 2010 | 152 | 268 | 3021 | 192.51 MB |
| 20 March 2010 | 148 | 279 | 2664 | 184.77 MB |
| 21 March 2010 | 122 | 265 | 2725 | 160.49 MB |
| 22 March 2010 | 162 | 301 | 3137 | 185.87 MB |
| 23 March 2010 | 136 | 266 | 2877 | 175.46 MB |
| 24 March 2010 | 117 | 212 | 2187 | 143.53 MB |
| 25 March 2010 | 126 | 245 | 2341 | 165.79 MB |
| 26 March 2010 | 121 | 207 | 2264 | 129.48 MB |
| 27 March 2010 | 101 | 155 | 1761 | 86.40 MB |
| 28 March 2010 | 418 | 839 | 8477 | 583.84 MB |
| 29 March 2010 | 313 | 674 | 6642 | 451.56 MB |
| 30 March 2010 | 228 | 398 | 4187 | 217.76 MB |
| 31 March 2010 | 165 | 318 | 3205 | 161.60 MB |
| Average | 547.45 | 1046.71 | 10725.58 | 683.95 MB |
| Total | 16971 | 32448 | 332493 | 20.17 GB |

*Table 4. Number of Hits on the website (Inter country comparison)*

| Countries | Pages | Hits | Bandwidth |
|---|---|---|---|
| India | 27897 | 285187 | 18.32 GB |
| United States | 2182 | 22439 | 1.04 GB |
| Canada | 339 | 388 | 231.51 MB |
| Australia | 235 | 2385 | 149.39 MB |
| Great Britain | 214 | 2358 | 104.84 MB |
| Japan | 167 | 1005 | 59.27 MB |
| United Arab Emirates | 159 | 1642 | 118.81 MB |
| Saudi Arabia | 135 | 1259 | 85.81 MB |
| New Zealand | 89 | 398 | 30.17 MB |
| Germany | 85 | 1095 | 48.27 MB |
| Singapore | 73 | 756 | 35.19 MB |
| European Country | 67 | 832 | 43.83 MB |
| Kuwait | 56 | 523 | 38.33 MB |
| France | 53 | 469 | 28.77 MB |
| Qatar | 53 | 669 | 33.12 MB |
| Malaysia | 42 | 498 | 23.49 MB |
| Hong Kong | 39 | 484 | 23.43 MB |
| Bangladesh | 34 | 137 | 28.45 MB |
| Oman | 30 | 362 | 15.88 MB |
| China | 27 | 323 | 18.31 MB |
| Bahrain | 27 | 269 | 17.91 MB |
| Sweden | 24 | 280 | 8.44 MB |
| Taiwan | 23 | 231 | 10.32 MB |
| Ireland | 22 | 234 | 8.87 MB |
| South Korea | 21 | 229 | 10.83 MB |

# Chapter 8
# Rice Husk Power Systems:
## Exploring Alternate Source of Energy

**Pulkit A Gupta**
*IMT Ghaziabad, India*

**Vedant Sharma**
*IMT Ghaziabad, India*

**Mohan Krishna Gade**
*IMT Ghaziabad, India*

## ABSTRACT

*In this chapter, the impact of rising cost of fuel and inability of government to supply electricity round the clock leading to spurt in frugal innovations utilizing alternative sources of energy has been analyzed. Rice is one of the prime crops of India, Rice husk, perceived as waste by many, being abundant and available at low cost can be major contributor in alternate energy. Due to lack of awareness of the potential of rice husk it is discarded as waste and results in waste disposal problem and methane emission. The use of rice husk for electricity generation in efficient manner has potential to transform agricultural waste into a valuable fuel and could help in boosting farm economy. This study explores the usage of rice husk and its untapped potential as a major fuel source. The target markets are villages in India with 400-500 households having ample biomass feedstock.*

## INTRODUCTION

In India power supply comes mostly from non-renewable energy resources, a lot of which is bought from international markets. Moreover, non-renewable energy resources combustion is associated with pollutants of $CO_2$, SOX and NOX leading to environmental impacts. The proposed solution for these problems is using alternative power instead of traditional (fossil) resources of power. Rice husk is considered to be source of an environment friendly energy because it can minimize $CO_2$, SOX and NOX pollutants when compared with traditional energy.

DOI: 10.4018/978-1-4666-8259-7.ch008

The majority of population in the rural areas of Uttar Pradesh lives below the poverty line and has limited access to electricity. As per Census 2001, Uttar Pradesh has a total of 97942 inhabited villages, and as per the report released by Central Electricity Authority, Ministry of Power, Government of India on 31 Oct, 2013 there a total of 32119 villages which are not electrified yet(Central Electricity Authority, Ministry of Power, Government of India, 2013). 33% i.e. 10856 of those villages are from Uttar Pradesh which needs immediate attention as this has affected the development of the state to a large extent. The need of these villages has been understood by an innovative system to generate power from rice husk, when used in efficient gasification or combustion systems, has potential to generate power. Rice Husk Power System used waste rice husks to produce and deliver electricity to off-grid villages in the Indian 'Rice Belt' region in Bihar. Rice is the main crop of Bihar, which falls in the rice belt of India, on an average, produces 47.14 lakh metric tonnes of rice per year and about 13.4 lakh metric a tonne of rice husk goes waste per year (GreenPeace India, 2010). Rice paddy has essentially two by-products, rice husk and rice bran.

Husk or hulls consists of the outer shell covering the rice kernel. Rice husk refers to the by-product produced in the milling of paddy which is 16-25% by weight of the total weight of paddy. India alone produces around 104.32 million tonnes of rice paddy per year, giving around 21.38 million tonnes of rice husk per year (Indian Agribusiness Systems Private Limited, 2013). Farmer's income would be increased if economically profitable means of utilizing rice husk generated are utilized in industry.

There are many other uses of rice husk such as a fuel in brick kilns, furnaces, rice mills for boiling process, raw material for the production of ethanol and acetic acid, as a cleaning or polishing agent in metal, in the manufacturing of building materials (Govindarao, 1980). Despite having so many well established uses of rice husk, little portion of rice husk is utilized in a significant way, remaining part is burnt, dumped as a solid waste or as a cattle feed. Some reasons for rice husk not being utilized effectively prior to this innovation are:

- Lack of awareness of its potential
- Socio-economic problems
- Penetration of technology
- Lack of interest
- Lack of environmental concerns

Its usage as a fuel in boilers is crux of our research with the possibility to have it implemented in villages in and around Ghaziabad. Also, the ash obtained post combustion of rice husk is silica rich and has been lately used as an important component of bricks.

## LITERATURE REVIEW

Important renewable sources of energy such as coal, diesel, kerosene, petrol are on the decline which leads us to the need for exploring non renewable energy sources. Biomass is one of these. Rice husk (form of biomass) is a product obtained on rice milling and has a huge calorific value and high silica content. It is used as a fuel in variety of furnaces such as rice mill furnaces, boilers, rice husk gasifier and in household stoves. In rural villages where power produced from plants fails to meet demand, rice husk gasifiers are being increasingly used to fill in the gap (Tanaka, Kjorven, & Yumkella, 2010). Also, rice husk is increasingly replacing cow dung/wood as fuel as there is high efficiency and almost nil smoke produced.

Lot of husk is thrown out as waste which results in waste disposal issue and methane pollutants. Moreover, the low solidity of grain husk can cause it to be air-borne easily leading to difficulty in respiration, if consumed. Rice husk can be transformed to a useful form of power to fulfil the thermal and mechanical power needed for the generators. This help in reduction of the waste and in addition to this also transform grain husk to an electricity source. Small mills can sell the husk to power plants. The major challenge is the cost of husk, which is increasing now due to its utilization for other programs such as; concrete preservative and poultry incubation etc., which makes the investment higher than before. Not only has this led to increased power production, but also has generated employment and a notable decrease in air pollution. Rice husk is easy to store, transport and has high combustion intensity. Rice is produced abundantly in states of Bihar, Orissa and Uttar Pradesh. These states are power deficient and rural people rely on kerosene lanterns for home lighting and diesel generators for irrigation and commercial power. Both these methods are not cost effective and detrimental in terms of increasing air pollution(Nerenberg, 2011).

The usage of rice husk for power generation has many benefits. Firstly it is a carbon-neutral and is renewable source of energy thus decreasing the emission of greenhouse gases resulting in decline of sulphur and other pollutants emissions which are associated with usage of fossil fuels. This enables to develop economy by creating a market for rice husks which is formerly treated as a waste to monetary product. Rice Husk meets the thermal energy requirements of industry in cost-effective manner and generates employment at the local level for collection and supply of rice husks promoting inclusive growth.(Chungsangunsit, Gheewala, & Patumsawad). In addition, steam which is by-product of power generation can also be used for paddy drying operations, thus increasing local incomes and reducing the dependency on imported fossil fuels.

Transport of husk to power plant has major impact on climate change as it leads to Global warming, at very long transportation distances which will never happen in exercise because the cost of transportation will be too much. The impact evaluation outcomes display that the impact of Global Warming potential of rice husk power (17.16 kg $CO_2$- eq/MWh) is less than the combined of non-renewable power plants (734.37 kg $CO_2$-eq/MWh) because $CO_2$ from biomass is regarded as greenhouse gas neutral. Sulphur and nitrogen material in rice husk is fairly less in contrast to fossil fuel and oil. Moreover, the combustion temperature of husk is less than 900°C, avoiding the development of thermal NOX. Hence, acidification and nitrification possibilities of grain husk plant (1.06 kg $SO_2$-eq/MWh and 0.39 N-eq/MWh) are smaller than combined of fossil run power plant (2.34 kg $SO_2$- eq/MWh and 0.73 N-eq/MWh) even though fossil fuel plants have NOX and SOX elimination devices set up. Photochemical oxidant development is from CO pollutants of rice husk power plant (0.34 kg $C_2H_2$-eg/MWh) and is greater than the combined of fossil based power plant (0.08 kg $C_2H_2$-eg/MWh). This is due to the low combustion efficiency of the husk power plant leading to part from the high moisture content in rice husk. Both bottom and fly ash are used and hence, not going to the dump.(Chungsangunsit, Gheewala, & Patumsawad)

The $CO_2$ emissions produced from rice husk plant gets re-absorbed by the biomass carbon cycle. Thus global warming potential would come only from fossil fuel consumed for transportation and CO from incomplete combustion. The amount of carbon emission contributing to global warming is about 1.38% of total carbon input. (Chungsangunsit, Gheewala, & Patumsawad)

Rice husk is used as fuel for power generation through steam or gasification process. For small scale power plant, gasification is preferred as small steam power plant is inefficient and is difficult to maintain due to the boiler. For rice mills running with diesel engines, gas produced from rice husk can be used in the current engine in a dual fuel operation.

The concept behind power generation technology from Rice husk gasification is that it converts biomass to green electricity. Power plant does not cause pollution because of biomass as fuel material. Biomass resource in general achieve high utilization of efficiency .Gasification process is reacting material at high temperatures (>700°C), in absence of combustion with a regulated amount of oxygen or steam. The gas mixture is called syngas (from synthetic gas) or producer gas and is a fuel. The power derived from gasification and combustion of the resultant gas is the source of renewable energy. (Pradhan, Ali, & Dash)

Biomass consists of carbon, hydrogen and oxygen. Biomass energy is formed from five energy sources: garbage, wood, waste, landfill gases and alcohol fuels. Wood energy is formed from use of harvested wood and from wood waste streams as a fuel. Waste energy is the second-largest source of biomass energy. The main contributors to waste energy are municipal solid waste (MSW), manufacturing waste, and landfill gas. Ethanol or Alcohol fuel is derived from sugarcane and corn. It can be used directly or as an additive to gasoline. Biomass can be converted to other forms of energy like methane gas, ethanol and biodiesel. (Pradhan, Ali, & Dash) Rice straw can be directly used or can be mixed with other biomass materials as a fuel. In this technology, boilers are used in conjunction with steam turbines to produce electricity. The energy content of rice straw is around 14 MJ per kg at 10% moisture. The by-products are fly ash and bottom ash, having economic value in cement and/or brick manufacturing, construction of roads and embankments, etc.(Zafar, 2013)

Rice husk enters circulation fluidized bed gasification furnace via feeder. With high- temperature, recycling and heating materials, rice husk in gasifier meets air from bottom and goes into hydrogenation and gasification reactions, rice husk gets converted into fuel gas. The composition of fuel gas is CO, $H_2$, $CH_4$ etc. Calorific value is approximately 1450 kcal/ m3. Using fuel gas purification technology, dust, tar present in fuel gas can be treated and collected to achieve the demand of internal combustion.

The advantages of the gasifier system are:

1. It uses wastes in rural areas to fuel engines that drive Generators.
2. Operation can be done continuously
3. It can be adopted with spark-ignition engine, readily available in the locality.
4. This technology can be locally produced making use of available fabrication resources and skills.
5. It can be scaled up to meet the power demand
6. Investment and operation costs are at the reach of the local community. (Pradhan, Ali, & Dash)

Husk Power System (HPS), started in 2007 is currently catering to 200,000 villagers in Bihar through its 84 plants across 300 villages and employing 350 people for operating these mini power plants (Chandra, 2011). Each plant typically has the potential to serve around 400 households, saving approximately 18,000 litres of diesel and 42,000 litres of kerosene per year(Husk Power System, 2013). According to Kyoto Protocol (1997), the plant can claim Rs 847.5 per one ton reduction in carbon dioxide. They made a significant distinction in the lifestyles of non-urban Indians by developing a sequence of tactically placed mini-power plants in distant villages. Kids now had adequate illumination to do their preparation in the evening and villagers revealed an enhanced feeling of security: When light came to a town, even reviews of dog attacks and reptile attacks dropped.

By the time OPIC discovered about the company in 2008, it was a simple start-up, providing energy to only to two non-urban towns of about 1,000 people, but the founders had programs to flourish into thousands of extra villages over the next few years. In July of 2009, OPIC provided $750,000 as loan to Husk Power for the growth of an extra 36 grain husk-powered generation plants. Although this deal was a relatively small financial commitment for OPIC, it was crucial to Husk, which had been incapable to acquire adequate financing from the Indian Government or other private players to enhance its pilot project to commercially viable project . Because the technological innovation used to turn rice husks to power is pretty affordable on an individual foundation, the OPIC money could be used to set up plants in many villages.

Husk Power distributes electricity through a "point-to-point" program that joins each family or company straight to the energy grid through a main line. A village manager reports the likely energy intake of each customer based on their illumination and equipment specifications and this calculation is used to figure out an appropriate pre-payment. The primary connection by Husk power provides a family with two 15-watt light weight CFL together with cell phone charging port throughout the period each day that the plant operates (up to eight hours in the evening). Households and company can also pay more for a higher power connection, however the system is designed such that fuse blows if the customer attempts to use more than the agreed-upon amount. Each mini-power plant facilitates about 500 houses. HPS provides electricity in 3-phase, 220V 50Hz. They also install low cost smart pre-paid meters. Husk Power System works strategically to locate plants in remote villages where they can reach a large number of households. It has achieved an average penetration rate of 75% within the first two months in a new village. One of Husk's value propositions is to develop plants that are simple to function and sustain.

There are several subsidies given by the Government of India like, accelerated depreciation on high efficiency equipment, tax benefits for five years and 30% exemption for next five years, exemption on central excise duty for renewable energy devices, including raw materials, components and assemblies. According to statistics available rice husk can be made available throughout year in the Northern, Southern, North-eastern and Eastern regions baring Western region. In case, availability of rice husk reduces for some reason other biomass like bagasse and other can be used in the multi-fuel combustion boilers.

The effects are evident in these villages – women need not work towards collecting firewood, activity increased beyond day time, reduced pollution etc. HPS creates income generation opportunities to farmers and entrepreneurs around each plant (The Hindu, 2010). This enables sustainable development within the communities HPS serves.

## THEORETICAL FRAMEWORK

Some of the problems to be addressed are:

- Rural electrification in India has been facing an acute problem as a total of 32,119 Indian villages are currently un-electrified (Central Electricity Authority, Ministry of Power, Government of India, 2013) leaving over 33% of the population without any access to reliable source of energy. (The Climate Group, 2013)
- Villagers are using kerosene lanterns and diesel generators which are health hazard since there isn't any reliable source of electricity (Energy Map, an Initiative of the Center for Science, Technology, and Society. Supported By Applied Materials, 2010).

## RESEARCH OBJECTIVE

To explore the possibility of extending the utility of rice husk as a high intensity fuel in the village of Tatarpur lallu in Bijnor district of Uttar Pradesh. The objective is to replicate the model adopted in villages of Bihar and customize it according to the geography, topography and economical conditions of this village.

## AREA PROFILE

Uttar Pradesh contributes 12014 thousand tonnes a year which is more than 10% to the total rice production in India. Bijnor, a district is the highest rice producers among all the districts in Uttar Pradesh approximately 2800 kg/hectare. Tatarpur Lallu is a small village in Najibabad Tehsil of Bijnor district located at 467 kms from the state capital Lucknow. Tatarpur Lalu is surrounded by Kiratpur Tehsil towards west, Kotwali Tehsil towards south, Mohammedpur Deomal Tehsil towards west, Nehtaur Tehsil towards south.

One more reason for choosing this village was optimum population compared to other villages. Our planned husk power plant can be a good testifier before being spread to other villages. From our research we found that this region boasts of one of the highest yield of rice in the country per hectare. There are many rice mills present close by this village which also gives an added strategic advantage with respect to the availability of the cheap rice husk required for production of electricity.

## RESEARCH METHODOLOGY

Research design is the collaboration of surroundings information for compilation and analysis of data in a manner that aims to combine the significance to the research purpose with economy in course of action. The research design used in this study was Descriptive Research. Descriptive Research, also known as Statistical Research, depicts characteristics and data about the inhabitants or observable fact being studied. Even though the data description in the case is factual, accurate and systematic, the research cannot describe what caused a situation.

Both primary and secondary research method will be used. Primary research is a research, conducted to answer specific issues or questions. It could involve interviews, questionnaires or surveys with individuals or small groups. A Primary research was conducted in Tatarpur Lallu, a small village in Najibabad Tehsil of Bijnor, Uttar Pradesh. For Primary Survey, we visited the village and asked questions to the Village panchayat and 25 other villagers and assessed the needs of the villagers.

The important point which arose out of discussion with the panchayat and the villagers was that they were bearing with untimely and long power cuts. This hampered their lifestyle most important being improper irrigation of paddy and other crops. It is well known fact that paddy requires large quantity of water which needs to be pumped into the fields. Lack of electricity was hampering their productivity and lowering their yield. This encouraged us to do secondary research regarding village profile, climate and rice productivity.

Secondary research or Desk Research makes use of selective information beforehand researched for other purposes and which is publicly available. Secondary research done for the project includes information from published research papers in a library and online. It also includes reports produced by councils, government agricultural and electricity departments, NGO's and other business magazines.

## DATA ANALYSIS

From Table 1 it can be seen that around 300 kg of rice husk per day can generate 32 KW of energy, which can easily illuminate 400 households for 8-10 hours every day. Rice husk is priced at Rs 1-1.5 for every kg. Company installs separate meter to quantify the electricity drawn by consumer, for this they charge Rs 100 initially from consumers. They have their own distribution network, due to high potential gradient between power from Grid and power from Husk based power. They charge Rs 80-100 base price from the consumers, wherein they can illuminate two CFL bulbs of 15 W each and one mobile charging point. Around 4 local villagers receive two month long training regarding work in plant and after completion of training is employed by power plant. The salary paid to these villagers is Rs 3000 per month per villager. The Rice Production in Eastern India per year is close to 50-60 tonnes. The amount of Rice husk, deemed as waste, generated is 15 tonnes. The waste obtained from plant operation, Rice Husk Ash is used for making rubber, candles and used as manure. The company also earns from the reduction of carbon credit. Every plant boasts of reduction of carbon dioxide to the tune of 125-150 tonnes.

The different Revenue Streams for the power plant:

- Sale of generated power to villages
- Sale of Rice Husk Char products
- Carbon Credits
- Sale of electrical appliances and fast moving consumer goods from corporate partners to end consumers in villages

The table shows the yearly statement of the plant build, with a onetime installation cost considering the present dollar rate (Rs. 60 per $).

*Table 1. Detailed Analysis*

| Cost Of Rice Husk (Rs / kg) | Quantity required(kg) | Day's cost of rice husk |
|---|---|---|
| 1-1.5 | 300 | 375 |
| No of households to receive power | Number of hours for which power is supplied | Charge Rates(Rs) |
| 400 | 8 - 10 hours | 80 – 100 |
| Local Villagers Employed | Local villagers employed for utilising waste products | Monthly earnings per rural household |
| 4 for each plant | 1200 | 3000 |
| Rice Production in Eastern India per year | Amount of Rice that goes to waste per year | Reduced Emissions of Carbon Dioxide (tonnes) |
| 50-60 tonnes | 15 tonnes | 125-150 |

*Table 2. Financial Viablity*

| Cost Centers | Amount (in Rs) | Total (in Rs) |
|---|---|---|
| **Material Cost** | | |
| Cost of Husk per kg | 1.25 | |
| Weight of Husk required in kgs | 108000 | |
| | | 135000 |
| **Labor Cost** | | |
| Wage rate per day | 150 | |
| Number of employees | 4 | |
| | | 219000 |
| Other Expenses | 35400 | |
| Total Variable Cost | | 389400 |
| **Income** | | |
| Electricity | 864000 | |
| Carbon Credit | 105000 | |
| | | 969000 |
| Profit | | 579600 |

One time Installation Cost/ Investment = Rs. 2340000

Subsidy from the Indian Government on the whole plant = Rs. 480000

Total onetime cost = Rs. 1860000

From Table 2, the yearly profit is evaluated to be Rs.579600 which can cover up the investment and break even in 3-4 years. This investment, thus, is a win-win situation for both the investors and the villagers in the long term.

## Application of Rice Husk Ash (RHA)

Using rice husk in generating power with high combustion efficiency and temperature below 600 °C leads to highly valuable by product, amorphous silica rich Rice Husk Ash (RHA). The quality of RHA depends on composition of ash, predominantly silica content, which varies from 85%-95%. There is huge potential for RHA, containing mainly amorphous silica as a commercial product. RHA has high average market value of US$200/tonne in India and is very important material in several industrial applications. Some of them are:

- As a Replacement to Silica Fume This finely grained RHA can be potential replacement of silica fume in the manufacture of high performance concrete. Silica content in RHA generally varies from 85% to 90%. RHA is suitable to replace silica fume, this has been confirmed by American Society of Testing and Materials (ASTM),which placed RHA in same class as silica fume.
- As a Tundish Powder in Steel Casting Industries RHA is used by the steel industry for the production of high quality flat steel. RHA is an excellent insulator, having low thermal conductivity, high melting point and high porosity. It is due to insulating property that makes it an excellent tundish powder, which is used to insulate and prevent speedy cooling of the steel and ensure uniform solidification. Approximately 0.5 to 0.7 kg of RHA is used per tonne of steel produced.

- As an admixture in Low Cost Concrete Block Manufacturing Ordinary Portland cement (OPC) is expensive and unaffordable to produce low strength concrete block. Sometimes it becomes economically feasible to produce low strength concrete block for masonry work. RHA is mixed with lime and gypsum and aggregates and cast of the required shape and sizes. Generally, around 7 MPa strength is achieved in 14 days. RHA as binder material along with some admixtures. Amorphous RHA is preferred for its use in the concrete manufacture.
- Manufacturing Refractory Bricks One of the potentially profitable use of RHA is in manufacture of refractory bricks. Due to the insulating properties, RHA has been used in the manufacture of refractory bricks. These are suitable for furnace bricks. Such bricks normally contains 80-98% ash.
- Control of Insect Pests in Stored Food Stuffs RHA has been found to be an excellent material to protect food produce from pests and insects. RHA includes a large amount of needle like particles, which may trigger a physical reaction on the skin of insects, resulting physical disturbance may cause their death. The use of RHA enables farmers to store their produce on a small scale and for a low cost.
- As a Flue Gas Desulphurization Absorbent In coal fired boilers of power plants, fly ash is used for the preparation of absorbents for flue gas desulfurization. Lower hydration period and temperature favour the formation of absorbent with higher surface area. Absorbent prepared from RHA does have a high capacity in gas absorption especially sulphur dioxide.

Despite having so many well established uses of Rice Husk Ash, it is perceived to be waste product where large quantity is generated.Power plants based on rice husk as a fuel should be installed not only to generate electricity but to generate high quality rice husk ash as well. This would further increase the financial benefits and would help tremendously in waste management. The competitive environment for the Rice Husk will be helpful to fetch higher prices of the rice husk for farmers.

## RESULTS AND FINDINGS

Rice husk, the hard protecting coverings outside grains of rice, generally considered as waste by many, has various supplementary benefits in addition to protecting rice during the growing season. Rice hulls or husks can be used as fertilizer, insulation material, or fuel for generating electricity. Rice husk is an important waste product generated by agricultural activities. It can be obtained at a price as low as Rs 1-1.5 per kg.

Rural electrification in India has always been facing an acute problem as a total of 32,119 Indian villages are currently un-electrified (Central Electricity Authority, Ministry of Power, Government of India, 2013) leaving over 33% of the population without any access to reliable source of energy. (The Climate Group, 2013). Out of the total un-electrified villages in India, a major chunk that is more than 34% of the un-electrified villages is in the state of Uttar Pradesh itself. Central Government of India as well as State Government of Uttar Pradesh are facing various problems in fulfilling the needs of the inhabitants in these villages. These problems could be catered with the help of Rice Husk power systems. A single 32KW power plant can enlighten approximately 400-500 households in a village and its surroundings. The beneficiaries could receive continuous power for 8-10 hours at monthly cost of Rs. 100-125. The power provided would be sufficient to illuminate two CFL's of 15 W each and to support a mobile charging point in each of the households.

A rice husk power plant would not only provide electricity to the residents but also provide them with many different sources of income. The Rice husk power plant would itself employ at least 4 local villagers, who would be engaged in running the power plant round the clock. Apart from the employment, by products of the power plant fuel such as Bio-char which is a waste product of the gasification process could be used to make incense sticks and char briquettes. Husk power plant would employ a group of women from the local villages for this activity providing them with income generating opportunities. Small programmes could also be monitored to train local electricians to assemble simple innovative electronic products which would not only enhance their knowledge but also increase their revenue generating source.

The different sources of revenue for Husk Power plant would be sale of generated power to villages, sale of Rice Husk Char products such as incense sticks and char briquettes made from Bio char, an industrial waste. Power plant would also provide solution to displace the use of kerosene lamps and diesel based generators. This can help in the saving of precious non-renewable source of energy and economically it has implication to improve the current account deficit. Each plant would avoid approximately 125 to 150 tonnes of $CO_2$ per year which could be monetised through Certified Emission Reductions (CERs). With help of all the revenue sources mentioned above, the break even period for power plant would be roughly about 3-4 years.

## LIMITATIONS

For this model to work seamlessly, the demand of rice husk should be met round the year. This is very challenging because of the typical demand and supply constraints which depends on seasonal variation as well as expectation of seller of price hike seeing the utility of the product. The financial analysis and thus breakeven period calculated for fixed value of rice husk, any variation on this would hurt the financial viability. This model works on the affordability, since the target market consists of villages with low paying capability, any hike in raw material would in turn require to raise the monthly bill. Other challenges include the proximity of the project to the rice mill, since the maximum limit up to which electricity distribution can be economically done is 2km, often the rice mills are not at sufficient distance which in turn raises the transportation cost of raw material. Also the attrition among the labour in-house trained is one of the major cost center.

## CONCLUSION AND FUTURE IMPLICATIONS

1. Rice husk is majorly considered as a waste product of agricultural activities. Implementing innovative idea of HPS can enable power generation for rural households.
2. Rice husk based power systems hold a great amount of promise for the bottom of pyramid users and reduces emission of carbon dioxide up to125-150 tons per year per plant.
3. We suggest that this innovation should be encouraged by private players by investing into this project. Whole model can be envisaged wherein private players would be supporting the local farmers helping them in improving yield of crops and strategically locating rice mills. Then the investors can go for franchisee model partnering with Husk Power System and in turn selling electricity to local villages.
4. The future of Husk Power plants looks very bright. The ever increasing demand by future generations for rice and energy can be achieved by this model.

## REFERENCES


Authority, C. E. Ministry of Power, Government of India. (2013, October 31). *Progress report of village electrification as on 31-10-2013.* Retrieved Dec 2013, from Central Electricity Authority, Ministry of Power, Government of India: http://www.cea.nic.in/reports/monthly/dpd_div_rep/village_electrification.pdf

Chandra, K. K. (2011, june 3). *The Weekend Leader*. Retrieved from http://www.theweekendleader.com/Innovation/515/Illuminating-villages.html

Chungsangunsit, T., Gheewala, S. H., & Patumsawad, S. (n.d.). *Emission Assessment of Rice Husk Combustion.*

Govindarao. (1980). Utilization of rice husk-preliminary analysis. *J. Science Industrial Research*, 495-515.

GreenPeace India. (2010, October). Empowering Bihar. In *Case studies for bridging the energy deficit and driving change*. GreenPeace India Society.

Husk Power System. (2013). *Our Solution*. Retrieved 2013, from Husk Power Systems: http://www.huskpowersystems.com/innerPage.php?pageT=Our%20Solution&page_id=77

Indian Agribusiness Systems Private Limited. (2013). *Agriwatch*. Retrieved 2013, from http://www.agriwatch.com/grains/rice/

Map, E. an Initiative of the Center for Science, Technology, and Society. Supported By Applied Materials. (2010). *Husk Power System*. Retrieved Dec 21, 2013, from http://energymap-scu.org/husk-power-systems/

Nerenberg, J. (2011, January 5). *Husk Power Systems wants to lead "A Revolution in Electricity"*. Retrieved from www.fastcompany.com: http://www.fastcompany.com/1714395/husk-power-systems-wants-lead-revolution-electricity

Pradhan, A., Ali, S., & Dash, R. (n.d.). *Biomass Gasification by the use of Rice Husk Gasifier*. Academic Press.

Tanaka, N., Kjorven, O., & Yumkella, K. K. (2010). *Energy Poverty: How to make modern energy access universal.* UNIDO.

The Climate Group. (2013, August 16). *As India revives US$8.7 billion clean energy grid upgrade, off-grid projects also on rise*. Retrieved Dec 2013, from The Climate Group: http://www.theclimategroup.org/what-we-do/news-and-blogs/as-india-revives-us87-billion-clean-energy-grid-upgrade-off-grid-projects-also-on-rise

The Hindu. (2010, July 26). *Rice husk power to light up villages.* Retrieved from The Hindu: http://www.thehindu.com/news/national/article533665.ece

Zafar, S. (2013, August 21). *BIO Energy Consultant*. Retrieved from http://www.bioenergyconsult.com/tag/energy-potential-of-rice-husk/

## KEY TERMS AND DEFINITIONS

**CFL:** Compact Fluorescent Lamp.

**Fuel Source:** Source of energy.

**Husk Power System (HPS):** Power system that provides power to rural Indians using cost effective technology and biomass gasifier that creates fuel from rice husks.

**Ministry of Power:** It is a ministry mainly responsible for the fulfillment of the demand of electricity.

**OPIC:** The U.S. Government's development finance institution which mobilizes private capital to help solve critical development challenges.

**Ordinary Portland Cement (OPC):** Most common cement used in general concrete construction when there is no exposure to sulphates in the soil or groundwater.

**Rice Husk Ash (RHA):** Combustion of rice hulls yields rice husk ash.

**Rice Husk:** A left-over product of the rice hullers that separate the husks as chaff from the rice.

**Rice:** A staple food in the region.

**SOX/ NOX:** Sulphur and Nitrogen oxides respectively.

# Chapter 9
# Talent Management

**Jaya Chitranshi**
*Jaipuria Institute of Management, India*

## ABSTRACT

*Changing of the world scenario, blurring boundaries in international and national markets and shifts in demographic profile of people have opened a new chapter of management thinking on 'strategies for retention of talent'. Skill unavailability, employee poaching, high costs of training and development, absolute necessity of international exposure are the alarming signals for organizations to shrug off their complacency-nap and get going for talent management. Talent Management is a wide function encompassing strategic planning, talent staffing, development-focus, performance management, compensation management etc. to manage retaining talent in the organization. This review paper is an attempt to throw some light on this vista.*

## INTRODUCTION

'Talent management' is becoming an area of growing concern in the field of human resource management. Retention of good employees and the role that various factors have in an employee's decision to stay or leave an organization are much sought-after themes of contemporary management research. Talent management is an espoused and enacted commitment to implementing an integrated, strategic and technology-enabled approach to human resource management. This commitment stems in part from the widely-shared belief that human resources are the organization's primary source of competitive advantage; an essential asset that is available in increasingly short supply every passing day!

Talent management refers to the anticipation of required human capital for an organization and the planning to meet those needs. The field increased in popularity after McKinsey's 1997 research and the 2001 book on *The War for Talent*. Talent management is the science of using strategic human resource planning to improve business value and to make it possible for companies and organizations to reach their goals. Talent Management refers to the process of attracting, selecting, training, developing and promoting employees through an organization. In other words it is the process of creating tenacious (T), alluvial (A), laborious (L),empowered(E), noteworthy(N) and trained(T) workforce members. The organizations aims to develop people who are persistent in their efforts, whose potential is cultured over

DOI: 10.4018/978-1-4666-8259-7.ch009

years, who are hard-working, who can be given power, who make notable contributions and who are mentored and trained by the organization as its valued members. Managers who focus on developing talent in-house ensure their employees have the tools and resources they need to perform well, receive proper compensation and transition to leadership roles. Internally developed leaders are valuable assets because over time they have developed the necessary core competencies and internalized company values. A talent-management strategy needs to link to business strategy to make sense.

From a talent management standpoint, employee evaluations concern two major areas of measurement: 'performance' and 'potential'. Current employee performance within a specific job has always been a standard evaluation measurement tool of the profitability of an employee. However, talent management also seeks to focus on an employee's potential, meaning an employee's future performance, if given the proper development of skills and increased responsibility.

This term "talent management" is usually associated with 'competency-based management'. Talent management decisions are often driven by a set of organizational core competencies as well as position-specific competencies. The competency set may include knowledge, skills, experience, and personal traits (demonstrated through defined behaviors).

A talent marketplace is an employee training and development strategy that is set in place within an organization. It is found to be most beneficial for companies where the most productive employees can pick and choose the projects and assignments that are ideal for the specific employee. An ideal setting is where productivity is employee-centric and tasks are described as "judgment-based work," for example, in a law firm. The point of activating a talent marketplace within a department is to harness and link individuals' particular skills (project management or extensive knowledge in a particular field) with the task at hand. Examples of companies that implement the talent marketplace strategy are American Express and IBM.

In adverse economic conditions, many companies feel the need to cut expenses. This should be the ideal environment to execute a talent management system as a means of optimizing the performance of each employee and the organization. Selection offers are large return on investments. Job analysis and assessment validation help enhance the predictive power of selection tools. However, within many companies the concept of human capital management has just begun to develop. With more companies in the process of deepening their global footprints, more questions have been asked about new strategies and products, but very few on the kind of leadership structure that will bring them success in their globalization process. "In fact, only 5 percent of organizations say they have a clear talent management strategy and operational programs in place today."

The environment for most organizations today is global, complex, dynamic, highly competitive, and extremely volatile, and is likely to remain so for years to come. In addition to these external conditions, most organizations are also facing several global challenges including those related to: talent flow; the managing of two generations of employees, viz., older or mature workers and younger workers; and a shortage of needed competencies. One major result of these challenges for organizations is that they have to be global and that they have to be systematic in managing their human capital if they wish to have any hope of gaining and sustaining a competitive advantage in the years ahead. Many human resource practitioners, academicians and consultants are now recognizing this. The new area is referred to as "global talent management".

Effective, practical and holistic people strategies that address key skills' retention, employee engagement, employee motivation and attendance gaps, with a view to positively impacting on organization costs, productivity and business performance are in acute shortage and demand today. There is need to examine the value of assessment and feedback in talent engagement and retention, and to look at developing employees via experience-based development initiatives.

The benefits of an effectively implemented talent management strategy include improved employee recruitment and retention rates, and enhanced employee engagement. These outcomes in turn have been associated with improved operational and financial performance. The external and internal drivers and restraints for talent management are many. Of particular importance is senior management understanding and commitment.

Managerial, job-related learning is confirmed as an important antecedent for the intention to stay/leave one's current organization. The differential meaning of learning and commitment across generations needs to be better understood in order to develop effective strategies for the retention of talent in all generations. In particular, differences in the psychological contract between organizations and their managers need to be understood. Alessia D'Amato & Regina Herzfeldt(1986) found that younger generations are less willing to remain in the same organization and have lower organizational commitment. The youngest generations (Early and Late Xers, born 1960 and after) show stronger learning orientation and lower organizational commitment than older generations (Early and Late Boomers, born 1946-1959).

## ESSENTIAL TOOLS OF TALENT MANAGEMENT

There's a problem that small-to-midsized but fast-growing private companies often do not realize the significance of talent-management until the damage is done. Namely – they don't recognize until it's too late just how much value is being lost owing to immature talent development, retention, evaluation and recruitment processes.

There are many reasons for this phenomenon. Prioritization tops the list. The very nature of high-growth means that a company is so focused on opportunities that it often does not notice the ways that sub-optimal talent processes nibble or even bite at performance. The pace of change is also an important factor. The fact is, with each new surge in sales, de facto, the organization responds and a new company is formed. Or in other cases, the owners and managers simply have no formal experience in organizational performance. They do not understand how talent lapses limit or damage performance and growth. In short, they cannot know what they do not know.

And as highlighted in *The Talent Imperative*, a recently-released report from Forbes Insights and BMO Harris **HRS**-0.42%, that damage, at least at first, is hidden by overwhelming success in other aspects of the business. The opportunity is so lush that any organization can find ripe pickings, regardless of the preparation of its individual people for their roles, or the overall integration of talent and strategy as a whole.

The shift from an ad hoc to a strategic talent management program can greatly aid a company in the achievement of its business objectives. And while there is no one-size-fits-all solution for talent optimization, leaders should consider implementing elements such as:

- **Objective metrics:** The need for metrics seems obvious. However, amid high-growth, job descriptions are often in flux, as is the nature of the associated opportunities. But regardless of these challenges, no company will ever be able to get the most out of its workforce without clearly defining roles and goals as well as addressing issues such as incentive compensation and advancement. What is it that defines success in this role? How is performance measured? Every employee should have a clear understanding of how they fit in. (Too often, they do not.)
- **Strategic alignment:** Talent, too often, is treated as an afterthought. According to the survey conducted for *The Talent Imperative*, fewer than one in ten executives from midsized private companies say their talent strategies are intimately aligned with overall strategic planning. This can be a critical mistake, as any strategic plan must be executed by people. So incorporating the views of HR – injecting talent into strategic planning – becomes an essential and relatively easy to use tool for optimizing overall performance.
- **Targeted training and development:** As talent and strategy become more closely aligned, companies will begin to get a better handle on their specific talent challenges. Often topping the to-do list: enhancing training and development.

One way to get things going quickly is to establish a *mentoring program.* Here the company assigns a more senior and experienced executive to develop a relationship with one or more high-potential individuals within the organization. Another tried and true means is to implement *rotational assignments.* Here, high-potential employees are exposed to a range of functions in the organization.

Another cost-effective means of training and development is to partner with local schools to develop – or merely refine existing – courses to meet the needs of the employer. Companies can also encourage more experienced workers to develop training videos.

- **Key talent identification/retention:** Going hand-in-hand with talent training and development, fast-growing companies need to make sure that their most valuable employees are engaged and satisfied: with work/life balance, compensation, strategic direction and a host of related variables. Once dissatisfied, it is often too late to turn things around. Companies need to make a concerted effort to proactively identify and work to satisfy the needs of their most critical talent.
- **Career-pathing:** As talent processes mature, companies can begin to add elements that can lead to anything from performance improvement to breakthrough. Providing each worker – particularly their most valuable employees – with a clear job description and performance metrics is only a start. The most enlightened companies take matters a step (or two) further. That is, they engage with each employee to get a sense of personal abilities, aspirations and needs to develop a growth and development plan within the organization.

Where do they want to go in their career? What can they do for the organization? What can the organization do to improve the work/life balance? What training or work experience will they need? If employers can better align the interests of individuals with those of the broader organization, employee engagement and performance are enhanced.

- **Talent mapping:** Talent mapping is a formalized process of linking the talent on hand to the talent that will be needed to support growth in order to assess shortfalls or gaps. As companies pursue greater alignment between talent management and strategic planning, they begin to see increasingly greater value in talent mapping.
- **Prioritizing efforts**

A sophisticated, comprehensive and value-generating talent function will not arise overnight. Rather, as talent and strategic and operational planning become more entwined, the most pressing opportunities become more visible. Start with those areas determined to be of the most critical importance, and build overall talent capabilities over time. Again, the biggest mistake being made is ignoring talent altogether. Once genuine awareness sets in, the talent equation will begin to optimize itself.

## CRUCIAL FACTORS FOR EMPLOYEE RETENTION

In a workplace characterized by market-driven turnover, organizations attempting to retain those employees considered core to their purpose and continued success (referred to as 'talent') face a huge challenge in determining the factors instrumental in minimizing turnover amongst this group. Birt, M.; Wallis,T.& Winternitz, G. (2004) discovered the relative importance of intrinsic and extrinsic variables to South African talent, particularly when these are considered as factors in their decisions to leave the organization. They found that South African talent placed great importance on intrinsic variables, although market opportunities were also considered highly significant in employees' decisions to leave. The variable of 'Concern with employment equity and affirmative action' was revealed as a specifically South African variable, but it was not ranked as one of the participants' top five most important variables influencing retention. Kerr-Phillips, Berenice Thomas, Ade le (2009) using a web-based survey placed on eight New Zealand sites, explored the reasons for emigration of South African talent during the period 1994-2006. They found that reasons for emigration (macro issues) included uncertainty about the future of the country, job insecurity and fears regarding both corruption and violent crime. Reasons for talent loss amongst identified top talent (micro issues) were found to be linked to leadership, organisational culture and employment equity.

Towers Perrin (2005) highlighted that for many companies in the United States, the changing demographics of the labor force and looming exodus of retirement-eligible employees pose significant challenges and opportunities in terms of talent retention, acquisition and management (Towers Perrin;2005).

Stahl, Günter and Björkman, Ingmar and Farndale, Elaine and Morris, Shad S. and Paauwe, Jaap and Stiles, Philip and Trevor, Jonathan and Wright, Patrick (2012) tried to determine how leading companies in North America, Europe, and Asia develop and sustain strong talent pipelines. The research investigated talent management processes and practices in a sample of 37 multinational corporations, selected on the basis of their international scope, reputation, and long-term performance. The research identified various effective practices that can help companies attract, select, develop, and retain talent. The results suggested that competitive advantage comes not primarily from designing and implementing best practices but rather from the proper internal alignment of various elements of a company's talent management system, as well as their embeddedness in the value system of the firm, their links to business strategy, and their global coordination.

Saket Jeswani & Souren Sarkar (2008) focused on how talent engagement is an antecedent of job involvement and what should a company do to make the talents engaged. They discussed the importance of talent retention strategies with special reference to the leadership style of the superiors within the organization. They suggested a Talent Engagement Model, which explains the process of engagement, psychological ownership, performance and retention of talents and their relative relationships, which can help not only to retain the talents but also to increase the performance for the overall development of both the talents and the organization.

Michael Hay, (2002) observed that one-third of employees plan to resign from their jobs within the next two years quoting a new international report and discussed the Retention Dilemma, by Hay Group. He added that however, with economists forecasting a downturn, this is not good news for companies struggling to stay successful. He explored the phenomena further. Ibraiz Tarique (2009) highlighted several selected challenges in global talent management, and several drivers of those challenges and the potential role of IHRM activities in addressing those selected challenges.

Margaret Deery, (2008) focused on job attitudes such as job satisfaction and organizational commitment, personal attributes such as positive and negative affectivity, the role of Work-life Balance in employee turnover and the strategies provided to alleviate high turnover rates.

Jyotsna Bhatnagar, (2007) found that a good level of engagement may lead to high retention, but only for a limited time in the Information Technology Enabled Services' sector. The need for a more rigorous employee engagement construct is also indicated by the study.

Julia Christensen Hughes, Evelina Rog, (2008) suggested to align talent management with the strategic goals of the organization; establish talent assessment, data management and analysis systems; ensure clear line management accountability; and conduct an audit of all HRM practices in relation to evidence-based best practices.

Chris Ashton, Lynne Morton, (2005) highlighted the importance of getting the right people in pivotal roles at the right time.

Sunley, J. (2006) discussed the top five key things that people want from their employer, namely, communication, a career path, learning and development, leadership, and values.

Clayton Glen, (2006) suggested that one must take a holistic view of the key elements of the business most likely to impact team engagement, motivation, attendance and retention, link individual assessment directly to the key drivers of the business, and recognize that key talent is likely to thrive on experience-based career leverage opportunities.

Heather A. Earle, (2003) examined the characteristics of the different generations that currently make up the workforce and discussed what they, as well as new recruits, expect from their employers and from their work environments in Canadian Federal Government. They also delved into the role the workplace plays in recruitment and retention and the way in which it can be used to improve an organization's corporate identity. They looked at what types of perks are actually valued most by employees, and explored how the physical environment can be aligned to help shape a company's organizational culture and facilitate the communication, teamwork and creativity that are necessary to sustain a culture of continual innovation.

Kamel Mellahi, David G.Collings (2010)) studied Talent management failure by multinational enterprises (MNEs) . They examined barriers to corporate advancement of talents located in subsidiaries and more specifically on promotion of talent already employed by the MNE to be part of the upper echelon management team at its centre(Kamel et. Al; 2010)

Today, organizations around the globe are operating in an unprecedented, highly competitive seller's market. The global workforce is now more mobile than ever before, meaning that companies are no longer simply competing for talent nationally, but rather on an international level. There is need of a positively oriented 'psychological ownership construct' that can be utilized by managers and human resource professionals as a potential guideline to facilitating talent retention and productivity in the current work environment. Many scholars, consultants and practitioners have recently focused their attention on 'ownership' as a psychological, rather than just a business phenomenon. Psychological ownership is defined as a state in which individuals feel as though the target of ownership or a piece of it is 'theirs' (that is 'It is mine!'). It suggests that, the presence of psychological ownership among employees can have a positive effect on organizational effectiveness.

The role of the corporate human resource function regarding global talent management is also being studied from two perspectives: increasing global competition for talent, and new forms of international mobility. New corporate HR roles are identified which show how these issues might be addressed considering the major future challenges facing corporate HR.(Elaine Farndale, Hugh Scullion, Paul Sparrow (2010)

## TALENT MANAGEMENT STRATEGY TO CREATE A HIGHER-PERFORMING WORKFORCE

Executives and HR management have always been focused on basic talent management—acquiring, hiring and retaining talented employees. But, to drive optimal levels of success, business leaders need engaged, high-performing employees. The key to inciting a workforce to greatness is to align your with company strategy, define consistent leadership criteria across all functional areas, and identify specific competencies (analytical, technical, education, experience) to cultivate for continuing growth.

Business leaders who implement the best talent management processes are more prepared than their competitors to compete in the global economy and capitalize quickly on new opportunities. True success is only available when companies do more than adapt to long-term trends; they must be able to anticipate and jump on new opportunities before the rest of the market. A strategic talent management plan allows you to:

- Become "proactive" versus "reactive". Fill your critical talent management needs and address company and industry changes promptly;
- Identify essential skills to be developed in all employees, and minimize training costs by focusing on key development areas; and
- Improve your recruiting process by identifying high-quality candidates using job descriptions based upon the expertise of your high performing employees holding uniquely valued company or industry competencies.

### Align Individual Goals with Corporate Strategy

The best talent management plan is closely aligned with the company's strategic plan and overall business needs. Goal alignment is a powerful management tool that not only clarifies job roles for individual employees, but also demonstrates ongoing value of your employees to the organization. When you engage employees in their work through goal alignment, you create greater employee ownership in your company's ultimate success; they become more committed to your company and achieve higher levels of job performance.

To achieve "goal alignment" in your organization, you must first clearly communicate your strategic business objectives across the entire company. By allowing managers to access and view the goals of other departments, your organization can greatly reduce redundancy. Goal sharing also helps departmental heads find ways to better support each other, as well as identify areas where they may be unintentionally working at cross purposes. With everyone working together toward the same objectives, your company can execute strategy faster, with more flexibility and adaptability. Essentially, goal alignment strengthens your leadership and creates organizational agility by allowing managers to:

- Focus employees' efforts on your company's most important goals;
- Understand more clearly all responsibilities associated with specific goals; and
- Strengthen accountability by assigning measurable and clearly articulated goals that are visible company-wide.

## Create Highly-Skilled Internal Talent Pools

Strategically minded organizations are able to change ahead of the curve when it comes to planning and developing a workforce with the right competencies. They have deeper strategic insight into their employees, and use that insight to proactively put the right workforces in place to effectively respond to urgent marketplace needs.

At one time or another, most companies will find themselves faced with a situation with limited time to assess viable candidates due to a planned (or unplanned) change in leadership or industry conditions. For many of these businesses, a prolonged leadership void is too risky. It raises questions about a company's internal talent pool. Is it robust enough? How much attention has been given to developing internal talent, starting at the senior executive level? Are there ready candidates at every key position?

A critical element of a successful talent management program is the generation of "talent pools" within a company—a reliable and consistent internal source of talent and a valuable piece of the succession planning process. The development of skilled talent pools makes it easier to develop desirable skill sets in a broader group of employees, resulting in higher performance across all levels and functions. By cultivating talent pools internally you are ensuring that you will have experienced and trained employees prepared to assume leadership roles as they become available.

## Break Down Information Silos and Develop Collaboration

To drive success, business leaders must do whatever they can to overcome the organizational silos that prevent the flow of information throughout the organization. For companies to perform faster and with more flexibility, knowledge and experience must be readily available—or, even better, proactively delivered - to the right people at the right time. In many cases, the innovation required to meet a new marketplace challenge exists somewhere in the organization; the challenge is tapping into it.

In order to cultivate a collaborative atmosphere, management needs to align the metrics for success—if success is based only on individual performance, you will be sending mixed messages to your employees. Beyond simply encouraging collaboration, organizations need to provide the tools to facilitate easier collaborative efforts. To drive better collaboration across an organization, employees and management need access to rich employee data, including experience, interests and special skills, such as language abilities. Centrally locating this robust information drives greater success companywide —employees can reach across departments or offices to tap into a knowledge base and collaborate easily, while managers can use the information to make informed talent management decisions to increase business performance.

### Create a Pay-for-Performance Culture

In a pay-for-performance culture, managers gain easy access to all the information they need to reward individuals for actual performance—, metrics, review data and performance notes taken throughout the year. This allows managers to make consistent, quantifiably fair decisions, thus avoiding improper compensation.

Many companies use employee assessments to help them motivate their employees to reach their full potential. This provides better results as each employee's reason for working is unique. Addressing each individual's needs in the organization will create a highly motivated workforce that strives for the best as a whole.

By measuring the essential factors that mark the difference between success and failure in specific jobs, your organization will be able to put the right person into every position, allowing them to utilize their talents without limitations. This leads to greater job satisfaction, improved morale and employee retention because your organization is staffed with a workforce of people who are highly productive, skilled and committed to doing their very best.

Businesses that outperform their competition know that strategic talent management is essential in building the right workforce necessary for precise business execution. Executives use analytics and diagnostic tools to move beyond generalities or "gut feelings" into detailed analyses of workforce performance drivers.

The ability to rapidly train and retrain employees according to business need, create opportunities for real-time collaboration, and support the workforce with better analytics are all benefits of a strategic talent management process that will drive true business success.

Without a doubt talent management can create long-term organizational success. Leaders must align talent management strategies to business goals, integrate all related processes and systems and create a "talent mindset" in their organization for the éclat.

## REFERENCES

Ashton, C., & Morton, L. (2005). Managing talent for competitive advantage: Taking a systemic approach to talent management]. *Strategic HR Review*, *4*(5), 28–31. doi:10.1108/14754390580000819

Bhatnagar, J. (2007). Talent management strategy of employee engagement in Indian ITES employees: Key to retention. *Employee Relations*, *29*(6), 640–663. doi:10.1108/01425450710826122

Birt, M., Wallis, T., & Winternitz, G. (2004). Talent retention in a changing workplace: an investigation of variables considered important to South African talent. *South African Journal of Business Management*, *35*(2), 25-31.

Chantal, O., Plessis, D., & Yvonne. (2012). *Psychological Ownership: A Managerial Construct for Talent Retention and Organizational Effectiveness*. Academic Press.

Clayton, G. (2006). Key skills retention and motivation: The war for talent still rages and retention is the high ground. *Industrial and Commercial Training*, *38*(1), 37–45. doi:10.1108/00197850610646034

D'Amato, A., & Herzfeldt, R. (1986). Learning orientation, organizational commitment and talent retention across generations: A study of European managers. *Journal of Managerial Psychology*, *23*(8), 929–953.

Deery, M. (2008). Talent management, work-life balance and retention strategies. *International Journal of Contemporary Hospitality Management*, *20*(7), 792–806.

Farndale, E., Scullion, H., & Sparrow, P. (2010). The role of the corporate HR function in global talent management. *Journal of World Business*, *45*(2), 161–168. doi:10.1016/j.jwb.2009.09.012

Hay, M. (2002). Strategies for survival in the war of talent. *Career Development International*, *7*(1), 52–55. doi:10.1108/13620430210414883

Heather, A. (2003). Building a workplace of choice: Using the work environment to attract and retain top talent. *Journal of Facilities Management*, *2*(3), 244–257. doi:10.1108/14725960410808230

Hughes, J., & Rog, E. (2008). Talent management: A strategy for improving employee recruitment, retention and engagement within hospitality organizations. *International Journal of Contemporary Hospitality Management*, *20*(7), 743–757. doi:10.1108/09596110810899086

Jeswani, S. & Sarkar, S. (2008). Integrating Talent Engagement as a Strategy to High Performance and Retention. *Asia pacific Journal of Management Research & Innovation*, *4*(4), 14-23.

Mellahi, K., & Collings, D. (2010). The barriers to effective global talent management: The example of corporate elites in MNEs. *Journal of World Business*, *45*(2), 143–149. doi:10.1016/j.jwb.2009.09.018

Millar, B. (2013, April 24). *Essential Tools of Talent Management*. Retrieved March 15, 2015 from http://www.forbes.com/sites/forbesinsights/2013/04/24/essential-tools-of-talent-management/

Phillips, K., & Berenice, T. & Ade le. (2009). Macro and micro challenges for talent retention in South Africa: Original research. *South African Journal of Human Resource Management*, *7*(1), 1–10.

Stahl, G., Björkman, I., Farndale, E., Morris, S. S., Paauwe, J., Stiles, P., & Wright, P. et al. (2012). Six principles of effective global talent management. *Sloan Management Review*, *53*(2), 25–42.

Subotnik, R.; Duschl, R. & Selmon, E. (1993). Retention and attrition of science talent: a longitudinal study of Westinghouse Science Talent Search winners. *International Journal of Science Education*, 15(1), 61-72.

Successfactors. (n.d.). *Talent Management*. Retrieved March 15, 2015 from http://www.successfactors.com/en_us/lp/ppc/talent-management.html?Campaign_ID=21941&TAG=Q114_APJ_Google_PPC_India&CmpLeadSource=Search%20Engine&source=Google_ppc&kw=Talent%20Management&ad--id=35149490117&adgroup=Google&gclid=CNaA3q32rL4CFUwpjgodCHUAVwhttp://en.wikipedia.org/wiki/Talent_management

Successfactors. (n.d.). *Talent Management Strategy to Create a Higher-Performing Workforce*. Retrieved March15, 2015 from http://www.successfactors.com/en_us/lp/articles/strategic-talent-management-training.html

Sunley, J. (2006). New ideas on talent retention. *Hospitality*, *1*, 26-28.

Tarique, I., & Schuler, R. S. (2009). Global talent management: Literature review, integrative framework, and suggestions for further research. *Journal of World Business*, *45*(2), 122–133. doi:10.1016/j.jwb.2009.09.019

Towers, P. (2005). The Business case for workers age 50+: planning for tomorrow's talent needs in today's competitive environment. In *AARP Knowledge Management* (p. 96). Washington, DC: AARP.

## KEY TERMS AND DEFINITIONS

**Corporate Priorities:** The corporates should define their strategic focus and talent management is an essential area.

**Employee Motivation:** Employee should feel motivated as he sees his career growth, commensurate reward-system, employee-friendly work culture etc.

**Employee Retention:** Retaining talented people in the organization viz-a-viz phenomena like demographic shift, exodus of retirement-eligible employees etc.

**Job Attitudes:** Nurturing job attitudes like commitment, involvement, satisfaction, engagement etc.

**Organizational Success:** The organization has a pool of talented employees who help the organization to achieve its objectives and vision in the long-run.

**Talent Management:** Managing talent within the organization so that the organization achieves its purpose with the help of talented employees.

**Tools of Talent Management:** Role and significance of strategic alignment, talent identification, career pathing, targeted training and development etc. in talent management.

# Chapter 10
# Rural Outreach for Banks: Challenges and Possible Solutions

**Subhankar Halder**
*IMT Ghaziabad, India*

**Krishan Kumar**
*IMT Ghaziabad, India*

**Prashant Chandrashekhar**
*IMT Ghaziabad, India*

**Gandharvika Choudhary**
*IMT Ghaziabad, India*

**Ayush Asthana**
*IMT Ghaziabad, India*

**Allu Reshma**
*IMT Ghaziabad, India*

## ABSTRACT

*The intention of this chapter was to explore the reasons as to why the poor in Indian cities shun banking services. On the basis of a survey of 25 low-income daily wage earners, it was noted that although there is awareness about banks, strict ID card requirements and corruption are the major explanations of this sociological happening. Further, in this chapter, the authors have tried to document the steps taken by the Serva UP Gramin Bank to address this issue. Finally, based on the results of a research survey and field visits to the Serva UP Gramin Bank, recommendations of encouraging private banks to compete in the rural market and increasing the reach of the bank branches have been enumerated.*

## OBJECTIVE

Low-income villagers often leave their homes for the cities to earn a better living. However, once they earn money, they rarely use the services of the bank to remit the amount to their villages. In fact, most of them hardly have any bank accounts. The objective of this project was to explore this social phenomenon and to identify the reasons as to why these individuals fail to have a bank account or use bank remittance services. Additionally, the role of the banking sector in addressing these concerns was also examined. Based on this primary research, recommendations have been suggested so that the banks can better serve the underprivileged society.

DOI: 10.4018/978-1-4666-8259-7.ch010

## CASE DESCRIPTION

Technology has become so dramatically revolutionary that one can transfer money from one part of the world to the other through a click on the computer. Today, banks have record low processing transaction times that make banking services more efficient. However, it seems that rural India and people of the low-income category have eschewed modern-age banking facilities.

An interesting sociological phenomenon exists in this country, which sets the background for this case. Men from near and distant villages move to the cities in search of work often leaving their families behind. These men belong to the low-income segment earning around Rs. 50/- per day. They earn in the cities and take their compensation back to the villages or pass the amount through a friend/relative travelling that route. Nevertheless, these men hardly have any bank accounts or use the services of a bank to remit the money. At times, it seems counterintuitive to reject the services of a financial firm. The organized banks provide a great deal of security to the funds and transfer the money instantaneously. However, the reasons that were found for such an action were mostly "structural" in nature.

## LITERATURE REVIEW

In recent times, the banking sector in India has experienced phenomenal growth in terms of geographical reach and credit disbursal. However, penetration into the hinterlands of rural India is still, largely missing (Christabell & Vimal, 2012). As a result, especially for the rural poor, core banking services, such as, credit facility and amenities for deposits and withdrawals of money are absent. According to All Indian Debt Investment Survey in 2002 (Christabell & Vimal, 2012), nearly 111.5 million households did not have access to bank credit. Additionally, 17 million household owed money to moneylenders. As per 2011 census, 58.7% of households were availing banking services at that time (Bhaskar, 2013). Further, in 2013, CRISIL published its own financial inclusion index called "Inclusix" (Bhaskar, 2013). This index took into account three vital parameters: (a) Branch penetration (b) Credit Penetration and (c) Deposit Penetration. For 2011, the score of Inclusix was 40.1 (on a scale of 100) (Bhaskar, 2013), suggesting enormous room for improvement. With a view of making financial services available to all sections of the society, the Indian government has taken steps towards "Financial Inclusion" of the entire country. These steps may be viewed in the following three phases (Memdani & Rajyalakshmi, 2013):

- *First Phase (1969-1991)*: This phase included the period of nationalizing banks in India. This was done with a view of providing financial services to all society strata. Primarily, the following strategies were incorporated as a step towards financial inclusion: Lead Bank Scheme, Priority Sector Lending Norms, and Interest Rate Caps for poor clients.
- *Second Phase (2005-*2006): Although nationalization fell out of favor, RBI (The Reserve Bank of India) issued a policy circular in 2006 urging banks to form strategies with a view of achieving financial inclusion. Further, RBI advised banks to start No Frills Account for the rural poor and provide for easier and transparent KYC norms.
- *Third Phase (Rangrajan Committee)*: The Rangrajan Committee suggested the development of a National Rural Financial Inclusion Plan, whose aim would be to provide financial services and products to approximately 50% of the rural Indian population. This committee also proposed that

the government take initiative and form an association called the "National Mission on Financial Inclusion". The objective of this group would be to bring together stakeholders and deliberate on policies to attain financial inclusion.

The role of RBI towards the objective of achieving financial inclusion has been substantial. As noted earlier, the central bank has taken a series of initiatives in guiding banks towards the goal. Some of the major measures taken by RBI are (Infosys Finacle, 2012):

- *Overcoming Language barrier*: India being a diverse country is home to various languages. The rural people are necessarily not conversant with either English or Hindi. RBI has asked banks to provide for forms (disclosure forms, account opening forms, etc.) in regional languages.
- *No Frills Account*: RBI has made mandatory for banks to have no-frills account for people from the weaker sections of the society. Accordingly, these account do not require any minimum balance. Further, reasonable transaction fee are charged and facility of overdraft for small amounts is also provided.
- *KYC Norms*: A major issue for the poorer Indians during opening bank accounts is the lack of any relevant government identity documents. As such, inability to comply with compliance forces banks to reject these clients. However, RBI has initiated measures to simplify KYC norms for the clients. Small accounts (with minute deposit money) can be opened as a result of an introduction of the client from another account holder and some basic ID. The accounts ideally have balances less than Rs. 50,000/- as deposit money and an upper limit credit facility of Rs. 1,00,000/-.
- *Rural Intermediaries*: A model to expand into the rural cores of the country is to allow intermediaries to conduct financial transactions on behalf of the bank. In 2006, RBI allowed banks to conduct their business through intermediaries such as, NGOs, SHGs, Micro Finance Organizations and Civil Society Bodies. These intermediaries can be in the form of (a) Business Facilitators and (b) Business Correspondents (BC). Business facilitators educate the public about the banking services whereas correspondents can collect deposit and engage in money lending on behalf of the bank.
- *Easy Credit:* Banks are allowed to provide general Credit cards (GCC) for easy credit to the rural clients. These credit cards have an upper credit limit of Rs. 25,000.
- *Simple authorization for bank branches:* The RBI has made it easy for the banks to freely open branches in Tier 3 and Tier 4 Indian cities. In certain districts, banks can open branches without taking permission of the RBI.

Presently, the process of financial inclusion in India, as of 2012, has been impressive. As of March 2012, nearly 80% of rural India was under the Business Correspondents (BC) model of financial inclusion (Dangi & Kumar, 2013). In the financial year 2012, commercial banks have opened a total of 6,503 bank branches, out of which, 2,051 are in the rural villages. Moreover, Regional Rural Banks (RRBs) and Public Sector Banks have started 43,000 ultra-small bank branches in India so as to increase the reach of organized financial services. Additionally, in the year 2011, 14,365 new ATM branches were added (Dangi & Kumar, 2013). Nevertheless, financial inclusion depends on both demand and supply side factors. On one hand, demand side factors of low-income customer groups limit inclusion. On the other, supply side aspects such as high transaction costs, inconvenient products and non-customized finance services hurt rural finance penetration (Chakrabarty, 2011).

Although the banking scenario of India has improved over the past years, specialized formal banking services like money remittance looms large for the rural population. Money remittance is the immediate need for various migrant working people in India. Besides transferring money, remittance services promote the usage of deposit accounts and thereby have a positive impact on the objective of achieving financial inclusion. Further, it has been found that remittances might increase the demand for savings instruments and decrease the requirement for external financing from banks and other financial institutions (Anzoategui, Demirguc-Kunt, & Peria, 2011). This financial service is not available to the migrant working people due to mostly (a) KYC norms, and (b) Small Ticket Size (Mohapatra & Kumar). As a result, a variety of illegal, informal channels have come up to provide such services. One of the popular remittance conduits is the "Hawala" system. These are run by money changers who charge exorbitant service fee (Mohapatra & Kumar). Such systems exploit the poor living in cities as they try to remit their money home. Further, these channels are known for sponsoring money laundering and terrorist financing activities (Financial Action Task Force, 2013).

A research study conducted by the global think-tank Analysys Mason found that the total transaction value of domestic transfer of money (remittances) in 2010 was $13 billion (Roy, 2013). Moreover, 80% of these remittances were directed towards rural areas. Growing at a CAGR of nearly 12%, this market size was expected to increase to $20.3 billion in 2014. Another survey noted that the states of Bihar, Uttar Pradesh and West Bengal are the major state beneficiaries of the domestic remittances whereas; Gujarat, Delhi and Maharashtra are the major regions of the source of the remittances (Roy, 2013). It was found that Uttar Pradesh was the largest beneficiary state with 20% of the domestic remittances transferred to the residents of the state. Further, the unorganized sector accounts for 70% of these domestic remittances. In comparison, in China, unorganized labor constitutes only 25% of domestic remittances (Roy, 2013). The Planning Commission of India has recommended changes/improvements in organization structure, risk mitigation steps, technology, infrastructure and literacy to achieve financial inclusion. Some of these recommendations are to (a) Have a decentralized banking sector at the lower wherein small banks be allowed to thrive (b) Designing customized health and life insurance products for the poor and needy (c) Reducing transaction costs through ICT (Information and Communication Technology) and (d) Run Financial educational programs through TV Channels (Planning Commission Government Of India, 2009).

## SURVEY

To grasp the reasons as to why people of the lower income group do not use the services of the bank to remit money from cities to villages, a qualitative research survey was conducted. 25 men doing various jobs as pulling rickshaws and selling tea by the road in Ghaziabad and earning a daily wage of less than Rs. 100/- were identified. A convenient sampling technique was incorporated to achieve this sample. Fig. 1 exhibits the various work demographics of the respondents. All the survey subjects had families in the villages and were living alone or with roommates in the cities. They hailed from villages near Ghaziabad and from far-off states like Madhya Pradesh, Bihar, Jharkhand, Assam and Orissa. 9 of them have been residing in Ghaziabad for more than 10 years. Varied questions were asked to them as to whether they were aware of banking services, did they have bank accounts etc.

*Figure 1. Work Demographics of the Respondents of the Survey*

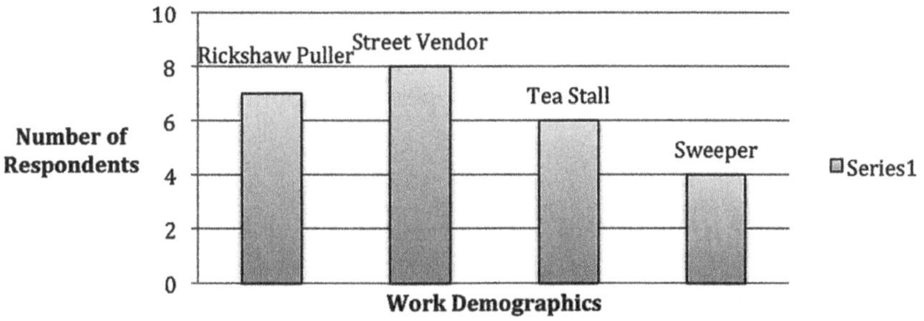


*Figure 2. Number of Respondents who want/do not want a bank account*

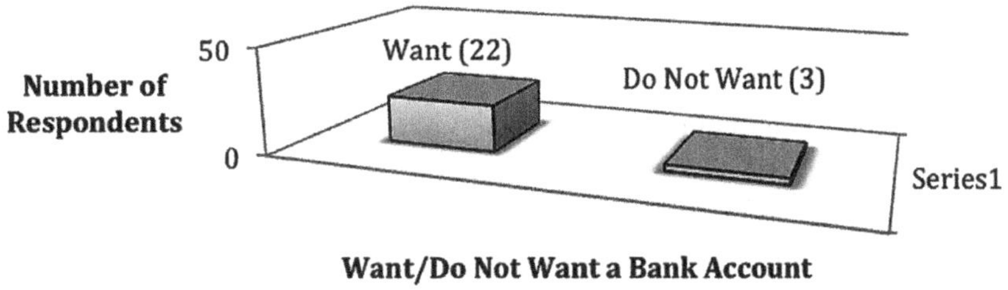


From Fig. 2, one can note that most of the respondents favored having a bank account. Further, the respondents were aware of the benefits of depositing money in the bank and the advantages of money transfer services. The three of them that didn't were of the view that their villages were only a two-hour drive from the city and they could take the money to their families themselves. One can infer that there's definitely awareness about banks and their services among the people surveyed.

Yet, only 7 of them actually have a bank account (Fig. 3)!

The main reason the respondents gave for their inhibition of opening bank accounts was the requirement of an ID card to open an account or avail any of the banking facilities. Since all of the respondents were high school dropouts, they didn't have even a high school certificate. Further, some respondents claimed that the government officials charged huge bribes when they sought to make a government ID (ration cards, BPL card). Inability of the respondents to pay such exorbitant amounts led them to not having any ID card.

*Figure 3. Number of Respondents who actually have/do not have a bank account*

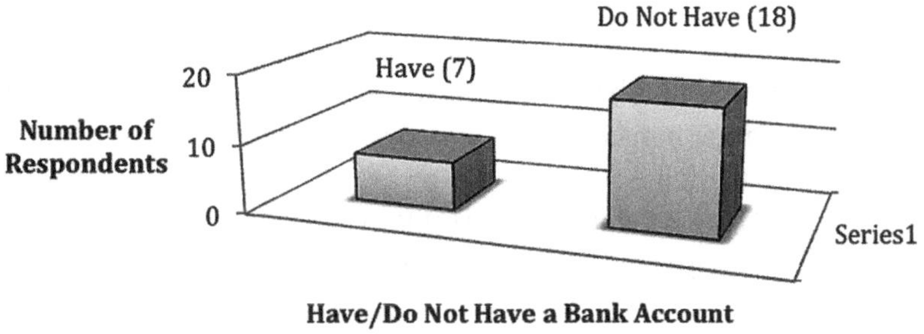

A bank, at the least, requires a guarantor (who has a account with that bank) to process any request for a bank account. One of the respondents recently opened a bank account at the Oriental Bank of Commerce with his friend as his guarantor. Interestingly, before this, he had tried his luck to open his account with eight different banks but had failed to open an account!

## PERSPECTIVES FROM THE BANKING SECTOR

### Serva UP Gramin Bank

Serva UP Gramin Bank is a RRB (Regional Rural Bank) and its motto is to stay "Committed to Rural Development". RRB's were established on 2nd Oct 1975 by the Indian Government to provide financial benefits to the people in rural India. Serva UP Gramin Bank was formed in 2007 after merging of four banks; namely: Uttar Pradesh Gramin Bank Meerut, Kisan Gramin Bank Baudan, Rani Lakshmi Bai Gramin Bank Jhansiand and Davi Patan Gramin Bank Gonda (Serva UP Gramin Bank, 2013). Initially these banks were heavily focused on rural development with no impetus on profit. However, over the few years, profit has become essential for the survival of the banks. Through various field visits to the Serva UP Gramin Bank, the authors came to know about the basic functioning of the bank. According to the executives of the Serva UP Gramin bank, the bank serves primarily three segments of customers: (a) Premium section (b) Middle class section and (c) The Weaker section of society. The segments constitute 10%, 65% and 25% of their total customer respectively. It has branches across Uttar Pradesh and it seeks to provide services to their customers at an affordable cost. The bank's chief focus is to elevate rural India by:

(a) Providing loans to farmers for their agricultural needs. Interest rates could be as cheap as 4.5%.
(b) Providing crop insurance facilities to the farmers.
(c) Providing loans to the farmers who are already burdened under the debt of non-institutional lender to mitigate their stress.
(d) Providing loans for purchase of tractors and farm machinery.
(e) Providing high deposit interest rate.

Thus, the outlook of the Serva UP Gramin bank is exclusively directed towards the rural society and their financial improvement.

### Money Transfer Services

According to an executive of the Serva UP Gramin Bank, money transfer services are extremely important for the rural people. Quite a good number of customers come to the Gramin Bank to avail remittance services. The bank helps them by transferring money through the NEFT (National Electronic Money Transfer) channel. In NEFT, the maximum amount a person can send without having an account in the Ghaziabad branch of the Gramin Bank is Rs 10,000/-. If someone wanted to transfer more than ten thousand then he/she ought to have a bank account. The bank charge is nominal and is Rs 2.80/- for each transaction. The benefit of using the NEFT channel is that money can be easily transferred from one bank to the other. However, the issue is that the NEFT receiver **must** have a bank account.

*Figure 4. Major reasons for not using banking services*

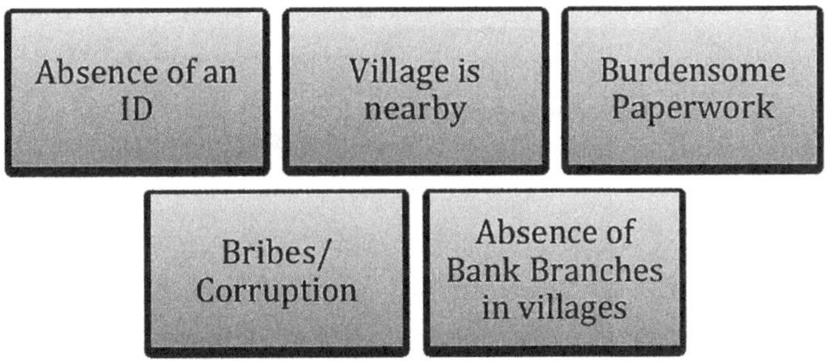


Additionally, the Gramin bank is in collaboration with Western Union Money Transfer Service for money remittance services. The bank uses this process to remit money to the remotest part of India. This service is most used by Indian laborers in Dubai to send their remuneration to their families in India.

The money transfer service does need improvement. Nowadays, the bank is looking to reduce the money tranfer cost as much as possible. An improvement in technology would enable them to have a "Bank account portability system". This system would be similar to a mobile number portability service such that a person can transfer accounts across geographical areas from one branch to another in India. This would allow people to stay in touch with the banking services wherever their go and would eleminate the cost to transfer money (since their would be no transaction cost as the account would be portable). Further, rural banks often merge with one other. This helps to increase the reach of bank branches into rural India.

### ID Proof Requirements

The Gramin Bank requires an ID Proof for opening up of a bank account and is quite strict about it. Additionally, there is rampant migration of people form neighbouring countries like Nepal and Bangladesh. To exclude these people form the Gramin bank system, the bank strictly adheres to the process of opening up of bank accounts. In fact, one needs an ID card, an address proof and a telephone or electricity bill to open an account. If someone does not have an ID, the bank can accept a recommendation from the "Sarpanch" of one's village. They would still require an address proof and a telephone/electricity bill.

## ANALYSIS OF THE CHALLENGES

Figure 4. notes the major reasons for the survey respondents' inability/inhibition to either open bank accounts or remit money via a bank. Based on the answers, the challenges of the financial firms to include the low income segment people in their fold can be divided into two different areas: **Individual** and **Structural** (Fig. 5). The **Individual** zone includes the challenges emanating as result of the individual's own choice to not open an account nor use banking services. These decisions are based on the proximity to family and villages and presenting the money personally to the family. To leverage these reasons and convert such people to potential customers of banks would entail innovative marketing on the part of the banks to sell their services.

*Figure 5. The challenges can be divided in two major areas*

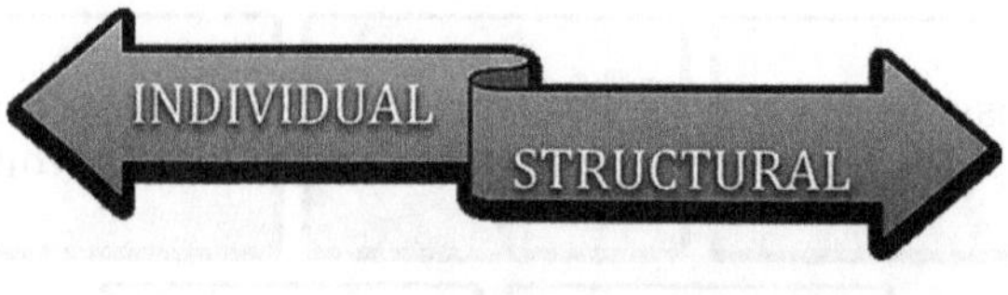


From the Supply side it is clear that a combination of operational and attitudinal issues like low business significance, possible crowding out of high net worth customers, profitability considerations, attitude regarding small customers, and network/staff limitations restricts the scope of the service that banks are willing to offer to low income groups such as migrant workers. However, the **Structural** zone is where improvements are needed. According to the survey most of the respondents wanted to open a bank account and avail its services. However reasons arising due to the structure of the financial sector inhibit them to use any of them. Requirements of an ID, onerous paperwork, absence of bank branches in the villages are structural challenges that the banks have to work on so that those individuals can avail basic banking services. Mahajan and Ramola (Mahajan & Ramola, 2013) argue that many such structural problems in the financial products also prevent financial inclusion. For example, they argue that getting credit for artisans and landless are still a problem. From Table 1, one can also note that the amount of saving deposits as a percentage in the rural areas has fallen since 2000. This could be a sign that banks are focusing more on customers in urban areas rather than the rural countryside.

## RECOMMENDATIONS

This study revealed some of the major problems plaguing the banking system. Based on the prevalent issues the following recommendations could be taken to improve the current system:

*Table 1. Percent of savings deposits according to geographical segmentation (Reserve Bank of India, 2013)*

| (Percent) | | | | |
|---|---|---|---|---|
| **Year** | **Rural and Semi-Urban** | **Urban** | **Metropolitan** | **Total** |
| 1 | 2 | 3 | 4 | 5 |
| 1991 | 42.7 | 25.7 | 31.6 | 100 |
| 1995 | 39.3 | 24.4 | 36.3 | 100 |
| 2000 | 40.1 | 25.4 | 34.5 | 100 |
| 2005 | 39.2 | 26.1 | 34.6 | 100 |
| 2009 | 36.2 | 26.1 | 37.8 | 100 |

## (a) Depoliticize the Rural Banking System

An innovative way is to be enforced to do away with corruption and governmental bureaucracy. Private banks should be encouraged to enter this market and competition between banks should be persuaded so that the low income customers can benefit from market competition.

Steps have already been taken by RBI towards this direction. According to the New Indian Express news (Natti, 2013), RBI has mandated that all new financial services have to open a bank branch in rural India for every four branches started in the semi-urban/urban areas. Since nearly six lakh Indian villages do not have even a single bank branch, this policy could be favorable for improving banking services in India. According to Uday Kotak (Natti, 2013), chief of Kotak Mahindra Bank, by increasing competiton between the banks, customer service would improve and would lead to better banking facilities.

Even banks are gung ho about penetrating the rural market segment. Axis Bank, one of the leading private banks in India, plans to open 100 branches in India under their "**RURAL BANKING STRATEGY**" (Axis Bank, 2013). They are offering basic banking services in these bank branches such as deposit facilities and microfinance. They are targeting Tier III, IV and V villages with a population density of ten thousand to fifty thousand people. They already have opened branches in 14 villages ranging from Palladam in Tamil Nadu to Bagasara in Gujrat. Additionally, Ms. Bindu Ananth (Ananth, 2013), a columnist for Forbes India, considers private banks to be more efficient in providing rural banking services as compared to the public sector ones. According to her research paper, the cost of providing a loan of Rs 10,000 by a private bank in rural India is Rs. 3210. Comparitively, it costs the public sector bank Rs. 4150 to provide the same service.

## (b) Find Better Ways to Seek Identification

A government ID is one of the major reasons why people prefer not to have a bank account. Better ways for identification process would be to leverage/stress more on a recommender's (guarantor's) letter. This could be followed by a bank official's verification of the residence of both the recommender and the prospective client to substantiate the identity.

## (c) Increase Reach of Bank Branches

Many respondents of the survey still believed that there hardly were any bank branches in their villages. Increasing bank branches would certainly help. Further, the banks could take help from the Self Help Groups and NGO's to raise awreness of their presence in these villages. Since it is important for the reciever to have a bank account to receive money via the NEFT channel, it is extremely important for the families of the bread-earners to open their bank accounts to receive money.

ICICI Bank has started "BANK LINKAGE PROGRAM – SHG (Self Help Group)" to organize self help groups in villages (ICICI Bank, 2013). In this program, nearly ten to twenty rural individuals form a group to save money. When a member requires some amount, the SHG internally lends the money from the amount saved by the group. Further, NGO's arranged by the bank teach these skillsets to the individuals in the SHG for earning a livelihood and impart knowledge about managing books of accounts. Such groups assist the rural folk in gaining knowledge about banking services and managing their financial lives better.

### (d) A Strong and Effective Steering Structure

A steering structure should be created that includes all stakeholders and follows a clear vision, mission and mandate. Representatives from Cooperative credit structure, rural banks, selected public sector banks and India post can form a steering committee that will be headed by RBI while NABARD will provide the secretariat. The Steering Committee would serve as a mechanism to guide and monitor small-value money transfer endeavours across the country, develop a dialogue with other countries, and derive recommendations to be brought forward to the GoI.

### (e) Models of Inter-Institutional Money Transfer

In order to provide adequate services, the core systems need to be revamped and used. At the bank and bank branch levels, the CBS and NEFT as well as the RTGS, should be implemented and their compatibility with the Business Correspondent (BC) and other banks should be ensured. Compatibility among banks and BCs will make banking easier and more customer friendly.

### (f) Driving the Business Correspondent Model

As the business correspondent model is fundamental to providing financial services, including remittances, to low-income households, the model has to be adapted in order to suit the opportunities and nature of individual banks, whose services it extends. It is important to provide information on past performance of the BC model, encourage the banking industry to follow a BC strategy and provide need-based solutions at the operational level. Furthermore, selected individuals or institutions which qualify as a BC and are in the position to serve the target group responsibly and sustainably will need more support. Banks can raise awareness and clarity among banks, guide and provide needs-based support to BC partaking institutions or individuals. Support in marketing strategies, for instance, could facilitate the banks' involvement in the model. Additionally, training needs could be reassessed and adapted if necessary. Together with primary agricultural credit societies, Self Help Groups and MFIs acting on behalf of banks greater reach can be achieved at lower costs.

### (g) Sensitising Bank Employees Towards Lower Income Groups

Training programs ought to be there that would sensitize bank employees towards the needs of the low-income customers. This would allow employees to serve them better.

### (h) Encouraging Industry/Employers to Facilitate Financial Inclusion

Large numbers of migrant workers are outside the ambit of formal employment arrangements. Migrants are recruited through intermediaries and contractors who negotiate the terms of their wage employment with the principal employer. Depending on the nature of employer/employee work arrangements, employers, intermediaries and labour recruiting agencies could become active participants in the drive for financial inclusion of migrant workers – their participation can range from a corporate social responsibility (CSR) type of partnership to acceptance of a financial inclusion code for industry in relation to the workers.

### (i) Demand-Oriented Product Development, and Linking Remittances with Other Financial Services

Remittance products should be clear and simple, easily applicable for migrants. All branches should be familiar with the products. They could be similar to a standing order, always connecting the same two bank accounts or even mobile phone numbers, with the option to enter different amounts and with a flexible sending date. The remittance could be limited to a particular amount say Rs 10,000. These products should be well marketed and it could be compulsory for all banks to make such a provision. The products should be available via any account. A one-time set-up of the sending and receiving account will facilitate any remittances to follow. For users of the products, KYC norms should be relaxed. Banks applying the BC model may opt for a BC delivery channel. Banks may opt for a model that allows door-step services. The possibility for a remittance without a bank account could be explored at a later stage. Along with easy access to simple remittance services, migrants also need other financial services. Financial inclusion could be more effective and sustainable, if banks offered a variety of products as per their interests and the customers' needs.

## CONCLUSION

It ought to be noted that over the past few years remitting money through RRBs (regional Rural banks) and other commercial financial institutions has become quite popular. Strong technological advancements along with simpler documentation requirements and a robust network have bolstered domestic remittances through legal channels. Earlier, methods of Post Office (PO) money orders, Hawala and local courier services were channels through which the migrant population sent their money. And, even today, many workers would either individually go home to transfer the money or transfer it through some relative/friend. There are important insights to be gained from these informal money transfer channels. Firstly, the residents value door –to – door remittance services. Secondly, migrant workers use the time to not only transfer money but also visit family and perform various social obligations. On the other hand, for the migrants, banks are paved with strict bureaucratic systems. Bank branches are established only when a significant population necessitates one. Additionally, banks are plagued with strict working hours (inflexible for the clients), KYC norms and form filling (documentation bureaucracy), and long queues. Such environment conditions make it difficult for the weaker sections of the society to carry out banking activities.

The rise of the BC model shows promise in this regard. They combine the flexibility along with traditioanl bank's safety and effieicy. The business correspondents build a social raport with their cleints, assisting them in their banking needs. Such partenership would help the banks and financial insitutions increase their reach and provide financil services to a greater number of Indians.

An important proviso applies for financial inclusion (and specialized services such as, remittance) to be successful. The condition is that of a constant upgrade of two-way knowledge. Awareness programs should be developed for the rural, migrant and weaker sections of the society that educates them of the benefits and requirements of availing banking services. Since many are illiterate, initiatives should be taken to advertise these facilities through word-of-mouth. Similarly, banks should conduct studies that comprehend the benefits of the informal banking channels and try to assimilate these advantages into the banks' daily business methods. Periodically, banks and financial firms should try to ascertain the needs of the migrant population and offer them the relevant financial products.

## REFERENCES


Ananth, B. (2013, October 17). *How much do rural bank branches cost the financial sector?* Retrieved October 17, 2013 from Forbes India: http://forbesindia.com/blog/economy-policy/how-much-do-rural-bank-branches-cost-the-financial-sector/

Anzoategui, D., Demirguc-Kunt, A., & Peria, M. S. (2011, October). *Remittances and Financial Inclusion: Evidence from El Salvador.* Retrieved May 9, 2014 from World Bank Policy Research Working Paper: http://elibrary.worldbank.org/doi/pdf/10.1596/1813-9450-5839

Axis Bank. (2013, October 17). *Rural Banking Initiatives*. Retrieved October 17, 2013 from Axis Bank Microfinance and Rural Banking: http://www.axisbank.com/agri-rural/microfinance/rural-banking-initiative/rural.aspx

Bhaskar, P. V. (2013). *Financial Inclusion in India - An Assessment*. MFIN and Access-Assist Summit.

Chakrabarty, K. (2011, November). Financial Inclusion and Banks: Issues and Perspectives. *RBI Monthly Bulletin*, 1831-1838.

Christabell, P. J., & Vimal, R. A. (2012). Financial Inclusion in Rural India: The role of Microfinance as a tool. *IOSR Journal of Humanities and Social Science (JHSS), 2*(5), 21-25.

Dangi, N., & Kumar, P. (2013). Current Situation of Financial Inclusion in India and Its Future Visions. *International Journal of Management and Social Sciences Research, 2*(8).

Financial Action Task Force. (2013, October). *The Role of Hawala and other similar service providers in money laundering and terrorist financing*. Retrieved May 10, 2014 from http://www.fatf-gafi.org/media/fatf/documents/reports/Role-of-hawala-and-similar-in-ml-tf.pdf

ICICI Bank. (2013, October 17). *Self Help Groups*. Retrieved October 17, 2013 from ICICI Bank Rural Banking: http://www.icicibank.com/rural/microbanking/shg.html

Infosys Finacle. (2012). *Measures for achieving financial inclusion in India.* Retrieved May 10, 2014 from http://www.infosys.com/finacle/solutions/thought-papers/Documents/measures-for-achieving.pdf

Mahajan, V., & Ramola, B. (2013, September 03). *Financial Services for the Rural Poor and Women in India: Access and Sustainability.* Retrieved September 03, 2013 from MicroFinanceGateway.Org: http://www.microfinancegateway.org/gm/document-1.9.24472/2147_file_Financial_Services_f.pdf

Memdani, L., & Rajyalakshmi, K. (2013). Financial Inclusion in India. *International Journal of Applied Research and Studies, 2*(8).

Mohapatra, N., & Kumar, P. (n.d.). *Pillars of Financial Inclusion: Remittances, Micro Insurance and Micro Savings.* Retrieved May 8, 2014 from http://skoch.in/images/stories/Governance_knowledge/Pillars%20of%20Financial%20Inclusion%20Remittances_Micro%20Insurance%20and%20Micro%20Savings.pdf

Natti, S. (2013, July 7). *India to be rich with new banks*. Retrieved October 17, 2013 from The New Indian Express: http://newindianexpress.com/thesundaystandard/India-to-be-rich-with-new-banks/2013/07/07/article1670918.ece

Planning Commission Government of India. (2009). *A Hundred Small Steps*. New Delhi: Sage Publications.

Reserve Bank of India. (2013, September 3). *Deregulation of Savings Bank Interest Rate*. Retrieved September 03, 2013 from RBI: http://www.rbi.org.in/Scripts/bs_viewcontent.aspx?Id=2344

Roy, A. (2013, October 13). *FINO may change remittance business in India's hinterland*. Retrieved May 9, 2014 from Live Mint: http://www.livemint.com/Industry/d5Q76nkacb1ZUTcS3OlC7H/FINO-may-change-remittance-business-in-Indias-hinterland.html

Serva UP Gramin Bank. (2013, October 7). *Serva UP Gramin Bank*. Retrieved October 7, 2013 from UPGB.com: http://www.upgb.com/keyfigures.htm

## KEY TERMS AND DEFINITIONS

**BC (Business Correspondents) Model:** This a model followed by banks to increase reach into the rural parts of the country. This involves correspondents to execute banking transactions such as deposit handling, credit lending on behalf of the banks. Such correspondents are useful in places where there are no bank branches.

**BPL Cards:** BPL stands for Below Poverty Level. BPL Cards are provided by the governement to low-income Indian families so as to provide them with government aid.

**Hawala Channel:** This is a network of money transfer brokers tranfering money at high service charges. This system is based on the honor system and doesn't have a legal track of financial records. This network has been known to sponsor illegal activities such as, money laundering and funding for terrorism.

**NEFT:** NEFT stands for National Electronics Fund Transfer. This framework facilitates the interchange and transfer of funds throughout the commercial banks in India. This remittance service is available for one-to-one funds transfer.

**Regional Rural Bank (RRB):** These are banks that operate in the rural areas of India. These banks are primarily devoted to providing loans to low-income groups. The government of India notifies the area of operation of these banks.

**Self Help Groups (SHG):** Self Help Groups are financial associations composed of mostly women. These members save capital and lend small loans to each other.

**Sarpanch:** Sarpanch is the head of the panchayat – the local village government institution.

## APPENDIX

Questionnaire for the research survey to 25 low-income daily wage earners:

1. What work do you do? How much do you earn per day?
2. From where do you hail/come from?
3. Are you aware of banks and their services?
4. Do you believe that having bank accounts and their services will help you?
5. Do you have bank accounts? If not, why?

# Chapter 11
# Role of Dairy Farming in Rural Development

**Siraj Raja**
*IMT Ghaziabad, India*

**Sanya Sehgal**
*IMT Ghaziabad, India*

## ABSTRACT

*Dairy farming is one of the growing industries. It offers multiple opportunities to people and leave a sustainable impact on society, environment and economy. In this chapter we discuss about its reach and establishment in rural areas and how this industry can play an instrumental role in rural development. The present case captures and reviews the functioning of a dairy farm situated in Ghaziabad, Uttar Pradesh, a state in India. The chapter narrates the role of various heads working at this farm and elaborates the steps involved from procuring the dairy products to its treatment and finally to its catering to the consumer, this case is developed through a rigorous literature review. To assess and establish the role of dairy farming in rural development, this chapter discusses the three tier AMUL model of Gujarat, India is also reviewed. This model by now is the most structured one and lays the foundation for dairy farming in the country. It also demonstrates that dairy farming can become instrumental in rural development.*

## INTRODUCTION

Dairy farming from being customary family run organizations, today has become a specialized and well established dairy industry with mechanical intrusion in all its functions. We have seen growth in dairy farming supplies which help current dairy farmers to take care of cows and buffaloes. This support in the business has made considerable contribution by generating alternative occupations for individuals. Consequently a large number of dairy farmers run dairy farms, especially in towns and supply the dairy products to expansive organizations, to be finally offered as retail product to consumers.

In the process of generating quality product, the best approach for the dairy farmer is to operate his dairy farm that gives greatest benefits to the end organization using his produce. Additionally, it should also be able to sustain the impact of dairy farms on situations and creatures for an extended period.

DOI: 10.4018/978-1-4666-8259-7.ch011

## DAIRY FARMING IN INDIA

As indicated by ASSOCHAM report (2010) milk handling in India is liable to achieve 190 million tons by 2015 (ref. Tables 1 and 2 for current production capabilities) with a yearly turnover of Rs.5 Lakh Cr. With planning commission focusing on 4.5 to 5% development for Animal farming in the twelfth arrangement and the World Bank's contribution of Rs1584 Cr to National Dairy plan, the division is going to witness sound development in the years to come. Further a plan of Rs17, 300 Cr. National Dairy Plan by NDDB for the next 15 years will be propelled soon. It is speculated that the first stage will have Rs 2000 Cr as opening balance.

As one of the significant hotspot for employment in rural regions, animal farming receives prime significance. To make animals division more profitable creature administration frameworks and creation efficiencies need to be moved forward. Separated from presenting new types of animal Government of AP arrangements to create grub nurseries, bund manor, lasting feed harvests and grain protection over next 4 years.

*Table 1. Current production capabilities: India's Milk Production by species in tons (FAOSTAT, 2013)*

| Year | Country | 2005 | 2006 | 2007 | 2008 | 2009 | 2010 | 2011 |
|---|---|---|---|---|---|---|---|---|
| All Milk Production in tons | India | 95619000 | 99348000 | 105712000 | 108618000 | 11493000 | 116904000 | 119444000 |
| | USA | 80254500 | 82463000 | 84189100 | 86177400 | 85880500 | 87474000 | 89015200 |
| % Difference between India & USA | | 19% | 20% | 26% | 26% | 30% | 34% | 34% |
| Cow Milk Production | India | 39759000 | 14148000 | 44601000 | 47006000 | 47825000 | 49960000 | 52500000 |
| | USA | 80254000 | 82463000 | 84189100 | 86177400 | 85880500 | 87474400 | 89015200 |
| % Difference between India & USA | | 102% | 100% | 89% | 83% | 80% | 75% | 70% |

*Table 2. Current production capabilities: Milk production in India and the United States of America (FAOSTAT, 2013)*

| Year | Country | 2005 | 2006 | 2007 | 2008 | 2009 | 2010 | 2011 |
|---|---|---|---|---|---|---|---|---|
| All Milk Production in tons | India | 95619000 | 99348000 | 105712000 | 108618000 | 11493000 | 116904000 | 119444000 |
| | USA | 80254500 | 82463000 | 84189100 | 86177400 | 85880500 | 87474000 | 89015200 |
| % Difference between India & USA | | 19% | 20% | 26% | 26% | 30% | 34% | 34% |
| Cow Milk Production | India | 39759000 | 14148000 | 44601000 | 47006000 | 47825000 | 49960000 | 52500000 |
| | USA | 80254000 | 82463000 | 84189100 | 86177400 | 85880500 | 87474400 | 89015200 |
| % Difference between India & USA | | 102% | 100% | 89% | 83% | 80% | 75% | 70% |

In today's mechanical world there have been numerous developments in current dairy cultivation. It is now accepted that a beneficial business such as dairy farming in India need diligent work, authentic positioning and a dynamic and extremely cautious directors and managers.

## DAIRY INDUSTRY IN INDIA

The Indian dairy industry is growing rapidly, keeping pace with the technical advancements as far and wide as possible. Today, India is recognized as 'The Oyster' of the worldwide dairy industry. It offers vibrant opportunities to people around the world, who wish to explore one of the world's biggest and quickest developing markets for milk and milk products. Numerous gainful alternatives and opportunities galore for Indian dairy farmers with the expansion of this industry and its foreign operations to India. The international dairy industry may exchange engineering, sign mergers or use India as a sourcing place for local fares. The liberalization of Indian economy supports and lures MNC's and remote moguls alike.

India's dairy division is working to triple its handling in coming 10 years in perspective of growing potential for fare to Europe and the West. With anticipated WTO regulations, that will come into power in impending years, all the nations which are among enormous dairy product exporters, might need to withdraw the backing and subsidy to their domesticated milk items segment. Likewise India today is the most reduced expense maker for every liter of milk on the planet, at 27 pennies, contrasted and the US' 63 pennies, and Japan's $2.8 [National Dairy Development Board, 2013]. Additionally to exploit this least cost of milk generation and expanding processing in the nation, multinational organizations want to extend their exercises here. Some of these milk makers have effectively acquired quality standard authentications from the powers. This will help them in showcasing their items in outside nations in transformed structure.

## OPERATION FLOOD

Government is heartily supporting the dairy division by actualizing different plans. Everything began with the White Revolution under the title Operation Flood (OF) Program started in 1970. By advertising Anand Pattern of dairy cooperatives, OF visualized growth in resource gainfulness, acquired repute of perfection in enhanced personal satisfaction of milk makers and guaranteed supply of value milk and other dairy items to shoppers at sensible cost in a free nature's domain. Taking after the cooperative way, market turned milk handling and modernization of dairying, milk generation, preparing and showcasing grew significantly.

The goals of Operation Flood were:

- To increased milk processing ('a surge of milk')
- To augment country earnings
- To ensure reasonable costs for customers

In OF zones, the nation has more than 1 lakh composed essential town dairy cooperatives at present with a total enrollment of 1.1 Cr. Producers. These primaries are unified into 170 region helpful milk unions and further to state agreeable dairy alliances. The dairy helpful system is evaluated to have gathered near 229 lakh kilograms for every day in 2007-08 ensuing in the installment of a total sum surpassing Rs.7000 Cr. to the milk makers throughout the year. It is seen that 14 significant dairying states viz. Uttar Pradesh, Punjab, Andhra Pradesh, Gujarat, Maharashtra, Madhya Pradesh, Karnataka, Haryana, Tamil Nadu, West Bengal, Bihar, Kerala and Orissa represent 92% of India's milk creation.

## IMPROVEMENT IN RURAL LIVELIHOOD THROUGH DAIRY FARMING

The sustenance of country employments is right now in question than any other time in the recent past, in the face of investment liberalization. Employment choices are contracting in rustic ranges, more so in eco-delicate areas, for example, dry spell, desert inclined mountainous zones and other immature/regressive locale. Quickly developing markets for domesticated animals items and dairy items specifically (owing to climb in for every capita earnings) are opening new roads for improving country livelihoods. Dairy farming plays huge part in supporting the rustic livelihoods, despite the fact that farmer suicides, relocation, ailing health/sick wellbeing are broadly common in India. In any case, a percentage of the dairy based dry spell inclined areas make fast strides in improving neediness by significantly helping the District/State farming economy.

## EMPLOYMENT

Livestock animals segment gives job to 18 million individuals and about 70% of them are ladies. Further, dairy part is the significant wellspring of salary for an expected 27.6 million individuals. Around these, 65 to 70% are small, peripheral farmers and land-less workers. The dairy part backs around 10 million parts/ agriculturists through one lakh helpful social orders existing in the nation. Separated from livelihood created by rearing of animals, the obtainment of milk and its preparing additionally gives significant vocation. Case in point is Punjab, MILKFED, with its system of in excess of 5,000 town Milk Producers' Agreeable Societies, underpins in excess of 3 lakh Milk Producers. Further, MILKFED and its units have a work power of about 5,000 workers and offers occupation to an alternate 10,000 specialists who work for milk obtainment and specializes in segments such as include supply and delivery to retail outlets. Comparable number of workforce is utilized in all the milk leagues. Further, under SGSY (Swarnajayanti Gram Swarojgar Yojana), the main independent work program for country zones, something like 35% swarojgaries selected dairy cultivating as pay producing movement. The incremental work chart included 11 man-days for every month and the incremental net pay created was Rs. 865 for every month for every individual. (Nationwide Study, 2005).

## CONTRIBUTION TO INDIAN ECONOMY

Dairying has turned into an essential auxiliary wellspring of pay for a huge number of country families and has accepted a paramount part in giving work and salary. Indian Dairying is novel in more than one ways. The extraordinary characteristic of the framework is that about 120 million rural families are occupied with milk preparation exercises as against huge specific dairy farmers in the west. Throughout the post freedom period, advancements made in dairy area has been stupendous. Milk preparation has expanded more than four folds. This noteworthy development exertion talks volume about the co-facilitated deliberations of vast number of milk generating farmers, researchers, organizers, NGO's and industry in accomplishing independence in milk handling.

Dairy industry is of urgent vitality to India. The nation is the world biggest milk maker, representing more than 13% of world's aggregate milk creation. It is the world's biggest buyer of dairy items, expending very nearly 100% of its own milk preparation. Dairy items are a real wellspring of shabby and nutritious nourishment to a huge number of individuals in India. Furthermore the main adequate wellspring of creature protein for huge veggie lover portion of Indian populace, especially around the landless, small farmers and ladies.

Dairying has been recognized as one of the exercises pointed at allaying the neediness and unemployment particularly in the provincial ranges in the sprinkle bolstered and dry season inclined areas. In India, around three-fourth of the populace live in provincial territories and about 38% of them are poor. Thus effects of Dairy Industry might be categorized into having:

- Social raise
- Economic development
- Impact on foundation
- Impact on enhanced nourishment support security

These effects can be gathered from the following existing benefits of Dairy Farming:

- Not dependent on rainfall
- Causes less pollution and is eco-friendly
- Skilled labor is not a constraint as its requirement is relatively less.
- Active Dairy product market
- Raw materials need not be stocked in huge quantities
- Shifting to a new location is relatively easier in case of any unfortunate event
- Less requirement of energy. Maximum energy can be obtained from Biogas plant fed with cow dung for daily requirements of the farms
- Fixed Selling rate of milk
- Assurance of regular income
- No control on the sale prices by the middlemen
- Increasing Demand for Milk

## PLANNING A DAIRY FARM

To plan and start a new dairy farm, the following points must be considered:

a. Nourish Resources Available
    - Pasture touching area
    - Green grain accessible and deficiencies in supply
    - Availability of dry grain
    - Concentrate, sort and expense, quality, brand

  - Mineral blender
- b. Classifications of Holdings
  - Land less horticultural specialists, minor, little, medium and substantial farmers.
  - Extent of usage of Natural Resources like land, human (work), capital and business endeavor.
- c. Existing Infrastructure offices
  - Veterinary doctor's facilities, dispensaries, and provincial veterinary dispensaries (veterinary essential wellbeing focuses)
  - Semen banks – semen gathering, assessment and solidifying, offices with satisfactory offices for putting away, of solidified semen.
  - Cooperatives – essential/ optional social orders for taking care of the farmers' requests and procurement of inputs comprehensive of delicate term, fleeting and medium term credits.
  - Extension administrations – Animal cultivation and dairying.
  - Chilling focuses – milk gathering and chilling units and transportation to preparing units.
  - Feed plants – assembling of intensified food.
  - Manpower accessibility.
- d. Generation of Milk Products and their Demands and Supply
  - Production of milk for every year for every animal and for every one thousand person.
  - Facilities for storage of milk
  - Actual provincial interest (utilization)

### Initial Preparations: Visit to a Dairy Farm

While visiting a dairy farm, the dairy farmer should

- Focus on the aims and objectives of the farm mainly on breeding and production
- Visit to commercially based dairy farms for a discussion with experienced farm owners.
- Study feed and fodder's market and its difficulties
- Choose experienced and reliable persons as a team for the specific jobs.
- Observe animals on sale in the market
- Study the patterns on rearing of dairy animals and manufacturing of milk as mentioned by National Dairy Research Institute (NDRI), Karnal (Haryana)

## DAIRY FARM: KIRPA RAM DAIRY INDUSTRY, UTTAR PRADESH

The dairy owns about 150 cows. All the cows are milked at an average of 5 minutes. Hormones are injected into them at regular intervals to increase their milk yields.

On asking the contact person, Mr. Amit Gupta, we came to know that the life expectancy of cows is about 15 years. The milk production drops to a large extent after 10 years, after which these cows are slaughtered for meat. The cows give birth to calves after nine months which are shipped to the veal industry if it is a male calf as it is of no use to the dairy industry. The cows are inseminated at regular intervals for proper milk yield.

Things that are kept in mind:

- Choosing the proper breed of animals for maximum productivity
- Construction of proper Cattle Sheds
- Proper nutrition as far as feeding is concerned and other management practices
- Adequate health Management practices for prevention of diseases in the farm
- Generation of profits by production of milk and its byproducts etc.
- Enhancement of productivity which will help farmers get more milk.

## Feeding Practices (Vetbharathi, 2011)

Dairy animals need to be fed for proper maintenance of their body and production of milk. Extra feeding is required in case of pregnancy for good health of the calf.

- Mineral mixtures and fresh drinking water must be fed to the animals of all age groups and health conditions
- Fodder, concentrates (mixture of grains and legumes seeds/urea)
- The dry matter content in various foods are as follows:
    a. Concentrates: 70%
    b. Green Fresh fodder: 10%
    c. Green dried in air / sun: 20%
    d. Dry fodder / crop residues: 85%
- Dry matter requirement should be made with 1/3rd of green fodder 1/3rd from concentrates and 1/3rd from dry fodder.
- Homemade concentrates can be used: mainly leguminous seeds and food grains mixed in the proportion of 40: 60 along with oil cakes and bran in small quantity. The protein content in leguminous seeds is 20-24%, food grains is 8 – 12% and oil cakes is 24%
- To provide energy to the animals, food grains can be fed which are the best source of proteins and fats.
- Mineral mixtures are essential especially in growing and pregnant animals.

# STAGES OF DAIRY FARMING (KIRPA RAM DAIRY INDUSTRY, UTTAR PRADESH)

## Step 1: Rearing

Dairy cows ordinarily use their days consuming, resting, and ruminating or biting their cud. They also meander around and consume new grass (i.e. brushing). In different farms, they are bolstered grain, feed, or silage (saved search) and stay throughout the day around other people known as restricted cattle nourishing operations (Cafos), some of which house many creatures.

Farmers also use development hormones and anti-infection agents throughout the raising methodology to falsely expand a cow's milk preparation and to decline the spread of irresistible ailments around their cows.

## Step 2: Harvesting

Cows are ordinarily milked at any rate twice a day. Milking time takes about five minutes for every dairy animals relying upon the kind of machine and the measure of milk the cow is transforming. Milking machines mirror the movement of a junior calf by making a throbbing vacuum around the teat, which causes the milk to be discharged from the udder.

## Step 3: Storing

Milk stockpiling vats or storehouses are refrigerated and come in different shapes and sizes. Milk is normally put away on the farm at 39 degrees Fahrenheit, or colder, for close to 48 hours. Vats and storehouses are fomented to verify that the whole volume stays icy and that the milk fat does not separate from the milk. After milk has been gathered, stockpiling vats and stainless steel funnels are completely cleaned before the agriculturist milks once more.

## Step 4: Transportation

Milk is gathered from the farm each 24 or 48 hours. The tankers that are utilized have extraordinary stainless steel bodies which are vigorously protected to keep the milk cool throughout transportation to the transforming manufacturing plant. Milk tanker drivers are licensed milk graders, qualified to assess the milk before gathering. Tanker drivers grade and if essential reject milk focused around temperature, sight, and odor. An agent example is gathered from each one farm pickup preceding being pumped onto the tanker. After accumulation, milk is transported to production line destinations and put away in refrigerated storehouses before preparing.

## Step 5: Lab Testing

Samples of milk are taken from homestead vats before gathering and from the mass. Tests from the mass milk tanker are tried for anti-toxins and temperature before the milk enters the manufacturing plant transforming zone. Farm milk specimens are tried for milk fat, protein, mass milk cell check and microscopic organism number. On the off chance that milk does not meet quality principles it is rejected. Most farmers are paid on the quality and piece of their milk.

## Step 6: Processing

Whole milk, once approved for use, is pumped into storage silos where it undergoes pasteurization, homogenization, separation and further processing.

- Pasteurization Involves heating every particle of milk to a specific temperature for a specified period of time and cooling it again without allowing recontamination.
- *Separation* Includes turning milk through an axis to divide the cream from the milk. After separation, the cream and remaining milk are remixed to give the craved fat substance to the distinctive sorts of milk being prepared.

For "entire milk," the cream is reintroduced until the fat substance achieves 3.25%. For "low fat drain," the fat substance is 1%. For "skim milk" (some of the time called nonfat milk) the fat substance is .05%.

### Step 7: Packaging

Now the milk is ready to be bundled for conveyance to the stores. The milk ventures out through funnels to the programmed bundling machines that fills and seals the milk into paper containers or plastic containers. As the holders travel through the sequential construction system, a date is printed on each of them to show to what extent the milk will stay new.

## RECOMMENDATIONS

To have safe, good quality milk from healthy animals, sustainable management practices can be adopted that are good for the animals from a social and economic perspective. Dairy farmers can implement the following measures to achieve the desired outcome:

- *Animal Health*: Healthy Animals that produce milk can be taken care of with effective health care programs.
- *Milking Hygiene*: Prerequisites to keep milk in hygienic conditions are proper harvesting and storing conditions. Equipment that can be used to harvest and store milk should be suitable and well maintained.
- *Nutrition (Feed and Water):* Products of suitable quality should be used to feed the animals need to be fed and watered.
- *Animal Welfare*: Animals should be kept free from thirst, malnutrition, discomfort, injuries, disease, pain and fear.
- *Environment*: Surroundings, which can balance the local environment around the farm, should be adopted for better milk production.
- *Socio-Economic Management*: Dairy farming can help by benefitting the farmers and other communities in both economic and social sector. These practices can also help to manage the social and economic risks to the enterprise.

## LIMITATIONS AND CONSTRAINTS

### How to Improve Dairy Farming Practices in Rural India

There is wide variety in (a) agro-climatic condition, (b) biodiversity and environment (c) socio budgetary and social foundation of individuals, (d) sorts/types of dairy cows raised. It is therefore important to get ready for dairy advancement particular to every micro level, viz., a piece, a town, a taluk and a locale. This arrangement enhances ideal use of nearby assets and guarantees better suitability of the projects and higher expense profits degree. Before defining and proposing dairy improvement programs, it is important to think about natural effect (water bodies' contamination, over munching of meadows, debasement of watersheds, deforestation). These days, saving the environment and nature is truly pushed by the private gatherings and multinational organizations while subsidizing the creature cultivation ventures. However for the healthy growth of dairy industry, the following measures are needed:

- Embrace the accompanying tips for proficient recognizable proof and plan of creature cultivation and veterinary ventures.
- Recognizing such innovations, which request less capital, less time and least operations.
- Explore the conceivable outcomes of giving advances at the most minimal investment rates with subsidies for dairy advancement exercises.
- Gradual change of existing indigenous types of animals.
- Gradual evacuation of futile stock and supplanting with high yielding predominant quality creatures.
- Gradual control in farming practice for enhancing creature benefit and reception of biotechnological mediations in food and grain, propagation and development perspectives.
- Support from Government in enhancing the supply of inputs and administration to dairy farmers/ beneficiaries at their doorsteps with least cost.
- Contribution from different nongovernmental organizations/association to straightforwardness the issues of farmers in acquaintanceship with the legislative offices.
- Create suitable agriculturist's cooperatives social orders/ leagues like, milk makers helpful social orders at town and locale levels, alliances, sheets and enterprises.
- Synchronous advancement of cool chain stockpiling and advertising offices are required, particularly for milk and milk items.
- Activation of different information administrations from various agencies.

## IMPACT OF DAIRY FARMING ON RURAL INDIA

### Social Impact

Since social participation interests all, absence of separation, existing doctrine, sexual orientation and budgetary status has succeeded in breaking down hindrances for those with milch creatures. Surprisingly new mindfulness has been produced and seen around the makers.

### Resolving Social Inequity

Social disgrace still exists in numerous parts of country India. At all the collection centers, morning and night, many grown-ups and also the youngsters of milk makers having a place with all positions come and stand in queue to deliver their milk produce, creating a propensity of discipline. The mix of different ethnic and social gatherings twice a day for a typical reason and to their shared change has brought about lessening social inequity.

## Superstitions

There were overall convictions in the greater part of the provincial ranges that drain is a sacred ware and is not intended to be sold and that certain infectious infection, for example, rudderpost ought not to be dealt with on the grounds that they are a condemnation of God. Normal pay and veterinary help through cooperatives have helped parts leave such superstitions behind.

## Health Care

The benefit of gathering the milk from parts puts a commitment on the cooperatives to give inputs to build the milk handling. If required, the unions work with veterinary administrations at their doorstep to deal with dairy cattle wellbeing. Presentation to different advanced innovations and their requisitions by the veterinarians to treat their family members as well.

## Impact on Infrastructure

Taking an interest farmers have gotten mindful of their obligation to the group. Consistently they liberally help a part of their agreeable benefit towards the general advancement of the town, for example,

- Improving the town approach way condition
- Providing offices to youth through making town libraries
- Contributing to instructive organizations and town essential wellbeing focuses
- Providing and redesigning regular information by putting TV sets in DCSs
- Providing a phone office to parts for better and quick correspondences
- Contributing to making the drinking water supply framework in the town.
- Cooperative dairying has in this manner demonstrated a noteworthy socio-investment sway in rural improvement.

## Impact on Improved Food Aid and Nutrition

A few studies have uncovered that India is better-off now in the region of preparation of sustenance grains, then in the recent past. The genuine issue however, is that even with extra grain accessibility, lack of healthy sustenance continues on the grounds that those in genuine need have lacking acquiring power. The milk producers' associations (Mpos) do make a commitment towards producing extra pay for these poor gatherings and help manufacture an advantageous relationship between animal and crop husbandry; wage created from one makes interest for the yield of the other, as such, yield of one gets sustain for the other. The essential impacts of Mpos are to give more terrific salary to the partaking families. As every capita use expands, so does the use on sustenance items. As such, there is a proportionate expand in the utilization of sustenance as using force increments. Subsequently, extra salary gave by Mpos to families beneath the destitution line really helps them build their nourishment consumption.

Mpos gave salary at standard interims; normally every day, yet once in a while additionally when a week. Given the low buying force of provincial family units, things of crucial utilization not processed by the families themselves, for example, salt, sugar, vegetable oils, flavors, lentils and vegetables, must be acquired every day. The procurement of extra money salary day by day or week by week undoubtedly helps the families expand

## Income from Dairy Farming

The ultimate goal of dairy farming is generating income and employment. Dairy farming has been able to reduce rural poverty as it ensures constant income and provides security to the family members. Selling of milk, dung, stock, milk products are the various sources of income from dairy farming.

Farmers get around 50% of the income from dairying and livestock. The price of buffalo milk is more than cow milk; hence the level of milk yield from buffalo's milk will be greater than the yield from cow's milk. Apart from this, the maintenance cost of crossbred cows is more than that for buffalos.

## THREE-TIER AMUL MODEL: A BENCHMARK

The highly successful AMUL (Anand Milk Union Limited) program sets the yardstick for almost all dairy organizations in the country. It is a three-tier structure at the town level, district level and the state level. A Dairy Helpful Society at the town level is associated with a Milk Union at the District level which then is further merged into a Milk Federation at the State level. This three-level structure makes the collection, treatment and delivery of dairy products easier, thereby making the process much more systematic. The milk collection is done at the Village Dairy Society, Milk Procurement & Processing at the District Milk Union and Milk & Milk Products Marketing at the State Milk Federation. This helps in dispensing with inward rivalry as well as guaranteeing that economies of scale are accomplished. As the above structure was initially developed by AMUL in Gujarat and from that point imitated everywhere throughout the nation under the Operation Flood Program, it is known as the 'Amul Model' or 'Anand Pattern' of Dairy Cooperatives.

### Roles and Responsibilities of Village Dairy Cooperative Society, District Cooperative Milk Producers' Union and State Cooperative Milk Federation

Structurally, the AMUL model comprises of collection, treatment and packaging of the dairy products. The segment wise responsibilities for each of these is given below:

#### Village Dairy Cooperative Society (VDCS)

The milk makers of a town, having surplus milk after own utilization, come together and structure a Village Dairy Cooperative Society (VDCS). The Village Dairy cooperative is the essential pop culture under the three-level structure. It has participation of milk makers of the town and is legislated by a selected Management Committee. This committee comprises of 9 to 12 representatives of the milk union focused around the rule of one part, one vote. The town public opinion further selects a Secretary (a paid representative and part secretary of the Management Committee) for administration of the normal capacities. It additionally utilizes different individuals for supporting the Secretary in achieving his/ her every day obligations. The VDCS is responsible for:

- Collection of surplus milk from the milk makers of the town & installment taking into account quality & amount

- Providing help administrations to the parts like Veterinary First Aid, Artificial Insemination administrations, steers nourish deals, mineral mixture deals, grub & feed seed deals, leading preparing on Animal Husbandry & Dairying, and so forth.
- Selling fluid milk for nearby buyers of the town
- Supplying milk to the District Milk Union Accordingly, the VDCS in a free element oversaw provincially by the milk makers and aided by the District Milk Union.

## District Cooperative Milk Producers' Union (Milk Union)

The Village Societies of a District (going from 75 to 1653 for every Milk Union in Gujarat) having surplus drain after nearby deals meet up and structure a District Milk Union. The Milk Union is the second level under the three-level structure. It has enrollment of Village Dairy Societies of the District and is legislated by a Board of Directors comprising 9 to 18 chose agents of the Village Societies. The Milk Union further selects an expert Managing Director (paid worker and part secretary of the Board) for administration of the regular capacities. It additionally utilizes different individuals for aiding the Overseeing Director in finishing his/ her every day obligations. The principle responsibilities of the Milk Union are:

- Procurement of milk from the Village Dairy Societies of the District
- Arranging transportation of crude milk from the VDCS to the Milk Union.
- Providing information administrations to the makers like Veterinary Care, Artificial Insemination administrations, steers encourage deals, mineral mixture deals, grub & feed seed deals, and so on.
- Conducting preparing on Cooperative Development, Animal Husbandry & Dairying for milk makers and leading specific aptitude advancement & Administration Development preparing for VDCS staff & Management Committee parts.
- Providing administration backing to the VDCS alongside normal supervision of its exercises.

## State Cooperative Milk Federation (SCMF)

The Milk Unions of a State are unified into a State Cooperative Milk Federation. The federation is the summit level under the three-level structure. It has participation of all the helpful Milk Unions of the State and is administered by a Board of Directors comprising of one chose illustrative of each one Milk Union. The State Federation further designates an Overseeing Director (paid representative and part secretary of the Board) for administration of the normal capacities. It likewise utilizes different individuals for helping the Managing Executive in achieving his day by day obligations. The fundamental capacities of the Federation are as takes after:

- Marketing of milk & milk items transformed/ produced by Milk Unions.
- Establish dispersion system for promoting of milk & milk items.
- Arranging transportation of milk & milk items from the Milk Unions to the market.
- Creating & keeping up a brand for promoting of milk & milk items (brand building).
- Providing help administrations to the Milk Unions & parts like Technical Inputs, administration help & consultative administrations.
- Pooling surplus milk from the Milk Unions and supplying

## CONCLUSION

Apart from cooperatives, the dairy segment is still described by little scale, scattered and chaotic milch creature holders; low gainfulness; lacking and improper creature nourishing and human services; absence of guaranteed year-round gainful maker costs for milk; insufficient fundamental framework for procurement of generation inputs what's more administrations; deficient essential framework for obtainment, transportation, handling and advertising of milk and absence of expert administration. In spite of every last one of issues it confronts, the dairy division holds high guarantees as a reliable wellspring of business for the dominant part of the country poor in India. ***The AMUL model of little scale dairy generation and advertising***, as it has developed and been refined in the course of the last 50 years, likewise holds high assurances for smallholder dairy improvement in India. Liberalization of world exchange dairy items under the new exchange administration of the WTO postures new difficulties and has opened up new fare open doors for the dairy business in India. It necessities to upgrade focused monetary preference in dairy items regarding both quality, expense and its validity in global markets. Milk yield needs to build in order to decline the for every liter expense of handling, quality needs to be upgraded with the selection of the most recent transforming and bundling engineering will expand fare of dairy items.

## REFERENCES

About.com. (n.d.). *Got Pasteurized Milk?* Retrieved October 8, 2014 from http://infectiousdiseases.about.com/od/prevention/a/pasteurization.htm

COM. M. (n.d.). *Guide to good dairy farming practice.* Retrieved September 10, 2014 from http://www.milkproduction.com/Library/Editorial-articles/Guide-to-good-dairy-farming-practice/

Department of Animal Husbandry. Dairying & Fisheries, Ministry of Agriculture, GoI. (1995-2015). *Milk Production in India.* Retrieved October 12,2014 from http://www.nddb.org/English/Statistics/Pages/Milk-Production.aspx

Feeds and Feeding Practices in Dairy Animals. (n.d.). *Thread: Feeds and Feeding Practices in Dairy Animals.* Retrieved September 21, 2014 from http://www.agricultureinformation.com/forums/consultancy-services/60410-feeds-feeding-practices-dairy-animals.html

Goswami, B. (2007). *Can Indian Dairy Cooperatives Survive in the New Economic Order? Session on Supply Management in Support of Rural Livelihoods under the WTO in Forum for Biotechnology & Food Security.* Retrieved October 10,2014 from www.wto.org/english/forums_e/public_forum2007_e/session11_goswami_e.pdf

National Bank for Agriculture and Rural Development. (n.d.). *Nationwide Study on SGSY, NIRD, 2005. Opportunities and Challenges in the Indian Dairy Industry.* Retrieved December 8, 2014 from www.nabard.org/fileupload/DataBank/.../issue9td-6.pdf

Vet Helpline India (P) Ltd. (n.d.). *Starting a Dairy Farm in India.* Retrieved December 8, 2014 from http://www.vethelplineindia.co.in/starting-a-dairy-farm-india/

## ADDITIONAL READING

Boden, E. (Ed.). (1998). *Black's Veterinary Dictionary*. London: A & C Black.

India Report, A. S. S. O. C. H. A. M. (2012). Rural development in India: State level experiences. The Associated Chambers of Commerce and Industry of India, New Delhi. Available: http://www.assocham.org/arb/general/Rural_Development_in_India_state_level_Exp-2012.pdf

Indian Council of Agricultural Research. (1962). Handbook of animal husbandry. Retrieved from http://icar.org.in/en/node/6639

Kumbhakar, S. C., Biswas, B., & Bailey, D. (1989). A Study of Economic Efficiency of Utah Dairy Farmers: A System Approach. *The Review of Economics and Statistics*, *71*(4), 595–604. doi:10.2307/1928101

Lund, V., & Algers, B. (2002). Research on animal health and welfare in organic farming. Livestock Production Science, 80(2003), 55-68.

Reinhard, S., Lovell, C. A. K., & Thijssen, G. (1999). Econometric estimation of technical and environmental efficiency: An application to Dutch dairy farms. *American Journal of Agricultural Economics*, *81*(1), 44–60. doi:10.2307/1244449

Sastry, N. S. R., & Thomas, C. K. (1991). *Livestock Management*. Delhi: Kalyani Publishers.

Singh, K., & Pundir, R.S. (August 2000). Co-operatives and Rural Development in India. Anand: Institute of Rural Management.

Sundaresan, D. (1975). *Principles of livestock breeding*. New Delhi: Vikas.

Verma, M. P. (1994). *Drugs and animal diseases*. KAS Publishers.

## KEY TERMS AND DEFINITIONS

**Dairy Farming:** A form of agriculture for production of milk for commercial purposes.

**Farming Practices:** The methodologies practiced in dairy farming.

**Milk:** Milk is a white liquid; India is the world's largest producer and consumer of milk, it has various health benefits.

**Operation Flood:** White Revolution under the title Operation Flood (OF) Program started in 1970.

**Rural Development:** The process of improving the quality of life and economic well-being of people living in villages in India.

# Chapter 12
# Solar Micro Grids:
## Impact and Future in Rural Uttar Pradesh – Case Study on MGP

**Rahul Singh**
*IMT Ghaziabad, India*

**Amanpreet Kaur**
*IMT Ghaziabad, India*

**Anirban Sharma**
*IMT Ghaziabad, India*

**Mansi Gupta**
*IMT Ghaziabad, India*

**Kannan TS**
*IMT Ghaziabad, India*

## ABSTRACT

*Like most of the developing countries, India also has a large number of off-the-grid villages. In spite of government's efforts at rural electrification, many villages cannot hope for grid power in the near future because the cost of setting up the distribution infrastructure. But when these villages come on grid, they place an additional demand on the distribution network and most states are already facing several hours of power cuts because conventional electricity is scarce. Thus these villages remain un-electrified for the simple reason that electricity is not available. This case study deals with the innovative business model of the company "Mera Gao Power" which sets up "Solar Micro Grids" in villages. It further analyses the impact of Solar Power on the socio-economic parameters of the villages where the project has been implemented. Further it discusses the various challenges faced by MGP in sustaining and expanding this business model.*

*"When you have your first idea, know that it will not work but do it anyway. Because in the middle of it you will get to know what will." (R. Singh, A. Sharma, A. Kaur, M. Gupta, & K. TS, personal interview)*

*Nikhil Jaisinghani, Co-Founder Mera GAO Power*

DOI: 10.4018/978-1-4666-8259-7.ch012

## INTRODUCTION

Energy is one of the important factors for social, economic, educational development for any country. It is very important for the sustainable growth and improvement of the lives of people living in a particular area. In a country like India with the majority of the population living in villages there are still thousands that are not connected to the main power grid. And even if they are connected, they lack an uninterrupted power supply. A rough estimate states that more than half of the 1.2 billion plus population of the country does not have access to electricity. At present there are 6, 40,867 villages and out of them 1, 07,452 are in Uttar Pradesh. Ministry of Power data puts the percentage of villages in Uttar Pradesh with electricity at less than 42% in 2006 and household electrification percentage figure even lower. Off-grid demand of power still continues to be unmet and communities use low quality sources of energy such as kerosene, wood, diesel, disposable batteries etc. When compared to the traditional power sources micro-grid provides efficient, reliable services to the end users and also helps in overcoming the various hurdles caused due to power shortage. Micro-grids are small-scale modern versions of centralized electricity system and are mostly developed to achieve local goals and help in production, distribution and regulation of flow of electricity to consumers locally. Globally the capacity of Micro-grid power is supposed to grow at a CAGR of 17% and will attain a total capacity of 22GW by 202210. (Census India, 2011)

## SOLAR POWER IN INDIA

Due to the huge energy crisis in the country there is in an increasing need to tap the energy from renewable forms of energy like wind and solar. In India sun shines for almost 300 days per year and receives on an average over 4500 trillion kWh of pure solar energy which is far greater than the annual energy requirement of the country. Thus the geographical location is ideal for tapping the solar power. The problem, however, is the high installation cost of solar energy systems as compared to the installation of conventional fossil fuel energy system. So, the future of solar power is basically dependent on the reduction in cost to a certain extent because in countries like India low cost is one the main factors when it comes to production of energy. Grid parity, which is the point when traditional and solar energy are equivalent in cost, will have to be reached for sustainable use of this power source. (Markets and Markets, 2013)

But in recent years it can be seen that solar power is slowly finding its way in the country. India has installed 1.8 Gigawatt solar plants in past three years and the government is working on approving projects for 2.3GW more over the period of next six months. States are pitching in large multinationals like SunEdison, Welspun Energy and Azure to install more solar capacity in the coming years. Central Government of India launched Jawahar Lal Nehru National Solar Mission in 2010, targeting a production of 20,000 MW of solar power by 2022. The first phase i.e. installation of 890 MW of solar energy capacity has been completed till date and this has made solar power much cheaper than what it was two years back. The same energy which was available at Rs. 15 per unit is now available at Rs. 7 per unit.

Gujarat was amongst the first state to come out with a solar policy and has solar energy capacity of 800 MW, closely followed by Tamil Nadu. Other states like Karnataka, Punjab and Andhra Pradesh have also developed respectable solar energy capacity in the last few years. Government of India has also recently launched the ambitious project of setting up the world's largest solar power plant in India which will generate 4000 MW (three times the present total solar energy) of energy from sunlight near

Sambar Lake in Rajasthan and plans to sell electricity at an estimated rate of Rs. 5.50 per unit. (Biswarup G 2013) Looking at the above factors it seems that solar power energy has finally arrived in India as the next big thing. (Majumder, 2013)

## POWER GRIDS IN INDIA

The potential market for micro grids in India is already huge and rapidly growing. By illuminating an entire village at once, a micro grid can spread light more quickly than hand-outs of solar-powered lanterns. It can also scale up far faster than traditional power lines, which are often promised in India but seldom delivered. By deriving their power from biomass or solar panels, micro grids raise the possibility for large regions to stay off coal-fired power grid forever, thus saving a significant chunk of the world's future carbon budget. Whoever finds the business model for providing cheap, reliable, local power will help pull 300 million Indians from the darkness of 19th century into the 21st century, with vastly expanded opportunities for education and commerce. These sectors are presently being targeted by private-sector players and profit-motivated enterprises with a drive for tapping the social cause. The leaders include small start-ups hoping to do social good, multinational solar power companies, and veterans of the cell-phone industry. But their prospects might be extinguished in a moment if regular power lines marched into the villages. However this seems least likely to happen as the electrical grid in India is already overtaxed; an estimated 25 percent of India's power generation capacity is underutilized because of fuel shortages and other problems. In India almost all micro grids are powered by solar photovoltaic panels. Only 20 to 30 networks in the states of Karnataka and Uttarakhand, run on hydropower utilizing the rivers in the Himalayas and the Eastern Ghat mountain range. At present, just a tiny fraction of India's overall power demand is supplied by micro grids and no comprehensive statistics are available regarding the number of micro grids present and running. A rough estimate on a conservative basis shows that at least 125,000 households in India are provided by Microgrid power. And these grids are divided mostly between large, government-sponsored projects in Chhattisgarh and West Bengal and private ventures centred on Uttar Pradesh and Bihar. In India, Uttar Pradesh and Bihar are among the least electrified states—*a countryside packed with tens of millions of people, united by darkness.* (Deccan Herald, 2011)

Microgrid installation may be easy, but that is often where the simplicity ends. Some high-caste farmers demand electricity lines to be rerouted because they can't bear to have electricity flowing from the house of the low-caste cobbler next door. At places some Hindu neighbourhoods don't want to be on the same grid as Muslims. One resident who breaks the rules and takes too much power, for a ceiling fan or television, can make the whole grid crash at times. But the biggest difficulty by far is getting paid for the power. India's farmers have irregular incomes and aren't used to monthly bills. In tiny hamlets, forgiving one person's debt means that next month no one will pay. This has forced Microgrid entrepreneurs, many of whom got in the business for social good, into uncomfortable new roles as debt collectors. In response they have sought out new models that assure payment, from installing meters that dole out electricity in chunks like a prepaid cellphone, or hiring local franchisees who can use their stature to bring deadbeats into line. (Debi Prasad Dash, 2013)

## MERA GAO POWER (MGP): A BRIEF OVERVIEW

In rural Uttar Pradesh, Mera GAO Micro Grid Power Pvt Ltd (MGP), has changed the lives of people by providing electricity for lighting and mobile charging facilities to the households disconnected from the central power grid. Established in the year 2010 by two entrepreneurs Nikhil Jaisinghani and Brian Shaad the company currently serves more than 65,000 people and roughly 13,000 households being present in more than 500 villages in Sitapur District of Uttar Pradesh, India. The company builds, owns and operates micro grids and is tapping into the huge off grid energy market of the country. In just 4 years of operations their low cost design and sustainable business model has made it a commercially viable energy solution for its consumers. In its initial years development agency USAID awarded MGP a grant of USD 300,000 to build and operate micro grids in 40 off-grid villages of Sitapur district, Uttar Pradesh. At the same time MGP also partnered with The University of California Davis' D-Lab to increase focus on innovative technologies and business models that allow people at the bottom of the pyramid to save or earn more money. (Mera Gaon Power, 2013)

Staff at MGP consists of 60 employees on permanent salary basis. They are mostly involved in fee collection, management and maintenance. For each grid construction the employee gets INR 200 and they construct a maximum of 300 grids per month. The company currently employs 10 collectors, 10 people for power grid construction, 10 people for maintenance, managers at different blocks levels and 1 hub manger handing all the block managers. The company is managed by the founders themselves but as the business matures they are planning to appoint a CEO from India to handle the operations in the country. Presently Nikhil is handling the technical and the finance departments while Brian heads the research and development wing. Sushil is the Hub manager under him there are 5 block/branch managers operating. While selecting the staff they look for people who are hardworking and are willing to opt for the particular post. Initially they are given on the job training for a month before they can start. However there is a need for skilled workers in the collection and construction departments.

The company believes that they are unique due to the fact that they are providing Micro Grid as a service to the customers and not as a product. They have done an excellent work in gaining insights into people's need and their energy usage patterns. Thus they are successful in crafting a model which is dependent on people's need and as is with all kinds of services, once the demand is created it never goes away. MGP is different from others in the same field in terms of their focus. They have always focused on fulfilling the basic energy needs and are not distributing power for other advanced usage like powering up television sets, refrigerators etc. which has a highly fluctuating demand depending on the earning capacity of the individual. The technology that the company uses along with the design of the micro grids is feasible in terms of ROI. In other words, the technology is compatible with the functions that it needs to serve. Initially

MGP used to charge INR 100 on a monthly basis, but this left an excessive number of villagers unwilling to pay or defaulting a lot. Then they realized that for a normal villager shelling out INR 100 at the end of a month creates a lot of discomfort and inconvenience. After looking into the matter closely they changed their money collection mechanising to a weekly one where villagers were asked to pay an amount of INR 25 per week. Also for each new connection consumers have to pay INR 50 in the form of security deposit to the company.

When the company started its operations the founders did not have a lot of knowledge about how the business works in India. For the reason they had partners for handling various aspects of the job. But having too many partners was proving to be a major hurdle as it was making things complicated resulting in lost control over key operations. Within a few months into the business they let go of their partners and brought the entire process, from setting up to collection, under their control. Presently under every branch of the company there are 8000 customers and the company has 5 such branches with the sixth one coming up in the next few months.

MGP's Micro Grid was included as one of the '10 Most Important Technology Milestones of the Last Year' by MIT's Technology Review in 2012, and was invited to attend White House event on 'Innovations for Global Development' in February 8, 2012. They were also identified as 'WWF Green Game Changer' in 2012 and were the finalist for the 'Wantrapreneur 2011' business plan competition. (Smart Grid for India, 2013)

## OPERATIONAL SETUP

The flow of events right from recognizing a village till setting up new connection is random in nature. MGP does not follow any formal procedure to identify potential villages for installing micro grids. It is done by visiting multiple villages and identifying whether or not the people there are willing to get the plant set up and this process takes usually one week. After identifying a particular location the company scans it for political, social, communal indifference's etc. Once found clear they set up engagement meetings with the villagers to increase awareness of the services provided by MGP. Once the viability of setting up the project in a village is assessed, then actual installation can be completed in as little time as a day by a team of 3 technicians. Unlike the process of rural electrification which needs elaborate infrastructures such as installing posts, drawing of cables over long distances, setting up of transformers etc., setting up a micro grid is pretty simple process. Setting up new connections and identification of villages is a parallel activity and goes on side by side.

A house, which is located almost at the centre of the village, is chosen for installing the solar panels. Four panels are sufficient to provide power to a village of around 100 households. The power produced during daytime is stored in batteries and from there it is distributed to individual houses through cables. Each household is given one light and mobile charging point. Following the smart way, MGP promotes

*Figure 1. A Typical microgrid power network*

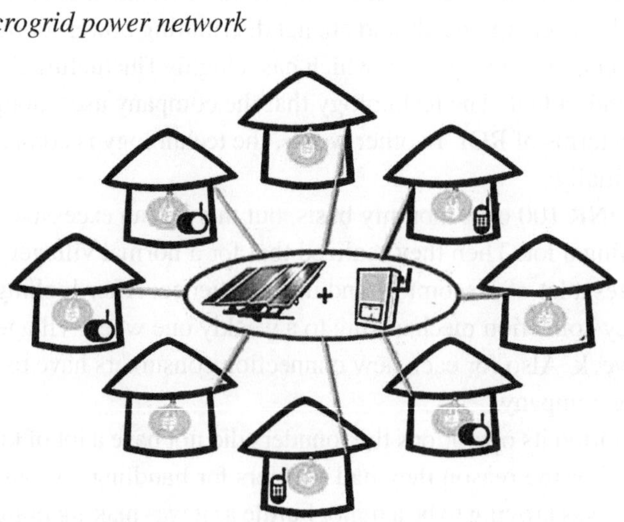

*Figure 2. MGP Microgrid*

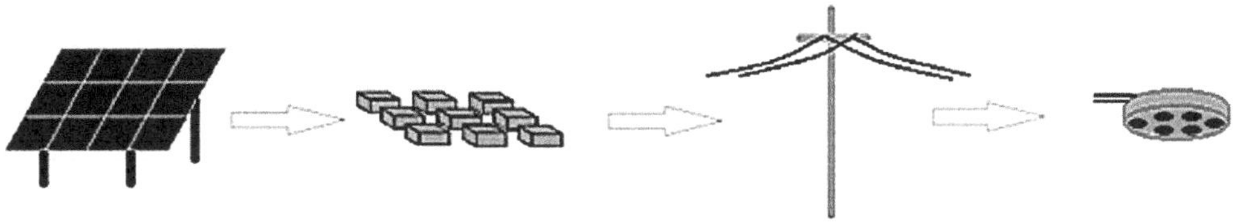


the use of LED lamps which are highly energy and cost efficient in the longer run. The distribution system is switched on and off automatically by timer controlled circuits. The supply is switched on at a specific time in the evening and switched off at a specific time in the morning. Thus the system does not need an operator to take care of it. It is completely self-sufficient and does not require any daily maintenance. An MGP technician who visits once in 15 days carries out periodic maintenance. Another aspect of the micro grid technology is that, if the village gets electrified in the future in the traditional way, then it is very easy to dismantle the MGP setup and move it to another location. Thus the fixed assets are kept to a minimum. The panels are installed on top of existing households and no separate structures are built either for installing the panels or the battery packs.

Mera GAO Power conducted a detailed survey covering 12 villages in 3 blocks of Uttar Pradesh. The total population of these villages were about 4800 and the total number of families 1065. Table 1. Details of the villages surveyed. Each family was interviewed by the team in end 2011, to assess their need and their problems. Table 2. Questionnaire surveyed. Basic objective of the survey was to determine the expense incurred by each of the households on lighting in the night and the inconvenience faced by the villagers. The average expenses were thus very useful to fix the rate for the solar grid power.

*Table 1. Details of the villages surveyed*

| Area | | No of Families | No of Persons | | |
|---|---|---|---|---|---|
| Block | Villages | | Male | Female | Children |
| Reusa | Chak | 94 | 229 | 189 | 227 |
| Reusa | Nibiyapur | 108 | 144 | 123 | 258 |
| Reusa | Moji purwa | 74 | 134 | 89 | 155 |
| Reusa | Jafarpur | 78 | 111 | 99 | 133 |
| Reusa | Kalepurwa | 105 | 208 | 154 | 256 |
| Reusa | Medai purwa | 88 | 124 | 104 | 227 |
| Reusa | Nirmal purwa | 67 | 110 | 95 | 145 |
| Reusa | Godiyan purwa | 97 | 121 | 104 | 216 |
| Reusa | Tipari | 63 | 88 | 63 | 137 |
| Pisawan | Barahamau | 88 | 315 | 238 | 376 |
| Pisawan | Mirjapur | 100 | 172 | 123 | 208 |
| Biswan | Kosalyapur | 103 | 135 | 122 | 213 |

*Table 2. Questionnaire surveyed*

| Household Information |
|---|
| Village |
| Block |
| Name of Respondent |
| 1.1 *Main Source of Income (A/W/S/O) |
| 1.2 Details of Family Member |
| No of Male |
| No of Females |
| No of children |
| 1.3 Monthly expenses (in Rs.)for light/ energy |
| Fuel |
| Wood / cooking gas |
| Battery charging |
| Mobile charging |
| Solar Light |
| Baseline Indicators |
| 2.1 Education |
| 1. No. of school going children |
| 2. How many hours do the children study in the light of kerosene lamp or other lighting sources not operated by electricity? |
| 3. What are key problems they experience in their study in the light of kerosene lamp or other lighting sources not operated by electricity? *KL= Kerosene Lamp |
| 2.2 Health |
| 1. Family members who suffered respiratory problem in the family in the past month among |
| Male |
| Female |
| Children |
| 2. Number of visits made to private and public clinics in the past month to consult for respiratory problems |
| 3. Number of visits made to local doctor in the past month to consult for respiratory problems |
| 4. Expenditure of the family on medication for respiratory problems in the last month |
| 2.3 Others |
| 1. What income generating work does the family do in the evening and early morning? |
| 2. What is the constraints family experience while doing income generating processes in the light of kerosene lamp or other lighting sources not operated by electricity? |
| 3. How much money did the family earn last month? |
| 4. How much money did the family earn last month specifically from this work done in the evening and early morning? |
| 5. Number of light hours per day required for sorting produce, grain cleaning and other agricultural activities? |
| 6. Type of incidences/risks/experienced by household members |

## ABOUT NIKHIL JAISINGHANI

After graduating as a software developer in the year 1997, he worked for three years in a software firm in the United States. Being bored by the mundane routine and work of the industry he left the job and joined a social organization. While working he was sent for social work to a village in Nepal as a math teacher. The village was nearly a couple of day's walk from the nearest town as there was no transportation available. The village did not have electricity and only alternative was to use kerosene lamps. In his two years he realized the importance of basic necessities like electricity, drinking water and connectivity to help solve the problems of this world.

Coming back to the US he completed his post-graduation and joined the US government as a part of the donor wing. He later on moved to Nigeria to start a business of his own with his colleague and friend Brian Shaad. The plan was to capture the natural gas ejected from oil production plants and use it as an energy source for electrifying adjoining villages. But this process required a very big capital investment, ranging in millions of dollars in the initial phase itself. They realized this venture can never be a successful as the benefits will not reach the people at a cheap and affordable price. Thus they dropped that idea and Nikhil came to India where he later on started MGP with Brain

## BUSINESS MODEL OF MGP

Looking at the financial aspects, the cost of installing the entire micro grid setup in a village is around INR 50, 000. Consumers are provided with 7 hours of power supply after dawn, sufficient to light a few lamps and for mobile charging. The maintenance charges are almost negligible in this case and there are no additional costs, such as fuel cost, which would have been there in case of other conventional power sources. All households are charged INR 25 per week. It is interesting to note that there are no energy meters installed to measure the usage at each home. This is partly to reduce cost and partly to induce community pressure to prevent excessive usage. All users pay the same rate irrespective of the amount they use. If one person uses more power, then everyone will fall short as the amount of supply is limited. This builds a social pressure to use power judiciously and leads in less grid failure.

For MGP a village of 100 households generates revenue of INR 10,000 per month. In this way they are able to recover the costs and break-even in 5 to 6 months' time. Thus MGP ensures that their business model is sustainable and does not depend on subsidies or support for its daily operations.

## ADVANTAGES FOR VILLAGERS

In case of micro grid power per unit cost is higher than those villages electrified by the grid. But the villagers know for a fact that grid electrification is a long way to go in most of the cases. Hence they find this an affordable as well as efficient alternative. Moreover by using this power they are able to cut down the amount spent on kerosene and other fuels, which used to be source of lighting previously. Besides many village households have mobile phones and they used to charge these when they travelled to the nearest town at a cost of about INR 60 to 80 per month, which can be saved now. Thus even without considering the secondary benefits of electricity the villagers save on their expenses in the longer run.

*Figure 3. Baseline indicators and results of surveyed village*

| | Avg Expense on kerosene | Avg expense phone chargin | Sum | Kids in school | Hours study at night |
|---|---|---|---|---|---|
| **Chak** | 67.85106383 | 21.69892473 | 89.54998856 | 1.361702128 | 1.881355932 |
| **Nibiya pur** | 77.65740741 | 20.38888889 | 98.0462963 | 0.805555556 | 2.302325581 |
| **Moji purwa** | 88.06849315 | 19.60273973 | 107.6712329 | 0.794520548 | 2.571428571 |
| **Jafar pur** | 66.76923077 | 19.87179487 | 86.64102564 | 0.846153846 | 2.243243243 |
| **Barahamau Khurd** | 130.980198 | 61.34653465 | 192.3267327 | 1.514851485 | 3.166666667 |
| **Mirja pur** | 100.452381 | 56.54761905 | 157 | 2.023809524 | 3.738461538 |
| **Tepri** | 38.31746032 | 57.38095238 | 95.6984127 | 0.857142857 | 2.137931034 |
| **Koshallya Pur** | 37.30208333 | 36.40625 | 73.70833333 | 0.791666667 | 4.076923077 |
| **Kalepurwa** | 49.93650794 | 12.20634921 | 62.14285714 | 0.936507937 | 5.509567812 |
| **Medai purwa** | 29.52272727 | 4.465909091 | 33.98863636 | 0.443181818 | 1.962962963 |
| **Nirmal Purwa** | 96.01980198 | 22.27722772 | 118.2970297 | 0.821782178 | 2.534883721 |
| **Godriyan purwa** | 69.66019417 | 28.23300971 | 97.89320388 | 0.281553398 | 2.473684211 |

In addition to the major cost savings due to reduced kerosene and fuel consumption there are three major secondary advantages, which can be identified after the adoption of micro grid power.

These include:

1. Better facility for education of the children
2. Better respiratory health of family members due to reduced exposure to kerosene smoke
3. Improved earning potential for businesses and housewives

## MAJOR RESULTS

### Impact on Education

The uninterrupted and bright LED lights are enabling children to read effortlessly at night for hours. This fact was evident from the results obtained by comparing the progress made by villages before and after they were electrified. Electricity is thus a major turning point in the improvement of education and other related social standards of the village. The impact on education thus creates a chain reaction leading to a number of related impacts on the society, economy, heath etc.

### Impact on Respiratory Health

Most of the houses in the villages have an average of one or two rooms and a kitchen. These rooms are small in size, usually with low ceilings. So when a kerosene lamp is lighted in the room, the soot from the lamp essentially goes into the respiratory system of the persons and creates health complications. This is mostly harmful for children and aged people as it causes respiratory problems. It is even worse for people with other respiratory problems such as asthma, lung complications etc. This issue can be totally eliminated by the use of MGP electric lights. The actual improvement made will only be visible after extensive research over years but the primary studies done showed a positive trend, as the number of hospital visits with respiratory ailments decreased after the electrification.

## Impact on Earning Potential

The primary source of income is agriculture related activities with no major industries in these non-electrified villages. The womenfolk usually engage in several activities like sewing, handicrafts and embroidery works etc. and there are some people involved in business activities like selling groceries, eatables and other essential items. But all these have to suffer due to unavailability of power leading to limited business hours and profits. With micro grid power the womenfolk in these villages are able to work at night and this in return increases their earning potential. Also the people with small businesses are able to keep their shops open for a longer duration resulting in increased earning than what they used to do.

## Plans for Expansion

Currently the company is planning to expand its operations within Uttar Pradesh itself as there are a lot of off grid villages in this part of the country. Presently their operations are mostly concentrated on Eastern UP but the company feels that Northern UP can be a potential market for expansion in the next 5year's time. In 2014, they target to rapidly scale up their operations and expand their customer base to add another 45,000 customers by the year end.

Apart from physical expansion they want making more payment options available to customer is one of the important things on their minds. MGP is seriously looking at mobile payment methods, like phone banking etc., to make the process convenient for both the customers as well as the company. Collection through mobile and correspondence banking can be looked as a feasible option. Though it is too early to comment on the feasibility of these options as these need an extensive development in terms of infrastructure and technology.

# CHALLENGES

Although MGP has come a long way forward in bringing the lives of thousands of people, there are a number of challenges it might have to face in the future. The energy needs of people always increase by an upward trajectory. Thus the power generated for the off-grid villages might be sufficient to fulfil their present demands but will be insufficient and fall short in case the villages develop in future. Currently only a mobile charging point and a lighting point are provided to the households. Also as children are being educated, their demand for power might also increase for various reasons. With the current setup, MGP cannot meet this increased demand for power. Though this will provide an opportunity to expand, but the infrastructural and technological challenges have to be taken care of to be able to cope with these challenges.

Secondly, MGP is not the only company which uses micro-grids to provide solar power to off-grid villages. There are many companies do the same but use a different kind of business and operational model. MGP thus might face increased competition from these companies. The services provided by the company needs to be updated from time to time to stop losing out to competitors.

A major issue that has come up was, money collection was taking a lot of manpower and resources but still the company has failed to efficiently carry it out. Villagers do not have a constant source of income thus many of them were defaulting in times of payment. Expanding their reach to several villages has resulted in shortage of trained work force for MGP.

Most of the people recruited by the company are the village locals. These people are not accustomed to a hectic work life and have instead a laid back behaviour. Even though the company pays them decent salary, it is very difficult to retain them because of their attitude towards work. Continuously motivating them and educating them seems to work at times but not always.

The revenue model which they use needs a large number of households to operate and even then it takes around 6 months to recover the initial costs and start making profit. If MGP increases the unit power prices, then the model will become costly for the villagers and they might be unwilling to be a part of the model. It will also increase the chances of regularly missing out payments by the villagers as they might not be able to support it economically. But on the other hand these low charges leave MGP with little margin for profits and further expansion and growth of the business.

As the company grows and expands its presence these challenges will keep on hindering the opportunities of growth Thus it is very crucial to find solutions to these problems in an effective way. The major questions are:

1. How should MGP go about expanding both its range of services and the geographies it is serving to? Will expanding operations to Northern UP will be a viable move right now for the company or should they just to stick to their current market?
2. How can the company use technology and manpower to make money collection a convenient process for both the customer as well as its employees?
3. Should MGP be worried about the competitors in the market or is their business model unique enough to kill competition if any in their territory?
4. Is increasing the per unit price of energy the only way to arrange capital for growth or should they be looking at other options like government grant, venture capitalist funding etc.?
5. Getting access to skilled and motivated work force is raising some major questions on the sustainability of their business model? Should they collaborate with local partners mainly EPC contractors, MFIs, NGOs to outsource their various activities?

## REFERENCES

*EcoSeed*. (n.d.). Retrieved December 25, 2013, from http://www.ecoseed.org/renewables/16922-why-energy-storage-is-important-for-micro-grids-in-india problems of micro grid

*Frequently Asked Questions about Smart Microgrids*. (n.d.). Retrieved December 25, 2013, from http://galvinpower.org/resources/microgrid-hub/smart-microgrids-faq/

Majumder, S. (2013, August 16). *Indian villages lit up by off-grid power*. Retrieved December 21, 2013, from http://www.bbc.co.uk/news/world-asia-india-23613878

Mera Gao Power. (n.d.). *Mera Gao Power: Providing Solar Lighting to Villages*. Retrieved August 22, 2013, from http://meragaopower.com/news

*Mera Gao Power*. (n.d.). Retrieved from http://meragaopower.com

*Micro grids offer solution to 400 million 'powerless' people*. (n.d.). Retrieved September 2, 2013, from http://www.deccanherald.com/content/203669/micro-grids-offer-solution-400.html

*Microgrid Market by Type. (Hybrid, Off-Grid, Grid Connected), Component (Storage, Inverter), Technology (Fuel Cell, CHP), Consumer Pattern (Urban, Rural), Application (Campus, Commercial, Defense), and Geography - Global Forecast to 2022*. (n.d.). Retrieved December 25, 2013, from http://www.marketsandmarkets.com/Market-Reports/micro-grid-electronics-market-917.html

*Rural Urban Distribution of Population*. (n.d.). Retrieved December 26, 2013, from http://censusindia.gov.in/2011-prov-results/paper2/data_files/india/Rural_Urban_2011.pdf

*Smart Grid for India*. (n.d.). Retrieved August 22, 2013, from http://smartgrid-for-india.blogspot.in/2012/05/mera-gao-microgrid-power-among-10.html

*Solar energy startups out to power rural India with cost-effective and less toxic solutions*. (n.d.). Retrieved September 25, 2013, from http://articles.economictimes.indiatimes.com/2013-10-02/news/42617599_1_azure-power-helion-venture-partners-power-company

## KEY TERMS AND DEFINITIONS

**EPC Contractor:** The EPC contractor (EPCC) agrees to deliver EPC, which stands for engineering, procurement and construction. It is a common form of contracting arrangement within the construction and manufacturing industry.

**MFI:** Microfinance institution is a source of financial services for entrepreneurs and small businesses lacking access to banking and related services.

**Micro Solar Grid:** An energy grid consisting of 10 to 15 houses or consumer with a single source, which converts solar energy to electricity and stores in a battery.

**Off-the-Grid:** The term off-grid refers to not being connected to a grid, mainly used in terms of not being connected to the main or national electrical grid.

**USAID:** United States Agency for International Development is the United States federal government agency primarily responsible for administering civilian foreign aid.

# Chapter 13
# Study of Carbon Footprint in Organizations

**Kapil Mendiratta**
*IMT Ghaziabad, India*

**Subhadeep Bhattacharyya**
*IMT Ghaziabad, India*

**Grandhi Venkata Abhinav**
*IMT Ghaziabad, India*

## ABSTRACT

*With the ever increasing intrusion of humans in the environment, it is imperative that individuals and organizations as a unit contribute to an ecologically sustainable environment. With the awareness about carbon emissions and their long term effects increasing; more and more companies are investing in achieving greener ways of production This chapter aims to study how socially/ environmentally conscious today's corporations are, and what courses of action are being taken towards a greener and carbon neutral society in terms of saving basic equivalents of resources such as paper, water, electricity etc. In this chapter we have conducted a survey to analyze the major sources of carbon emission in corporate offices and discuss how corporations can be engaged in contributing to a greener environment.*

## INTRODUCTION

During the early part of the 21st century, there were many articles, blogs and journals which spoke of measures that organizations could take to ensure a healthy path towards a carbon neutral society. Most of such measures included reducing usage of items like paper, water, electricity & fuel. This project will look at how many of these measures are being followed and how much is the scope of further improvement. The total carbon footprint of the entire world in 2013 was 2150 Giga tons of $CO_2$ equivalents, whereas the same was around 350 Giga Tons of $CO_2$ equivalents in 1990. (Global Carbon Project, 2013) The period from 1980 to 2013 has seen a massive jump in the global carbon footprint compared to the years prior to 1980. Fossil fuels and Conversion of land from forests to pastures and crop lands are the

DOI: 10.4018/978-1-4666-8259-7.ch013

two major reasons for the massive jump in carbon footprint of the earth in the recent years. Amongst the two, burning of fossil fuel is responsible for more than two thirds of the global carbon footprint and a major contributor to the remaining one third of global carbon footprint is the land conversion. Looking at region wise contributors to carbon footprint, one can observe that Europe and North America contribute to more than 50% of world's total carbon footprint. The two most populous countries in the world viz. China and India account for around 13% of world's total carbon footprint. Around half of the carbon emissions from human activities go to the atmosphere whereas the remainder of emissions goes to oceans and land parts almost equally. The emissions which stay in the atmosphere are responsible for the warming of the planet in general and also for other climatic changes that are occurring simultaneously. (Global Carbon Project, 2013). However looking at per capita emissions the region wise top contributors change, Oceania and North America would form the top contributors to territorial emissions with the per capita emissions being 14 & 13 $tCO_2$ per person and the same for an average Asian would be 4.1 $tCO_2$ per person, Africa being the lowest per capita contributor has its average individual contributing only 1.1$tCO_2$. However, per capita emissions from burning gases show that Europe and North America contribute the most with 1970 $MtCO_2$ per person and 1696 $MtCO_2$ per person respectively; Asia is at a close third with 1360 $MtCO_2$ per person whereas Central America and Oceania are the most conservative contributors with 48 & 68 $MtCO_2$ respectively. (Roberts, 2013) In 2012, Schneider Electric presented 5 CIOs of the country with the Green Crusader award. The award was given for steps taken by the CIOs in ensuring greener methods of using office resources thereby reducing their organizations' carbon footprint. Following are the winners of the 2012 Green Crusader Awards and the actions they took as CIOs for carbon reductions.

## Baljinder Singh – CIO, EXL Service

Awarded for taking the initiative of moving the entire organization base to a dynamic cloud based environment which covered all the IT aspects of the organization including desktop, datacenter, network, applications, tools and products.

## Bhujay Kumar Bhatta – Operation Manager; IT Shared Services, ITC Ltd.

Awarded for taking the initiative of decentralizing the software platforms used for critical applications like ERP & CRM in the organization. This step moved ITC closer to a cloud like environment and thus helped them in reducing their carbon footprints.

## Damon Frost – CIO, Proctor & Gamble, India

Damon was responsible for the successful integration of all departments under one IT infrastructure which was to be a cloud environment. This again led P&G to be recognized as an organization that does focus on its carbon footprint as a corporate citizen.

### Sachin Jain – CIO, Evalueserve

Awarded for the initiative he took for changing the traditional way of managing data centers. This led to a massive reduction in using physical technological assets in the company, thereby directly saving electricity. This movement led to the creation of an in-house clod environment with just 4 physical servers from the earlier 100 (more than 100) and also saved the company on power by approximately 60%.

### V.C. Kumanan – Senior Director, IDFC

Awarded for envisioning the idea of having high quality data centers which were carbon friendly and for conceiving the idea of having a carbon audit in place for the company for better governance and sustainability (CIO, 2012)

## LITERATURE REVIEW

Carbon Footprint (also called Carbon Profile) is defined as the overall quantity or overall amount of $CO_2$ and other GHG emissions that are related to a product during its entire life cycle starting from its supply-chain to usage and its disposal. The relative effect of other Green House Gases in comparison to the effects from $CO_2$ is done using quantifiable indicators such as Global Warming Potential. (Joint Research Centre European Commission, 2007). Environmentalists and researchers in the field have done a lot of research on how commuting adds to the carbon footprint of the entire globe and have been suggesting companies to cut down on business travel. A report from U.S. Environmental Protection Agency details the methods of estimating/measuring the extent of carbon emissions emanating from an employee's business travel; be it through bus, airline or railways. Reports also talk about how employee's commuting to workplace can also add to the carbon footprints and how work-from-home or telecommute strategies adopted by companies can help them reduce such carbon footprints. (United States Environmental Protection Agency, 2008). A report from Evantage Consulting talks about Fuel/Natural Gas, Electricity, Industry Waste and Employee commuting as 4 major areas of improvement for organizations to work on in order to reduce their carbon footprint. (LBM Direct Marketing Ltd, 2009). A report from the UK Committee on Climate Change categorizes the sources of carbon emissions into Production emissions & Domestic Consumption Emissions. The Production emissions typically include Electricity & Power related emissions, Fossil fuel usage related emissions & emissions related to industrial waste. (Committee on Climate Change, 2013) A similar research white paper on Carbon footprint from IBM which talks about the carbon footprints in the IT industry explains about the power consumption as a major source of carbon emissions. (International Business Machines, 2007). Another study by V. Ryan (2009) indicates fuels, electricity, paper & water as the sources of carbon emissions.

The literature review suggests various parameters that contribute majorly to the carbon footprint and should be looked after. The key parameters thus identified include Commuting, Use of fuels, Paper, Water and Electricity.

For the purpose of this study, some of the aforementioned parameters have been enlisted as the key parameters that could be looked after by organizations in order to reduce their carbon footprints. These include Commuting, Use of Fuels, Paper and Electricity. Respondents were asked objective and subjective questions that helped us to quantitatively and qualitatively identify the usage patterns of paper, electricity & fuel.

Some key facts that arose from the study in terms of Carbon emissions are as mentioned below

For one year's food supply for one person; an individual having an average diet which includes an equal mix of vegetarian and non-vegetarian food contributes 3174 Kg $CO_2$e of carbon footprint to the environment; an individual who primarily eats non-vegetarian food contributes 4193 Kg $CO_2$e of carbon footprint to the environment and an individual who either eats mostly vegetarian food or only vegetarian food contributes the least carbon footprint to the environment at 2602 Kg $CO_2$e. (Eden Project, 2013)

This basically suggests that the amount of carbon footprint contributed by an individual has a direct correlation with the amount of non-vegetarian content in his/her food. In other words, non-vegetarians contribute the most to carbon footprint than people with a mixed diet (a mix of vegetarian and non-vegetarian) and similarly individuals with a mixed diet contribute more carbon footprint than their pure vegetarian counterparts.

For a long distance travel of 500 – 600 Km travel for one person; if the individual travels via an airplane he / she would contribute approximately 549 Kg $CO_2$e to the environment; if the individual travels via a small Hatchback car he / she would contribute approximately 330 Kg $CO_2$e to the environment; for a SUV / 4X4 he / she would contribute 1100 Kg $CO_2$e; For a Train he /she would contribute 119 Kg $CO_2$e and via Bicycling he / she would contribute 192 Kg $CO_2$e to the environment. (Eden Project, 2013)

This basically suggests that for long distance travel, trains are the most eco-friendly in terms of contributing to the carbon footprint that the personal vehicles. Although various studies have shown bicycling to be the most carbon friendly mode of commuting; it turns out that for long distance travels bicycling is not a carbon friendly option when compared with a train. However; for commuting short distances, bicycling is certainly the best mode to commute if the objective is to reduce the carbon footprint.

For travelling 1,00,000 miles in a new car; if the new car is a Small Hatchback a long drive of 1,00,000 miles would typically contribute approximately 41,880 Kg $CO_2$e to the environment; For a Sedan the number would be approximately 61,520 Kg $CO_2$e and for a SUV / 4X4 the drive would contribute approximately 96,940 Kg $CO_2$e to the environment. (Eden Project, 2013) This basically suggests that for commuting via personal vehicles; it is best to travel in a small hatchback car than in sedan or worst in a SUV / 4X4. Of course; it goes without saying that personal vehicle travels should be avoided and public transport be used as and when possible to move towards a more ecologically green environment.

For communicating messages; It has been found that for communicating standard messages an SMS contributes very minimal of 0.000014 Kg $CO_2$e of carbon footprint to the environment; a standard mobile phone calling for the similar amount of message would contribute 0.19 Kg $CO_2$e; An email to send the similar amount of message would contribute 0.004Kg $CO_2$e and a letter written on a piece of paper would contribute 0.2 Kg $CO_2$e to the environment. (Eden Project, 2013) This basically suggests that various modes of communication exchange also contribute to carbon footprint. It can be observed that telecommunicating which includes the use of IT for communication has largely reduced that carbon footprint when compared with communication hard copy letters. It is observed that while emails and SMS' are very economical to carbon footprint and contribute almost negligibly to it; a standard telephone call may contribute almost equally to carbon footprint when compared with the written paper mode of communication.

More-so a laptop emits approximately 80% less carbon equivalents than a desktop for similar usages. (The Ecologist, 2013) This presents a challenge for those who are concerned with the carbon footprint. It is difficult to enforce the entire organization to use laptops instead of desktops for the simple reasons that the organization would then have to invest more on the employee as laptops are costlier.

## RESEARCH OBJECTIVE

The objective of the project is to study and analyze the major sources of carbon emissions (or other sources of environmental hazards) in corporate offices, the steps these companies are taking to tackle such issues and what can be done to overcome this issue for a greener and a better planet.

## RESEARCH METHODOLOGY AND DESIGN

The study involved identification of key areas which companies can work upon to reduce their carbon footprint and to understand if there any other factors that can be looked into for a company to reduce its carbon footprint. After the parameters were identified based on the literature study, an elaborate survey form was constructed to ask the employee about his individual usages of the key parameters identified viz. Paper, Water, Electricity & Fuel. The survey also asked users to qualitatively inform us about key areas where they see a need for change in order to see a possible reduction in carbon footprint. The construction of this survey form went through a number of iterations and test surveys before actually releasing it to the target employees. The survey was to be released by way of sending to 1, 2 or 3 Points of contacts in each of the organizations and circulating it to the organizations' employees thereafter. The following companies had been contacted and 95 responses were received.

The following organizations were surveyed

- Infosys
  - Infosys is a famous Indian Multinational providing Information Technology, Business Consulting & Outsourcing services to multifarious clients across the globe. Infosys also happens to be one of the leading players in the IT sector in India.
- Accenture
  - Accenture is an Irish Multinational and one of the global leaders in Management Consulting & Technology Services. It also comes in the list Fortune 500 companies. With clients in 56 countries, Accenture is the world's largest consulting firm by revenue.
- Snapdeal
  - Snapdeal.com is a popular Indian e-commerce company selling a whole list of consumer goods to online consumers in India. Growing at a very rapid pace, Snapdeal is the second largest e-commerce website in India.
- Evalueserve
  - Evalueserve is an Indian multinational and a premier name in the Knowledge Process Outsourcing sector, providing Business & Technology Research, Data Analytics, Investment research, Financial & Legal services to clients across the globe.

- Tata Consultancy Services
    - Tata Consultancy Services is an Indian multinational IT service, business solution provider and a consulting firm belonging to the Tata group of companies. Similar to Infosys, Tata Consultancy Services happen to be the leading player in its sector in India.
- Tata Global Beverages Ltd.
    - Tata Global Beverages is an Indian Multinational organization that deals in the manufacturing and marketing of non-alcoholic beverages across the globe with the products offered being Tea, Mineral Water & Coffee. Belonging to the Tata Group of Companies, Tata Global Beverages is also the leading player in the tea segment in India, and the second biggest player in tea worldwide.
- Deloitte Touche Tohmatsu India Pvt. Ltd.
    - Deloitte Touche Tohmatsu India is the India wing of Deloitte Touche Tohmatsu Ltd, and is a large player in providing audit, tax, consulting and financial services to clients across the globe. Deloitte is also one amongst the world famous "Big Four" Audit firms and the largest of the four firms by revenue.
- Hyundai Motors
    - Hyundai Motors is a South Korean Multinational and is the second largest auto-maker in the whole of Asia. The company also has significant presence in India. Hyundai also happens to be the fifth largest auto maker globally with a wide range of car offerings mostly in the hatchback and sedan segments.

Five of the eight companies namely Infosys, Accenture, Evalueserve, Tata Consultancy Services & Deloitte Touche Tohmatsu India Ltd. belong to the Services Sector. Of the remaining three companies; Hyundai motors belongs to the automotive sector, Tata Global Beverages ltd. belongs to the FMCG sector and Snapdeal is an online retailer and belongs to the emerging e-commerce sector.

The survey carried out was through an online questionnaire in the form of a Google form; the link to the survey given below was circulated to all the companies mentioned above

## DATA ANALYSIS

The survey response of 95 respondents was split across the surveyed organizations as shown below (Figure 1 shows the number of respondents from each organization). Accenture, Infosys & Snapdeal employees were the major contributors to the survey with 17, 17 & 16 responses respectively.

The employees of the above chosen organizations who worked in the office premises were surveyed by means of the online questionnaire.

The employees seems quite pleased to respond to our survey and one of the respondents also pointed out that this survey is not only helpful for the academic research purpose but also it gives the respondent a time to think and invest time to understand the mechanics of implications of carbon footprint.

A few key pie charts below summarize the survey responses and indicate the level of Employee awareness, Paper usage, Power consumption & Fuel usage.

*Figure 1. Number of respondents split by the organization*

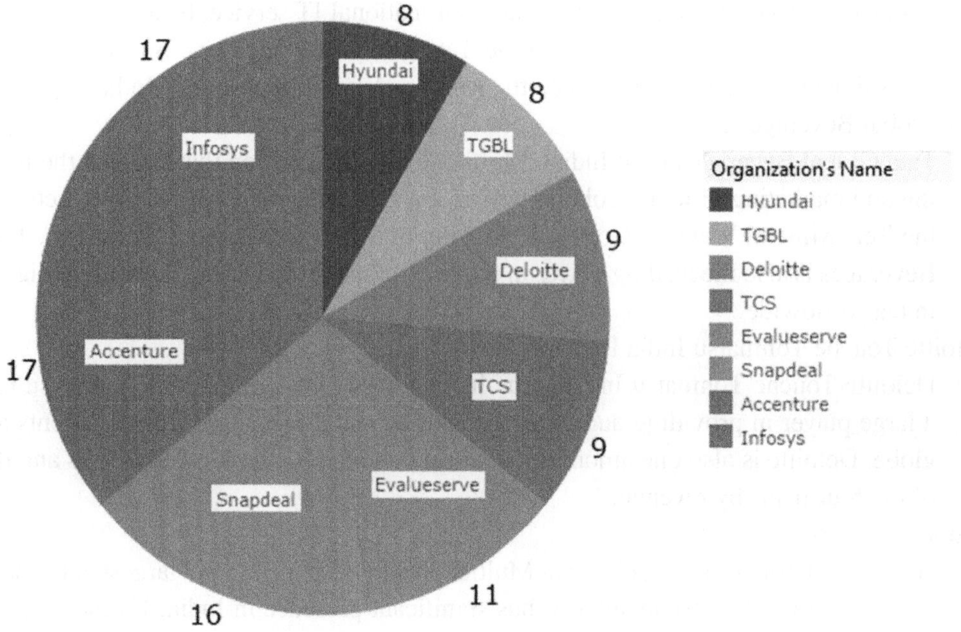


## Awareness

The respondents were asked questions in order to judge their awareness of the issue of the rising carbon footprints and organizations being responsible for a good chunk of it. The respondents were asked are about whether they were aware about the fact that they could estimate their personal contribution of carbon footprint to the environment through online websites (Figure 2 shows the number of respondents who have measured carbon footprints online). On a similar note they were asked about whether their organization used recycled paper at all (Figure 3 shows responses about usage of recycled paper)

## Paper Usage

Paper wastage is a major and a common phenomenon contributing to the carbon footprints in organizations. In many cases it is very easy for the individual to take print-outs for convenience in working, and it is also difficult to do the same work on a computer compared to making notes. The respondents were asked questions to ascertain their usage patterns for paper in two categories – Paper for printing and Paper cups.(Figure 4, 5 shows response of respondents) The respondents were asked about the frequency of their usage of paper cups and the frequency of their printing papers.

## Fuel Usage

Fuel Usage & Modes of Commuting were identified as the major contributors to carbon footprint. In order to estimate the fuel usage patterns of the employees, they were asked questions pertaining to their modes of commuting to their workplace (Figure6 shows, the mode of commute used by employees); and if they had a personal vehicle to commute to their workplace they were asked about the kind of vehicle they owned from amongst a Hatchback, a Sedan & a SUV / 4X4 (Figure 7 shows the different types of vehicles that are used).

*Figure 2. Ever measured your carbon footprint online?*

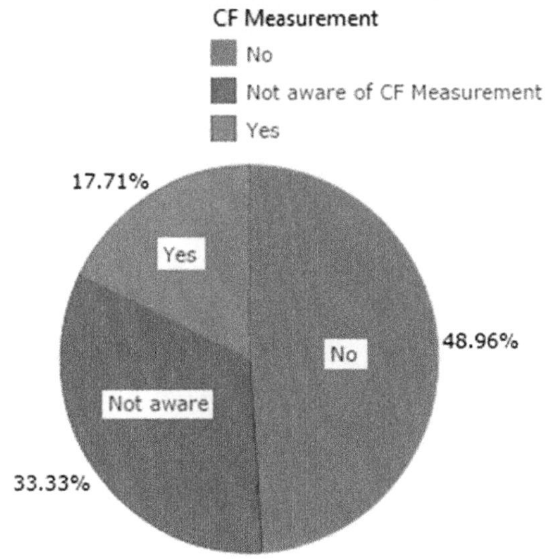


*Figure 3. Does your organization use recycled paper?*

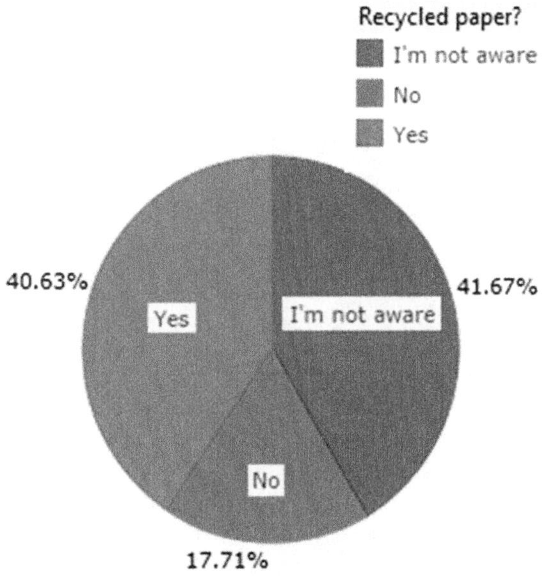

*Figure 4. How many paper cups do you use per day?*

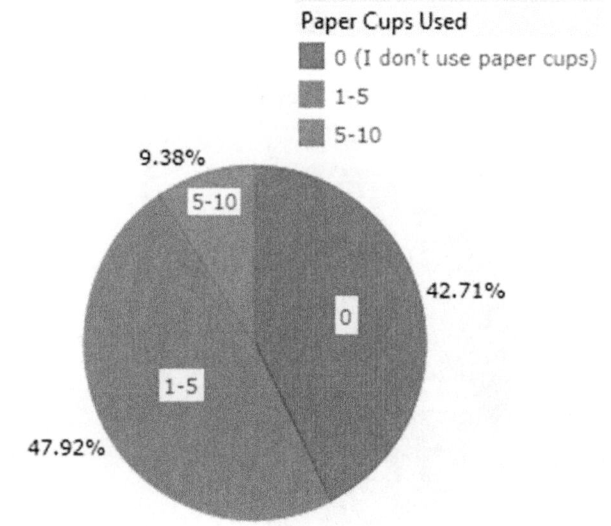


*Figure 5. Number of print-outs taken in a week?*

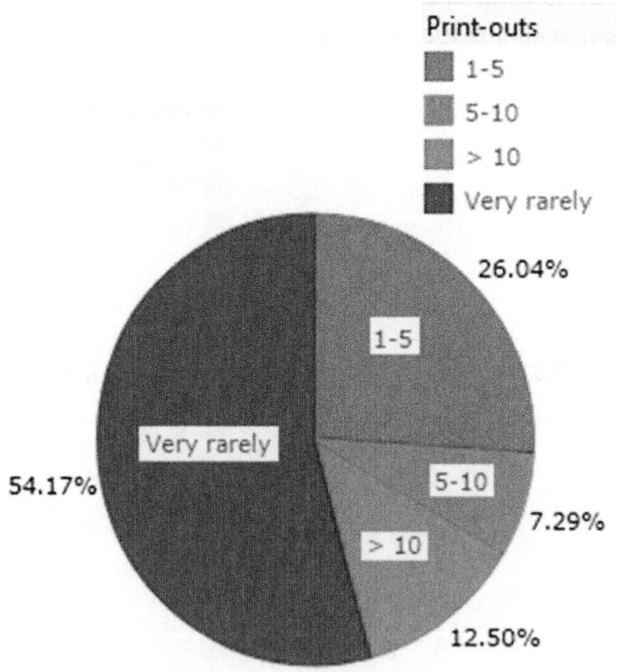

*Figure 6. Mode of commuting to office?*

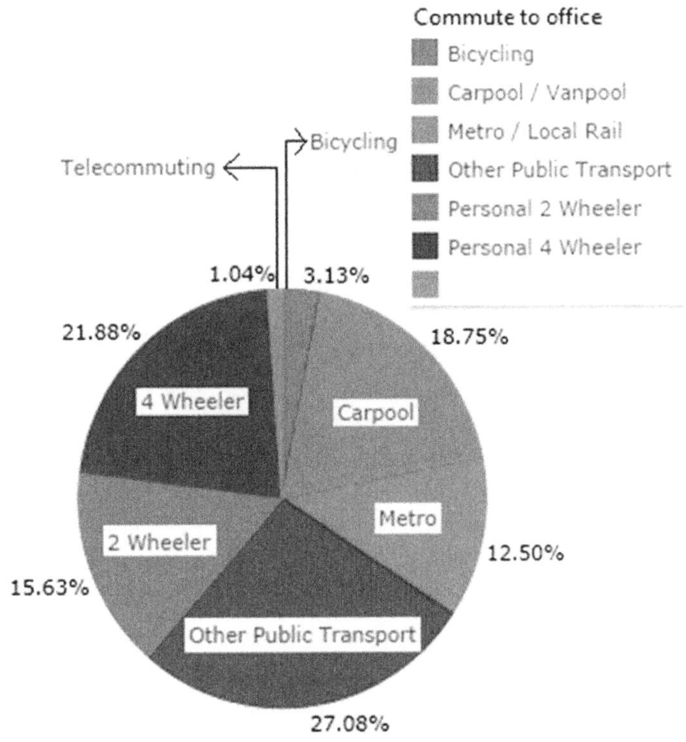


*Figure 7. Which vehicle type? (if personal 4-wheeler used)*

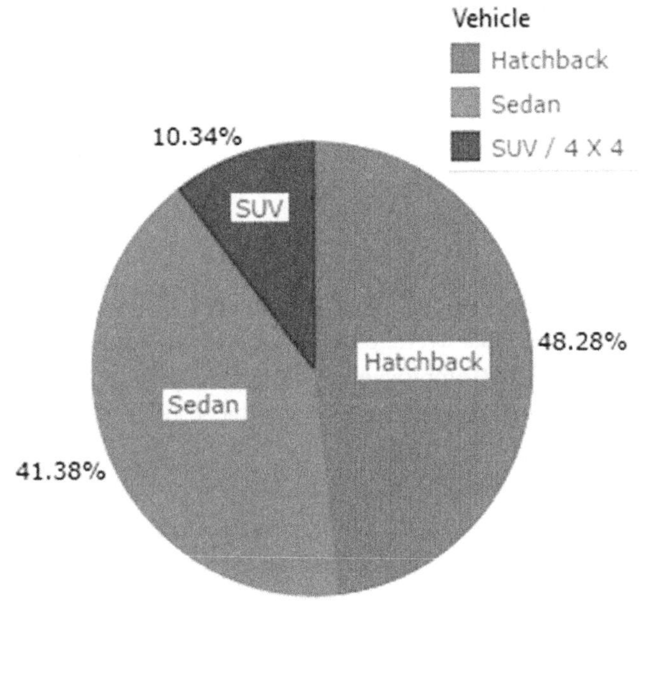

*Figure 8. Which computer type?*

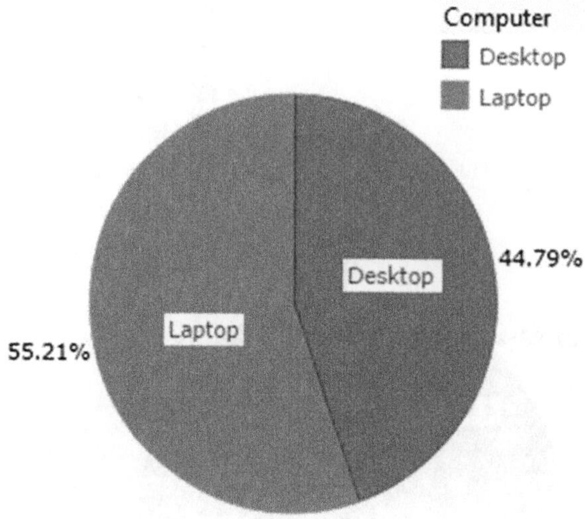


## Power Consumption

Electricity also formed a major contributor to carbon footprint according to our literature review. Through our survey tried to estimate the power usage patterns by asking them about the frequency of them shutting down their work systems before leaving for the day(Figure 10 shows how frequently respondents shut down their systems). As laptops contribute much lesser in terms of carbon footprint to the environment, the respondents were asked as to whether they used a laptop or a desktop for their regular work(Figure8 shows the type of computer that respondents use) .To judge their consciousness about the fact that power contributes to carbon footprint, the respondents were asked about the frequency of usage of elevators(Figure 9 shows the frequency of elevator usage) and correlated the results with the floor in which their work office was located. The objective was to identify if people who worked in the $1^{st}$ or the $2^{nd}$ floors tried avoiding the elevators at times.

# RESULTS AND FINDINGS

## Paper Usage

The survey shows that on an average an employee uses 2 paper cups every day. If employees who don't use paper cups at all are excluded, that average number comes around to be 5 cups a day. This implies that an organization with around 2000 employees would typically waste 14.6 Lac cups every year. Paper cups are used for convenience and can very easily be replaced by ceramic reusable mugs. This would help save massive amounts of paper every year.

The survey also establishes that the key paper wastage is by way of print outs in these organizations. The survey reveals that more than 54% of the employees take print-outs very rarely and that is a very positive sign. However, because of those who do take print-outs on a regular basis, the average amount

*Figure 9. How frequently do you use the elevator?*

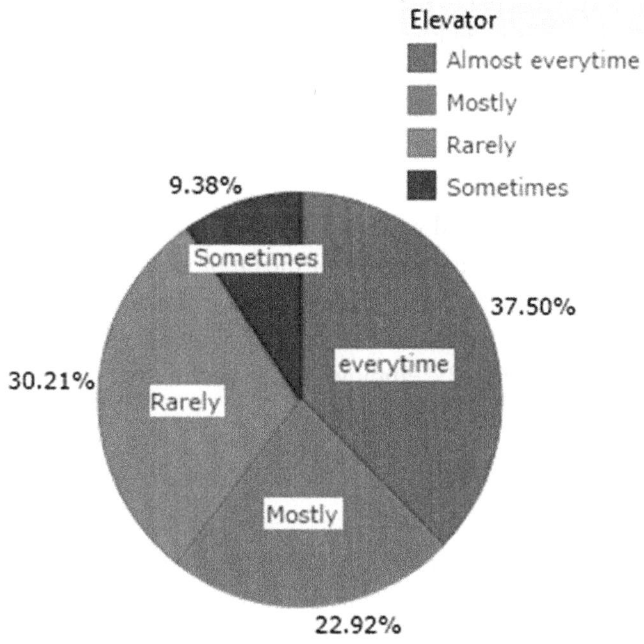


*Figure 10. How frequently do you shut-down your systems before leaving for the day?*

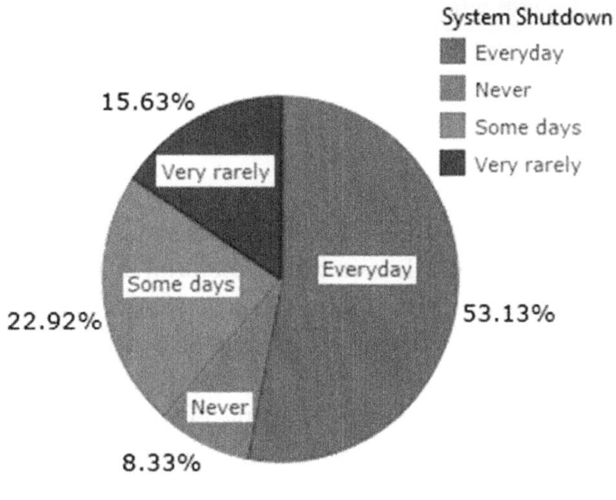

of paper printed per employee in a week comes out to be just a little more than 3 pages per week, and this amounts to approximately 3 Lac pages being printed in an organization of 2000 employees. Qualitative survey also reveals that most of such print-outs can be avoided and hence organizations have a large scope of working on printing paper wastage.

## Awareness

A mere 17.71% of the employees surveyed were aware of the online carbon footprint measurement and had done the measurement. The remaining 82.29% of the employees had either no idea of the presence of the online carbon footprint measurement or had not taken it. There is a real big gap in terms awareness of such critical issues and needs attention.

Similarly there were approximately 42% employees who had no clue whether their organizations use recycled paper or not.

## Fuel Usage

Commuting to workplace was fairly distributed between personal transport & public transport, with around 37.5% of the employees using their own personal vehicle to commute, while others were distributed between various modes or public transport or car-pooling.

From amongst those 37.5% employees using their personal mode of commuting; there are roughly half the people using either a Sedan or a SUV, both being major contributors to carbon emissions when compared to their hatchback counterparts. Although the choice of vehicle is an individual's choice and has a lot of parameters to do with when choosing between a Sedan, SUV or a Hatchback; there still needs to be a comprehensive education for the consumer about the carbon footprints being emitted by each of the categories.

## Power Consumption

The survey revealed positive results with 55.71% of the employees using a laptop rather than a desktop and given the fact that a laptop emits 80% less on carbon footprint than a desktop. The results however, might be skewed owing to the employees being surveyed, a qualitative interview with one of the organizations revealed that the number of desktops used in the organization was much more than the number of laptops used.

The survey also revealed that approximately 60% of the employees are frequent users of the elevators. However, a closer study on the data revealed that more than 90% of such elevator users had their offices on or above the $4^{th}$ Floor. Also, majority of the people who had office on or below the $3^{rd}$ floor did exercise the option of not using the lifts on many occasions. This showed a rational behavior in terms of elevator usage and thus is a positive sign for carbon footprint reduction.

While there were 53.13% of the employees who did shut-down their systems below leaving the workplace on a daily basis, the remaining 47.87% didn't. This is one clear area which needs improvement, as a system which is not shut keeps consuming electricity and is still emitting carbon equivalents. Approximately 24% of the people would rarely shut-down their systems whereas the remaining 24% would shut-down some days and leaving the systems on for the other days.

## QUALITATIVE SURVEY: KEY POINTS TO NOTE

The Avenues where Employees Find Their Colleagues and the Organization as a Whole in Wasting Any of the Three Viz. Paper, Water & Electricity

- Tissue papers in washrooms can be replaced with a hand dryer
- People take print-outs of presentations for proof-reading purposes
- The whole floor is lighted – even though there are 2-3 employees working out of shifts
- People use more than one paper cup for single time use, to avoid the heat conduction
- People sometimes don't take back-to-back print-outs
- Paper is wasted to promote organizational policies by way of posters/pamphlets
- Many employees don't shut-down their systems before leaving for the day, since it helps them regain from where they left for the next day
- Unnecessary wastage of electricity in meeting rooms which are not regularly used
- Even though the shredder is present, hardly any one puts it to proper use

Steps that Organizations have Taken to Reduce the Wastage of Paper, Water & Electricity

- Lights being dimmed or shut between 1 pm and 2 pm every day to allow natural light to take charge
- Emails sent to educate employees to use paper for print-outs judiciously
- Use of paper shredding machine
- Regular switching off of the lights and ACs as company policy every day after working hours
- Annual statistics of paper consumption is provided to the employees in numbers of tree that had to be fallen to create awareness amongst employees
- Sensor based taps to avoid water wastage
- Offices shifting towards energy efficient LED & CFL Lights
- Auto-shutdown of workstations after a certain time of the day
- Default printing is set at print on both sides for all systems

The subjective responses given by the respondents indicates that instances of printing presentations for discussions have become commonplace and can most certainly be avoided. Some organizations followed a strict policy of shutting down work systems after work hours, most organizations didn't and this is a step which can be implemented throughout. Certain organizations are taking steps like shutting out unnecessary lightings after a specified time during the day and this is also a policy that can most certainly be incorporated by one and all.

## CONCLUSION

As more and more organizations are becoming aware of issues on sustainability, there are a lot of cases where organizations have taken a step towards a greener planet. However, there is still a long way to go. A lot of such issues can be taken care of, with the employees individually being environment conscious and being aware of the issues and their corresponding long term hazards. Paper, Fuel, Water & Electricity form very basic parameters that can be looked at by the corporate offices, but it is the employee awareness on all these parameters and their actions about the same that will lead to a more sustainable future.

The project led to an elaborate study on how organizations have improved or can improve when it comes to saving on carbon footprint and working on the Planet aspect of the triple bottom-line. Few important points that arose from this study and which could be laid down as recommendations & basic guidelines for corporates on the key fronts Awareness, Paper & Electricity as measures for a sustainable future are as mentioned below

### Awareness

- Organizations should send emails discouraging people to take print-outs
- Annual statistics of the amount of pages printed and the equivalent trees felled for it needs to be circulated to the employees
- Employees should be educated on how electricity, print-outs, diets & mode of commuting contribute towards the carbon footprint of the entire organization as a whole

### Paper

- Double sided prints should be set as default on all systems
- Paper cups should be avoided in offices, employees should use personal mugs which can be reused
- Tissue papers in washrooms can be done away with, by having a hand dryer in place of it
- Print-outs for posters of Organizational policies should be done through emails
- Presentation print-outs for proof reading purposes should be discouraged
- Paper Shredders should be available for the employees (the shredded papers should be sent for recycling purposes)

### Electricity

- Organizations should promote switching off lights in personal cabins and meeting rooms, when the rooms/cabins are not in use
- Alternate forms for lighting – solar lights or energy efficient LEDs & CFLs should be used
- Auto-shutdown of workstations, ACs, Lights should be there after office hours
- The employees should be educated for shutting down of their systems before leaving for the day

## REFERENCES

CIO. (2012). *Green Crusader Awards - Schneider Electric*. Retrieved from http://www.cio.in/cio100-2012/special-awards-green-crusader

Collier, U. (2013). *Reducing the UK's Carbon Footprint*. Retrieved from http://www.theccc.org.uk/wp-content/uploads/2013/04/Reducing-carbon-footprint-report.pdf

Eden Project. (2013, August). *What's your Carbon footprint?* Retrieved from http://www.edenproject.com/whats-it-all-about/climate-and-environment/online-tools/whats-your-carbon-footprint

Freya, R. (2013, November). *5 Facts about Europe's Carbon Emissions*. Retrieved from http://www.carbonbrief.org/blog/2013/11/5-facts-about-europes-carbon-emissions/

Global Carbon Atlas. (2013). *Global Carbon Project*. Retrieved from http://www.globalcarbonatlas.org/?q=outreach

International Business Machines. (2007). *Cutting the Carbon Footprint of IT*. Retrieved from http://www-05.ibm.com/innovation/uk/green/pdf/SOLUTION_IT_cutting_the_carbon_footprint_of_it.pdf

Joint Research Centre, European Commission. (2007). *Carbon Footprint - what it is and how to measure it*. Retrieved from http://www.envirocentre.ie/includes/documents/Carbon_Footprint-what_it_is_and_how_to_measure_it-JRC_IES-Feb09-b[1].pdf

LBM Direct Marketing Ltd. (2008, June 1). *Carbon Footprint Profile*. Retrieved from http://www.lbm.co.uk/Public/content/about/LBM%20Carbon%20Footprint%20report.pdf

Ryan, V. (2009). *World Association of Technology Teachers. How can we reduce our carbon footprint?* Retrieved from http://www.lbm.co.uk/Public/content/about/LBM%20Carbon%20Footprint%20report.pdf

The Ecologist. (2013, October). *Carbon Footprint*. Retrieved from http://files.theecologist.org/resources/carbonfootprints.html

United States Environmental Protection Agency. (2008). *Optional Emissions from Commuting, Business Travel & Product Transport (Publication No.EPA430-R-08-006)*. Washington, DC: Office of Air and Radiation.

## KEY TERMS AND DEFINITIONS

**Car Pooling:** Sharing car journeys by the employees to and from workplace.

**CIO:** Chief Information Officer – The Chief Executive officer in an organization responsible to for heading information technology.

**Data Center:** A data storage facility used to house computer/server machines that store major information for the organization.

**GHG:** Green House Gas.

**Global Warming:** The persistent rise in average temperature of the climate system of the earth.

**IT:** Information Technology.

# Chapter 14
# NGO Sudhaar:
## Empowering the Livestock Dependents

**Pragun Aggarwal**
*IMT Ghaziabad, India*

**Ronit Anand**
*IMT Ghaziabad, India*

## ABSTRACT

*This chapter discusses the analysis of opportunity to setup a milk production and distribution system in Badalpur and Sakipur, two remote villages in Uttar Pradesh. Sudhaar, a regional development organization, is a group of corporate professionals who joined hands in 2003 to work on grassroots to bring in a positive change in rural/semi-urban strata. The chapter details the challenges faced by dairy farmers in rural India and proposal laid by NGO to revamp the existing business model to make it more financially viable.*

## INTRODUCTION

It's early June 2013, a hot summer afternoon in Greater Noida, India, Mr. Nagesh along with his team are going through the data collected for the new business model. The model's primary focus is a collection of milk and establishing its distribution network in the nearby Tier II & Tier III cities. The system is to be run by the villagers for the urban milk consumers being the primary consumers. The point of differentiation for the business model is supply of good quality milk to the consumers at a cheaper price and at the same time to empower the families employed in the milk business.

Mr. Nagesh is convinced that this business model would completely revamp the traditional business by subduing its shortcomings and become a lucrative deal by providing a dependable source of income for rural households. But there was a critical issue in hand which had to be dealt with. He is concerned that he lacked a clear strategy on how to enter this market and where to start from. He realized his decision would have immediate effects, thus considering the constraints involved he ponders: How to venture into the "Milk-Business"?

DOI: 10.4018/978-1-4666-8259-7.ch014

## NGO SUDHAAR

Females in households in Gulawati today are busy managing their families and their business together. Every alternate day they devote 4 hours in setting up the recipe of the traditional sweet, Furfuri, which was in great demand and used to be sought by the people from nearby towns to such an extent that they didn't mind travelling 25-30 km every other weekend. But now people do not need to travel so much as furfuri is now available in a number of reputed sweet shops across the nearby towns. The rural households were provided with a regular and stable source of income along with the development of women of the families. All this was made possible by a group of professionals who had identified this business opportunity and had done the cumbersome task of convincing the families of this business and chalking and implementing out the marketing plan. These people find themselves as a part of Sudhaar – the game changer.

Sudhaar is a regional development organization touching the lives of more than 25000 underprivileged families annually in the suburbs of NCR by introducing in areas of education, healthcare and youth employability in its 10 years of existence. A few young professionals who shared the common belief of 'Self-help is the best help', joined hands in 2003 to set up Sudhaar to work on grassroots level and bring in a positive change in the rural/semi urban strata. The vision of the organization is to work as a catalyst in bringing about a transformation in the lives of the underprivileged and marginalized.

The work approach was initially based on the concept of social venture philanthropy in line with venture capital. To offer support to the bottom of the social-economic pyramid of the country by identifying earning opportunities for the marginalized by enabling genuine grass root NGO in capacity building and empowerment in area of their work. Gradually the organization has started concentrating on other important aspects of overall development – education, healthcare and women empowerment by involving NGO active at a level at the very bottom of the pyramid.

The modus operandi of the organization works on a no profit no loss basis. Out of the 40 employees that the NGO has, 40% are graduates hired from respectable educational institutions of the country who wish to gain experience in the social entrepreneurship sector or want to do some social work before taking up a corporate life. The organization's source of funds is mainly CSR funds that it gets by pitching in to the big corporate houses. Companies want to generate generously to organizations like Sudhaar which they believe will use their money in the development of the society. Big names like Barclay's, Cairn, SAIL, Indian Oil and Siemens are associated with Sudhaar. Donations from people, societies are also a part of the funding.

## LIVESTOCK WITH AN INDIAN PERSPECTIVE

India, the second most populous country in the world, is home to over 1.2 billion people. Out of which nearly 72.2% reside in rural areas with agricultural activities being their primary source of income. 18.0 million People out of the total rural population of India depend on livestock dairying and animal husbandry to earn bread for their families *(National Institute of Rural Development [NIRD], n.d.)*. Numerous socio-economic development schemes, launched extensively in the poor parts of the country, are a failure if their impact does not reflect in the betterment of lives of these dairy farmers.

The knowledge of the fact that animal husbandry and dairying contributed to almost 4.68% of the total GDP of the country and the potential in this sector to create self-employment opportunities motivated Nagesh to channel all his resources in formulating a strategy for the development of livestock and people involved in this business. His research team's findings revealed that India is the second largest home to livestock population in the world with livestock population of 529.7 million spread across 100 million households.

The population under the scope are totally dependent on the agricultural sector to earn their bread and butter. Three fourth of this rural population either have no land ownership, or devoid of fertile soils and regular water supply for irrigation. Thus for such families livestock, primarily cattle and buffaloes, plays an integral part in running their households by selling the milk produced and also consuming the left over. However irrespective of the criticality of this sector with an economic point of view, it never really took off as compared to other sectors of the economy. Lack of integration with the market and unavailability of basic requirements of livestock farming prove to be the major reasons behind this sector being an under achiever.

A lot of researches already conducted, point out towards a common set of problems. These include shortage of health care services, unavailability of healthy feed and fodder, farmers' lack of awareness on healthy breeding practises, exploitation of locals by traders, farmers' lack of knowledge of utilizing cattle dung for energy needs, no reach of modern farming technologies to the rural and last but not the least the pricing of milk which is more favourable to the consumers and gives less benefit to the producer *(National Institute of Rural Development [NIRD], n.d.)*. Nagesh acknowledged the fact that this is one sector which despite of its huge potential to grow and prosper has not been able to deliver promising results. India, the largest milk producer in the world, is far behind in the yield efficiency of its livestock which is one-fifth of its foreign counterparts. Such inefficacy is due to poor health of livestock, poor handling, and unhygienic environment. Organizing a competent distribution system to do away with inefficiencies is very critical in the process of improving the productivity and thus profit margins for the rural households.

## MILK BUSINESS

Nagesh who is one of the newly recruited graduates from Delhi University has worked on this project for quite some time now. His team paid frequent visits to Sakipur and Badalpur villages and interacted with the milk producing families to collect information on all aspects of the business as well as the problems or constraints they faced.

Bamul, an established milk brand which is the current market leader in the packaged milk industry poses a serious challenge to the proposed business model. Bamul followed a very structured approach to its business. It had separate departments with predefined roles. The organization was a 3 tier structure with dairy co-operatives at village, district, and state level. The village cooperatives collected milk from the rural producers and paid them according to the amount and quality of the milk supplied (the purity of milk along with cream content was also tested before accepting the milk), provided support services like veterinary emergency care, sale of mineral compositions, sale of hygienic fodder feed, providing guidance on healthy and efficient animal husbandry and dairying practises, supply of milk to district co-operative societies.

The district cooperatives run chilling centres and dairy plants for collecting and processing the milk received from the villages. The state cooperatives were responsible for marketing of milk processed by milk unions, set up a distribution network and arranging transportation for the same.

The traditional producer in these villages followed a two-step approach:

- Step 1: Milking of cattle in the morning and evening. *Table 4: Essential details about Livestock.*
- Step 2: Distribution of milk is done on cycle/motorcycle which consumes a lot of time or some customers take it directly from the milkman's house. This demanded the customer to cover a lot of distance.

A detailed gap analysis of the prevailing unorganized village practises brought to light numerous shortcomings in the system. Firstly, milk supplied by the local milkmen suffered inconsistent supply as their mode of commute was cycle or motorcycle as against the 24x7 availability of the packaged milk in the markets. This proved to be an added advantage for the working class especially people who were living alone as they could fetch milk as per their convenience.

Secondly, lot of customers were sceptical about the adulteration issues of milk and water and it's true that some milkmen resorted to such unethical means of mixing. Also irregular price fluctuation as against the market determined fixed price of the established brands proved to be a major setback for the demand of milk of rural milk vendors.

Finally modern consumers were very well aware of the practises exercised by both the local villagers and the company and their apprehensions over the quality of milk versus the tested quality standards of branded milk were justified. Fifthly, the milk supplied by the local milkmen were unpasteurised milk which needed to be boiled before use whereas the milk supplied by Bamul and other established brands were sold in pasteurized form and could be consumed directly from packet.

## RECYCLING AND GREEN ENERGY

Biogas is considered one of the cheapest form of renewal energy. Surprisingly it is the fourth largest source of energy in the world. A total of 12% of world's energy is met by biogas plants. According to International Energy Agency, one-fourth of the world's transportation fuel demand can be fulfilled by biogas plants. Denmark is known for its agricultural practises and lately government has announced that 50% of the total cow dung will be converted into biogas *(The Official Website of Denmark, n.d.).*

Biogas plants in India use cow dung, agricultural waste and human waste as raw materials and operate at very low efficiency. *Table 5: Manure / 10 animal unit.* Very few plants operate at its total capacity. The primary reason behind this lag in efficiency is the lack of raw materials and unawareness about the benefits of running a biogas plant. The data collected by Nagesh showed that number of biogas plants in India recorded negative growth of 9% in the past two years. *Table 6: Energy crops per ha.*

## NAGESH'S PROPOSAL

The business model, implemented to perfection, was ought to deliver promising results. The model works on a vertical approach where the producer would be involved from the point of produce to the point of sale.

Milk collection centres or the co-operatives for each village would be set up at a convenient location for all the milk producers. Each farmer can come at the co-operative with his produce for a collective collection of milk at one place. This can be done twice a day depending upon the amount of milk produced. The milk would then be loaded into tankers for distribution to the nearby cities. Two persons would be appointed, one by the NGO and other by the villagers themselves, who would accompany the truck driver to do the money collection. The trucks that carry milk collected from the villages would reach the nearby city at a set place every day at a set time. The customers who will be informed of the schedule can come collect their milk and pay for the same then and there. The money collector would then pay each villager for his produce on returning to the village at the milk cooperative. This way cash flow would keep running. The transportation facility would be availed on monthly rent.

For any business to be successful it is very important that the consumers realize great benefit out of the product. The suppliers too need a profitable stream of cash flows to keep the business running. The business model proposed would take care of both the consumers as well as the suppliers interests. The consumers, if provided with an easily available, best quality and low cost product, would definitely want to purchase it. Nagesh proposed to price the milk 4-5 INR per litre lower than the packaged branded milk. This was possible for there would be no advertising expenses, negligible salary pay-off, considerably low transportation and overhead costs as compared to established market players. The customers are now willing to pay 10%-15% higher for fresh cow milk and so such low pricing would drive up the sales immensely. Though it would be required to make the customers believe that there is absolutely no adulteration in the milk and they are getting it completely fresh. Once the people start realizing the health benefits of consuming fresh milk in the long run, they would then become villagers' loyal customers. Fresh milk is always preferred over packaged milk provided it is easily available. Easy availability would be achieved by employing efficient workforce to deliver the milk at set locations and time every day. The rationale behind the successful implementation of this business is providing these solutions to the customers.

The other side of the business which includes the producers also do have a lot in it for them. A regular and timely delivery system would be achieved by employing the service of trucks for supply of milk to the cities. The villagers who now deliver the milk to their customers on their 2-wheelers or bicycles would save a lot of time and energy with the implementation of this project. They would also be spared of the task of finding customers who often have to change their milk vendor due to adulteration issues. The villagers can thus utilize their time in other activities for generating more income. Lower selling price would not affect their margins since carrying out operations in an organized way would lessen the overhead costs including their daily travelling expenses.

Milk quality testing centres, one each, would be established in both the villages to remove any anomalies in the milk procurement process. The complete check process would be explained to each producer in order to remove any dilemmas regarding the quality results generated. This would ensure supply of unadulterated milk to the customers. Seasonal variation in the milk produce is also reported by the farmers. A team would be set up to study the factors responsible for the varying production level and find out measures to lessen the variation. The producers would be compensated in cash on daily basis in accordance with the quantity and quality of their milk. Tankers used in transportation of milk will be monitored for regular maintenance and service to eliminate any leakages and hygiene issues from the mind of the customers.

A substantial decline in fodder availability is observed in the country to compensate which commercial feed is used. It is not just costly but also mixed with urea and other artificial milk boosters. This delivers a double blow due to higher cost of milk and negative impact on milk quality and livestock health.

A solution to this problem has been identified in form of plant Azolla, which promises to be a sustainable source of livestock feed. Azolla is a floating fern which hosts symbiotic blue green algae and is high on protein content. It is also rich in essential amino acids, vitamins, growth promoter intermediaries and minerals like calcium, phosphorous, potassium, ferrous, copper, magnesium etc. the composition of nutrients makes it an effective livestock feed. Livestock digest and quickly get used to it. Moreover it is economical and easy to grow *(Rajamony, Premalatha, & Pillai, 2005).*

Azolla cultivation has been taken up widely in countries like China, Vietnam, and the Philippines. Use of Azolla is found to increase milk yield by about 15% when fed with regular feed. Dairy farmers in Badalpur and Sakipur who do have too little land for production of fodder will be trained and entertained to practise Azolla production which is likely to improve both productivity and quality.

The second step consists of installation of a biogas plant in the villages. A campaign will be launched to educate dairy farmers and their families coming to the milk collection centres to spread awareness on the benefits of renewal energy. All farmers will be advised to deposit the cow dung produced in their animal shelters and the raw material collected will then be used at the biogas plant proposed. Farmers depositing cow dung and other agricultural waste will be either given monetary benefits or supplied with fuel produced at the biogas plant. Nagesh plans to hold talks with the authority concerned in the Government of India to fund the installation of biogas plant. Cow dung which cannot be used as raw material will be used as a fertilizers. The added avenues of income in form of money or fuel will further enhance the sustainability of the business model.

## THE CHALLENGES

### Absence of Funds and Insurance

The milk producing households face financial problems as there are not enough government plans to support their livelihood. The plans which were commissioned were either not implemented properly or were trampled in bureaucracy. Milk and its products which constitute a major part of food diet play a favorable part in such conditions. It comes second to cereals in terms of items consumed. So it becomes all the more important for poor rural households to maintain good health of their livestock. The milk produced can be sold to realize monthly income plus the leftover milk and its products can be substituted for cereals.

The Government of India realizes the fact and has come up with various subsidy and low interest rate loan schemes via NABARD. But the implementation part has not been able to complement the planning part. All loans whether agricultural or livestock need to be routed through commercial banking facilities which do not pass a loan application without taking collateral since complete onus of loan recovery is on them and NABARD has no role to play in it. And over 60% of households engaged in livestock farming own no land which makes them ineligible for any loan or subsidy. Farmers who do get loans keep on applying and getting further loans irrespective of non-payment of previous dues. Banks are secured by both collateral as well as the periodic government schemes to waiver off agricultural loans in bad times. Farmers in fact keep taking loans until a bad year arrives when there is a crop failure.

The livestock farmers are not that fortunate for no Indian government has yet waivered their loans. The rationale behind this as per the farmers is that unlike crop milk production can be low but not fail totally. There is no scheme under which the livestock itself can be taken as collateral for loan. It's partly because animals are not insured due to lack of insurance plans. The helpless farmers left with no option go to private parties for loans. These middlemen exploit the situation by charging exorbitant interest rates up to 60% per annum. The more likely scenario of farmers not being able to pay back the amount lead to dispossession of their livestock which further aggravates the situation.

The root of the problem lies in counting livestock loans under agricultural loans. Banks meet their obligation of disbursing agricultural loans and livestock segment may still remain loan deficient. There is no separate division to cater to livestock farming loan disbursement.

Maintenance of livestock was not cheap and untimely death further dampens the financial status of the households since most of there is hardly any insurance coverage. Milk producing households lose a considerable chunk of their income with demise of their livestock. The problem lies in absence of insurance schemes for the livestock farmers. Insurance cover is either not available on the livestock or the premium demanded is too high.

One of the many possible explanations to this scenario in the livestock insurance segment lies in the farmers' awareness of insurance plans. A study on the villages showed 83% households are not even aware of livestock insurance while the number for crop insurance is just 49%. Other findings from the study included the lack of understanding of the judicial terms used in the documentation which was faced by 91% of the households. The unavailability of insurance caused a chain reaction from lower size of the herd to loss in finances ultimately leading to weak household financial position.

## Lack of Awareness of Medical Needs of Cattle

It is very well known that dispensing timely, affordable and of course best healthcare facilities is one of the major drivers needed for the upliftment of the sector. This would result not only in production of clean milk but also prove to be economically less burdensome on the farmers in the long run. But still Badalpur and Sakipur lack a major portion of healthcare measures that need to be implemented for prosperity of the livestock farming sector.

In Badalpur and Sakipur there is no provision for regular vaccinations which is imperative to stymie the outbreak of any major diseases which can prove to be a setback in the future. *Table 2: Procurement and maintenance charges in Rupees.*There is total lack of communication between the labs setup at the district level for disease investigation and the veterinary doctors posted on government rolls. There is no setup at the village level which would ensure sale purchase of healthy disease free cattle and prevent farmers from being cheated by unfair trade practices.

In addition to the above there are very few qualified veterinary doctors to cater to the needs of the livestock in the region thus resulting in lack of timely and efficient medical facilities both at the time of emergency and for regular checkups as well. Less milk, bad health, economic burden on families, are some of the immediate consequences of having not enough medical facilities.

Health camps are a means to spread awareness about the medical needs of cattle and ensure their good health by conducting proper and regular checkups. The villagers have no clue of when was the last time a national, or state, or district level campaign was organized in their village. The villagers who already lack the right know how of managing the medical needs of their cattle keep on postponing the health check-ups till the time there is an acute emergency. And this they do it in order to save funds. Such practises negatively impact the cattle health which either leads to less production of milk or sometimes in the untimely death in the worst case scenario.

## Switch Over to Other Professions

The villagers involved in this business have been found switching to other professions. Those who have not yet regret their decision. After doing all the hard work of managing their livestock, owners hardly break even and most of them who do make a meagre 2000- 3000 INR per month. *Table 2: Procurement and maintenance charges in Rupees.* The numbers shared by the village 'Panchayat' reveal the number of households involved in livestock farming to have dwindled down to 50% of what it was 2 years ago. *Table 1: Approximate number of people involved in milk production.*

Bir Singh, a resident of Badalpur, had 2 cows and 1 buffalo. His livestock on an average produce 30 kg of milk daily. His sales proceeds from selling price which is 35INR and 42INR per litre for cow and buffalo's milk respectively was merely enough to cover his operating expenses and interest on debt combined. And when the labour put up by Bir Singh and his elder son is taken into picture the meagre savings would turn into red. His son tells that his family were having troubled times affording 3 meals a day. Bir Singh now works in Delhi as a contract labourer and sold his livestock to the village Sarpanch. He earns 350INR in daily wages which his son believes is not possible to earn in the milk business. Of course he does consider the living expenses in the metropolitan city.

Some other households which are no longer into the milk business find this work demeaning as it involves working in an unhygienic environment. Adding to that they do not get rewarded for their efforts and physical labour put in. Thus they preferred jobs in cities where they are able to earn considerably more than their previous jobs. Moreover working in the cities give these villagers a sense of pride and self-esteem which kind of reinforces their decision to move to the city in search of a job.

The villagers who own land in the village and use it for livestock farming are becoming part of the land acquisition drive carried out by the State Government of Uttar Pradesh. The government has been acquiring a lot of land lately to carry out development projects which have led to surge in land prices. Prices have increased by almost 10 times. The steep rise in land prices has caused villagers to look at the commercial value of the land and they are either leasing it to private players for hefty sums or carrying out construction activities to realize more value on selling the developed land. This directly hampers the milk business. Livestock farming requires good measure of open area which is now being given out for construction purpose. This has a negative effect on the livestock and the milk produced.

## Unavailability of Genuine Cattle Feed

Healthy and nutritious feed for the cattle ensures higher yield of milk and a healthy life as well. This lessens the economic burden on the family by enhancing the efficiency of operations. Notwithstanding there are very few sources of good quality cattle feed and fodder in either of the villages and the nearby region. There are even fewer production facilities and distribution units of seeds of good quality. Villagers generally take their cattle for grazing in the open fields and do not use the fodder which is prescribed by experts. Figure 2. Traditional process

A lot of factors are responsible for the unavailability of good quality fodder. Storage of fodder after its harvest is a critical activity to maintain its nutritional value in fact to enhance it. There is hardly any promotion of technologies to do so. Thus the fodder which is served is mostly nutrient deficient. Also it is found that farmers tend to serve damp fodder to their cattle in rainy days due to lack of storage space in their premises. *Table 3: Prescribed diet chart and price break-up.* Lack of funds with the milk producers due to their weak finances is one big concern in this respect. This forces them to either serve poor quality feed or not serve at all. Selling adulterated fodder to the farmers is also prevalent in the local market. All these factors combined result in poor livestock health, reduced milk production and aggravates financial burden on the rural families.

## Poor Market Access and Low Value Appreciation

Realization of an appropriate price and adding value to the produce are two very important parameters for the development of livestock sector to take place. Milk which is perishable in nature needs facilities near the villages for collection in time. Studies reveal that less than 35% of the milk is distributed via organized channels and which makes it all the more important to organize the operations of the rural livestock owners.

In the current scenario farmers are unable to fetch a decent deal for their milk either due to their lack of awareness or use of power and influence by the middlemen. Absence of any dairy co-operative has made the situation even tougher since the farmers have to themselves travel long distances to sell their produce.

Adding value to the product has now become a continuous practice in every business around the world to keep selling. But this is found to be lacking in the milk business of Badalpur and Sakipur. Milk quality assessment facility which should be a prerequisite to judge the best price is not setup in any of the two villages. Farmers have hardly any knowledge of the methods to maintain a low count of bacteria and produce clean milk. Milk products which offer a lucrative business opportunity form a meager part of the sales proceeds probably due to lack of storage facilities.

## Decision Time

Mr. Nagesh and his team were in the process of designing a full-proof business plan to set up the rural dairy model. They had made good progress but the scale of the project was so large that they were running out of time and resources. They had very less time in their hands to finalize their work and deliver a complete report to the senior management. Only time would tell whether Nagesh was correct or not in anticipating the huge potential of this business model and the dairy sector. You being a consultant need to work upon the viability of the project and come up with your own findings.

*Table 1. Approximate number of people involved in milk production*

| | Badalpur | Sakipur |
|---|---|---|
| Number of Families | 600 | 400 |
| Average number of Member involved per family | 3 | 4 |
| Average Number of cattle per family | 4 | 5 |

Source: Field data collected from study villages

*Table 2. Procurement and maintenance charges in Rupees*

| | Cow | Buffalo |
|---|---|---|
| Purchasing Cost | 40,000 -- 50,000 | 45,000 -- 70,000 |
| Selling Price of Milk per litre (open market) | 35 | 42 |
| Selling Price of Milk per litre (Co-operative society) | 26 - 28 | 28 - 30 |
| Medical Expenses per month | 1500 | 2000 |
| Fodder Cost per day | 145 | 200 |

Source: Field data collected from study villages

*Table 3. Prescribed diet chart and price break-up*

| Types of fodder | Cow | Buffalo |
|---|---|---|
| "Bhusa" Consumption per day (in Kg) | 6-7 | 9 - 10 |
| "Bhusa" Price break up (per Kg) | Rs.5 | Rs.5 |
| "Hara-chara" Consumption per day (in Kg) | 20 | 30 |
| "Hara-chara" price | Re 1 / kg | Re 1 /kg |
| Khal + chokar + chana + churi +chilka (in Kg) | 4-6 | 7-8 |
| Khal + chokar + chana + churi +chilka price | Rs 15/ kg | Rs 15 /kg |

Source: Field data collected from study villages

*Table 4. Essential details about Livestock*

| | Cow | Buffalo |
|---|---|---|
| Milk Production per day (in litres) | (8 - 14) | (12 - 20) |
| Age at which production starts | 3 years | 4 years |
| Life span | 22 years | 24 years |

Source: Field Data collected from Study villages

*Table 5. Manure / 10 animal unit*

| Input | Substrate Mass [kg/a] | Dry Substance [%] | Biogas Output [m2/t] | Methane Concentration [%] | Output of BHKW [kW/a] |
|---|---|---|---|---|---|
| **Cow manure** | 96 | 10 | 5267.4 | 55 | 1.13 |
| **Pig manure** | 171.36 | 7.5 | 8589 | 58 | 1.94 |
| **Poultry manure** | 161 | 27 | | 58 | 5.08 |

Source: Biogas Polygeneration for Romania. (n.d.). What outputs does a biogas plant have?. Retrieved September 01, 2014, from http://www.probiopol.de/12_What_outputs_does_a_biogas.50.0.html

*Table 6. Energy crops per ha*

| Input | Substrate Mass [kg/a] | Dry Substance [%] | Biogas Output [m2/t] | Methane Concentration [%] | Output of BHKW [kW/a] |
|---|---|---|---|---|---|
| **Beets** | 58.4-80 | 12-23 | 5300-10664.6 | 53 | 0.87-1.99 |
| **Beet leafs** | 23.1-45 | 11-18 | 2930-4704 | 56 | 0.23-0.63 |
| **Maize** | 500-700 | 30-36.5 | 11594 | 53 | 2.2-3.9 |
| **Gras** | 8-9 | 20-40 | 900-1900 | 56 | 0.042-0.2 |
| **Hay** | 4.5 | 90 | 2000 | 55 | 0.38-0.45 |
| **Sunflower** | 15.9 | 34.8 | | | 0.44 |
| **Millet** | 12.7 | 25 | | | 0.4 |
| **Straw** | 6-7 | 89-91 | 2000-2700 | 52 | 0.5 |

Source: Biogas Polygeneration for Romania. (n.d.). What outputs does a biogas plant have?. Retrieved September 01, 2014, from http://www.probiopol.de/12_What_outputs_does_a_biogas.50.0.html

*Table 7. Income and Expense*

| | |
|---|---|
| Number of families involved in business | 1000 |
| Livestock per family | 4 |
| Milk per livestock per day - kg | 12 |
| Total milk production- kg | 48000 |
| | |
| **Annual expenses (Rs)** | |
| Food cost per livestock per day | 200 |
| Total food cost per year | 292000000 |
| Medical cost per livestock per month | 500 |
| Total medical cost per year | 24000000 |
| Financial cost per livestock per month (bank interest 1.5% over Rs 100000) | 1500 |
| Total financial cost per year | 72000000 |
| Insurance premium per livestock per month | 500 |
| Total insurance premium per year | 24000000 |
| Total annual expenses | 412000000 |
| | |
| **Annual income (Rs)** | |
| Selling price of milk per kg | 38 |
| Milk Sale receipts | 665760000 |
| Dung price per kg | 0.5 |
| Dung sale receipts | 8760000 |
| Total annual earnings | 674520000 |

Source: Financial workings on field data collected from study villages

## Solution

The financial modelling of the proposed business as given below in the table gives an insight of the costs involved and expected earnings from the same. *Table 7: Income and Expense.*

The expenses include the food, medical, interest, and insurance costs which need to be incurred by the households in livestock management. The earnings constitute the proceeds from sale of milk plus the dung produced. The difference of the two provides a rough estimate of expected annual profits.

## CONCLUSION

The case sheds light on the fading traditional rural businesses like the dairy business. Slowly and gradually people have been either migrating to cities in search of employment or shifting all together with their families. The case discusses the challenges faced by the villagers in the milk business and aims to do a feasibility check of setting a sustainable milk collection and distribution system from the rural households and by the rural households to the nearby cities.

## REFERENCES

Ghosh, N. (2012, June). Biogas Production and Power Generation Simulation: Research & Training in Perspective. *E Newsletter of Biogas Forum – India*, 3. Retrieved August 15, 2014, from http://web.iitd.ac.in/~vkvijay/June%202012_Enewsletter.pdf

Mondal, P. (n.d.). *Sanitary Production of Milk and Method of Milking*. Dairy Farm Management. Retrieved August 1, 2014, from http://www.yourarticlelibrary.com/dairy-farm-management/sanitary-production-of-milk-and-method-of-milking-2/36374/

National Institute of Rural Development (NIRD). (n.d.). *A study on improvement in rural livelihoods through dairy farming*. Retrieved August 20, 2014, from http://www.nird.org.in/nird_docs/ven_finrepo.pdf

Rajamony, S., Premalatha, S., & Pillai, P. K. (2005, September). Azolla a sustainable feed for livestock. *Leisa, 21*(3). Retrieved August 10, 2014, from http://www.agriculturesnetwork.org/magazines/global/small-animals-in-focus/azolla-livestock-feed

Yadav, A., Gupta, R., & Garg, V. K. (2013, October). Organic manure production from cow dung and biogas plant slurry by vermicomposting under field conditions. *International Journal of Recycling of Organic Waste in Agriculture*. Retrieved August 10, 2014, from http://www.ijrowa.com/content/2/1/21

## KEY TERMS AND DEFINITIONS

**Azolla:** An economical and sustainable green source of livestock feed.

**Bhusa:** A Hindi word meaning chaff, separated from grain, used to feed cows and buffaloes.

**Co-operative Society:** A group of people who cooperate, for their mutual benefit, in running an enterprise engaging in supply of goods or services.

**Land Acquisition:** It is taking over possession of land for public use by a government institution from individual landowners, after paying compensation fixed as per law.

**NABARD:** A development bank in India, which stands for "National Bank for Agriculture and Rural Development", focussed on rural upliftment by increasing credit flow to agricultural sector.

**Socio-Economic Development:** Process of identification of social and economic necessities within a community and their upliftment thereafter.

**Sudhaar:** A Hindi word meaning an act of improvement from the existing state.

# Chapter 15
# Mapping the Rural Retail of India

**Aditya Vashisth**
*Institute of Management Technology Ghaziabad, India*

**Parul Gupta**
*Institute of Management Technology Ghaziabad, India*

**Aparajita**
*Institute of Management Technology Ghaziabad, India*

**Pravin Patil**
*Institute of Management Technology Ghaziabad, India*

**Rohit Agarwal**
*Institute of Management Technology Ghaziabad, India*

## ABSTRACT

*The case here tries to sensitise its readers towards what is one of the largest privatized and yet highly unorganised retail store formats in the world. The case in question talks about how the backward integration and adoption of set standards by the small time retailers can in turn benefit the end consumer tangibly as well as intangibly. Our research, first entailed, outlining the methodology and the singling out the markets of Greater Ghaziabad catchment areas in Uttar Pradesh for our research. The study is diversified according to various parameters like the age of business, & the customers these businesses are targeting. All in all the chapter tries to communicate to its readers, the importance of understanding the dynamics of doing business in rural retail sector of India, whether relatively organised or unorganised.*

## INTRODUCTION

The centre of attraction of the world economy is continuously shifting from the developed economies of Europe & US to the developing economies of Asia Pacific. Among these developing economies, India is one of the fastest growing economies. Over the last 15 years, India has grown much more rapidly than that predicted. Structural changes and competition in the market has raised the bar in terms of consumer expectation. Retail happens to be the largest private sector industry in India. Retailing includes all the activities involved in selling goods and services directly to the final Consumers for personal, non-business use (Kotler, Keller, Brady & Goodman, 2009).

DOI: 10.4018/978-1-4666-8259-7.ch015

One of the major changes affecting retail is the changing consumer behaviour. The outlook of consumer is rapidly shifting from traditional to modernize traditional. Earlier the focus of consumer was to meet their functional requirements but for the past few decades there has been a shift of consumer behaviour towards lifestyle oriented approach. Due to the increased income and higher employment in the India, the buying capacity and demand for diverse and innovative products has increased manifold. This has further shifted the limelight towards retail.

## Need for Rural Retail

Rural market of India offers ample opportunity for the retail sector as rural India accounts for 55% of the private retail consumption. Rural retail market presents a tremendous growth opportunity which needs to be tapped with care. The IMD report 1998 of National Council of Applied Economic Research suggest that there are 742 million consumers across 638,000 villages. These villages account for more than half of the total wealth (Bansal, Maan & Rajora, 2013). Thus by reaching out to these villages total opportunity can be tapped in the rural retail sector. As urban markets are on the verge of saturation rural retail market is the next target of big retail companies. Now B.O.P. markets are looking very lucrative to companies who want to explore new turf.

Since rural retail forms the pillars of Indian economy so it becomes very important to understand them better. This segment is still unexplored and is considered to be a virgin market. Retailing is a part time job in rural India and has low maintenance cost. Penetration in rural India is low as there are high transportation and travelling costs involved. Penetration of big retail companies has happened only through intermediaries and most of the rural retail in handled by local mom and pop stores only.

# CREATING EFFICENT ECOSYSTEMS

The idea of creating sustainable ecosystems stems from the facts of big businesses creating deep impact whether it is Hindustan Unilever's Shakti Amma programme or the ITC-e-Choupal Sanchalak programme, both identify with the idea of developing business and taking social development in the catchment areas as a necessary step. These programs are part of integration strategy of large corporations to develop markets following an inclusive approach. To make these ideas work, there is a need to identify the opportunity within the constraints of the B.O.P. The key questions which can be raised are: How does innovation play at the B.O.P. level and how the services and products need to be reinvented keeping the four A's at B.O.P. level: Awareness, Access, Affordability and Availability? How much can our solutions be scaled to include small scale mom and pop stores to be a part of changing culture to buy groceries in a much better, organized and informed manner? What is price performance code which our catchment area stores can sustain in long run? How can modern technology be of help in undertaking dramatic cost and business reduction exercises?

## NATURE OF RURAL RETAIL

Rural retail or let's take the superset the Bottom of Pyramid exhibits characteristics that are different to the rest of the middle class market or more varied than the typical hypermarkets of the urban centres of India. Saying this shall not in any way mean that these characteristics cannot be mapped from the perspective of prospective mom and pop store owner.

Let's break the first myth, the dominant assumption that people at B.O.P. have neither the purchasing power nor do they represent a viable market is a direct assumption why most of retailers have not entered the market altogether. The idea is to unlock the latent potential which present due the vast penalty the poor pay due to product being available only for the middle or upper segments. The value paid is in multiples of the value the rich pay, which shall basically motivate the mom and pop retailers to form a cohort and make themselves available to microfinance organizations which can fund their expansion or rejuvenation plans.

Coming to myth number two, poverty does not spring brand desires, well myth is partially correct as to luxury brands do stand irrelevant to masses but the aspirational element behind these brands is key. The desire to grow and aspire for a progressive quality of life harbours this frame of mind of consumers. The way to grow for our retailers in the catchment market might be harnessing this potential desire. The supressed margins from regular usage products will mean that consumers demanding for better products and in the end getting up scaled to the aspirational brands. Our retailers need to keep this view point in mind whilst planning ahead for their stores.

The third myth is regarding the information network seeping down to B.O.P. market and how well the technology is being used by the market. Well it was believed that the technology and poverty two different ends, but soon with the meteoric rise of mobile telephony and the interconnected social structure as a result, we see technology as a solution to alleviating whole countries from poverty. The technological scope is today reaching far beyond what we as a country set out to achieve. Close to a billion mobile phone connections and World's fastest growing internet economy, we are taking the services to masses. Hence, in all probabilities, the idea to achieve sales from B.O.P. market via harnessing these information networks is right and feasible to all extents. The arguments in the other direction are valid but these have to be seen from the perspective of political class of India not being receptive to technology. Close to end of the 20th century, the politicians have started to see India as a major player in technology sector and now the next generation is eager towards policy implementation of information networks and making the same available to common audience at low to very low prices.

The fourth and final assumption which has to be foregone before we delve into specifics is that B.O.P. markets are inaccessible. Again, the assumption is challenged by the third myth broken, the rural markets in totality have been 'Media Dark' which has made access to these markets problematic at the very least. But with the mobile telephones reaching the masses and connecting each and every corner of the country, the accessibility issues tend to exist but to a lesser extent.

The point to be analysed here is that not a single distribution network but a multi-pronged strategy is used by giants to tame the B.O.P. market. If the giants are using a multiple point approach, the same applies to the mom and pop store owners to reach their end customer. Simply, catching eyeballs from the shop is not the solution to low sales, reaching out to consumers by making services available as a cohort might be the way forward, and certainly the mom and pop store owners will need to partner with for example: FMCG giants to create more distribution points for products and services alike.

## OBJECTIVE

The prime motive behind our study is to analyse the business as well as accounting practices prevalent in the rural India. The major business practices taken into consideration for this include supply chain management, inventory management and accounting and billing practices.

The major motivation is to showcase the efficient/inefficient systems which are hindering the next level of retail growth in India's hinterland. For rural markets, Reach is the key, and the study shall help us in order to identify factors driving financial health of the rural Mom and Pop stores and how these factors affect the financial health of retail shops in rural India.

This is followed by a detailed analysis of the study and finally provides recommendations and suggestions. In future, we plan to assist the rural retailers in implementing some of our recommendations and study the outcomes so obtained.

## METHODOLOGY

The overall methodology used in the project can be broadly classified into two phases. These include the planning phase and the execution phase.

The Planning phase can be demarked with the following pointers:

- **Target Geography:** The first task was to collect data of 30 rural mom and pop shops from different geographies. We chose 3 villages from Ghaziabad, U.P. area for the survey.
- **Research objectives:** To identify the supply chain management; inventory management and accounting and billing practices prevalent in Mom and Pop stores in rural India and to study their effect on the financial health and profitability of such stores.
- **Secondary data research:** This includes a broad study of the rural markets by studying the Mom and Pop stores in Rural India. The main sources of information for this include Census of India and NCAER.
- **Primary Data Collection:** This includes the collection of preliminary on-site data, which is done through the following methods:
    - **Sampling:**
        - **Village Sampling:** Process included selection of the villages from which data has to be collected. The villages were selected in such a way that they provided an appropriate level of diversity as far as demographics, psychological and other factors are concerned.
        - **Respondent Sampling (Rural Retailers):** From the selected villages, we identified the particular mom and pop stores from where data has to be collected. For this purpose, we identified three types of stores big, small and medium scale stores based on the criteria of per day sales.
        - **Sample size determination:** We identified a sample size of 30 for our research project i.e. data from thirty stores across three villages are being collected.
    - **Data Collection Method:** Process included the actual collection of data from the targeted geographies. We planned to collect data through the following methodology:
        - **Interviews:** By interviewing the shop owners and customers on one-to-one basis.

- **Focused GD's:** By carrying out group discussions at the Nukkads, Tea stalls and other joints where people gather, in order to know the general opinion of people.
- **Questionnaire:** Targeted Questionnaire aiming to study the particular identified parameters that we plan to study namely supply chain management, inventory management and accounting and billing.

Execution Phase includes the following stages:

- **Categorize retail shops:** Segregated on the basis of size, sales volume and number of years in business.
- **Survey:** Focusing business practices(supply chain management, inventory management and accounting and billing) and financial health (profitability of the shop)
    - Identify the goals and aspirations of shop owners
    - Study their attitude towards customer and suppliers
    - Cause- Effect analysis of financial health
    - Identify factors that are drivers of financial health
    - Suggestions
    - Monitor the implementation of suggestions.

## Data Analysis

The survey of 3 Ghaziabad villages included a list of 30 small retailers. The data collected was comprehensive with the questions ranging from whether the store is their only source of income to whether the retail stores owners had any basic education or not.

## Insights: The Shift towards Retailing in Rural India

The data analysis thus reports that 46s.67% of the shop owners have put up their shops in last 2 years which shows a significant increase in number of new businesses being owned by population. Further, when we drilled this fact qualitatively, close to 20% of the shop owners actually switched from a manufacturing based business to a retail store as a faith reposed in the strength of USD 470 Billion Indian retail sector. Out of this 46.67% of new shop owners, 64.28% of population has this store as their only source of income and all the new shop owners are the ones to work in their stores as a primary resource.

Out of total survey population, only 20% of the stores were found to be in the bracket of 2-5 year old with the same number of stores in 5-10 year old business bracket and 13.33% of the survey population did actually have a business of more than 10+ year old. Out of those with 2-5 year old, 95% of the stores are now managed by family members as well. But, out of the 10 + year old bracket, 75% of the stores now also involve labourers generating employment for the area.

The major point of importance over here was how to diversify the sources of income to the retailers as the businesses get old the sources of income do increase and the retail stores do stop getting the lesser amount of precedence in terms of business importance. The marked trend with these questions suggest that villages in Ghaziabad area have very short lifecycles and as the businesses get hold they tend to lose customers to new competitors. Also, the strong emergence of new businesses suggests a surge in growth of discretionary income of village population in Ghaziabad.

## The Financial Accounting Practices

Coming to the financial accounting practices of the rural retail stores, 36.67% of the businesses do actually maintain record for business transaction and 50% of the survey population does keep records of goods purchased, and most importantly 66.67% of the transaction made with suppliers are documented as these transaction are bulk in nature as suggested by business owners. Also 50% of the population has credit sales accounted for which increases the risk of payments given the small scaled nature of business and the daily capital requirements of these businesses being volatile.

## Sourcing for Rural Retailers

About one-third of the store owners' contact with the suppliers only by phone, which decreases their chances of maintaining healthy relation with suppliers and also decreases chances to a part of any future schemes. Unanimously, the kinds of suppliers to buy from are completely local. Out of 3, every 2 store owners are in the habit of stock keeping and 50% of the survey population is in the habit of buying goods only when they about to go out of stock. The very basic nature of the retail business is forecasting customer demands. With no astonishment only 36.67% of the owners are keeping a documented track of the product requirement of specific customers. This practice is still found in old businesses but the new store owners do not maintain a record of customer requirements which suggest a lack of connection between customers and new business owners in the village areas of Ghaziabad. As we drilled further into his practice, we found a high disconnect in terms of offering of products as only 46.67% of the store owners were changing products stocked according to customer requirements.

Now, here the first stakeholder at play is the wholesaler who supposedly takes up the sourcing orders from the retailers. As the store owners (66.67%) are in habit of stock- keeping, the turnover time for the wide variety of goods is large, which does not take into account the larger benefits with respect to pricing sensitivity to the retailers. The retailers are not able to pass on the price fluctuation from the market to the consumer as a benefit and in the long run suffer from the loss in increased sales. The major point over here as the Indian cash and carry markets develop is whether to maintain or not maintain the stock keeping which also increases the costs by close to 5% and also forms a part of leakage in sales to the tune of 12.5%. With the decrease in stock- keeping, the retailers can further reduce the turnover time of products, bring in the fresh products from the markets, and in turn reduce costs substantially. If retailers use the wholesalers as stakeholders to their advantage and carry the costs backwards in the chain, things can turnaround on the cost front.

## The Products Sold at the Rural Retail and Customers Who Buy Them

In consumption section, mapping the rural customer, we found demand ranging from 65% to 80% of customers across categories such as Household, personal care, packed food items, loose items, beverages, groceries, and some store owners were bundling the products even with stationery. On an average day, the daily footfall at the stores is approximately to 43.33% for the bracket of 0-50 customers. 30% of the surveyed population, records 50-100 customers daily, and 16.67% records 150-300 customers daily.

Here, again the sources play the key, the long term idea of any retailer shall be to source as much from the producer/plant as possible i.e. move backwards in the value chain. The ITC e-choupal and H.U.L.'s shakti amma program can go the distance (considering the cash pool these multinationals are piling on) in solving the problem of going to retailers directly cutting the intermediaries in process. The idea from ITC and H.U.L. viewpoint is to increase revenues and from small retailers viewpoint to cut costs and pass on benefits to consumer. This level of backward integration can solve two major concerns of rural markets:

1. Price Frugality
2. Price sensitivity

From the product point, big time F.M.C.G. players have introduced frugal innovation at various points to stimulate the rural market. The discretionary spending increase seen during recent years and the brick & mortar channels in place for these firms, time is ripe to deliver on the integrated markets goal and trickle down chain benefit to customers.

### Record Keeping: Challenges and the Way Out

Over 50% of the store owners are in the habit to buy on bill and about the same number of sales are on bill which is pretty low considering the advantages of book keeping are not transforming into real numbers. The optimism over return on investment is high, 2 out of every 3 respondents do recognize the fact that returns on investment is high and they are banking on the future to turn the table around even in a gloomy economy.

Now, coming to transaction record keeping, new businesses ranging from 0-2 years old and 2-5 years old are in a habit of daily record keeping whereas this business practice is adopted on weekly basis in 5-10 year old businesses. However, the time scale zooms to monthly record keeping for 10+ year old businesses.

Coming to net income levels, 50% of the respondents concluded with a 0- 5000 bracket and the other big bracket are 5000-10000 for net income on a monthly basis. The margins, however, are highly suppressed for the majority with 0-5% and 5-10% holding margin levels. The frequencies of supply updates are very low due to their non-existent relations and networking capabilities. The previous year and current financial year performance record keeping is low with percentage of 16.67 only able to keep a sufficient data in terms of financial. In terms of education of store owners, 36.67% of the owners are under qualified to run a business with less than 10$^{th}$ class education background. The lack of primary education and training seems to be taking a toll on business performance as notified by the survey. With this, the new shop owners in the bracket of 0 to 5 years old businesses would like to be provided with some basic primary training regarding best practices to be adopted and further improve their overall business efficiency.

## PROPOSED MODEL FOR BEST PRACTICES IMPLEMENTATION

### What Are the Best Practices These Mom and Pop Stores Should Follow?

Post the data analysis stage, we would now like to propose some key models to be adopted for the desirable profits and to create sustainable business environment via the route of best business practices. Along the lines of 2003 study by Pirog and Benjamin, we would like to propose a weighted average source distance (WASD) which shall cover the key product mileage of the offerings of mom and pop stores.

Products travelled in different routes log different mileages. The mileage has been expressed in kilometres; "minimum" mileage is the shortest distance travelled by a product and "market" mileage is the average mileage of the same product. The minimum mileage distance is contributed by very small quantity, which is less than 0.7% of the daily transactional volume. The product mileage values are for customer's destination at Ghaziabad.

Key Product Mileage (KPA) or Weighted Average source of distance for any product P can be defined as:

$$K.P.A. = \frac{\sum \text{(Volume of product)} \times \text{(Distance travelled by the product)}}{\sum \text{(Volume of product)}}$$

Currently, only organized retailers such as Reliance Fresh (Reliance Retail Ltd) follows a Value Chain business model (VCM). Organized retailers who adopt VCM procure the produces directly from farmers and sell to customers by avoiding intermediaries. This model is based on its core growth strategy of backward integration and progressing towards building an entire value chain starting from the back. The backward integration allows better forecasting of the customer demand and allows for business to be dynamic according to demand.

In value chain model for mom and pop stores we shall calibrate the performance according to business performance as required across 4 categories of store owners.

Some of the larger businesses require establishment of consolidation centres where they can devise there stock in accordance with the customer demand. The basic problem with the value chain model in small businesses is the over leveraging of processes which we shall tweak by making the practices more dynamic according to consumption and geographical demands.

The cluster formation shall allow us to innovate more in terms of overall product penetration thereby increasing revenues for the mom and pop stores. The suppressed margins game can only be covered by volumes as rural market is price conscious and scale is achievable only via certain advancements in products are made available to end consumers. Hence, another point in value chain model to be taken care of is the supplier-owner engagement. This type of engagement model tends with good consolidation centres catering to customer demand help in building everlasting relationships and a sustainable business environment which is our basic aim of study. The end point to be taken care of is financial reporting and accounting. As an emergency measure, providing short term help in accounting is necessary in plugging leakages in money cycle. But on a longer term, primary training of accounting practices is necessary to achieve scale as funds and debt do increase the tendency to grow which is lacking in the aspirations of store owners. A robust financial practices model shall help them in leveraging their business to right amount in coming future.

## THE BEST PRACTICES FOLLOWED BY THE THREE DIFFERENT MOM AND POP STORES I.E. ESTABLISHED, SMALL SCALE AND STARTER MOM AND POP STORES

The model that has been discussed above cannot be implemented by all the three kinds of stores and only the established stores are in a position to implement this. Hence we propose that these stores apply the model. Further the three important parameters that are the basis of our study i.e. Inventory management, Account management and Supply chain management are the parameters which the established stores are in position to improve. For e.g. these stores can maintain the supply chain by keeping in constant touch with the suppliers who will be happy to supply to these stores as the turnover is large. Also since the turnover is large they should maintain the inventory level and keep records of it to further smoothen the business. And as the supply chain and inventory is being managed it is important that accounts be maintained by these retailers. So we propose that the 5 established stores we studied should follow all these three practices.

### Small Scale

For small scale Mom and pop stores we propose that since the level of customers is not that much and the turnover is not that high as compared to the established stores managing a healthy supply chain is not possible and even not required. Although if these stores follow them it is going to be beneficial but before they follow the best practices for managing the supply chain it is essential for them to focus on the improvement and implementation of best practices for managing their accounts and keeping record of their inventory. Hence we propose that all the 20 small scale Mom and pop stores that we studied should follow the best practices for Accounts management and Inventory management.

### Start-Ups

For a start-up Mom and pop stores we suggest that they do not need to implement Supply chain management or inventory management as the level of business is not that high and the turnover is not that much. Hence the initial thing that these stores can do is that follow the practices for managing Accounts so that at least they will be in a position to know that what the income is or are they running in loses or they have started earning profit. They can get to know the breakeven point for their business. Once the stores grow then they can further follow other best practices and hence all the 5 stores that we studied should manage their Accounts.

## RECOMMENDATIONS

Considering the extensive data analysis of the surveyed data and the proposed business improvement model, various solutions were identified and evaluated. The solutions which are of critical importance for the rural Mom and pop shop owners have been recommended. Thus, following recommendations are of immense importance for the Mom and pop shop owners to make their business more profitable and make it sustainable over long term.

### Recommendations Based on the Age of the Mom and Pop Store

- Majority (i.e. 64.28%) of the owners with ownership between 0-2 years which are more dependent on the shop as source of income should follow the improvement strategies or could adopt the business improvement model to make the business more profitable and sustainable in the long term. Practices adopted like basic accounting books and using low cost mobile technology for repletion of supplies to store can go a long way in modernising the customer experience. Once the data is available for the next 3 years, harness the same to develop a strategy by sitting down with wholesalers and intermediaries to trade-up the consumption pattern in the long run.

- Majority of the owners with ownership of greater than 10 years and are less-dependent on the shop as source of income as they have peaked or diversified into other businesses, should adopt the business improvement model mentioned in the analysis to improve on present efficiency. The data availability with this category is huge and serves as an indicator to multinationals about the growing demand from rural India. However, with the indicated model, the system can integrate the various synergies like trust of long time consumers to trade-up the consumer in a 6 month to 2 year period.
- The owners with ownership between 10+ years should opt for volume based strategy with fewer margins and act as a supplier to new entrants to be more profitable, acquire larger market share and also generate close distance option for new shops.
- The owners should be discouraged from employing children below 18 years as labour by educating the owners of Governments legal initiatives about child labour laws.

## Recommendations for Accounts and Billing System

- Shop owners across categories should be encouraged to keep accurate and clear records of purchase from suppliers as it's of critical importance for them to decide upon competitive pricing strategy of goods and not just passively taking prices from big players.
- To improve book keeping the shop owners should try to make sales to customers with billing.
- Shop owners across categories especially new shop owners should try to refrain from selling on credit as it has been identified as a major component leading to not only losses but also bitter relations with customers.

## Recommendations for Inventory Management

- The owners, with ownership between 0-2 years which always lag to fulfil seasonal demands, should think of early stock option to avoid buying at higher prices during high seasonal demand for product with higher price variation. The whole planning in short run should be such to display as much as possible to consumer and use the wholesaler logistics for daily stocking of products to estimate turnover of S.K.U's.
- The shop owners, with ownership 0-2 yrs., 2-5 yrs. should consider an option of buying in bulk together to purchase goods at fewer costs and compete with big retail shops. But in the long run, the best practice shall be to sustain the warehousing requirements for perishable products from the cash & carry stores which shall sprout up as the sector opens to Retail giants like Walmart. The buying in bulk option is only sustainable for products with sustainable demand, but across categories innovation renders products incapable of sustaining long run into the markets. Hence, taking the storage backwards is the best possible solution to deal with rising costs.

## Recommendations for Social Factors

- The uneducated or less educated shop owners should be educated about efficient business practices and the business improvement model proposed.

## CONCLUSION

Rural mom and pop stores have indicated their approach towards their business to be ad-hoc and their proclivity to develop network within their work environment as non-existent. However, with a tightened local economy and larger number of new players entering the market and with bigger corporate houses also taking rural retail as next big revenue maker, the pressure is undoubtedly on the local mom and pop stores to institutionalize their business practices and shaping the business in a more organized way even if it starter in the market.

The big idea by which rural retailers can actually improve their presence in the market is by playing a pivotal role in the social life of a village and find out a way to become part of the local social environment. The internal practices as suggested include all aspects via backward integration which include financial accounting, supply chain modelling for established players, financial health reporting and analysis using different parameters. Institutionalizing this idea and leveraging the robust internal business practices as proposed in the model for established, small scale and starter category stores, retailers can assure a sustainable business environment and can play a huge role in improving rural economy.

## REFERENCES

Bansal, P., Maan, V. K., & Rajora, M. (2013). Article. *International Journal for Advanced Research in Computer Science and Software Engineering*, *3*(11).

Kotler, P., Keller, K. L., Brady, M., & Goodman, M. (2009). *Marketing Management* (2nd ed.). New York: Pearson Education.

## ADDITIONAL READING

Gupta, K. L. (2011). In proceedings of RIED conference retailing in India: Emerging dimensions to explore rural potential. RIED Conference.

Kashyap, P., & Raut, S. (2010). *The Rural Marketing Book*. New Delhi: Biztantra.

Koli, Amita & Jadhav, Amrita (n.d.).Retailing-the rising sector in Rural India. Journal of Research in Commerce and Management, 1(2).

Modi, A. (2013, August 4). Lost in the Outback: Cracking the rural market has turned out to be a tough task for organised retail chains. Business today. Retrieved from http://businesstoday.intoday.in/story/cracking-the-rural-market-organised-retail-chains/1/196804.html

Srinivas Rao, P. (2013).Innovation and Creativity in Rural Retail Marketing. Global Journal for Research Analysis, 2(3).

Wanmali, S. (1981). *Periodic Markets and Rural Development in India*. New Delhi: B R Publishing Corporation.

## KEY TERMS AND DEFINITIONS

**Bottom of Pyramid (B.O.P.):** Bottom of the Pyramid (BOP) is a socio-economic concept that allows us to group that vast segment (estimated to be 4 Billion) of the world's poorest citizens constituting an invisible and unserved market blocked by challenging barriers that prevent them from realising their human potential for their own benefit, those of their families, and that of society's at large. Technically, a member of the BOP is one who lives with less than $2.50 a day and is excluded from the modernity of our globalised civilised societies.

**H.U.L.:** Hindustan Unilever.

**Key Product Mileage (K.P.A.):** Used to measure the average travelling distance of the product from the source of production.

**Media Dark:** Phrase used to highlight the fact of non-coverage of populace with respect to proper channel.

**Mom & Pop stores:** A conversational term for a small, independent, family-owned business. Unlike franchises and large corporations, which have multiple operations in various locations, mom and pop shops usually have a single location that often occupies a physically small space.

**N.C.A.E.R.:** National Council of Applied Economic Research.

**Stock Keeping Units (S.K.U.):** is a distinct item for sale, such as a product or service, and all attributes associated with the item that distinguish it from other items.

**Value Chain:** The complete transaction level detail with respect to retail business outlining the value created at each step.

# Chapter 16
# Revitalizing ICDS: India's Flagship Child Care Program

**Jeremiah Jacob**
*Institute of Management Technology Ghaziabad, India*

## ABSTRACT

*ICDS-Integrated Child Development Services is India's only government program for combating the rampant malnutrition prevalent in young children. In this chapter, the authors aim to examine the need and scope of ICDS scheme, its services and countrywide reach; considering that every fifth child in the world lives in India, this scheme is critical to ensuring that today's children who are our citizens of tomorrow are well nurtured and nourished, thus securing the country's future. Also its efficacy in achieving stated objectives is assessed through analysis of vital parameters such as nutritional status, mortality rates etc. Further, the bottlenecks facing the scheme such as lack of adequate sanitation facilities and supervisory staff etc. are studied and the initiatives taken by the government to revitalize it are also examined. The transformation into Mission Mode has ushered in programmatic, institutional and management reforms and renewed thrust on creating awareness through an Information, Education and Communication (IEC) campaign.*

## INTRODUCTION

**ICDS-Integrated child development services** is the world's largest programme that caters to development of young children with the noble objective of investing adequate early childhood care, nutrition and immunization, thus ensuring their health and emotional well being. Launched on 2nd October, 1975 it is one of the most unique programmes for meeting challenges of morbidity, malnutrition, mortality and also providing pre-school education to children. ICDS is a Centrally-sponsored Scheme implemented through the State Governments or UT Administrations.

The services offered by ICDS converge at the AWC(Anganwadi Centre) (a village courtyard), which is the central platform for delivery of services. These AWCs have been set up in every village in the country. Present government is taking steps to set up an AWC in every human habitation/ settlement. The number of AWCs presently reaches almost 1.35 million.

DOI: 10.4018/978-1-4666-8259-7.ch016

The anganwadi worker is one of the most important frontline workers who owns a major responsibility for delivering an integrated package of services to children and women and building up capacity of community, especially of mothers for child-care and development.

ICDS provides a host of services which include:

1. Supplementary nutrition,
2. Immunization,
3. Health check-up,
4. Referral services,
5. Pre-school non-formal education and
6. Nutrition & health education

## LITERATURE REVIEW

First it is imperative to examine the effectiveness and impact of ICDS in India by analysing data obtained from Family health surveys. Awofeso and Rammohan (2010) made an attempt to examine the various issues plaguing the scheme and suggests strategies for effective capacity building.[1] By examining scheme coverage, malnutrition data and the dynamics of the health workforce, the paper concludes by stating that over the three decades of its existence the scheme has failed to achieve its intended objectives. In spite of government spending for the program increasing from $35 million in 1990 to $170 million in 2000, growing agricultural output and high growth rates of the economy, India accounts for 50% of the world's hungry, and it occupied 134th rank in the UN Millenium Development Goals (MDG) in 2009. The theme is that the management of the scheme is insufficient to achieve its large scale objectives. The lack of safe drinking water and proper sanitation facilities in rural areas is identified as a major cause of child mortality, thus highlighting the need for proper infrastructure to be provided through the scheme. The coverage of the scheme is termed modest with respect to the need and gender inequality in terms of nutritional status also is a persistent issue with substantial increase in nutritional outcomes of boys than that of girls. Further wide regional differences in the compensation or pay structures of Anganwadi Workers(AWW) is seen as being one of the factors leading to demotivation and impaired performance. This is particularly important in view of the minimum wage specifications put in place by the MGNREGA Act. The central government is observed to be isolated in its functioning and decision making from state level bodies and private health players like NGOs, and more emphasis is placed on food supplements to children above the age of three years rather than to newborn infant feeding and maternal care. Lack of timely breastfeeding, coupled with persistent deficiency of crucial vitamins like vitamin A and minerals like Iron lead to diseases like anaemia, causing malnutrition and maternal mortality. The research finally suggests that capacity building of the system is an appropriate solution to the problems facing the scheme and it should focus on structural factors beyond the scheme itself such as tackling the socio-economic, cultural and attitudinal hurdles such as corruption, neglect of girl child etc. Some solutions suggested include decreasing poverty though government programs in areas with high malnutrition (keeping in view the high correlation between poverty and undernutrition), allocating the charge of the supply of ICDS food to local women's groups instead of corrupt contractors, improving the training provided to the AWWs etc.

In addition, gaping holes exist in the monitoring aspect of the scheme as was revealed by a survey conducted by NIPCCD(National Institute of Public Cooperation and Child Development) in Himachal Pradesh where many vacancies for posts of CDPO(Child Development Project Officers) remained unfilled. This has an adverse impact also on the efficacy of the AWTC (Anganwadi Training Centre) which is reflected in the absence of monitoring committees. Hence a supervisory committee comprising of CDPO, DPO and NGO coordinators is extremely important to not only effectively coordinate daily activities but also to ensure that grants and funds allocated are appropriately passed on to the AWTC. Another curtailment on effective functioning of the scheme is the lack of funds or allowances for petrol, diesel and other fuels needed for vehicular travel, especially constraining the Block Medical Officers and divisional doctors from visiting AWCs located far away from the PHCs (primary health centres) and the CHCs (community health centres). This problem is observed to be particularly rampant in Orissa and not only results in unavailability of one of a fundamental ICDS service but also hinders supervisory officers from travelling and doing surveillance as one CDPO needs to handle many blocks due to shortage of staff.

The AWWs view data recording and collection as loathsome and boring in spite of its great importance in monitoring and evaluation purpose by program managers. Lack of computerization further perpetuates the system of manual recording in registers etc. Hence it is quintessential to provide adequate quantity of computers to the CDPOs, also softwares for analysis of collected data so that efficient steps for solving the analyzed problems can be taken in earnest.

The HUNGaMA (Hunger and Malnutrition) Survey Report (2011) and released by the prime minister brought to light that 42 per cent of children surveyed in 112 districts across nine states were undernourished. The Report of the Inter Ministerial Group on ICDS Restructuring (2011) highlights the need for reforms in the programme and its management by pointing out the existing gaps in implementation. The absence of quality human resource and community participation, lack of an MIS for maintaining data, ignoring of working women's needs have been identified as some programmatic drawbacks. Some major operational issues pointed out were lack of revision of program and nutrition costs according to the inflation in fuel, food and transport prices, lack of efficiency and transparency in operations at various levels etc. The compensation of AWWs and AWHs has been recently doubled in 2011 and minimum working hours of 6 hours as opposed to the earlier prevailing norm of 4 hours has been prescribed. This is expected to improve quality and enhance commitment of AWWs and AWHs. It lays out a detailed proposal for strengthening and restructuring the scheme by not only allocating increased budgetary spending but also facilitating comprehensive institutional and management reforms. It focuses on early childhood care and community mobilisation and decentralisation by transforming ICDS into "Mission Mode".

## RESEARCH OBJECTIVE

This paper aims to research on the following areas:

1. The need and scope of ICDS scheme in India
2. The challenges faced by ICDS and the reforms being instituted to counter them

## ICDS: A LIFELINE OF INDIA'S UNDERNOURISHED CHILDREN

It is a well known fact that the average child in India has numerous struggles during childhood. One in four newborn children is underweight, approximately 46% children have the luxury of proper breastfeeding for the first six months of life and every second young child in India is malnourished. With infant mortality rate at 47 deaths per 1000 live births and under-five mortality rate of 64 for Indian children, monumental steps needed to be taken to improve the life of children and provide them with a strong foundation for future development.

In addition, the malaise of rampant poverty and lack of adequate sanitation facilities accentuated the crisis faced by children. The preference for the boy child and other discriminatory practices against girls led to a decline in sex ratios and neglect of girls with respect to nutritional and educational privileges.

The early childhood years are crucial in laying the foundation for the cognitive, emotional and linguistic development of a child. Almost 80% of brain development happens during the first three years, and the positive impact created by adequate nutrition lasts a lifetime. Thus to ensure proper child development through adequate nutrition and immunization and secure the future of India's young children, ICDS was launched in 1975 with financial and technical assistance from UNICEF.

The following services are provided at the AWC:

### Supplementary Nutrition

This includes supplementary feeding and growth monitoring; and prophylaxis against vitamin A deficiency and control of nutritional anaemia. Children below six years of age, pregnant & nursing mothers are provided supplementary feeding support for 300 days in a year. In this way, the Anganwadi tries to match up to the nationally recommended intake level of children and women in economically weak and underprivileged communities.

Growth Monitoring of children is carried out by weighing children below three on a monthly basis and children 3-6 years of age on quarterly basis. Supplementary feeding is provided to malnourished children. They are also referred for medical check-ups.

### Immunization

Protection of children from six diseases-poliomyelitis, tuberculosis, diphtheria, pertussis, tetanus and measles is carried out by immunization of pregnant women and infants. Such activities help in preventing child disability, incidence of particular diseases, malnutrition and mortality. Immunization of expecting women against tetanus also lowers maternal and neonatal mortality rates.

### Health Check-Ups

It comprises health care of children below six, prenatal care of expecting women and postnatal care of nursing mothers. The various anganwadi workers and Primary Health Centre (PHC) staff provide a host of health services to children like- regular medical check-ups, malnutrition control, weight measurements, immunization, de-worming and distribution of basic medicines etc

## Referral Services

Sick or malnourished children requiring immediate medical consideration, are alluded to the medical officers of Primary Health Centre/subcentre. The anganwadi worker is also trained to detect disabilities in infants. She keeps a record of such cases and those are referred to the medical officers of the Primary Health Centre or its sub-centre.

## Non-Formal Pre-School Education (PSE)

PSE focuses on all round development of the child, below six years of age, mainly from the underprivileged sections of society. It is the most joyful play-way daily activity, sustained for three hours a day. Its programme for the three-to six years old in the anganwadi is aimed at providing and securing a joyful and stimulating environment, with focus on essential inputs for optimum development. It provides a foundation for preparation for primary education and offers substitute care to younger siblings. This also helps in keeping the older ones free to attend school.

## Nutrition and Health Education

Nutrition, Health and Education are key elements of the work of the anganwadi worker. This has the objective of capacity-building of women – particularly in the age group of 15-45 years – so that they can look their own health and nutrition needs as well as that of their children.

## Challenges Faced by ICDS

ICDS today is able to extend its services to 7.5 crore young children below 6 years of age which is less than half of the the total of 15.88 crore. An appraisal of ICDS performance outcomes three decades after its inception which was conducted by NIPCCD(National Institute of Public Cooperation and Child Development) has revealed that although ICDS has made a positive contribution in reduction of mortality rates, percentage of malnourished children and resulted in higher prevalence of immunization, there are several issues which need to be addressed.

Some facts emerging from the survey are:

1. A significant percentage of AWCs studied have no toilet facility (69%) and in many AWCs this facility was found to be unsatisfactory.
2. Around 75% of AWCs have pucca buildings;
3. Large shortage of supervisory staff – vacancies for CDPO/ACDPO are as high as 32%, for Supervisors is 34%, AWWs (8%) and AWHs (8%)
4. 44 per cent AWCs covered under the study were found to be lacking PSE kits;
5. Disruption of supplementary nutrition was noticed on an average of 46.31 days at Anganwadi level. Major reasons causing disruption was reported as delay in supply of items of supplementary nutrition
6. 36.5 per cent mothers did not report weighing of new born children;
7. 29 per cent children were born with a low weight which was below normal (less than 2500 gm);

8. 37 per cent AWWs reported non-availability of materials/aids for Nutrition and Health Education (NHED).
9. The coverage of the scheme is inadequate in the northern Indian states of Bihar, Uttar Pradesh which have the highest prevalence of underweight and stunted children
10. Coordination lapses occurred between stakeholders at the micro level which was mainly due to lack of enthusiasm of supervisors. AWWs and community NGOs rarely preferred working under panchayats.
11. Early marriage and frequent pregnancy was cited as a cause for malnutrition in tribal people
12. In the case of Supplementary Nutrition, the greater share of benefits went to boys than girls in spite of greater number of girls enrolled for the scheme.
13. Only about 51.5% immunization was achieved in tribal children as opposed to 71.6% in rural children and 65.7% in urban children.
14. Close to half (49%) of AWCs lack the requisite floor area or space required for outdoor and indoor activities as envisaged in scheme guidelines.
15. Significant number of disabled children are unable to benefit from the ICDS initiatives.
16. Very poor attendance was observed at NHED (Nutrition and Health Education) sessions conducted in urban, tribal and rural areas with a meagre 18.68% mothers in attendance.
17. Only 14% AWCs are functional in Bihar, with a significant percentage of children suffering malnutrition and coverage of children by government crèches was very poor and NHED sessions were hardly conducted
18. The data in Table 1 and Figure 1 clearly implies that rural areas in the country are facing a bigger challenge in terms of number of children being stunted (inadequacy of height with respect to age), underweight or wasted (inadequate weight for a given height) than urban areas.
19. The **HUNGaMA (Hunger and Malnutrition) Survey Report-2011** published by Naandi Foundation and released by the prime minister brought to light that 42 per cent of children surveyed in 112 districts across nine states were undernourished.
20. Following data in Table 2 and summarised in Figure 2 clearly shows the extremely high prevalence of malnourishment in eastern states of Bihar (highest), Odisha in addition to NCR Delhi, Andhra Pradesh etc. Thus high priority should be given on effective ramp up and monitoring of ICDS services in these areas.
21. The under-five mortality rates are also a critical indicator of the schemes success. Measured in rates per 100 live births, this indicator, statistics of which are shown in Table 3, has been showing a steadily decreasing trend, falling from as high as 125 in 1990 to 59 in 2010 as per Annual Health Survey 2010-11 as observed in Figure 3. Thus although considerable improvement has been brought about which clearly underscores the scheme's efficiency, the task remains still arduous and compelling.
22. One clear area of failure of the scheme is highlighted in the declining sex ratio (girls per 1000 boys) of children over the last four decades as seen in Figure 4 when the overall sex ratio of the population has been showing an increasing trend. Thus this indicates that not only are overall demographic changes in the population composition underway, it is a direct pointer to the high post natal mortality of female infants in age group of 0-6 years. Hence the scheme needs to focus more on girl child related measures and creation of awareness about female foeticide. Census 2011 data shows that child sex ratio in rural areas witnessed a decline which was three times that witnessed in urban areas.

23. Maternal mortality ratio (also called MMR, which is the no. of women dying due to pregnancy complications or during childbirth per 1 lakh live births) has fallen by about 16% from a level of 212 in 2007-09 to 178 in 2010-12 as shown in Table 4. This can be attributed as a success point for the pre natal and post natal care provided by ICDS. Further analysis of data presented below reveals the following trends: Figure 5. shows that southern states have far lower mortality than EAG (Empowered Action Group) states, Assam and other states. Kerala is the best and Assam the worst in terms of MMR.
    a) The reduction in MMR has been generally uniform across the country, In EAG states and Assam, a 16% reduction from form 308 to 257 was witnessed. It was 17% in southern states (from 127 to 105), and 15% in other states (149 to 127).
24. Beneficiary mothers said that the supplementary foods provided were of inferior quality with little oil and pulse components, causing children to dislike it . Lack of variety in the food was another factor.
25. The Anganwadi workers (AWW) were overburdened with handling paperwork and attending workshops, thus impairing effective dispensation of core du
26. Anganwadi workers suffered from lack of motivation as they were paid as casual staff and not treated as government workers or paid pensions. There are wide regional differences in AWW pay and also a wide gap between least paid government worker and the AWW (since the minimum national wages have increased post the roll out of MGNREGA scheme). Table 5 shows there is high incidence of anaemia in women and young children with anaemia accounting for 20% of total maternal deaths.

## SIMILAR PROJECTS WORLDWIDE

In this section, we look at child care schemes in two of the most developed economies of the world, the USA & the UK, and go on to highlight lessons for India to learn.

In the United States, there is a federal agency by the name of United States Children's Bureau under the United States Department of Health and Human Services' Administration for Children and Families. Its operations cover all matters of children's welfare such as infant mortality, birth-rate, orphanages etc.

Also, under the United States Department of Health and Human Services (HHS) is a division called The Administration for Children and Families (ACF) that oversees child care, welfare, support, adoption, assistance and deals with child abuse.

Under the ACF is an Office of Child Care or OCC that enlists several initiatives like *Let's Move* Child Care program or LMCC that focuses on encouragement of healthy nutrition practices and more of physical activity in early care of children.

OCC also runs an Emergency Preparedness Programme that which is essentially a web page or portal of emergency preparedness resources for grantees and child care providers.

There is also a Tribal Maternal, Infant, and Early Childhood Home Visiting Program wherein grants or cooperative agreement funds are awarded by the ACF to consortia of tribes and tribal organizations. It is this program that supports maternal and child health, child abuse prevention and early childhood programs for American Indian and Alaska native families.

*Table 1. The state wise percentage of underweight children in urban and rural areas of India as of 2006*

| State-wise Percentage of Underweight Children (under 5 Years) in Urban and Rural Areas of India (2005-2006) | | | |
|---|---|---|---|
| **States/UT** | **Urban** | **Rural** | **Total** |
| Andhra Pradesh | 28 | 34.8 | 32.5 |
| Assam | 26.1 | 37.1 | 36.4 |
| Bihar | 47.8 | 57 | 55.9 |
| Chhattisgarh | 31.3 | 50.2 | 47.1 |
| Delhi | 26.5 | 22.5 | 26.1 |
| Gujarat | 39.2 | 47.9 | 44.6 |
| Haryana | 34.6 | 41.3 | 39.6 |
| Himachal Pradesh | 23.6 | 37.8 | 36.5 |
| Jammu and Kashmir | 15.8 | 27.9 | 25.6 |
| Jharkhand | 38.8 | 60.7 | 56.5 |
| Karnataka | 30.7 | 41.1 | 37.6 |
| Kerala | 15.4 | 26.4 | 22.9 |
| Madhya Pradesh | 51.3 | 62.7 | 60 |
| Maharashtra | 30.7 | 41.6 | 37 |
| Odisha | 29.7 | 42.3 | 40.7 |
| Punjab | 21.4 | 26.8 | 24.9 |
| Rajasthan | 30.1 | 42.5 | 39.9 |
| Tamil Nadu | 27.1 | 32.1 | 29.8 |
| Uttar Pradesh | 34.8 | 44.1 | 42.4 |
| West Bengal | 24.7 | 42.2 | 38.7 |
| **India** | **32.7** | **45.6** | **42.5** |

*Figure 1. Graph showing the distribution of stunted, wasted and underweight children in rural and urban areas of India*

*Source: http://www.indiastat.com: Lok Sabha Unstarred Question No. 4481, dated on 07.09.2012*

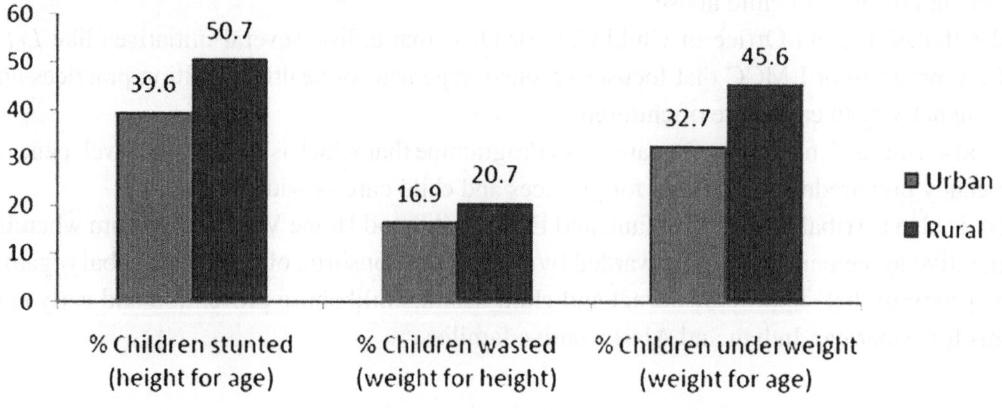

*Table 2. The state wise number of malnourished children as of 2011*

| Selected State-Wise Nutritional Status of Children under Integrated Child Development Services (ICDS) Scheme in India (2010-2011) (Figures in Lakh) | | | | | | | |
|---|---|---|---|---|---|---|---|
| **States/UTs** | **Total Children Weighed** | **Normal Number** | **Percent** | **Grade I and II (Moderately Malnourished)** | | **Grade III and IV (Severely Mainourished)** | |
| | | | | **Number** | **Percent** | **Number** | **Percent** |
| Andhra Pradesh | 50.21 | 25.75 | 51.28 | 24.42 | 48.63 | 0.04 | 0.08 |
| Assam | 19.09 | 13.11 | 68.68 | 5.89 | 30.86 | 0.09 | 0.46 |
| Bihar | 64.15 | 11.47 | 17.88 | 36.04 | 56.17 | 16.64 | 25.94 |
| Chhattisgarh | 20.13 | 12.38 | 61.53 | 7.35 | 36.5 | 0.4 | 1.97 |
| Gujarat | 38.71 | 23.7 | 61.23 | 13.24 | 34.21 | 1.76 | 4.56 |
| Haryana | 20.49 | 11.69 | 57.05 | 8.79 | 42.9 | 0.01 | 0.05 |
| Himachal Pradesh | 4.48 | 2.95 | 65.76 | 1.53 | 34.18 | 0 | 0.06 |
| Jammu and Kashmir | 1.98 | 1.36 | 68.88 | 0.61 | 31.06 | 0 | 0.06 |
| Jharkhand | 27.19 | 16.31 | 60 | 10.68 | 39.3 | 0.19 | 0.7 |
| Karnataka | 33.3 | 20.15 | 60.5 | 12.21 | 36.66 | 0.95 | 2.84 |
| Kerala | 18.61 | 11.74 | 63.08 | 6.86 | 36.83 | 0.02 | 0.08 |
| Madhya Pradesh | 73.97 | 52.89 | 71.51 | 19.69 | 26.61 | 1.39 | 1.88 |
| Maharashtra | 61.3 | 47.01 | 76.68 | 12.7 | 20.71 | 1.6 | 2.61 |
| Odisha | 42.42 | 21.03 | 49.57 | 21.09 | 49.71 | 0.31 | 0.72 |
| Punjab | 21.24 | 14.1 | 66.37 | 7.13 | 33.59 | 0.01 | 0.05 |
| Rajasthan | 39.19 | 22.29 | 56.87 | 16.78 | 42.8 | 0.13 | 0.33 |
| Tamil Nadu | 41.98 | 27.2 | 64.78 | 14.78 | 35.2 | 0.01 | 0.02 |
| Tripura | 1.97 | 1.25 | 63.11 | 0.72 | 36.54 | 0.01 | 0.35 |
| Uttarakhand | 4.5 | 3.38 | 75.07 | 1.07 | 23.74 | 0.05 | 1.19 |
| West Bengal | 53.07 | 33.48 | 63.08 | 17.48 | 32.93 | 2.12 | 3.99 |
| Delhi | 3.1 | 1.56 | 50.09 | 1.55 | 49.87 | 0 | 0.03 |
| **India** | **782.29** | **460.27** | **58.84** | **296** | **37.84** | **26.02** | **3.33** |

*Figure 2. Prevalence of Malnourishment in Indian children*
*Source: http://www.indiastat.com: Report of the Comptroller and Auditor General of India. (14212)*

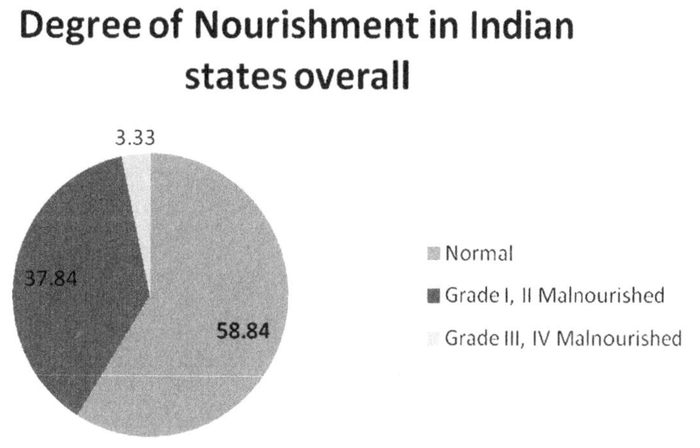

*Table 3. Under five mortality rate composition in India*

| India | | | Rural | | | Urban | | |
|---|---|---|---|---|---|---|---|---|
| Total | Male | Female | Total | Male | Female | Total | Male | Female |
| 59 | 55 | 64 | 66 | 61 | 71 | 38 | 36 | 40 |

*Table 4. MMR rates across India*

| Region | MMR | Maternal Mortality Rate | % to Total Maternal Deaths |
|---|---|---|---|
| INDIA | 178 | 12.4 | 100.0 |
| EAG AND ASSAM | 257 | 23.3 | 61.5 |
| SOUTH | 105 | 5.9 | 11.3 |
| OTHER | 127 | 7.8 | 27.1 |

*Figure 3. Declining trend in under five mortality rates*
*Source: National Family Health Survey*

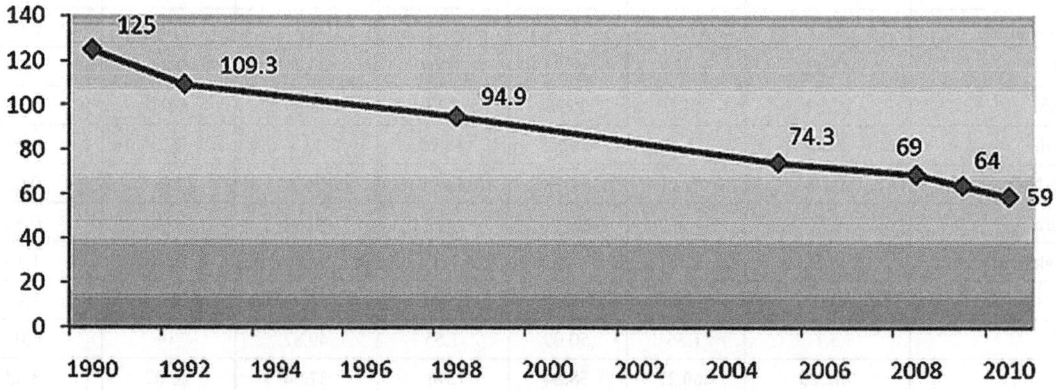


*Figure 4. Comparison of sex ratio variation in Indian children and Indian population*
*Source: Census, India, Office of Registrar General of India*

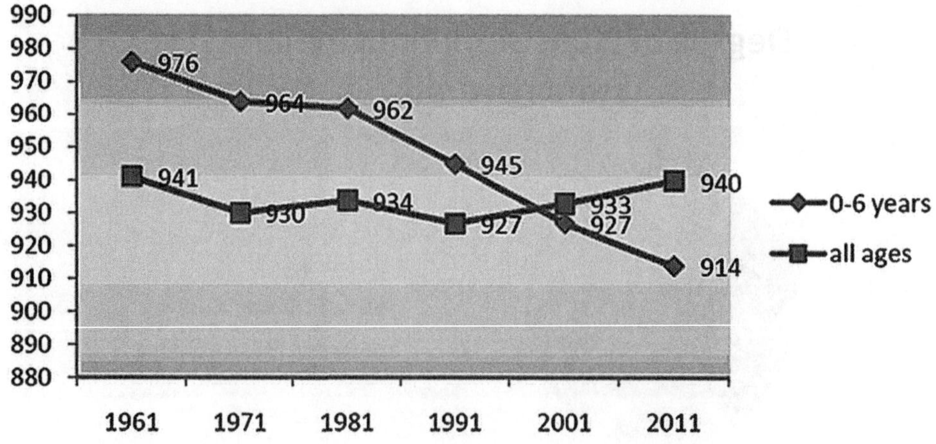

*Figure 5. Representation of MMR Levels By Regions 1997-2012*
*Source: Census, India, Office of Registrar General of India*

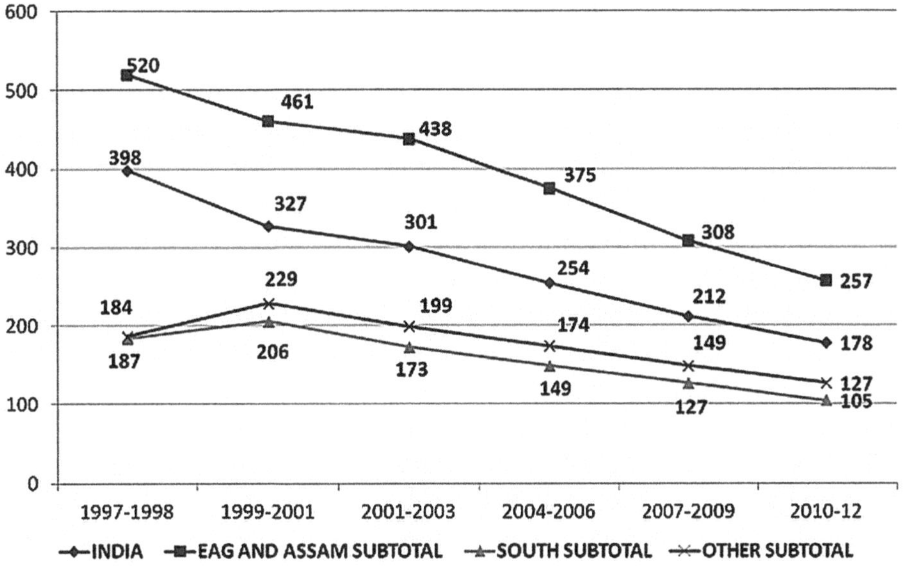


*Table 5. The prevalence of anaemia in various age groups of women and young children in India*

| State-wise Percentage of Anaemia among Children and Adults in India 2007 | | | | |
|---|---|---|---|---|
| **State/Uts** | **Children Age 6-59 Months Who are Anaemic** | **Ever-Married Women Age 15-49 Who Are Anaemic** | **Pregnant Women Age 15-49 Who Are Anaemic** | **Ever-Married Men Age 15-49 Who Are Anaemic** |
| Andhra Pradesh | 70.8 | 62.9 | 56.4 | 23.3 |
| Assam | 69.6 | 69.5 | 72 | 39.6 |
| Bihar | 78 | 67.4 | 60.2 | 34.3 |
| Chhattisgarh | 71.2 | 57.5 | 63.1 | 27 |
| Gujarat | 67.7 | 55.3 | 60.8 | 22.2 |
| Haryana | 72.3 | 56.1 | 69.7 | 19.2 |
| Himachal Pradesh | 54.7 | 43.3 | 37 | 18.9 |
| Jammu and Kashmir | 58.6 | 53.1 | 54 | 19.5 |
| Jharkhand | 70.3 | 69.5 | 68.4 | 36.5 |
| Karnataka | 70.4 | 51.5 | 59.5 | 19.1 |
| Kerala | 44.5 | 32.8 | 33.1 | 8 |
| Madhya Pradesh | 74.1 | 56 | 57.9 | 25.6 |
| Maharashtra | 63.4 | 48.4 | 57.8 | 16.8 |
| Orissa | 65 | 61.2 | 68.1 | 33.9 |
| Punjab | 66.4 | 38 | 41.6 | 13.6 |
| Rajasthan | 69.7 | 53.1 | 61.2 | 23.6 |
| Tamil Nadu | 64.2 | 53.2 | 53.3 | 16.5 |
| Uttar Pradesh | 73.9 | 40.9 | 51.6 | 24.3 |
| West Bengal | 61 | 63.2 | 62.6 | 32.3 |
| Delhi | 57 | 44.3 | 29.9 | 17.8 |
| **India** | **69.5** | **55.3** | **57.8** | **24.2** |

Source: http://www.indiastat.com: Ministry of Health and Family Welfare, Govt. of India.

Under the OCC is also a Child Care & Development Fund or CCDF that provides child care assistance every month to around 1.5 million children in around 903,500 low-income families. These subsidies were paid to child care centres or home-based child care providers for care of infants, toddlers, pre-schoolers and school children.

The above facts highlight that in the USA, there are several dedicated programs targeting various aspects or different schemes of child care, health and welfare – from a targeted program for tribals to a fund for monthly disbursements. Additionally, electronic and mobile reporting of licensed child care centres and home-based child care providers, have increased the proliferation of the child care network.

All of this is a clear explanation to the data that Maternal Mortality Ratio in USA was 6 in 2013 while it was 41 in India (World Bank). The figures are the same for Infant Mortality ratio as well.

In the UK, the government in 1998 initiated a child care, education and health support area-based programme by the name of Sure Start that was followed up by an 'Every Child matters' programme which started the funding for Children's Centres which provide child and family health services like antenatal and postnatal support, integrated early learning and childcare, specialist support etc.

Additionally, there is a Healthy Child Programme under the Department of Health that runs a program of screening, immunisation, and health in early life stages.

The infant mortality rate in 2008 was the lowest ever recorded in England, with fewer than 5 deaths per 1,000 live births.

In view of the above, it is imperative that India launch a plethora of targeted programs under the umbrella of the ICDS – ranging from early child care to early child education and support, prevention of child abuse etc.

## ICDS STRENGTHENING AND RESTRUCTURING: RESOLVING THE CHALLENGES

This is sought to be accomplished by the following reforms:

1) Programmatic reforms:
   a) First step towards this involves **repositioning the AWC as a vibrant, child friendly ECD centre (Baal Vikas Kendra)** and women in the community will be taking the lead in ownership and functioning.
   b) provision of adequate infrastructure (4 lakh AWC buildings as shown in Table 6), facilities such as safe drinking water, toilets, hygienic nutrition, toys and play environment for children. The government has mandated 600 sq. Ft as the minimum area of an AWC and planned contruction of 200000 AWCs during the 12th Five Year Plan according to the plan.
   c) Crèche services are planned to be offered in almost 70,000 AWCs under **AWC cum Crèche scheme** which will enable working mothers to leave their children at the AWC and thus enable their proper care and monitoring . This will be in coordination with Rajiv Gandhi National Crèche Scheme of the CSWB (Central Social Welfare Board)
   d) Enhancing nutrition levels through revised norms, starting pilot community kitchens.
   e) **Sneha Shivirs**: These are 12 day Nutritional counselling and care sessions for moderate and severe underweight children, with feeding demonstrations for prevention of nutritional deterioration and referral support for severely undernourished children in high burden pockets.

Learning By Doing approach is emphasized using positive role model mothers/peers whose children are growing well for demonstrating cooking and optimal feeding behaviours. There is 100% weighing of all eligible children and identification of underweight children, followed by referral to NRCs(Nutrition Rehabilitation center) under NRHM for children requiring medical attention.

f) **ECCE (**Early Childhood Care and Education) will be repositioned as catering to holistic development of 3-6 year olds and under 3 year olds by highlighting the following:
   1. Early stimulation programme and early detection of delayed developmental faculties of children, early intervention for children with disabilities/impaired faculties
   2. 4 hours of play and activity based non formal preschool education for 3-6 year olds
   3. Development of appropriate ECCE curriculum imparted through PSE(Pre school education) kits worth Rs 3000 and activity books
   4. School readiness interventions for children 5 plus years of age, collocation of ICDS AWCs with schools
   5. Additional AWWs in 200 high focus states/districts to spearhead this effort
   6. **Monthly fixed Village ECCE Days will be conducted** for community and parent involvement and advocacy.

2) Management Reforms
   a) The program will be decentralised to enable state specific Annual Programme Implementation plans (APIPs), regional and community level indicators which will be linked with state awards such as Nirmal Gram Puruskar.
   b) Reducing workload of AWW and redefining roles of AWW/ANM/ASHAs through improved Human Resource Management
   c) Providing for better monitoring of ICDS training activities with support form Voluntary Action Groups and NGOs
   d) To foster innovation and address area specific needs while ensuring quality improvement, operation of upto 10% of ICDS projects will be done in partnerships with civil society groups
   e) Following measures have been implemented which will leverage community participation through involvement of Panchayati Raj Institutions(PRIs) to create complete awareness about ICDS initiatives:
      1. Under restructured ICDS, Common Village Health Sanitation and Nutrition Committees (VHSNC) are planned to be created which will be recognised as sub committee of panchayats.
      2. Constitution of Anganwadi Management Committees, with members including mothers and ASHAs, with defined roles and linked to common VHSNCs, chairperson will be a Gram Panchayat/ Ward member (preferably woman member)
      3. Sharing of nutritional status of children at gram sabha meetings, conducting **Monthly Fixed Village Health and Nutrition Days**
   f) Resources of national schemes and missions like MGNREGA, NRHM will be utilised for ICDS to bring about convergence with these related sectors such as collocation of schools and AWCs wherever feasible
   g) Improved real time data availability for assessment, analysis of key performance indicators will be made possible through **Management Information System (MIS). Mother & Child Protection Card** which is an extremely important tool for identification as well as to take

follow up action for malnutrition and key health interventions. Mother Child cohort tracking using an ICDS NRHM joint card (with new WHO child growth standards) is being planned to be distributed to mothers. Child nutrition and development outcomes would be made visible to families and communities through the card and display of community charts.

3) Institutional Reforms

a) ICDS in Mission Mode The govt decided to **transform ICDS into a "Mission Mode" decentralised programme** like NRHM with monitorable and measurable outcomes with AWC being rebranded as an institution owned by the community. This is in contrast to the earlier strategy which was a one-size-fits-all viewpoint which resulted in a rigid programme structure and left no scope for district specific planning.

1. Better training at the State level will be provided by setting up of a Training Cell in each state which will envision capacity building for training. Also **State Training Institutes (STIs)** will be instituted in 10 states for block level officer training
2. The **State Mission Steering Group** as shown in Figure 6, headed by the Chief Minister will provide policy guidance and **State Empowered Program Committee** headed by the Chief Secretary of the state will assume the role of highest technical authority for planning and monitoring of scheme implementation.
3. The blocks within a district will each have a **Block ICDS Mission** and will be headed by the Panchayat chairman and meetings of the committee convened by the CDPO. Tracking of nutritional parameters of children will be done and proper distribution and supply chain management to AWCs will be done, facilitate public community participation for feedback assessment
4. In 10% of blocks, a **Block ICDS Resource Centre (BIRC)** will be instituted as a pilot project with a Nutritional Helpline intended to to provide counseling over phone and this will promote exclusive breastfeeding for first six months (thereafter which complementary feeding is allowed) and effectively disseminate best practices. Two models will be used for testing the efficacy of this pilot: NGO led model (where the Nutrition and IYCF training will be executed by the NGO) and Project Led Mode (CDPO aided by contractual staff will be responsible for providing the required implementation of services)

b) **"Mission Mode"** creates a flexible implementation framework and provides scope for state / district specific approaches/models. Under this strategy, State/District level Annual Programme Implementation Plans (APIPs) will be prepared, powers will be devolved to Panchayati Raj Institutions and Urban Local Bodies who will be supported by village level functionaries in overseeing AWC functioning such as Village Health Sanitation and Nutrition Committees (VHSNCs) as Sub-committee of PRIs.

c) Public Accountability, Reviews and Evaluation Jan Sunwai or Public Hearing is a process by which people who may be affected by a particular action or decision have the opportunity to ask questions, make submissions or register objections to a panel of experts. The panel may comprise of elected representatives, government officials, non-government organizations, experts from the field, media, etc. It is a formal meeting or a social audit designed to provide the public with an opportunity to express their support or opposition for any project of ICDS scheme in an open forum.

d) Community owned ICDS accreditation system with grading of AWCs, sectors, block/projects, districts, based on child related outcomes. Formation of Citizen's charter based on service guarantees for promoting quality.
e) Enhanced budgetary allocation: An average annual GoI expenditure of about Rs. 35,000 crore would be required for effectively implementing ICDS in Mission Mode to achieve the above mentioned goals and objectives with the expected total requirement for the 12th Five Year Plan calculated to be Rs. 1,83,778 crore.
f) Increased community awareness: **IEC(Information, Education and Communication) Campaign against Malnutrition** Launched on 19th November 2012 by Shri Pranab Mukherjee, in response to the major challenge of rampant malnutrition, it is a key decision of Prime Minister's Council on India's Nutrition Challenges, organised by the Ministry of Women and Child Development. This campaign has actor Shri Aamir Khan as brand ambassador with technical support being provided by UNICEF. The prime objective of the nationwide campaign is to address issues pertaining to status of women, the care of pregnant mothers and children under two, breastfeeding and highlighting the importance of balanced nutrition, health. A sample advertisement created by the Directorate of Advertising and Visual Publicity (DAVP) for the Ministry of Women and Child Development is shown in Figure 7. The nationwide campaign has been designed in four stages covering 34 weeks in 18 different languages. The media channels used include television, radio, electronic print, outdoor and digital media besides the traditional methods of folk and field publicity.

## CONCLUSION

ICDS has witnessed expansion from its early reach of 4891 AWCs and 33 community development blocks; to acquire a coverage of as high as 14 lakh AWCs through 7076 approved projects across the country with final phase of universalization being approved in 2008-09. An ICDS MIS has been implemented for better monitoring by establishing key indicators of performance, this also has resulted in reducing the number of registers maintained at AWCs for record keeping. This web based MIS design is being scaled up after the initial pilot launch. This has been followed up with setting up a Digital Nutrition Resource Platform (NRP) which not only acts as a document management system but also as an e-forum and provides end user mobile telephony based services. Ensuring good governance by involving PRIs and

*Table 6. Plan for additional AWC Construction during the 12th Five Year Plan*

| Details of Construction of AWCs in a Phased Manner | | | | | | | |
|---|---|---|---|---|---|---|---|
| **S No.** | **Particulars** | **Year-1** | **Year-2** | **Year-3** | **Year-4** | **Year-5** | **Total** |
| 1 | Total AWCs to be constructed | 0 | 20,000 | 50000 | 60000 | 70000 | 200000 |
| 2 | % wrt total | 0 | 10 | 25 | 30 | 35 | 100 |
| 3 | Construction in other states | 0 | 18500 | 46250 | 55500 | 64750 | 185000 |
| 4 | Construction in North Eastern states | 0 | 1500 | 3750 | 4500 | 5250 | 15000 |

Source: Ministry of Women and Child Development, Govt. of India.

*Figure 6. The plan of institutional arrangements under ICDS Mission with authority being delegated by the National Mission Steering Group (headed by Minister I/C WCD) and Empowered Committee*
*Source: Report of the Inter Ministerial Group on ICDS Restructuring Chaired by Member Planning Commission Dr. Syeda Hameed, Planning Commision(2011)*

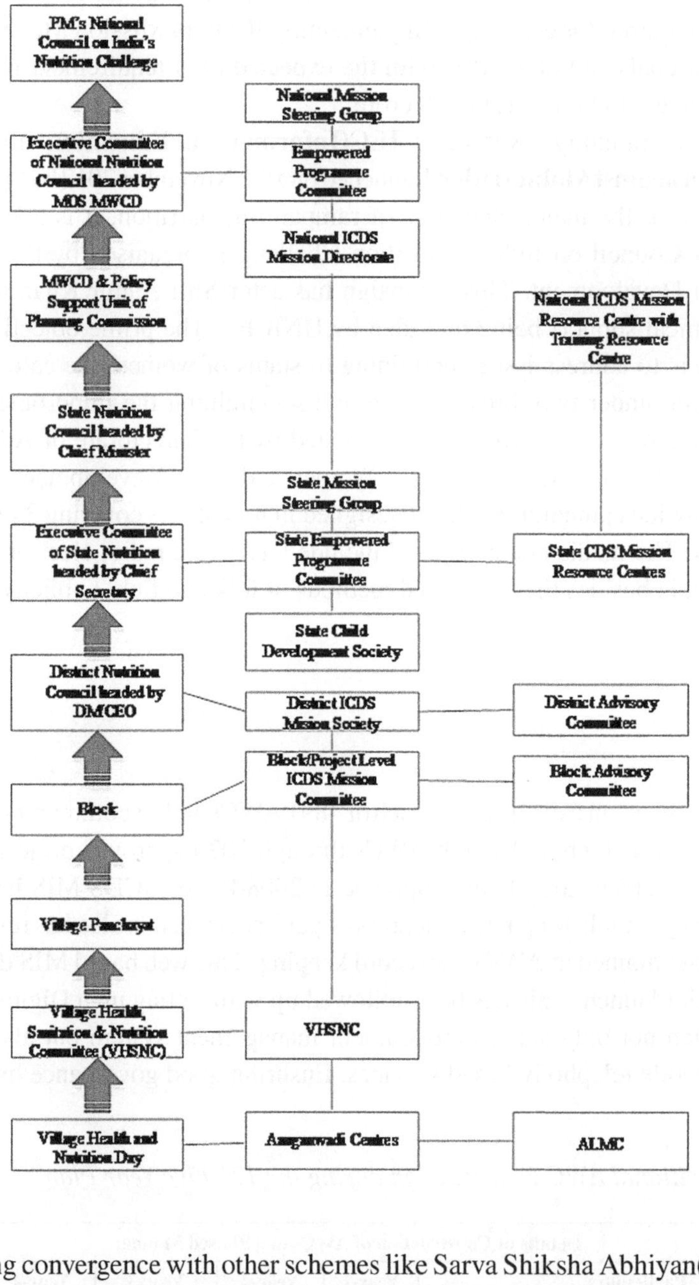


civil society, ensuring convergence with other schemes like Sarva Shiksha Abhiyan(SSA), Reproductive and Child Health Program (RCH) of the NRHM; will definitely strengthen the scheme at the grassroots. Also the new structure of the ICDS mission envisages a decentralised financial management with better flow of funding by improving the accountability and transparency. The national training resource centres which are sought to be established will ensure capacity building of functionaries at all levels. All these initiatives combined will indeed revitalise and improve the operational efficiency of this most crucial welfare scheme ie. ICDS.

*Figure 7. A sample ad highlighting best practices to be followed in child care six months from birth*
*Source: Directorate of Advertising and Visual Publicity(DAVP), Ministry of Women and Child Development, Government of India(2013) http://poshan.nic.in/jspui/index.html*

But it will take dedicated policy implementation and supervision by the government in order to be able to achieve the realisation of these new goals. Ever since the scheme was universalised in 2008-09, it essentially required fast expansion of AWCs to reach the revised coverage targets. New challenges of resource requirements, delivery and management skills, quality compliance etc are now more pronounced and need to be tackled efficiently. It is imperative to improve the supply chain to provide continuous, undisrupted distribution to the AWCs. The huge vacancies in CDOs should be filled at the earliest to address the skill deficit being faced by the scheme. The engagement with the respective state governments for proper planning, monitoring, implementation of service delivery should be done with greater focus and intensity through use of latest data/information systems for analysis. The vision for the revitalised program should be that children's rights to survival and development are inseparable from their right to receive adequate nurturing and care and the national goal of inclusive growth has to begin with its young children.

## REFERENCES


Awofeso, N., & Rammohan, A. (2011). Three Decades of the Integrated Child Development Services Program in India: Progress and Problems. Health Management - Different Approaches and Solutions. doi:10.5772/19871

Department of Health. Govt. of UK. (2014). *Healthy Child Program.* Retrieved September 23, 2014 from https://www.gov.uk/government/publications/healthy-child-programme-pregnancy-and-the-first-5-years-of-life

Directorate of Advertising and Visual Publicity (DAVP) for the Ministry of Women and Child Development, Government of India. (2013) *IEC (Information, Education and Communication) Campaign against Malnutrition.* Retrieved October 12, 2013 from http://poshan.nic.in/jspui/index.html

IndiaStat. (2013) *State wise percentage of underweight children in urban and rural areas of India as of 2006: Lok Sabha Unstarred Question No. 4481, dated on 07.09.2012.* Retrieved October 12, 2013 from www.indiastat.com

IndiaStat. (2013). *State wise number of malnourished children as of 2011: Report of the Comptroller and Auditor General of India (14212).* Retrieved October 12, 2013 from www.indiastat.com

IndiaStat. (2013) *Prevalence of anaemia in various age groups of women and young children in India: Ministry of Health and Family Welfare, Govt. of India.* Retrieved October 12, 2013 from www.indiastat.com

Ministry of Women and Child Development, Government of India. (2013). *Plan for additional AWC Construction during the 12th Five Year Plan.* Author.

Ministry of Women and Child Development, Government of India. (2013). *Integrated Child Development Services (ICDS) Scheme.* Retrieved October 9, 2013, from http://wcd.nic.in/icds.htm

Naandi Foundation. (2012). The HUNGaMA (Huger and Malnutrition). *Survey (London, England),* Report–2011.

NIPCCD (National Institute of Public Cooperation and Child Development). (2009). *Research on ICDS: An Overview (1996-2008).* New Delhi: Hauz Khas.

Planning Commision. (2011). *Report of the Inter Ministerial Group on ICDS Restructuring Chaired by Member Planning Commission Dr. Syeda Hameed.* New Delhi: Yojana Bhavan.

Planning Commision. (2011). Institutional Arrangements under ICDS Mission, Report of the Inter Ministerial Group on ICDS Restructuring Chaired by Member Planning Commission Dr. Syeda Hameed. Author.

Sure Start Services. Govt. of UK. (2014). *Sure Start Services.* Retrieved September 23, 2014 from http://www.nidirect.gov.uk/sure-start-services

UNICEF. (2013) *India: Statistics.* Retrieved October 11,2013, from http://www.unicef.org/infobycountry/india_statistics.html

US Department of Health and Human Services. (2014). *Administration for Children and Families, ACF Programs for Children and Youth.* Retrieved September 23, 2014 from http://www.acf.hhs.gov/program-topics/children-youth

## KEY TERMS AND DEFINITIONS

**Accredited Social Heath Activist (ASHA):** A trained female community worker of the National Rural Health Mission of the Government of India in every village working as an interface between the village community and the public health system. She facilitates access to Anganwadi/sub-centre/primary health centers for health services being provided by the government. She is also the village distributor of essential health care provisions like ORS, Disposable Delivery Kits, oral pills etc.

**Early Childhood Development (ECD) Centre or Baal Vikas Kendra:** An AWC for children below eight years of age with the objective of providing them sound and balanced emotional and psychological development through an enriching and stimulating psycho-social and physical environment that facilitates cognitive and brain development.

**Empowered Action Group (EAG):** A committee comprising participants from the Ministries of Health and Family Welfare, Women and Child Empowerment, Rural Development of the Government of India, and representatives of the Voluntary Health Association of India and the Family Planning Association of India, set up to prepare area-specific population stabilization programmes in eight States, namely, Bihar, Jharkhand, MP, Chhattisgarh, Orissa, Rajasthan, UP and Uttaranchal.

**Grade I & II Malnutrition:** WHO classifications of malnutrition for wasting (weight below median weight for height) / stunting (height below median height for age). Grade I & II stands for moderate malnutrition.

**Grade III & IV Malnutrition:** WHO malnutrition classification for severe wasting/stunting.

**Panchayati Raj Institutions (PRI):** A decentralized governance system for inclusive growth and development in rural India wherein all states with a population in excess of 2 million have a 3-tier administration comprising of village panchayats, panchayati samitis, and zilla parishads.

**Pre-School Education (PSE) kit:** The Early Childhood Care & Education initiative provides kits for children containing building blocks/dolls/stuffed toys/colour-number-alphabet matching cards etc for cognitive and psycho-social development of toddlers.

# Chapter 17
# Feasibility of Implementation of Solar Bottle Bulb in Urban Slums of India

**Akshay Maggu**
*Institute of Management Technology Ghaziabad, India*

**Jaideep Garg**
*Institute of Management Technology Ghaziabad, India*

## ABSTRACT

*Reach of undisrupted electricity is a perennial problem that is faced by urban slums in India. Through this chapter, the authors aim to study the feasibility of implementation of a ground breaking idea that will help in fighting this problem in a cost effective way and that has already been implemented in Philippines on a large scale. Further, given the present scenario of development in India, this chapter also tries to focus on the ways in which this product can be introduced on a commercial level covering one slum at a time. Also, this chapter revolves around the usability and identification of the most suitable and cost effective way to implement this idea in the desired target group. The chapter ultimately hopes to drive its readers to find the best solution to the proposed problem.*

## SOLAR BOTTLE BULB: LIGHT AND HOPE FROM WASTE

Kartik Jayraman and Prashant Sahni, members of Social Welfare Society- Sudarshana of Management Institute Ghaziabad (MIG) were putting the final touches on a presentation to the society's heads concerning the launch of their latest innovation targeted for slum dwellers of urban India. Solar Bottle bulb was an unconventional lighting solution for the people living in slums of urban India who have always faced problems of irregular power supply. The product could generate a light of close to 55-60 watts just by harvesting sunlight and without use of any electricity. Also, it could be a remarkable product owing to the fact that it could be made available at a meagre price of Rs.80 which was well under the purchasing power of the targeted segment. Its life is around one year and after that it'll need a fresh mixture of water and bleach along with a changed bottle which will cost around Rs. 20. Both of them were excited

DOI: 10.4018/978-1-4666-8259-7.ch017

but nervous at the same time because Mr Pramod Banerjee, Director of MIG would also attend the meeting along with representatives of some NGOs[a] working in and around New Delhi. The only problem which they faced at that moment was scalability. They knew that it was an exceptional product and one that could bring remarkable changes in the lives of slum dwellers. But the question was how they would make this product available at a large scale to slum dwellers, and once made available how they would coerce the people to use this product? Whether NGOs would come in for help or venture capitalists or for that matter their institute?

## URBAN SLUMS IN INDIA: THE TARGET

Approximately 68 million Indians are living in slums[b], according to a government census in 2011. One in six urban Indians lives in slum housing that is cramped, unclean, not properly lit even during the day. The report prepared from data collected for 2011 national census looks at urban slums in around 4000 towns across India. The electricity being used in these households are mostly illegal – electricity supplies.

Three types of slums have been defined in Census, namely, Notified, Recognized and Identified.

i. All notified areas in a town or city notified as 'Slum' by State, Union territories Administration or Local Government under any Act including a 'Slum Act' may be considered as **Notified slums.**
ii. All areas recognised as 'Slum' by State, Union territories Administration or Local Government, Housing and Slum Boards, which may have not been formally notified as slum under any act may be considered as **Recognized slums.**
iii. A compact area of at least 300 population or about 60-70 households of poorly built congested tenements, in unhygienic environment usually with inadequate infrastructure and lacking in proper sanitary and drinking water facilities may be considered as **Identified slums.** (See Figures 4 & 5: Slum reported towns & slum wise population in India)

Mumbai leads the chart for slum dwellers: 41% of its 20.5 million people. But in percentage terms, the coastal city of Vishakhapatnam overtakes the financial capital. (See Figure 6: Distribution of slums in India). According to that report one-third of studied slum households in India do not have toilets, but have mobile phones and televisions. This statistics shows an essential characteristic of general masses that live in slums. Lack of education and awareness hampers their growth prospects and they give more importance to not so important commodity like a mobile phone over a greener and cheaper source of power. In the future, this mind-set of slum dwellers could create a problem in reaching to them for implementation of Solar Bottle Bulb.

Both of them knew that this was quite an untapped market because they had come across a census report which read that out of 1.73 crore census houses reported, 1.37 crore are slum households. Need of cheap source of lighting wold be very high in this segment of population because of frequent power cuts? The issue of affording uninterrupted power supply was also a major concern because of low income levels of this segment. Most importantly 90% of slum households use electricity as the main source of power, out of which 20% is the stolen power supply

## Power Theft

Prashant came across a study which stated that India faces huge distribution loss in form of thefts. India is a power deficit country and it's appetite for energy is increasing every day. However, the distribution companies loose approximately Rs.70,000 crores due to power theft. This value is approximately 20% of the total electricity produced by the country. A significant part of this theft is done by urban slums dwellers. These cramped slums are so dingy that dwellers light their homes even in the day time from unauthorized power. The availability of Solar Bottle Bulb would free the slum dwellers from this dependence on stolen electricity during day time. Resulting which the government will not have to incur significant revenue loss. This will have significant benefit on the exchequer of the government of India. Both the students thought that the Ministry of Power can also be interested in implementation of this product. (See Figure 7: Target users in India)

## SUDARSHANA, MANAGEMENT INSTITUTE GHAZIABAD (MIG)

Sudarshana—the social welfare society of Management Institute Ghaziabad(MIG) of which Kartik and Prashant were members was established in order to promote social entrepreneurship through innovation and capacity building. Management Institute Ghaziabad is a reputed business school in India which was established in 1975. Over the years it has built a significant reputation in industry for continuously producing excellent management and research graduates who have excelled in various industries. Sudarshana was established in year 2001 at MIG and over the years it has developed relationships with number of NGOs and aid releasing agencies like the Ministry of Tribal Affairs, WHO etc.

The society encourages the business school students to take up projects that will bring a positive impact in the lives of those who are at the bottom of the pyramid by helping them in building sustainable businesses and exploring job opportunities for them. This is facilitated by providing mentorships and financial help to the students of the institute to go ahead with their ideas of social business ventures. Only the best from the institute get the opportunity to work with the reputed faculty associated with this society.

The society in the past has been successful in launching number of entrepreneurs, financing award winning documentaries and providing consultancy services to a number of NGOs.

## ENERGY POVERTY: A CURABLE MENACE?

Since electricity has now become a basic necessity, various organizations around the globe, primarily in developing and under-developed nations have taken the charge of illuminating those areas which are untouched by industrialization and hence are still devoid of electricity and its benefits. Thanks to technological advances, simple solar lamps which are portable and easy to manufacture have given the gift of light to millions in India and Africa. In wealthy countries, where access to cheap fossil-fuelled[c] electricity from the grid is nearly universal, solar electricity is still seen as an expensive energy option. That's particularly true when considering that a rooftop photovoltaic installation of sufficient size to power an electronics- and appliance-packed home costs tens of thousands of dollars. But the calculus is much different when bringing electricity for the first time to homes and communities that have none, with an aim of providing basic needs such as lighting and cell-phone charging. Development organizations are finding that solar energy is one of the most cost-effective options for providing not only power, but also a better livelihood.

Private companies and non-profits are tapping into this enormous global need. An estimated 1.6 billion people, or more than one-fifth of the world's population, don't have access to a public electricity grid and instead rely on other means of lighting such as kerosene and candles. Nearly 600 million of the energy-poor live in Africa. Buying kerosene fuel can strain already tight household budgets, often meaning little or no light for key evening and night time stretches when children could be studying and parents could be working indoors.

Kerosene also produces toxic smoke and soot, which damages lungs and causes other serious health problems. Kerosene lamps, especially makeshift ones, also are dangerous-tens of thousands of children and adults in the developing world die or are seriously burned in kerosene accidents each year.

It's unclear how fast the solar lamp market is growing, but India's 2011 census alone estimated 1.1 million homes with solar lighting devices.

## THE JOURNEY OF SOLAR BOTTLE BULB

### Solar Energy

The students were keen on working with solar energy due to a number of reasons. Solar energy is clean and renewable. It is abundant in tropical countries. Most prevalent use of solar energy currently is through solar cells[d] and also the cost of harvesting solar energy through solar cells is decreasing, however, the solar cells are themselves polluting. Unhealthy chemicals are used in solar panel manufacturing, including arsenic, cadmium telluride, chromium, and lead. These toxic metals will enter the environment when the solar panel is no longer useful. The solar cells manufacturing requires manufacturing of plastics which are not biodegradable. Further, the efficiency of solar cells decreases over time. The fluorescent bulbs that are connected to the solar cells to produce electricity are further polluting as they contain heavy metals like mercury. Solar bottle bulb directly harvests the energy of sun without the use of solar panels making it a better and environmental friendlier source of lighting.

### Why This Product?

Access to indoor lighting and its affordability is a growing problem and this has led to renewed interests in studies of solar lights. Especially in developing countries, access to electricity for indoor lighting is very important for growth, both socially and economically. The availability of light enhances the opportunities for a better education, a healthier life-style, and an extended amount of leisure time. These were the reasons which imbibed a thought in their mind to find a product which caters to all these needs. After a lot of hours spent on reading journals and using their experience in Sudarshana, they found this product designed by the students of Massachusetts Institute of Technology (MIT). They had devised a soda bottle solar light made from a 2 litre plastic soda bottle filled with water and bleach. The bottle bulb was inspired by engineer Amy Smith, from the D-Lab in MIT. The device when inserted through the roof of a house with almost half the bottle inside and half exposed to sunlight, manipulates the ultraviolet rays of the sun, resulting in an omnidirectional light source emitting light equal to a bulb of 50 or 60 watts.

## Philippines Story

Philippines is very similar to India in a number of aspects; both countries are developing and have large number of urban slums.

Sheila Guirreo, her husband, her mother and two young daughters lived in a single-room cement apartment in a poor neighbourhood in Manila, Philippines. Their tiny house sat less than a meter from a two-story building under construction and among close, cramped units. Like many such homes, it was mostly dark during the day, except for a small ray of sunlight that enters through an open front door.

But this was about to change.

On a lovely morning, volunteers of My Shelter Foundation (discussed in next section) arrived to hang low-tech solar bottle bulbs from the corrugated metal roof. The workers cut a circle exactly the size of the bottle's diameter into the corrugated metal roof. Then one litre bottle, filled with water and two caps-full of bleach- to keep it clean and clear- was placed inside the hole. The bottle stayed in place with sealant and to keep rain out and a small metal brace that was hammered into the roof. The liquid inside refracts sunlight and disperses light that is equivalent to about 55-watts bulb into the house.

Throughout the Philippines, solar bottle bulbs were being used by people who were not able to access or afford electricity for indoor lighting. There were national development programs that had been working on increasing the accessibility of electricity to other areas.

## My Shelter Foundation

My Shelter Foundation was established by Illac Diaz in 2006 to create a system of sustainability and reliability through its capability-building and employment-generating projects. This was one of their most ambitious projects in recent times. As of July 2011, the organization had installed 10,000 bottles in the Philippines and shortly thereafter reached 15,000 installations and their goal for 2012 was to reach 1 million homes. In order to help the idea to grow sustainably, they had implemented a "local entrepreneur" business model, whereby bottles were put together and installed by locals who can in turn earn a small income for their work.

The foundation, instead of working towards windmills and solar panels worked towards solar bottle bulbs because they wanted to tap the unexplored arena of huge demand of power in poor countries. They thought this product could be made available easily at a very low price to its targeted segment. Also, it would produce less carbon dioxide, one of the gases that cause global warming[d]. "If you multiply that by a million bottles, it will save more carbon than one huge windmill which costs more to run."

MyShelter Foundation also established a training center that conducts workshops with youth, business companies, and other groups who are interested in volunteering their time to build lights in their communities. Diaz's organization had been singled out for praise from the United Nations for its ability to upscale and reach so many people. In this regard, Diaz said one of the keys to his success was using the Internet to make people aware of the solar bottle while also giving them a solution online so they could immediately begin installing lights on their own.

*It's safer. It's healthier. It's brighter. And the funny thing is, the light bulb actually comes from the place you'd least expect it, which is the trash bin. So it's the cheapest light bulb in the world.*

*- Illac Diaz, MyShelter Foundation*

*Figure 1. Approximate cost of assembling and installing a Sola Bottle Bulb.*

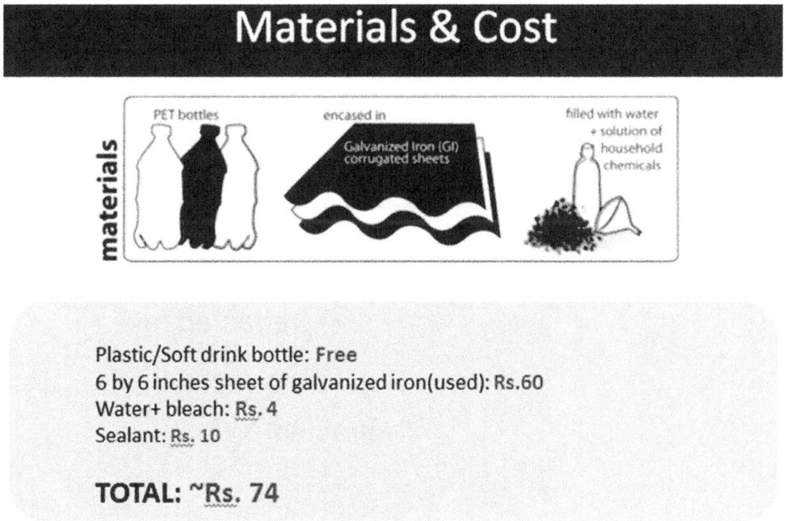


## SOLAR BOTTLE BULB

### Materials and Cost

Prashant estimated that the cost of constructing solar bottle bulb is very low and it could be made with the use of such material that is otherwise considered waste. A Solar Bottle Bulb requires 1 litre PET Bottle, galvanised iron corrugated sheet (approx. size 6" x 8"), household bleach, sealant, sand paper, pliers and filtered water. Please see Figure 1 for approximate cost of installing a solar bottle bulb.

### Assembly and Installation

The assembly of solar bottle bulb is quite easy; it had taken the students just an hour to construct a prototype for the first time. With skilled hands it may not even take 15 minutes to assemble and install it.

The assembly requires just three steps. Firstly, cut approximately 6" x 8" inches of galvanized iron sheet and at the centre of the sheet, draw two concentric circles with outer circle having radius just 1 cm longer than the bottle's radius. Secondly, cut the 1 cm difference radially, making strips and bend upwards, perpendicular to the GI sheet. Then insert the bottle into the GI sheet until the upper third. Thirdly, now apply rubber sealant on the strips above and around the area below and fill the bottle with the mixture of bleach and water.

The solar bulb is now ready for installation!!

Installation requires only two steps. Firstly, one needs to create a hole in the roof then fix the above assembly on the roof using nuts and bolts. Secondly, apply sealant on all sides of the GI sheet of the bulb to avoid leakage. (See Figure 8 for pictorial representation)

*Figure 2. Refraction properties of water*

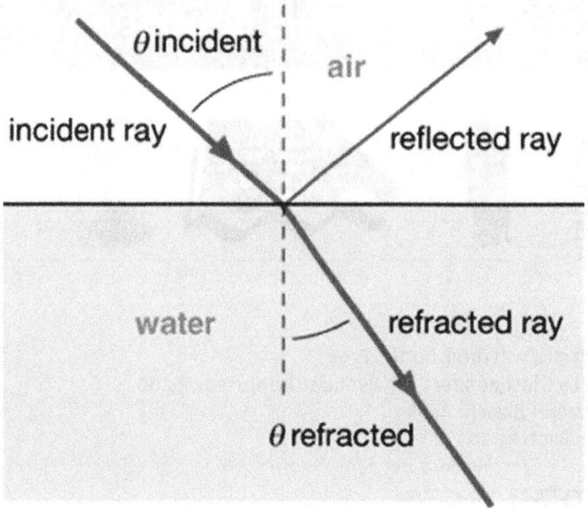


## Working

A solar bottle bulb works on the basic phenomenon of reflection and refraction of light (Snell's law) [e]. Also, water has an inherent property of dispersing light in all directions. So, when a light ray enters the bulb from above the roof, the water inside the bulb disperses the light in an omnidirectional manner sending light to every corner of the house. (See Figure 2) Addition of bleach helps in making the water clearer so that its refraction properties get enhanced. Bleach also helps in avoiding algae formation in the water and elongates the life of solar bottle bulb. Though the bulb needs sunlight to function at its best but in a clear night sky, it can emit measurable amount of light with the help of moon light. The colour of light emitting is a shade of white as in a household tube light and its intensity is apt to light up an average slum. Unlike the strong yellow/orange light of electrical bulbs, this light is soothing to eyes.

The light moving through air enters into water which is a denser material than air, its direction gets changed. The light changes the direction in such a way that it travels more directly in the water. This phenomenon is used by the solar bottle bulb to disperse more light into the slum. (See Figure 3)

*Figure 3. The difference in lighting conditions inside a small house with just a hole vis-à-vis a solar bottle bulb installed.*

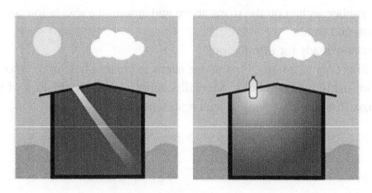

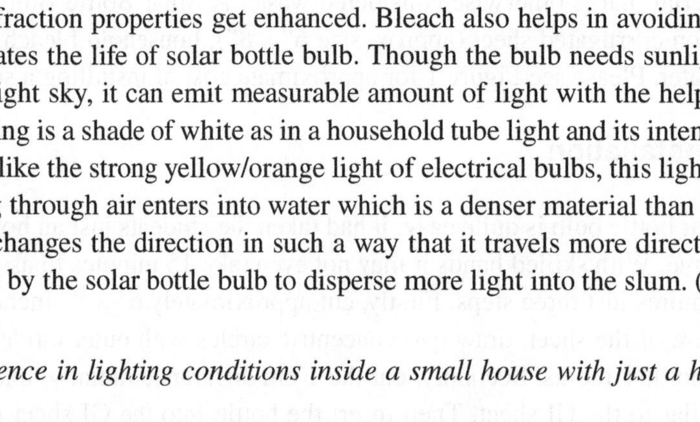

*Figure 4. Number of statutory and slum reported towns with type wise slum population*

**Number of Statutory and slum reported towns with type wise slum population**

| Name of State/ Union territoryt# | Towns | | Type wise Slum Population | | | |
|---|---|---|---|---|---|---|
| | Statutory towns | Slum reported towns | Total population | Notified slums | Recognised slums | Identified slums |
| **INDIA** | **4041** | **2,613** | **6,54,94,604** | **2,25,35,133** | **2,01,31,336** | **2,28,28,135** |
| Jammu & Kashmir | 86 | 40 | 6,62,062 | 1,62,909 | 1,36,649 | 3,62,504 |
| Himachal Pradesh | 56 | 22 | 61,312 | 60,201 | 0 | 1,111 |
| Punjab | 143 | 73 | 14,60,518 | 7,87,696 | 1,93,305 | 4,79,517 |
| Chandigarh | 1 | 1 | 95,135 | 95,135 | 0 | 0 |
| Uttarakhand | 74 | 31 | 4,87,741 | 1,85,832 | 52,278 | 2,49,631 |
| Haryana | 80 | 75 | 16,62,305 | 14,912 | 0 | 16,47,393 |
| NCT Delhi* | 3 | 22 | 17,85,390 | 7,38,915 | 0 | 10,46,475 |
| Rajasthan | 185 | 107 | 20,68,000 | 0 | 0 | 20,68,000 |
| Uttar Pradesh* | 648 | 293 | 62,39,965 | 5,62,548 | 46,78,326 | 9,99,091 |
| Bihar | 139 | 88 | 12,37,682 | 0 | 0 | 12,37,682 |
| Sikkim | 8 | 7 | 31,378 | 31,378 | 0 | 0 |
| Arunachal Pradesh | 26 | 5 | 15,562 | 0 | 0 | 15,562 |
| Nagaland | 19 | 11 | 82,324 | 0 | 48,249 | 34,075 |
| Manipur | 28 | 0 | 0 | 0 | 0 | 0 |
| Mizoram | 23 | 1 | 78,561 | 0 | 78,561 | 0 |
| Tripura | 16 | 15 | 1,39,780 | 0 | 1,24,036 | 15,744 |
| Assam | 88 | 31 | 1,97,266 | 9,163 | 70,979 | 1,17,124 |
| West Bengal | 129 | 122 | 64,18,594 | 48,918 | 37,03,852 | 26,65,824 |
| Jharkhand | 40 | 31 | 3,72,999 | 64,399 | 59,432 | 2,49,168 |
| Odisha | 107 | 76 | 15,60,303 | 0 | 8,12,737 | 7,47,566 |
| Chhattisgarh | 168 | 94 | 18,98,931 | 7,13,654 | 7,64,851 | 4,20,426 |
| Madhya Pradesh | 364 | 303 | 56,88,993 | 19,00,942 | 25,30,637 | 12,57,414 |
| Gujarat | 195 | 103 | 16,80,095 | 0 | 0 | 16,80,095 |
| Daman & Diu | 2 | 0 | 0 | 0 | 0 | 0 |
| Dadra & Nagar Haveli | 1 | 0 | 0 | 0 | 0 | 0 |
| Maharashtra | 256 | 189 | 1,18,48,423 | 37,09,309 | 34,85,783 | 46,53,331 |
| Andhra Pradesh | 125 | 125 | 1,01,86,934 | 83,38,154 | 8,77,172 | 9,71,608 |
| Karnataka | 220 | 206 | 32,91,434 | 22,71,990 | 4,45,899 | 5,73,545 |
| Goa | 14 | 3 | 26,247 | 6,107 | 0 | 20,140 |
| Lakshadweep | 0 | 0 | 0 | 0 | 0 | 0 |
| Kerala | 59 | 19 | 2,02,048 | 1,86,835 | 8,215 | 6,998 |
| Tamil Nadu | 721 | 507 | 57,98,459 | 25,41,345 | 19,78,441 | 12,78,673 |
| Puducherry | 6 | 6 | 1,44,573 | 70,092 | 73,928 | 553 |
| Andaman & Nicobar Is. | 1 | 1 | 14,172 | 0 | 0 | 14,172 |

## Sustainability

The Solar Bottle Bulb is an environmentally-friendly, zero carbon emitting alternative to the daytime use of incandescent light bulbs and kerosene. The plastic bottles and the other materials used in the technology are easily available eliminating the need for energy-intensive processes involved in gathering, manufacturing and transporting new bottles. Coupled with the simple assembly, this means that even people in the most deprived neighbourhoods can install and enjoy the benefits that are associated with access to better lighting. The affordability of the technology means that the majority of slum households can install it with the assistance of entrepreneurs in the informal settlements who stand to benefit from having a new source of income. Although it is virtually free, once installed the bottle is estimated to continue producing light for a period of five years before having to be replaced reinforcing the project's economic sustainability. According to MyShelter Foundation, the GHG emissions savings accumulated from substituting an incandescent bulb with the Liter of Light and using it for the same number of hours during the day are substantial, especially when considered over the 5-year lifetime of the latter technology.

## Implementation: Pilot Project

It was going to be a herculean task to implement their idea in their target group. Slum dwellers knew their ways of stealing electricity from nearby connections and lack of awareness was also a hindrance in taking the ir product into the slum dwellers' lives. Hence, it was important to understand the psyche of slum dwellers as it would have helped them note down some common issues they might face while implementation of the project. In order to do this it was required that Kartik and Prashant had one on one interaction with the targeted users. To introduce slum dwellers to the idea of implementation of solar bottle bulb in their houses, a prototype was constructed from cardboard. It was a 4X2X2 ft box with a hole at its top to fit a small solar bottle bulb. Intensity of light inside the box was recorded in different positions under the sunlight. Videos were created of this exercise with background voice in 'Hindi' explaining about the solar bottle bulb and its uses & benefits.

The students visited a number of slums around the institute. In these slums the prototype was shown along with the videos. At first they had to face reluctance because slum dwellers thought that it didn't concern them but later they became responsive to the explanation. The benefits of the product were explained to them. There initial reactions were recorded and concerns raised by them were registered. Nearly all the respondents were sceptical about the working of the bulb. Though they liked the videos but did not seem very confident of using it. Having slums made with galvanized iron roofs was an important pre-requisite to using this bulb, and this had become a road-block to expansion of reach as many slum houses were made of other materials such as raw bricks or 'khapra' as they called it.

Also, there were concerns over drilling a hole into their homes' roofs as they feared that roof formed the most important part of their house and if it wasn't sealed properly, their homes would be filled with water during the rainy season. A few said that the bulb would not emit light during night when it is needed the most so there was no use of it. Some said that they had kerosene lamps for night and they didn't need light in the day as sunlight was enough for them. Initial touch point of the product with its users revealed mixed reactions; some were a little reluctant to the idea whereas some were equally excited and ready to install the solar bottle bulb. The million dollar question was now who will take up this project to the next level and how?

*Figure 5. State Share of Slum population to total slum population of India*

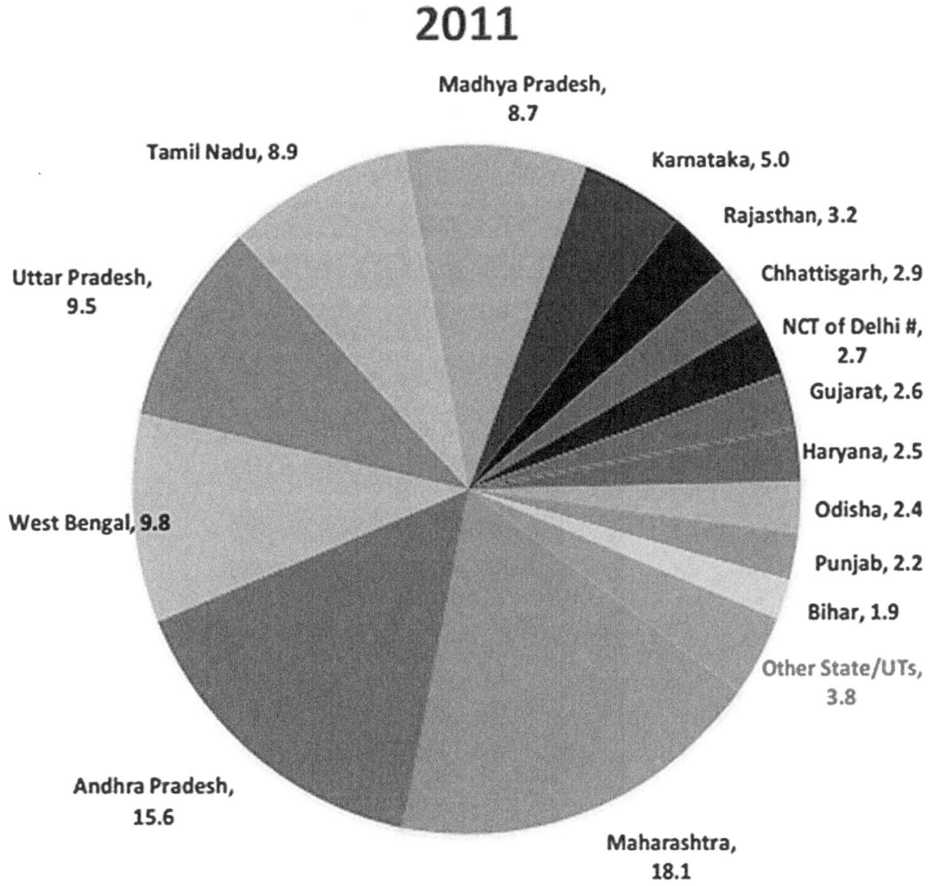


## COMPETITION

Seeing this huge demand and supply gap, many players had entered in this category and had come out with innovative products which use solar energy to provide light in rural parts of India. Some of these successful projects are:

### 1. TERI Solar Lantern

The Lighting a Billion Lives (LaBL) initiative launched by The Energy and Resources Institute (TERI) aimed to replace kerosene-based lighting with cleaner, more efficient, and more reliable solar lighting devices. LaBL employed an entrepreneurial model of last mile energy delivery to establish micro solar-enterprises in un-electrified or poorly electrified villages. The initiative had reached to around half-a-million people in 1860 villages across 22 states of India. In 2007, at the Clinton Global Initiative annual meeting, TERI committed to bring light and socio-economic development to one million rural people in India.

*Figure 6. Distribution of Slums in India*

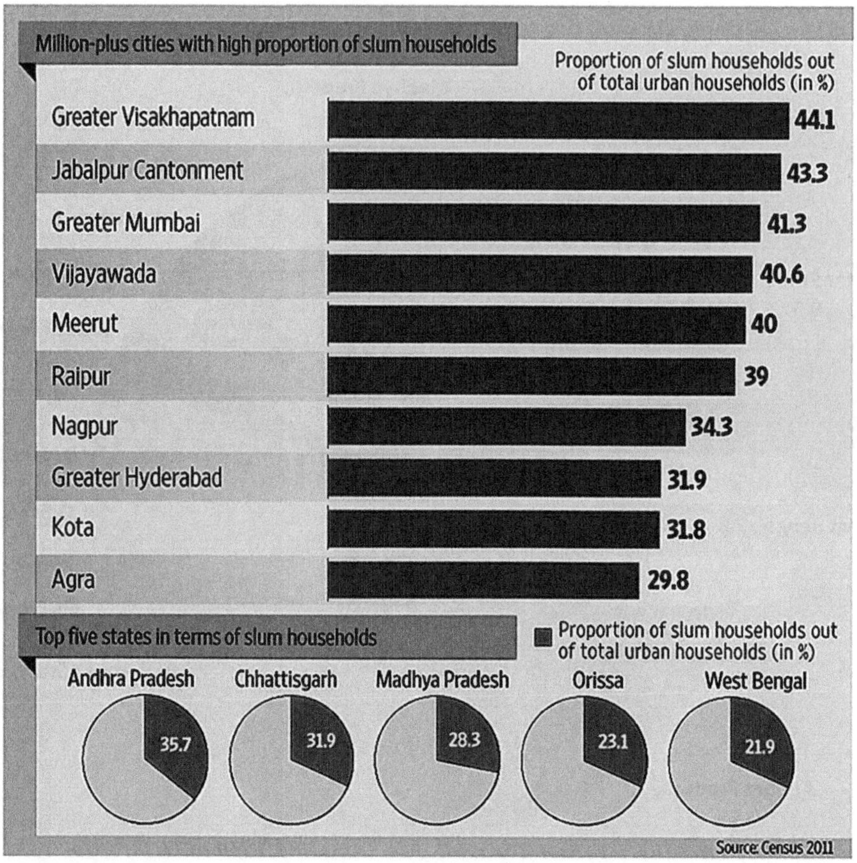


LaBL was based on an entrepreneurial model of energy service delivery which seeks to provide high-quality and cost-effective solar lamps, disseminated through micro solar enterprises set up in un-electrified or poorly electrified villages. These enterprises were operated and managed by a local entrepreneur trained under the initiative, who rents the solar lamps every evening, for an affordable fee, to the rural populace. The approach includes:

- Fee-for-service model: This approach made solar lighting affordable to the poorer sections of society with the user paying only a nominal daily rent. Capital costs were supported to a large extent by grants.
- Loan finance model: This provided an option for operators to start solar enterprises as their own business by facilitating loans (through financial institutions) and subsidizing some of the cost of the enterprise (via TERI and/or the partner organizations, including government agencies).

*Figure 7. Target Users in India*

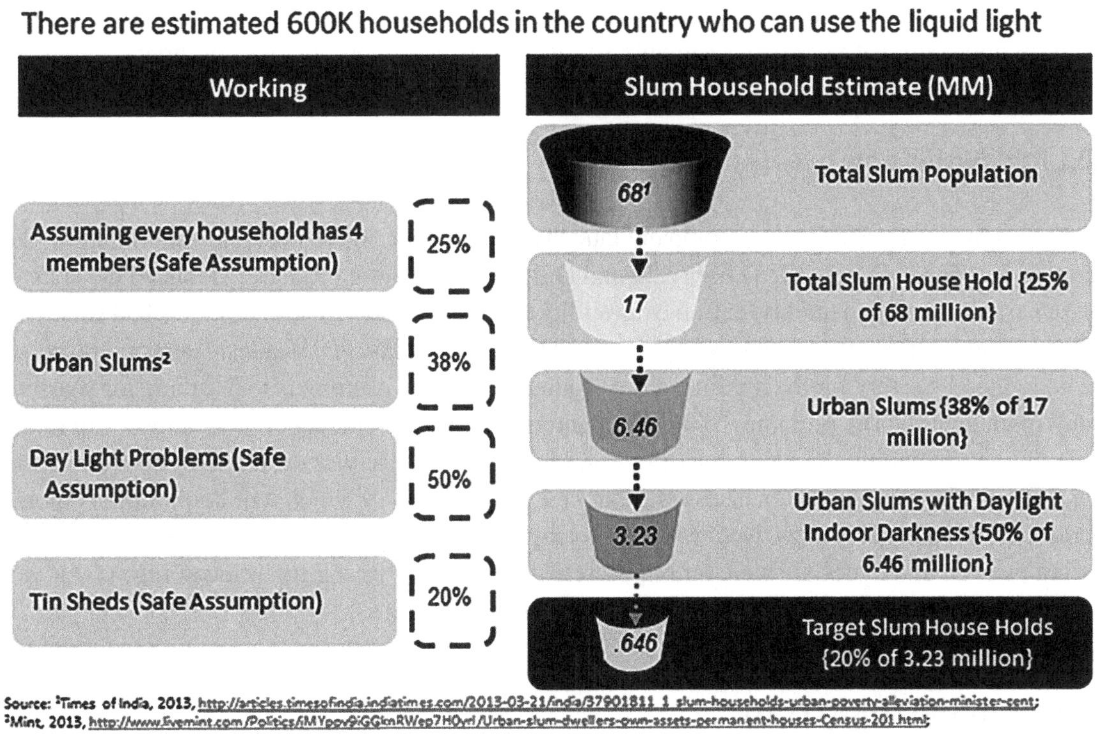
There are estimated 600K households in the country who can use the liquid light
Working
Slum Household Estimate (MM)
Total Slum Population
68[1]
Assuming every household has 4 members (Safe Assumption)
25%
17
Total Slum House Hold {25% of 68 million}
Urban Slums[2]
38%
6.46
Urban Slums {38% of 17 million}
Day Light Problems (Safe Assumption)
50%
3.23
Urban Slums with Daylight Indoor Darkness {50% of 6.46 million}
Tin Sheds (Safe Assumption)
20%
.646
Target Slum House Holds {20% of 3.23 million}
Source: [1]Times of India, 2013, http://articles.timesofindia.indiatimes.com/2013-03-21/india/37901811_1_slum-households-urban-poverty-alleviation-minister-cent;
[2]Mint, 2013, http://www.livemint.com/Politics/iMYpov9iGGknRWep7H0yrI/Urban-slum-dwellers-own-assets-permanent-houses-Census-201.html;

*Figure 8. Assembly and Installation*

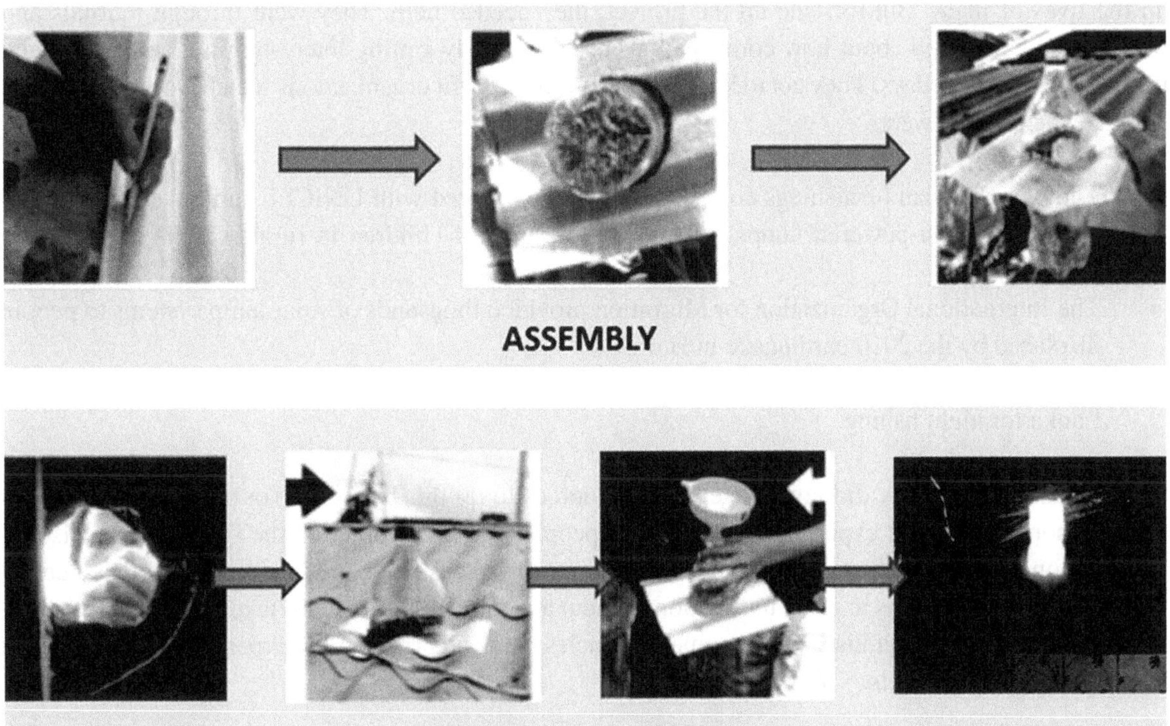
ASSEMBLY
ROOF INSTALLATION

The LaBL initiative was helping to address critical clean and sustainable energy challenges while spurring innovations that help enable energy access for all. The campaign had adopted a localized, bottom-up approach that provided a valuable set of lessons and good practices on how to address the challenges of providing clean lighting to billions of people that are at the bottom of the pyramid.

## 2. D.Light Solar Lamp

D. light design, an American based company launched its product line of portable solar lamps in 2013. It came in 3 variants; D.light S2, D.light S20 and D.light S300. These products advanced the social enterprise's tradition of high quality, extreme durability and affordability. These products had solar panels that charge more efficiently on cloudy days and LEDs that could last for decades. Battery replacements were no longer necessary for the lifetime of the products, allowing customers to use them for years without any maintenance. The premium S300 solar lantern and mobile charger could charge a full range of mobile phones, including the latest smartphones. Each solar lantern was designed to be more resistant to dust, impact, insects and water. These were priced at Rs 399 or $9 which will help millions more access the benefits of solar energy. Note with the average income of a majority of Indians being $2 a day, solar lamps even at $20 dollars were an impossible dream. By lowering the price point to $9,it would help get more at the bottom of the pyramid to buy these solar lamps.

## THE PLAN: DISTRIBUTION

Kartik and Prashant knew that it was a great idea and if implemented well, it can bring drastic changes in the lives of many. But to scale up the project, they needed help. They went through journals and websites which talked about how companies were increasingly getting interested in Corporate Social Responsibility these days. They got to know of various non-profit organizations which worked in similar area. Few examples were:

- The Scandinavian furnishings company Ikea had partnered with UNICEF and Save the Children to provide solar-powered lamps to tens of thousands of children in rural schools in India and Pakistan.
- The International Organization for Migration provided thousands of solar lamp systems to people displaced by the 2010 earthquake in Haiti.
- Non-profit organization EMACE, Sri Lanka had distributed 172 solar lamps to fishermen in Sri Lanka for night fishing.

The institute's society did not have enough resources to do this by itself. Not only were they looking for monetary aid but experienced and trained people who had worked in the field of channels and distribution of products. Since, the project would have started covering one slum at a time; they needed identify their target slums in order to function without any hassles. They could take help of NGOs, self-help groups, venture capitalists or government agencies who had prior market experience or would have worked in similar projects.

Any organisations that would tie-up with the project would bring in their volunteers who had goodwill in the local urban slum community. Introduction of the bulb through these volunteers would be more acceptable to slum dwellers as they were already not so sure of getting a hole drilled in their rooftops. As the process of assembling was simple, this could be easily taught to the volunteers who would initially install it. Once enough interest was created in the community, then they could transfer their skills of manufacturing and installation of the bulb to the local youth in the community. They thought that this may even create the installation of solar bottle bulb a micro-business [f] within the community.

## WAY FORWARD

The dilemma which both the students faced was the issue of Scalability. They had done thorough research on their part with all the required facts and figures. All they needed was a fool-proof marketing and implementation plan of their product. They knew that since the demand of electricity was rising in the urban slums, solar bottle bulb could be a blessing for the slum dwellers. Also, the cost factor was a big positive point of the bulb considering the low income level of target population.

It could be a luring proposal for the electricity department of different stated of India since the solar bottle bulb could save up to Rs.18 cr. every year. In addition it would help in reduction of pollution and reduce electricity theft. Both the students were very confident about the idea of getting NGOs on board to fund the whole project. Sudarshana had contacts with various small and large scale NGOs which had been involved with the society in earlier projects.

Identifying the NGOs and convincing them to implement solar bottle bulb in urban slums had number of conflicting challenges. Larger NGOs would be difficult to approach and would have number of projects in pipeline. They would be reluctant to accept any external proposal whereas smaller NGOs would be interested to be a part of this project in order to be associated with the prestigious Management Institute Ghaziabad. In addition, larger NGOs would have resources and capabilities to take up this project which in turn would have reduced the time required for the benefits to reach the maximum population. However, these NGOs often did not have strong community connection in comparison to the smaller NGOs. The product introduction required building of trust from the end users with the NGOs as the matter was important to users because it directly dealt with the roofs over the heads of the users. Other option that could be explored was roping in a number of NGOs for different regions.

There were some expectations which these creators had from the NGOs. The NGOs selected should have had the capability of identifying different processes that were required for the implementation of this product and also the zeal to continuously keep improving them by emulating the best industrial practices. Moreover, selected NGOs' goals and values should be in sync with Sudarshana for better transfer of knowledge and skills leading to mutually beneficial relationship that would last up to full implementation of the project.

Solar Bottle Bulb had to compete with other products in the same category which were targeted to the same consumers. Some of these were Solar D.light, TERI solar lantern, hand crank lantern and kerosene lamp. The benefits of bulb over these similar products needed to be highlighted to the NGOs. How solar bottle bulb was better than other products, needed to be logically explained to NGOs. The battery life of the solar lantern, the cost and high probability of the mechanical failure of the hand crank lantern, and the pollution caused by the kerosene lamp were some of the drawbacks of these products. D light came in three variants and all of them were costlier than solar bottle bulb. Also, the solar panel used in D.light was made of heavy metals like arsenic, cadmium etc. In addition, the awareness of the non-apparent ill effects like the blue spectrum light emitted by LEDs had to be increased in order to promote the solar bulb.

## REFERENCES

Bergen, I. A. (2013). Selling Solar Power in India's Slums. *The Atlantic Cities*. Retrieved September, 24, 2013 from http://www.theatlanticcities.com/jobs-and-economy/2013/04/selling-solar-power-indias-slums/5153/

Ganesh, J. (2013). *Data on Indian Slums, Searchlight South Asia*. Retrieved October, 01, 2013 from http://urbanpoverty.intellecap.com/?p=879

Goldena, R., & Min, S. (2012). *Theft and Loss of Electricity in an Indian State*. Retrieved September, 14, 2013 from http://www.theigc.org/sites/default/files/Golden%20and%20Min_Electricity%20theft.pdf

Grayson, T. (2013). Eco Etiquette: How Green Are Solar Panels? *Huffington Post*. Retrieved October, 11, 2013 from http://www.huffingtonpost.com/jennifer-grayson/eco-etiquette-how-green-a_b_554717.html

Maken, A. (2013). 68 million Indians living in slums. *The Times of India*. Retrieved September, 06, 2013 from http://articles.timesofindia.indiatimes.com/2013-03-21/india/37901811_1_slum-households-urban-poverty-alleviation-minister-cent

Malakunas, R., & France, P. (2011). Philippine solar light bottles offer hope. *Inquirer News*. Retrieved October, 02, 2013 from http://newsinfo.inquirer.net/103043/philippine-solar-light-bottles-offer-hope

Oredain, K. (2013). Soda Bottle Solar Bulbs Bring Light to Thousands in the Philippines. *Voive of Americe*. Retrieved September, 12, 2013 from http://www.voanews.com/content/soda-bottle-solar-bulbs-bring-light-to-thousands-in-the-philippines-134766408/168250.html

Orendain, K. (2013). In Philippine Slums, Capturing Light in a Bottle. *NPR*. Retrieved October, 15, 2013 from http://www.npr.org/2011/12/28/144385288/in-philippine-slums-capturing-light-in-a-bottle

Rehmaan, D. (2013). India's Slumdog census reveals poor conditions for one in six urban dwellers. *The Guardian*. Retrieved October, 02, 2013 from http://www.theguardian.com/world/2013/mar/22/india-slumdog-census-poor-conditions

Sethi, J. (2013). Urban slums data reinforces India's consumption story. *Mint and the Wall Street Journal*. Retrieved September, 16, 2013 from http://www.livemint.com/Politics/jMYppv9iGGknRWep7H0yrI/Urban-slum-dwellers-own-assets-permanent-houses-Census-201.html

## KEY TERMS AND DEFINITIONS

**A micro-enterprise (or microbusiness):** is a type of small business, often registered, having five or fewer employees and requiring seed capital of not more than Rs.50,000.

**A solar cell:** (also called a photovoltaic cell) is an electrical device that converts the energy of light directly into electricity by the photovoltaic effect.

**Fossil fuels:** are hydrocarbons, primarily coal, fuel oil or natural gas, formed from the remains of dead plants and animals.

**Global warming:** refers to an unequivocal and continuing rise in the average temperature of Earth's climate system.

**Non-governmental organizations (NGOs):** are legally constituted corporations created by natural or legal people that operate independently from any form of government.

**Slum:** defined as a human settlement of at least 20 households with a collection of poorly built tenements, mostly of temporary nature in a small area usually unfit for human habitation.

**Snell's law:** is a formula used to describe the relationship between the angles of incidence and refraction, when referring to light or other waves passing through a boundary between two different isotropic media, such as water, glass and air.

# Chapter 18
# Business, Government, and Society Synergy for Sustainable Livelihood:
## A Case Study of Sabars from Jharkhand

**Ranjana Agarwal**
*IMT Ghaziabad, India*

**Parag Agarwal**
*IMT Ghaziabad, India*

## ABSTRACT

*In the post globalization era, synergy of Business, Government, and Society (BGS) forces is paving the way for development. This chapter gives an example of a case where BGS forces work together for development. The chapter discusses livelihood issues of Sabars, a tribal group from Jharkhand, located in Eastern India. A local NGO was working for upliftment of tribal people.. The Sabars were given training in making handicrafts under a project under Government of India. The focus of the training programme was on creating marketable handicrafts based on tribal's inherent art and culture. Problems were faced in marketing the products. Students from MBA College were roped in to provide solutions for marketing. The chapter discussed how social issues can be tackled collaboratively by all sectors of society. This chapter is based on primary data and is primarily qualitative in nature.*

## INTRODUCTION

Globalization, liberalization and Privatization forces have brought about paradigm shifts in society. The role of the three sectors, Business, Government and Society has changed considerably in the post globalization era. Changing paradigms in society has ushered an era where the government is no longer a key player. Earlier, the onus of development was on government. The role of government is now of a regulator. It is instrumental in implementing changes in society through public policy and regulation. The government assists society in which businesses operate through economic and social policies.

DOI: 10.4018/978-1-4666-8259-7.ch018

Changing global political and economic structures have paved the way for civil society development. An important aspect of civil society development is the growth of large number of Non-Governmental Organizations – NGOs. The civil society referred to as the third sector is today a sizeable force in society. The third sector has today assumed the role of a watchdog and is also playing an important role in development aspects in context of receding role of state.

Businesses have tremendous power to change society. They affected society by changing ideas, institutions and materials things. Post globalization, the receding role of state has accorded it higher power than earlier. Many corporations may be larger than small governments. Steiner and Steiner (2012) go on to explain that given the magnitude of power the businesses command in society, the onus of development is now falling on business. In India, The Company's Act 2013 is now made it mandatory for large companies to work and spend compulsorily on developmental activities under the mandate of Corporate Social Responsibility.

The three elements or spheres of society, the Business, the Government and Civil Society have different roles and functions. Each one has its distinctive strengths and weaknesses. All sectors have realized the strengths and weaknesses of each other and are combining together to get the best results. The work of Lawrence and Weber (2012) shows the strength and weaknesses of each sector. It is the synergy of forces of Business, Government and Society (BGS), which is paving the way for development.

This case study highlights how forces of Business, Government and Society joined hands for upliftment of Sabar tribes, in Jharkhand, in the state of Eastern India. Sabar tribes are classified as, primitive tribal group (PTG) now renamed as particularly vulnerable tribal group (PVTG). The Sabar tribes in Jharkhand were given training in making handicrafts under, IAP, a project under Planning Commission of India in the district of Saraikela Kharsawan. The project was executed by the state Government of Jharkhand. The major focus of the training programme aims at creating marketable handicrafts based on tribal's' inherent art and culture. These handicrafts, if adapted to modern designs, have huge perceived value and utility. The training is given in making goods based using "Kansi Grass" (an indigenous grass) and "Bamboo" as raw material which is found in abundance in this region. However, training continued for 8 months and goods were made. Problems were being faced in marketing these products.

To find solutions to these marketing problems, students from MBA College were roped in the project. The Government of Jharkhand also joined hands with an NGO Ambalika for the cause of tribal community. As a result, efforts were made to market the products. The management students also advocated the cause of continuation of training programme. The students also suggested how digitization tools could be used for marketing the products, their areas of operation and the lacunae they can fill in promotion of these handicrafts.

This chapter is based on primary data. Observations, Questionnaires and interviews were used to collect data. The study is exploratory in nature. The author's own experiences are the major source of data collection. After discussing Business, Government and Society relationships, the paper discusses the issues of tribal community and their life style. It then discusses the role played by each of 3 sectors in working for the cause of tribes. The last section concludes the paper.

## BACKGROUND: THE BUSINESS – GOVERNMENT – SOCIETY RELATIONSHIP

As stated above, all 3 sectors have unique strengths and weaknesses. Post globalization, it is the development of collaborative, multi-sector partnership which has led to solving particular social problems (Lawrence and Weber 2012). As highlighted by Lawrence and Weber (2012), the core competencies of all 3 sectors of Business, Government and Society can be combined to solve social issues as each sector has its unique attributes.

Businesses have technical know-how, capital assets and production skills. The government has regulatory and enforcement power and can also implement social and economic policies beneficial to society. Civil society has community support and inspirational leadership. A combination of unique capabilities of all sectors can bring manifold changes in society. The strengths of one sector can counterbalance the weaknesses of other sectors. Businesses have short term motives while government sector is highly bureaucratic. Society is amateurish and lacks financial resources. Government sector weaknesses can be neutralized by bringing professional approach from business. Society and government can focus on long term prospects. Development issues can be solved through BGS synergy.

A method of implementing the BGS synergy is the public private partnership mode (PPP). On examining Research and survey series by Ockleford (2000) show that tri – sector partnerships have been instrumental in implementing water sanitation projects as Colombia, Angola and Philippines. The PURA model of development in India is also based on (PPCP) Public Private Community Partnership model as discussed by Kalam and Singh (2011).

Steiner and Steiner, (2012) elaborate four different models of Business, Government and Society relationship. As per the Stakeholder model, the corporation is at the center of an array of mutual relationships with persons, groups and entities called Stakeholders. Stakeholders are those whom the corporation benefits or burdens by its actions and those who benefit or burden the firm with its actions.

In India too, the concept of tri- sector partnership has emerged in various sectors. The development of tribal community in Jharkhand is an example of 3 sector collaboration. The Planning Commission and Govt. of Jharkhand were forces of government and were imparting training in handicrafts to tribals. The NGO Ambalika was the element of Civil Society. The MBA students from IMT Ghaziabad played the role of business as well as society.

## LIVELIHOOD ISSUES FOR SABAR TRIBE

Tribals constitute around 28% of total population of the state of Jharkhand, which is around 8% of total tribal population of India. 9 tribes have been identified as PVTG or PTG primitive tribal groups in Jharkhand namely Asur, Birhor, Birajia, Korwa, Parahiya (Baiga), Sabar, Mal Pahariya and Souriya Pahariya and Bil Kahria. The tribal's have the inherent art of rope making, basket making and weaving. One option for livelihood is handicrafts, which holds great potential but has to be redesigned as per modern day requirements.

Sabar are primitive tribes in Eastern India mainly residing in Jharkhand. Their main economic activities are basketry, collection of minor forest produce from forest, lac cultivation and agriculture. Their total population in Jharkhand as per Census 2001 is 3014. Sabars constitute .05% of tribal population in Jharkhand. The Sabar have the concept of village Panchayat where all heads of family are the members. The village head is called "*Manjhi*" who holds rent free land for his service. As per 2001 census, Sabars occupy 0.05% of the total Tribal population in Jharkhand.

Although these tribal people have the potential to make handicrafts with high demand potential, they were plagued with several problems. Their lifestyle is extremely backward. They are not educated, extremely poor, and have no economic resources. They lack awareness regarding social and economic issues. They need to be handled tactfully and carefully integrate in the larger section of society without endangering their ethnic identity.

Drinking is a part of tribal culture. Drinking is a major problem which affects their lifestyle behavioral patterns. Substance abuse of harmful Mahua and Hadia (local liquor) leads to health problems as well contributes to their economic degradation. The tribal people are short-sighted and could visualize only the immediate need.

Lack of suitable job opportunities is another problem. They have no option, apart from wood cutting and gathering from forests. There is a middleman to whom they sell their goods. The profits are taken away by the middleman and very little money comes in the hands of the tribal people.

The cause of Sabars were taken up by an NGO called Ambalika. It was working for development of livelihood by giving training in handicrafts. It was working for marketing of handicrafts made by the tribal people.

## Role of NGO: Ambalika

Ambalika is an NGO which was incorporated and registered under the Societies Registration Act XXI of 1860 on 17th of January, 2002. One main objective is to train artisans and craftspersons from the PTGs to improve their skills, increase their productivity through design and development of their products and finally sell the products for livelihood. Ambalika has adopted three tribes viz, Sabars, Birhors and Paharias, in the villages of Chilgu, Asanboni, Makula, Kamjhor, Kadambjhor, Chakulia, Sumanpur and Bhangat under Chandil and Nimdih blocks of Saraikela-Kharsawan district of Jharkhand. Ambalika has started working for economic development of PTG's artisans and craftpersons by reviving and upgrading their age-old dying craft with the help of Designers from National Institute of Fashion Technology (NIFT), Delhi and Kolkata. The designers from NIFT, Kolkata and Delhi were invited to stay with these tribes in their villages as to understand their art, crafts and culture. The aim was to impart training to improve their skills and efficiency by way of introducing new design and technology in order to modernize their products and make them marketable.

Ambalika has organized several Design Development workshops in the villages of Nimdih and Chandil Blocks in which 210 craft persons including 85 women from Paharia and Sabar primitive tribes participated. These Workshops were organized especially in the crafts like Papier Mache, Terracota, Bamboo, Kansi Grass and Palm leaves which are found in abundance in this area. On the recommendations from the District Admin, Ambalika got some support from Bihar State Export Corporations, Ministry of Culture, Office of DC Handicraft and Rural Development, Government of India and some local corporate Houses as a part of their CSR programme. However, the support from these Ministries proved to be inadequate and unsustainable. Some efforts were made to create self-help groups (SHG) of the women folk of the PTGs under Development of Women and Children in Rural Areas (DWCRA) programme of the State Government but that could not last long because of lack of continuous and sustained support.

When Ambalika organized Design and Development Workshops in these areas, with the support from NIFT, the products developed under these workshops were highly appreciated. The PTG artisans were invited to participate in India International Trade Fair 2011 at Pragati Maidan, New Delhi by Department of Industry, Government of Jharkhand. These artisans were adjudged best among all craftsmen, participated in Jharkhand Pavilion. Their work was highly appreciated by Honorable Welfare Minister, Government of Jharkhand, Sri Ranjan Chatterjee, Senior Consultant, Planning Commission, Mrs. Snehlata Kumar, Additional Secretary, Ministry of Tribal Affairs, Government of India and many others.

The Senior Consultant from Planning Commission of India was very much impressed with the work of the PTGs and efforts made by Ambalika. He offered to lend support to carry out this project through Integrated Action Programme (IAP).

## Role of Government: Training Module

Training in handicrafts was given by the government under IAP, Integrated Action Plan, (Planning Commission initiative) to Sabars PTG. The training named as "Design Enhancement and Development Training" started in an area of Nimdih block in Saraikela Kharsawan district in 3 modules. The first Module was from 12 March, 2012 to 12 June, 2012 oand trained 55 craftsperson. 20 artisans worked on Bamboo craft while 35 worked on Kansi grass handicraft. The second Module began on 4 May, 2012 and continued to 4 August, 2012 for 62 craftsperson. 20 worked on Bamboo craft and 42 worked on Kansi grass handicrafts. The third Module was also held in the same year and trained 61 craftsmen on the same lines as before.

The implementation of IAP plan was through the state government of Jharkhand. A Committee headed by District Collector/District Magistrate, Superintendent of Police of the District and the District Forest Officer were responsible for implementation of this scheme. The District-level Committee had the flexibility to spend the amount for development schemes according to need as assessed by it.

The aim of the IAP training programme was to:

a. Involve the whole tribal community, preserving their ethnic identity keeping in mind the objective of inclusive growth.
b. Make the system stable and self-sustainable without influence of any outside body.
c. Make sure the profits earned goes back to tribal society and for their advancement to further enhance their growth.

*Area of Study* - Saraikela-Kharsawan district (formerly the Princely State of Seraikella/Saraikella) is one of the twenty-four districts of Jharkhand state in eastern India. This district was carved out from West Singhbhum district in 2001. Nimdih block is located in district Saraikela Kharsawan. The district has an overall literacy rate of 68.85%, where Male literacy rate is 81.01% and Female literacy rate is 56.19% as per 2011 census.

The training was in batches under Integrated Action Planning (IAP) by Planning Commission in 2012. This was a pilot training module which trained around 168 tribal people in handicrafts made from Kansi grass and bamboo. The funds were allocated under the office of District Magistrate. An officer working with government of Jharkhand was instrumental in pushing the programme forward.

Training was given by a designer from NIFT in making around 120 products. The existing production range consisted of Baskets, Jewellery Boxes and Small utility products. Some of the main products developed were Show Pieces (peacock, mask), Night lamp, Table lamp, Wooden clock, Bags, Hats, Pots, Hand fans , Tea plates, Optical cases , Boxes, Pen stand and File folders. The Costing of goods is based on 3 parameters: Raw material (negligible), Man power (Rs. 120 per day) and Profit margin (10-15% or perceived value).

These artisans were sourcing the raw materials locally from the nearby forests and other areas around water bodies. Basic tools & equipment were used by artisans as a small needle made locally using umbrella spooks. as well as a pair of small scissors. The steps of the production process were very simple. It started with sourcing of the grass and date leaves and then moved on to drying the kansi grass. This was followed by sizing and removing waste from the grass. After this, the artisans weaved the product using date leaves. Finishing of the product was given due importance. Artisans were paid Rs 120 per day for training. Food and transport were also the perks given for on the job training.

## Role of IMT Ghaziabad: Business Solutions for Society, a CSR Initiative

The training programme continued for 8 months and was discontinued in March 2012. An officer from Govt. of Jharkhand continued working for the cause of tribes. Some efforts were made to sell the handicrafts in India International trade Fair (IITF) and Delhi Haat. However, only limited marketing of goods was done. The officer from govt. of Jharkhand was working with an NGO Ambalika which had earlier given training to artisans. Now the main aim of NGO was selling of products. However, they received a feedback that the prices of goods were too high. Substantial corrections were required as far as pricing was concerned. Marketing the products was a major problem. Hence, they approached IMT Ghaziabad as it was felt that MBA students could provide solutions for marketing of products.

A team of 1 faculty member and students started working on marketing of Kansi grass products made by primitive tribal groups. The team mapped different Stages of handicraft development under IAP training programme for sustainable development.

A. Training Programme
B. Making of goods
C. Proper Pricing of goods
D. Finding suitable markets for goods
E. Creating local managers
F. Creating a sustainable livelihood option

The team from IMT was working with Govt of Jharkhand as it was Delhi based. This team realised that their strengths lay in mainly stage C and D, which was mainly proper pricing of goods and finding suitable markets for goods. The team realized that although the training programme was an initiative of high quality, enough efforts were not put in marketing. The whole effort was on training programme only. The customer, who is the last mile linkage, has been totally neglected. The customer has to be kept in mind also while designing the products. Also, Marketing requires sustained efforts, to get returns in initial period. Due to certain reasons marketing of products could start only after 7 months of training programme. Exhibitions were put up in Delhi haat and India International Trade Fair (IITF) for 30 days only which was too less a time period. Awareness about such products was missing. They decided to make use of new information and communication technologies for marketing purposes.

They initially proposed solution for above issues. They decided that Proper test marketing of the products should be done. They recommended that a permanent outlet needs be set up where there was high footfall. They decided that exhibition should be organized at least monthly, so as to create awareness among the people.

*Test Marketing* - To start with, the team decided to test market the products. For this purpose, an exhibition was organized in the Jawaharlal Nehru University Campus (JNU), Delhi. Test marketing of the products was started on Gandhi Jayanti, 2nd October, 2012. It was immediately realized that prices were too high. However, the response in JNU was lukewarm and a sale of only Rs.5000/- was made. The team received a feedback that the products were very good but the prices were too high.

Certain lessons were learnt in this exhibition. It was seen that there were several issues regarding Pricing of the product. It was seen that Consumers do not buy goods on basis of emotion. They buy goods only if they feel they are worth the price. Innovation was required in many goods for increasing market share. Many competitors were already there in the market who were creating goods with more aesthetic appeal. Their presence could be ignored. It was recommended that Focus should be given on volumes to generate profits. As per the response of the customers, Polishing of products would have to be given emphasis..

So, it was felt that the root cause of low response in this exhibition was exorbitant pricing. Pricing has to be redone after covering for cost of raw material and labour costs. There was a need felt for proper marketing of the goods to create awareness and build a brand value for the products.

*Innovations and finishing in making of goods* – The student team gave recommendations regarding finishing of products. The goods were finely made and the work was neat. However, some corrections were required. The students also suggested some innovations for handicrafts to be more appealing to the customer.

*Pricing* – As part of corrective action, the team went for re-pricing of the goods. Suitable prices were set on labour charge basis (Rs 120 per day). Earlier prices set by the IAP implementers were considered too high by the customers and products were not selling. It was later seen that after setting suitable prices, the goods were well accepted by the market. It was felt that Focus should be on volumes to generate profits. Total Revenue is price multiplied by quantity demanded (TR = P X Q). For increasing total revenue, quantity sold has to be increased. To reach the level of efficiency, large volumes have to be sold. The management students identified that ICT should be used to play a role in selling large volumes.

*Branding* - Brand name *Palash* was given to the products and the logo was prepared. Proper promotion was done through Social media and other channels like Print media, exhibitions etc. But, still there are a lot of gaps, which needs to be bridged, for successful implementation of this project. The photo displays the logo as prepared by the team.

*Marketing of products through exhibitions* – After re-pricing of goods, a series of exhibition were held. Exhibitions were held at office of Jharkhand on 4 August 2013and 28 August 2013. The first exhibition on 4 August was a huge success and goods worth Rs 15,000 were sold. The team realized that they had set suitable prices which led to huge sales. The second exhibition had low sales due to thin footfall. Efforts were made to identify potential markets with huge footfall. The student team identified Dastkar craft centre as a potential market. Negotiations by the team led to display of tribal goods for 10 days in during September 2013. The display led to sales of Rs 22,000. Also, direct selling was done and awareness was created through word of mouth. The goods received good response from the market, and a sale of around Rs. 65,000/= was made during August – September 2013. A few orders were also received. A few goods were sold out completely as Potli bags, Pen-stand, Lotus Diya, etc.

The student team made recommendations regarding the goods to be produced as demanded by customers. Among 120 type of products, those goods were identified which were in great demand. Suggestions were made to produce those goods in large numbers which were more in demand. However, this was a case of test marketing. The customer base was restricted to a small segment of society. The team felt that Digital marketing has to be used for selling large volumes and reach a wider range of markets.

*Promotions* – The team realized that awareness on products made by craftsmen was missing. Creating awareness was one of the key issues which needed to be worked upon. Technology was used through usage of one of most popular forms of social media, Facebook. A page was specially created for spreading awareness about the tribes, the Facebook page, "*A languishing Tribe of Jharkhand – Sabar*". The goods made have been displayed on the website.

*Plan for digital marketing* - The management students mapped out a plan for digital marketing. The management students felt that was a wide gap in the awareness level of the people, about the handicrafts and where to procure them. The marketing and promotion of the handicrafts was not in the right place. It was felt that ICT can bring a significant change in the destiny of handicrafts, being made by the tribal people. Currently, tribes are working in an unorganized manner, with no demand-supply equivalence being maintained. It was suggested that a website be created showcasing the whole catalogue of handicrafts available. The website will act as a Vertical Market Portal (sometimes referred as Destination Sites or Vortals) for the affinity group of customers, to attract the highly focused group of individuals having a deep interest in the handicrafts. The website will give brief information about the tribes and their livelihood. The awareness about the handicrafts is to be created on a global scale, as these products have received appreciation of being of world class quality by certain dignitaries.

Moreover, this website will act as an e-commerce portal for the sale of handicrafts on a global scale. Initially there can be a tie-up with other e-commerce websites like Jharcraft.org, TribesIndia.com, Craftsvilla.com, FabIndia etc to leverage their marketing platform. These websites have a higher reach, as they cater to various clusters of artisans. The promotion of various events and fairs could be done through this website, by the use of Banner Advertising and subscribe options, where users can register as loyal customers, and they could be given regular updates about the upcoming events.

Tribal artisans make a wide portfolio of goods, but all of them are not sellable in the market. 120 types of products were made under IAP. The product range can be finalized depending on the taste and liking of people of various cultures and demographic locations. ICT can play a major role in the selection of the products to be made by them. Due to presence of ICT, various catalogues of handicrafts can be checked in the portals like Craftsvilla.com, TRIFED, and Hast Karigar Society etc. Regulation of Supply Chain and elimination of middleman can take place through usage of ICT.

The blogs and articles about the handicrafts can be written, so as to have a wider reach to people and attracting them towards the website, ultimately resulting in the sales of goods. Social media influences customers in a big way. Now, organizations are harnessing the digital technology in making strategies about the marketing and promotion. The Facebook page should be strengthened more by linking to various pages like Indian Handicrafts, Tribal Art etc. Various MBA graduates can discuss the shortcomings on the blog, and suggest a suitable strategy to be followed to overcome the hurdles coming in the way.

The products could also be pitched to B2B customers like Hotels, Branded houses and Government undertakings like ONGC, SAIL etc. Marketing should also be done through the various exhibitions, haat and fairs organized in the country on a regular basis. This can only be done, when the products have a presence on the web, and anybody can access and get them whenever required. In the long run, the products can be sold to Incredible India, by showcasing the mythological connect of the tribes in Jharkhand.

The officer from Government of Jharkhand also made efforts in marketing of products. An order was received for bags to be made for an international conference held on 21-22 November 2013, in Delhi, India. Orders worth Rs 4 Lacs were received for this conference. This gave a boost to sales of tribal handicrafts and created awareness about their traditional art and craft.

## RESULTS AND FUTURE RESEARCH DIRECTIONS

As a result of collaboration of sectors, it was seen that the goods made by tribal population reached the urban markets of Delhi region and customers could buy traditional handicrafts. The revenue generated from sale of these handicrafts was given as salary to the tribal artisans. As a good start, it was seen that livelihood options were being generated due to involvement of all three sectors. The programme is in the implementation stage. If continued on the same lines, more business solutions can be attained. A fully sustainable model can be achieved with business solutions from management schools.

The case is a replicable model and can be an example for other development projects also. Many training programmes are being conducted for tribals all over the country by different organisations. The journey from training programme to marketing handicrafts to sustainable livelihood is a long one. The forces of business, government and society need to be integrated at various points of sustainable livelihood process. Training is provided by government organisations as TRIFED. Several NGO's as TCS is also providing training to tribal community in making handicrafts. Organisations as TRIFED and TCS also need to integrate with business and society sectors for better results of their training programmes. The knowledge of Academia and Management students can be harnesses to address similar social issues.

More research is required in the area of BGS synergy for development issues. Tribal people face several problems regarding marketing Handicrafts. They get very little compensation as major part of money is taken by middlemen. More research is required on marketing solutions for tribal handicrafts through BGS synergy.

## CONCLUSION

It is seen that all 3 sector of society combined together to work for cause of sustainable livelihood. Each sector used its core strengths. The government had resources and influenced public policy to provide for training of tribal people. The NGO was working for promotion of tribal community. The management team had skill sets which were harnessed for providing marketing solutions. They had knowledge about usage of technology and suggested ideas for promoting the livelihood issues. The synergy of 3 sector forces has started bringing small changes. If continued, this will help promote the cause of marginalized sections of society.

However, it seems to be a long journey ahead in this direction.

## REFERENCES

Agarwal, R. (2013). Sustainable Livelihood Options through Training in Handicrafts: A Study of Primitive Tribal Groups in Jharkhand. CRICKET, Centre for Research for Rural Innovation, Capacity Building, Knowledge Management, Entrepreneurship and Technology, IMT Ghaziabad.

Agarwal, R. (2013). CSR for Sustainable livelihood. *CSR Mandate*, *1*(June – July), 46–49.

Census of India. (2011). *Vital Statistics*. Retrieved 13 December, 2012, from http://www.censusindia.gov.in/2011-common/vitalstatistics.html

Company's Act. (2013). *Corporate Social Responsibility*. Retrieved on 5 January 2015 from www.mca.gov.in/Ministry/pdf/CompaniesAct2013.pdf

Dillihaat. (2014). *History of Dilli Haat*. Retrieved 14 November, 2014, from http://www.dillihaat.net.in/

GOI. (2007). *Scheme Of Development Of Primitive Tribal Groups (PTGs), F.NO.22040/58/2007-NGO*. Government of India.

Kalam, A. P. J. A., & Singh, S. P. (2011). *Target 3 Billion*. Delhi: Penguin Publishers.

Lawrence, A., & Weber, J. (2012). Business and Society: Stakeholders, Ethics, Public Policy. New Delhi: McGraw Hill Education (India Pvt Ltd.).

Lussier, R., & Sherman, H. (2014). *Business, Society and Government Essentials: Strategy and Applied Ethics* (2nd ed.). Routledge Publications.

Ockleford, J. (2000). *Research and Survey Series: Tri-Sector Partnerships Beyond those of Participating Groups in the BPD Cluster*. Retrieved 16 Jan, 2014, from www.bpd-waterandsanitation.org

Steiner, J., & Steiner, G. (2012). Business, Government and Society: A Managerial Perspective. New Delhi: Mcgraw Hill Education (India Pvt Ltd.).

TRIFED. (2014). *Introduction to TRIFED*. Retrieved 10 October, 2014, from www.trifed.in/trifed/.../about_trifed.aspx

Tulder, R., & Zwart, A. (2006). *International Business-Society Management: Linking Corporate responsibility and Globalization*. London: Routledge.

## KEY TERMS AND DEFINITIONS

**Company's Act 2013:** Companies Act, 2013 is an Act of the Parliament of India which regulates incorporation of a company, responsibilities of a company, directors, dissolution of a company. As per Section 135, every company having net worth of rupees five hundred crore or more, or turnover of rupees one thousand crore or more or a net profit of rupees five crore or more during any financial year shall constitute a Corporate Social Responsibility Committee and spend a mandated amount on developmental activities.

**Delhi Haat or Dilli haat:** Dillihaat, is an open air craft bazaar cum food plaza situated in Delhi. It was established and opened in 1994 with the joint venture of Delhi Tourism (DTDC), D.C (Handicrafts), NMDC, D.C. (Handlooms) and Ministry of Tourism and Textile, Government of India. The Dilli haat Tourism provides the craftsmen who are registered with the Handicrafts to directly place their things in the market, eliminating the middleman.

**IAP (Integrated Action Plan):** was launched in February 2009 by the Indian Central government. The aim was to deal with Naxalite (lawlessness) problems in 9 states. This plan included funding for grass-root economic development projects in Naxalite affected areas, as well as increased special police funding for better containment and reduction of Naxalite influence in these areas.

**Kaansi Grass:** Kaansi Grass is a special type of grass grown in Eastern India and is stiffer as compared to other grasses. This helps in making the handicrafts stronger and better.

**PTG or PVTG (The Primitive Tribal Groups or Particularly vulnerable tribal groups):** According to Government of India, there are 622 kinds of notified Tribes in India. It was observed all tribal communities were not at the same level of development. In order to foster the same, certain groups were identified as Primitive Tribal Groups or PTGs. Identification of PTGs was on following fixed criteria: Pre-agricultural level of technology, Very low level of literacy and Declining or stagnant population. 75 communities have been identified as PTGs. The nomenclature PTG was later in changed to PVTG.

**TCS (Tribal Cultural Society):** is a non-profit organization,located in Eastern India in the city of Jamshedpur. It is equipped with expertise and financial resources to make a difference in the lives of marginalized tribal communities. The society focuses on three important issues: a. education b. improvement of livelihood opportunities c. preservation of the ethnic identity of the tribal community.

**TRIFED (Tribal Cooperative Marketing Development Federation of India Limited):** It was formed by Government of India under Ministry of Tribal Affairs in 1987.The objective of TRIFED is socio-economic development of tribal people in the country by way of marketing development of the tribal products. The lives of tribals depends heavily on tribal products as they spend most of their time and derive major portion of their income.

# Chapter 19
# An Empirical Investigation into the Key Characteristics of Socio-Technical Societies:
## Social Identity, Social Exchange, and Social Vicinity

**Shailja Agarwal**
*IMT Ghaziabad, India*

## ABSTRACT

*The Internet has moved human interaction to a virtual dimension where users connect with each other through social networks. A social network comprises users and relations between these users (Wasserman & Faust, 1994), wherein relations connote "the collection of connections between members of a group" (Wasserman & Faust, 1994). This chapter looked to explain the reasons behind using social networking sites. Analysis of the collected data used a factor analysis to study the characteristics of the emerging socio-technical society amongst the students. The chapter identifies social identity, social exchange and social vicinity as the key characteristics of the emerging socio-technical societies. A gradual but paradigm shift from traditional societies to knowledge based societies was observed. While on one hand, a high dependency and usage of social networking websites (SNWs) was observed, on the other hand, the level of trust and dependency between the community members was found to be diminishing. The chapter reveals the emergence of a socio-technical community amongst students which is characterized by the need to create a social identity, a change in the style of social exchange and expansion of social vicinity. The findings suggest directions for future research.*

## INTRODUCTION

The Internet has moved human interaction to a virtual dimension. The World Wide Web has helped create online communities that link to one another and form a complicated web of interactions. The year 2005 witnessed online social network sites like MySpace and Facebook becoming common destinations the youth worldwide. The young generation, cross the globe, was logging in, creating elaborate profiles,

DOI: 10.4018/978-1-4666-8259-7.ch019

publicly articulating their relationships with other participants, and writing extensive comments back and forth. The extensive adoption of social network sites by the youth and middle aged generation raised some important questions. Why do users flock to these sites? What are they expressing on them? How do these sites fit into their lives? What are they learning from their participation? Are these online activities like face-to-face friendships – or are they different, or complementary? The goal of this chapter is to address these questions, and explore their implications for youth identities. While particular systems may come and go, how youth engage through social network sites today provides long-lasting insights into identity formation, status negotiation, and peer-to-peer sociality.

A knowledge based society, apart from demanding technical skills and access to information technologies, also makes it necessary for people to have diversified and supportive social connections. Although resources and opportunities may be available, one may not necessarily be aware of their existence, or even have direct access to them. In those cases, knowing people from different backgrounds, grades of expertise, and social levels turns out to be essential. This is where social networking sites enter the scene and provide necessary information through online networking. Corporations that operate in these environments have begun to listen to the 'voice' of their communities and participate in their 'conversations' (Srividya, 2006). The genX is showing a strong presence in multiple aspects of socio-technical networking. They have expanded their repertoires beyond mere email by joining list servers, maintaining their own web pages and blogs, sending instant messages (IM) and becoming a part of virtual communities and online networking sites. Their online lives are as full and complete as their offline lives (Dixon, 1996). This intense usage of social network and its analysis has offered a plethora of opportunities to modern organizations. On one hand, it has given an insight into how informal organizations influence the formal ones; while on the other hand, it has established the pattern of human interactions (Steiny & Oinas-Kukkonen, 2007). In other words, this rapid development in digital technology has impregnated network awareness. This network, which has reduced the cost of communication (Yoo, Lyytinen & Boland, Jr., 2008),can be defined as "a multileveled concept that includes people's awareness of the networks around them, the strategy of becoming more aware of networks, and the processes and tools to help aid this strategy" (Steiny & Oinas-Kukkonen, 2007).

## LITERATURE REVIEW

Networking can be explained as either being a technical process, the methods for successful operation of which are straightforward, or it being as a completely non-technical process, involving organizational, interpersonal and social interactions (McMurdo, 1996). A social network comprises users and relations between these users (Wasserman & Faust, 1994), wherein relations connote "the collection of connections between members of a group" (Wasserman & Faust, 1994). When a computer network connects computers via cables and electrical networks, it becomes a 'computing network', and when it connects people, it creates a 'social network' (Raghavan, 2006). Simply put, social networking is a platform for one person to meet up with other people on the Net. These people could be existing friends, acquaintances or starngers on the net. Social networking sites, created to assist in online networking, are generally communities created to support or be a part of a common theme. Given the immense communication opportunities, surpassing geographical and time constraints, social networking sites are expected to transform the world in an unprecedented manner. Social networking sites such as MySpace, Twitter, LinkedIn, Facebook etc. give individuals opportunities to meet new people and friends in their own and also in the other diverse communities across the world. Users have the option of becoming friends or fans of other users, and are continually updated on current events, specials, and other essential information that the masses would like to share. Traditionally speaking, this kid of interaction was virtually impossible due to lack of technological advancement; however; gradual evolvement of technology has liberalized people to communicate and network to the desired extent. Social network promises to be very informative, entertaining and knowledge disseminating. This social network is seen to be mediating between the individual and society (Dixon, 1996) and such social network websites (SNWs) pave a new way to steer and maintain an egocentric social network. It needs to be seen if they are a mere fad or precursors of an entirely new social world (Judith, 2007).

## Social Identity

Haythornwaite observed that the inherent need to create a social identity compels users to integrate Internet applications, by way of becoming a part of online social networks, in their personal and professional environments (Haythornwaite, 2001). These online networks connect people in various forums on multifarious subjects like politics, music etc (Rice & Love 1987), thus creating networks of relationships that evolve from 'conversations' among people who share common interests (Kimball & Rheingold, 2000). This has culminated in the formation of "communities and societies", (Piselli, 2007) which is the coming together of people with similar interests, beliefs, and ideas. The extensive use and collective time spent on these sites causes users to create online self-presentations in order to participate in the discussions. Some features of socio-technical networking, such as anonymity and desired self-presentation, make these online social groups a welcome alternative to traditional networks within the face-to-face environment (Turner, Grube, & Meyers, 2001; Walther & Boyd, 2002). The power to cultivate an image is inherent in software use. Users have an option to either reinforce their real-life image or cultivate an entirely new and different image, one preferable to their real-life image. They accomplish this by portraying themselves in the light they would like to be known. The power and alternative to control over self-representation brings certain autonomy to them as an individual. They are able to construct and live-up to a particular image, which has the ability to fulfill their personal needs which are otherwise forcefully crushed by them. The impression the users' profile carries to fellow users, be it networked friends or unknown participants, is of high significance to them. In a way, it aids their identity construction and maintenance. This takes place through comments and other details posted by friends in the user's network. Curiosity drives users to gather information that can lead to entertainment, the ability to cultivate an image, ego boosts, and social contact. Also, by being part of online communities people join discussion groups on various topics like social, political, etc and thus, united by the same interests, form "virtual communities that give them emotional support, friendship, and a sense of belonging and free them from all constraints imposed by their geographical location." (Mu & Artemio, 2006)

## Social Exchange

Social exchange of ideas and beliefs between like-minded people, with no prior acquaintance, who live far away from each other and who are provided with a setting that is conducive to friend and family interaction, is another factor that pulls people to online communities. Anybody with an ability and desire to access them is welcome to join in (Mu & Artemio, 2006). Respondents are individuals who use social networking websites to communicate with others about their shared interests and concerns. (Ye, 2006)

Users integrate the Internet their lives as the incessant growth of online technology has created endless possibilities for communication (Dixon, 2006) on information sharing about various issues like travel, recreation, economy etc that would otherwise be difficult to obtain. People with physical or psychological difficulties have been able to receive advice, support and help. It has aided all kind of communication, fulfillment of every kind of experience, both individual and collective (Smith & Kollock, 1998).

### Social Vicinity

Social network sites have helped in building human relationships (Birnie & Horvath, 2002) by way of maintaining old ties and establishing new ones. Similar to other electronic media like telephone etc., the SNWs aid by expanding opportunities for interaction, allowing communication across time and space. Unlike traditional face-to-face networking, online networking does not depend on physical closeness. (Ye,2006). Studies reveal that the major part of online communication, through networking sites, takes place among people who are prior acquaintances living at far- off distances from each other. These networking sites enable users to maintain relationships with people with whom they might otherwise lose contact, thus, reinforcing distant friendships. Consequently, they provide the same support and solidarity as direct contacts do (Haythornthwaite & Wellman, 1998).

## RESEARCH OBJECTIVES

This empirical exploration attempts to study the emerging socio-technical environment and understand the changing nature of socialization. Specific objectives are:

- To identify the characteristics of a socio-technical society.
- To explore whether students use social networking websites to create an identity for themselves.
- The understand the impact of social vicinity on the students use of social networking websites
- To study the emerging style of socio-technical exchange

## METHODOLOGY

The arguments made in this exploratory study are based on primary data collected from users of social networking sites. An exploratory study, on a sample of six-hundred-sixty B-school students, was undertaken. The survey instrument, which was a questionnaire, was developed and a pilot study on 29 respondents was conducted. The pilot study helped the researchers refine the questionnaire towards improvement of the collected data. Based on the responses received in the pilot study, the questionnaire was appropriately revised, two variables were removed, and data was then collected. Through a convenience based sampling, data was collected both online and offline.

The target sample for this survey was college students/millennial across India. The logic behind choice of millennial (people born between 1980---1995) and college students was due to the time in which they grew up. For quite a few of them, social networking sites would have been a part of their socialization process and a part of their daily activities. It was assumed that this target population would be familiarized with social networking sites and thus would be able to provide the most accurate measurements for the study. The goal for this survey and study was between 500---600 respondents. The sample size was aimed to be large since this was an exploratory study and to arrive at reliable conclusions, it was important that the sample size be large. The response rate for this survey was 75% (751 out of 1000), while the sample size finally used in the analysis is 660; excluding incomplete submissions.

A total of 751 responses were received, out of which 91 were rendered unusable. The final data size comprised 660 responses. A five-point Likert scale was used to understand participants' motivations behind using social networking sites, where 1 = most negative response and 5= most positive response. Analysis of the collected data used a factor analysis to study the characteristics of the emerging socio-technical society amongst the students.

## ANALYSIS OF RESULTS

An immediate analysis of the descriptive statistics revealed some interesting facts. Approximately 80% of the students did not want their profile to be public while almost 50% believed that privacy of exchange was not maintained on SNWs. 87% of the respondents said that they did not post false profile information on the SNS. 65% of the students found exchange of information on SNS safe, almost 50% opined it to be truthful and 45% felt that the information was also dependable. A large percentage, i.e. 75% felt that the information exchanged on the SNWs could be misused and was risky. These figures suggest that interactions through SNWs are still cast with a suspicious eye, when it comes to trust, as compared to offline interactions since exchange of information on SNWs is not perceived to be safe and chances of information to be misused are considered to be high. While almost 75% of the students were frequent visitors to SNWs, almost 74% had created a profile on a SNS. Table 1 illustrates the descriptive statistics about the reasons behind usage of SNSs.

*Table 1. Descriptive Statistics*

| | Mean | S.D. |
|---|---|---|
| To Understand business Environment | 3.1845 | .95740 |
| To create an identity and sense of belongingness to a community different from your real life | 3.1905 | 1.02933 |
| To better your job prospects | 3.0500 | 1.02863 |
| To keep yourself updated on current events | 3.1346 | 1.07989 |
| To be part of a formal discussion forum | 3.7212 | .79387 |
| To entertain yourself | 3.3107 | 1.01004 |
| To stay in touch family/friends/contacts you see a lot | 3.1827 | 1.20488 |
| To make plans with your friends/contacts | 2.2816 | 1.21605 |
| To build opinions | 3.8269 | .78136 |
| To get in touch with like minded people across the globe | 3.5096 | .92427 |
| To seek help from people | 3.3981 | 1.04168 |
| To make new friends/contacts | 3.7143 | .97778 |
| To share opinions | 3.6442 | .83513 |

*Table 2. Total Variance Explained*

| Factor | Extraction Sums of Squared Loadings | | | Rotation Sums of Squared Loadings | | |
|---|---|---|---|---|---|---|
| | Total | % of Variance | Cumulative % | Total | % of Variance | Cumulative % |
| 1 | 4.259 | 28.391 | 28.391 | 3.157 | 31.044 | 31.044 |
| 2 | 2.251 | 25.004 | 53.395 | 2.431 | 26.209 | 57.253 |
| 3 | 1.332 | 18.88 | 72.275 | 2.253 | 15.021 | 72.275 |

*Note.* Kaiser-Meyer-Olkin Measure of Sampling Adequacy = .72;
Bartlett's Test of Sphericity = 452.08 (df = 105, p = .00).

A **factor analysis** (Table 2, 3 and 4) was conducted to study the characteristics of the emerging socio-technical society amongst the students. The total variance, shown in Table 2, accounted for by each of the three components, explains approximately 73% of the variability in the original 15 variables. Hence, the original data set can be reduced by using these three components (Eigen values greater than 1 as shown in Table 2) with only 27% loss of information.

Table 4, presenting the rotated factor matrix, shows three factors (which represent the three characteristics of the networked society) derived from 13 variables (which represent the purpose of using social networking websites). As **Table 3** shows the variables which are loaded to **factor 1** are related to social identity, hence, this factor has been labeled as 'social identity' through social networking websites. The

*Table 3: Rotated Component Matrix*

| | Significance | Factor 1 | Factor 2 | Factor 3 |
|---|---|---|---|---|
| Factor 1: Social Identity | | | | |
| 14. To understand business Environment | .370 | 0.687 | 0.082 | 0.188 |
| 15. To create an identity and sense of belongingness to a community different from your real life | .001 | 0.792 | 0.102 | -0.1 |
| 16. To better your job prospects | .695 | 0.557 | 0.153 | 0.015 |
| 17. To keep yourself updated on current events | .409 | 0.819 | 0.106 | 0.145 |
| 18. To be part of a formal discussion forum | .088 | 0.618 | 0.272 | -0.017 |
| Factor 2: Social Exchange | | | | |
| 19. To make plans with your friends/contacts | .034 | 0.162 | 0.432 | -0.219 |
| 20. To build opinions | .065 | 0.109 | 0.595 | 0.465 |
| 21. To share opinions | .090 | 0.102 | 0.634 | 0.477 |
| 22. To seek help from people | .252 | 0.27 | 0.726 | -0.073 |
| Factor 3: Social Vicinity | | | | |
| 23. To make new friends/contacts | .048 | 0.258 | -0.104 | 0.552 |
| 24. To stay in touch with family/friends/contacts | .421 | -0.061 | -0.003 | 0.842 |
| 25. To entertain yourself | .110 | -0.083 | 0.151 | 0.653 |
| 26. To get in touch with like minded people across the globe | .075 | 0.106 | 0.19 | 0.687 |

*Table 4: Correlations between the Internet usage, degree of sociability, personal disclosure, frequency of visiting social networking websites and social identity (regression factor score 1), social exchange (regression factor score 2), social vicinity (regression factor score 3).*

| | | Regression Factor Score 1 | Regression Factor Score 2 | Regression Factor Score 3 |
|---|---|---|---|---|
| Internet Usage | Pearson Correlation | .189 | -.059 | .209(*) |
| | Sig. (2-tailed) | .046 | .572 | .042 |
| Degree of sociability | Pearson Correlation | -.013 | .180 | .092 |
| | Sig. (2-tailed) | .904 | .032 | .373 |
| Personal disclosure on SNWs | Pearson Correlation | -.143 | -.033 | -.205(*) |
| | Sig. (2-tailed) | .166 | .750 | .036 |
| Frequency of visiting social networking websites | Pearson Correlation | -.242(*) | -.063 | .226(*) |
| | Sig. (2-tailed) | .021 | .553 | .032 |

** Correlation is significant at the 0.01 level (2-tailed).
* Correlation is significant at the 0.05 level (2-tailed).

components of **factor 2** are related to social exchange; therefore this factor has been labeled as 'social exchange' through social networking. The variables of **factor 3** are primarily related to social vicinity; therefore this factor has been labeled as 'social vicinity' through social networking websites.

The networked society is characterized by: social identity, social exchange and social vicinity (Table 3). It was found that the respondents use SNW for creating a social and professional identity for themselves. The components of factor 1 reveal that in the global world of today, social identity is not just personal in nature but an identity which fits the contemporary knowledge society.

The type of social exchange has also changed. While, traditionally social exchange was more of personal nature and for entertainment, the social exchange through a social networking website is characterized by sharing of information and understanding the business world. It is not limited to exchange of information only but also to extend professional advice and help.

There was found to be a significant relationship between the extent of Internet usage and social vicinity (Table 4). The reason for this could be that as Internet crosses boundaries there is a merging of the geographical boundaries and thus social vicinity is expanding.

A significant relationship between the extent of personal disclosure on the Internet and the social vicinity was also observed. This could be attributed to the fact that as social vicinity expands, control over vicinity reduces and so the respondents feel more insecure in disclosing personal information on SNWs in comparison to the close knit society of yesteryears.

A significant correlation existed between frequency of visiting social networking websites and social identity. The results show that social vicinity expanded with frequency of visiting social networking websites.

A discriminant analysis was conducted to find out the impact of social identity, social exchange and social vicinity on the frequency of visiting social networking websites. The results reveal that almost 71% of the cases were classified correctly. The discriminant function was found to be significant (Table 6). The results of Hosmer and Lemeshow test indicated that the model had a high goodness - of- fit (sig. > .05, indicates high goodness –of-fit) (Table 8). There was found to be a high impact of social identity on

*Table 5: Summary of canonical discriminant functions (eigen values)*

| Function | Eigenvalue | % of Variance | Cumulative % | Canonical Correlation |
|---|---|---|---|---|
| 1 | .124(a) | 100.0 | 100.0 | .332 |

*Table 6: Summary of Canonical Discriminant Functions (Wilks' Lambda)*

| Test of Function(s) | Wilks' Lambda | Chi-square | df | Sig. |
|---|---|---|---|---|
| 1 | .690 | 10.096 | 3 | .018 |

*Table 7: Summary of Canonical Discriminant Functions (Structure Matrix)*

| | Function |
|---|---|
| | 1 |
| REGR factor score 1 for analysis 2 | .710 |
| REGR factor score 3 for analysis 2 | .659 |
| REGR factor score 2 for analysis 2 | .180 |

*Table 8: Hosmer and Lemeshow Test for goodness –of-fit*

| Step | Chi-square | df | Sig. |
|---|---|---|---|
| 1 | 12.232 | 8 | .141 |

*Table 9: Logistics Regression Model summary*

| Step | -2 Log Likelihood | Cox and Snell R Square | Nagelkerke R Square | Sig. |
|---|---|---|---|---|
| 1 | 101.755(a) | .232 | .288 | .000 |

*Table 10: Logistic Regression Hosmer and Lemeshow Test*

| Step | Chi-square | df | Sig. |
|---|---|---|---|
| 1 | 4.401 | 8 | .819 |

*Table 11: Logistic Regression beta coefficients and significance of variables*

| | | B | S.E. | Wald | df | Sig. | Exp(B) |
|---|---|---|---|---|---|---|---|
| Step 1(a) | FAC1_2 | .744 | .258 | 8.307 | 1 | .004 | 2.103 |
| | FAC2_2 | .232 | .250 | .862 | 1 | .353 | 1.261 |
| | FAC3_2 | .397 | .240 | 2.738 | 1 | .098 | 1.487 |
| | Constant | .995 | .251 | 15.747 | 1 | .000 | 2.706 |

the discriminant function (Table 7). The impact of social vicinity on the discriminant function was found to be second highest. There was found to be no significant impact of social exchange on the frequency of using social networking sites.

The results of the logistic regression between the usage of social networking websites to create a social identity and the characteristics of a socio-technical society show that there is a significant impact of the nature of socio-technical society on the need for creation of a social identity (Table 11). Also Table 10 shows a high goodness-of-fit (sig. > .05, indicates high goodness –of-fit), which seems to indicate that the need for creating a social identity leads to the adoption of socio-technical networks.

## DISCUSSION

The traditional Indian society is hierarchical in nature with the elders having more say in the society. It is predominantly unacceptable to vociferously voice out difference of opinions with elders. Social identity is an extension of the family identity. In a traditional society, the exchange gets limited by geographical boundaries and only those people form part of the society, who are accessible in terms of geography, also known as neighborhood. The emergence of the society is more on the basis of nearness and accessibility of the social members. As a result, social identity is also limited to the geographically placed social circle. In the socio-technical society of today, the geographical boundaries are diminishing and there is a coming together of people from various countries, culture and races but who are similar in thinking and tastes. It also reveals that the power distance that a traditional offline identity adheres to, due to complex Indian social ties, has been diluted to a great extent in the online social identity.

The study shows that there is a significant usage of social networking websites for social communication amongst the student community. Traditional social networking was limited by geography and thus the 'circle of interaction' was small in size. The local social community could only accord the members of the community a local presence. With the advent of the Internet and the increasing dominance of SNWs the 'circle of interaction' has expanded with members as people of the socio-technical community belonging to different countries and cultures. In contrast to the traditional social community, which is a coming together of the people in the geographical neighborhood, a social-technical community was a coming together of the people of similar thinking likes and dislikes from various cultures and backgrounds.

Traditionally the size of the community was small and thus the expanse of the social identity was also small. Since the need to create a global identity is what is driving the wave of socio-technical networking, there was found to be a significant relationship between social identity and frequency of visiting social networking websites. Students who participated in discussion forums and chat groups were found to be more frequent users of social networking websites than those who were simply using social networking websites to get in touch with friends and colleagues. Also, because the students were participating in discussion forums and chat groups they needed to be aware of the current business environment and technology innovations. In a socio technical network 'social identity' becomes a 'knowledge identity' (Table 3-factor 1).

There was found to be a significant correlation between personal disclosure on the Internet and social vicinity. The concept of social vicinity plays an important role in the building of a community. The results indicate that there is a significant impact of the socio-technical networks on the social vicinity. The SNWs have afforded a very convenient medium for social interaction and made the network neighborhood global in nature and extent. The global communities of today allow the students a common platform to exchange opinions and information with their global counterparts. The study also indicates that the type of social exchange, which was traditionally personal in nature, has changed to an information exchange. Thus we can say that the 'social community' has become a 'knowledge community'.

The social exchange in a socio-technical society is characterized by chat groups and discussion forums. The style of socio-technical networking is sharing and building opinions and sharing knowledge. The study found that the need for creating a global, social and knowledge based presence was perceived as the usefulness of social networking websites. The style of social exchange was found to be significantly correlated with the degree of sociability of an individual. This could be attributed to the fact that the style of social exchange of students who were traditionally more social was more on the lines of building and sharing opinions and sharing knowledge.

There was found to be a significant negative correlation between social vicinity and personal disclosure on a social networking website. The reason for this could be that as the social vicinity increases in size, personal control over the network decreases. As a result trust over the community decreases. Also since the community members belong to different countries and culture, there was a significant lack of trust between the community members with the increase in socio-technical networking. Thus we can say that although the adoption of socio-technical networking is growing day-by-day, the trust between the community members is reducing. The socio-technical society is thus changing its base from a trust based society to an information based society.

## CONCLUSION AND IMPLICATIONS

The study reveals the emergence of a socio-technical community amongst students which is characterized by the need to create a social identity, a change in the style of social exchange and expansion of social vicinity. The socio-technical communities offer a very conducive environment to the students for exchange of ideas and opinions and thus support their information needs. The present study has explored the gradual but paradigm shift from traditional societies to knowledge based societies. The contrary greyer shade to the adoption of socio-technical networking is the diminishing trust and dependence amongst the community members. Research needs to further take into account the reasons behind this diminishing trust and dependence, despite the increasing dependence on virtual communities and SNWs. The virtual world and consequently the knowledge communities would be greatly benefited if research is able to suggest measures to reestablish and restore this trust on networks in a social context.

## REFERENCES

Birnie, S., & Horvath, P. (2002). Psychological predictors of Internet social communication. *Journal of Computer-Mediated Communication*, *7*(4). Retrieved from http://jcmc.indiana.edu/vol7/issue4/horvath.html

Dixon, J. (1996). Uses and gratifications theory to predict use of computer-mediated communications. *International Journal of Educational Telecommunications*, *2*(1), 3–27.

Faust, K., & Wasserman, S. (1994). *Social Network Analysis*. New York, NY: Cambridge University Press.

Haythornthwaite, C., & Wellman, B. (1998). Work, friendship and media use for information exchange in a networked organization. *Journal of the American Society for Information Science*, *49*(12), 1101–1114. doi:10.1002/(SICI)1097-4571(1998)49:12<1101::AID-ASI6>3.0.CO;2-Z

Haythornwaite, C. (2001). The Internet in everyday life. *The American Behavioral Scientist*, *45*(3), 363–384. doi:10.1177/00027640121957240

Judith, D. (2007). Signals in Social Supernets. *Journal of Computer-Mediated Communication*, *13*(1), 231–251. doi:10.1111/j.1083-6101.2007.00394.x

Kimball, L., & Rheingold, H. (2003). *How Online Social Networks Benefit Organizations*. Retrieved April 8, 2011, from www.groupjazz.com

McMurdo, G. (1996). Networking for trust in tribal organizations. *Journal of Information Science*, *22*(4), 299–314. doi:10.1177/016555159602200407

Mu, H., & Artemio, R. Jr. (2006).Who, how and with whom: An exploration of Social Internet use and loneliness. In *Proceedings of the Annual Meeting of the International Communication Association*, 2006, 1-35.

Piselli, F. (2007). Communities, Places, and Social Networks. *The American Behavioral Scientist*, *50*(7), 867–878. doi:10.1177/0002764206298312

Raghavan, S. (2006). Blogs and Business Conversations. *Journal of Creative Communications*, *1*(3), 285–309. doi:10.1177/097325860600100305

Rice, R. E., & Love, G. (1987). Electronic Emotion: Socioemotional Content in a Computer-Mediated Communication Network. *Communication Research, 14*(1), 85-108.

Smith, M., & Kollock, P. (Eds.). (1998). *Communities in cyberspace*. London: Routledge.

Steiny, D., & Oinas-Kukkonen, H. (2007). Network awareness: Social network search, innovation and productivity in organizations. *International Journal of Networking and Virtual Organisations*, *4*(4), 413–430. doi:10.1504/IJNVO.2007.015723

Turner, J. W., Grube, J. A., & Meyers, J. (2001). Developing an optimal match within Online Communities: An exploration of CMC support communities and traditional support. *Journal of Communication*, *51*(1), 231–251. doi:10.1111/j.1460-2466.2001.tb02879.x

Walther, J. B., & Boyd, S. (2002). Attraction to computer-mediated social support. In Communication Technology and Society: Audience Adoption and Uses (pp. 153–188). Cresskill, NJ: Hampton Press.

Ward, C. (1996). Acculturation. D. Landis & R. Bhadat (Eds.), Handbook of Intercultural Training (pp. 124–147). Thousand Oaks, CA: Sage.

Wellman, B., Salaff, J., Dimitrova, D., Garton, L., Gulia, M., & Haythornthwaite, C. (1996). Computer Networks as Social Networks: Collaborative Work, Telework, and Virtual Community. *Annual Review of Sociology*, *22*(1), 213–238. doi:10.1146/annurev.soc.22.1.213

Ye, J. (2006). Traditional and Online Support Networks in the Cross-Cultural Adaptation of Chinese International Students in the United States. *Journal of Computer-Mediated Communication*, *11*(3), 863–876. doi:10.1111/j.1083-6101.2006.00039.x

Yoo, Y., Lyytinen, K., & Boland, R. J. (2008), Distributed Innovation in Classes of Networks. In *Proceedings of the 41st Hawaii International Conference on System Sciences*. Waikoloa: HI: IEEE.

## KEY TERMS AND DEFINITIONS

**Communities and Societies:** The coming together of people with similar interests, beliefs, and ideas.

**Computing Network:** Connects computers via cables and electrical networks.

**Knowledge Based Society:** Needs a user to be possessing technical skills and access to information technologies and to have diversified and supportive social connections.

**Networking:** Could be both – a technical or a non-technical process, involving organizational, interpersonal and social interactions.

**Social Exchange:** Exchange of ideas and beliefs between like-minded people.

**Social Network:** Connects people of a shared network and defines the relationship between these people.

# Chapter 20
# Rural Innovations:
## Text and Cases

**Roopesh Rao**
*Shri Ramdeobaba College of Engineering and Management, India*

## ABSTRACT

*In a country like India innovations are more referred as "jugaad". Though the dictionary does not explain such kind of words, but every person in India understands the importance of jugaad. India has one of the largest systems for agricultural research in the world. However this system has focused predominantly on strengthening of cereal production under irrigated conditions. It would be essential that they participate in all decision making which cater to overall development of rural india. India also needs to increase its efforts to tap into the rapidly growing stock of global knowledge through channels such as FDI, technology licensing, importation of capital merchandise that embody knowledge, as well as advanced products, components, and services. This chapter analyses and focuses on various innovative practices done with the help of Government, Public Private Partnership, private Players, Individuals, NGOS, etc*

## BACKGROUND

*"Innovation is increasingly being seen as the currency of 21st century. The future prosperity of India in the new knowledge economy will increasingly depend on its ability to generate new ideas, processes and solutions, and through the process of innovation convert knowledge into social good and economic wealth." - India Innovation Portal Decade of Innovation 2010-20*

India lives in numerous villages scattered thorough out the country. Rural areas are nearly three-fourth of the country of India and accounted for more than half of economic consumption. In spite of urbanization about 63 percent of population will continue to live in rural areas in year 2025. And the total potential of Indian rural market will reach to about 500 billion by 2020. According to 2011 census there is 640000 villages in India. India has substantial population below poverty line and having literacy level.

DOI: 10.4018/978-1-4666-8259-7.ch020

## INNOVATION

"The process of translating an idea or invention into a good or service that creates value or for which customers will pay. To be called an innovation, an idea must be replicable at an economical cost and must satisfy a specific need. "Innovation involves deliberate application of information, imagination and initiative in deriving greater or different values from resources, and includes all processes by which new ideas are generated and converted into useful products. In business, innovation often results when ideas are applied by the company in order to further satisfy the needs and expectations of the customers. 'Innovation is defined as a process by which varying degrees of measurable value enhancement is planned and achieved, in any commercial activity. This process may be breakthrough or incremental, and it may occur systematically in a company or sporadically; it may be achieved by introducing new or improved goods or services and/or implementing new or improved operational processes and/or implementing new or improved organizational/ managerial processes in order to improve market share, competitiveness and quality, while reducing costs.' Business Dictionary (2014) Innovation and competitiveness have a dynamic, mutual relationship. Innovation thrives in a competitive environment and in turn, plays a key role in the achievement of such an environment. Innovation generates economic value, new jobs in the economy and cultures of entrepreneurship. By virtue of its relationship with competitiveness, Innovation emerges as a factor in promoting economic growth. Given the fact that the Indian economy is growing at 6-8% per year, while exports are growing at 30% Cumulative Annual Growth Rate (CAGR), India Innovation (2014) and many Indian firms are successfully competing against international firms and brands, it can be concluded that this has been made possible by a combination of factors, including enabling environment, rising capital and labor productivity as well as improved quality of goods and services at lower costs. In a social context, innovation helps create new methods for alliance creation, joint venturing, flexible work hours, and creation of buyer's purchasing power. Innovator need not be a person who comes from a wealth background, with a huge credential and qualification. Innovation can be done and are happening at grass-root levels. The story of Mandar Talukar, a small town boy from Nagpur winning the "best innovator in the world" award at USA for his innovation mobile shoe charger, show that innovators are not born; they are developed in adversity thus proving that "necessity is the mother of invention". Rao et al (2012)

In a country like India innovations are more referred as "jugaad". Though the dictionary does not explain such kind of words, but every person in India understands the importance of jugaad. The classic examples of jugaad are the use of washing machine to make huge amount of "lassi" (sweet butter milk, sold in northern part of India), pressure cooker used for making espresso coffee, etc.

As we can see India is the land of innovation (jugaad) and innovation is here to stay for a long time. Innovations have become a way of life and life without innovations is unimaginable. To its credit, India has been taking bold steps to strengthen its R&D infrastructure, developing technological innovations and altering the mind-set of its people toward better creation, acquisition, and use of technology. It is endowed with a critical mass of scientists, engineers, and technicians in R&D and is home to dynamic hubs of innovation, such as Bangalore and Hyderabad. It also has vast and diversified publicly funded R&D institutions, as well as world class institutions of higher learning, all of which provide critical human capital. India is also emerging as a major global R&D platform; about 100 multinational corporations (MNCs) have already set up R&D centers in the country, leading to the deepening of technological and innovative capabilities among Indian firms.

*Figure 1. An ATM (automated teller machine) in a small village in INDIA*

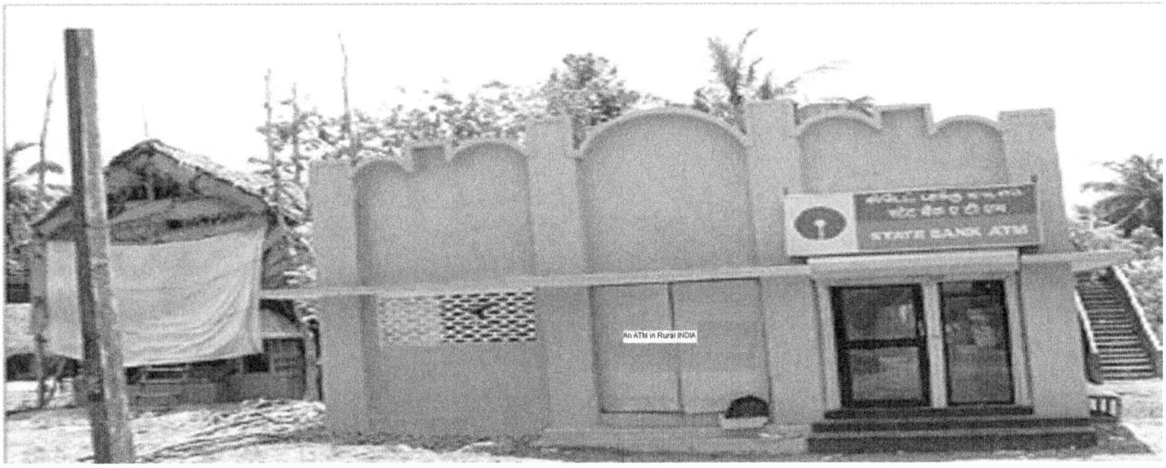


## AUTOMATED TELLER MACHINES IN RURAL PARTS OF INDIA

Though it has given its remarkable footprints in rural development but still there are some parts were there are lack of facilities in rural parts and remote areas. When studied awareness of ATM facilities in rural part we come to know that, within two decades, ATM technology development is happening at an alarming rate. Qureshi, Kumar, Jhunjhunwala (2002). Gone are the days when customers were limited to only withdrawing cash from ATM's. We have now reached an era, where we can use multi function and biometric ATM, (See Figure 1) equipped with touch sensitive and user friendly options to transfer funds, book air and train tickets, go for mobile recharge, and even deposit cheque with scanning.

The consumers in the rural areas lack awareness about various schemes and e-banking services of bank. The emergence of new technology allows to access the banking service without physical direct re-course to the bank premise by the customer at present atm is city oriented in the country. Agarwal (2012) The growth of rural it industry fosters financial inclusion by providing financial services to people in the farthest reach of the country. Qureshi, Kumar, Jhunjhunwala (2002)

Rural marketing plays an important role in development strategy, particularly in the areas of diversification, modernization, globalization and self-reliance. 70% of Indian population belongs to rural part of the country.

When it specifically comes to contribution of information technology ATM (automated teller machine) had played a very important role in rural development. The emergence of new technology has effect the consumer awareness in rural parts to a remarkable extent. (Srinivasa Rao, 2013) (See FIGURE 2)

It has also give awareness and education to undeveloped part of the region. It has also influenced over the population with financial support. Agarwal, Dadhich (2012)

India lives in numerous villages scattered thorough out the country. Rural areas are nearly three-fourth of the country of India and accounted for more than half of economic consumption. In spite of urbanization about 63 percent of population will continue to live in rural areas in year 2025. And the total potential of Indian rural market will reach to about 500 billion by 2020. According to 2011 census there is 640000 villages in India. India has substantial population below poverty line and having literacy level. Rural banking system with emergence of information technology is influencing the population

*Figure 2. A solar operated ATM – innovation for greener tomorrow*

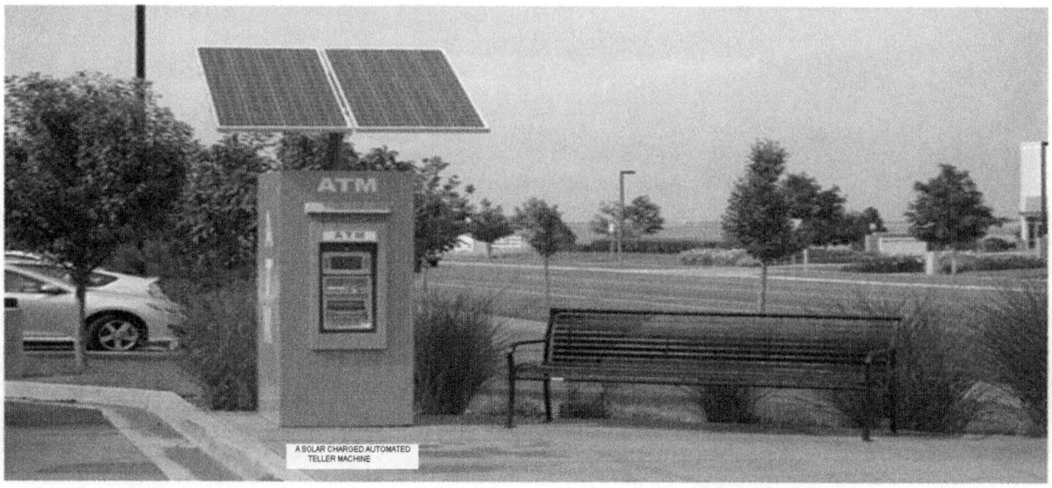


towards banking services like ATM cards, credit cards and other quick and easy services. Even now, rural development defies any clear definition as it has gone through a number of changes over a period of time. Persuasive communication for rural development has been given highest priority for bringing about desirable social and behavioral change among the most vulnerable rural poor and women. Initially, the approach lacked gender sensitivity and empathy of the communicators and development agents who came from urban elite homes. Agarwal, Dadhich(2012) Added to these constraints is political will that still influences the pace and progress of rural development. We are one of the world's oldest and ancient civilizations that evolved, matured and decayed over several millennia.

After independence we have been experimenting and carving a path of revitalization for development through democracy. The existing sharp divide between the small but economically, politically and socially "rich elite ruling class" and a very big but "economically poor and socially deprived" continue to persist as a legacy of the past.

After independence, the government took upon itself the major responsibility of development. Hence, the central and state governments carried out development projects. The experiment was carried out from February to April 1956 in five districts of Maharashtra state by all India radio (air). Rao (2013)

Rural listener groups were organized, who would listen to radio broadcasts twice a week. The summative impact evaluation indicated positive outcome of radio rural forum. Impressive knowledge gains as a result of radio listening were reported across illiterates and literates, agriculturists and non-agriculturists, village leaders and others. Almost all healthcare projects for rural poor, especially women and children have used demand driven social marketing approach for rural the development.

## HDFC Bank 'Project Jharkhand' – An IT enabled Financial Inclusion program

HDFC Bank, launched 'Project Jharkhand' a financial inclusion program. As part of the program, the Bank launched its world class services at a Common Service Center in Kanke comprising over 1.5 lac households spread across 100 villages in 30 Panchayats. The Bank also adopted Chakala village near Ranchi as part of the Common Service Center program. Under Project Jharkhand HDFC Bank will look to cover over 45 lac households in the state through both the Common Service Center and village adoption models, subject to regulatory provision.CSC is an integral component of the Central Government's National e-Governance Plan (NEGP) that seeks to set up over 5000 CSCs in Jharkhand and about 100,000 in the country.

These Common Service Centers will make available to the rural population a slew of services ranging from public information services, e-governance services, educational services to agri related and financial services. Common Service Center will also work like a 'Human ATM" that the rural people can use to withdraw and deposit cash. (HDFC Bank launches 'Project Jharkhand 2008, http://www.hdfcbank.com/htdocs/common/pdf/Project_Jharkhand.pdf)

## TRANSFORMING RURAL INDIA THROUGH AGRICULTURAL INNOVATION

"Agricultural jeopardy is related with undesirable outcomes that shoot from badly expectable biological, climatic, and price agents. These variables include natural calamities and climatic factors not within the control of agricultural producers." Shanmugam, Chandrasekaran, Vijayasarathy. (2011)

They also include adverse changes in both input and output prices. To set the stage for the discussion on how to deal with risk in agriculture, we classify the different sources of risk that affect agriculture. Agriculture is often characterized by high variability of production outcomes or, production risk. Unlike most other entrepreneurs, agricultural producers are not able to predict with certainty the amount of output that the production process will yield due to external factors such as weather, pests, and diseases. Agricultural producers can also be hindered by adverse events during harvesting or collecting that may result in production losses. Agriculture community (2014)

Input and output price volatility is important sources of market risk in agriculture. Prices of agricultural commodities are extremely volatile. Output price variability originates from both endogenous and exogenous market shocks. Segmented agricultural markets will be influenced mainly by local supply and demand conditions, while more globally integrated markets will be significantly affected by international production dynamics. In integrated markets, a reduction in prices is generally not correlated with local supply conditions and therefore price shocks may affect producers in a more significant way. Another kind of market risk arises in the process of delivering production to the marketplace. The inability to deliver perishable products to the right market at the right time can impair the efforts of producers. The lack of infrastructure and well-developed markets make this a significant source of risk in many developing countries. The ways businesses finance their activities is a major concern for many economic enterprises. However, in this respect, agriculture also has its own peculiarities. Many agricultural production cycles stretch over long periods of time, and farmers must anticipate expenses that they will only be able to recuperate once the product is marketed. This leads to potential cash flow problems exacerbated by lack of access to credit and the high cost of borrowing. These problems can be classified as financial risk. Agriculture community (2014)

Another important source of uncertainty for agricultural producers is institutional risk, generated by unexpected changes in regulations that influence producers' activities. Changes in regulations can significantly alter the profitability of farming activities. This is particularly true for import/export regimes and for dedicated support schemes, but it is also important in the case of sanitary regulations that can restrict the activity of producers and impose costs on households.

*Figure 3. Some Agricultural Innovations*

Like most other entrepreneurs, agricultural producers are responsible for all the consequences of their activities. However, the growing concern for the impact of agriculture on the environment, including the introduction of genetically modified organisms (GMO), may cause an increase in producer liability risk. Finally, agricultural households, along with other economic enterprises, are exposed to personal risks to the wellbeing of people who work on the farm, and asset risks, the possible damage or theft of production equipment and assets. With a majority of its population living in villages, rural poverty is a major problem in India. The disparity between the urban and rural incomes is also on the rise. This leads to migration to urban areas resulting in urban blight as well. Therefore addressing the problem of rural poverty assumes urgency. Agriculture community (2014)

Rural innovations has been involved in a range of interventions—infusion of technology, soil enrichment, efficient farm and water management, improved cattle development, functional literacy, rural sanitation and public health, human resource development, establishment of self-help groups particularly among women, self-employment opportunities and facilitating institutional credit—to address the problem of farm productivity in India.Rural innovations focus on the poor and marginal farmers, women, unemployed youth, and depressed communities. Rural innovations work in about 250 villages in tamil nadu and have reached 30,000 rural families. A large part of rural innovations' effort with farmers is to help break their initial emotional barriers to new technologies. This has provided the platform to launch into other initiatives. The success of these measures has had a demonstrative impact on the farmers' willingness to adopt and internalize new technologies. This may be considered an attitudinal breakthrough. (Figure 3)

Another initiative, the center for rural development (CFRD), a training cum village knowledge center, has been established in illedu village of kancheepuram district with classrooms, computer lab with internet facilities, input and product handling center, farm machinery workshop, model experimental farm, residential complex for trainees and an open air theatre to cater to the needs of various sections of rural community. Rural innovations also helps in housing a comprehensive soil testing laboratory, food safety and standards laboratory and a plant tissue culture lab to provide agriculture support services.

Agriculture productivity improvements through resource conserving "lean farming": paddy (55%), groundnut (113%), vegetables (116%), sugarcane (40%), and corn (150%). Through successful lead farmers, technology transfer has been effected over an area of 10,000 acres with a "lead farmer—lead village" concept. Addressing the agriculture value chain—soil testing, facilitation of inputs and credit, market linkage, and field advisory services—is part and parcel of agriculture development initiatives. Promotion of climate resilient agriculture, resource conserving technologies and promotion of use of information communication technology (ICT) in agriculture are being attempted too. Watershed and natural resource management initiatives have resulted in increase in water table ranging from 3.5 meters to 5 meters in the project area of over 6,000 hectares. Cropping intensity has been doubled (two crop cultivation in a year instead of one crop) and about 20% additional area which had been left fallow has also been brought under cultivation. Soil erosion, nutrient loss, damage due to flooding during rainy seasons has reduced significantly. Agriculture community (2014)

To sustain the benefits derived, the social development initiatives of rural innovations have helped village communities in establishing community-based institutions like farmers clubs, self help groups and joint liability groups, farmers producer organizations, watershed committees, etc for collective decision and action.

India has many of the key ingredients for making this transition. The time is very appropriate for India to make its evolution to the knowledge economy—an economy that creates, disseminates, and uses knowledge to enhance its growth and development. It has a critical mass of skilled, English-speaking knowledge workers, especially in the sciences. Its local market is one of the world's largest. The knowledge economy is often taken to mean only high-technology industries or information and communication technologies (ICTs). It would be more appropriate, however, to use the concept more broadly to cover how any economy harnesses and uses new and existing knowledge to improve the productivity of agriculture, industry, and services and increase overall welfare. In India, great potential exists for increasing productivity by shifting labor from low productivity and subsistence activities in agriculture, informal industry, and informal service activities to more productive modern sectors, as well as to new knowledge-based activities—and in so doing, to reduce poverty and touch every member of society. India should continue to leverage its strengths to become a leader in knowledge creation and use. To get the greatest benefits from the knowledge revolution, the country needs to press on with the economic reform agenda that it put into motion more than a decade ago and continue to implement the various policy and institutional changes needed to accelerate growth. It has a large and impressive Diaspora, creating valuable knowledge linkages and networks. The list goes on: macroeconomic stability, a dynamic private sector, institutions of a free market economy, a well-developed financial sector, and a broad and diversified science and technology(S&T) infrastructure. In addition, the development of the ICT sector in recent years has been remarkable. India has created profitable niches in information technology (IT) and is been remarkable. India has created profitable niches in information technology (IT). Rapid advances in ICTs are dramatically affecting economic and social activities, as well as the acquisition, creation, dissemination, and use of knowledge. The use of ICTs is reducing transaction costs and lowering the barriers of time and space, allowing the mass production of customized goods and services.

Some of the examples of rural innovations which are changing the lifestyle, business and way of life are as follows

## INFORMATION AND COMMUNICATION TECHNOLOGY (ICT) GYANDOOT

Situated in Dhar district of Madhya Pradesh, Gyandoot is an Intranet based Government to Citizen (G2C) service delivery portal it was launched in January 2000. Gyandoot aims to create a lucrative, replicable, economically independent and financially viable model for the rural population to take the benefits of Information and Communication Technology (ICT). Gyandoot: The Purveyor of Knowledge (2014)

## E-CHOUPAL BY ITC

Choupal is a Hindi word which means "village meeting place". Market is a meeting place where vendors and customers come together to do transactions. e-choupal is a virtual market place where farmers can transact directly with a processor and can realize better price for their produce. The main charisma of e-choupal is that it can be used for connecting large producers/small producers and small users/large users, thereby eliminating the need for chain of command of brokers.

Geographical distances do not restrict participation in the e-choupal. E-choupal has the advantages of the market but spans very large varieties of vendors and customers. The main disadvantage of Traditional market is that information asymmetry is inherent in the market where as e-choupal provides for transparent transactions. This enables the participation of smaller as well as larger players. Exclusion of intermediaries allows for larger share of profits to reach the bottom end of value chain.(https://www.echoupal.com/)

## UNIQUE IDENTIFICATION PROJECT

In a country like India, absence of social security number or its equivalent has made more than 380 millions of poor suffer in the hands of the existing corrupt system because they are unable to participate in the official financial system of the country. The government of India's Unique Identification (UID) project has created avenues for this people to become a part of the different projects and plans developed for self sufficiency, growth and improvement in living standards. This innovation has revolutionized the way Identification is done. The linking of bank account to the card has helped government send direct subsidy to the poor and the needy, thus removing the middle men and barriers. The gas subsidy is directly transferred to the card holders every time they purchase a cylinder thus creating a barrier for black marketing of gas cylinders. Adhar card (2014)

## INNOVATION FOR IMPROVING HEALTH IN RURAL INDIA

Innovation is required to address health needs at the bottom of the pyramid. Delivering affordable and quality health care to India's billion-plus people presents enormous challenges and opportunities. Innovations could be a way out for a large number of people get quality care at a cost that the nation can afford.

Addressing healthcare challenges in rural India is a complex proposition. Healthcare starts with generating awareness of risk factors, disease symptoms and the benefits of healthy living to the rural masses for the betterment of the rural population. Measures are taken to convert these messages into actions resulting in the prevention of disease or morbidity. Patients suffering from disease would then require provision of primary, secondary or tertiary care. This is followed by protection of patients from relapse or future risks through management of disease, regular monitoring and health maintenance. Addressing this continuum of care is more complicated owing to the 'double burden of disease' i.e. the co-existence of both communicable and non-communicable diseases. While the country is still dealing with the issue of communicable diseases, the share of non-communicable diseases is also increasing rapidly requiring the health system to come up with a wide range of diverse interventions to address the varying financing, prevention, provision and protection needs of the diseases. Governments schemes (2012)

In addition, a number of other external factors have a bearing on health and health seeking behavior. Recent research increasingly relates health inequalities to social factors such as poverty, nutrition, hygiene, water and sanitation, education, empowerment of women and living space. This would mean that to make any lasting impact on population health outcomes, addressing issues along the complete gamut including these social determinants of health is essential.

## TOTAL SANITATION CAMPAIGN

In spite of noteworthy investments over the last 20 years, India faces the most daunting sanitation challenge in any region in the world. The Total Sanitation Campaign in Ahmednagar (Maharashtra) has bought innovation into Sanitation systems. Innovation in the Ahmednagar pilot project is in its use of conditional financial incentives. Most sanitation front individual household subsidies used to assist private toilet construction. Yet stopping open defecation requires collective action, which suggests that the financial incentives would be more effective if used to encourage the attainment of community, rather than individual, goals. In Ahmednagar, every household has to fund its own toilet. Governments schemes (2012)

However, the BPL households do so on the understanding that they will be paid US$ 8.10 if everyone builds a toilet and the community is declared 'open defecation free'.

The remainder of the TSC subsidy (US$ 2.69 per BPL household), paid to the GP on achieving universal access, thus acts as an incentive for the GP to assist in stopping open defecation, including the promotion and facilitation of the construction of toilets by the landless, the very poor, and those unwilling to invest. A similar financial incentive is provided to the NGO working in the village. It is paid US$ 1.07 commission for every household that builds a toilet (from the IEC funds), but does not receive any of this money until the village is declared 'open defecation free'.

For more than 800 million men, women and children across India living on USD 1-3 a day, the idea of accessible and affordable medicines is often as remote as their rural homes.

**Arogya Parivar ("Healthy Family" in Hindi)**: A social initiative developed by Novartis to reach the underserved millions living at the bottom of the pyramid in rural India.

After just five years, Arogya Parivar is proving to be both a force for improving health in rural communities and a sustainable business. Arogya Parivar provides opportunities to expand business in an innovative and responsible way. The program offers education on diseases, treatment options and prevention as well as increases access to affordable medicines. Health educators, usually local women, raise awareness about local diseases and preventive health measures. They also refer sick people to doctors and cooperate with local NGOs to further spread their message. Each educator covers a few villages every day, with an Arogya Parivar branded cap, shirt and banner, making them easily recognizable. Sales supervisors serve as the initiative's local sales force. They interact with local pharmacies and collaborate with doctors, hospitals and NGOs to organize health camps where villagers can receive treatment and preventive care. Arogya Parivar focuses on the diseases most prevalent in rural India. Further, products and services are tailored to meet the needs of underserved rural populations with a low disposable income, usually earned on a daily basis. Novartis arogya (2014)

## IKURE TECHSOFT

Delivering affordable healthcare to the doorsteps of rural masses, India continues to face enormous challenges. With a population over one billion, rural India comprising of 840 million people are served by only 30 per cent of the country's combined medical force. Out of which, three per cent of India's physicians live in rural areas, and 25 per cent in semi-urban areas. This is disproportionate, and an example of the Pareto Principle – where 20 per cent of the doctors serve 80 per cent of the population.

This is disproportionate, and an example of the Pareto Principle – where 20 per cent of the doctors serve 80 per cent of the population. Moreover, the morbidity rate in people reporting the same, in rural areas increased to 70 per cent in 2011 against 64 per cent in 2004. Rural India is critically flawed with inefficient heath care system. They either remain short of medical personnel or untrained officers. According to NRHM report, out of 22,000 primary healthcare centers, eight per cent do not have a doctor, 39% remain unattended without a lab technician and 17.7% without a pharmacist, and this is when, each primary health center is supposed to have at least one medical practitioner. Based in Kolkata ikure sets up rural health centers across India. with an initial funding of Rs 45 lakh from Intellecap Impact Investment Network and Calcutta Angels; Rs 70 lakh from WEBEL iKure Techsoft has built a network of rural health centers where doctors are available through the week and pharmacists dispense only ac. (http:/www.**ikuretechsoft**.com)

## DRINKING WATER QUALITY IN RURAL INDIA: ISSUES AND APPROACHES

The rural population of India comprises more than 700 million people residing in about 1.42 million habitations spread over 15 diverse ecological regions. It is true that providing drinking water to such a large population is an enormous challenge. Our country is also characterized by non-uniformity in level of awareness, socio-economic development, education, poverty, practices and rituals which add to the complexity of providing water.

The health burden of poor water quality is enormous. It is estimated that around 37.7 million Indians are affected by waterborne diseases annually, 1.5 million children are estimated to die of diarrhoea alone and 73 million working days are lost due to waterborne disease each year. The resulting economic burden is estimated at $600 million a year. The problems of chemical contamination are also prevalent in India with 1,95,813 habitations in the country are affected by poor water quality. The major chemical parameters of concern are fluoride and arsenic. Iron is also emerging as a major problem with many habitations showing excess iron in the water samples. Transforming rural India, (2014)

The provision of clean drinking water has been given priority in the Constitution of India, with Article 47 conferring the duty of providing clean drinking water and improving public health standards to the State. The government has undertaken various programs since independence to provide safe drinking water to the rural masses. Till the 10th plan, an estimated total of Rs.1,105 billion spent on providing safe drinking water. One would argue that the expenditure is huge but it is also true that despite such expenditure lack of safe and secure drinking water continues to be a major hurdle and a national economic burden.

## COMMUNITY BASED MAINTENANCE OF WATER SOURCES MAINTENANCE OF WATER SOURCES

Ramakrishna Mission Lokasiksha Parishad (RKMLP) is one of the biggest units of the Ramakrishna Mission Ashram, Narendrapur. It has done remarkable work in the field of maintaining water sources and has successfully demonstrated community based maintenance of 800 hand pumps in Medinipur. To carry out this process, a seven-member 'water committee' with four female and three male members from the beneficiary families were formed for each hand pump. These members were trained in operation and maintenance by the RKMLP. A maintenance chest fund was developed for individual pumps, with each family contributing one rupee per month. The money is collected once or twice a year depending on the paying capacity of the family. An innovative strategy developed is to collect the money during religious ceremonies after the harvest season as people have money during this time of the year. In this way, the water committee was able to collect Rs. 300-500 from the beneficiary families. The members of the committee also organized awareness generation activities relating to safe collection, storage and handling of drinking water simultaneously promoting sanitation and personal hygiene practices. Transforming rural India (2014) & Indian rural water supply (2014)

## DUAL WATER SUPPLY AND WASTE WATER TREATMENT

To reduce the burden on fresh water sources, the option of dual water system is being worked out in several parts of the country. The success of this system lies in the fact that filtered purified water is used only for drinking purposes while other source of water may be used for purposes other than drinking. This is also is cost saving measure as resources spent on providing clean water is saved by using alternate sources. Waste water treatment can also be another effective means of reducing the burden on freshwater sources. The treated waste water can be used for purposes other than drinking. One example of effective wastewater treatment is in Mehsana district of Gujarat where wastewater from homes in villages is used for agriculture. The wastewater coming out of homes is collected in a pond which is then auctioned to farmers for use in agriculture.

Magod Dungri village in Valsad district in Gujarat has a population of 4,264. An old well served as a water source, but the water was saline and not potable. In 2006, this village was brought under the Bigri Malwan group water supply scheme of the GWSSB and it started getting safe drinking water. But in-village distribution of water continued to pose difficulty. Under the Swajaldhara programme, the village community decided to develop a system of household connections. The entire community made a 10 per cent contribution towards capital costs and the responsibility of collecting the contribution was taken up by one individual in each habitation. In the process, a 5,000 liter water tank in the village school, electricity connections, a 2,208 meter distribution pipeline, a 318 meter gravity pipeline and 15 stand posts were made. Out of a total expenditure of Rs.5, 20,000, the community contributed Rs.80,000. The foremost priority of the village was to get regular and safe water to meet their drinking water requirements. As far as water for other purposes was concerned, this need could easily be met from the village well. For drinking water, the villagers make use of the treated water supplied through the regional water supply scheme. This is accessed from the 15 stand posts constructed in the 15 habitations in the village. Drinking water is received for about 30-45 minutes every day Thus by making use of dual sources of water, the community has ensured that treated water is not wasted and is used only for drinking purposes. Indian rural water supply (2014)

The villagers regularly pay water tariff fixed by the Pani Samiti. The Pani Samiti regularly pays Rs 14 per person as water tariff to the water supply department and if need be the villagers are ready to contribute more. The villagers also contribute Rs.16 per person towards electricity and maintenance charges.

## SOLAR HOME SYSTEMS FOR RURAL ELECTRIFICATION

Lack of access to electricity is one of the biggest issues facing the world's poor, with over 1.6 billion left in the dark globally. The vast majorities of these people live in rural areas of developing countries because they are too poor and may be in too remote a location to be reached by the national grid. For their lighting needs they rely on candles, kerosene lanterns, and firewood which results in a daily expense that is expensive in the long run. Furthermore, this type of indoor lighting causes indoor pollution and chronic lung problems. Long-term, solar energy is the most practical and economical way of bringing power to poor and remote communities. Small-scale, distributed solar home systems provide an effective and affordable way to bring light to people without electricity. A basic system consists of a small solar panel, a battery, a charge controller, LED lights, and a universal outlet for charging cell-phones or other small appliances.(See Figure 4) A basic system can be made affordable through microfinance options. Partnering with local banks and/or microfinance organizations to create payment plans can help overcome the large initial investment associated with purchasing a system. Energy savings result from not having to buy candles or kerosene fuel, and can make the monthly payments affordable. When proposing this technology to a new area, it is important to target a community that has expressed a need and desire for solar electricity. Identifying and allying oneself with a respected community leader who is receptive and supportive is a good idea.

*Figure 4. Some Solar Instruments for electrification*

Solar Pannels and Euipments for Lighting Using Solar Energy

## THE CLASSIC CASE OF SELCO IN SOLAR ELECTRIFICATION

SELCO's pioneering efforts with microfinance in rural India is a large reason why they have become a world leader in the field. However, their case also brings to light another issue relating to "free riders." Innovative companies willing to be first in the game can be put at a competitive disadvantage when they spend resources on innovation and capacity building. This is due to other companies taking advantage of their earlier efforts, getting a "free-ride." For example, after SELCO spent many years and dollars on developing India's rural financial infrastructure, other companies benefited from it. There were even some banks that, after giving out successful loans for SELCO systems, started selling their own systems for personal social development programs. Broadly speaking this isn't a bad thing, as it results in greater adoption of the technology and increased electrification for the poor. However, it does result in a decreased incentive for individual companies to innovate if their competitors are accruing benefits from their investment. To overcome the free-rider problem, governments and non-profit development institutions should provide funding and incentives for enterprises to innovate. This could be in the form of technical and financial support for businesses entering a not served geographical area. Furthermore, a government or non-profit could provide financing for early-stage systems, which would allow local banks in the private sector to see the technology successfully implemented before they decide to take on the risk of loans. (http:/www.**selco**-india.com)

### Sunkalp Energy

A solar power company Sunkalp Electricity is launching a project called Solar Soldiers to involve people in Rural Electrification in Uttar Pradesh through the innovative use of Solar Power. A number of corporate are stepping up the green ante this day. This is what Sunkalp asks, "No TV. No internet. No AC. In fact, no LIGHT!!! Can you imagine a world without electricity? Not for a minute, an hour– but for 25 years. This Indian village in Uttar Pradesh has lived without power for so long that they can't remember what electricity means. We are here to bring them back from the past."Hence the idea is to rescue a forgotten community from the clutches of darkness. With this mission, it is building a solar mini-grid to power the lives of around 200 villagers without access to electricity. About 93% of the villagers in Gulabganj have already signed up for an electricity connection from the mini-grid. Sunkalp Energy has developed a low cost micro grid tailored to the needs of off-grid villages. Sunkalp Energy is constructing and will operate a pilot project initially in a small village of 25 households and will approximately extend to 4 new village-level micro grid lighting facilities to reach 300 new customers and 1,800 new beneficiaries in Hamirpur districts of Uttar Pradesh, India.(http:/www.**sunkalp**.com)

## DRAWBACKS OF RURAL INNOVATION

While innovation helps in attaining cost efficiency, reliability and ease of use, the investment in terms of land, labor, machinery and other fixed assets may be huge. As far as Innovations in electrification and water purification is concerned, it requires huge initial investments. Implementation part is also a major concern when it comes to government policies. Challenges are huge when we talk about the implementation part. How much work is actually done on ground will be a million dollar question. Moreover if private investors are encouraged to invest in these rural innovations sector will inculcate in drawing quickly the return on their investment. This may hamper the main concern of helping the rural people for which the process was started altogether. Moreover less private players would like to put their liquidity into these matters as they may not find the area interesting for their bottom line. Minor drawbacks can be catered to in long term but projects like solar electrification, water purification and rural electrification may also lead to environmental hazards which can be cause of great concern.

## CONCLUSION

So after going through various context, cases, contention and issues we can conclude that many innovations are coming up for the agricultural sector but they are not widely known nor have they been systematically monitored and evaluated. Many of the innovative models are still relatively new, but through time and the use of appropriate systems to monitor and evaluate their achievements, we will be able to draw more complete lessons that can help in scaling up and replicating them. This will help us better understand what works and what does not, and under what conditions. What seems to be missing at this point is some repository of innovative models, systems to monitor, and methodologies to evaluate them. In addition, we need to think of incentives to strengthen existing innovative models and also promote further innovation

As said early in the chapter 'Innovation is defined as a process by which varying degrees of measurable value enhancement is planned and achieved, in any commercial activity. This process may be breakthrough or incremental, and it may occur systematically in a company; it may be achieved by introducing new or improved goods or services and/or implementing new or improved operational processes and/or implementing new or improved organizational/ managerial processes in order to improve market share, competitiveness and quality, while reducing costs.' India has one of the largest systems for agricultural research in the world. However this system has focused predominantly on intensification of cereal production under irrigated conditions. There has been criticism that this research system enabled an exploitative agriculture without a proper understanding of the various consequences of every one of the changes introduced into traditional agriculture. So it becomes imperative, based on previous experience of change in Indian agriculture to empower the resource poor smallholder and marginal farmers to be able to negotiate with stakeholders to their development their needs for political, social, economic and technological development. It would be essential that they participate in all decision making. The technologies they need will not therefore be limited to those related to agriculture alone but also to politically, socially and economically aggregate and collectively decide. Those who will generate enable adoption and, if need be, adaptation and innovation, will need to understand how development works along with how technology works and adapt each other for success. The has to be focus on innovation and the rebuilding will be based on social research of the needs of small holder farmers and that includes the study of socio-economics of the new technologies of Agriculture, ICT, Irrigation technologies, Solar Electrification that are developed to meet the needs of smallholder farmer. But, more important, it will be important to understand how development and technology, with all its facets and components, work side by side. And within this context, this would need entire communities, especially agricultural, to be included in decision making through participation.

In cases where the total sanitation approach had been used, program managers and local government officials were aware that their main objective was to stop open defecation, and that this required community-wide action, universal toilet use, and hygiene behavior change. Opinion was divided as to how these changes should be effected, but there was little argument about the approach. In this respect, the 'total sanitation' concept is a major step forward, as this level of shared understanding and purpose was sadly lacking in many earlier sanitation programs. It would be also important to redirect research for agriculture so that its purpose is to provide the innovations needed by small holder farmers as a direct product and not as a spillover or trickledown effect. The system has to recognize that a large number of technologies influencing each other and working together and in tandem contribute to agricultural development and all these need to be brought about appropriately. It can also be concluded that no single innovation can be considered the miracle or "silver bullet" solution, and this is despite the various calls over time to come up with grand schemes and search for big solutions. Creation of a forum of large agri-businesses that could be encouraged to leverage their networks in emerging markets and create openness that could be encouraged to leverage their networks in emerging markets and create opportunities for attracting financial institutions that could fund parts of their value chain, like local small traders, processors, farmers, etc. Financing could be linked and become the catalyst for technology improvements and promotion of environmental and social standards along specific value chains.

Based on the current state of healthcare system in rural part of Indian States the scope for Innovation is there. Through Government sponsored schemes, private sector interventions and the recent string of PPP Projects are intervening and trying to build up an infrastructure to make possibilities of inroads for betterment of facilities, it is understood that there is still a long way to go in terms of uplifting of the healthcare sector and reaching the desired health goals. It is very much evident that huge investment will be required in developing upgrading of healthcare infrastructure, in order to improve accessibility and quality of care. The private sector must consider this as business opportunity to establish their presence and expand their operations/ market share in the healthcare delivery market in India either by partnering with the different state governments or pursuing a pure private model. The government at the same time needs to understand the issues faced by private sector currently (working independently or in the existing PPP programs) and take measures to improve the investment climate in the respective states. The states will need to put in place clear policies and guidelines in the healthcare sector which will enable to attract large private investments in the health care industry

In the end it can be concluded that Rural Innovation will envision what is there in store for India as a country to develop as the next super power which will dominate the Subcontinent and create inroads and benchmarks for countries to follow. Under developed countries in Africa and other parts of the world are looking forward towards India to create a magnum opus so that the same model can be followed and replicated in their countries.

## REFERENCES

*Adhar card*. (2014). Retrieved from, http:/www.uidai.gov.in

Agarwal, M. D. (2012). Online banking services: An empirical study of banker's and customer's awareness about obs. *Journal of Exclusive Management Science*, *1*(7), 25–35.

*Agriculture community*. (2014). Retrieved from http://data.gov.in/community/agriculture-community/blog/national-agricultural-innovation-project

*Annual Report of State Bank of India 2011-2012*. (n.d.). Retrieved from http://www.sbigroup.co.jp/english/investors/library/filings/pdf/2012_en.pdf

Bhatnagar, S. C. (2004). *E-Government: From Vision to Implementation – A Practical Guide with Case Studies*. New Delhi: SAGE Publications Pvt. Ltd.

*Echoupal, I. T. C.* (n.d.). Retrieved 2 July 2014 from https://www.echoupal.com/)

*Governments schemes*. (2012). Retrieved from http://yojana.gov.in/CMS/(S(y4dqrc55g1m1qhnd4soqih45))/pdf/Kurukshetra/English/2012/January.pdf

*Gyandoot: The Purveyor of Knowledge*. (2014). Retrieved from http://gyandoot.nic.in/

*HDFC Bank launches 'Project Jharkhand' – an IT enabled Financial Inclusion program*. (n.d.). Retrieved from http://www.hdfcbank.com/htdocs/common/pdf/Project_Jharkhand.pdf

iKure. (2014). *Solar Soldiers*. Retrieved from http:/www.ikuretechsoft.com

*India Innovation*. (2014). Retrieved from http:/www.IndiaInnovationPortalDecadeofInnovation2010-20.com

*Indian Rural Water Supply*. (2014) Retrieved from, http:/www.worldbank.org/projects/.../india-rural-water-supply-sanitation-project

*Innovation*. (n.d.). Retrieved from) http:/www. Businessdictionary.com

Kumar, R., & Jhunjhunwala, A. (2002). *Taking Internet to Village: A case study of Project at Madurai Region*. TeNeT Group of IIT Madras.

*Novaritis arogya*. (2014) Retrieved from www.novartis.com/downloads/corporate.../arogya-factsheet.pdf

*Planning Commission. Government of India*. (n.d.). Retrieved 2 July 2014 from http:/www.planning-commission.gov.in

Qureshi, T. M. (2008). Customer Acceptance of Online Banking in Developing Economies. *Journal of Internet Banking and Commerce*, *13*(1), 13–20.

Rao, C. S. (2013). Consumer awareness in rural India with special reference to E-Banking services in SBI. *Indian Journal of Research*, *2*(2), 46–48.

*Rural Finance Learning Center*. (n.d.). Retrieved 2 July 2014 from http:/www.ruralfinance.org

Satyanarayana, J. (2004). *E-Government. The Science of the Possible*. New Delhi: Prentice Hall of India Pvt. Ltd.

SELCO. (2014). *Rural financial infrastructure*. Retrieved from http:/www.selco-india.com

Shanmugam, T. R., Chandrasekaran, M., & Vijayasarathy, K. (2011). *Economic Analysis of Farm and Market Risk*. Saarbrücken: LAP Lambert Academic Publishing.

*Sustainable Access in Rural India*. (2014) Retrieved from http://www.tenet.res.in/rural/sari.html

*The World Bank*. (n.d.). Retrieved 2 July 2014 from http:/www.worldbank.org

*Transforming rural India*. (2014). Retrieved from http://blogs.hbr.org/2014/02/transforming-rural-india-through-agricultural-innovation/

*United Nationals Conference on Trade and Development*. (n.d.). Retrieved 2 JULY 2014 from http:/www.unctad.org

*White paper*. (n.d.). Retrieved from http://edevelopment.media.mit.edu/SARI/papers/uncrd_report.pdf

Rao, R., Menaria, D., Maurya, A., & Parashar, A. (2012). *Video Case on Social Innovation*. Retrieved from https://www.youtube.com/watch?v=CA4Q2sEcsg0

## KEY TERMS AND DEFINITIONS

**ATM- Automated Teller Machines:** Machines with the help of which money can be stored by a bank and retrieved by the customer of a bank without any human intervention.

**ICT:** Information communication technology helps in connecting people with the help of tools like telephone, mobile phones and Internet.

**Innovations:** Innovation is defined as a process by which varying degrees of measurable value enhancement is planned and achieved, in any commercial activity.

**Rural Innovations:** Innovations happening in underdeveloped and rural parts of a country.

**Sunkalp Energy:** A solar power company Sunkalp Electricity is launching a project called Solar Soldiers to involve people in Rural Electrification in Uttar Pradesh through the innovative use of Solar Power.

**UID- Unique Identification Project:** The government of India's Unique Identification (UID) project has created avenues for this people to become a part of the different projects and plans developed for self-sufficiency, growth and improvement in living standards.

# Chapter 21
# Organic Farming:
## Growth and Issues

**Aditya Vikram Agrawal**
*Institute of Management Technology Ghaziabad, India*

**Siddharth Jindal**
*Institute of Management Technology Ghaziabad, India*

**Charu Sharma**
*Institute of Management Technology Ghaziabad, India*

**V. Raghavendra**
*Institute of Management Technology Ghaziabad, India*

**Neha Joshi**
*Institute of Management Technology Ghaziabad, India*

**Vaibhav Kango**
*Institute of Management Technology Ghaziabad, India*

## ABSTRACT

*India practised organic farming in early centuries but Green revolution lead to shift of farming to fertilizer based farming. So, in this chapter the focus is to elucidate the idea of organic farming and its growth over the years across the countries with focus on India. Organic farming is a type of farming method where the crops are sowed and raised by using organic wastes instead of the regular use of pesticides and insecticides. This method has been quickly accepted and adopted by most of the countries across the world with the number being 144 in the year 2010 with major percentage being practised in developing nations. Out of this, India has just about 0.03 percent of the total land under organic farming across the world. India has witnessed a significant growth in organic farming since the last few years, keeping in sync with the world market.*

## INTRODUCTION

Organic Farming is based on various principles. The primary principle states that nature is the best role model for farming, as it neither uses any inputs nor demands unreasonable quantities of water. The entire system of organic farming is thus, based on an intimate understanding of the ways of nature. The system discourages the mining of soil for nutrients, and its degradation keeping in mind today's needs is avoided extensively. This leads to the soil being considered as a living entity, rather than as a necessary material.

DOI: 10.4018/978-1-4666-8259-7.ch021

Microbes and other living organisms, which make the living population of soil, are important contributors to its fertility, on both strength and sustainability basis. These organisms need to be protected and nurtured for the long term sustainability of soil and farming in itself (Yadav, 2011). The protection of the total environment of the soil, right from its structure to its cover, is important. This in principle leads to the system of farming termed as organic farming ("The world of Organic Agriculture in India", n.d.).

In today's terminology, organic farming is a method of farming system which primarily aims at cultivating the land and raising crops in such a way, as to restore and rejuvenate the soil by primarily using organic wastes (crop, animal and farm wastes, aquatic wastes) and other biological materials along with beneficial microbes (bio-fertilizers) for a sustainable production in an eco-friendly pollution free environment with the release of the nutrients.

India has its roots based in organic farming. In the earlier days, India was primarily an organic based farming nation, but later on due to the problems of population boom and scarcity of the food it had to shift to synthetic fertilizer based farming. With the current wave of rising awareness to preserve environment and food quality consumer, both the farmers and government are shifting towards organic food and farming ("Organic Farming an Overview", n.d.).

Few of the major advantages that organic food has over the normally produced food are listed as follows -

1. Organic food is less toxic as compared to normally produced food.
2. Taste giving ingredients like fat, carbohydrates, etc. are found to be higher in quantity in organic food.
3. Organic food is comparatively much less adulterated and mainly available in pure form.
4. Organic food is found to be superior in nutrients than normally produced ones.

Organic farming is primarily growing crops with the help of bio fertilizers and organic waste to keep the soil nutrients intact. The present scenario in India is one in which the government is providing aid to the farmers to produce organic food ("The world of Organic Agriculture in India", n.d.). The farmers are also reciprocating by showing interest towards it. But, contrary to popular perception, there are three main reasons for farmers to shift to the organic farming –

1. A sector of farmers does not have access to the normal farming resources like fertilizers and seeds and shifted towards organic farming.
2. Reduction in soil fertility and food toxicity due to excessive use of the fertilizers and also increasing cost of production and loans has shifted another sector towards it.
3. Increasing growth opportunity and high revenue margins in organic farming is a primary contributor towards farmers adopting it.

India has almost 1 million hectare land under organic farming and 340000 organic producers and is one of major contributor in organic food. But, still there are some areas which need to be developed and worked upon to promote awareness about organic products among consumers and farmers.

The purpose of this research is to study the problems and constraints faced by Organic farming. These problems are analysed both from the perspective of operational issues and also government policies. The research studies the growth of Organic farming and then goes onto look into the constraints, followed by measures that can be taken up by all stakeholders for its growth.

The background research of the objective was done using secondary data sources. This secondary information was used to study the growth of organic farming and the issues faced for its expansion. Further, primary research was done to meet the research objective. This research was done by meeting Government officials and farmers to understand the issues faced at the ground level and while implementation of government policies.

## BACKGROUND

The concept of organic farming has been there since ancient times. Earlier, farmers and scientists condemned the use of chemicals or artificial fertilizers. In the early 1990s, a concept of humus farming emerged in Europe and America. Humus farming had at its root the well-being of soil as it was considered the lifeline of the plants. A sustainable plantation method with regeneration of soil led to saving of natural resources. The term 'organic farming' was coined in the 1940s by Lord Northborne. This terminology was used since he believed the plants to be a sort of organisms with nutrients and energy in them. In the 1960s, the use of organic fertilizers for faring was encouraged with the 'be natural' approach. The practice of organic farming was brought to Australia from Europe in the 2000s.

The organic farming in India has been a part of its ancient culture. Ever since the fertilizers used in India were all organic and not chemical. In the 1950s and 1960s, natural calamities struck the nation and its ever increasing population added to the calamities. To add on to the production of food grains during the period, the Government had to give a push to the agriculture and thus set up chemical fertilizer factories. Though this shift was required at the time, it resulted in loss of fertility of soil and immunity of pests. Since then, Indian farmers have been shifting to a more sustainable form of organic farming.

In India, organic food market is currently valued at a gross of 1000 crore INR, growing with a CAGR of 20-22%. The global trend is pretty much the same, with global organic food and beverages market expected to grow from $57.2 billion in 2010 to $104.5 billion by 2015. Total of 154 countries with 35 million ha land and 1.4 million producers are involved in organic farming. Region wise land under organic farming is Oceania 12.1 million ha, Europe 8.2 million ha, Latin America 8.1 million ha. India is the leading producer with respect to number of producers, with 340000 producers, which is followed by Uganda, having 180000 producers, and Mexico with 130000. Around 12 million ha land involved in organic farming is located in the developing countries. In contrast to this consumer demand is concentrated in North America and Europe with 97% of global revenue is generated from these areas. Asia, Latin America and Australia are important producers and exporters of organic food (Reddy B.Suresh, 2005). By March 2010 India had brought 4.48 million ha land under organic certification process. Every year approximately 60 million tonnes of organic material is exported out of India, the total value of which exceeds 700 crore INR. In India organic farming is most prevalent in Gujarat, having almost 0.7 million hectare under organic farming (Gupta M. L., Garg Rekha, 2012). Cotton is the most popular organically cultivated commodity, having a production of approximately 380,000 million tonnes annually. Total area under organic farming in Uttar Pradesh is pegged at 112,000 hectares and is growing at a rate of almost 500% annually.

*Figure 1. Histogram showing the growth of agricultural market from 2010-15 (Source: Data from World Bank Database)*

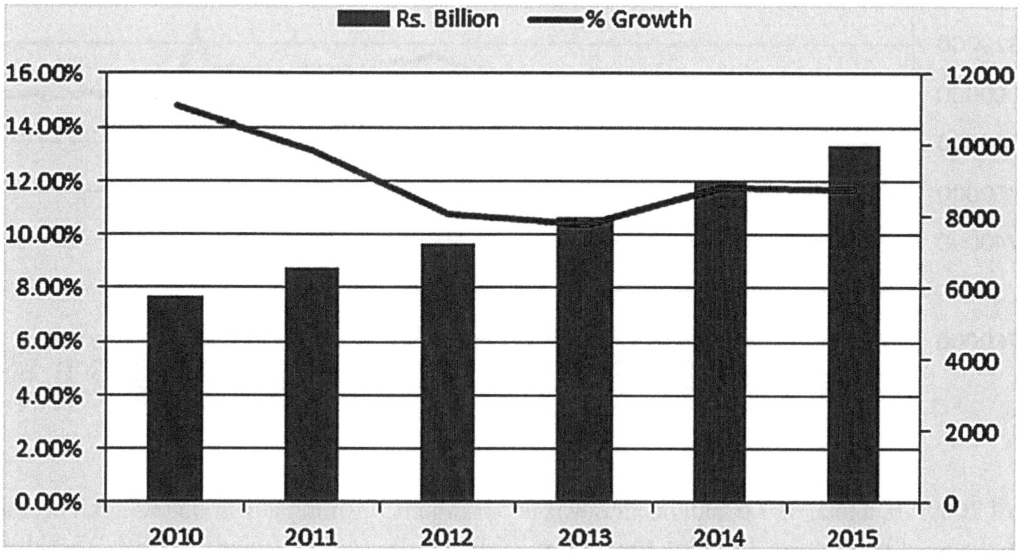


## AGRICULTURAL GROWTH

India was historically an agriculture driven economy. The phase of globalisation changed the contours, as the service industry became the primary driver of the economic growth of India. The last 20 years has seen the contribution to GDP almost getting halved from about the 30% level to nearly about 15% contribution to GDP level presently.

But, at the same time the agricultural produce of India has also been increasing. The agricultural market for the period 2010-13 with a projection for 2014-15 is shown in Figure 1. The Indian agricultural products market had total revenue of Rs 5800 billion in the year 2010, which had grown at a CAGR of 12.5% in the previous 5 years. Furthermore, this market is expected to grow at a CAGR of 11.5% for the next 3 years, to have a total value of approximately Rs 10,000 billion by the end of 2015.

The area of land under agriculture had seen a low growth during the period of 1961-90. It has been at a pretty much a constant figure since then, with a slight decrease, if at all. As of 2011, approximately 17.5 million hectares of land is used for agriculture in India. The figures of land under agriculture are shown in Figure 2.

## GROWTH OF ORGANIC FARMING

Organic farming has been growing at a rapid pace, with over 141 countries having started to commercially produce organic farming as back as in 2010. Even during the year 2007, approximately 32.2 million hectares of land was being utilized for organic farming worldwide. A concern though that remains is that over 65 percent of the total organic produce is done in the developing countries. In 2004 India contributed just 0.03 percent of the total land under organic across the world ("Agricultural Products in India", 2011).

*Figure 2. The increase in agriculture lands over years (Source: Data from World Bank Database)*

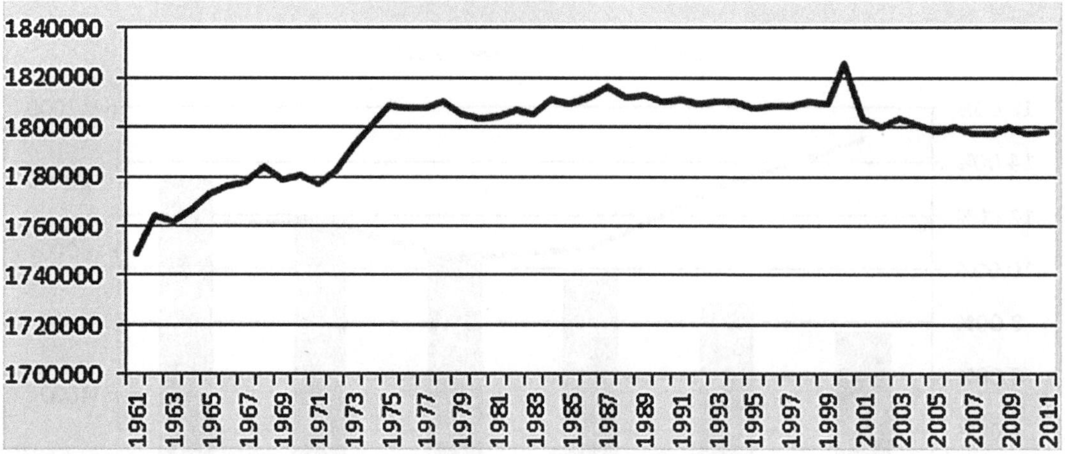


As of 2009-10, a total of 7.6 lakh hectare was under organic farming and about 3.3 lakh hectares was in the process of conversion, bringing the total to 10.9 lakh hectares. A total of about 3.5 lakh farmers had adopted organic farming and a further 2.5 lakh farmers were in the process of converting to the practices of organic farming, as of 2009-10. The total produce of organic products for the year 2010-11 stood at 3.88 million tonne. The figure of total land under organic farming rose to approximately 55.5 lakh hectares by the end of 2011-12. As can be seen from the Figure 3, there has been a meteoric growth in the total area under organic farming in India. Also the break-up of production under organic farming of various products can be found for the year 2010-11 in Figure 4.

## ROLE OF GOVERNMENT IN ORGANIC FARMING

The national legislation has increased over the years to promote the growth of organic agriculture production and trade in order to set the minimum requirements for organic agriculture and create the institutional framework for certification. This has provided greater credibility to labels provided to the

*Figure 3. Histogram of area under organic farming (Source: Data from World Bank Database)*

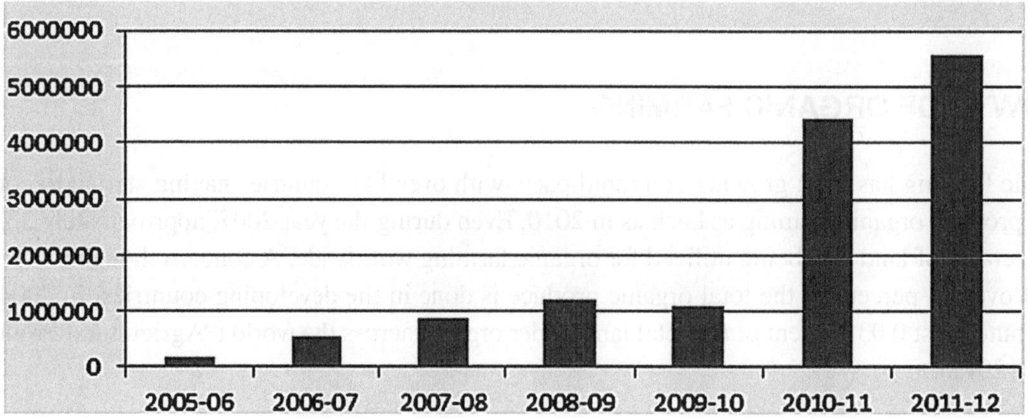

*Figure 4. Pie chart of various agricultural products share for 2010-11(Source: Data from" National Project of Organic Farming, Annual Report", 2010-2011)*

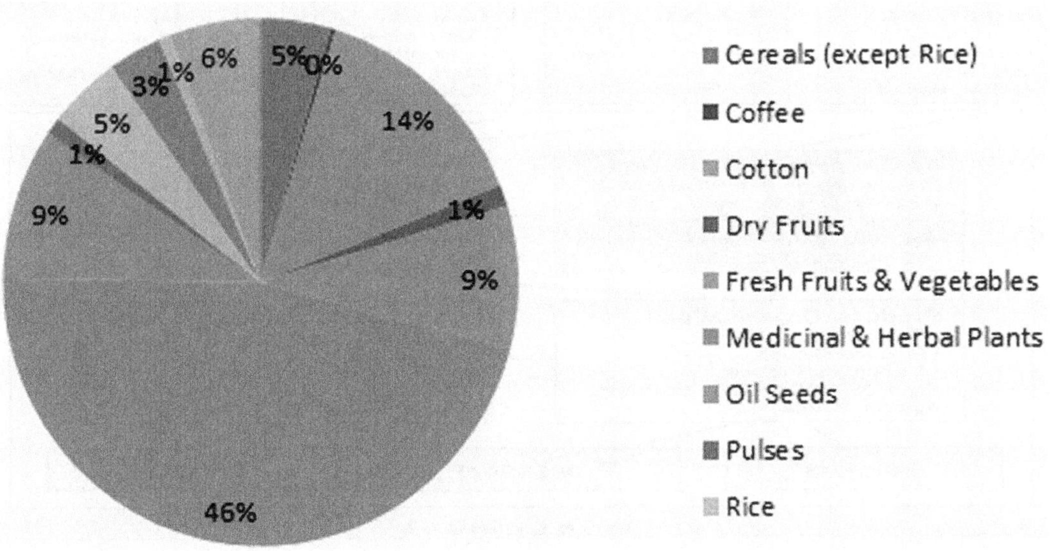


organic products. In order to promote equivalence with other nations for international trade and facilitate fair competition among producers the legislation by the Indian Government has been improvised upon over the years by introducing several policies and forming special departments for looking after organic farming. Because of the health and environmental benefits and trade opportunities associated with organic agriculture, governments sometimes pass regulations that encourage farmers to shift to organic methods, through tax reductions/exemptions, subsidies, or support in research and marketing. The framework of the activities and actions looked after by the government and other agencies have been shown in the Figure 5.

Regulatory mechanisms in India have developed an internationally acclaimed certification – Indian Organic for export, import and domestic market. These regulations are categorized under various programmes and policies. The most prominent of these policies is that of the National Programme on Organic Production (NPOP). This regulation guides the policy of organic farming under both export and import separately. This followed by the policy under the Foreign Trade Development and Regulation Act (FTDR). The FTDR is under the Ministry of Commerce (Commission, 2001) and is responsible for the export requirements. It is granted equivalence from both the European Union and Sweden. Other primary policies are that of the Agriculture Produce Grading, Marking and Certification Act (APGMC) and the National Accreditation Body (NAB). The APGMC is under the Ministry of Agriculture (Department of Agriculture & Cooperation, 2005), which is notified by the NPOP. It regulates the requirements for the import and domestic markets. The NAB is responsible for the accreditation of Certification and Inspection Agencies.

The requirements for the certification process are being looked after by 18 accredited certification agencies out of National Project on Organic Farming Department of Agriculture and Cooperation, Government of India and the National Centre of Organic Farming, Ghaziabad. Out of these 18 agencies, 4 agencies are under the public sector while the remaining 14 are under private management ("National Project of Organic Farming, Annual Report", 2011-2012).

*Figure 5. Support given by Government for the consumers*

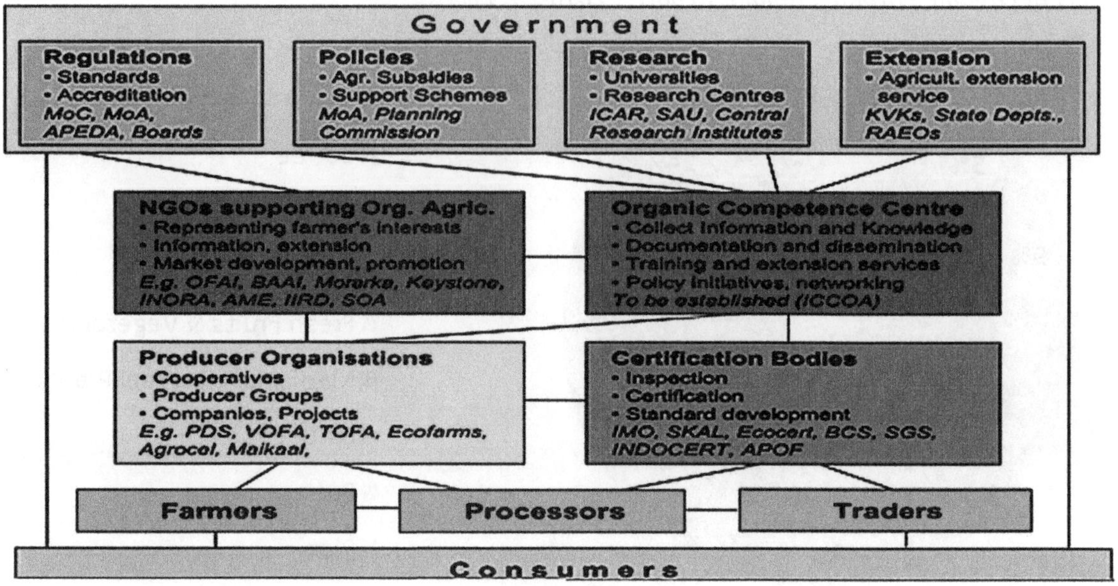


The Certification for Organic food and process is done to compete on the global level, and its basic requirements are:

1. Avoidance of use of synthetic chemical inputs
2. Farms to be maintained free from chemicals for number of years
3. Detailed written production and sales record
4. Periodic inspection of the farm

Post the development and adoption of organic farming culture by the government there has been active participation of private players in the various processes of organic culture but these involve very few players who either have gained profitability due to their presence across several regions or have been based on only the notions of social welfare. The major initiatives that have had the maximum private player presence include:

1. Export Hubs: There are several hubs which have been established over the time to procure, store, process and export from a single location. These help in demand servicing as well as act as major centres to promote the exports of organic crops across the nations. They also help in establishing linkages and securing linkages for both the forward as well as backward paths. The value chain due to such centres remains sustained and there is a provision of providing end to end solutions to all the stakeholders during any processing.
2. Infrastructural facilities: In order to reduce the chances of the perishable items getting damaged over the period of time, the government promotes the establishments of warehouses and other storage centres across the regions to minimize the risk of crop spoilage due to storage or other kind of calamities. They have also been formed as a part of the Food Park initiative of the government under the Mega Food Parks Scheme announced by MoFPI which aims at scaling up the organic farm architecture in India

3. Extension Services like Training on PPP Model: Due to the lack in technological development in this area, government has started promoting private participation in the extension services related to the organic farming architecture. Many of the major players like Mahindra and Reliance have already implemented projects based on the implementation of the current and upcoming technical and automation practices in organic agriculture. Several social players like Upasna Seva have integrated with the government to provide training to the farmers on the new organic farming techniques. Poabs Organic and Phalada Agro Research Foundation are few other key players who help in the distribution of organic crops amongst farmers across India

## INDIAN COMPETENCE CENTRE FOR ORGANIC AGRICULTURE

Established in the year 2003, International Competence Centre for Organic Agriculture was formed after a number of NGOs, farmer organizations, companies, research institutions and government agencies took the initiative of forming an organization to provide services to the organic farming and organic stakeholders in India. This competence center was registered under the Karnataka Societies Registration Act 1960 with a joint vision and road map for building this Centre for the development of Organic Agriculture in Indian Region. ICCOA's mission is to help build the competence of individuals and organizations of the Indian region in organic agriculture and thereby contribute to building ecologically, economically and socially sustainable agriculture and organic business.

The work of ICCOA includes the integration of a range of tasks in order to facilitate the development of organic culture in India. Some of its tasks are highlighted in Figure 6.

To have consonance with these international standards, India had to take steps to identify organic products. As a result in 1985 Agricultural and Processed Food Products Export Development Authority Act was passed. Along with that, two authorities have also been established to regulate the organic agriculture field. These include the following:

*Figure 6. The channel of ICCOA (Indian Competence Centre for Organic Agriculture)*

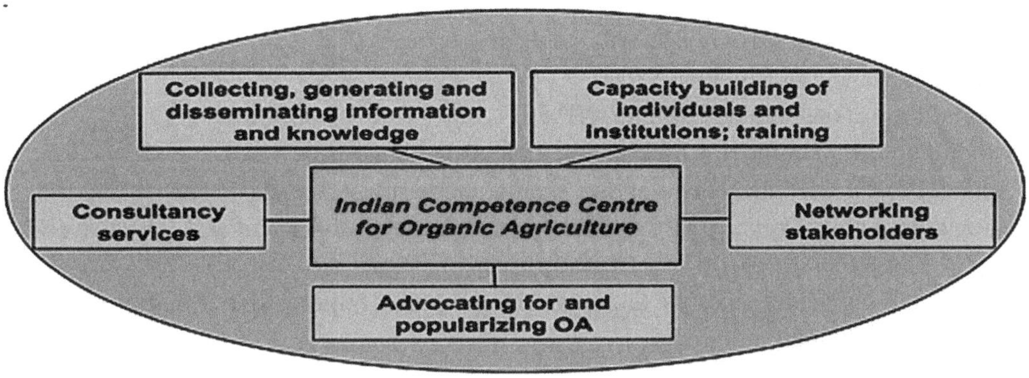

## 1. The Agricultural and Processed Food Products Export Development Authority (APEDA)

APEDA was established under the Agricultural and Processed Food Products Export Development Authority Act, passed by the Indian Parliament in December 1985. The primary function of the APEDA revolves on the promotion of export oriented production and development of scheduled products (including fruits, vegetables, meat, dairy, cereal, cacao products and non-basmati rice). This promotion is done vis-à-vis the growing demand of organic products outside of India. It also functions to fix standards and specifications for the scheduled products for the purpose of exports. Considering the global scenario, there is a high amount of focus on maintenance of standard for the products. This is followed diligently across the developed economies and has a high relevance in the United States. The APEDA thus functions as the body which provides for providing standards which are on an equal footing across the world. This is followed by the third activity of the APEDA, that of, carrying out inspection of meat and meat products for quality purposes and other matters. Only products certified by accredited bodies as conforming to national organic standards may be marketed as organic in India.

## 2. National Programme on Organic Production (NPOP)

In 2000, the Ministry of Commerce (Commission, 2001) and Industry of India launched the National Programme on Organic Production (NPOP). It was formed with the following objectives and principles:

- To provide the means of evaluation of certification programmes for organic agriculture and products as per approved criteria
- To accredit certification programmes
- To facilitate certification of organic products in conformity to the National Standards for Organic Products
- To encourage the development of organic farming and organic processing.

Besides the certification, the Central government and the state governments provides many various other aids to the farmers and bio fertilizers producers to promote organic farming. These aids come under the following various schemes –

- Rashtriya Krishi Vikas Yojna (RKVY)
- National Horticultural Mission (NHM)
- National Project on Organic Farming (NPOF)
- Horticultural Mission for North East and Himalayan States (HMNNEH)
- National Project on Management of Soil Health and Fertility (NPMSHF)
- National Project on Organic Farming under Indian Council of Agricultural Research (ICAR)

Along with these schemes and aids, there is various capacity building opportunities provided by the government through training programs.

## EXISTING PROBLEMS AND CONSTRAINTS

The major issue, proving to be a road block in the growth of organic farming is the inability of the government to come out with appropriate policies to promote the organic culture. The unavailability of financial and technical support from the government both at the Centre as well as the Panchayat level has led to the sustained resistance from farmers' to use the available organic method of farming. Some of the major areas that serve as a hindrance to the growth of organic farming in India are –

### Lack of Awareness

A majority of the farmers across the country are unaware about the use and advantages of organic farming against the conventional farming methods. Moreover, there is unwillingness amongst the farming community for the use of bio-fertilizers and bio-pesticides. There is lack of knowledge about the usefulness of supplementary nutrients to enrich the soil which are used to increase productivity of the land. In addition to this, there is lack of knowledge about the usage of modern techniques for compost making. There is a need for proper training of the farmers on the use of vermin-compost and their applications, which requires appropriate knowledge before use.

Though the NPOP was adopted in the year 2000, yet there is a huge scarcity of green markets to sell the products. Appropriate trade channels are in the nascent stage and poor infrastructure facilities make it impossible for the farmers to practice organic farming. There is a need for the state government to come into action and implement much needed policies and plans to help build the supporting infrastructure.

### Lack of Financial Support

One of the biggest existing problems is the lack of financial support from both the State as well as the Union Government. This is in sharp contrast to large subsidies provided to the conventional farming methods. As pointed in discussions by Dr A. K. Yadav (Yadav, 2011), ex-Director National Centre of Organic Farming, the Union Government has provided close to 700-800 crore for the development of organic farming in the last five years. This figure though may seem to be big, turns out to be peanuts in comparison to the subsidy provided to the conventional methods, especially the fertilizers industry, which was close to about 100,000 crore for the last five years. It is seen that the financial support for organic farming is just about 7-8% of the conventional one, which is very low for its adequate and necessary growth.

Furthermore, there is a high fee charged by the respective agencies for developing the practice of organic agriculture, which prevents the small farms from adopting this technique. There is also a high amount of cost involved for the certification, from inspection agencies, for the farmers which will carry out periodic inspections for standards. An additional cost is also incurred for the implementation and maintenance of standards which would be upto the national required standards.

Due to the rise in costs of organic inputs like groundnut cake, neem seed and cake, vermi-compost, silt, cow dung, other manures, etc. used as organic manure, the farmers prefer using chemical fertilizers and pesticides which are comparatively cheaper. As said by Dr. Yadav (Yadav, 2011), farmers are forced towards using chemical fertilizers considering the huge difference in prices. Considering the subsidy provided to the fertilizer industry the cost for organic manure turns out to be close to double of the normal fertilizers. Because of this there has been a rise in the move towards conventional farming techniques. For those who still practice organic farming, use of local or own farm renewable resources and implementation of agricultural practices in an ecologically friendly environment is the only way out to save costs.

## Inability to Meet the Export Demand

The demand for organic products is high in the advanced countries, like USA, European Union and Japan. It is reported that US consumers are ready to pay a premium price of 60 to 100 per cent for the organic products, due to the present wave of health consciousness present there. A market survey done by the International Trade Centre (ITC) during 2010 indicated that the demand for organic products is growing rapidly in many of the world markets while the supply is unable to match it.

India is known in the world organic market as a tea supplier, and there is great potential to export a wide array of products. Some of the most significant ones are coffee, vegetables, sugar, herbs, spices and vanilla. Dr. D. S. Yadav (Yadav, 2011), Research Officer National Centre of Organic Farming, points out in discussion that in spite of several initiatives India was able to export just about 70,000 tonnes of its annual organic produce. This is approximately just about 4-5% of the total produce of India for the year. He also states that demand is not a constraint for organic products in the international markets, and India can export close to almost 85 per cent of its production. This huge shortage in export quantity is primarily due to quality concerns of the food produced.

## Low Yields

There is a huge debate existing on the issue of production taking a huge hit on conversion to organic farming practices. Dr A. K. Yadav says that production though low, is only during the gestation period of conversion of the farm from conventional farming methods to an organic based one. Under the normal circumstances it is expected for a farmland to take a couple of years to realise the complete fruits of organic farming. It is not unnatural for farmers to experience some loss in yields due to the conversion of their farming method from conventional to organic. This is due to the existent harm done to the farmland with continuous usage of pesticides and fertilizers ("Raychaudhuri, S., Mausumi Raychaudhuri, Ngachan, S. V. and Yadav, A. K.", 2005).

But, he goes on to say that normal restoration of biological activity in terms of growth and produce is seen after the gestation period is over. He also says that there are existing methods to overcome this deficit in yield during this period, but the costs involved in implementing it serves as a hindrance to farmers to implement them. He says that the absence of appropriate schemes from the Government to compensate the losses suffered by the farmers during this gestation period prevents them practicing organic farming, as it is only logical for farmers to not want to undergo losses by shifting to a different production method compared to their normal one.

## Non-Standardization of Quality for Bio-Manures

Both the financial inability as well as the lack of availability of organic manures, forces the farmers to go for chemical fertilizers which is readily available. The increasing pressure of population and disappearance of the common lands have made the availability of waste very difficult. The waste which at times is used to produce the organic manure by converting it into bio-mass can also be collected from the locality. Also, most of the farmers are not informed that nutrients adequate for their land can be made available by the organic materials. The crop residues used as fodder and fuel and vermi-compost can be removed after harvest. They also increase productivity of the soil once ploughed back into it.

There is a growing need for fixing standards and quality parameters for bio-fertilizers and bio-manures, due to the increasing popularity of organic farming in the country. Most farmers are not aware of the harms of using the commercially available bio-manure products. While organic farming in itself puts great stress on the manures produced on the farm and the households of the farmers', branded products available in the market are quite often not truly organic ("Organic Farming Policy", 2005). Even though farmers are using manure produced by different methods, proper parameters for bio-manure is yet to be finalized.

## Marketing Problems of Organic Inputs

There is a lack of marketing and distribution network for the most important organic inputs i.e. bio-fertilizers and bio-pesticides. The high costs of these inputs and poor demand forces the retailers to deal in chemical fertilizers and pesticides, which are heavily advertised by their manufacturers and dealers. In addition to this the margin of profit earned is higher in case of chemical products as compared to the organic ones. Furthermore, low awareness of organic methods and erratic supplies adds to the problem. This is in its totality has created a situation wherein organic inputs are unavailable to the farmers who are inclined towards organic farming.

The marketing of the organic crops is a major issue. It needs to be insured that organic produce is sold at a premium over the conventional produce, due to the higher cost involved in their production. The inability to obtain a premium price is a huge setback for the farmers, more so when this is the case during the period where they aim reach the productivity level equivalent to the conventional crop. Organic produce are by nature not as good looking from the exterior as conventionally produced ones. This leads consumers to believe that the quality of these produce are not as good as the conventional ones. There is a need to educate consumers regarding the benefits of consumption of organic food and the basic difference of look which will exist for the organic produce. Lack of private players in the organic food sector has further deteriorated the popularity and availability of organic food to the consumers. This is due to the higher costs that would have to be shelled out by the private players for implementing an organic food network.

## Problems with Certification Process

The certification process currently present in India is a very complex one. As already mentioned the certification is divided into two parts. One notified by the FTDR, under APEDA, looks after the certification for exports produce. The second notified by the APGMC, under the AMA, looks after the certification for domestic markets. This has created a situation wherein farmers would have to go through two certifications for export. Furthermore, the annual costs involved for these certifications would be a hindrance for the farmers to opt for it. In addition to this, the amount of time a farmer would have to devote towards the certification process is too huge and unnecessary for the whole process. The amount of data required to be submitted by the farmers may not be available, or be feasible to find out, during a number of scenarios.

Dr A. K. Yadav (Yadav, 2011), in further discussions, brings forth an apathy wherein a there is a situation that there is almost 30-35% unlisted sales made every year, which are outside the purview of the certification process. There is an increasing majority of situations wherein the farmer is able to sell his produce in the vicinity of his farmland. This creates a situation where he sees no requirement or use of undergoing the certification process. These uncertified farmlands may not be producing at the proper quality standards, and thus there will be no possible method available for their standard checks.

## Political and Social Factors

Both political and social factors have a major role to play in determining the future of agriculture in India. Subsidies and other supports from government, government controlled prices of inputs like chemical fertilizers, production of fertilizers, government set prices for agricultural products, free supply or subsidized rates for inputs like power and water, etc. are the tools often used by the government to drive votes. Any movement for the promotion of organic farming in India will face opposition from all these major forces which benefit from such policies in the conventional farming system. This deadlock of resistance has to be broken by the government looking at the broader perspective of the future of India and steps need to be taken towards implementing organic farming. Also, the major issue of corruption drives costs of organic production up, as costs get escalated from the policies in place to the benefits that actually are derived by the famers.

## Farmers' Perspective

If we change our perspectives towards the farmers, we find that there is a continuously increasing popularity amongst the farmers towards organic production. It is seen at various places that farmers have started practising organic production on a small patch of farmland, which is sufficient for their personal usage, and continue with the conventional farming process in the remaining farmland. This they say is due to the wide acceptance of conventionally produced food products and the readily available returns that are derived from it.

During discussions held with organic farmers, Bharat Bhushan Tyagi, an organic farmer from Bheta village, points out that the government has implemented various schemes for the promotion of organic production, but there is no proper implementation of these schemes. He says that there are training programmes organised for the display of organic production methods, but there is no account of the existing season taken into account while holding these sessions. For, e.g. a session on organic production of winter crops is taken during the monsoon season, when such a demonstration would be redundant and useless. There also seems to be no coordination between the Union government and the State government on organic materials. It is seen that materials tend to arrive on time when being processed by the Union government, but are traditionally always late when it is being processed by the state government. Thus, there are various loopholes that need to be filled in for the effective growth of organic production in India.

# SOLUTIONS AND RECOMMENDATIONS

It has been very well understood that organic farming need support from private players to overcome its constraint. Though organic farming is getting very minimal support from them due to before mentioned problems, there are few models related to traditional agriculture which can be used as a base to build upon solution for organic farming. Improving certification process and developing infrastructure is a time taking procedure. The Government needs to give more visibility and help to organic farming. The Government has started with the certification process, but a general lack of awareness towards it and the highly complicated procedure has led to nearly as much as 30-35% of the farmers not being certified. Moreover with non-organic fertilizers being considerably cheaper and productivity being higher, there is a greater demand towards it. Promoting organic fertilizers and giving financial aid and resources to the farmers will help growth of organic farming.

Private players are not active in organic farming products as they are costly and private players get very low margins. The supply chain for organic production is weak and most of the organic product is distributed in the nearby areas to the production itself. Government provides aid to the farmers but puts in a very low contribution into the creation of an effective supply chain and distribution network. Both private and public players have to come together to take organic farming forward. Furthermore, Consumers are primarily unaware about the benefits of organic products and do not demand for good quality certified food. Also, farmers are small, and produce a very low amount of produce which is normally of a low quality. If the consumers are made aware of the benefits and quality of organic food, there will be a sustained demand for better quality goods, and this would invariably lead the farmer has to produce better quality organic product.

Also, this can be taken a step further by the implementation of an online portal. E-commerce has been growing at very fast pace and is ubiquitous and reachable. This platform can be used to promote organic farming and deliver product to the target customer group. Developing basic processing unit and basic delivery infrastructure similar to "Mother Dairy – Safal" can add to the network. www.Isayorganic.com is an example which is implemented in South Delhi and Noida region. Through this portal, they provide organic products at the door step of the people and provide all after sales service as well.

Another step which can be taken is the implementation of a network to reach the market. This can be modelled on the Akshamaala – Unnati model. Akshamaala is an initiative to bridge gap between farmers and market. It provides production, sales and processing support to the farmers using latest technical and analytical techniques. This has proved efficient and empowered farmers. Similar model can implemented to boost organic farming. Using this model, it would become easy to reach market and provide their products to the desired target group.

## FUTURE RESEARCH DIRECTIONS

The government has already introduced several programs in association with National Centre for Organic Farming. In order to increase consumer confidence in the organically produced products several initiatives have been launched which can be used for the certification of these products. The agents appointed under these programs have been expected to test at least 6% of the organic farms and businesses and provide certification to the same. According to the Organic Monitor (2010), mergers and acquisitions led to consolidation, with large companies emerging at every level of the supply chain. Many new entrants and small companies in the organic industry had to focus on niche segments/sectors.

Today the population no more remains blind to the harms that the technology has caused to our health and it is time that action is taken without waiting for the irrefutable scientific proof of such harms. The change from conventional to organic farming is going to be gradual yet the transformation is much needed given the benefits that organic farming offers. This opens a further research area, wherein the impact of technological advances vis-a-vis the changing demographics of government policies can be looked into. Further, the gap between communications and the ground realities is one of the potential fields to be looked into.

## CONCLUSION

Organic farming comes a distant second to the traditional farming methods in India. But, the organic farming landscape across India has been changing at a phenomenal rate. This can be seen as a step in the right direction for a green and better environment. There are visible roadblocks in the path, both at an administrative level and at the implementation level. There has been considerable action towards the streamlining of efforts to resolve all issues. But, as is the nature of the world, issues don't get resolved at once and is a continuous process of upheaval. There is also a lack of active communication between the farmers and the government, which serves as a roadblock. But, amongst all the gloom surrounding it, there is the beacon of hope with organic consumption on the rise worldwide. This has instilled a sense of motivation amongst everyone involved to make this a success. India is also leaving no stone unturned with its policies, certification schemes, etc. to invigorate what will be the future of farming in the years to come.

## REFERENCES

Commission, P. (2001). Organic Farming and Biodynamic Farming for the 10th Five-year plan. New Delhi: Government of India. Retrieved from planningcommission.nic.in/aboutus/committee/wrkgrp/wg_organic.pdf

George Kuepper, Kerr Centre for Sustainable Agriculture. (2010). *A brief overview of the History & Philosophy of Organic agriculture*. Retrieved from http://www.kerrcenter.com/publications/organic-philosophy-report.pdf

Gupta, M. L. (2012). *Garg Rekha*. Problems & Prospects of Agricultural Exports in the Emerging Scenario.

Kaur, G. (2013). Sustainable Development in Agriculture & Green Farming In India. *Oida International Journal of Sustainable Development*, *6*(12), 59–64.

Kaur, G. (2014). Sustainable Development in Agriculture & Green Farming in India. *Oida International Journal Of Sustainable Development*, *7*(3), 59–64.

Ministry of Agriculture. Department of Agriculture & Cooperation, National Centre of Organic Farming, Sector 19, Hapur Road, Ghaziabad. (n.d.). *Organic Farming Policy 2005*. Retrieved from http://ncof.dacnet.nic.in/Policy_and_EFC/Organic_Farming_Policy_2005.pdf

National Centre of Organic Farming. Sector 19, Hapur Road, Ghaziabad. (n.d.). *The world of Organic Agriculture in India*. Retrieved from http://ncof.dacnet.nic.in/OrganicFarmingAnOverview/TheWorldofOrganicAgricultureinIndia%202010.pdf

National Centre of Organic Farming. Sector 19, Hapur Road, Ghaziabad. (n.d.). *Organic Farming an Overview*. Retrieved from http://ncof.dacnet.nic.in/OrganicFarming-AnOverview/OrganicFarmingAnoverview.pdf

National Centre of Organic Farming. Sector 19, Hapur Road, Ghaziabad. (n.d.). *National Project of Organic Farming, Annual Report 2011-2012*. Retrieved from http://ncof.dacnet.nic.in/AnnualReports/AnnualReport2011-12.pdf

Panneerselvam, P. P., Hermansen, J., & Halberg, N. (2011). Food Security of Small Holding Farmers: Comparing Organic & Conventional Systems in India. *Journal of Sustainable Agriculture*, *35*(1), 48–68. doi:10.1080/10440046.2011.530506

Purushothaman, S., Patil, S., & Francis, I. (2012). Impact of policies favoring organic inputs on small farms in Karnataka, India: A multi criteria approach. *Environment, Development and Sustainability*, *14*(4), 507–527. doi:10.1007/s10668-012-9340-1

Raychaudhuri, S., Mausumi Raychaudhuri, Ngachan, S. V., & Yadav, A. K. (2005). Organic Farming – Management and Practices. ICAR Research Complex for NEH Region, Manipur Centre, Imphal.

Suresh, R. B. (2005). *Organic Farming: Status, Issues & Prospects – A Review*. Agricultural Economics Research Paper.

The Organic Institute. (n.d.). *History of the Organic Movement*. Retrieved from http://theorganicsinstitute.com/organic/history-of-the-organic-movement/

*WWOOFindia*. (n.d.). Retrieved from http://www.wwoofindia.org/history.htm

Yadav, A. (2011). *Organic Agriculture in India*. Retrieved from National Centre of Organic Farming: http://ncof.dacnet.nic.in/Training_manuals/Training_manuals_in_English/Organic_Agriculture_in_India.pdf

## ADDITIONAL READING

Commission, P. (2001). Organic Farming & Biodynamic Farming for the 10th Five-year plan. New Delhi: Government of India; Retrieved from planningcommission.nic.in/aboutus/committee/wrkgrp/wg_organic.pdf

Commission Regulation (EC) No 889/2008 (2008): Commission Regulation (EC) No 889/2008 of 5 September 2008 laying down detailed rules for the implementation of Council Regulation (EC) No 834/2007 on organic production & labelling of organic products with regard to organic production, labelling & control.

Cooper, J., Niggli, U., & Leifert, C. (2007). *Handbook of Organic Food Quality & Safety*. Abington: Woodhead Publishing.

Figge, F., & Hahn, T. (2004a). Sustainable value added – measuring corporate contributions to sustainability beyond eco-efficiency. *Ecological Economics*, *48*(2), 173–187. http://www.researchgate.net/profile/Tobias_Hahn5/publication/222425875_Sustainable_Value_Addedmeasuring_corporate_contributions_to_sustainability_beyond_eco-efficiency/links/0deec5212398be67f3000000 doi:10.1016/j.ecolecon.2003.08.005

Greenhouse Gases per Life Weight. (2006). *Dalgaard et al. (2006), Olesen et al. (2006), Petersen et al. (2006)*. Syvasalo et al.

Hughner, R. S., McDonagh, P., Prothero, A., Shultz, C. J., & Stanton, J. (2007). *Who are organic food consumers?* A compilation & review of why people purchase organic food. *Journal of Consumer Behaviour*, *6*(2/3), 94–110. doi:10.1002/cb.210

Kleijn, D., & Sutherland, W. J. (2003). How effective are agri-environment schemes in maintaining & conserving biodiversity? *Journal of Applied Ecology*, *40*, 947–969. onlinelibrary.wiley.com/doi/10.1111/j.1365-2664.2003.00868.x/pdf doi:10.1111/j.1365-2664.2003.00868.x

Makatouni, A. (2002). *What motivates consumers to buy organic food in the UK?* Results from a qualitative study. *British Food Journal*, *104*(3/4/5), 345–352. www.emeraldinsight.com/doi/full/10.1108/00070700210425769 doi:10.1108/00070700210425769

Narayanan, S. (2005) Organic Farming in India: Relevance, Problems & Constraints, Occasional Paper No. 38, Department of Economic Analysis & Research, National Bank for Agriculture & Rural Development, Mumbai.

Rajendran, A. T. P., Venugopalan, B. M. V., & Tarhalkar, C. P. P. (2008) Organic cotton farming in India, Review of Organic Farming/ Organic Cotton Cultivation – A culmination of non- chemical pest management, New Delhi.

Rajendran, S. (2002) Environment & economic dimensions of organic rice cultivation in South India, Paper presented at the *International Conference on Asian Organic Agriculture*, Suwan, Korea. 12-15 November.

Ramesh, P., Singh, Mohan & Subba Rao, A. (2005). Organic farming: Its relevance to the Indian context. *Current Science*, *88*(4).

Reddy Suresh, B. (2010b). *Assessment of Economic & Ecological Returns from Millet- based Bio-diverse Organic Farms vis-à-vis Conventional Farms, CESS Monograph Series No.8*. Hyderabad: Centre for Economic & Social Studies.

Sanghi, N. K. (2007) Beyond certified organic farming: *An emerging paradigm for rainfed agriculture*, Proceedings of the National Workshop on New Paradigm for Rainfed Farming: Redisgning Support Systems & Incentives, 27-29 September, IARI, New Delhi.

Schmid, O., Dabbert, S., Eichert, C., Gonzálvez, V., Lampkin, N., Michelsen, J., & Zanoli, R. et al. (2008). *Organic Action Plans. Development, implementation & evaluation. A resource manual for the organic food & farming sector. Research Institute of Organic Agriculture, Frick, Switzerland & European Union Group of the International Federation of Organic Agriculture Movements*. Brussels, Belgium: IFOAM.

Sharma, S. (2005). Contour cultivation based natural farming technique. *Organic Farming Newsletter*, *1*(2), 3–6.

Smit, A. H., Driessen, P. J., & Glasbergen, P. (2009). Conversion to organic dairy production in the Netherlands: Opportunities & constraints. *Rural Sociology*, *74*(3), 383–411. doi:10.1526/003601109789037286

Wander, M. M., Traina, S. J., Stinner, B. R., & Peters, S. E. (1994). Organic & conventional management effects on biologically-active soil organic-matter pools. *Soil Science Society of America Journal*, *58*(4), 1130–1139. doi:10.2136/sssaj1994.03615995005800040018x

Watson, C. A., Atkinson, D., Gosling, P., Jackson, L. R., & Rayns, F. W. (2002). Managing soil fertility in organic farming systems. *Soil Use and Management*, *18*(3s1), 239–247. doi:10.1079/SUM2002131

Willer, H., & Klicher, L. (Eds.). (2009). *The World of Organic Agriculture: Statistics & Emerging Trends. IfOM, Bonn, FiBL, Frick*. Geneva: ITC.

Wood, R., Lenzen, M., Dey, C., & Lundie, S. (2006). A comparative study of some environmental impacts of conventional & organic farming in Australia. *Agricultural Systems*, *89*(2-3), 324–348. doi:10.1016/j.agsy.2005.09.007

Woodward, L. (1996). *Can Organic Farming Feed the World?* Newbury, UK: Elm Farm Research Centre.

## KEY TERMS AND DEFINITIONS

**APEDA:** Agricultural and Processed Food Products Export Development Authority. It is responsible for promoting and setting of standards for export oriented organic produce.

**Bio-Fertilizers:** It is a substance which contains living microorganisms, which when applied to seeds and plants promotes their growth.

**Bio-Manure:** It refers to plants which are mostly planted for adding nutrients and organic matter into the soil. They are generally planted for a fixed period of time, post which they are ploughed into the soil, while they are still green.

**Bio-Mass:** It generally refers to a material derived from living or recently living organisms. A popular form of bio-mass is wood, which is used for energy production.

**Bio-Pesticides:** Bio-pesticides in the broad term include several types of pest management methods. These are typically harmless, non-detectable residues which are more effective than chemical pesticides.

**Certification:** It is the process being certified that the produce from the farm is upto the necessary standards of quality for its respective usage area, internally or export.

**Gestation Period:** It is the period during which the farm is being converted from a fertilizer based farm to an organic based farm. Yields are typically low during this period.

**NCOF:** National Centre for Organic Farming. It is responsible for the promotion of organic farming by capacity building and quality control, under its central sector scheme.

**NPOP:** National Programme on Organic Production. It is responsible for accrediting and evaluating certification programmes of organic farms.

**Organic Farming:** It is the form of farming which relies on crop-rotation, compost, green manure, etc., rather than fertilizers. Organic farming is referred to over here as that done on Indian soil.

**Traditional Farming:** It is the general popular form of farming that is followed in India. It depends heavily on fertilizers.

**Vermi-Compost:** It is the product formed by composting various types of worms to create a mixture. Its usage shows greater soil and product enrichment than otherwise.

# Chapter 22
# Jugaad Inc:
## Evolution of Frugal Entrepreneurship and Lean Start Ups

**Neelendra Nath**
*IMT Ghaziabad, India*

**Sayantan Saha**
*IMT Ghaziabad, India*

**Somtirth Chaudhuri**
*IMT Ghaziabad, India*

**Bineydeep Singh**
*IMT Ghaziabad, India*

**Parikshit Sarkar**
*IMT Ghaziabad, India*

**Neha Bhardwaj**
*IMT Ghaziabad, India*

## ABSTRACT

*The essence of an entrepreneur's effort lie in finding solutions to challenges. Monetary profit is a by-product of entrepreneur's success and not the main agenda or measure of it. This bare nature makes entrepreneurship a risky business. In spite of all the rigor and challenges, entrepreneurs never cease to exist; in fact now we are seeing an unprecedented surge in their numbers. This surge has changed the whole dynamics of the entrepreneurial environment. A study of changing norms, style and sentiment of entrepreneurs is in order. In this chapter we study changing times and style of entrepreneurship; the evolution of new age entrepreneurs and their approach. Is this trend lasting or will burst like a bubble? Is it increasing uncertainty at conventional jobs or people have developed a deep lust for entrepreneurship? With so many startups coming up these days, how to evaluate them? These are the few questions which have risen and await adequate response.*

## INTRODUCTION

As with the time people have evolved thus their needs. An entrepreneur is someone who works with the objective of bridging the gap of need and availability; hence it is natural that they also evolve with changing time. Entrepreneurs have been around since there was some need unfulfilled or some advancement seemed possible. They work with the idea of adding efficiency and simplifying life. To commence a discussion on entrepreneurship, it is necessary to answer two basic questions. Who is an entrepreneur

DOI: 10.4018/978-1-4666-8259-7.ch022

and how are they different from businessmen? The difference would lie in the objective they frame in their mind and parameter on which they adjudge their success. Once that is set, we could move ahead talking about the evolution over time. For convenience sake, we can assume a time line marked with other historical events and evaluate the evolution at all these junctures. In recent time, specially post liberalization and recent global slowdown, we have seen a sudden surge in number of people turning to entrepreneurship. This has forced the whole entrepreneurial environment to change radically. A lot of concepts and practices are born to understand the practices the multitude of first generation entrepreneurs are bringing in. Start up, venture capitalist, equity pitch and taking the plunge has become the new buzz words. What was earlier considered as a choice to make when all other doors are close; has now become probably the most respected career choice. Barriers have always been there for most who decided to take a plunge and they still are. So, what could be the reason of this changing scenario? While the barriers mostly remains as they were, new age entrepreneurs found a way around them. Frugal entrepreneurship & lean startup is a couple of new age terms defining approach taken by first generation entrepreneurs to stay competitive in the market with the minimal cost or fund they could arrange for. Though the concepts were born out of approach taken by few enthusiastic and prudent entrepreneurs, it has also become a reason for a lot of people considering taking a plunge. A wheel has been set in motion, but now the question rises in wake of a lot of traditional business housed not doing well and most of startups closing down in first couple of years; are these new approaches really a torch bearer to the future or just a short term hysteria working just on speculative success of model? Such examination can be done only by doing a comparative study of new organizations and developing a frame work which could evaluate them.

## BACKGROUND

### Evolution of Entrepreneurship

The first entrepreneur was probably the caveman engineer, who invented wheel, while other dwellers logged their load around on slabs. They saw a need of better transport system and thus came up with the idea of wheel. This example adequately explains the motivation of an entrepreneur – to bridge the gap, to improve the quality of existence. Monetary profit is often a byproduct of idea acceptance and implementation for an entrepreneur. This motivation led them to go places where conventional businessmen would not wander. The zeal of doing the new and unwarranted by entrepreneurs has shaped the world we see today. From the Phoenician traders to Roman merchant, all of them moved out of their comfort zone to find, buy and trade in commodity in places where they were not known; Idea was to make the world know what exist beyond their knowledge and not to let them miss out on those things. The explorer – preneurs of renaissance age and the innovator of colonial America were all entrepreneurs while being a lot of other things. The mid 1800s saw the rise of gold rush after which entrepreneurs saw digging for minerals as an opportunity and we entered an era of oil rush from gold rush. Utilitarian Entrepreneurs were a breed which developed in early 1900s. They say a need of innovation which could improve the daily life of mass. From here entrepreneurs never stopped, from things of daily utility to luxury – they were finding gap in every segment and bridging them. No opportunity was missed. There was just one thing common in all of them – zeal to make their idea work and guts to take the plunge without safety net. It was their risk taking appetite which gave us technology which looks so common place these days, computers. That was the era of 1980s when probably for the first time world was seeing a bunch of young college students going unconventional and taking huge risk for their mission of changing the world as they saw it. Steve Jobs and Bill Gates remains the role model of many such youth even today who think their creation has the ability to revolutionize the world.

Business scene in India during 1900s was mostly dominated by huge business houses. It was very difficult for new entrepreneurs to enter market and compete with them. Entry barriers have always been huge in Indian market whether the dominant status of big business houses or license raj policy of government. Except for Reliance, pre-liberalization era did not see much rise of entrepreneurship in India. Entrepreneurs limited themselves to open up retail stores or home based small business. They also were done in very traditional way in conventional market. No path breaking enterprise could come up before that. After 1991 with advent of liberalization, the scenario changed in India. A rapid change in the Indian business landscape happened with coming of Internet. In 1990s India saw a lot of IT entrepreneurs. Under the relaxed norms of government and an expanding market called a lot of people and with that India became a major IT hub for the world. This boom kept going for a long time and this market is still not saturated. World stage was also seeing a lot of ideas and innovations happening on internet arena – social media opened a completely new Pandora box. The global economic slowdown made people aware of the uncertainty attached with tradition jobs. This period encouraged a lot of people to take up to their own business instead of working for others. Through late 1990s and early 2000s the number of entrepreneurs continuously rose in India. Bangalore and Pune rapidly became entrepreneurs' hub and a huge number of youth started choosing it as their first career option. Internet market and virtual world are ever expanding and has a plethora of services to offer. Entrepreneurs are daily finding new ways of exploiting and exploring internet and presenting them in front of people to use. As the technology is new and better understood by young people, we started seeing a lot of young entrepreneurs in the business scene. These were not the traditional business, so the ways they were being done was also not traditional. These new entrepreneurs were also not riding on huge capital and mostly started with meager startup money. They had to find a way to start and expand cheap. The process of starting a business has also become quick, because market was moving faster than before. If a business gets delayed in starting they would see no market for them when they will commence. The whole environment changed in this era, the new entrepreneurs were making their own rules and playing the game. Focus was being shifted from competency to market requirement. Since 1990, over 3402 new product startups (Figure 1) have come up in India – which translates to roughly 1 company every other day. These figures have been on a continuous rise since 2005 except for 2009 slowdown.

In the recent time on an average over 412 technology companies are formed in India annually out of which only 154 has received any sort of funding. This shows a trend shift of from a cautious capital intensive well planned business entity to quick money crunch business entities (Mohan, 2012). In recent times another trend which became evident was of youth moving to starting own company. Data shows that of approximately 1200 companies started between 2010 & 2012; almost over 300 were founded by people which work experience less than 3 years (Figure 2). (Best Engaging Communities, 2012)

The changing trend called for new practices and born out of these trends are the concept of Frugal Entrepreneurship and method of Lean Startup.

*Figure 1. Indian new product startups fig1*

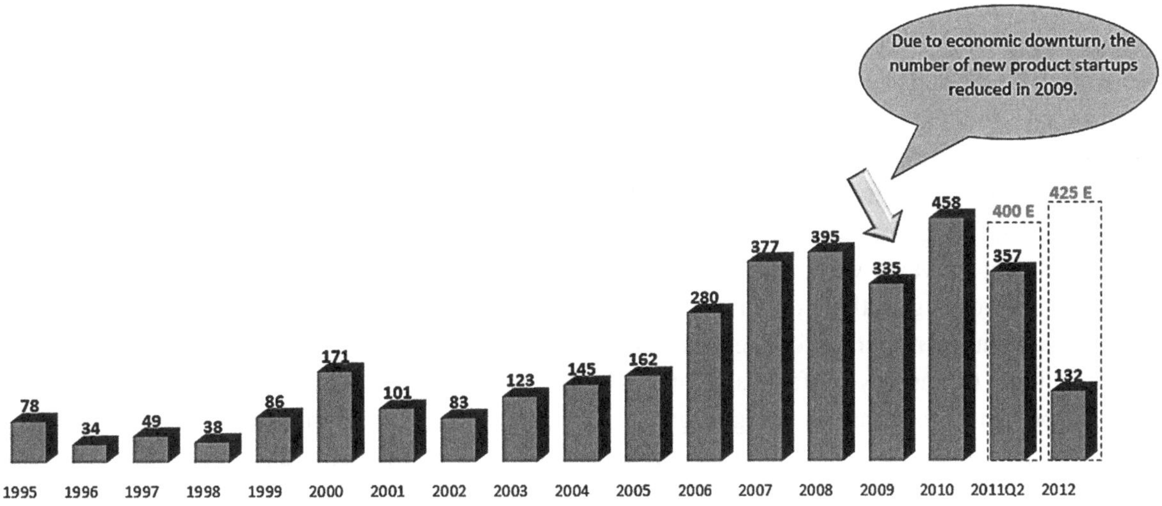


## Frugal Entrepreneurship

"Smart entrepreneurs are doing more with less," says Joseph R. Cardamone, president of the U.S. Federation of Small Businesses. "With diminished cash flow and tight credit, only those businesses that operate efficiently will survive this economic downturn, which may last several years." (Cardamine, n.d.)

Frugal entrepreneurship is a lifestyle which has become prevalent among the young entrepreneurs taking the plunge. Frugality is often attached with money crunch and low budget, though for entrepreneurship it is more of a culture. Changing market environment, consumer behavior and competition has compelled entrepreneurs not only be innovative with product but also with how they do business. Frugality is a concept which encompasses all those innovation – cash, resource, time and energy crunch is just tip of the frugality iceberg. Frugal entrepreneurship builds on the concept of market focus growth than competency focus. Traditionally basis of going into the business used to be core competency of the founder or founder's group and need of such competency in the market. This approach often is a slow

*Figure 2. Work experience of Startup Founder*

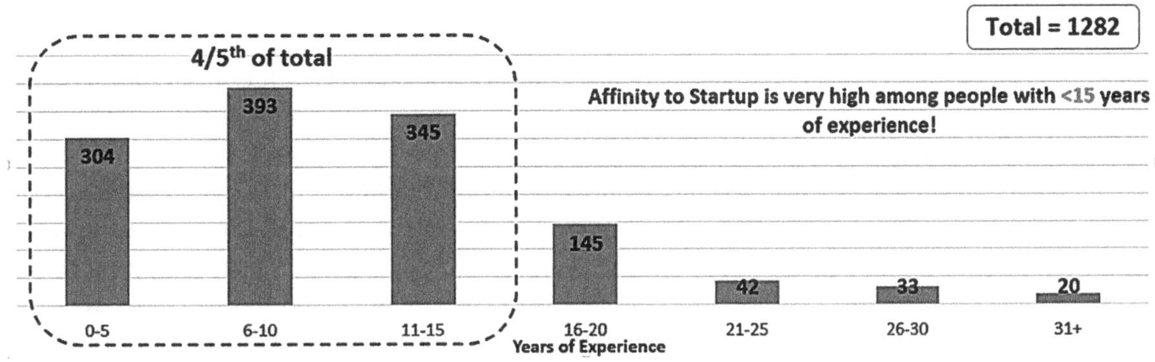

Elephant, bulky in planning and expensive to sustain. In the swift rabbit market, which changes track continuously an Elephant approach is a certain way to hit a dead end where no consumer stay. This led entrepreneurs today to take up approach which ensures that they if not ahead of the market remain at par with the market. They were not expected to provide product/services to market only based on their competencies but they were required to have customized services or product as consumer demands. This also called for rapid diversification event into category which is not part of logical extension of current product or service line. In traditional approach this would be highly resource and cash intensive thus not something first generation entrepreneurs could do. Unless, they could develop a way of providing service/product in which you could maintain profitability and more important sustainability without scaling. This would give them opportunity to jump sector and category without completely changing focus or duplicating resources for every diversification they do.

Frugality in technology is often associated with innovative product development and low cost quick fix solutions. In here, we are adopting frugality in entrepreneurship as an innovation to process and approach. Starting a new business is often associated with bulky, non-productive and non-returning activity. Most of these activities are actually associated with drawing constraints around enterprise and defining boundary. In another word, it is spending more for less. Most of the startups shut down or fail because they run out of money even before sufficiently producing their saleable product in the market and in many cases even before identifying their saleable product. A frugal approach proposes to cut down these costs and also the boundaries we create by spending them. These costs are often associated with brand definition and structure designing. Incorporating an entity seems very fascinating at early stage, which also cost a lot of money often leave entrepreneur with changing their memorandum or status at a later stage when they realize the actual scope of business. In current times, entrepreneurs have identified the constraint a very strong legal document can create for their business and they are opting more for open or more flexible structures until they identify their actual business scope. This reduces the initial cost of business and also allows the startup to explore market and products beyond their own imagination. This is one example of frugality in approach; it saved time, money and effort of altering and re-altering hard deed documents. As new age entrepreneur are identifying processes which are more of hurdle than help, they are looking for a way across them and building their business on core of offerings and customer feedback rather than legal documentation and constraints.

Frugality in the approach helps enterprises retain cash, time and energy to make required business iteration when they deem time to be right or find a void in marketplace. The flexibility of structure and focus on offering solution gives them more opportunity to be successful. They are doing horizontal expansion without building vertical potential unless they see a void big enough to park themselves. Diversification gives them security from sector wise barrier of entries and also able them to make a raw network of offerings which they might be able to integrate in future. The whole model is like creating a web at a very small scale and then expanding it up to the size. In traditional setup we see just opposite, where an entity will first bring itself to size and then build an integrated or diversified network around it. If the entity fails in building its own size they would never realize what part of network could have help them survive. For the new age entrepreneur who often find themselves in a David fighting Goliath situation, a diversified network works as a cushion to support the fall of one single node, or fast moving network pulls along with it a stayed behind node. Inclusive development is a straight outcome of it.

Frugality in entrepreneurship thus can be defined as freedom of doing business without being constrained within sector or category with minimal indulgence in cash, resource, time and energy. Frugality has brought back the world oldest business style – barter and trade. They are single point method of reducing cost across the startup where they exchange product, service or marketing for what they seek. If this system effectively allows them to hold cost, then an opportunity to diversify opens automatically. The system also effectively provides the effect of scale of economy without scaling up as barter ration remains same irrespective of number of units in question.

Frugality has opened a door which sees entry of a lot of new players. This has suddenly made the startup market a very busy place. But, there are a lot of questions attached with it. Is it a sustainable model, will it keep going when forerunners mature or become established big firms? Is it an evolutionary step or just a bubble which is riding on trend cycle and will hurt a lot of people when it will burst? But, for now this concept has allowed a lot of first generation entrepreneurs to take plunge and keep their hold in the market. It has also, not just stopped there but is forting on its base. Lean Startup is one such method of organization which tries to make the concept of frugality more concrete and gives us a hope that frugality is the way ahead when it comes to startups and entrepreneurs of future.

## Lean Start Up

Eric Ries in 2011 proposed a method for developing businesses and products – it was called "Lean Startup". At the core of the concept, idea was to reduce the product development cycle by adopting a combination of business – hypothesis – driven experimentation aided with iterative product releases. He termed this sequence as "validated learning". Ries claims that this method can actually reduce market risk and avoid a need of large amount of initial project launch and extensive knowledge repository while entering an alien product business. Lean startup necessarily comprise of process where the enterprise launches product/service at a very early stage to a select consumer base and then seek validation from market before further going ahead with it. Market here by itself works as a filter in deciding what product or service is to be taken up and to what scalability. The method develops an environment of 'in market dynamic learning', thus allowing a frugal entrepreneur to go beyond their own competency and safety net and explore a demand of market which they could not have in traditional business method.

The lean startup philosophy finds its origin in lean manufacturing method – a streamlined production method to reduce the resource and time employed and waste generated. Lean startup philosophy focuses on developing consumer solutions based on learning through feedback through beta stage and reducing the cost and time while creating the consumer value. In the HBS – Lessons from the classroom article ' Teaching a Lean Startup Strategy', author Carmen Nobel (Nobel, 2011) quoted Thomas Eisenmann stating, most startup fail because they waste too much time and money building the wrong product before realizing what the right product should have been. The article mentions some key concepts from this lecture:

- Rather than spending months in stealth mode, a lean startup launches as quickly as possible with a "minimum viable product" (MVP), a bare-bones product that includes just enough features to allow useful feedback from early adopters. The company then continues hypothesis testing with a succession of incrementally refined product versions.
- Lean startup executives do not invest in scaling the company until they have achieved product marketing fit (PMF); that is, the knowledge that they have developed a solution that matches the problem.

- In lean startup lingo, "pivoting" refers to a major change in a company's direction based on user feedback. Eisenmann's students discuss how entrepreneurs can stay true to their vision while still maintaining the flexibility to pivot.
- Adhering to a lean startup strategy is especially challenging for companies that require a great deal of time to launch a workable product, such as clean-tech or biotech companies.

Steve Blank in his HBR article 'Why the Lean Start-Up Changes Everything" (Blank, 2013) has drew a parallel in traditional startups and lean startups and demonstrated the difference between the two. In strategy stage, while traditional entrepreneur develops an implementation – driven business plan, a lean entrepreneur goes for hypothesis-drive. New product development process in the way they are developed and presented to market; wherein a lean approach looks at customer development and hypothesis testing, traditional approach is that of product management and linear step by step development. Similar differences are visible in engineering, organization, financial reporting, speed and failure. While product development in lean process is iterative, traditional approach will look at end product specified at the beginning method. Organizational development in lean startup happens through developing agile flexible team with hiring happening for learning, nimbleness and speed where as traditional structure would be that of departmentalization and hiring for experience and execution ability. Important feature of financial reporting for a lean startup would be customer acquisition, lifetime value and viralness whereas traditionalist sticks to balance sheet and cash flow.

Very important differences two approaches have are in terms of failure and progression or speed. While failure in traditional approach hit hard and may lead to firing, disinvestment etc. for a lean startup failure is part of profess which can be managed by iterating other ideas and pivoting away from the one which did not work. Progression of work or speed, in traditional set up are well measured and happen with the complete data, a lean startup whereas moves on with good enough information and thus have a rapid speed.

For a frugal entrepreneur essence of lean startup lies in two benefits they get out of it –

1. Reduced cash and resource deployment while developing solution for consumer and ease of shifting with market sentiments.
2. Reduced time between ideation and product placement in the market thus giving them flexibility and early mover advantage. This also enables them to gain dynamic learning to improvise on their offering without spending a lot on nonessential market study and business intelligence.

Lean startup method is a go ahead strategy which has enables frugal entrepreneurship to come alive from a philosophy to practice.

## Literature Review

Cambridge dictionary defines an entrepreneur as *"someone who starts their own business, especially when this involves seeing a new opportunity"*. Praag and Versloot (2007) have defined entrepreneurs as those who are self-employed owner-managers of their own incorporated businesses. In such a case, the size of the firm is not a factor and employees are in control of such an organization. They have also given a definition of what they term as an entrepreneurial firm. They have defined an entrepreneurial firm as one which meets the following criteria:

- Less than 100 employees.
- Less than 7 years old.
- New entrants into the market.

On the other hand, Aswath Damodaran (2009), in his research paper titled "*Valuing, Young, Start-up and Growth Companies: Estimation Issues and Valuation Challenges*" has given the following characteristics of an entrepreneurial firm:

- New entrant in the market.
- Small or no revenues, accompanied by operating losses.
- Almost completely funded by private equity.
- A small number of such firms actually survive beyond 7 years.

Saras D. Sarasvathy (2001), in her research paper *"What makes entrepreneurs entrepreneurial?"* submitted to The Harvard Business Review stated that all young entrepreneurs begin with three categories of means:

1. Who they are – their character, abilities and traits.
2. What they know – their education, experience, training and expertise
3. Whom they know – their social and professional network.

From our studies, it is clear that there are different challenges when it comes to evaluating start-ups. Such challenges may range from lack of information to the problem in the structure of the firm.

Aswath Damodaran has also pointed out the different issues that analysts and valuation experts face while valuating a start-up. He has pointed out that lack of credible financial statements, lack of growth assets makes it difficult to do due diligence. Furthermore, the lack of historical data and the fact that these companies have very large operating expenses as compared to more matured companies makes it even more challenging. He opined that the traditional way of estimating a company's value is flawed when it comes to start-ups and young enterprises. He provided a framework in this research paper on how to analyze such companies and come up with a sound and credible rating system.

Aswath Damodaran mentions that the value of a firm is actually its capacity to generate future cash flows and the assets it holds. However in cases of new firms, the cash flow may be negative but the value of the firm may not be so. Further a company does not own many assets at the outset, so it is difficult to estimate the value of the firm. Thus he states that a start-up could not be valued using the same principles as the established companies. An evolved and more practical method thus needs to be developed for valuing start-ups.

In the publication Hypothesis – Driven Entrepreneurship: The Lean Startup authors Thomas R. Eisenmann, Eric Ries, et al. defined a lean start up as firms which follow hypothesis driven approach. As per the paper entrepreneurs in these startups put their vision in form of falsifiable business model hypothesis and then test them using a series of "minimum viable products". A minimum viable product has been put across as a product which represents the smallest set of features or activities needed to validate the solution being offered by the startup or product. This publication necessarily is an extension to the idea earlier presented by Eric Ries in his book 'The Lean Startup' which extensively talked about future being created in dorm rooms of colleges and how the new generation innovators approaching the solution to the problems of world.

The Lean Startup has taken its name from the lean manufacturing revolution of Toyota, created by Taiichi Ohmo and Shigeo Shingo. The management world owes a lot to lean manufacturing revolution, through it came out just – in – time production, batch size shrinking, inventory control and acceleration of cycle times among many other tenants. World had learnt the difference between value creating activity and waste activity. This revolution has shown a way of inside out development of qualities in products. Lean Startups have adapted these ideas to entrepreneurship – they propose a different parameter to judge progress and success than other ventures. They call it 'validated learning'. The central idea here is to validate every little progressive step through a feedback channel and differentiate between value creating feature & waste.

Steve Blank in his Harvard Business Review article "Why the Lean Start-Up Changes Everything" talks about the hypothesis approach, the fallacy or the Perfect Business Plan and declining popularity of Stealth Mode. He talks about experimentation over elaborate planning, customer feedback over intuition and iterative design over traditional "big design up front" development. He indicates that even though philosophy of lean start up pretty new, it's fundamental concepts – minimal viable product and pivoting have already taken deep roots and being brought in execution by many a new age entrepreneurs. These approaches according to him are going to change everything.

Frugal Engineering and many terms pointing to it was coined by Carlos Ghosn, the joint chief of Renault and Nissan. He defined frugal engineering as achieving more with fewer resources. Since then the word has taken many form, appearing and reappearing in many works. Essentially it was always attached with creating more in scarcity of resources. The most used and famous for the word has taken is 'Frugal Innovation'. Yassir Ahmad Bhatti in his paper, "What is Frugal, What is Innovation? Towards a Theory of Frugal Innovation", develops a theoretical model by applying existing theories to emerging market context. It talks about the idea of frugal innovation as the intersection where technology innovation, institutional innovation and social innovation merges. (Bhatti, 2012)

Preeta M. Banerjee and Ana Leirner, in Handbook of Research on Techno-Entrepreneurship, edited by Francois Therin discuss the idea of frugal innovation and returnee-diaspora entrepreneurship. They have stated frugal innovation as a means to end for returnee – diaspora entrepreneurship.

While the focus of all literature till now on frugality has been in terms of innovation and technology, there certainly is a link of it with process innovation. If lean startup is a way of minimal viable product development through consumer feedback channel and iteration, frugality in entrepreneurship itself is the way to manage that startup with minimal and only necessary resource usage.

## Research Methodology

The objectives of this research are:

1. To study the evolution of entrepreneurship over ages and the recent development.
2. Establish the concept of Frugal Entrepreneurship
3. Study method of Lean Startup and its implication on frugal entrepreneurship
4. Develop evaluation matrix for early startups

The research method involved reaching out to early startups and investigating them on certain parameters and interviewing them to understand following about them to initially establish if they fall into the category of frugal entrepreneurship as defined in this literature work. This was essentially done

*Table 1. List of Participating Startups*

| Name of The Start Up | Service/Product Category | Funding Status | City |
|---|---|---|---|
| Rattle | Diversified | Not Funded | Pune |
| Quizot | Web Based Quizing | Not Funded | Delhi |
| Brandunia | Brand Placement | Not Funded | Noida |
| Funza | Career Services | Not Funded | Hyderabad |
| Walker Styleways | Online Footware | Not Funded | Delhi |
| Cardback | Loyalty Service | VC Funded | Delhi |

though a questionnaire response by 30 entrepreneurs who claimed to believe in the philosophy of frugal entrepreneurship. Further to develop in depth understanding of purpose, motivation and process in these entities close investigation was done on their working style, organizational structure and founder's profile. Evaluation matrix was developed by combining these responses with financials of the enterprises. Of the investigated six entities, one was selected to do detailed study to understand lean startup philosophy and rapid diversification as a response to market demand.

## CASE INVESTIGATION

To validate philosophy of frugal entrepreneurship, an open investigation through web based questionnaire was run. Thirty valid responses was recorded and evaluated against a score based system to recognize their level of frugality. This survey mostly had questions revolving about frugal utilization of resources to develop and market product in a startup environment. Further to validate the extension of the philosophy as provided in this report and engaging lean startup concept with frugal entrepreneurship detailed case investigation was undertaken. Six startups (Table 1) thus investigated are:

The investigation of these six entity revolved around four fundamentals i.e.

1. The Entrepreneur: Need for achievement, locus of control, risk-taking propensity, and previous work experience
2. The Environment: Venture capital availability, presence of experienced entrepreneurs, accessibility of customers or new markets, and proximity of universities
3. The Organization: Type of firm, entrepreneurial environment, partners, and strategic variables: cost, differentiation, and focus
4. The Process: The entrepreneur locates a business opportunity; the entrepreneur markets products and services. (Gartner, 1985)

Further the financials were considered to develop complete evaluation matrix validating efficacy of the frugal structure. Rattle Lifestyle Private Limited was studied in details to investigate lean startup methodology efficacy for frugal entrepreneurship and also market initiated demand based diversification. Appendix has the attached questionnaire used for investigate the frugality of enterprise.

*Figure 3. Frugality score of startups included in survey*

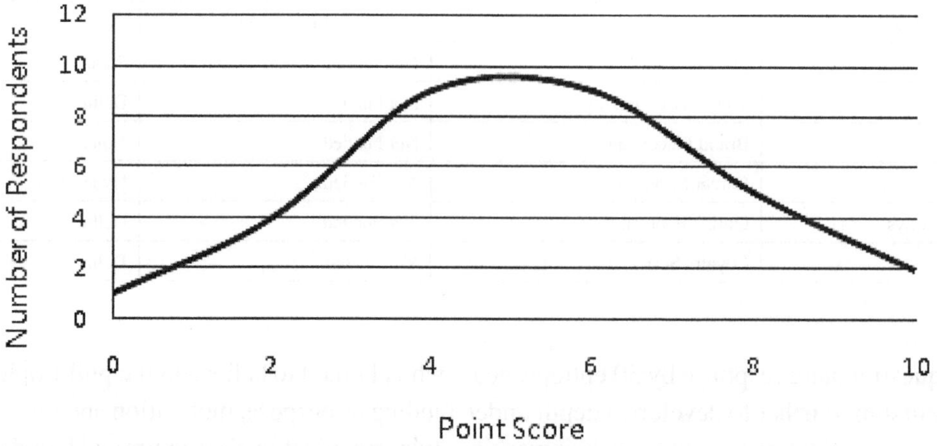


## FINDINGS AND ANALYSIS

Frugality was analyzed using a 10-pointer scale resulting from a Yes/No survey of 5 questions. From the 30 respondent who claimed that they follow frugal approach we could lean down to 7 which could stand the claim under our study. Graph of the scores (Figure 3) plotted resulted in an almost normal distribution of score across the startup, hence representing the actual startup environment scenario.

This result was crucial from the point of view of the perception of startups and entrepreneurs when it comes to taking up frugal and lean start up approach. Many who thought that they were being frugal in approach figured out they ranked in lower half on frugality chart. From the seven startups which were rated frugal, six (as mentioned in Table 1) agreed to go further with the study.

*Figure 4. Key lean startup principle responses*

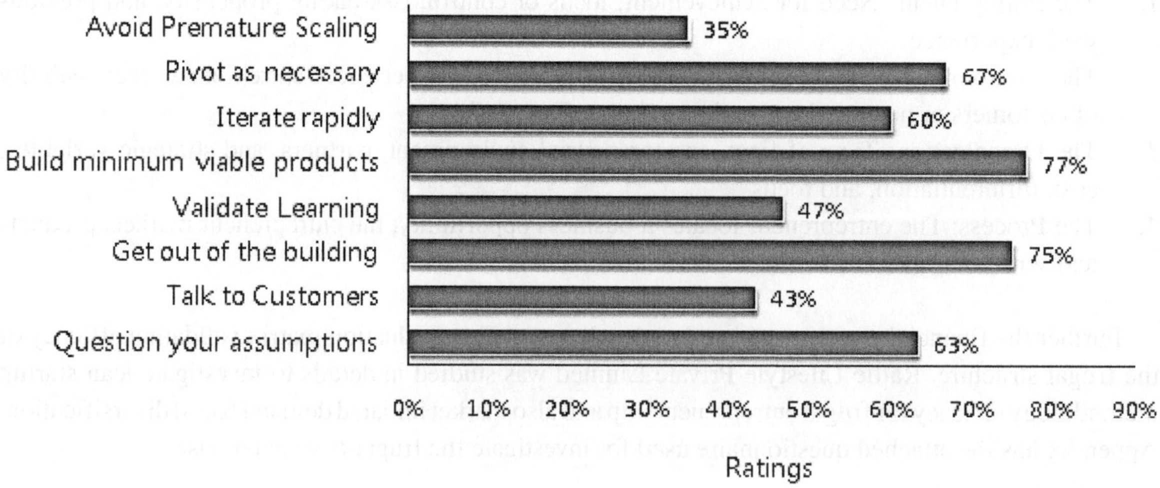

Six startups further questioned on lean startup principles (Kählig, 2011) being followed by them. Building the minimum viable product at a time and going out to the market with it was rated as the most important and highly followed principle (Figure 4). Rapid iteration and pivoting was close behind. This validated what we were seeking as a new age definition of frugality in approach of entrepreneurs.

Rattle Lifestyle Private Limited was picked from the lot to further investigate implications and sustainability of frugal approach with help of lean methodology. It formed a good cased study because of its rapid growth, consumer centric approach, iterative method for product development and quick pivoting. RLPL has been steadily growing over past 2 years, first as a partnership and then as a private limited company. They have diversified in five verticals what they call as Rattle's FLAME – Foundation, Lifestyle, Adventure & Sports, Media & Advertisement and Entertainment.

Rattle started off as a cause based networking website couple of years ago, a business which never took off. But, while they were trying to get a hold in web based business, an opportunity presented itself – to make merchandise for a potential client. They applied the first principle of frugal approach – quick diversification without cost scaling. On minimal margin they entered the market and rapidly grew in Pune merchandising scene. It was a $100 company which they had founded and mostly worked on credit clearance system. They played along a low margin for a long time supplying as the demand and going off primary product to cater whatever client demanded. Diversification in other three verticals was just a natural progression for them by filling wherever they saw a supply gap. Two basic principles they were following throughout their growth were – reducing resource duplication while diversifying, avoiding unnecessary scaling and crunching cost instead of increasing margins. Core competency of the employees was found necessary in managing clients and developing business and not for the product or service delivered. They placed themselves somewhere between manufacturer – trader line and employed barter – trade system. The approach made them a very appropriate case to study frugality in entrepreneurship and develop base principles of it.

## Evaluation Matrix

Through the study an evaluation matrix was developed to analyze and evaluate an early startup over six point principles of frugal entrepreneurship thus developed through following the practices surveyed unconventional startups are following. The matrix evolved from the conventional measure of startup revolving around the entrepreneur, the venture and the environment. When we introduce principle of frugality in this ecosystem, we extend the matrix and add one more parameter –the process. A qualitative, quantitative, strategic and ethical assessment of all these factors would paint a picture of growth and sustainability of the frugal entity in question. A frugal enterprise is always a cash crunch and resource crunch organization, at times diversified beyond its own size. Thus a mere quantitative analysis based on venture focus and development could not be representative. Strategic and ethical analysis gives us more insight about the strength of organization which can carry it on through the early uncertainties. Hence, the extended matrix (Figure 5) could be a good measure of the anticipated sustainability and growth of early frugal startups.

*Figure 5. Proposed evaluation metrics*

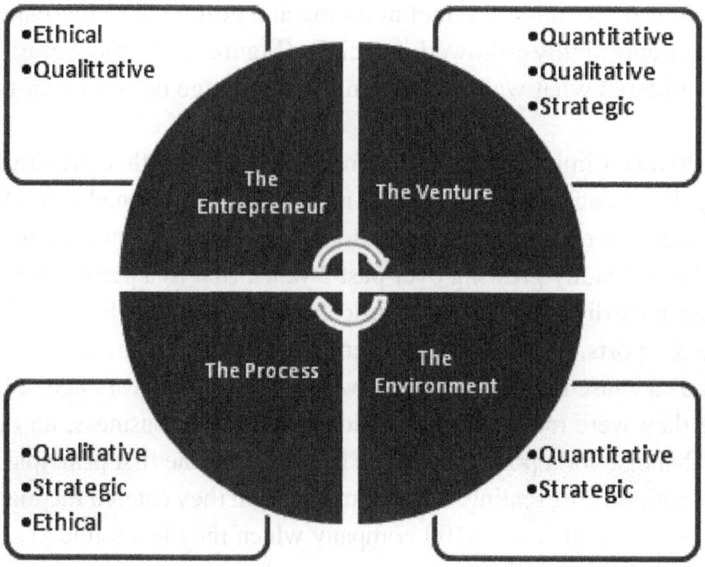


## CONCLUSION

The study has ascertained the paradigm shift in the way new age entrepreneurs are approaching the startup scenario in India. With advent of more young and penny less entrepreneurs – new approaches are flourishing daily. It's a disruptive innovation in progress in entrepreneurial arena in terms of approach and processes undertaken by new age first generation entrepreneurs. It is identified that it is necessary to develop an understanding and standards for approach to be able to aptly speculate direction in which startup are moving. One of these approaches is termed 'Frugal Entrepreneurship' here. This principle extends the definition of frugal from being cash, resource, time and energy crunching to process extension, rapid pivoting and quick response & diversification as per market shift. Thus, through the study we propose a six pointer principle defining frugal entrepreneurship approach which is certainly here to stay and change the complete entrepreneurial ecosystem. The principles of 'Frugal Entrepreneurship' are:

1. Adopt dynamic learning instead of pre surveying market and developing plan
2. Market Research & Business plan turns obsolete with ready to diverse flexible enterprise
3. Core competency of Organization lies in delivering solutions and developing business not in developing solutions and delivering business
4. Manufacture – Stock – Sell cycle is to be replaced by Identify – Barter – Trade cycle
5. Replace vertical scaling by rapid diversification and pivoting
6. Work on cost efficiency & resource allocation instead of increased margin and economy of scale

Enterprises following these principles are getting a very unique advantage of staying away from competing eyes as they do not scale vertically in initial stage and their horizontal diversification makes core companies in the field to take them as a short term opportunistic trader. But, away from prying eyes they keep growing in this competitive market in direction which offers even a small void and when they would scale up they will take the market by surprise.

## REFERENCES

*Best Engaging Communities*. (2012, September). Retrieved October 15, 2013, from Best Engaging Communities: http://beaforceofgood.files.wordpress.com/2012/09/snippets_product-startup-landscape-in-india_2012.pdf

Bhatti, Y. A. (2012). *What is Frugal, What is innovation? Towards a Theory of Frugal Innovation. Said Business School, Oxford Centre for Entrepreneurship and Innovation*. Oxford, UK: University of Oxford.

Blank, S. (2013, May). Why the Lean Start-up Changes Everything. *Harvard Business Review*, 3–9.

Cardamine, J. R. (n.d.). Retrieved October 15, 2013, from www.entrepreneur.com: http://www.entrepreneur.com/article/200102

*Frugal Entrepreneurship Survey*. (n.d.). Retrieved September 9, 2013, from Inc.com: http://www.inc.com/articles/1999/11/15720.html

Gartner, W. B. (1985). *A Conceptual Framework for Describing the Phenomenon of New Venture Creation*. Academic Press.

Kählig, C. (2011). *Facilitating Opportunity Development: Increasing Understanding of the Lean Startup Approach in Early Stage High-Tech Entrepreneurship*. Academic Press.

Mohan, M. (2012, September 19). *Best Engaging Communities*. Retrieved October 15, 2013, from Best Engaging Communities: http://bestengagingcommunities.com/2012/09/19/technology-product-startups-angel-and-venture-market-comparisons-us-and-india/

Nobel, C. (2011, April 11). Teaching a 'Lean Startup' Startegy. *HBS Working Knowledge*, 1-2.

## KEY TERMS AND DEFINITIONS

**Entrepreneurship:** Entrepreneurship is the process by which a new business venture is identified and started, the capital and other resources required for it are put into place and the entrepreneur carries both the risk and reward associated with it.

**Frugality:** In business terms, frugality is the quality of being prudent in the use and consumption of valuable resources, resulting in lesser waste and leakages.

**Lean Start Ups:** A lean start-up is a start-up with minimal resources and is frugal in its approach to achieve its long term goals.

**Venture Capitalist:** The one who provides initial capital assistance to high growth, high risk and high potential start-ups in their early stages.

**Innovation:** An innovation is something that is new, original and an improvement over the current system and generally considered important to whatever market or society it breaks into.

**Evaluation:** It is a systematic organized and scientific determination of a subject's merit based on some pre-defined rules or standards.

# Chapter 23
# Tackling Energy Issues in Rural India

**Riju Antony George**
*IMT Ghaziabad, India*

**Vijayshree M.**
*IMT Ghaziabad, India*

**Pavan Dev Singh Charak**
*IMT Ghaziabad, India*

**Kaustubh Singh Rana**
*IMT Ghaziabad, India*

**Shagun Agarwal**
*IMT Ghaziabad, India*

**Ambadipudi Venkata Sai Dhiraj**
*IMT Ghaziabad, India*

## ABSTRACT

*India is an energy deficient country and this deficiency is more felt in the rural villages of India. More than half of the villages are not electrified. Villages have many renewable resources and if these resources are put into effective use, the energy crunch can be mitigated. Such a renewable resource is rice husk which is perceived as a waste product. In this chapter, the authors have studied the potential of rice husk as a source of electricity for the rice producing villages of India. A particular village in the state of Uttar Pradesh was chosen to conduct the research to analyze the viability of a rice husk power plant. Various methods of converting biomass into energy have been discussed and based on research the biomass gasification method has been suggested as the most appropriate. The various advantages and challenges of using this technology, uses for by-products are discussed in this chapter. A workable business model has also been outlined along with future strategies and implications.*

## ENERGY ISSUES IN RURAL INDIA

India is a growing economy and it requires more and more energy to sustain its growth. It is imperative that India meets its growing energy necessities to sustain this growth. Even today, vast majority of people living in rural India do not have access to commercial forms of energy like electricity. This indeed is one of the key challenges faced by the energy sector in India. Most of the people in rural India depend on wood, dung and crop residue and they use primitive and inefficient technologies to harness power. Rural electrification is a must to facilitate inclusive growth and socio economic development of a country.

DOI: 10.4018/978-1-4666-8259-7.ch023

In India, 72% of people live in villages and they use only 33% of the generated electricity (Y, April 2012) as shown in figure 1. Electrified households in rural India gets only limited hours of electric supply. It generally varies from 9 to 11 hours per day. Voltage fluctuation and below voltage distribution is a common phenomena in rural India. A village is deemed to be electrified if 10% of household have access to electricity (Rural Electrification Policy, 2006). As per rural Electric Corporation, 78,743 villages are not electrified as on 31st December 2011 (Prem K. Kalra, 2007). This means that more that 78,000 villages do not have even 10% of its household electrified. As per the criteria of rural electrification, if we look into the number of households in rural India, more than half the number of households does not have electricity connection.

Biomass is the major source of energy used in rural India. Almost 75% of energy used in rural households is extracted from biomass. When it comes to rural industries (Pottery, brick making, smithy etc), biomass is used for more than 95% of energy requirement (Ramachandran, 2012). Traditional biomass fuels used are wood, animal dung, crop residues and charcoal. Other energy sources used in rural India are Bagasse, bio diesel with solar photo voltaic cells, Micro hydro power, wind turbines etc. Most of the rural households use kerosene for cooking and lighting purposes.

Indoor air pollution is another major issue faced by rural India due to the use of inefficient methods to extract energy from biomass. It majorly affects women and children in the household. According to a WHO (World Health Organization) study, 1.3 million people in India die due to Indoor air pollution which is more than double of the outside air pollution. Almost 27.5% of 'under five' mortality is also because of indoor air pollution as per TERI (The Energy and Resource Institute). India does not have any norm for indoor air pollution (Chauhan, 2013).

## RESEARCH OBJECTIVE

The objective of the research is to check the feasibility of rice husk technology for production of electricity, availability of rice husk in certain parts of rural India and how this technology has been successfully implemented in other parts of the country to resolve the energy crisis.

*Figure 1. Population percentage in rural and urban India and their electricity consumption*

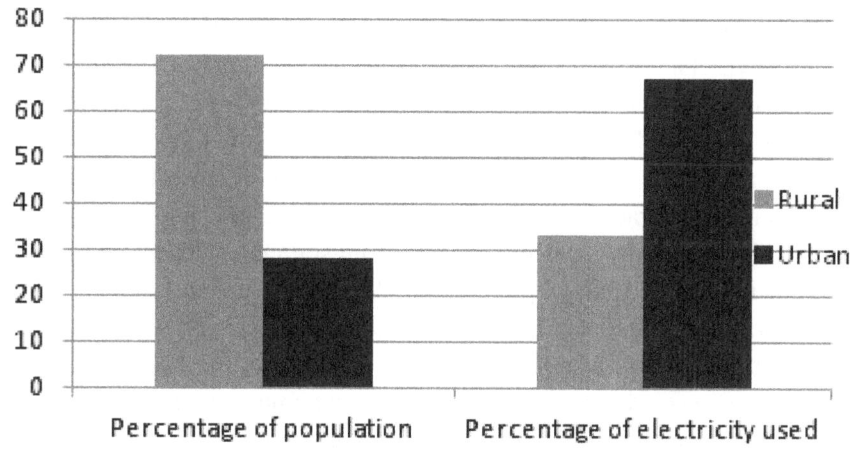

## RESEARCH METHODOLOGY

The first step in the research was of visiting a village in Uttar Pradesh to look into the renewable resources available. The team was looking for villages where paddy cultivation is extensive so that they can do the feasibility study of setting up a rice husk generator. They selected 'Sujaanpur Akhaada', a village in Hapur district of Uttar Pradesh where 30% of the land is used for paddy cultivation. After doing the feasibility study, they researched about the technology used in rice husk power generator, the amount of electricity it produces for a given quantity of husk, the usability of by products, how can it be set up as a business model and the advantages and the challenges.

## FEASIBILITY STUDY

Uttar Pradesh is considered as one of the worst power deficit states in India according to Associated Chambers of Commerce and Industry of India (ASSOCHAM). In 2010, UP had a power deficit of 1351 million units against an average all India power deficits of 8980 million units (Maharashtra, UP worst power deficit states: ASSOCHAM, 2010). 80% of its population resides in rural areas and almost 75% of its total workers are into cultivation or farming directly or indirectly. Agriculture is the main source of income for families in UP. Rice is the major crop in Uttar Pradesh and is grown in about 5.90 million hectares which comprises of 13.5% of total rice in India (Status paper on Rice in Uttar Pradesh, 2012). UP is the third largest rice producing state in India. In UP rice production is present in all the 72 districts of UP. It is grown on majority of the rural farms and it is part of almost every meal of its residents. Annual rice production in UP is around 12 metric ton in 2012 as per the status paper on rice in Uttar Pradesh.

There are three rice growing seasons in UP. They are Kharif season (wet season) which is from June - July to October, Boro season (winter season) which is from October – November to April – May and the Zaid season (summer season) which is from February to May - June. Majority of rice cultivation happens in the Kharif season followed by the Zaid or summer season. In Kharif season rice is cultivated in almost 5.90 million hectare where as in Zaid season; it is only 35000 – 40000 hectare. Around 98% of the rice is grown in the Kharif season which includes early, medium and long duration varieties (Status paper on Rice in Uttar Pradesh, 2012). In Kharif season, rice is cultivated in almost all parts of the state. Boro rice is cultivated only in flood prone areas of the state. The average productivity of rice in UP is 2 ton per hectare which is similar to national average. The overall rice production and productivity depends upon the rainfall and its distribution during the period in which crop is grown. In drought years, productivity has decreased and the state has witnessed high production and productivity in years in which adequate rainfall was received. In UP, rice is produced in five ecological conditions. They are favorably irrigated land, unfavorable rain fed upland, rain fed lowland, deep water and flood prone areas and in inland salinity conditions. As per cultural practices, direct seeding is done in rain fed areas whereas transplanting is practiced in irrigated and favorable low land. Almost 50% of the rice is cultivated in areas which are favorably irrigated. The main sources of irrigation are via canals, which are fed by medium and minor irrigational projects which are also rain dependent.

As a part of the first step of the research, the team visited Sujaanpur Akhaada, a village in Hapur district in Uttar Pradesh. The main occupation of the inhabitants of the village is agriculture. A small percentage of people work as clerks or attendants and they are employed in industries and colleges near Ghaziabad. The main produce of the village are sugar cane and paddy. The type of soil in Hapur district is Alluvial. Almost 70 percentage of the agricultural land are used for sugar cane cultivation and rest 30 percentage for paddy. Rice is cultivated in this village in areas which are favourably irrigated. Sugarcane residue, rice husk and dung are the main renewable resources available in the village. Sugarcane residue is chopped using a milling machine and is given as fodder for cattle. Dung is dried and used as an energy source by villagers. But there was no effective use of rice husk in the village. Rice along with rice husk is separated from paddy by beating the paddy so that rice, which weighs more, gets separated from the plant. This rice along with the husk is given to the rice mills which process them. Most of the rice mills see the rice husk as waste with no use. Since most of the rice husk was left unused here, this village was chosen to be a part of the research.

The village boasts of hundred percentage electrification. But electricity is available only for 12 to 14 hrs per day. Villagers face constant voltage fluctuation. They use electricity for irrigation, lighting and for other day to day activities. Villagers are proud to tell that they can manage without electricity for 2 to 3 days. Even diesel and kerosene is used to power motor for irrigation. They use kerosene lamps in case electricity is not available. A rice husk power plant can make the village self sufficient in terms of electricity and can supply 24 hrs of electricity without fail.

70% of village households have LPG (Liquefied Petroleum Gas) connection. Indane and HP cater LPG to the village households. Even the households having LPG uses a mix of LPG, wood and dung for cooking. Even though there are chances for indoor air pollution, the village has not reported any causalities or health hazards because of air pollution.

There are many reasons associated with the ineffective utilization rice husk. They include lack of awareness regarding the potential usage of rice husk to the village community, lack of information regarding technology, lack of environmental concerns, lack of interest, lack of information regarding its proper usage etc.

The rice husk power plants have advantages such as lower emission of green house gases, renewable energy source, carbon neutral process etc. The main threat that these power plants face is the low availability of rice husk or other biomass resources. Some of these plants had to rely on coal for production due to the lack of sufficient rice husk. The production of rice is seasonal and hence stock need to be kept for the non seasonal period for the production of electricity. Hence small scale off grid power plants are better with long term strategic sourcing of rice husk from the farmers in the village. Instead of the grid connected power plants, it is better to have a decentralised electricity supply to the households and small scale industries in the village.

## BY PROUCT OF RICE AND THEIR USAGE

The by-products of rice milling industries consist of rice husk, rice barn, rice straw and broken rice.

- Rice husk – Rice husk are the hard protecting coverings, the outermost layer of protection encasing grains of rice. It is used as the boiler fuel wherever rice is subjected to paraboiling. Paraboiling improves the quality of rice and consist of three steps; soaking, steaming and drying. Paraboiling is very common in eastern Uttar Pradesh. Rice husk is tough due to its silica cellulose content. Hence it is perceived as waste and does not find any industrial use.

- Rice bran – Rice bran is the hard outer layer of cereal grain. This is considered as the most valuable by-product of the rice and is obtained while milling in the production of white rice. Rice bran consists of pericarp, aleurone layer, germ and a part of endosperm. Rice bran is a potential source of vegetable oil. Refined vegetable oil is edible. Crude bran oil contains high free fatty acids and is used for manufacture of soap and fatty acids. De-oiled or defatted bran is used as fertilizer.
- Rice straw – Rice straw is the dry stalks of cereal plants, after the grain and chaff have been removed. It is used as cattle feed, thatching roofs and by cottage industry.
- Broken rice - This is another by-product of rice milling industry. There is no difference between the nutrition content of whole rice and broken rice. But quality wise, broken rice is inferior due to admixture with grit, stones and clay particles. So they are cleaned and used for the preparation of south Indian dishes such as Idli, Dosa etc in which rice flour or wet-ground rice paste is needed.

## COMPOSITION OF RICE HUSK

Our rural villages have many renewable resources that can be used to harness power. Extracting energy from these resources efficiently using advanced technologies is imperative as India is an energy deficient country with rural villages having limited access to commercial energy such as electricity. One of those resources we identified which has got the potential to produce electricity and other high value industrial product is rice husk. Rice hulls (or rice husks) are the hard protecting coverings, the outermost layer of protection encasing grains of rice. Rice husks are perceived as a waste in rural India without much use. Rice husks are difficultly biodegradable. Discharge of these husks accruing in numerous rice mills causes serious environmental problem.

About 78% of weight of paddy is received as rice, broken rice and bran. Rest almost 22% of the weight of paddy is received as husk (Rice husk Technology, 2010). Rice husk consist of 75% of organic volatile matter and the rest 25% of the weight of husk is converted into ash during the firing process. These compositions are shown diagrammatically in Figure 2. Rice husk has significant calorific value and a high percentage of amorphous silica. With the use of innovative technology, rice husk can be used for solving the above mentioned environmental problems and at the same time can be used for producing electricity and other industrial products. Almost 105 million tonnes of rice was produced in 2011 – 2012. So India produced almost 23 million tonnes of rice husk in that year. Rice husks are low in density and unusually shaped. So it poses storage and transportation challenge.

## BIOMASS CONVERSION TECHNOLOGIES

Biomass resources are divided into primary, secondary and tertiary sources of biomass. Primary biomass resources are resources which are available or taken directly from the land. They are produced directly from photosynthesis. The examples of primary biomass resources include perennial short-rotation woody crops and herbaceous crops, the seeds of oil crops, and residues resulting from the harvesting of agricultural crops and forest trees (e.g., wheat straw, rice husk, corn stover, and the tops, limbs, and bark from trees).

*Figure 2. Percentage composition in paddy and rice husk*

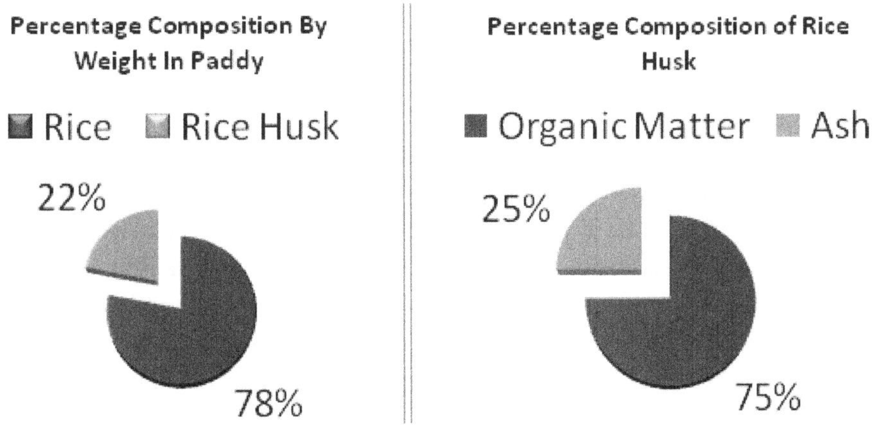


Secondary biomass resources are obtained by processing of primary biomass resources. Processing can be physical, chemical or biological. Example for physical processing can be the production of saw-dust in mills. Extraction of black liquor from pulping is an example of chemical processing. Biological processing can be the manure production by animals.

Tertiary biomass resources are residues which are obtained post consumer use. It can be expelled animal fats and greases, used vegetable oils, packaging wastes or construction and demolition debris.

There are various conversion technologies that are used for converting biomass resources into power, heat and fuels for potential use.

## Electricity Production Using Combustion

Renewable biomass fuels such as rice husk can be converted to heat and electricity using processes similar to those employed with fossil fuels. At present, electricity is generated from biomass primarily through combustion or direct-firing (Sustainable Bioenergy Development in UEMOA Member Countries, 2008). These combustion systems which produce electricity and heat are similar to that of power plants in which fossil-fuels are used as the fuel. The biomass fuel, Rice husk is burned in a boiler to produce high-pressure steam. This high pressure steam is introduced into a steam turbine. The steam flows over a series of turbine blades, which causes the turbine to rotate. The rotation of turbines powers an electric generator which is connected to it. The electric generator rotates and this produces electricity. This is a widely available, commercial technology. Combustion boilers are available in different designs in order to suit for different application and biomass characteristics. The main options to burn the biomass are the following. One is to burn the biomass on a grate which is fixed or moving. Other is to fluidize the biomass with air or some other medium. This will help in even and complete burning. The design of steam turbine also varies in terms of their application. Condensing turbines are used to maximize power production. This is achieved by cooling the steam.

These power plants convert only one third of the fuel energy into electricity. Two third of the power is wasted as heat. This is considered as major disadvantage of using combustion power plants. At this time of rising fuel cost and energy deficiency combustion based power plants are not recommended.

## Combined Heat and Power Facilities

Combined heat and power (CHP) facilities make use of the heat generated by power plants and put that for effective use. These kinds of power plants are mainly useful for power plants which are located at industrial sites and which has a steady supply of biomass (Sustainable Bioenergy Development in UEMOA Member Countries, 2008). These factories can be the ones which make sugar and/or ethanol from sugarcane at pulp and paper mills. At these factories, the waste heat from the steam turbine can be recovered and used for meeting industrial heat needs—further enhancing the economic attractiveness of such plants. These facilities are also called as cogeneration facilities. These facilities are resource efficient compared to normal combustion power plants as they can provide increased levels of energy services per unit of biomass consumed. Conventional thermoelectric stations as the one mentioned in the above section convert only about one-third of the fuel energy into electricity and the rest is lost as heat. This is detrimental in light of rising fuel costs and the adverse effect on the environment through wasteful use of power. CHP facilities provide efficient use of energy through the production of electricity and effective use of heat for industrial applications. In a CHP facility, more than four-fifths of the biomass fuel's energy is converted into usable energy, resulting in both economic and environmental benefits.

Cogeneration is termed as the simultaneous production and exploitation of two energy sources, electrical (or mechanical) and thermal, from a system utilizing the same fuel. The heat produced from a CHP facility can be used to produce cooling via absorption cycles. This cooling can be used for refrigeration and air conditioning.

## ELECTRICITY PRODUCTION USING BIOMASS GASIFICATION TECHNOLOGY

First of all, impurities are separated from rice husk before combustion. Rice husk can be most effectively used to produce electricity using biomass gasification technology (Wang, 1998).

Gasification is the process by which carbon solid fuel is converted into clean combustible gas by partial oxidation. Figure 3 is the schematic diagram of how gasification process works. The air to fuel ratio of biomass required for complete combustion is 6:1 or 6.5:1 where as in gasification the air to fuel ratio is 1.5:1 to 1.8 to 1. The gas obtained is producer gas whereas the apparatus used is the gasifier. Here in rice husk power generators, rice husk which is rich in silica is used as the fuel. The ash or slag which is a by product of the process is rice husk ash which finds huge industrial use.

Biomass gasification technology is carbon free green technology which can be operated by unskilled labor. The objective is to convert rice husk using biomass gasification into combustible gases like methane, hydrogen etc. However it requires very rigorous safety and health procedures for the operator and regular maintenance of the plant to ensure regular supply of electricity. It consists of a gasifier; a husk feed system, an ash discharge system, a tar absorber and internal combustion engine. Rice husk is poured at the rate of 100 pounds per hour into a gasifier which needs to be preheated at 773K in the nitrogen atmosphere. This causes rice husk to decompose into a mix of combustible gases. Heating results in the production of producer gas along with tars. Rice husk is also used as adsorbent (can be recycled) in the reduction of tar content .The gas produced is then used to run internal combustion engine which generates electric energy. Power produced is then distributed using village based grid to all the subscribing households, farms and business. Furthermore the residual from gasifier is a black ash which can be used for producing components which has significant industrial value. The flow diagram of how a rice husk generator works is shown in figure 4.

*Figure 3. Gasification (bioenergy technologies office, 2013)*

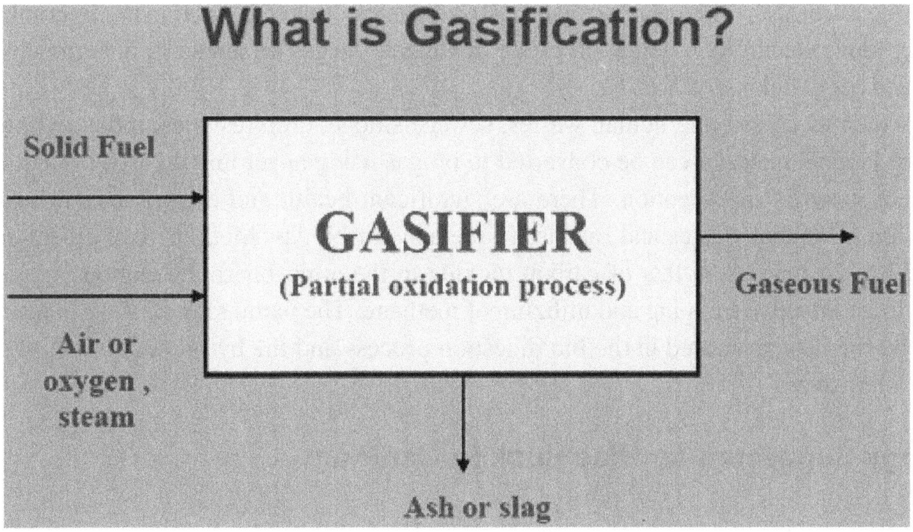


## Anaerobic Digestion

Anaerobic digestion is a series of biological processes in which microorganisms break down biodegradable material in the absence of oxygen. This technology is a commercially proven and is widely used for recycling and treating wet organic waste and waste waters (Sustainable Bioenergy Development in UEMOA Member Countries, 2008). Livestock manure, municipal wastewater solids, food waste, high strength industrial wastewater and residuals, fats, oils and grease (FOG), and various other organic waste can also be used as the energy source. It is a type of fermentation that converts any of these organic ma-

*Figure 4. Flow diagram – how a rick husk generator works*

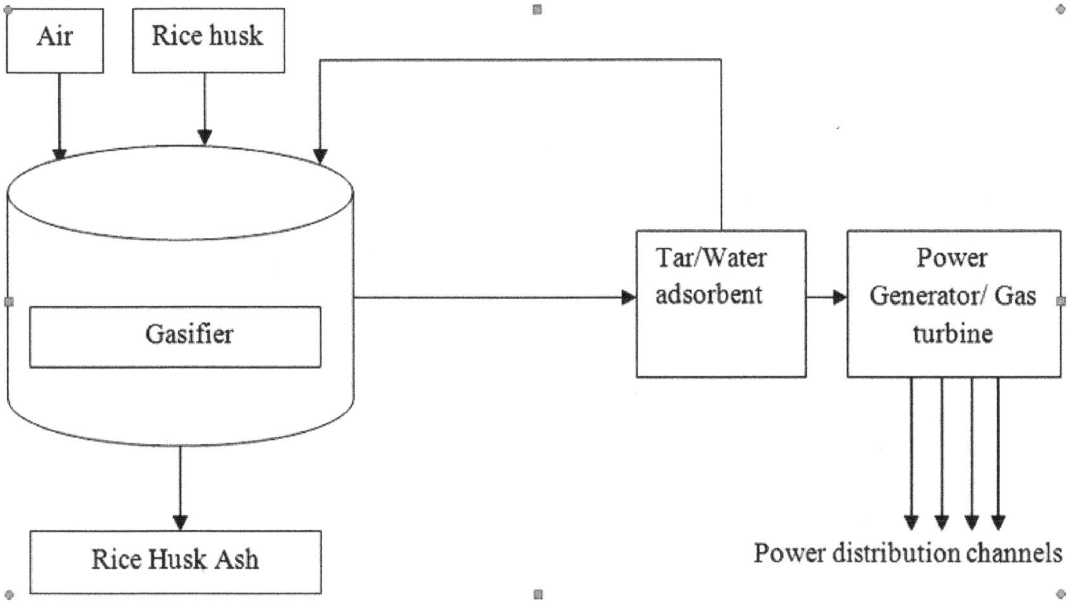

terials into biogas, which mainly consists of methane and carbon dioxide. Methane will be approximately 60% and carbon dioxide will be approximately 40%. This gas can be burned using internal combustion engines to produce electricity. After appropriate treatment, the gas produced by anaerobic digestion can be used directly for cooking or heating.

Biomass such as animal and human wastes, sewage sludge, crop residues, industrial processing by products and landfill material can be converted to biogas using anaerobic digestion. Lignin is a major component of wood is an exception. There are significant health and environmental benefits due to the conversion of animal wastes and manure to methane or biogas. Methane is a greenhouse gas that traps heat 22 to 24 times than that of carbon dioxide in the atmosphere. Greenhouse gas impacts are avoided with the effective trapping and utilizing of methane. The pathogens existing in manure are also eliminated by the heat generated in the bio digestion process and the by product is used as a valuable, nutrient-rich fertilizer.

## Technology Suggested for Rice Husk Power Plant

Biomass gasification technology is suggested for Rice Husk power plant as it is the most effective technology to produce electricity using biomass (Wang, 1998). A combined Heat and Power facility (CHP) outweighs combustion facilities in the production of electricity. CHP facilities are better suited for power generation facilities in industries than for a village, because the heat generated can be used for industrial applications. Anaerobic digestion is better suited for wet organic waste and waste water. Hence biomass gasification technology is suggested for rice husk power plant in Indian rural villages.

The advantages of using biomass gasification technology are

a. High efficiency: An integrated gasification combined cycle power plant offers efficiencies better than coal power plant. If the power plant has a carbon dioxide capture and sequestration process, the efficiency will be improved as the energy required to remove carbon dioxide is less due to high pressure and temperature of the producer gas.
b. Usability of variety of feed stock: A variety of feed stocks with carbon content can be used as raw material for the power plant. These raw materials include wood, grass and woody plants, food crops, agriculture and forest residues and organic components of industrial and municipal waste. Various gasifier designs are available, which can accommodate various grades of coal in addition to the biomass varieties discussed.
c. Emission control: Emission control is easier in gasification compared to combustion as the producer gas produced is at higher pressure and temperature. This higher temperature and pressure facilitates easier removal of sulfur and nitrous oxide, traces of mercury, cadmium, selenium etc. Similar to this, it is easier to remove carbon dioxide due to the high pressure and temperature of the producer gas.
d. Less water requirement compared to direct combustion and heat and power facilities. (ADVANTAGES OF GASIFICATION, 2010)

The open top, twin air entry, re-burn gasifier developed at Combustion, Gasification and Propulsion Laboratory (CGPL) of Indian Institute of Science (IISc) is unique in terms of generating superior quality producer gas compared to other biomass gasification technologies in the world (Biomass gasification, 2011). The twin air entry together with the design ensures production of combustible gas with low tar content at different throughputs. The combustible gas is re-burnt and is allowed to stay in high temperature environment in order to ensure cracking of higher molecular weight compounds. This improves the overall efficiency of gasification process to 75% to 85%.

The special features of twin air entry gasifier system developed by IISc are

a. Better thermal environment compared to conventional closed top model. This ensures higher through put and better producer gas quality.
b. The modules are available from 5kg/hr to 1100 kg/ hr. Hence the gasifier module can be brought as per availability of the biomass in a particular village.
c. Multi fuels as discussed can be used for production of electricity.
d. Gasification efficiency of 75% to 85%.
e. Superior gas quality.
f. Environmentally sound.
g. Value added products such as activated carbon is a byproduct (Biomass gasification, 2011).

## EFFECTIVE USE OF BY-PRODUCTS

Rice husk ash which has tremendous industrial value is received as a by-product after generating power. The ash produced will have 5% to 40% of carbon content depending upon the combustion process used. The other components of ash are amorphous silica, crystalline silica and some inert. Liquid sodium silicate, powdered activated carbon and precipitated silica can be produced from rice husk ash using certain chemical processes. These three products are used in industries widely (Rice husk Technology, 2010).

1. Industrial use of Liquid sodium silicate
    a. Used in detergents and cleaning compounds
    b. Used in adhesives and cements
    c. Used in paints and coatings
    d. Used in pulp and paper processing industries
    e. Used in ceramics and binders
    f. Used in water treatment
    g. Used in Textile processing
    h. Used in Mining and metal processing
    i. Used in petro chemical processing
2. Industrial use of activated carbon
    a. Used for decolouring in food and beverages
    b. Used as sweetener
    c. Used in pharmaceutical industry
    d. Used for air purification
    e. Used in water purification
3. Industrial use of precipitated silica
    a. Used for reinforcing rubber
    b. Used in solar panels
    c. Used for Plastic reinforcement

d. Used in animal food
e. Used in Food, healthcare, cosmetics industry
f. Used as a Catalyst
g. Used in Pulp and Paper processing
h. Used in Detergents and soaps
i. Used as Adsorbents
j. Used as Anti caking agent for packing

## BUSINESS MODEL

The electricity produced can be supplied to the grid in case the village is electrified. In case the village is not electrified, a distribution system should also be there in place. 'Pay for use' service approach can be used for raising revenue.

Rice husk power system is already implemented in Bihar, India. As per them, 300kg of rice husk is required to produce 40MW of electricity. This much electricity is sufficient to cater to 500 households for 8 to 10 hours. Only 400W to 600W is expected to be used by each household. Rice husks can be procured from rice mills for Re 1 per kg (Waste to Energy, 2007). Low cost pre paid metres need to be installed in all households. Consumers can be charged depending upon the amount of electricity used by them. The entire business model is shown in figure 5. An electrician needs to be employed to look into the issues if any in the distribution system and a bill collector need to be employed for issuing and collecting monthly bill.

### Advantages of Rice Husk Technology

Implementation of rice husk power plant will improve the socio economic indicators of the rural India. Here are some of the advantages of introducing such technologies.

a. Enhanced energy security – India is an energy deficient country and more than half of the village households are not electrified. A power plant can enhance the energy security and provide uninterrupted power to villagers.
b. Effective waste management – Rice husk which is perceived as a difficultly biodegradable waste can be used for producing electricity and other industrially useful products.

*Figure 5. Business model*

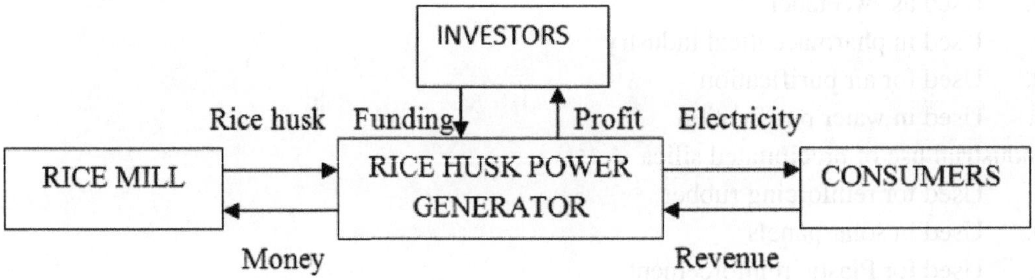

c. Help to increase employment – Villagers can be trained and employed for maintaining and operating the power plant. The availability of power can stimulate the introduction of small scale industries in the village. In effect it can generate both direct and indirect employment.
d. Lead to significant improvement of rural economy – The availability of electricity can in effect improve the economy of village. Employment will improve the living standard of villages and overall it will lead to overall development of village.
e. Save valuable foreign exchange – This initiative can indirectly save foreign exchange for the country. India can become self sufficient in energy by the introduction of rice husk power plants in large scale. Also by products can be used in lot of industrial applications. In effect, it leads to reduced import bills as less electricity and chemicals need to be imported.

## CHALLENGES AND SOLUTIONS

a. Rice husk is unusually shaped and low in density. Because of this it takes so much of space while packing and transporting. In order to mitigate this issue, rice husks are powdered and packed (Ricehusk.com, 2013).
b. Rice husk need to be burned in a controlled way in the gasifier in order to produce rice husk ash with the appropriate silica content (75% amorphous silica). If it is over burned, the synthesis of industrial components from rice husk ash will be difficult.
c. Electricity can be produced from rice husk using steam turbine power plant and gasification power plant. A gasification power plant gives more power output compared to a turbine power plant.

## SUGGESTIONS AND FUTURE IMPLICATIONS

Effective use of rice husk in villages using rice husk technology has the power to transform our villages. It provides enhanced energy security, effective waste management, provides employment and all together leads to significant improvement of rural economy.

a. Villages can be made energy self-sufficient with the help of rice husk power plants. Small plant for 2 or 3 villages depending upon the availability of rice husk will be an effective way to produce electricity. This will decrease the transportation cost of rice husk. It is always better to powder and transport rice husk in order to transport more as the density of rice husk is very less.
b. Rice husk power plant makes use of rice husk which was perceived as a waste. Use of such technology helps to reserve the non-renewable limited fossil resources. In India, major electricity production is using coal. Extensive use of rice husk technology in rice producing villages will decrease the dependency on coal and other fossil fuels for power generation.
c. Availability of electricity in rural India can encourage small and medium scale industries in rural India. Presently non availability of electricity is one of the dampening factors which prevents launch of industries in rural India. Availability of electricity will lead to more small and medium scale industries in rural India. This further increases employment and overall development of rural India. This will reflect on GDP and economic indicators of the country positively.

## REFERENCES

*Advantages of Gasification.* (2010). Retrieved September 22, 2014, from US Department of Energy: http://www.netl.doe.gov/research/coal/energy-systems/gasification/gasifipedia/Advantage-of-Gasification

*Bioenergy Technologies Office.* (2013). Retrieved October 1, 2013, from Office of Energy Efficiency and Renewable Energy: http://www1.eere.energy.gov/biomass/large_scale_gasification.html

*Biomass Gasification.* (2011). Retrieved September 22, 2014, from http://www.netl.doe.gov/research/coal/energy-systems/gasification/gasifipedia/Advantage-of-Gasification

Chauhan, C. (2013, February 22). *Indoor air pollution kills a million people every year in India.* Retrieved October 8, 2013, from Hindustan Times: http://www.hindustantimes.com/India-news/NewDelhi/Indoor-air-pollution-kills-a-million-people-every-year-in-India/Article1-1015749.aspx

*Maharashtra, UP worst power deficit states: ASSOCHAM.* (2010). Retrieved December 10, 2013, from India Today: http://indiatoday.intoday.in/story/Maharashtra,+UP+worst+power+deficit+states:+Assocham/1/95124.html

Prem, K., & Kalra, R. S. (2007). *Electrification and bio-energy options in rural India.* Retrieved October 22, 2013, from india infrastructure report 2007: http://www.iitk.ac.in/3inetwork/html/reports/IIR2007/iir2007.html

Ramachandran, G. (2012). *Integration of energy issues in rural development planning in India.* Retrieved October 1, 2013, from http://www.unescap.org/esd/Energy-Security-and-Water-Resources/energy/policy_and_planning/integration/egm/documents/G_Ramachandran_paper.pdf

*Rice Husk Technology.* (2010). Retrieved August 10, 2013, from http://www.poerner.at/fileadmin/user_upload/pdf/Brochure_Grimma_Rice_Husk_090615_web_e.pdf

*Ricehusk.com.* (2013). Retrieved October 8, 2013, from http://www.ricehusk.com/faq

*Rural Electrification Policy.* (2006, August 23). Retrieved October 1, 2013, from Ministry of Power: http://www.powermin.nic.in/whats_new/pdf/RE%20Policy.pdf

*Status Paper on Rice in Uttar Pradesh.* (2012). Retrieved December 10, 2013, from http://www.rkmp.co.in/status-paper-on-rice-in-uttar-pradesh

*Sustainable Bioenergy Development in UEMOA Member Countries.* (2008). Retrieved December 10, 2013, from http://www.globalproblems-globalsolutions-files.org/gpgs_files/pdf/UNF_Bioenergy/UNF_Bioenergy_full_report.pdf

Wang, K. S. (1998). *A process development for gasification of rice husk.* Retrieved October 8, 2013, from http://myweb.ncku.edu.tw/~wanghp/A%20process%20development%20for%20gasification%20of%20rice%20husk.pdf

*Waste to Energy.* (2007). Retrieved October 8, 2013, from http://www.devalt.org/knowledgebase/pdf/Case%20Study-3.pdf

Y, K. G. (2012). Rural Electrification in the Changing Paradigm of Power Sector Reforms in India. *International Journal of Electrical and Computer Engineering (IJECE)*, *2*(2).

## KEY TERMS AND DEFINITIONS

**Amorphous Silica:** Amorphous silica is the non-crystalline allotropic form of silica with the chemical formula SiO2. Silica is most commonly found in nature as quartz, as well as in various living organisms.

**Anti caking Agent:** An anti caking agent is an additive placed in powdered or granulated materials, such as table salt, to prevent the formation of lumps and for easing packaging, transport, and consumption.

**Bagasse:** Bagasse is the fibrous matter that remains after sugarcane or sorghum stalks are crushed to extract their juice. It is currently used as a bio fuel and in the manufacture of pulp and building materials.

**Biomass:** Biomass is biological material derived from living, or recently living organisms.

**Bran:** Bran is the hard outer layers of cereal grain. It consists of the combined aleurone and pericarp.

**Calorific Value:** The heating value (or energy value or calorific value) of a substance, usually a fuel or food is the amount of heat released during the combustion of a specified amount of it.

**Inert:** The term inert is used to describe a substance (here a gas) that is not chemically reactive.

**Renewable Resources:** A renewable resource is a natural resource which can replenish with the passage of time, either through biological reproduction or other naturally recurring processes.

**Rice Husk:** Rice hulls (or rice husks) is the hard protecting coverings of grains of rice. In addition to protecting rice during the growing season, rice hulls can be put to use as building material, fertilizer, insulation material, or fuel.

**Smithy:** A person skilled in many trades, primarily wood working, metal work, electrical, plumbing, and general handy work around the home.

# Chapter 24
# Waste Management Initiatives in Rural India

**Rishi Kumar**
*Institute of Management Technology Ghaziabad, India*

## ABSTRACT

*In this chapter, the author aims to present an overall view of the Waste Management practices employed in rural parts of India and their overall sustainability in terms of present scenario. It would discuss the successful models employed in some parts of the country and the reason, that why they are not prevalent or expand to the rest of the nation inspite of them being successful in their own territory. It would also discuss the various Initiatives taken by the government in this regard such as the Total Sanitary Campaign which aimed at bringing an improvement in the general quality of life by creating awareness on improving the sanitation facilities and providing health education in rural parts of the country. This chapter also suggests about the further improvements that can be done in the overall model by including other stakeholders like Local Gram Panchayats, NGOs and community people.*

## INTRODUCTION

The rural population in India exhibits unique waste management and resource utilization techniques in comparison to urban population. With the emerging concern on large quantity of the waste being produced both in the form of solid and liquid waste, the method and concept of waste management becomes one of the key focus of sustainable development principles. The need for genuine and organized initiatives in the rural waste management has been regularly voiced in India. The wastes produced from various sources are utilized effectively ranging from crop cultivation, rearing animals and liquid wastes produced domestically. In rural areas, compared to urban areas, land availability is not often a constraint.

Also, there are more options possible in rural areas for reuse of waste, such as composting of biodegradable material, which can be used in kitchen gardens, agricultural fields, and so on. With the increased number of Panchayats becoming open and free, necessity has risen to address the problems of solid and liquid waste management in rural communities in order to really make them clean and green. In Rural India Waste is a severe threat to the health and cleanliness to the people residing in villages and nearby

DOI: 10.4018/978-1-4666-8259-7.ch024

remote areas. It is estimated that 1 in every 10 deaths in Indian villages, is linked to poor sanitation and hygiene which are directly the result of improper disposal of waste in rural parts of the country. As per the study done by Indian Sanitation Portal (2013), the generation of solid waste in Indian villages has been expected to grow with 1.3 percent annually. The estimated generation of waste in 2025 will be around 700 grams per capita per day. As the quantity of Waste produced by society is increasing the composition of the waste is also becoming more and more diverse. Around thirty years ago, the composition of the solid waste generated by the Indian Farmer consisted of one-fifth of non-biodegradable waste and four-fifth of biodegradable waste. Currently, this ratio is about to reverse and mere 40% of all solid waste is biodegradable while 60% is non-biodegradable.

As per the study conducted by Ministry of Rural Development, Govt. of India (2010) more than two-thirds of all Indians are still impoverished, surviving on less than 2 dollars per day and also close to 70% of the Indian Population still lives in the Rural Areas. Consumption of unsafe drinking water, improper environmental sanitation and lack of personal and food hygiene have been major causes of many diseases in developing countries. In addition to these, many problems still prevails in Indian Society like Caste System, Poverty, Illiteracy which leads to inequality in the society, especially in the rural parts of the country. Poor and marginalized people lack the resources needed to reduce the negative effects of a degraded environment. Prevailing High Infant Mortality Rate is also largely attributed to poor sanitation. At the same time, they are usually directly dependent on their close natural environment for their daily survival.

This paper will discuss in detail the various kinds of wastes produced in Villages and rural areas, different methods employed to dispose them, various policies in place by the government to address the issues and further suggestions and future implications.

## LITERATURE REVIEW

Under this section we would discuss the previous researches done regarding rural waste management initiatives. A review of existing literature reveals that a great number of studies on Solid waste management have been undertaken. A study conducted by Hazra & Goel (2008) presented an overview on of current solid waste management practices in Kolkata, India and suggested solution to some of the problems. They stated that the collection process is deficient in terms of manpower and vehicle availability. Capacity of bins provided is adequate but locations were found to be inappropriate which contributed to the inefficiency in the process. Further, Hazra & Goel (2008) proved that there is no treatment was provided to the waste and it is dumped on land after collecting it. However, in order to improve these problems, authors provided some solutions for these problems. For instance, to improve collection and transportation at Kolkata city, PPPs can be a successful solution, with private agencies providing waste collection service at lower cost and greater efficiency (Hazra & Goel, 2008). It was proposed that it could also be replicated in other rural parts of the West Bengal once it shows results in Kolkota.

Niraj S. Topare et al. (2011) stated that users must concentrate their Sewage/Wastewater treatment process to ensure that it complies with regulatory guidelines. Sewage/Wastewater treatment operations are done by various methods in order to reduce its water and organic content, and the ultimate goal of wastewater management is the protection of the environment in a manner that commensurate with public health and socio-economic concerns. The paper discussed factors affecting selection and design of Sewage/Wastewater systems and also various techniques employed in many rural parts of India.

Another study conducted by Rashmi Shah et al. (2012) considered a cluster of villages near Tekanpur area located in Gwalior district of Madhya Pradesh. The study was based on a cluster of six villages. It showed that about 287 grams of agricultural/residential solid waste per capita is generated in these villages every day. They found that street sweeping, cattle dung, agricultural waste, grass cutting, drain and public toilet cleaning contribute most to waste generation in these villages.

Most common practices of waste processing are uncontrolled dumping which causes mainly soil and water pollution. The qualities of both liquid and solid wastes are increasing and if the wastes are disposed in an uncontrolled manner it may cause adverse impact on public health & environment. Therefore, the solid wastage is still a major problem in these areas. To overcome this, the researchers have proposed to implement vermicomposting as a waste management technique.

## RESEARCH OBJECTIVE

This paper would focus upon explaining the various types of Solid and Liquid Wastes produced in Rural India and what are the practices followed in their disposal and proper utilization. Also, the initiatives taken in this regard by the Central Government, Authorities operating at local village level who are responsible for the proper execution of the policies and also the further recommendations to improve the present scenario will be discussed.

## RESEARCH METHODOLOGY

The Methodology adopted to develop this paper is majorly based upon secondary research. The sources used were documents from Ministry of Urban Development, National Solid Waste Association of India. Few online database like EBSCO and Sage publication were also referred. Research papers published by Ministry of Rural Development and Ministry of Drinking Water and sanitation were also insightful in completion of the report.

The results and findings were concluded by analyzing three case studies which include implementation of waste management practices in different parts of the country

## PROBLEM ANALYSIS

The Rural Waste is a problem of the public health and cleanliness and the form of waste (both solid and liquid) generated in rural areas is predominantly organic and biodegradable yet becoming a major problem to the overall sustainability of the ecological balance. In reference to the report published by Water and Sanitation Program (2012), it is estimated that rural people in India are generating liquid waste of around 15,000 to 18,000 million liters and solid waste of around 0.3 to 0.4 million metric tons per day respectively. While the quantity of solid waste generated by society is increasing, the composition of waste is becoming more and more diversified, with increasing use of materials used in packaging which are made of both paper and plastic. Figure 1 shows the classification of various types of waste produced in rural India.

*Figure 1. Classification of types of waste produced in rural India*

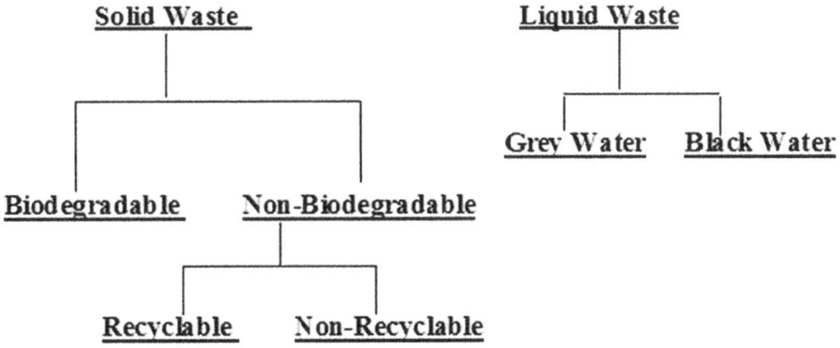


Absence of proper disposal of solid and liquid waste is leading to vector borne diseases such as Diarrhea, Cholera, Typhoid, Polio, Malaria, and other infections in many parts of Rural India. A recent study of Indian Sanitation Portal (2013) shows that around 88% of the total disease load is due to lack of clean water and sanitation and the improper solid and liquid waste management which intensify their occurrence, for example:

a) Close to 5 of the 10 harmful diseases (Polio, Diarrhea, Hepatitis Tuberculosis, Diphtheria etc.) of children aged 1-14 in rural areas are related to water and sanitation
b) According to the Technical note of UNICEF in Solid and Liquid Waste Management almost 1500 children die every day from diarrheal diseases.
c) The water and sanitation problems due to improper waste management not only affect the nutritional status of the children but also impact their attendance in the school. Nearly 50% of school-going children in rural areas do not reach class 5th.

1. SOLID WASTE: On the criteria of biodegradability, Solid Waste can be classified as:
   a) **Biodegradable:** Waste that are completely decomposed by biological processes either in presence or in absence of air are called biodegradable. E.g. animal dung, agricultural and kitchen waste etc.
   b) **Non-biodegradable:** Waste which cannot be decomposed by biological processes is called non-biodegradable waste. They are of two types:
      1) **Recyclable:** Waste having economic values but destined for disposal can be recovered and reused along with their energy value. E.g. plastic, old cloth, paper etc.
      2) **Non-recyclable:** Waste which do not have economic value of recovery e.g. thermo coal, carbon paper, tetra packs etc.

Solid waste management has become one of the biggest issues to handle in rural India. Due to changing practices of living and opening of many industries in rural parts of the country solid wastes poses a serious threat to human lives as improper disposal could lead to transfer of pollution to ground water and land, which makes the soil infertile. On the other hand, lack of knowledge on the unfavorable health outcomes of improper burning of solid wastes has increased the occurrence of diseases which are infectious, in many parts of the country.

2. LIQUID WASTE:_The unwanted water from factories nearby villages and the contaminated water collected from wastes from homes come under the category of liquid waste. Two of the types are:
   a) Black Water: It mainly consists of the waste contaminated by faeces and other bodily wastes. They contain bacterias which can be harmful to people as it is the water flushed out from toilets which contains human wastes and also pathogens. They are used in separate tanks for treatment purposes and their reuse is commonly in fertilizer purposes. It needs for more intense methods to be applied for refinement.
   b) Greywater: It consists of waste water generated in the kitchen, bathroom, bathing and dish-washing. It doesn't contain many harmful bacteria as compared to black water and can be treated easily by grey water treatment plants can be reused for various irrigation purposes.

Black water treatment methods make use of physical, biological, and chemical methods to treat the solid and liquid organic and inorganic waste. The different types of black water treatment include soil drain fields, septic tanks, cess pools, chemicals, composting toilets and black water recycling systems. Another efficient way of treating black water is using bio digesters. Bio digesters typically seek to make more efficient, effective use of anaerobic and aerobic digestion to treat black water.

Grey water has a relatively low nutrient and pathogenic content and reuse of grey water helps to reduce sewage generation and also covers for the fresh water requirement if treated properly in rural parts of the country. Another major use of treated grey water is for agricultural irrigation purposes. It is rich in nitrogen, potassium, phosphorous and which makes it a good nutrient or fertilizer source for irrigation. Due to lowering of groundwater table, decreasing availability of drinking water and increase in fluoride concentration in groundwater National Environmental Engineering Research Institute (NEERI) Nagpur and UNICEF Bhopal, Madhya Pradesh have tested and implemented grey water reuses systems for schools in rural areas of Western Madhya Pradesh.

Dhar and Jhabua are two districts of MP which suffer from recurrent water quantity and quality problems. The grey water treatment plants have been constructed in these areas and this process has resulted in use of treated grey water in flushing the toilets which were otherwise unclean and hence not used by the students. Eventually, this campaign has proved successful and is in process of being replicated in other schools operating in rural parts of India.

General Practices Employed in Rural Areas for Waste Management

## A) Vermi-Compositing

Vermi composting involves the stabilization of organic solid waste through earthworm consumption which converts the material into worm castings. It differs from composting in many ways .It is a mesophilic process, using microorganisms and earthworms that are active at 10-32 degree Celsius. The process is very much faster than composting, due to passing of material through the earthworm gut, a significant but not complete transformation takes place, whereby the resulting earthworm manure is rich in pest repellence attributes, and microbial activity and plant growth regulators. Microbial decomposition of biodegradable organic matter occurs through extracellular enzymatic activities whereas decomposition in earthworm occurs in elementary tract by micro-organisms inhabiting the gut which is secondary decomposition. Microbes such as fungi, protozoa, actinomycetes, etc. are reported to habit the gut of earthworms. Ingested feed substrates are aligned to grinding in the interior part of the worms gut and resulting in particle size reduction.

The technology comprises of a tripartite system which involves microbes, biomass and earthworms is influenced by the abiotic factors such as aeration, temperature, moisture etc. Microbial ecology changes according to change of abiotic factors in the biomass but decomposition never ceases. Conditions which aren't favorable to aerobic decomposition result in mortality of earthworms and subsequently no vermi -composting occurs.

Vermicomposting is a well-known technology and as a process for handling organic residuals, it represents a

suitable approach for solid waste management. It plays a significant role in improving growth and yield of different field crops, vegetables, fruit crops and flowers. However, Vermicomposting being an efficient process to produce richer compost in comparison to normal composting, a major drawback would be that it needs a vermi-tank or vermin-bed and worms need to be bought or grown which eventually increases its cost.

## B) Biogas Technology

When biodegradable organic solid waste is subjected to anaerobic decomposition, a gaseous mixture of Methane ($CH_4$) and Carbon-dioxide ($CO_2$) known as Biogas could be produced under particular set of conditions.

The decomposition of the waste materials are mainly done by the fermentation process which is carried out by different group of microorganisms like bacteria, fungus etc. The group of microorganisms involved for biogas generation is mainly the bacteria.

The process involves a series of reactions by several kinds of anaerobic bacteria feeding on the raw organic matter.

Biogas technology is a useful system in reference to the Indian rural economy, and can fulfill several needs of the people residing in the rural part of the country. In case of Anaerobic Digestion energy in the form of Biogas is produced. Biogas is useful as a fuel substitute for dung firewood, diesel, agricultural residues, petrol and electricity, depending on the nature of the task, and local supply conditions and constraints thus supplying energy for cooking and lighting.

A clean and particulate-free source of energy produced from Biogas also reduces the likelihood of chronic diseases, such as respiratory infections, ailments of the lungs; bronchitis, lung cancer, asthma. Benefits can also be scaled up and mounted when the potential environmental impacts are also taken into account; major reductions in emissions associated with the combustion of biofuels, such as nitrogen dioxide, sulphur dioxide, carbon monoxide (CO), total suspended particles, and poly-aromatic hydrocarbons are possible with the large-scale introduction of biogas technology. Anaerobic Digestion helps against the hazardous effects of burning the crop residues after harvesting, which is a common practice in many agricultural states of India. Also, burning of the standing crop also leads to volatilization of the soil nutrients, decreasing soil fertility. Cow Dung cakes are extremely popular among masses in rural part of the country as a cooking fuel. Burning of dung cakes leads to toxic emissions which are harmful for health and many studies have related the cow dung cake burning to cases of lung cancer, tuberculosis and many other respiratory diseases.

Biogas plants are economically cost effective and easily adaptable in households as well as many small scale industries.

The Anaerobic digestion process begins with bacterial hydrolysis of the input materials. Insoluble organic polymers, such as carbohydrates, are broken down to derivatives (soluble) that become available for other bacteria. Some of the advantages of anaerobic digestion are:

a) Total quantity of waste is reduced by nearly 60-90%
b) Need for huge requirement of land is obviated
c) Cost of transportation of waste to landfill sites is minimized, pollution of soil, water and air is arrested to minimum recovering of methane as renewable energy source and effluent as organic manure appears attractive, eco-friendly, cost-effective and sustainable.

Process of anaerobic digestion has the capability to meet the energy requirements of rural India, and also counter the harmful effects of burning of biomass resources. In reference to the report by Water and Sanitation Program (2012), the fuel efficiency of cattle dung is 11 percent whereas on the hindsight that of biogas from the same dung is approx. 60 percent. For a general purpose usage a 3 cubic meter capacity of a biogas plant is considered sufficient to meet the cooking and lightning needs of a rural family of 6 to 9 persons in India. Both Vermi-Composting and Anaerobic digestion are considered as the most suitable options to deal with organic fraction of municipal, household or industrial solid waste. Both of these methods reduces the environmental burden and helps in generating nutrient rich fertilizer.

The adoption of biogas technology is required for better utilization of renewable energy resources. But, there are certain factors which limits its widespread use in rural part of India. The most significant being the lack of awareness among farmers and lackadaisical attitude of the government towards providing easy funding to the farmers and household in rural India who cannot afford this technology from their own pockets. The federal and state government needs to be more proactive in providing easy access of these technologies to the poor farmers. The policies and support of the government are decisive in motivating the farmers to adopt such technologies and to make a transition from wasteful traditional approaches to efficient resource utilization.

## CASE ANALYSIS

Analysis in this study is done by on the basis of few caselets where various Waste Management Techniques were successfully implemented in different parts of the country, and discussing their salient features in detail.

### Caselet 1: Liquid and Solid Waste Management in Dhamner Village,Maharashtra

#### Background

Dharmner village in Satara Dist. having population of 2756, and around 488 households, received Nirmal Gram Puruskar from RGDWM from the Ministry of Rural Development, government of India for the substantial amount of work done in the village towards Waste Management. . It is remarkable that the Panchayat has not only achieved ODF (Open Defecation Free) status but has also been running a waste management program for more than seven years. This has been possible because of careful planning by the Gram Panchayat and the involvement of the community. To address solid waste, the GP provided one kuchrakundi (dustbin) for every five to 15 households and community kuchrakundis were placed at appropriate locations. The GP recruited two safaikaramcharis to collect waste from the kuchrakundis and transport it to a common treatment site. Here, waste is segregated and biodegradable waste is composted and non bio-degradable waste recycled.

## Salient Features:

### *Solid Waste*

Individual households dispose of their domestic solid waste (without segregation) in to a community Kutchara Kundi. GP has provided a kutchra kundi for every 5 to 15 households. Community kutchra kundis are placed at appropriate locations in the village. Wastes are segregated at treatment plant site (vermi composting). Non-biodegradable waste is sorted out in a pit of size 7ft (L) x 7ft (W) x 3ft (D) and biodegradable solid waste in an adjacent pit of same size. On an average 10 tons/year vermi manure is available from this vermi compost treatment unit. On an average 10 tons/year vermi manure is available from this vermi compost treatment unit (2 pits). During the last four years about 40 tons of vermi manure produced from this treatment unit 50% of the produced were used for gardening in the village and the balance 50% i.e. 20 tons were sold at the price of Rs. 10/- per kg and from this, GP earned about Rs 20,000/- from the sale of Vermi Composting.

### *Liquid Waste*

Gray water from households and effluent from a few septic tanks are collected and transported through underground drainage system with adequate slop (gravity flow) at a point outskirts of the village where waste water is treated with provision of a screen chamber followed by taken by gravity through underground pipes and disposed off in a soakage pit .Non-biodegradable waste is sorted out in a pit of size 7ft (in length)x 7ft (in width) x 3ft (in depth) and biodegradable solid waste in an adjacent pit of same size.

## Caselet 2: Nightsoil -Application of Biogas plant in Dehu Village Maharashtra

Dehu village of Pune district in Maharashtra, where some families allow their neighbours to use their toilets for a nominal maintenance charge making attached biogas plants economically viable. Currently, there are about 75 family-owned human nightsoil -based biogas plants in Dehu providing kitchen fuel for villagers. The strategy has also eased the village Panchayat's responsibilities for human nightsoil management and reduced environmental pollution due to open defecation.

Biogas generated from nightsoil serves a dual purpose of providing energy and helping manage human waste. biogas generated from nightsoil of community toilets, which are used by larger numbers of people, has proved viable, gas produced from individual toilets used by 5-10 persons is inadequate for any practical use.

## Salient Features:

Each new biogas system eliminates the need for one or more waste/manure/latrine pits, thereby substantially improving the hygienic conditions in the village concerned.

The processing animal and human excrements in biogas systems naturally improves sanitary conditions for the plant owners, their families and the entire village community.

The initial pathogenic capacity of the starting materials is greatly reduced by the fermentation process.

Since biogas systems do not attract flies or other vermin, the effect is to reduce the danger of contagious diseases for human and animals alike. Furthermore, eye aliments and respiratory problems attributable to soot and smoke from the burning of dried cow dung can no longer develop.

The gas generated from five persons using the toilet is sufficient to cook food for the family.

Using Human faeces and cowdung for Energy production helps in many advantages as displayed through the case above and the organic manure is also widely accepted by farmers as a rich source of natural fertilizer. The fully digested organic manure which comes out after 45-50 days is excellent for promotion of soil fertility and restore the land which has lost its productivity due to continuous application of chemical fertilizers. Both cow dung and human faeces are available easily in rural areas which saves a lot of time of people to arrange for their fuel source and also the maintenance of the plant is very simple, which can be learnt by any in the village or a group of people which could also train others to help them learn to run it.

## Caselet 3: Solid Waste Management- Alappuzha District in Kerala

Chunakkara is a backward Village Panchayat of Alappuzha district with 14 Wards covering 5411 households within an area of 17.32 km square. Management of Solid waste emerged as a major problem with waste piling up in all public places inviting the protest of the public. The water bodies got polluted and the canals became clogged. At this point, when the Village Panchayat was desperately searching for solutions, the Socio Economic Unit

Foundation (SEUF), which is a leading NGO in the sanitation sector, entered into a partnership with the Village Panchayat and decided to promote decentralized waste management with focus on the household through a process of intensive awareness building and community education .A trained resource group called the Programme Support Group (PSG) was setup. People were given the option of choosing from a variety of vermicomposting options – from standalone buckets for households to centralized composting pits for those who wanted to come together and manage them as a group. The emphasis on involving the community and public education before initiating SLWM was a key ingredient in the successful implementation of this initiative.

### Salient Features

Municipal Council and Socio and an NGO got into a partnership and initiated an Action Research Programme called “Women, Wellbeing, Work, Waste and Sanitation (4 W-S). After a small pilot, six Wards were identified covering 5624 households. The initial survey conducted by Suchitwa Mission, Government of Kerala (2013), indicated that only 10% of the households segregate their waste and 58% of the households burned their waste, while 16% threw them into their backyards and 15% resorted to dumping them in public places .A detailed Step-by-Step method was adopted as mentioned below:

1) Grassroots level mobilization and education of all stakeholders.
2) Capacity based building of the community with focus on women.

3) Household level processing of organic waste via various techniques like small homemade bio gas tanks, vermicomposting and collection and sale of recyclables.
4) Substitution of plastic bags with cloth and paper bags.
5) Dissemination of Information on cost effective technology.
6) Community policing to prevent people from violating the code of clean and maintenance of proper sanitation in and around their houses.

In a short span of time, 3350 households started vermi-composting. In 35 places common vermi-composting units were set up. Nearly two thousand families started organic farming in their compounds. Three units of paper bag have been started along with two Plant Nurseries. Through public action eight kms of canals and twelve ponds have been cleaned and rejuvenated. The Alappuzha experiment showed that through social engineering which involves committed professionals and elected leaders, even in an urban setting, community behavior can be changed for the better and improved version can be made.

## Total Sanitary Campaign (TSC)

The Programme was inaugurated in 1999 and termed as a demand-driven and people-centered sanitation program. It evolved from the limited achievements of the first structured programme for rural sanitation in India, the Central Rural Sanitation Programme, which had minimum community participation. It has a principle of "low to no subsidy" where a nominal amount of incentive is given to rural poor households for construction of toilets. Total Sanitary Campaign has given strong emphasis on Capacity building and Hygiene Education for effective behavior change with involvement of Panchayati Raj Institutions, NGOs etc.

The basis or concept of sanitation was earlier restricted to disposal of human excreta by cess pools, open ditches, bucket system, pit latrines etc. In the present scenario it relates to a comprehensive concept which includes food, personal, domestic and environmental hygiene. It also accounts for vast amount of liquid and solid disposal. Complete and proper sanitation is not only essential from the general point of health but also has a vital role to play in our individual and social life too. Sanitation is one of the basic determinants of quality of life and HDI (human development index).Advanced Sanitation practices help a great way in preventing contamination of water and soil and thereby preventing diseases and improving quality of life.

The Total Sanitation Campaign was later renamed as "Nirmal Bharat Abhiyan"and was effective from April 2012.

There is a lack of Operational guidelines or National level policy to address Solid and Liquid Waste Managementissues, therefore majority of the states have framed their initiatives under the guidelines as described under Nirmal Bharat Abhiyan. In reference to the Water and Sanitation Program (2012), the vision of Nirmal Bharat Abhiyan is enshrined in the Rural Sanitation and Hygiene Strategy 2012-2022. The three major goals set under the strategy of NBA are:

a) **Adopting Improved and Advanced Hygiene practices**: Population residing in the rural areas, especially caregivers and children, adopt safe and hygienic practices during all times. The Target year for this is set by 2020.
b) **Solid and Liquid Waste Management:** Effective Management of Solid and Liquid Waste to keep the village surrounding and environment clean and healthy. Target year - 2022.

c) **Creating Totally Sanitized Environments:** The mission to end open defecation and achieve clean and hygienic environment where human fecal waste is safely contained and disposed. Target year- 2017.

The main objectives and agendas covered under Nirmal Bharat Abhiyan are:

- Accelerate the sanitation coverage in rural areas to achieve the vision of Nirmal Bharat by 2022 with all Gram Panchayats in the country attaining Nirmal status.
- Motivate communities and Panchayati Raj Institutions promoting sustainable sanitation facilities through awareness creation and health education.
- Develop community managed environmental sanitation systems focusing on solid and liquid waste management for overall cleanliness in the rural areas.
- Encourage cost effective and appropriate technologies for ecologically safe and sustainable sanitation.
- To Bring about an improvement in the general quality of life in the rural areas.
- To cover the remaining schools which not covered under Sarva Shiksha Abhiyan and Anganwadi Centres in the rural areas with proper sanitation facilities and undertake proactive promotion of hygiene education and sanitary habits among students.

To motivate and encourage people residing in rural parts of the country many states have instituted rewards and recognition to organizations or individuals who contribute towards mission of Total Sanitation on the similar lines of Nirmal Gram Puraskar. State Government of Maharashtra has initiated a competition based campaign known by the name "Sant Gadge Baba Gram Swachata Abhiyan". Government of Tamil Nadu has also launched the "Clean Village Campaign" to increase the awareness related Improper Sanitation problems and encourage people to work towards better hygiene thereby improving the state of villages. There are also reward schemes for schools and Anganwadi centers. These types of initiatives help to grow awareness of sanitation issues and can be individually tailored to meet the needs of each State. A State supported initiatives also show a high level of willingness from States to prioritize sanitation issues with the overall aim of supporting the national vision which is of Nirmal Bharat.

## Some of the Proposals Specific to Solid and Liquid Waste Management Are

Panchayati Raj Institutions (PRIs) are required to put in place mechanisms for garbage collection and disposal and for preventing water logging. A research study by Ministry of Drinking Water and Sanitation, Govt. of India (2011) revealed that upto 10% of the project cost can be utilized for meeting capital costs incurred under this component. The pattern of fund sharing between the Centre, State and Panchayat / Community should be in the ratio of 60:20:20, as the Gram Panchayat plays a major role in executing the policies passed by the Central government and the State Government so an appreciable share should be handed over to Gram Panchayats. Under this component activities like common compost pits, system for collection, reuse of waste water, segregation, low cost drainage, soakage pits/channels and disposal of household garbage etc. may be taken up. Successful models may be further replicated dovetailing funds from other Rural Development programmes. Cooperation of NGO's may be sought to develop / test / document / replicate such models.

The project is there since a decade ago but wasn't successful Initially and had a revised version of Guidelines in 2010.Some of the observations were:

1) Better performing districts were not doing different things but are doing things differently within the TSC framework. As detailed, better performing districts use the opportunities for flexibility available within the guidelines to adapt implementation to their field realities and learn from successes and mistakes to scale up the programme.
2) National coverage has significantly scaled up to about 60 percent till March 2010. However, significant differences have been observed in the coverage between the states. While one state, Sikkim, has declared itself ODF (Open Defecation Free), some others have coverage of less than 30 percent.

### Business Integration Relevance of Rural Waste Management

According to India's Constitution, Solid Waste Management (SWM) falls under the purview of respective state governments. In most of the rural parts of India activities like processing, segregation and waste disposal is carried out by the respective municipal corporations and the state governments that enforce regulatory policies.

However, a new trend is being observed from past 3-4 years in this domain since the advent of private players in waste management. In many urban cities like Bengaluru, Mumbai, Hyderabad, Chennai, Ahmedabad, Delhi etc., garbage disposal is done by Public Private Partnerships (PPPs) and recently they are also showing interest in rural waste management. The private sector has been involved in door-to-door collection of solid waste,

Secondary storage and transportation and for treatment and disposal of waste. Some private firms are carrying out Integrated Municipal Solid Waste Management (IMSWM) which includes segregation & transportation, compost, collection, treatment, refuse derived fuel, and final disposal. Rural areas consume biodegradable waste more efficiently than urban areas but plastic and electronic waste has emerged as major problems in rural areas.

As of now there is a lot of focus of private players entering in urban waste management initiatives as it provides ease of operations with proper regulatory framework for sustainable projects.

Private players enter in any sector for profits and hence relevance and importance of waste management in rural India should be made realized to private players by various stakeholders involved in these initiatives which would be beneficial for both the local government and citizens.

This would probably encourage more participation from other players interested in this domain and also serve the environmental aspect of rural population in terms of proper management of waste. It would also open up new avenuess of employability and job creation for people residing in rural parts if government goes for the commercialization of waste management either through PPPs or inviting investments from private players.

## RESULTS AND FINDINGS

The Findings which were observed during the course of our research for this paper from various perspectives of all the stakeholders involved in Waste management Practices in Rural India are mentioned below:

1) With the growing technology and infrastructure, holistic approaches to treat waste management have evolved, but Indian waste management system has lagged in implementing them efficiently due to poor planning and support from Ministry of Rural Development. No Policy is made till date which perceives waste through a prism of overall sustainability. The new MSWM Rules 2000(issued under Environmental protection act,1986) effective from 2004, failed to manage proper waste management and recycling in the rural areas. Though Waste Management has been included under Total Sanitary Campaign but no sustainable model specific to Rural Waste Management has been into place till now.

2) A report published by Water and Sanitation Program(2012) highlights that many benefits and funds allocated towards Waste Management doesn't percolate to the grassroot level due to many governing bodies involved in the whole procedure. Policies are in place but their execution is a major problem. Also, It was found that lack of awareness and funds is a major problem in rural areas which hinders them to execute and plan their own waste management techniques and systems. Another major point associated is with the prevalence social stigmas and taboos in our villages which treats waste as something dirty which is only dealt by inferior people classified as dalits and untouchables. Lack of awareness and education is one of the major reason which is hindering in the growth of rural parts of our country which if improved and worked upon could help remove all these social stigmas and treat waste as a lucrative commodity as perceived by people in developed countries.

3) There is a huge role to be played by Panchayats in Villages where reach of government is limited per say and major control on policy making and execution lies on the shoulders of Panchayats. Panchayats and NGOs who are in the frontline of implementation have a key role in ensuring the proper execution of various schemes implemented at the National level. In the Total Sanitary Campaign these institutions have been extensively involved for the proper delivery of the model.It has been observed that NGOs not only play an important role in spreading awareness about various programmes and policies implemented by the government but also act as a bridge between Government and the local people as they are involved in activities like surveys, educating people to use various waste management techniques like biogas plants, vermi compositing techniques and proper management of liquid waste.

## SUGGESTIONS AND FUTURE IMPLICATIONS

The condition of Villages in India is not very promising inspite of so many policies and Institutions in place for Proper Waste Management and Disposal to maintain proper hygiene and sanitation. Some of the recommendations are:-

1) A report published by Suchitwa Mission, Government of Kerala (2013) highlights that waste generated in villages has a huge potential to be transformed into various sources of energy provided proper methods are adopted and proper execution of the applied methods takes place. Many villages and rural towns have implemented the method of homemade biogas plant which are small compatible systems, large enough to meet normal cooking fuel environments of an average household consisting of 5 members. This is only prevalent in few parts of South India like Yellur in Kerala, Hulikeri, Dundur in Karnataka and many parts of Southern India. There are few organizations like BIOTECH India, VK-NARDEP, ARTI working in this regard.BIOTECH India has also been Awarded by Ashden in 2007 for its Consistent Effort in this field by manufacturing homemade biogas tanks which are prevalent in southern parts of India and really successful to meet fuel and energy requirements from household waste itself. These Biotanks are very economical and costs from Rs.2,000 to Rs. 8,000 depending upon the Size of the biotank which helps a great way in fuel costs saving .

These Institutions need proper support which could be provided by collaborating with few NGOs operating in the local area to expand more rapidly and also support from their respective State Governments which could provide them monetary as well as strategic support to expand to other parts of the country as these are more prevalent in their own territories and specially in the Southern Parts of India.

People living in rural areas especially in northern part are almost unaware of such practices being followed in other parts of the country. So, innovative techniques of these sort which are really benefitting people in some parts of the country should be encouraged to expand in other parts too through various awareness programs and support programs from the Ministry of Rural Development and Governments operating locally.

2) Solid and Liquid Waste Management is a component of Total Sanitation Campaign. There is no extensive countrywide plan in with the government to be implemented in the rural parts for the proper Solid and Liquid Waste management. Role of various stakeholders like Local Government, GP(Gram Panchayat), community people is very important in proper execution of any programme. At the village level, the GP should ideally have the overall responsibility for ensuring safe management of waste. It should hold individual households and institutions in the village responsible for the management of their waste, through household, institutional or community waste management facilities. Only waste that cannot be managed at source should be managed by the community level waste management system. The GP, and households and institutions within it, should be responsible for the construction of SLWM facilities at village, household and institution levels, respectively. A GP can either assume responsibility for O&M (Operation and Maintenance) or engage another agency for all or part of this activity. GP-led O&M can include hiring workers and buying vehicles for collection and transportation of waste.

In those villages where all the waste cannot be managed at household level, non-managed and segregated household waste need to be transported either to the community bins at the village level or to the treatment plant sites at community level where household level bio degradable waste can be treated by community treatment plant and recyclable and non- bio degradable waste can be sorted out and sold to the kabadiwalas or raggpickers by gram panchayats.

Alternatively, a Community Based organization (CBO) (for example, youth club, and women's group), NGO or private operator may be engaged by a GP to undertake O&M.

3) Solid and liquid waste management involves a number of stakeholders from national, state and local government agencies and programs, NGOs, private sector players to Gram Panchayats. Major dearth is of lack of effective coordination between them which is necessary to make services work, both at the development stage and in the long term sustainability of the model. A need of effective policy which defines proper coordination mechanisms necessary at each level for service delivery, regulation and performance management, and monitoring is felt for better waste management in rural India. Coordination of funding arrangements and convergence with other funding programs will also be necessary to ensure efficient and effective disbursement of funds for the development.

One more point which needs focus here is the involvement of private sector in the area of rural development. These days focus of many private players is upon the rural sector due to saturation of market in urban and metropolitan cities, therefore improved sanitation and environment in terms of cleanliness and hygiene would augment business of private players in rural India operating in different sectors. Tata & Bhada (2012) examined the huge potential of energy arising out of waste generated in India. The only challenge is to positively engage private players in this sector. The physical capacity of service providers is available, people are willing to work in SLWM (Solid and Liquid Waste Management) sector and they can see the potential to make Waste Management into a business. Examples of successful

SLWM based businesses are already operating in rural parts of the country (especially for septic tank emptying, collection of paper, glass bottles, etc.). For medium sized operators, their financial capacity is boosted through bank loans and for small scale operators there are a number of NGOs and development programmes working to develop the idea of SLWM as a business. Technical capacity is available through machines, trucks and low-cost technologies are being developed by international organizations for services like pit emptying, decentralized treatment plants, prefabricated plants, etc.

4) An important step to motivate and engage the public is via continuous public awareness Campaigns .The Strategy which adopted by the government in this front is Conventional IEC programs (Information, Education, Communication) which has been observed that it fails to address and convince people to adopt safe waste management practices. Some of the Drawbacks of Conventional IEC systems practiced under TSC programme are:-

a) Messages are only determined and comprehended by external experts who are assumed to 'know better' and, therefore, may not be relevant or practical in the local context, for example, the messages tend to focus on teaching people about the health risks and diseases linked to poor waste management rather than focusing on people's priorities such as the inconvenience caused by choked drains or smelly garbage dumps.
b) Methods used to communicate 'tell people what to do' are such by which people do not get an opportunity to relate to their own concerns or experiences.
c) Conventional IEC assumes that if people are better educated or informed, they will change their behavior which is not the case in Rural parts of the country in India.

Suggestive corrective measures to deal with this issue could be introduce participatory approach .It seeks to 'find out' what causes people to change their behavior. Participatory methods are based on principles of adult education and have been field-tested extensively. Participatory tools help to encourage everyone to participate and, if facilitated well, can be more interesting than a lecture or discussion. From the program implementer's perspective, these tools help to gain insights into current practices and potential triggers for change in a relatively short time compared with regular IEC programs. Field experience has shown that community workers find use of participatory methods far more rewarding. Community workers who have tried participatory methods and found them worthwhile usually do not want to return to their earlier methods.

Also, Sustainable waste management and planning requires precise prediction of solid and liquid waste generation in a particular area of study, possible routes of collection optimum waste management, treatment and landfill capacity. These days Forecasting models are applied in many other developed countries .It comprises of Qualitative and Quantitative study. Qualitative methods are primarily based on survey, interview, observations and executive jury analysis whereas Quantitative methods are based on numerical and statistical analysis, such as trend or pattern analysis, regression analysis and so on. For example in "Forecasting 2020 waste arisings and treatment capacity" report of Department for Environment Food and Rural Affairs, Govt. of UK(2013) many methods have been used like Monte –Carlo Methods, Sensitivity Analysis Reports and standard approach to modelling to forecast capacity of waste arisings in 2020. It gave them an opportunity to plan for their future optimization of resources in order to minimize the waste arisings and build adequate treatment capacity.

The Study shows that Lack of Proper Execution of Policies at the Grass root level due to various issues as discussed in detailed in the paper which hinders proper replication of successful models in other parts of the country, lack of awareness among community members which leads to less of involvement of all the stakeholders involved in the proper functioning leads to improper waste management in rural part of India which could otherwise prove to be an asset if managed judiciously.

## REFERENCES

Department for Environment Food and Rural Affairs. Govt. of UK. (2013). Forecasting 2020 Waste Arisings and Treatment Capacity: Published October 2013, London: Author.

Indian Sanitation Portal. (2013), *Waste management*. Retrieved September 29, 2013, from website: http://indiasanitationportal.org/34

Ministry of Drinking Water and Sanitation. Govt. of India. (2011). Guidelines on CRSP. Nirman Bhawan, New Delhi: Author.

Ministry of Rural Development. Govt. of India. (2010). Guidelines on Central Rural Sanitation Programme Total Sanitation Campaign. Krishi Bhawan, New Delhi: Author.

Mission, S., & the Government of Kerala. (2013). *Total Sanitation Campaign*. Retrieved October 9, 2013, from website: http://indiasanitationportal.org/

Tata & Bhada, P. (2012). *The Potential for Waste to Energy in India*. Retrieved October 5, 2013, from website: http://www.waste-management-world.com/

Water and Sanitation Program. (2012). *Handbook on Scaling up Solid and Liquid Waste Management in Rural Areas*. New Delhi: Lodhi Estate.

## KEY TERMS AND DEFINITIONS

**Anaerobic Digestion:** Anaerobic digestion is a series of biological processes in which microorganisms break down biodegradable material in the absence of oxygen. It is a process that produces a gas principally composed of methane (CH4) and carbon dioxide (CO2) also known as biogas.

**PPPs:** Public Private Partnerships: Public Private Partnerships refers to an arrangement between the public and private sector with clear agreement on shared objectives for delivery of public infrastructure and services of which management is undertaken or investment are made by the private sector for the specified period of time.

**PRI:** Panchayati Raj Institutions: A decentralized governance system for inclusive growth and development in rural India wherein all states with a population in excess of 2 million have a 3-tier administration comprising of village panchayats, panchayati samitis, and zilla parishads.

**NGO:** Non-Governmental Organization: NGO is any non-profit voluntary citizen-based group that doesn't functions under the purview of any local or national government. NGOs are also termed as civil societies which are organized on community, national and international levels to serve various political and social purposes.

**HDI:** Human Development Index: The Human Development Index is a measure of average achievement by people of a country in key dimensions of human development such as life expectancy, education standard and standard of living. It determines the country's overall achievement in its social and economic dimensions.

**Gram Panchayat:** A Gram Panchayat is a village based local self-government organization in India .It is a grass root level statutory institution of rural self-government whose members are selected by public votes. The head of Gram panchayat is called Sarpanch.

**IEC Programs:** Information, Education and Communication (IEC) programme is used to create awareness about hygiene and effect behavioral changes. Activities under this programme are area specific and involve all sections of the rural population. The IEC also focuses on health and hygiene practices and environmental sanitation aspects.

# Chapter 25
# Capacity Building through Knowledge Management:
## How Vedic Concepts Can Interpret the Occurrences at Maruti Suzuki India, Manesar

**Shampa Chakraberty**
*NSHM Knowledge Campus, India*

## ABSTRACT

*This chapter talks about the history of Maruti which is marked by exploitation of workers through extraordinary work pressure, harassment by arbitrary issuing of show-cause notices and charge-sheets, transfers, suspensions, criminal intimidation, terminations without inquiry, reducing the labour costs by contractualisation of work-force, devising mechanisms to extract maximum work effort from workers, getting rid of the relatively older workers or those with disabilities or medical condition etc. are methods that act against the interest of workers. In this chapter one of the Vedic philosophy's systems namely Karma- Mimamsa is explained by the author who thinks that karma alone awards fruits to the performer of Vedic ritual and the reward is consistent with the karma of the performer of the ritual. Where there is good karma, there is good fruit and vice versa. Dharma comes from the Lord, karma comes from the Lord, but the fruit comes from karma itself.*

## INTRODUCTION

The word *karma* refers to any action that results in a reaction, whether it be good or bad. The word Mimamsa means to analyze and understand thoroughly. The philosophical systems of *karma-mimamsa* and *vedanta* are closely related to each other and are in some ways complimentary. *Karma-mimamsa* may be understood as a stepping stone to *vedanta*. Since *Karma-mimamsa* is to be taken up by householders as stated in the Vedas, its philosophy is to provide a practical methodology for the utilization of the Vedic religion (*dharma*) for the satisfaction of the urges for wealth (*artha*) and sensual pleasure (*kama*). In

DOI: 10.4018/978-1-4666-8259-7.ch025

so doing, *karma-mimamsa* provides a materialistic explanation of the Vedic rituals for persons whose material desires have blinded them to spiritual understanding. Many people are very concerned about their rights but little aware of their duties. Demanding rights without accepting duty leads to many problems, as is evinced by today's chaotic global society. The execution of duty handed down by higher authority is the path of honor in all human cultures; conversely, the path of dishonor is the neglect of duty for the satisfaction of animal urges. History teaches that when the family, society and nation fail to fulfill traditional duties and instead follow the whims of lust as their only value system, they are soon destroyed. All those activities that coordinate one's individual life with universal life constitute one's duty or *dharma*. Most people lack a positive attitude of inspiration toward their daily duties, performing them only to earn money or status. *Karma-mimamsa* explores the subtle levels of sound by delving into its origin. *Vak shakti* refers to both thought and expression and is actually a law of communication that is responsible for conveying thoughts and concepts, both individually and collectively. The urge to create wealth, as provided in Vedic literature as well as expansion into developing territory drew the Japanese to do business in India. Maruti was the result of this venture.

Maruti Suzuki India Limited commonly referred to as Maruti and formerly known as Maruti Udyog Limited, is an automobile manufacturer in India._It is a subsidiary of Japanese automobile and motorcycle manufacturer Suzuki. For carrying out business with a foreign partner both partners must be culturally tuned towards each other. However there is a huge socio-cultural abyss between the Indians and the Japanese. *Vak shakti* as stated in *Karma-mimamsa* was found to be absent here. The practice that increasing the productivity of workers by fair means or foul will generate increased production was a Japanese idea and is the very antithesis of the strategies a typical business firm in India follows namely corporate, business or functional strategy. This case study shows how and why certain strategies to boost productivity of workers failed. The execution of duty handed down by higher authority is the path of honor in all human cultures as stated in *Karma-mimamsa.* But the same execution was done without delving into the socio-cultural milieu of the Indian workers. The case study also sheds light on some of the region-specific socio-economic issues relevant to the company and why labour-management relations have to be handled with care taking into consideration the culture, region- specific features, the labour policies of the state, the education level of the workers etc.

## BACKGROUND

Maruti Suzuki manufactures and sells a complete range of cars for every segment of the population. As of November 2012[update], Maruti had a market share of 37% of the Indian passenger car market. Originally, 18.28% of the company was owned by the Indian government, and 54.2% by Suzuki of Japan. The BJP-led government held an initial public offering of 25% of the company in June 2003. As of May 2007[update], the government of India sold its complete share to Indian financial institutions and no longer has any stake in Maruti Udyog Ltd.

Maruti Udyog Limited (MUL) was established in February 1981, though the actual production commenced in 1983 with the Maruti 800, based on the Suzuki Alto kei car which at the time was the only modern car available in India, its only competitors- the Hindustan Ambassador and Premier Padmini were both around 25 years out of date at that point. The company's manufacturing facilities are located at two facilities Gurgaon and Manesar in Haryana, south of Delhi. It exports more than 50,000 cars annually and has domestic sales of 730,000 cars annually. Maruti Suzuki's Gurgaon facility has an installed capacity of 900,000 units per annum. The Manesar facilities, launched in February 2007 comprise a vehicle assembly plant with a capacity of 550,000 units per year and a Diesel Engine plant with an annual capacity of 100,000 engines and transmissions. Manesar and Gurgaon facilities have a combined capability to produce over 1,450,000 units annually. The company is 54.2% owned by the Japanese multinational Suzuki Motor Corporation. The rest is owned by public and financial institutions. It is listed on the Bombay Stock Exchange and National Stock Exchange of India.

The permanent workers in Maruti are qualified and have passed out of the ITI's (Industrial Training Institute). They were hired through campus interviews. However Maruti determined that Haryanvis were better workers hence most of the workers are from various places in Haryana. These workers were recruited in 2007 as trainees and became permanent in 2010. As batch after batch of trainees became permanent the demand to form a union was raised towards end of 2010 (*The Telegraph,* 20th October, 2011 p 01).

Since its founding in 1983, Maruti Udyog Limited experienced few problems with its labour force. The Indian labour it hired readily accepted Japanese work culture and the modern manufacturing process. In 1997, there was a change in ownership, and Maruti became predominantly government controlled. Shortly thereafter, conflict between the United Front Government and Suzuki started. Labour unrest started under management of Central government. In 2000, a major industrial relations issue began and employees of Maruti went on an indefinite strike, demanding among other things, major revisions to their wages, incentives and pensions.

Employees used slowdown in October 2000, to press for a revision to their incentive-linked pay. In parallel, after elections and a new central government led by NDA alliance, India pursued a disinvestments policy. Along with many other government owned companies, the new administration proposed to sell part of its stake in Maruti Suzuki in a public offering. The worker's union opposed this sell-off plan on the grounds that the company will lose a major business advantage of being subsidized by the Government and the union has better protection while the company remains in control of the government.

The standoff between the union and the management continued through 2001. The management refused union demands citing increased competition and lower margins. The central government prevailed and privatized Maruti in 2002. Suzuki became the majority owner of Maruti Udyog Limited_(Wikipedia-Maruti Suzuki- retrieved on 16th July, 2013).

## LITERATURE REVIEW

Each of the six schools of thought that propagated Vedic wisdom, did so from a different philosophical perspective. Each of these perspectives or *darshanas* is associated with a famous sage who is the author of a *sutra* (code) expressing the essence of his *darshana*. Vyasa's *Vedanta-sutra*, which carefully examines and judges the six systems of Vedic philosophy (as well as other philosophies), forms the third great body of Vedic literature after the *sruti-sastra* and *smrti-sastra*. This is known as the *nyaya-sastra*, "scripture of philosophical disputation." The *sad-darshana* (six philosophical views) are *nyaya* (logic), *vaisesika* (atomic theory), *sankhya* (analysis of matter and spirit), *yoga* (the discipline of selfrealization), *karma-mimamsa* (science of fruitive work) and *vedanta* (science of God realization). The study of the six systems of Vedic philosophy is itself a form of *yoga: jnana-yoga*, the *yoga* of theoretical knowledge. But from *jnana* one must come to *vijnana*, practical realization of the ultimate truth. The *sad-darshana* are six branches of theoretical dialectics (*sastratha*) that twist and turn from thesis (*purvapaksa*) to antithesis (*uttarapaksa*) to synthesis (*siddhanta*). *Vedanta* teaches that liberation is attainable only by knowledge of the Supreme Lord and by His Divine Grace. There is no possible harmony between *yoga* and *Vedanta* on the subject of liberation, which yoga claims is attained only through discrimination of spirit from matter. Yoga here simply means meditation. The *Yoga-smrti* (the *Patanjala Yoga-sutra* and allied writings) depicts: 1) depicts the individual souls and the Supreme Soul as being only all-pervading consciousness, with no further characteristics; 2) says that *prakrti* is the original independent cause of all causes; 3) says that liberation is simply the cessation of pain, obtainable only through the Patanjala system; 4) presents theories of sensory perception and the workings of the mind that are different from the explanations given in the *Veda. Vedanta-sutra* 3.2.41 cites the viewpoint of Jaimini (the author of the *karma-mimamsa* philosophy) on the fruits of *karma*. He thinks that *karma* alone awards fruits to the performer of Vedic rituals, because after an act is completed, it leaves behind a force called *apurva*. After a lapse of time, this *apurva* force gives the reward that is consistent with the *karma* to the performer of the ritual. Where there is good *karma*, there is good fruit. Dharma comes from the Lord, karma comes from the Lord, but the fruit comes from karma itself.

Now the *nyaya* system of philosophy which was established by the sage Gautama is primarily concerned with the conditions of correct knowledge and the means of receiving this knowledge. *Nyaya* is predominantly based on reasoning and logic and therefore is also known as *Nyaya Vidya* or *Tarka Sastra* -- "the science of logic and reasoning. This philosophy asserts that obtaining valid knowledge of the external world and its relationship with the mind and self is the only way to attain liberation. All six schools of Vedic philosophy aim to describe the nature of the external world and its relationship to the individual, to go beyond the world of appearances to ultimate Reality, and to describe the goal of life and the means for attaining this goal. In this attempt, the six philosophies divide their course of study into two major categories: the study of unmanifested reality, and the study of manifest reality. In *nyaya* philosophy, both aspects of reality are divided into sixteen major divisions, called *padarthas.* The Object of Knowledge or *Prameya* may be translated as "that which is knowable," or "the object of true knowledge." That which is the object of cognition is *prameya*, and whatever is comprehended or cognized by *buddhi* is categorized into the twelve objects of cognition known as the *prameyas*. These twelve divisions are: *atman*, the self; *sarira*, the body -- the abode of the experience of pain and pleasure that is the seat of all organic activities; *indriyas*, the five senses -- smell, taste, sight, touch and hearing -- which contact external objects and transmit the experience to the mind; *artha*, the objects of the senses; *buddhi*, cognition; *manas*, the mind -- the internal sense that is concerned with the perception of pleasure, pain, and all other internal experiences and that, according to *nyaya*, limits cognition to time and space. The mind is compared to an atom (not the atom of modern physics; see vaisesika philosophy) because it is minute, everlasting, individual, and all-pervading; *pravrtti*, activity -- vocal, mental, and physical; *dosa*, mental defects that include attachment (*raga*), hatred (*dvesa*), and infatuation or delusion (*moha*); *pretyabhava*, rebirth or life after death; *phala*, the fruits or results of actions experienced as pain or pleasure; *dukha*, suffering -- the bitter or undesired experiences of mind; and *apavarga*, liberation or complete cessation of all suffering without any possibility of its reappearance. Bondage is born of the misunderstanding of these twelve knowable objects, and one obtains freedom from bondage when he attains the correct know ledge of these twelve aspects of reality. Most of the time, however, this knowledge remains incomplete, and the means for attaining an integral comprehension of reality is not learned, so defective or invalid knowledge is maintained. In order to cast off this invalid knowledge, *nyaya* provides a profound method for determining valid knowledge.

Pramana -- The Sources of Valid Knowledge:The four pramanas are: perception (*pratyaksa*); inference (*anumana*); comparison (*upamana*); and testimony (*sabda*). Experiential knowledge is received through the four pramanas. Categories of knowledge can be divided into two parts: valid and invalid. In the language of *nyaya* philosophy, valid experiential knowledge is called *prama*, and nonvalid experiential knowledge is called *aprama*. *Prama* can be received through perception, inference, comparison, and testimony; therefore there are four types of valid knowledge based on these four means. *Aprama* is divided into doubt (*samsaya*), faulty cognition (*bhrama* or *viparyaya*), and hypothetical argument (*tarka*). According to *nyaya* philosophy true knowledge is that which corresponds to the nature of its object; otherwise the knowledge is false. To perceive a thing in its true nature is true knowledge. *Nyaya* philosophy says that the validity or invalidity of knowledge depends on its correspondence or non-correspondence to the facts. True knowledge leads a person to successful practical activity while false knowledge makes one helpless and leads to failure and disappointment.

Most people believe that whatever is experienced through perception must be true, and they do not further test the data that are received via the senses. *Nyaya* philosophy, however, is very critical in this respect and makes a thorough examination of perception. Perception is knowledge produced by the contact of the senses with the objects of the world. In *nyaya* philosophy, ordinary perception (*laukika*) is either indeterminate (*nirvikalpa*) or determinate (*savikalpa*). Indeterminate perception is the primary cognition of a thing before judgment is used to specify diverse characteristics.

*Nyaya* philosophy provides a detailed and systematic description of inference. Inference is the process of knowing something not by means of contact between the senses and the objects of the world and not by observation but rather through the medium of a sign, or *linga*, that is invariably related to it. Inference involves the process of analyzing memories, correlations, and uncontaminated arguments. The Sanskrit word for inference is *anumana*, and may be defined as "the cognition or knowledge that follows from some other knowledge." There are two kinds of concomitance: equivalent and nonequivalent. Equivalent *vyapti* (*samuvyapti*) is an invariable concomitance between two coexistent terms. Concomitance denotes a relationship of coexistence (*sahacarla*). According to *nyaya*, concomitance is established through the perception of classes (*samanya laksana perception*). The most crucial concern in any systematic inference is how to make certain that concomitance, the logical basis for the inference, is valid -- that is, free from limiting conditions (*upadhis*). *Nyaya* provides three general classification systems for inference. The first classification system is based on psychological grounds; the second is based on the nature of *vyapti* or the universal relationship between the middle and major terms; and the third is based on the logical construction of the inference. According to the first system of classification, there are two kinds of inference: *svartha*, meaning "for oneself," and *parartha*, meaning "for others." In *svartha*, the purpose of the inference is for one to gain correct knowledge by oneself and for himself. In this kind of inference, the whole process of reasoning is internal – one employs systematic logical reasoning to protect oneself from confusion and doubt and to arrive at correct inferential knowledge. In *parartha*, on the other hand, the inference is meant for others. Here someone is trying to prove the truth of his view. These Vedic concepts have been shown in the case study to indirectly affect the affairs of the company.

Ethics refers to the character or conduct of men and expresses it in value judgements of worth, duty or goodness (Banerjee, 2005). Ethics constitutes the values and social system for individuals and organizations. Ethics and values are deep rooted in our traditional heritage of culture and beliefs. It promotes an orderly corporate life and a disciplined society. Ethics is what an organization projects about its values and its commitments to its roles. It brings discipline and order and improves and strengthens relationships amongst superiors, peers and subordinates.

The central problem of many ethical theories is to determine the grounds for the valid use of the concept of "good" and to arrive at a reasoned synthesis of the things to which goodness intrinsically belongs. According to one view, good is relative to the individual; according to another view it is happiness or pleasure, wherever found, of the community or of mankind. The former was the doctrine of Epicurus (Laertius, 3 B. C.) while the latter owes its development to modern writers (Cumberland 1672, Shaftesbury, 1711, Butler, 1755, Hutcheson, 1725). Utilitarianism is a morality of consequence, finding the criterion of goodness in the kind of feeling which actions tend to produce in sentient beings. This feeling can only be ascertained by experience which is a subject of debate between the empirical and intuitive school of ethics. The latter school lays stress on the immediateness and universality of the moral judgements passed by each man's conscience. A doctrine of the moral sense, as a feeling or perception by which actions or motives were morally distinguished apart from their consequences, was developed by Shaftesbury and Hutchenson while Butler formulated the doctrine that conscience is the supreme authority as to what is right and wrong. However Butler's work talks about a calm regard to one's interest on the whole, is frequently spoken of as superior to conscience. In other works of Butler the actions which conscience prescribes is not coterminous with actions aiming at the good or happiness of the society. Hence Butler's severance from utilitarianism is complete though he may be regarded as the head of the 19th century intuitive school. The weakness of the intuitive position lies in the fact that the conscience is seldom brought into intelligible relations with the rational or spiritual nature of man.

The accepted practice that, increasing the productivity of workers by fair means or foul will generate increased production, goes against the very grain of the concept of human beings as resources, who by their very nature require different handling methods than other resources namely financial, material, machine, information etc. Since any business today is operating in a highly socio-political environment where social demands and political laws are constantly changing, management has to meet the demands of business and people by not just focusing on wealth creation but also by adding values to the system in which they are operating. Values are the beliefs that guide individual's actions. Values lay standards against which individual's behavior is judged. Although Indian management does not preach morality the problem lies elsewhere – it is how to implement good values in real life and yet become a great achiever. Indian managers practice how good values pay better dividends, how honesty helps to grow industry and business, how cooperation and not competition are better growth strategies. Typical values include trust, honesty, mutual respect, teamwork and customer focus (*The Economic Times Wealth*, 9th-15th December, 2013, p 27). Ethical violations, misconduct with colleagues, lapses of judgement and financial irregularities at the workplace are all over the news. Most employers today have become extremely serious about doing the right things in order to stay afloat (*The Economic Times Wealth*, 9th-15th December, 2013, p 27). However, some contemporary business and society seems to be deviating from the ethical precepts in their lust for maximizing their personal gains.

When we look at the ethical side of management various models are there to help us understand the qualities required by management to manage today's knowledge workers (Banerjee, 2005):

## The Jitatmananda model

1) Talks about the holistic paradigm which focuses on the following two concepts – a) since all minds and all lives are interconnected, a respectful attitude of honesty, help, care and encouragement are the only policy in management and b) since a living organism can regenerate himself a worker can regenerate himself more when he is offered empowerment, encouragement, trust, faith and sup-

port.The holistic paradigm teaches that love begets love, hatred begets hatred, trust begets trust, gratitude begets gratitude, respect begets respect, empowerment begets responsible productivity and meditation and spiritual practice bring internal growth and flowering of the higher personality.

2) Creation of ethical leaders – Such a leader must have the following essential qualities – a) evenness or equanimity of mind, b) attention to means as a road leading to the end,c) capacity to face adverse situation with strength and calmness, d) show respect to others and respect to all works, e) learn to be the servant to be able to rule, f) ability to make the place of work a place of worship, g) ability of creating the environment of a corporate family;
3) The leader is one who has learnt the art of drawing different kinds of people towards him and extracting the best from each one according to his qualities and aptitude – here the worker must know that the leader sincerely feels for them; the workers must see that the leader himself loves to share all the work that the workers do; the workers must see that the leader practices what he preaches and the leader must be pure in body and mind.
4) A creative leader must be both a visionary and a missionary – he must be a contemplative man, a quintessential thinker, a doer, a visionary with the power to envision and capacity to transmit that vision and spiritual dynamism into others.
5) Vedic idea of corporate culture – company is a family.

The manager as a leader holds centre stage in Jitatmananda's model. In this model the likely ill effect of competition on the company's ethical behavior is also shown. The pre-eminence given to the competitor in Japan today has subtly changed the ethos and culture of Japanese companies with deleterious results. If the end objective of excellence is higher profitability, competition is bound to have its ill effects on ethics.

So the seeds of ethical dilemma persist in this model. In case of a conflict regarding objectives and visions, an ethical manager may have to leave the company.

However an alternative model (Banerjee 2005) which stands on the twin foundations of, a) allowing the whole world to be happy – i.e. desire for the organization to spread happiness to all and b) encouraging the organization to aim at objectives and mission beyond mere profit. Hence the organization should pursue profit motive as a requirement for achieving the aforesaid super ordinate objective. The stakeholders expected return should be the furtherance of the organization's objectives.

The concept of human beings as machines gained ground with the sayings of Rene Descartes who stated that nature worked according to mechanical laws and everything in the material world could be explained in terms of the arrangement and movement of its parts. This view of the universe as a mechanical system provided scientific sanction for manipulation and exploitation of nature in a typical business scenario. The relentless search for raw materials and markets on the part of business has led to the following implications:

1. Continued notion of differentiating between brain and other motor organs like hands and feet have led to downgrading 'blue collar workers' as compared to management
2. The mechanistic model of the universe has generated a technology aimed at control, mass-production, standardization and centralized management that pursues the mirage of infinite growth

The concept of social Darwinianism held the belief that all life in society had to be a struggle for existence ruled by 'survival of the fittest'. Accordingly competition has been seen as the driving force of the economy and the 'aggressive approach' has become the ideal of the business world. Combined with the mechanistic model of the universe with its excessive emphasis on linear thinking, this attitude has produced a technology that is unhealthy and inhuman. This technology is aimed at control, mass production and standards and is subjected to centralized management that pursues an illusion of endless growth in which employees and management are expected and required to submerge their personal identities and adapt to the corporate identity and a prescribed behavior pattern; a situation and behavior pattern which has become typical of today's management.

According to Descartes's statement "I think, therefore, I exist" led to the development of a method of analysis and derivation of conclusion totally opposed to a holistic approach which had a profound influence on business and management thinking and attitude. He tried to explain nature as a perfect machine, governed by exact mathematical laws. This mission was fulfilled by Newton who said all physical phenomena are reduced to the motion of material particles, caused by their mutual attraction, i.e. by their force of gravity. These mathematical laws guiding the activities of the material universe had a great influence on the growth and character of the world of business.

The contemporary business environment is governed by selfish motives. Managers work to maximize business profits, workers want maximum wages, suppliers want high process for their supplies and shareholders want maximum dividend. Hence there is need to introduce a holistic approach to management. It advocates growth and prosperity for everyone and not any one stakeholder. The whole world is seen as a family and decision making process is not oriented to the interest of companies only. All corporate members work together for the good of all people. Holistic management is value-driven and based on ethics and values in business. Values are represented by ethics. Increasing profits at the cost of social benefits may be the economic values of one enterprise and sacrificing a part of profits for benefits of society may be the social values of another business enterprise. On the other hand business values are beliefs that develop a system, based on sound business principles. These values become guides for employees' actions. The business unit derives values from the nation where it is established, the industry to which it belongs and the people who constitute its workforce.

Ethical and value driven management is the result of the following factors:

1. Spirit – Corporate spirit is defined in the actions of its managers. A right decision for the benefit of all reflects decisions in the light of spirit of Dharma.
2. Righteousness – Right actions are those taken for the benefit of maximum people, based on ethics and values and hope to achieve objectives of the organizations in an optimum manner.
3. Fearlessness – Right actions create fearlessness in the managers.

## HISTORY OF UNREST AT MANESAR

In the year 2011-12 Maruti sold 12, 71, 005 cars and earned a profit of Rs. 3135 crores (before tax). This prompted the Chairman of Maruti to state that ".... producing 250,000 extra cars without any new additions to capacity was an outstanding achievement...." (Bhargava, 2010). Also, Maruti's expenditure on workers has continued to remain lower than that of almost all other automobile companies; thereby ensuring a consistently high degree of exploitation of workers. By the time the Manesar unit was opened the condition of the workers in Gurgaon unit had deteriorated considerably and the bargaining power of the workers became really low. In Manesar the company replicated the Gurgaon model but created harsher working conditions for the workers. Hence the structure, design, employment policy, high speed of production, intensification of work etc. at Manesar became the context of persistent labour unrest in the years to come.

There have been 7 strikes at Maruti factories in the last 16 years. The first occurred in April, 1995 for 3 days at Gurgaon when the demand was more wages. The second was in March, 1998 at Gurgaon factory for 2 days when some local issues was the reason. The third strike impacted Maruti for 89 days, the longest ever strike at any factory of Maruti where the demand was of more wages at the Gurgaon plant. The fourth was for 13 days at Manesar plant when the management did not allow the workers to form a new, independent union. The fifth strike was again of a long duration, for 33 days at Manesar when the workers were directed by the management to sign a "good conduct bond" and they refused. This bond was to seek an assurance from the workers that they will not resort to go-slow, sabotage production or indulge in activities which would hamper the normal production in the plant. The sixth strike was for 2 days in the sister concerns of Maruti who were supporting the Manesar workers. The seventh strike went on for 10 days at Manesar and the two sister concerns where the workers demanded restoration of the services of 1100 contract workers. The last two strikes resulted in the full closure of Suzuki Motor's Indian operations. The strikes at Manesar in 2011 portray a disturbed industrial relations scenario with demands of the workers ranging from formation of a new independent union to permanency of contract workers (*The Economic Times,* 17th October, 2011, p 04,).

## FACTORS CONTRIBUTING TO THE INDUSTRIAL UNREST

The 750 acre Manesar facilty of Maruti Udyog Ltd., a highly automated factory that produced 600,000 units for India's largest automaker each year was in the news for labour unrest that resulted in a number of strikes from 1995 to 2011. Maruti's record of following labour guidelines and practices has been far from remarkable. In the automotive industry, while Japanese peers like Honda and Toyota have managed to keep their workers happy, Maruti's labour trouble has been growing. Strikes and unrest have been growing with a rapid decline in workers' trust, keeping the labour situation at a low ebb. The company also failed to maintain agreements signed with workers on the creation of Works Committee and the Grievance Committee, which was part of the October, 2011 agreement and which has not yet been formed. While the formation of these committees would have increased the trust of the workers, it would have been a subtle weapon in the hands of the management while dealing with workers' grievances. The fragile industrial relations at the factory premises took a turn for the worse as an unrelenting management, a union lacking mature leadership and a dithering state government all contributed in lighting the fuse.

Since any business today is operating in a highly socio-political environment where social demands and political laws are constantly changing, management has to meet the demands of business and people by not just focusing on wealth creation but also by adding values to the system in which they are operating. Indian managers practice how good values pay better dividends, how honesty helps to grow industry and business, how cooperation and not competition are better growth strategies.

Yet these concepts were forgotten when Mr. M.M. Singh the then company's Head of Manufacturing commented, while addressing a meeting of the company's functional heads- "How did we lose the connect with our workers?", part of the answer might lie in measures he spearheaded in early 2010 when Maruti saw a spurt in demand which led to outstripping its capacity (*The Economic Times,*, 17th October, 2011, p 04,). Since longer waiting periods for Maruti cars meant that rivals will step in and start eating into its market share, Singh and his team put in place a series of measures to produce more. This included more frequent maintenance of machines, reprogramming robots that control the assembly line to squeeze out efficiency and implementation of a "flexi-line" that could produce multiple models. These measures resulted in creating a capacity of 350,000 cars per year as compared to 250,000 earlier (*The Economic Times,*, 17th October, 2011, p04,). Incentives of workers were aligned to production; in short life was like a machine on the shop floor with production accelerating by 40% at Manesar. Hence life on the shop floor took a turn for the worse.

One of the distinctive features of all Maruti plants is the absence of any declared daily target; the assembly line continues irrespective of how many cars are produced. Moreover the expected speed of production was also high. A worker was expected to check out 142 parts of a car in production in 42 seconds. Even at the end of a shift there may be a continuous schedule of work; once a shift gets over the worker cannot leave his station till the worker from the next shift takes over, but is not compensated for the extra time he spends at the machine beyond his shift duty, while half a day's salary is deducted from the worker who arrives late. The work pressure increased considerably with the passage of time.

According to the Vedic literature *nyaya-sastra,* every occurrence has to be judged from the perspective of the six philosophical views that is nyaya (logic), vaisesika (atomic energy), sankhya (analysis of matter and spirit), yoga (the discipline of self realization), karma- mimamsa (science of fruitive work) and Vedanta (science of God realization). However, from jnana one has to come to vijnana, practical realization of the ultimate truth (Suhotra Swami Ṣad-darśanam, 1997). Whatever decisions were taken for increased production at Maruti Suzuki were not the right ones; realization or vijnana of the ultimate truth did not happen, hence the above incidents occurred.

Major component of wages was determined by way of payment as incentive. Conditions of the 'incentive payment' were always decided by the management. Arbitrary revisions were often made in the norms of the incentive, which adversely affected the wages. In fact, changes in the norms of the payment of incentive bonus have been one of the first causes of discontent amongst the workers and remains so till date. Till 1995, the wages at the Gurgaon unit were determined by an original incentive scheme, according to which 65% of all saving in the labour cost above the norm set was distributed to workers as incentive bonus. In 1999, the union (Maruti Employees Union) demanded that the original scheme be restored with revised norms on account of increased production capacity due to mechanisation, etc. In response, the company brought in a new 'Productivity, Performance and Profitability Scheme'. According to this scheme, the incentive paid to the workers was to be calculated on the basis of sales of both cars and spare parts as well as the attendance record of the workers. The union opposed this scheme, quite legitimately arguing that the productivity incentive could not be linked to sale as the latter was not in their control. The strategy which was adopted here by the Production department was meant to achieve corporate and business unit objectives through maximizing resource productivity. This consists of nurturing a distinctive business competence to provide the company with a competitive advantage. The strategic decision taken here had no precedent among other Maruti Suzuki plants in India, leading to commitment of substantial resources and demanding a great deal of commitment from the employees at all levels.

In other words, this is the adaptive mode of strategic decision making as stated by Henry Mintzberg (1973), which is characterized by reactive solutions to existing problems. Strategy is adopted to move the corporation forward incrementally. The Maruti leadership took decisions in fits and starts based on the volume of cars selling instead of taking decisions based on a planning mode after gathering appropriate information, generating feasible alternative strategies and a rational selection of the most appropriate strategy. This strategy should include both the proactive search for new opportunities and the reactive solution of existing problems.

The unionization problem is predominant in the Manesar area where the Gurgaon-Manesar-Dharuhera-Rewari belt in Haryana employs about 400,000 workers in about 1000 companies. Here trade unions which are popular are the All India Trade Union Congress and the Hind Mazdoor Sabha. Since AITUC is a left leaning trade union it is thought to be prone to violence, so HMS is the lesser evil of the two. Apart from the above two unions, CITU and NTUI also enjoyed support among the workers. When workers wanted their matters to be taken up exclusively by a trade union, they first approached the Maruti Udyog Kamgar Union (MUKU), the Gurgaon based union recognized by the company as the union for all Maruti workers. However the workers demanded a separate union which the company bypassed by persuading the workers to join the Gurgaon based union. The company management also promised elections to the existing union while warning the workers not to form a second union in Manesar. Election eventually did take place in July, 2011 but the Manesar workers boycotted it. Management went so far as to force workers to sign a declaration that they were happy with the Gurgaon union and did not want a new one. The management on the other hand reiterated that they were stopping workers who were collecting signatures of all workers for the purpose of formation of an union during factory hours. This sort of faux pas by the management was further aggravated when management summarily dismissed workers for indiscipline including 4 office bearers of the new union whose application the workers had filed the day before. It seems childish on the part of the management to resort to such tactics to be one above the workers. The workers went on strike for 10 days from 10$^{th}$ of June, 2011 to 16$^{th}$ of June, 2011, at the end of which the dismissed workers were reinstated by the management. The loss of face suffered by the management was the result of indelicate handling of a volatile situation. As per the Industrial Disputes Act, 1947 the 5$^{th}$ Schedule deals with Unfair Labour Practices wherein it is stated that employers and employers' trade union, if they interfere, restrain, coerce workmen and do not allow them to engage in concerted activities, it will be treated as unfair labour practice. Violation of the Act will lead to penalty as specified under Section 25U, Chapter V-C of the said Act. Union leaders among them Amitabh Bhattacharya, General Secretary of Mazdoor Kranti Parishad who was a key figure in the Hindustan Motors strike in 2007 as well as in Mamata Banerjee's agitation against land acquisition at Singur for the Tata Nano factory was waiting in the sidelines ready to strike once the iron was hot. It was to the credit of the workers that they were receiving advice from all unions but they confided in none.

The societal environment in which Maruti Suzuki operated consisted of economic forces, technological forces, political-legal forces and socio-cultural forces. These forces do not generally influence the short-run activities but often influence the long-run decisions of an organization. Among these influences the impact of Generation Y boom is of importance because of the socio-cultural environment in which they have grown up. The Maruti workers are all in the age group of 18 to 30 and take decisions based on environmental factors. The changing pace and location of life results in instant contact and communication and this helps take fast decisions. Efficiency is at its best today and this was taken advantage of by the Maruti management. Also, in terms of socio-cultural variables Asian cultures are less concerned with the value of human rights which was amply demonstrated by the dictates of the Maruti Suzuki management and elaborated later on in the case study.

The Manesar plant draws its employees mostly from Haryana. The workers consist of 60% regular employees and the rest contract workers (*The Economic Times,* 17$^{th}$ October, 2011, p04,). Average age of the workers at Manesar is under 25. They became regular after three years of training entitling them to privileges which trainees and contract workers do not enjoy. The strategic decision to squeeze out more cars from existing plants involved adopting regressive policies which were harmful for the workers. For example, workstations have 40 seconds in which the worker has to do the job assigned to him.

This duration may be compressed or expanded depending on the production target. All Maruti workers are young and able bodied. Hence in an eight hour work shift workers get a 30 minute lunch break and two 7.5 minutes tea breaks. This is easier said than done because one has to remove the safety equipment, run 500 meters to grab tea and snacks, then run to the washroom 400 meters away and come back in 7 minutes, which becomes very tight at times (*The Telegraph,* 20th October, 2011, p01). The time for breaks may be reduced which does not give workers enough time to go to the washroom, change his clothes, run to the canteen 450 metres away and get back on the job before the belt starts running (*The Telegraph,* 20th October, 2011, p01). There is no scope for leaving the work station and no extra breaks are given; besides any absence from work results in a heavy pay cut. For example if an attendance reward of Rs 2000/- has accumulated in respect of a worker, he may forfeit the same if he is absent 3 days in the next month. Hence, for one day of leave a sum of Rs 1200-1500/- was deducted from the wages of a worker and this amount increased proportionately for every day of leave taken, although there may be very valid reasons for taking leave and the worker had also informed the company in advance about his absence. These wages were deducted from the incentive-linked part of the workers' wages. These measures speak of the stringent policies being implemented as part of the performance linked pay. However these measures were not properly explained to the shop floor workers but dictated by the demands of the assembly line. If a single worker does not do his part in the specified time the production halts. As the General Secretary of the proposed Maruti Suzuki Employees' Union, Shiv Kumar says that Maruti is like a family and all workers are willing to do their bit provided the management treats them with understanding and respect.

The nyaya system of philosophy established by the sage Gautama is based primarily on reasoning and logic wherein obtaining valid knowledge of the external world and its relationship with the mind and self is the only way to attain liberation. The object of knowledge or Prameya is categorized into twelve objects of cognition. Misunderstanding of these objects results in bondage and correct knowledge of these objects results in freedom. Most of the time this knowledge remains unattained which results in misunderstanding. True knowledge leads a person to successful practical activity while false knowledge leads to failure and disappointment (Suhotra Swami Ṣad-darśanam, 1997).

In the year 2001 and 2003 Voluntary Retirement Scheme was introduced which was seen by the workers as a move which the management initiated to replace permanent workers by contractual workers who are paid much less for the same work although the employees' cost to the total turnover was between 2.16% to 2.43% only. Here we are looking at a huge profit margin. The VRS was anything but voluntary. The active union members were targeted and forced to accept VRS. During the time between 2001and 2003 around 2500 permanent workers lost their jobs on account of VRS or dismissal. The workers who were forced to quit did so because they were questioned, threatened, arbitrarily transferred from one kind of work to another, intimidated (for physically challenged or ill workers) etc.

It was issues like the aforesaid ones which prompted the Maruti workers to demand a union to negotiate with the management. The workers first approached the Maruti Udyog Kamgar Union (MUKU) the Gurgaon-based union recognized by the company as the union for all Maruti workers. This happened sometime in end 2010 or early 2011. Maruti officials were reluctant to allow formation of another union so they persuaded the workers to join the existing one and promised elections to the existing union. However when elections did occur the Manesar workers boycotted it. In June, 2011 workers called a strike which went on for 13 days. The reason stated by the workers was that they were forced to sign an affidavit stating that they were happy with the Gurgaon trade union and did not want a new one although the management denies this stating some workers were forcing other workers to sign showing their consent to form a new union. The workers had filed an application with the Haryana labour department regarding formation of a new union, Maruti Suzuki Employees Union. As a result the management dismissed some workers for indiscipline which included the office bearers of the proposed union. However the management retreated from its aggressive stand and agreed to reinstate the dismissed workers.

After peace was made with reinstatement of the dismissed workers, these workers started flouting all rules of the company, appointing their own representatives in each machine area and encouraging workers to listen to only these representatives and not those of the management. Here the workers' views are different; they said that company officials started harassing and victimizing the workers through show cause notices, pay cuts, etc. (*The Economic Times,* 12th October, 2011, p05). The workers in turn resorted to go-slow policy.

There were various instances when management made a blunder in handling sensitive issues. The management of the auto giant made a major miscalculation in handling a labour incident, as a result of which violence broke out in the factory. Two office bearers of the workers' trade union were suspended following accusations of manhandling of a supervisor. They were let off after an oral apology; but in a similar incident in which an ordinary worker was involved in manhandling, the company launched disciplinary proceedings against him. This different treatment affected the morale of the workers (*The Economic Times,* 6th August, 2012, p 03,). Again there was an incident of scuffle of an ordinary worker with a supervisor and suspension and disciplinary proceedings followed, unlike what happened with the union office bearers. The case of the union office bearers were dealt with by bending some of the clauses of the Maruti's Standing Orders. Violence resulted leaving a senior company executive dead and many more injured (*The Economic Times,* 26th July, 2012, p 04,).

Nyaya philosophy provides a detailed description of inference or anumana and may be defined as " the cognition or knowledge that follows from some other knowledge". Nyaya provides three general classification systems for inference – the first is based on psychological grounds (swartha meaning for oneself and parartha meaning for others), second is based on universal relationship and the third is based on the logical construction of the inference. The above happenings at Maruti have a strong relationship with the concepts of swartha and parartha, wherein Maruti employees thought only about their immediate needs and not the consequences of violence. Violence begets violence and the Vedic scripts advises us to meditate (yoga or discrimination of spirit from matter) (Suhotra Swami Ṣad-darśanam, 1997).

Punitive measures introduced by Maruti meant that the workers suffered pay cuts. For example, for each day of strike in the year 2011 two days wages were deducted from the striking workers. Again, if the workers have come to work braving the strike they are locked out of the factory if they have not yet signed the "Good Conduct Bond". According to the workers while the annual remuneration of the CEO had increased from Rs.47.3 lakhs in 2007-08 to Rs. 2.45 crores in 2010-11 an increase of 419% from 2008 to 2011(*The Telegraph,* 20th October, 2011, p 01), while that of the workers had not, what with the punitive pay cuts.

There were questionable practices regarding corporate governance issues too (*The Economic Times,*, 7th Nov, 2011) at Maruti Suzuki, Manesar. It became apparent that 30 suspended workers were given a handsome package by the management in return for their exodus from Maruti Suzuki, Manesar. The package amount was from Rs 16-40 lakhs per worker and included the two union leaders Sonu Gujjar and Shiv Kumar. However the management said that the 30 workers had resigned from the company. Institutional investors were seriously condemning the Maruti management for handling the issue in this suspicious manner

Here the role of corporate culture comes into focus. Corporate culture is the collection of beliefs, expectations and values learned and shared by a corporation's members and transmitted from one generation of employees to another. It often includes a number of informal work rules that employees follow without question and these become part of a company's unquestioned tradition. The rules regarding increased productivity at the Maruti factory in Manesar fall in this category. The cultural intensity is the degree to which members of a unit accept the norms, values or other culture content associated with the unit. Corporate culture has a strong and powerful influence on the behavior of people at all levels and can strongly affect a corporation's ability to shift its strategic decisions. A strong culture should not only promote survival but it should also create the basis for a superior competitive position. If such a distinctive competence is embedded in an organization's culture it will be a form of tacit knowledge. This knowledge was present to a certain extent at Maruti Suzuki, Manesar; however due to environmental factors it could not be sustained and worked upon to the benefit of the company.

The societal environment has some important variables which affect the industries operating in the region. For the Manesar area some of the important variables affecting the functioning of Maruti Suzuki factory operations are:

1. Economic – wage/price controls, inflation, disposable and discretionary income: they affect the availability and cost of capital, influence the cost of production, prices and consumer demand. After liberalization, the Indian economy was opened up which also paved the way for foreign investments and entry of multinationals in a big way.
2. Technological – productivity improvements through automation: strategies developed on the basis of technological developments create a competitive advantage.
3. Political-legal – special incentives, laws on hiring and promotion, attitude towards foreign companies: a few of the issues under political-legal factors are legislations regulating wages, price control, import-export policies etc. Certain policy changes such as industrial policy liberalization in India has opened up enormous opportunities to Indian companies to expand but at the same time posed a serious threat of increased competition.
4. Socio cultural – lifestyle changes, career expectations, age distribution of population, regional shifts in population, consumer activism:
5. Demographic factors – size, growth rate, age and sex composition of the population, family size, education levels: companies have to adapt to automation, rationalization, downsizing etc. to remain competitive in the market economy which are opposed by labour, socialist and political groups.
6. Global factors – India is emerging as a super economic power and is having a major influence on world markets simply because of its very large consumer base and significant purchasing power. The demand for quality goods at competitive prices has shot up.

## FACTORS INDIRECTLY CONTRIBUTING TO THE INDUSTRIAL UNREST

### 1. Role of Trade Unions

About 400,000 workers are employed by about 1,000 companies in the Gurgaon-Manesar-Dharuhera-Rewari auto hub. Trade unions have had a mixed track record here. AITUC and HMS are the two most prominent trade unions operating here. AITUC is regarded as Left aligned and has a propensity for violence while HMS is more conciliatory. However in the run up to the formation of the new union the Maruti workers had grown close to the AITUC who helped them file the application for the new union. But there the role of the established union ended. A lot of unions started advising the Maruti workers. However the union leaders namely Gujjar and Kumar both remained indifferent to all the unions.

Here the issue of union leadership comes into focus. Initially the Gurgaon based union Maruti Udyog Kamgar Union (MUKU) looked after the affairs of the workers at Manesar. However the highly automated factory suffered a series of strikes in 2011 (*The Economic Times*, 14th June, 2011, p 05). When the workers were inclined to form a new union Mr. Gurudas Dasgupta of the AITUC helped them. He assumed the role of a mentor since he too had a stake in the Manesar pie. Union leaders of other unions such as CITU, NTUI etc. also started helping the young workers. The worker leaders listened to all of them but trusted no one. These young workers had managed to force the Maruti management to reinstate the sacked workers. Next they demanded a separate union, colouring their demand with aggression. The general secretary of Maruti Udyog Kamgar Union (MUKU), Kuldeep Jhangu originally organized the Manesar workers. But the workers were wayled by other forces and demanded a separate union. However the methodologies adopted by the workers of Manesar were too violent even for MUKU. Instead of starting with a tool-down protest and slowly progressing up to a full-fledged strike, they started off with a full strike; they also wanted the Gurgaon plant to shut down and join the strike, but when the MUKU general secretary refused, he became their enemy (*The Economic Times,* 26th July, 2012, p 04,). These workers were young, impressionable and eager to fight for what they felt was their right; the leaders of these workers namely Gujjar and Kumar too were raring to go. They were young and inexperienced. They were not elected leaders since they had boycotted the election process of MUKU, but nominated. The workers were angry young men and expected a lot from the union leaders. These young workers were aware that the production in India contributed to half of Suzuki's worldwide profits. They were disgruntled with the fact that there were massive salary hikes of the top management whereas workers' pay rose by barely 5%. However, these union leaders were new to their position and had little track record in leading workers as well as little acceptance among them. Hence they were being guided by unknown external leaders of various trade unions such as Hind Mazdoor Sabha, New Trade Union Initiative etc. The new union had the support of the management since it was set up with the cooperation of the management. It was also the union recognised by the management. The workers were a little wary about this. However the union leaders promised a lot but could not deliver that much; as a result workers became disgruntled (*The Economic Times,* 26th July, 2012, p 04,). The new leaders were impatient on the negotiating table, a fact that was noticed by the Haryana labour department officials. They were not as tactful and patient as was required under the circumstances. Veteran AITUC secretary D.L. Sachdev rued the fact that the leadership lacked maturity and this may lead to ultra-left elements misleading the workers (*The Economic Times,* 6th Nov, 2012, p 03). Unionisation raised expectations of the workers sky high. They expected the new union to deliver the goods, forgetting that union leaders tend to promise more than they can get out of the management. This resulted in the union leaders coming under constant pressure to be a more effective political force.

These union leaders are first-time leaders with little or no track record of sitting at a negotiating table. One cannot be impatient there as the HR managers are not authorized to take decisions on behalf of management. Hence one has to be tactful and patient. However the leaders were neither tactful nor patient and they failed to temper the expectations of the workers. These workers felt that they now had a recognized union that would represent them in the upcoming wage negotiations and they could negotiate with the management on equal terms. However the workers' unionization had exacerbated tensions on the shop floor. The worker-supervisor friction received a new twist with the union being a new variable in the checkerboard. Earlier, the relationship between the supervisors, who were more or less of the same social standing as the workers and the workers were cordial, it turned frosty with the new union being established and equations changing between the workers and the supervisors as a result.

## 2. Dependence on Contract and Casual Labour

The central government had identified the increasing reliance on contract and casual labour to get routine operational jobs done at cheaper costs, as the primary reason for the recent increase in labour strife and violence. This was done so that gratuity and provident fund benefits can be denied to these temporary workers. In the process the workers are losing out on many social security benefits which the company is committed to provide as per the labour laws of the country. Social security benefits are not reaching out to the casual workers and as a result this is leading to labour disputes and labour violence. They are victims of the system where the company is getting work out of them for half the wages. As per the Contract Labour (Regulation and Abolition) Act, 1971 if an organization has 100 or more permanent workers it has to seek the permission of the appropriate government in case it wishes to dismiss any permanent worker. Hence all the more it was easier to make do with contact labour where no questions would be asked if any of them were retrenched. These contract workers also have no job security and are denied benefits like gratuity, provident fund and health insurance. Necessary amendments to the Contract Labour (Regulation and Abolition) Act of 1971 where provisions for securing the rights of contract labourers have been identified have not yet seen the light of day. International Labour Office has recommended a nationally-determined social security floor for all workers, which is a comprehensive package consisting of medical aid, educational funds, old-age income security, gratuity, provident fund, etc. This has received support from India; it remains to be seen whether this can be put to practice in the form of a labour law by the Indian Parliament. The top demand of the Maruti union during this period of unrest related to contract workers. The union wanted higher wages for the contract labour and regularization of casual labour since they have strong ties of clan, caste and region with the permanent workers. A large number of them are related or have been employed through references from permanent workers to the labour contractors. But once on the shop floor they work together with very different terms and conditions and remuneration. After the violence the Chairman, Maruti Suzuki said that contract labour from contractors would be phased out and Maruti's own HR department would take in contract workers and give priority to them when permanent worker vacancies arise.

## 3. Fair Implementation of Labour Laws

The Gurgaon-Manesar-Dharuhera-Rewari belt in Haryana employs about 400,000 workers in about 1000 companies. Here a large number of companies have taken licences for contract labour but they are making the contract workers do work which should be done by the permanent workers. This violates provisions of the Contract Labour (Regulation and Abolition) Act, 1971. Minimum wages as per the Minimum Wages Act, 1948 are not being given, Employees State Insurance deductions and Provident Fund deductions are not being deposited – these are the grievances of the union leaders operating in the above belt. Maruti engages contractual workers and tries to ensure that they are paid at least the minimum wages by asking the contractor proof, which in turn allows the contractor to fudge. Workers' grievance is that the contractors bill the company more than what they pay the labourers and pocket the difference.

However Maruti's record of following labour guidelines and practices has been far from being remarkable. Strikes and unrest have been on the rise; the company has failed to maintain agreements signed with workers on the creation of the Works Committee as per The Industrial Disputes Act, 1948 and the Grievance Committee (*The Economic Times,* 6th August, 2012, p 03,). Following the strikes and unrest the management decided to introduce a 'good conduct bond' in August, 2011 wherein the workers would be promising to show good conduct during working hours.

## 4. Nature of Employment, Wages and Promotion

Recruitment of workers was done as apprentices or as contract workers. Apprentices would be paid half the salary of a contract worker of which as large portion was attached to his attendance and assigned to work as apprentice for a year. After a year the apprentice can apply for a contract worker's position which will depend largely on his performance which consists largely of his behavior – that is, whether he was a trouble maker, whether he has complained or asked questions or come late to work. If all is well he may be employed as a contract worker but he would do the same work. After a few years the contract worker can apply for the position of a permanent worker, where his past record would be looked at. To become permanent, a worker must become a trainee first, doing the same job. The technical trainee would then reach Level 1 (stay 3-5 years), then Level 2 (3-5 years) and so on till he reaches the last level. Criteria for promotion to these levels are "good behavior" and 95% attendance. After the agreement of September, 2012 the company said that those who became permanent workers will be initially be 'Company Trainees'(CT) for 2 years and work as CT1 and CT2, then would be promoted to Maruti Associate (MA) I,MA II,MA III after working at each level for 3 years. The MA I and MA II levels were not there earlier, so that now a worker would get promoted to MA III after 5 more years.

The composition of the workforce had changed recently. The workers comprise of fresh ITI apprentices, short term casual workers and helpers. Work which is of a perennial nature should be performed by the permanent workers as per the Contract Labour (Regulation and Abolition) Act, 1970. However at Manesar such work is being done by the contractual workers. Less than 25% of the workers were permanent at any point of time at Manesar. These contract workers are paid on a daily basis and do not get paid on the weekly leave i.e. Sunday. Also these workers had been employed as contract workers for four or more years hence it may be assumed that they were deliberately kept as contract workers so that wages and other benefits as eligible for permanent workers will not be required to be given. The wage gap between permanent and contractual workers is significant – the former get about Rs 29000/- – 30000/- per month whereas the latter gets between Rs 8000/- - 12000/- per month. These contract workers are neither given any appointment letter nor are there any time limit given for the contract period.

The contract workers were entitled to 2 days of leave per month but if they were absent beyond those two days they lost the entire incentive linked pay in one month (PUDR Report, 2013).

## RESULTANT EFFECTS OF THE STRIKE

Rising inventory, underused plants, idle workforce etc gave the vendors of spare parts and components sleepless nights. These vendors had invested more than Rs. 10000/- crores in capacity expansion in 2010-11 when car sales were growing by about 30%. 14 of these are joint venture companies setup exclusively for Maruti. They were allowed to supply to other car manufacturers' during the ongoing disturbances at

Maruti. However these vendors lost about 15-20% of their revenue or about Rs. 1400 crores during the ongoing dispute at Maruti Suzuki. These vendors were in a dilemma about whether to retain their temporary workforce, whether to give holidays to their permanent workers or whether to ask them to resign. Foreign car makers who source components from the Manesar auto belt were scared that the agitation could affect supplies. In order to de risk their business they were thinking of relocating to places like Gujarat, Rajasthan or even Thailand.

Scores of industries, including original equipment manufacturers (OEMs), component suppliers and other ancillary units spread out in the Gurgaon-Manesar belt are the life line of large manufacturers like Maruti Suzuki, Hero MotoCorp and Honda Motorcycles & Scooters India(HMSI).Some of these firms had called for an impartial enquiry into the recent violence at Maruti Suzuki's Manesar plant. They had the audacity to warn the law-enforcing authorities against harassing the Maruti workers. Their union leaders demanded fair implementation of labour laws by the companies operating in the region, housing facilities for workers and a rise in minimum wages of entry level workers from Rs 4850/- to Rs 15000/-. According to the General Secretary of Honda Motorcycle & Scooter India Employee Union, various companies were blatantly violating contract labour laws, not depositing provident fund and ESI of employees etc. Work done by the contract workers were actually the work assigned to the permanent workers.

The wage settlement at Maruti Suzuki, Manesar which expired in March 2012 was effective till a new settlement was put in place. The charter of demands of the Manesar union included the following (*The Economic Times,* 26th July, 2012, p 04,):

- Basic salary of at least Rs 25000/-
- All contract workers to be made permanent
- At least 20% annual hike till 2014 when the next agreement will be due
- D A of at least Rs 10000 a month
- HRA to be hiked to 60% of basic and DA
- Laundry allowance of Rs 3000 /-per month
- Child education allowance of Rs 8000/- a month
- Transport allowance of Rs 10000/-a month
- City compensatory allowance @ 40% of basic pay etc.

However the top demand of the union related to contract workers. The workers wanted higher wages and regularization of casual workers because even though the contract workers are not part of the union they have strong ties of clan, caste and region with the permanent workers. A large number of them are related or have been employed through references from permanent workers to labour contractors. But once on the shop floor they work alongside for very different terms and remuneration.

## MANAGERIAL IMPLICATIONS

Originally the six *darshanas* (six philosophical views) are *nyaya* (logic), *vaisesika* (atomic theory), *sankhya* (analysis of matter and spirit), *yoga* (the discipline of selfrealization), *karma-mimamsa* (science of fruitive work) and *vedanta* (science of God realization) were departments of study in a unified understanding of the *Veda*, comparable to the faculties of a modern university. But with the onset of Kali-yuga, the scholars of the *darshanas* became divided and contentious. Some even misrepresented

*Table 1. The agreement of September, 2012 resulted in the following increases in wages and other benefits:*

| Salary Component | Pre-Revision | Salary (in Rs.) After Revision |
|---|---|---|
| Basic Pay | 5150 | 8050 |
| Variable DA | | 133 |
| HRA | 1600 | 2200 |
| Uniform Maintenance | 260 | 2000 |
| Fixed DA | 250 | 1350 |
| Child Education Allowance | 200 | 200 |
| Shift Allowance | 525 | 250 |
| Conveyance Allowance | 1775 | 2000 |
| Special Allowance<br>Production Performance Reward | 583<br>8910 | 559<br>9350 |
| Additional Settlement Benefit | | 2000 |
| PPRS (In house spares) | | 3409 |
| TOTAL | 19253 | 31501 |

Vedic philosophy for their own selfish ends. *Nyaya* is predominantly based on reasoning and logic. It is a philosophy of life. *Karma* or action is viewed in the *vaisesika* school as being physical movement but the term physical here refers to more than just bodily movements because in *vaisesika* mind is also considered to be a kind of substance. Just like quality, the second category of reality, action also exists only in a substance. There are five kinds of action: upward, downward, inward, outward and linear. The action of perceptible substances like earth, water, fire, and air can be perceived by the five senses, but not all of the actions of tangible substances can be perceived.

The love and care which Maruti bestows on its customers is abundant but the same cannot be said with respect to its workers. Therein lies a history of coercion, denial of basic rights and the dehumanisation of labour by the company. The violent incident of July 2012 wherein the General Manager (HR) was killed was taken up by the management and the blame for the death was put squarely on the workers by the management. Actions taken by the management go against the grain of our Indian Constitution. The strong bondage which developed between the casual and the permanent workers speaks volumes of the democratic structures which were created among the workers. Management should take a lead from this and realize that unity is strength as enunciated in the idiom "United we stand divided we fall".

## CONCLUSION

Most of the Japanese companies in India are facing labour unrest – it has to be ascertained whether the reason is to do with the Japanese way of thinking which pushes workers limitlessly, with inflexible processes and uncaring attitude towards local nuances. According to Osama Suzuki, Chairman of Suzuki Motor Corporation cost reduction and improvement is a continuous process. However Japanese companies in India are nowhere near Japanese benchmarks on costs, shop-floor practices, the yen for hard work and perfection, discipline and consensual decision making. According to Soft bridge Solutions, a software and training company that handles Japanese companies and helps them bridge the socio-cultural abyss between Indians and Japanese, it is both to do with the peculiar Japanese way of thinking and the Indians inability to comprehend them. These Japanese firms invest a lot of money into our industries and if the market is capable of giving them these returns they will keep pushing relentlessly. This continuous improvement bore fruit in India as Maruti gained 50% of the market share. They could churn out light and fuel efficient cars by reducing the weight of car components every year. This fits into the continuous improvement framework of the Japanese. The Japanese abhor static situations hence are constantly trying to enhance intellectual property or increase profits for the parent company. If the Japanese are aware that the market is capable of giving them the required returns, they will keep on pushing relentlessly. The labour turmoil evident in most of the Japanese firms in India can be attributed to the punishing work ethic, unyielding deadlines, the widespread practice of unpaid overtime etc (*The Economic Times*, 27th March, 2014, p 14).

The same situation applied in India when Maruti Suzuki build a swanking new plant at Manesar. The workforce chosen were mostly the low cost, flexible options – of contractual workers hired through contractors. The Maruti management in Japan did not trouble to get acquainted with the local ethos and cultural mores. The young workers came from Haryanvi families and were placed in pressure cooker-like assembly line situations of high production efficiency. They stretched the idea of discipline to stupefying limits. Leave requests were disregarded, even toilet breaks were frowned upon. The typical Indian worker has high family ties and expects to be granted leave when he requests it. But the Japanese concept of strong family ties is shown by immersing oneself in work. The Suzuki management wanted the Manesar plant to be like the one in Kosai, Japan with all its best practices. But that fitting in did not happen as the Japanese had wanted it to. The diktat of churning out cars with high levels of attendance and discipline was resented by the Manesar workers since this coincided with a 25% spurt in demand for cars in India in 2011. A disaster was waiting to happen and it did happen in July, 2012 with the death of the HR manager.

Indian ethos is built upon Vedic knowledge which is called *apauruseya*, which means it is not knowledge of human invention. Vedic knowledge appeared at the dawn of the cosmos within the heart of Brahma. *Vaisesika,* one of the philosophical views of the Vedas engages the method of *nyaya* or logic in a deeper analysis of the predicament of material existence by showing that the visible material forms to which we are all so attached ultimately break down into invisible atoms. Through *yoga*, the soul awakens its innate spiritual vision to see itself beyond the body. *Karma-mimamsa* directs the soul to the goals of Vedic ritualism. The six systems of Vedic philosophy is itself a form of *yoga: jnana-yoga*, the *yoga* of theoretical knowledge. Indian ethos and culture breathes *yoga* in all activities. Interruptions occur when a foreign culture tries to envelope them and spread its tentacles over these ancient processes.

The above presented itself in the form of a communication gap or a listening gap between the Japanese management and the workers. The Japanese are afraid to interact with the Indian workers fearing that a wrong move will jeopardize their career and a recall to Japan. This in itself is a shameful thing for the Japanese who feel they cannot commit any mistake because of their Japanese upbringing. The Japanese spend an enormous amount of time in planning and seeking consensus on issues; but once this process is over they become very rigid and do not want to change anything as any change requires the same procedure followed earlier. Hence a Japanese Managing Director has very little leeway to act on his own even when situations outside the plan emerge; in this context he may be taken to be obstinate. The Japanese do not like to work with many variables as it impinges on quality.

The Japanese way of operating also gets a boost from the Indian managers – Indians are culturally attuned in such a way that they cannot say no to their bosses and just followed what the Japanese wanted. Since they are the interface to the Indian workers they too may be held responsible for the impasse in which the Japanese companies are in since whatever may be the ground realities Indian managers always say 'it can be done' (*The Economic Times*, 2014, 27th March, 2014, p 14,).

The *nyaya* system of philosophy has sixteen divisions of studying reality. To be free from bondage correct knowledge of the aforesaid divisions is necessary. *Samsaya* or "doubt" is the state in which the mind wavers between conflicting views regarding a single object. The mind becomes confused at that moment since *Samsaya* is not certain knowledge; neither is it a mere reflection of knowledge; nor is it invalid knowledge. The Indian managers worked under this state of mind at Maruti and gave in to the pressure tactics of the Japanese and allowed them to bully the Indians.

Most enterprises of today face conflicts, tensions, low efficiency and productivity, absence of motivation and lack of work culture etc. For them the underlying purpose in developing a strategy is to outperform the competitors over a sustained time period. Organizations today have realized that that they need to present a more positive image to the public and manage their human resources efficiently and carry out business so as not to harm others. Successful management means managing men, money and material in the best possible way according to circumstances and environment. In order to get an edge over their competitors Maruti Suzuki tried to enhance the productivity of its workers with Taylorian (Taylor, 1911) concepts of scientific management principles, leading to disastrous results. Such a sustainable competitive advantage cannot be achieved through operational effectiveness alone; a winning strategy considering the cultural, social and economic aspects need to be determined. Such a strategic plan requires tough managerial choices from among numerous good alternatives. The case study highlights that such decisions were taken but, at a much later date and somewhere along the way the leadership faltered when it could not match the cultural and social nuances of the Japanese with the Indian ethos. Vyasa's Vedanta-sutra talks about logic, discipline of self-realization, science of fruitive work and science of God-realization among other things - jnana and vijnana. If these philosophical views had any bearing on the work atmosphere of Maruti Suzuki India, the situation may have been drastically different.

## REFERENCES

Appa Rao, C., Rao Parvathiswara, B., & Sivaramakrishna, K. (2008). Strategic Management and Business Policy. New Delhi: Excel Books.

Banerjee, P. B. (2005). *Foundations of Ethics in Management*. New Delhi: Excel Books.

Bhargava, R.C., & Seetha. (2010). *The Maruti Story: How a Public Sector Company put India on Wheels*. Noida: Collins Business, an Imprint of HarperCollins Publishers.

Butler, J. (1729). *Fifteen Sermons Preached at the Rolls Chapel*. London: J and J Knapton.

Contract Labour (Regulation and Abolition) Act. (1971). *Indian Parliament at New Delhi Cumberland Richard (1672). De Legibus Naturare*. London: Ashgate Publishing Limited.

*Descartes Rene (1637). Discours de la méthode (Discourse on the Method). An introduction to the Essais, which include the Dioptrique, the Météores and the Géométrie. Discourse on the Method, Part IV.* (1998). 3rd ed.Cress, D. A., Trans.). Indianapolis: Hackett.

Hutcheson, F. (1725). *Inquiry into the Original of our Ideas of Beauty and Virtue*. Dublin: J. and J. Knapton.

Industrial Disputes Act, 1947. Citation: Act No. 14 of 1947; Enacted by Central Legislative Assembly, Government of India on 11 March 1947 and commenced on 1 April 1947. Indian Parliament at New Delhi

Jitatmananda, S. (2006). *Modern Physics and Vedanta*. Mumbai: Bharatiya Vidya Bhavan.

Laertius, Diogenes. (3 B. C.). *Lives of Eminent Philosopher.* Cambridge, MA: Harvard University Press.

Mehri, D. (2005). *Notes from Toyota-Land: An American Engineer in Japan*. Ithaca, NY: Cornell University Press, xviii.

Minimum Wages Act, 1948. Citation Act No. 11 of 1948 of the Government of India, enacted by the Parliament of India; date of commencement: 15th March 1948. Indian Parliament at New Delhi

Mintzberg, H. (1973). Strategy-Making in Three Modes. California Management Review.

People's Union for Democratic Rights Report. (2013). *Driving force- Labour Struggles and Violation of Rights in Maruti Suzuki India Limited*. Delhi: Secretary, People's Union for Democratic Rights.

Shaftesbury. (1711). Inquiry concerning Virtue and Merit. In *Characteristics of Men, Manners, Opinions, Times*. Oxford, UK: Oxford UP.

Suhotra Swami Ṣad-darśanam. (1997). *The Six Systems of Vedic Philosophies.* Mayapur: Bhaktivedanta Academy.

Taylor Fredrich Winslow. (1911).The Principles of Scientific Management. New York: Harper & Brothers.

Vasishth, N., & Rajput, N. (2012). *Business Ethics and Values*. New Delhi: Taxman's Publications Pvt. Ltd.

Wheelen, T. L., Hunger, D. J., & Rangarajan, K. (2010). Strategic Management and Business Policy. Noida, New Delhi: Dorling Kindersley (India) Pvt. Ltd, licensees of Pearson Education in South Asia.

## KEY TERMS AND DEFINITIONS

**Apurva:** Or force left behind after karma which gives reward consistent with one's karma.
**Artha:** Or wealth.
**Darshanas:** Or perspectives.
**Dharma:** Or one's ideology for living one's life.
**Kama:** Or sensual pleasure.
**Karma:** Or performance in one's lifetime.
**Karma-mimamsa:** Is the science of fruitive work.
**Mimamsa:** Is to understand and analyse thoroughly.

**Nyaya:** System of philosophy is concerned with the conditions of correct knowledge and the means of receiving this knowledge and is predominantly based on reasoning and logic.

**Prameya:** May be translated as "that which is knowable or the object of true Knowledge.

**Sad-Darshana:** Are six branches of theoretical dialectics.

**Sankhya:** Or analysis of matter and spirit.

**Vaisesika:** Or atomic theory.

**Vak-Shakti:** Refers to thought and expression.

**Vedanta:** Or science of God realization.

**Yoga:** Or the discipline of self-realization.

# Compilation of References


Abrahams. (2010). Technology adoption in higher education: a framework for identifying and prioritising issues and barriers to adoption of instructional technology. *Journal of Applied Research in Higher Education, 2*(2), 34 – 49.

Adelman, I., & Chenery, H. (1966). Foreign Aid & Economic Development: The Case of Greece. *The Review of Economics and Statistics, 48*(1), 1–19. doi:10.2307/1924853

*Adhar card.* (2014). Retrieved from, http:/www.uidai.gov.in

*Advantages of Gasification.* (2010). Retrieved September 22, 2014, from US Department of Energy: http://www.netl.doe.gov/research/coal/energy-systems/gasification/gasifipedia/Advantage-of-Gasification

Agarwal, M. D. (2012). Online banking services: An empirical study of banker's and customer's awareness about obs. *Journal of Exclusive Management Science, 1*(7), 25–35.

Agarwal, R. (2013). CSR for Sustainable livelihood. *CSR Mandate, 1*(June – July), 46–49.

Agarwal, R. (2013). Sustainable Livelihood Options through Training in Handicrafts: A Study of Primitive Tribal Groups in Jharkhand. CRICKET, Centre for Research for Rural Innovation, Capacity Building, Knowledge Management, Entrepreneurship and Technology, IMT Ghaziabad.

*Agriculture community.* (2014). Retrieved from http://data.gov.in/community/agriculture-community/blog/national-agricultural-innovation-project

Ali, A. (2003). Faculty adoption of technology: Training comes first. *Educational Technology, 43*(2), 51–53.

Allee, V. (1997). *The Knowledge Evolution, Expanding Organizational Intelligence.* Boston: Butterworth Heinemenn Publication.

Amiel, T., & Reeves, T. C. (2008). Design-based research and educational technology: Rethinking technology and the research agenda. *Journal of Educational Technology & Society, 11*(4), 29–40.

Ananth, B. (2013, October 17). *How much do rural bank branches cost the financial sector?* Retrieved October 17, 2013 from Forbes India: http://forbesindia.com/blog/economy-policy/how-much-do-rural-bank-branches-cost-the-financial-sector/

*Annual Report of State Bank of India 2011-2012.* (n.d.). Retrieved from http://www.sbigroup.co.jp/english/investors/library/filings/pdf/2012_en.pdf

Anupindi, R., Chopra, S., Deshmikh, S., Mieghem, J., & Zemel, E. (2004). *Managing business process flows.* New Delhi: Pearson Education.

Anzoategui, D., Demirguc-Kunt, A., & Peria, M. S. (2011, October). *Remittances and Financial Inclusion: Evidence from El Salvador.* Retrieved May 9, 2014 from World Bank Policy Research Working Paper: http://elibrary.worldbank.org/doi/pdf/10.1596/1813-9450-5839

Appa Rao, C., Rao Parvathiswara, B., & Sivaramakrishna, K. (2008). Strategic Management and Business Policy. New Delhi: Excel Books.

Ashton, C., & Morton, L. (2005). Managing talent for competitive advantage: Taking a systemic approach to talent management]. *Strategic HR Review, 4*(5), 28–31. doi:10.1108/14754390580000819

Authority, C. E. Ministry of Power, Government of India. (2013, October 31). *Progress report of village electrification as on 31-10-2013.* Retrieved Dec 2013, from Central Electricity Authority, Ministry of Power, Government of India: http://www.cea.nic.in/reports/monthly/dpd_div_rep/village_electrification.pdf

Awad, E., & Ghaziri, H. (2004). *Knowledge Management.* Singapore: Pearson Education International.

Awofeso, N., & Rammohan, A. (2011). Three Decades of the Integrated Child Development Services Program in India: Progress and Problems. Health Management - Different Approaches and Solutions. doi:10.5772/19871

Axis Bank. (2013, October 17). *Rural Banking Initiatives.* Retrieved October 17, 2013 from Axis Bank Microfinance and Rural Banking: http://www.axisbank.com/agri-rural/microfinance/rural-banking-initiative/rural.aspx

Babu, S. C. (2011). *Farmers' information needs and search behaviours: Case study in Tamil Nadu, India.* International Food Policy Research Institute. Retrieved October 7, 2013, from http://www.ifpri.org/sites/default/files/publications/ifpridp01165.pdf

Bachhav, N. B. (2012). Information Needs of the Rural Farmers: A Study from Maharashtra, India: A Survey. *Library Philosophy and Practice (e-journal).* Paper 866. Retrieved October 7, 2013 from http://digitalcommons.unl.edu/libphilprac/866

Balasubramanyam, V. N. (2003). *Foreign Direct Investment in India.* Lancaster University Management School, Working Paper, 2003/001

Banerjee, P. B. (2005). *Foundations of Ethics in Management.* New Delhi: Excel Books.

Bansal, P., Maan, V. K., & Rajora, M. (2013). Article. *International Journal for Advanced Research in Computer Science and Software Engineering, 3*(11).

Bergen, I. A. (2013). Selling Solar Power in India's Slums. *The Atlantic Cities.* Retrieved September, 24, 2013 from http://www.theatlanticcities.com/jobs-and-economy/2013/04/selling-solar-power-indias-slums/5153/

Besson, L., & Carot, D. (Producers), Bertrand, Y.A. (Director). (2009). *Home* [Motion picture]. United States: Elzevir Films Sub-District Details. (n.d.). Retrieved December 24, 2013, from http://censusindia.gov.in/PopulationFinder/Sub_Districts_Master.aspx?state_code=09&district_code=07

*Best Engaging Communities.* (2012, September). Retrieved October 15, 2013, from Best Engaging Communities: http://beaforceofgood.files.wordpress.com/2012/09/snippets_product-startup-landscape-in-india_2012.pdf

Bhargava, R.C., & Seetha. (2010). *The Maruti Story: How a Public Sector Company put India on Wheels.* Noida: Collins Business, an Imprint of HarperCollins Publishers.

Bhaskar, P. V. (2013). *Financial Inclusion in India - An Assessment.* MFIN and Access-Assist Summit.

Bhatnagar, J. (2007). Talent management strategy of employee engagement in Indian ITES employees: Key to retention. *Employee Relations, 29*(6), 640–663. doi:10.1108/01425450710826122

Bhatnagar, S. C. (2004). *E-Government: From Vision to Implementation – A Practical Guide with Case Studies.* New Delhi: SAGE Publications Pvt. Ltd.

Bhatti, Y. A. (2012). *What is Frugal, What is innovation? Towards a Theory of Frugal Innovation. Said Business School, Oxford Centre for Entrepreneurship and Innovation.* Oxford, UK: University of Oxford.

*Bioenergy Technologies Office.* (2013). Retrieved October 1, 2013, from Office of Energy Efficiency and Renewable Energy: http://www1.eere.energy.gov/biomass/large_scale_gasification.html

*Biomass Gasification* . (2011). Retrieved September 22, 2014, from http://www.netl.doe.gov/research/coal/energy-systems/gasification/gasifipedia/Advantage-of-Gasification

Birnie, S., & Horvath, P. (2002). Psychological predictors of Internet social communication. *Journal of Computer-Mediated Communication, 7*(4). Retrieved from http://jcmc.indiana.edu/vol7/issue4/horvath.html

Birt, M., Wallis, T., & Winternitz, G. (2004). Talent retention in a changing workplace: an investigation of variables considered important to South African talent. *South African Journal of Business Management*, *35*(2), 25-31.

Blank, S. (2013, May). Why the Lean Start-up Changes Everything. *Harvard Business Review*, 3–9.

Bolis, I., Brunoro, C., & Sznelwar, L. (2012). The workers role in knowledge management and sustainability policies. *Work (Reading, Mass.)*, *41*(1), 2713–2720. PMID:22317131

Bradley, A., & McDonald, M. (2011). *The social organization: How to use social media to tap the collective genius of your customers and employees*. Boston: Harvard Business Press.

Butler, J. (1729). *Fifteen Sermons Preached at the Rolls Chapel*. London: J and J Knapton.

Cardamine, J. R. (n.d.). Retrieved October 15, 2013, from www.entrepreneur.com: http://www.entrepreneur.com/article/200102

Census of India. (2011). *Vital Statistics*. Retrieved 13 December, 2012, from http://www.censusindia.gov.in/2011-common/vitalstatistics.html

Central Statistical Organization (CSO). (n.d.). *Database*. Retrieved from http://www.cso.ie/en/databases/index.html

*Centre for Monitoring Indian Economy*. (n.d.). Retrieved from www.cmie.com

Cervera, R. (n.d.). *Knowledge Process Management*. Retrieved March 10, 2013, from http://hosteddocs.ittoolbox.com/LC071805.pdf

Chakrabarty, K. (2011, November). Financial Inclusion and Banks: Issues and Perspectives. *RBI Monthly Bulletin*, 1831-1838.

Chandoevwit, W. (2003). Thailand's Grass Roots Policies, *TDRI. The Quarterly Review*, *18*(2), 3–8.

Chandra, K. K. (2011, june 3). *The Weekend Leader*. Retrieved from http://www.theweekendleader.com/Innovation/515/Illuminating-villages.html

Chantal, O., Plessis, D., & Yvonne. (2012). *Psychological Ownership: A Managerial Construct for Talent Retention and Organizational Effectiveness*. Academic Press.

Chauhan, C. (2013, February 22). *Indoor air pollution kills a million people every year in India*. Retrieved October 8, 2013, from Hindustan Times: http://www.hindustantimes.com/India-news/NewDelhi/Indoor-air-pollution-kills-a-million-people-every-year-in-India/Article1-1015749.aspx

Chouhan, R. S., Kumar, Dushyant, & Sharma, H O (2011). Performance of Kisan Call Center: A Case Study of Kisan Call Center of Indian Society of Agribusiness Professionals Bhopal (Madhya Pradesh). *Indian Journal of Agricultural Economics*. Retrieved October 9, 2013, from http://search.proquest.com/docview/912670940?accountid=50136

Christabell, P. J., & Vimal, R. A. (2012). Financial Inclusion in Rural India: The role of Microfinance as a tool. *IOSR Journal of Humanities and Social Science (JHSS)*, *2*(5), 21-25.

Chungsangunsit, T., Gheewala, S. H., & Patumsawad, S. (n.d.). *Emission Assessment of Rice Husk Combustion*.

CIO. (2012). *Green Crusader Awards - Schneider Electric*. Retrieved from http://www.cio.in/cio100-2012/special-awards-green-crusader

*Classroom Technology Reference Guide. EdTech Magazine by CDW-G*. (2013). Retrieved December 20, 2013 from http://www.edtechmagazine.com/higher/sites/edtechmagazine.com.higher/files/041713_rg_g_classroomtech_121833.pdf

Claymone, Y., & Jaiborisudhi, W. (2011). A study on one village one product project (OVOP) in Japan and Thailand as an alternative of community development in Indonesia. *The International Journal of East Asian Studies*, *16*(1), 51–60.

Clayton, G. (2006). Key skills retention and motivation: The war for talent still rages and retention is the high ground. *Industrial and Commercial Training*, *38*(1), 37–45. doi:10.1108/00197850610646034

Collier, U. (2013). *Reducing the UK's Carbon Footprint*. Retrieved from http://www.theccc.org.uk/wp-content/uploads/2013/04/Reducing-carbon-footprint-report.pdf

COM. M. (n.d.). *Guide to good dairy farming practice.* Retrieved September 10, 2014 from http://www.milkproduction.com/Library/Editorial-articles/Guide-to-good-dairy-farming-practice/

Commission, P. (2001). Organic Farming and Biodynamic Farming for the 10th Five-year plan. New Delhi: Government of India. Retrieved from planningcommission.nic.in/aboutus/committee/wrkgrp/wg_organic.pdf

Company's Act. (2013). *Corporate Social Responsibility.* Retrieved on 5 January 2015 from www.mca.gov.in/Ministry/pdf/CompaniesAct2013.pdf

Contract Labour (Regulation and Abolition) Act. (1971). *Indian Parliament at New Delhi Cumberland Richard (1672). De Legibus Naturare.* London: Ashgate Publishing Limited.

Crumpton, M. A. (2012). Innovation and entrepreneurship. *The Bottom Line: Managing Library Finances, 25*(3), 98 - 101.

D'Amato, A., & Herzfeldt, R. (1986). Learning orientation, organizational commitment and talent retention across generations: A study of European managers. *Journal of Managerial Psychology, 23*(8), 929–953.

Dangi, N., & Kumar, P. (2013). Current Situation of Financial Inclusion in India and Its Future Visions. *International Journal of Management and Social Sciences Research, 2*(8).

Darnton, G., & Darnton, M. (1997). *Business Process Analysis.* Boston: International Thompson Business Press.

Davenport, T. (2005). *Thinking for a Living: How to get better Performance and Results from Knowledge Workers.* Boston: Harvard Business Press.

David, H., & Ann, M. (2008). Making knowledge workers more creative. *Research Technology Management, 51*(2), 40–46.

Deery, M. (2008). Talent management, work-life balance and retention strategies. *International Journal of Contemporary Hospitality Management, 20*(7), 792–806.

Denpaiboon, C., & Amatasawatdee, C. (2012). Similarity and difference of one village one product (OVOP) for rural development strategy in Japan and Thailand. *Japanese Studies Journal.*

Department for Environment Food and Rural Affairs. Govt. of UK. (2013). Forecasting 2020 Waste Arisings and Treatment Capacity: Published October 2013, London: Author.

Department of Animal Husbandry. Dairying & Fisheries, Ministry of Agriculture, GoI. (1995-2015). *Milk Production in India.* Retrieved October 12,2014 from http://www.nddb.org/English/Statistics/Pages/Milk-Production.aspx

Department of Health. Govt. of UK. (2014). *Healthy Child Program.* Retrieved September 23, 2014 from https://www.gov.uk/government/publications/healthy-child-programme-pregnancy-and-the-first-5-years-of-life

*Department of Industrial Policy and Promotion, Government of India.* (n.d.). Retrieved June 28, 2010, from www.dipp.ac.in

*Descartes Rene (1637). Discours de la méthode (Discourse on the Method). An introduction to the Essais, which include the Dioptrique, the Météores and the Géométrie. Discourse on the Method, Part IV.* (1998). 3rd ed.Cress, D. A., Trans.). Indianapolis: Hackett.

Dhyani, S. (n.d.). *BPO Caretel announced the achievements of their "Kisan Call Center" project As Kisan Call Center completes its successful 5th Year.* Retrieved October 10, 2013 from http://www.indiaprwire.com/pressrelease/agriculture/20090117l8157.pdf

Dillihaat. (2014). *History of Dilli Haat.* Retrieved 14 November, 2014, from http://www.dillihaat.net.in/

Directorate of Advertising and Visual Publicity (DAVP) for the Ministry of Women and Child Development, Government of India. (2013) *IEC (Information, Education and Communication) Campaign against Malnutrition.* Retrieved October 12, 2013 from http://poshan.nic.in/jspui/index.html

Dixon, J. (1996). Uses and gratifications theory to predict use of computer-mediated communications. *International Journal of Educational Telecommunications*, *2*(1), 3–27.

Drucker, P. (2007). *Management Challenges for the 21st century*. Oxford: Butterworth-Heinemenn Publication.

Dutta, S. (2010). Community Radio: Revenue Structure and Possibilities in India. *Global Media Journal*, 1-1. Retrieved December 25, 2013, from http://www.caluniv.ac.in/Global mdia journal/Commentaries-june-2010/soumya datta.pdf

Dutta, S., & Manzoni, J. (1999). *Process Re-engineering, Organizational Change and Performance Improvement*. London: McGraw-Hill Publishing Company.

*Echoupal , I. T. C.* (n.d.). Retrieved 2 July 2014 from https://www.echoupal.com/)

*EcoSeed*. (n.d.). Retrieved December 25, 2013, from http://www.ecoseed.org/renewables/16922-why-energy-storage-is-important-for-micro-grids-in-india problems of micro grid

Eden Project. (2013, August). *What's your Carbon footprint?* Retrieved from http://www.edenproject.com/whats-it-all-about/climate-and-environment/online-tools/whats-your-carbon-footprint

Fagerberg. (2006). *Innovation, technology and the global knowledge economy: Challenges for future growth*. Paper presented at the "Green roads to growth" conference, Environmental Assessment Institute, Copenhagen, Denmark.

Fahmy, M. (2004). Thinking about technology effects on higher education. *The Journal of Technology Studies*, *33*(1), 53–58.

Farndale, E., Scullion, H., & Sparrow, P. (2010). The role of the corporate HR function in global talent management. *Journal of World Business*, *45*(2), 161–168. doi:10.1016/j.jwb.2009.09.012

Faust, K., & Wasserman, S. (1994). *Social Network Analysis*. New York, NY: Cambridge University Press.

Feeds and Feeding Practices in Dairy Animals. (n.d.). *Thread: Feeds and Feeding Practices in Dairy Animals*. Retrieved September 21, 2014 from http://www.agriculturereinformation.com/forums/consultancy-services/60410-feeds-feeding-practices-dairy-animals.html

Financial Action Task Force. (2013, October). *The Role of Hawala and other similar service providers in money laundering and terrorist financing*. Retrieved May 10, 2014 from http://www.fatf-gafi.org/media/fatf/documents/reports/Role-of-hawala-and-similar-in-ml-tf.pdf

Flynn, M., Doodley, L., & Cormican, K. (2003). Idea management for organizational innovation. *International Journal of Innovation Management*, *7*(4), 417–442. doi:10.1142/S1363919603000878

*Frequently Asked Questions about Smart Microgrids*. (n.d.). Retrieved December 25, 2013, from http://galvinpower.org/resources/microgrid-hub/smart-microgrids-faq/

Freya, R. (2013, November). *5 Facts about Europe's Carbon Emissions*. Retrieved from http://www.carbonbrief.org/blog/2013/11/5-facts-about-europes-carbon-emissions/

*Frugal Entrepreneurship Survey*. (n.d.). Retrieved September 9, 2013, from Inc.com: http://www.inc.com/articles/1999/11/15720.html

Ganesh, J. (2013). *Data on Indian Slums, Searchlight South Asia*. Retrieved October, 01, 2013 from http://urbanpoverty.intellecap.com/?p=879

Gartner, W. B. (1985). *A Conceptual Framework for Describing the Phenomenon of New Venture Creation*. Academic Press.

Gatlin-Watts, R., Arn, J., & Kordsmeier, W. (1999). Multimedia as an instructional tool: Perceptions of college department chairs. *Education*, *120*(1), 190.

George Kuepper, Kerr Centre for Sustainable Agriculture. (2010). *A brief overview of the History & Philosophy of Organic agriculture*. Retrieved from http://www.kerrcenter.com/publications/organic-philosophy-report.pdf

Ghosh, N. (2012, June). Biogas Production and Power Generation Simulation: Research & Training in Perspective. *E Newsletter of Biogas Forum – India*, 3. Retrieved August 15, 2014, from http://web.iitd.ac.in/~vkvijay/June%202012_Enewsletter.pdf

Global Carbon Atlas. (2013). *Global Carbon Project*. Retrieved from http://www.globalcarbonatlas.org/?q=outreach

GOI. (2007). *Scheme Of Development Of Primitive Tribal Groups (PTGs), F.NO.22040/58/2007-NGO*. Government of India.

Goldena, R., & Min, S. (2012). *Theft and Loss of Electricity in an Indian State*. Retrieved September, 14, 2013 from http://www.theigc.org/sites/default/files/Golden%20and%20Min_Electricity%20theft.pdf

Goswami, B. (2007). *Can Indian Dairy Cooperatives Survive in the New Economic Order? Session on Supply Management in Support of Rural Livelihoods under the WTO in Forum for Biotechnology & Food Security*. Retrieved October 10,2014 from www.wto.org/english/forums_e/public_forum2007_e/session11_goswami_e.pdf

*Governments schemes*. (2012). Retrieved from http://yojana.gov.in/CMS/(S(y4dqrc55g1m1qhnd4soqih45))/pdf/Kurukshetra/English/2012/January.pdf

Govindarao. (1980). Utilization of rice husk-preliminary analysis. *J. Science Industrial Research*, 495-515.

Grayson, T. (2013). Eco Etiquette: How Green Are Solar Panels? *Huffington Post*. Retrieved October, 11, 2013 from http://www.huffingtonpost.com/jennifer-grayson/eco-etiquette-how-green-a_b_554717.html

GreenPeace India. (2010, October). Empowering Bihar. In *Case studies for bridging the energy deficit and driving change*. GreenPeace India Society.

Gupta, M. L. (2012). *Garg Rekha*. Problems & Prospects of Agricultural Exports in the Emerging Scenario.

*Gyandoot: The Purveyor of Knowledge*. (2014). Retrieved from http://gyandoot.nic.in/

Harris, R. (1997). Teaching, learning and information technology: Attitudes towards computers among Hong Kong's faculty. *Journal of Computing in Higher Education*, *9*(2), 89–114. doi:10.1007/BF02948780

Hay, M. (2002). Strategies for survival in the war of talent. *Career Development International*, *7*(1), 52–55. doi:10.1108/13620430210414883

Haythornthwaite, C., & Wellman, B. (1998). Work, friendship and media use for information exchange in a networked organization. *Journal of the American Society for Information Science*, *49*(12), 1101–1114. doi:10.1002/(SICI)1097-4571(1998)49:12<1101::AID-ASI6>3.0.CO;2-Z

Haythornwaite, C. (2001). The Internet in everyday life. *The American Behavioral Scientist*, *45*(3), 363–384. doi:10.1177/00027640121957240

*HDFC Bank launches 'Project Jharkhand' – an IT enabled Financial Inclusion program*. (n.d.). Retrieved from http://www.hdfcbank.com/htdocs/common/pdf/Project_Jharkhand.pdf

Heather, A. (2003). Building a workplace of choice: Using the work environment to attract and retain top talent. *Journal of Facilities Management*, *2*(3), 244–257. doi:10.1108/14725960410808230

Hughes, J., & Rog, E. (2008). Talent management: A strategy for improving employee recruitment, retention and engagement within hospitality organizations. *International Journal of Contemporary Hospitality Management*, *20*(7), 743–757. doi:10.1108/09596110810899086

Husk Power System. (2013). *Our Solution*. Retrieved 2013, from Husk Power Systems: http://www.huskpowersystems.com/innerPage.php?pageT=Our%20Solution&page_id=77

Hutcheson, F. (1725). *Inquiry into the Original of our Ideas of Beauty and Virtue*. Dublin: J. and J. Knapton.

ICICI Bank. (2013, October 17). *Self Help Groups*. Retrieved October 17, 2013 from ICICI Bank Rural Banking: http://www.icicibank.com/rural/microbanking/shg.html

*IFFCO Kisan Sanchar Ltd*. (n.d.). Retrieved February 12, 2014, from http://www.iksl.in/

iKure. (2014). *Solar Soldiers*. Retrieved from http:/www.ikuretechsoft.com

*India Innovation*. (2014). Retrieved from http:/www.IndiaInnovationPortalDecadeofInnovation2010-20.com

*India: Issues and Priorities for Agriculture*. (2012). Retrieved October 7, 2013, from http://www.worldbank.org/en/news/feature/2012/05/17/india-agriculture-issues-priorities

Indian Agribusiness Systems Private Limited. (2013). *Agriwatch*. Retrieved 2013, from http://www.agriwatch.com/grains/rice/

*Indian Rural Water Supply*. (2014) Retrieved from, http:/www.worldbank.org/projects/.../india-rural-water-supply-sanitation-project

Indian Sanitation Portal. (2013), *Waste management*. Retrieved September 29, 2013, from website: http://indiasanitationportal.org/34

IndiaStat. (2013) *Prevalence of anaemia in various age groups of women and young children in India: Ministry of Health and Family Welfare, Govt. of India*. Retrieved October 12, 2013 from www.indiastat.com

IndiaStat. (2013) *State wise percentage of underweight children in urban and rural areas of India as of 2006: Lok Sabha Unstarred Question No. 4481, dated on 07.09.2012*. Retrieved October 12, 2013 from www.indiastat.com

IndiaStat. (2013). *State wise number of malnourished children as of 2011: Report of the Comptroller and Auditor General of India (14212)*. Retrieved October 12, 2013 from www.indiastat.com

Industrial Disputes Act, 1947. Citation: Act No. 14 of 1947; Enacted by Central Legislative Assembly, Government of India on 11 March 1947 and commenced on 1 April 1947. Indian Parliament at New Delhi

Infosys Finacle. (2012). *Measures for achieving financial inclusion in India*. Retrieved May 10, 2014 from http://www.infosys.com/finacle/solutions/thought-papers/Documents/measures-for-achieving.pdf

*Innovation*. (n.d.). Retrieved from) http:/www. Business-dictionary.com

International Business Machines. (2007). *Cutting the Carbon Footprint of IT*. Retrieved from http://www-05.ibm.com/innovation/uk/green/pdf/SOLUTION_IT_cutting_the_carbon_footprint_of_it.pdf

Jaiborisudhi, W. (2011). OVOP Network toward in East Asia and a Case study in Thailand: The authority between the government and the general public. *The International Journal of East Asian Studies*, *16*(1), 14–18.

Jefferies, P., & Hussain, F. (1998). Using the internet as teaching resource. *Education + Training*, *40*(8), 359–365. doi:10.1108/00400919810239400

Jeswani, S. & Sarkar, S. (2008). Integrating Talent Engagement as a Strategy to High Performance and Retention. *Asia pacific Journal of Management Research & Innovation*, *4*(4), 14-23.

Jitatmananda, S. (2006). *Modern Physics and Vedanta*. Mumbai: Bharatiya Vidya Bhavan.

Joint Research Centre, European Commission. (2007). *Carbon Footprint - what it is and how to measure it*. Retrieved from http://www.envirocentre.ie/includes/documents/Carbon_Footprint-what_it_is_and_how_to_measure_it-JRC_IES-Feb09-b[1].pdf

Judith, D. (2007). Signals in Social Supernets. *Journal of Computer-Mediated Communication*, *13*(1), 231–251. doi:10.1111/j.1083-6101.2007.00394.x

Kählig, C. (2011). *Facilitating Opportunity Development: Increasing Understanding of the Lean Startup Approach in Early Stage High-Tech Entrepreneurship*. Academic Press.

Kalam, A. P. J. A., & Singh, S. P. (2011). *Target 3 Billion*. Delhi: Penguin Publishers.

Kaoru, N., Kunio, I., Aree, W., Aree, C., Sombat, S., & John, T. (2011). One Village One Product - Rural Development Strategy In Asia: The Case Of OTOP In Thailand. *RCAPS Working Paper (11)*.

Karki, B. B. (2012). Doing business and role of government for entrepreneurship development. *Journal of Nepalese Business Studies*, *7*(1), 53–62.

Kaur, G. (2013). Sustainable Development in Agriculture & Green Farming In India. *Oida International Journal of Sustainable Development*, *6*(12), 59–64.

Kaur, G. (2014). Sustainable Development in Agriculture & Green Farming in India. *Oida International Journal Of Sustainable Development*, *7*(3), 59–64.

Kazuhiro, T. (2009). *Keizai Kaihatsu Seisaku Ron*. Tokyo, Japan: Kyoto University Press.

*KCC: Features, Directorate of Extension*. (n.d.). Retrieved October 10, 2013, from http://vistar.nic.in/training/locations.asp

Kessler, D. (1998). *Knowledge workers revealed: New challenges for Asia*. Hong Kong: Economic Intelligence Unit.

Kim, J., Gil, Y., & Spraragen, M. (2012). Principles for interactive acquisition and validation of workflows. *Journal of Experimental and Theoretical Artificial Intelligence, 22*(2), 103–134-103–134.

Kimball, L., & Rheingold, H. (2003). *How Online Social Networks Benefit Organizations*. Retrieved April 8, 2011, from www.groupjazz.com

Kirton, M. (1976). Adaptors and innovators: A description and measure. *The Journal of Applied Psychology, 61*(5), 622–629. doi:10.1037/0021-9010.61.5.622

*Kisan Call Center*. (n.d.). Retrieved May 5, 2013, from http://agricoop.nic.in/policyincentives/kisancalldetail.htm

Kotler, P., Keller, K. L., Brady, M., & Goodman, M. (2009). *Marketing Management* (2nd ed.). New York: Pearson Education.

Krentler, K. A., & Willis-Flurry, L. A. (2005). Does technology enhance actual student learning? The case of online discussion boards. *Journal of Education for Business, 80*(6), 316–321. doi:10.3200/JOEB.80.6.316-321

Krishna Reddy, P., & Ankaiah, R. (n.d.). *A framework of information technology-based agriculture information dissemination system to improve crop productivity*. Ministry of Communications and Information Technology, Department of Information Technology, New Delhi, India. Retrieved May 17, 2014, from http://www.currentscience.ac.in/php/toc.php?vol=088&issue=12

Kuhonta, E. M. (2004). The political economy of equitable development in Thailand. *The American Asian Review, 21*(4), 69–108.

Kumar, R., & Jhunjhunwala, A. (2002). *Taking Internet to Village: A case study of Project at Madurai Region*. TeNeT Group of IIT Madras.

Kumar, N. (1994). *Multinational Enterprises & Industrial Organization: The Case of India*. New Delhi, India: Sage Publications.

Kurokawa, K., Tembo, F., & Velde, D. W. T. (2010). Challenges for the OVOP movement in Sub-Saharan Africa-Insights from Malawi, Japan and Thailand. *JICA-RI Working Paper (18)*.

Laertius, Diogenes. (3 B. C.). *Lives of Eminent Philosopher*. Cambridge, MA: Harvard University Press.

Lawrence, A., & Weber, J. (2012). Business and Society: Stakeholders, Ethics, Public Policy. New Delhi: McGraw Hill Education (India Pvt Ltd.).

LBM Direct Marketing Ltd. (2008, June 1). *Carbon Footprint Profile*. Retrieved from http://www.lbm.co.uk/Public/content/about/LBM%20Carbon%20Footprint%20report.pdf

Lee, S. Y., Florida, R., & Gates, G. (2002). *Innovation, human capital, and creativity*. Working paper, Software Industry Centre, Carnegie Mellon University, Pittsburgh, PA.

Lee, S. Y., Florida, R., & Acs, Z. J. (2004). Creativity and entrepreneurship: A regional analysis of new firm formation. *Regional Studies, 38*(8), 879–891. doi:10.1080/0034340042000280910

Leidner, D. E. & Jarvenpaa, S. L. (1995). The Use of Information Technology to Enhance Management School Education: A Theoretical View. *MIS Quarterly, 19*(3), 265-291.

Lewis, K. (2004). Knowledge and Performance in Knowledge-Worker Teams: A Longitudinal Study of Transactive Memory Systems. *Management Science, 50*(11), 1519–1533. doi:10.1287/mnsc.1040.0257

Lussier, R., & Sherman, H. (2014). *Business, Society and Government Essentials: Strategy and Applied Ethics* (2nd ed.). Routledge Publications.

Mahajan, V., & Ramola, B. (2013, September 03). *Financial Services for the Rural Poor and Women in India: Access and Sustainability*. Retrieved September 03, 2013 from MicroFinanceGateway.Org: http://www.microfinancegateway.org/gm/document-1.9.24472/2147_file_Financial_Services_f.pdf

*Maharashtra, UP worst power deficit states: ASSOCHAM.* (2010). Retrieved December 10, 2013, from India Today: http://indiatoday.intoday.in/story/Maharashtra,+UP+worst+power+deficit+states:+Assocham/1/95124.html

Majumder, S. (2013, August 16). *Indian villages lit up by off-grid power*. Retrieved December 21, 2013, from http://www.bbc.co.uk/news/world-asia-india-23613878

Maken, A. (2013). 68 million Indians living in slums. *The Times of India*. Retrieved September, 06, 2013 from http://articles.timesofindia.indiatimes.com/2013-03-21/india/37901811_1_slum-households-urban-poverty-alleviation-minister-cent

Malakunas, R., & France, P. (2011). Philippine solar light bottles offer hope. *Inquirer News*. Retrieved October, 02, 2013 from http://newsinfo.inquirer.net/103043/philippine-solar-light-bottles-offer-hope

Manisha, M., & Deb, S. M. (2009). *Indian Democracy: Problems and Prospects*. Anthem Press.

Map, E. an Initiative of the Center for Science, Technology, and Society. Supported By Applied Materials. (2010). *Husk Power System*. Retrieved Dec 21, 2013, from http://energymap-scu.org/husk-power-systems/

Marx, S. (2005). Improving faculty use of technology in a small campus community. *T.H.E. Journal*, *32*(6), 21–43.

Massy, W., & Zemsky, R. (2005, June). *Using information technology to enhance academic productivity*. Paper presented at the Enhancing Academic Productivity Conference, Wingspread, WI. Retrieved November 16, 2013, from http://www.educause.edu/LibraryDetailPage/666&ID=NLI0004

McCormack, K., & Johnson, W. (2001). *Business process orientation: Gaining the e-business competitive advantage*. St. Lucie Press. doi:10.1201/9781420025569

McMurdo, G. (1996). Networking for trust in tribal organizations. *Journal of Information Science*, *22*(4), 299–314. doi:10.1177/016555159602200407

Megill, K. (2012). *Thinking for a living: The coming age of Knowledge Work*. Walter de Gruyter & Co. doi:10.1515/9783110289671

Mehri, D. (2005). *Notes from Toyota-Land: An American Engineer in Japan*. Ithaca, NY: Cornell University Press, xviii.

Melerdiercks, K. (2005). The dark side of Norzaidi, M.D., Chong, S.C. and Intan Salwani, M. (2008a). Perceived resistance, user resistance and managers' performance in the Malaysian port industry. *Aslib Proceedings: New Information Perspectives*, *60*(3), 242–264.

Mellahi, K., & Collings, D. (2010). The barriers to effective global talent management: The example of corporate elites in MNEs. *Journal of World Business*, *45*(2), 143–149. doi:10.1016/j.jwb.2009.09.018

Memdani, L., & Rajyalakshmi, K. (2013). Financial Inclusion in India. *International Journal of Applied Research and Studies*, *2*(8).

Mera Gao Power. (n.d.). *Mera Gao Power: Providing Solar Lighting to Villages*. Retrieved August 22, 2013, from http://meragaopower.com/news

*Mera Gao Power*. (n.d.). Retrieved from http://meragaopower.com

MICAVAANI. (2010). *Transmitting on 90.4 MHz*. Retrieved October 7, 2013, from http://www.mica.ac.in/home/introducing-mica/life-at-mica/student-committees/micavaani

*Micro grids offer solution to 400 million 'powerless' people*. (n.d.). Retrieved September 2, 2013, from http://www.deccanherald.com/content/203669/micro-grids-offer-solution-400.html

*Microgrid Market by Type. (Hybrid, Off-Grid, Grid Connected), Component (Storage, Inverter), Technology (Fuel Cell, CHP), Consumer Pattern (Urban, Rural), Application (Campus, Commercial, Defense), and Geography - Global Forecast to 2022*. (n.d.). Retrieved December 25, 2013, from http://www.marketsandmarkets.com/Market-Reports/micro-grid-electronics-market-917.html

Miguel-Ángel Galindo, María-Teresa & Méndez-Picazo, (2013). Innovation, entrepreneurship and economic growth. *Management Decision*, *51*(3), 501 – 514.

Millar, B. (2013, April 24). *Essential Tools of Talent Management*. Retrieved March 15, 2015 from http://www.forbes.com/sites/forbesinsights/2013/04/24/essential-tools-of-talent-management/

Miller, D., & Friesen, P. H. (1983). Strategy-making and environment: The third link. *Strategic Management Journal*, *4*(3), 221–235. doi:10.1002/smj.4250040304

Minimum Wages Act, 1948. Citation Act No. 11 of 1948 of the Government of India, enacted by the Parliament of India; date of commencement: 15th March 1948. Indian Parliament at New Delhi

Ministry of Agriculture. Department of Agriculture & Cooperation, National Centre of Organic Farming, Sector 19, Hapur Road, Ghaziabad. (n.d.). *Organic Farming Policy2005*. Retrieved from http://ncof.dacnet.nic.in/Policy_and_EFC/Organic_Farming_Policy_2005.pdf

Ministry of Commerce & Industry, Government of India. (n.d.). *SIA Newsletters*. Retrieved from http://www.sia-web.org/publications/sia-newsletter/

Ministry of Drinking Water and Sanitation. Govt. of India. (2011). Guidelines on CRSP. Nirman Bhawan, New Delhi: Author.

Ministry of Information Broadcasting, Govt. Of India (2011). *Community radio awareness*. Author.

Ministry of Rural Development. Govt. of India. (2010). Guidelines on Central Rural Sanitation Programme Total Sanitation Campaign. Krishi Bhawan, New Delhi: Author.

Ministry of Women and Child Development, Government of India. (2013). *Integrated Child Development Services (ICDS) Scheme*. Retrieved October 9, 2013, from http://wcd.nic.in/icds.htm

Ministry of Women and Child Development, Government of India. (2013). *Plan for additional AWC Construction during the 12th Five Year Plan*. Author.

Mintzberg, H. (1973). Strategy-Making in Three Modes. California Management Review.

Mission, S., & the Government of Kerala. (2013). *Total Sanitation Campaign*. Retrieved October 9, 2013, from website: http://indiasanitationportal.org/

Mohan, M. (2012, September 19). *Best Engaging Communities*. Retrieved October 15, 2013, from Best Engaging Communities: http://bestengagingcommunities.com/2012/09/19/technology-product-startups-angel-and-venture-market-comparisons-us-and-india/

Mohapatra, N., & Kumar, P. (n.d.). *Pillars of Financial Inclusion: Remittances, Micro Insurance and Micro Savings*. Retrieved May 8, 2014 from http://skoch.in/images/stories/Governance_knowledge/Pillars%20of%20Financial%20Inclusion%20Remittances_Micro%20Insurance%20and%20Micro%20Savings.pdf

Mondal, P. (n.d.). *Sanitary Production of Milk and Method of Milking*. Dairy Farm Management. Retrieved August 1, 2014, from http://www.yourarticlelibrary.com/dairy-farm-management/sanitary-production-of-milk-and-method-of-milking-2/36374/

Mu, H., & Artemio, R. Jr. (2006).Who, how and with whom: An exploration of Social Internet use and loneliness. In *Proceedings of the Annual Meeting of the International Communication Association*, 2006, 1-35.

Mukherjee, A. (2007). Fodder on the Line. *Business Today, 16*(9), 62. Retrieved October 8, 2013, from http://web.ebscohost.com/bsi/detail?sid=62b7dd32-2b33-47ea-9c6f-f67a8b588225%40sessionmgr14&vid=1&hid=19&bdata=JnNpdGU9YnNpLWxpdmU%3d#db=bth&AN=24844647

Murayama, H. (2011). OVOP Network toward in East Asia and a Case study in Thailand: The authority between the government and the general public. *The International Journal of East Asian Studies*, *16*(1), 63–65.

Naandi Foundation. (2012). The HUNGaMA (Huger and Malnutrition). *Survey (London, England)*, Report–2011.

Naikal, A., & Paloti, R. (2005). Knowledge Sharing: A Key For KM Success. In *Proceedings of 7th MANLIBNET Convention*. Kozhikode: IIM Kozhikode.

National Bank for Agriculture and Rural Development. (n.d.). *Nationwide Study on SGSY, NIRD,2005. Opportunities and Challenges in the Indian Dairy Industry*. Retrieved December 8, 2014 from www.nabard.org/fileupload/DataBank/.../issue9td-6.pdf

National Centre of Organic Farming. Sector 19, Hapur Road, Ghaziabad. (n.d.). *National Project of Organic Farming, Annual Report 2011-2012*. Retrieved from http://ncof.dacnet.nic.in/AnnualReports/AnnualReport2011-12.pdf

National Centre of Organic Farming. Sector 19, Hapur Road, Ghaziabad. (n.d.). *Organic Farming an Overview*. Retrieved from http://ncof.dacnet.nic.in/OrganicFarming-AnOverview/OrganicFarmingAnoverview.pdf

National Centre of Organic Farming. Sector 19, Hapur Road, Ghaziabad. (n.d.). *The world of Organic Agriculture in India*. Retrieved from http://ncof.dacnet.nic.in/OrganicFarmingAnOverview/TheWorldofOrganicAgricultureinIndia%202010.pdf

National Council of Applied Economic Research (NCAER). (2009). *FDI in India & its Growth linkages. Sponsored by Department of Industrial Policy & Promotion, Ministry of Commerce & Industry*. Government of India.

National Institute of Rural Development (NIRD). (n.d.). *A study on improvement in rural livelihoods through dairy farming*. Retrieved August 20, 2014, from http://www.nird.org.in/nird_docs/ven_finrepo.pdf

Natti, S. (2013, July 7). *India to be rich with new banks*. Retrieved October 17, 2013 from The New Indian Express: http://newindianexpress.com/thesundaystandard/India-to-be-rich-with-new-banks/2013/07/07/article1670918.ece

Nerenberg, J. (2011, January 5). *Husk Power Systems wants to lead "A Revolution in Electricity"*. Retrieved from www.fastcompany.com: http://www.fastcompany.com/1714395/husk-power-systems-wants-lead-revolution-electricity

Neuhaus, M. (2006). The Impact of FDI on Economic Growth- An Analysis for the Transition Countries of Central & Eastern Europe. Physica-Verlag, Springer Co ltd.

NIPCCD (National Institute of Public Cooperation and Child Development). (2009). *Research on ICDS: An Overview (1996-2008)*. New Delhi: Hauz Khas.

Nobel, C. (2011, April 11). Teaching a 'Lean Startup' Startegy. *HBS Working Knowledge*, 1-2.

Norzaidi, M. D., Chong, S. C., Azizah, A., Intan Salwani, M., Rafidah, K., & Rohana, Z. (2007a). The effect of students' backgrounds and attitudes on computer skills in Malaysia. *International Journal of Management in Education*, *1*(4), 371–389. doi:10.1504/IJMIE.2007.015198

Norzaidi, M. D., Chong, S. C., Intan Salwani, M., & Rafidah, K. (2008b). A study of intranet usage and resistance in Malaysia's port industry. *Journal of Computer Information Systems*, *49*(1), 37–47.

Norzaidi, M. D., Chong, S. C., Murali, R., & Intan Salwani, M. (2007b). Intranet usage and managers' performance in the port industry. *Industrial Management & Data Systems*, *107*(8), 1227–1250. doi:10.1108/02635570710822831

*Novaritis arogya*. (2014) Retrieved from www.novartis.com/downloads/corporate.../arogya-factsheet.pdf

Ockleford, J. (2000). *Research and Survey Series: Tri-Sector Partnerships Beyond those of Participating Groups in the BPD Cluster*. Retrieved 16 Jan, 2014, from www.bpd-waterandsanitation.org

Oguz, F. (2001). How entrepreneurs learn? A practical interpretation. *METU Studies in Development*, *28*(1/2), 183–202.

Oita OVOP International Exchange Promotion Committee. (2010). *OVOP Movement: Fruits of OVOP*. Retrieved from http://www.ovop.jp/en/index.html

Oredain, K. (2013). Soda Bottle Solar Bulbs Bring Light to Thousands in the Philippines. *Voive of America*. Retrieved September, 12, 2013 from http://www.voanews.com/content/soda-bottle-solar-bulbs-bring-light-to-thousands-in-the-philippines-134766408/168250.html

Orendain, K. (2013). In Philippine Slums, Capturing Light in a Bottle. *NPR*. Retrieved October, 15, 2013 from http://www.npr.org/2011/12/28/144385288/in-philippine-slums-capturing-light-in-a-bottle

*Over 300,000 MP Farmers Indian used Kisan Call Center: Report, Asia Pulse Pty Ltd*. (2010). Retrieved October 10, 2013, from http://search.proquest.com/docview/759359583?accountid=50136

Ozowa, V. (n.d.). *Information Needs of Small Scale Farmers in Africa: The Nigerian Example*. Retrieved December 24, 2013, from http://www.worldbank.org/html/cgiar/newsletter/june97/9nigeria.html

Panneerselvam, P. P., Hermansen, J., & Halberg, N. (2011). Food Security of Small Holding Farmers: Comparing Organic & Conventional Systems in India. *Journal of Sustainable Agriculture*, *35*(1), 48–68. doi:10.1080/10440046.2011.530506

Parker, B., & Burnie, D. (2009). Classroom Technology in Business Schools. *AACE Journal*, *17*(1), 45–60.

Park, R., Burgess, E., & McKenzie, R. (1925). *The City*. Chicago, IL: University of Chicago Press.

Peluchette, J. V., & Rust, K. (2005). Technology use in the classroom: Preferences of management faculty. *Journal of Education for Business*, *80*(4), 200–205. doi:10.3200/JOEB.80.4.200-205

People's Union for Democratic Rights Report. (2013). *Driving force- Labour Struggles and Violation of Rights in Maruti Suzuki India Limited*. Delhi: Secretary, People's Union for Democratic Rights.

Phillips, K., & Berenice, T. & Ade le. (2009). Macro and micro challenges for talent retention in South Africa: Original research. *South African Journal of Human Resource Management*, *7*(1), 1–10.

Phonsuwan, S., & Kachitvichyanukul, V. (2010). *Management System Models to Support Decision-making for Micro and Small Business of Rural Enterprise in Thailand*. Paper presented at 2nd International Science, Social Science, Engineering and Energy Conference.

Piselli, F. (2007). Communities, Places, and Social Networks. *The American Behavioral Scientist*, *50*(7), 867–878. doi:10.1177/0002764206298312

Planning Commision. (2011). Institutional Arrangements under ICDS Mission, Report of the Inter Ministerial Group on ICDS Restructuring Chaired by Member Planning Commission Dr. Syeda Hameed. Author.

Planning Commision. (2011). *Report of the Inter Ministerial Group on ICDS Restructuring Chaired by Member Planning Commission Dr. Syeda Hameed*. New Delhi: Yojana Bhavan.

Planning Commission Government of India. (2009). *A Hundred Small Steps*. New Delhi: Sage Publications.

*Planning Commission . Government of India*. (n.d.). Retrieved 2 July 2014 from http:/www.planningcommission.gov.in

Poell, R., Van, F., & Krogt, V. (2003). Learning strategies of workers in the knowledge-creating company. *Human Resource Development International*, *6*(3), 387–403. doi:10.1080/13678860210136080

Popper, M., & Lipshitz, R. (1998). Organizational learning mechanisms: A structural and cultural approach to organizational learning. *The Journal of Applied Behavioral Science*, *34*(2), 161–179. doi:10.1177/0021886398342003

Pradhan, A., Ali, S., & Dash, R. (n.d.). *Biomass Gasification by the use of Rice Husk Gasifier*. Academic Press.

Prem, K., & Kalra, R. S. (2007). *Electrification and bio-energy options in rural India*. Retrieved October 22, 2013, from india infrastructure report 2007: http://www.iitk.ac.in/3inetwork/html/reports/IIR2007/iir2007.html

Purushothaman, S., Patil, S., & Francis, I. (2012). Impact of policies favoring organic inputs on small farms in Karnataka, India: A multi criteria approach. *Environment, Development and Sustainability*, *14*(4), 507–527. doi:10.1007/s10668-012-9340-1

Qureshi, T. M. (2008). Customer Acceptance of Online Banking in Developing Economies. *Journal of Internet Banking and Commerce*, *13*(1), 13–20.

Raghavan, S. (2006). Blogs and Business Conversations. *Journal of Creative Communications*, *1*(3), 285–309. doi:10.1177/097325860600100305

Rahul, A. (2011). *Kisan Call Center: Bridging the information gap*. Retrieved October 10, 2013, from http://www.thebetterindia.com/2304/kisan-call-center-bridging-information-gap/

Rajamony, S., Premalatha, S., & Pillai, P. K. (2005, September). Azolla a sustainable feed for livestock. *Leisa*, *21*(3). Retrieved August 10, 2014, from http://www.agriculturesnetwork.org/magazines/global/small-animals-in-focus/azolla-livestock-feed

Ramachandran, G. (2012). *Integration of energy issues in rural development planning in India*. Retrieved October 1, 2013, from http://www.unescap.org/esd/Energy-Security-and-Water-Resources/energy/policy_and_planning/integration/egm/documents/G_Ramachandran_paper.pdf

Rao, R., Menaria, D., Maurya, A., & Parashar, A. (2012). *Video Case on Social Innovation*. Retrieved from https://www.youtube.com/watch?v=CA4Q2sEcsg0

Rao, S., & Sharma, V.P. (n.d.). *Tele-Agri-Advisory Services for Farmers: a Case Study of Kisan Call Center in Andhra Pradesh*. Academic Press.

Rao, C. S. (2013). Consumer awareness in rural India with special reference to E-Banking services in SBI. *Indian Journal of Research*, *2*(2), 46–48.

Raychaudhuri, S., Mausumi Raychaudhuri, Ngachan, S. V., & Yadav, A. K. (2005). Organic Farming – Management and Practices. ICAR Research Complex for NEH Region, Manipur Centre, Imphal.

Rehmaan, D. (2013). India's Slumdog census reveals poor conditions for one in six urban dwellers. *The Guardian*. Retrieved October, 02, 2013 from http://www.theguardian.com/world/2013/mar/22/india-slumdog-census-poor-conditions

Reserve Bank of India. (2013, September 3). *Deregulation of Savings Bank Interest Rate*. Retrieved September 03, 2013 from RBI: http://www.rbi.org.in/Scripts/bs_viewcontent.aspx?Id=2344

*Rice Husk Technology* . (2010). Retrieved August 10, 2013, from http://www.poerner.at/fileadmin/user_upload/pdf/Brochure_Grimma_Rice_Husk_090615_web_e.pdf

Rice, R. E., & Love, G. (1987). Electronic Emotion: Socioemotional Content in a Computer-Mediated Communication Network. *Communication Research, 14*(1), 85-108.

*Ricehusk.com* . (2013). Retrieved October 8, 2013, from http://www.ricehusk.com/faq

Routray, J. K. (2007). One village one product: strategy for sustainable rural development in Thailand. *CAB (College of agricultural banking) Calling, 3*(1), 30-34.

Roy, A. (2013, October 13). *FINO may change remittance business in India's hinterland*. Retrieved May 9, 2014 from Live Mint: http://www.livemint.com/Industry/d5Q76nkacb1ZUTcS3OlC7H/FINO-may-change-remittance-business-in-Indias-hinterland.html

Rukmani, R. (n.d.). *Measures of Impact of Science and Technology in India: agriculture and rural development*. Retrieved May 21, 2014, from http://www.currentscience.ac.in/Downloads/download_pdf.php?titleid=id_095_12_1694_1698_0

*Rural Electrification Policy*. (2006, August 23). Retrieved October 1, 2013, from Ministry of Power: http://www.powermin.nic.in/whats_new/pdf/RE%20Policy.pdf

*Rural Finance Learning Center*. (n.d.). Retrieved 2 July 2014 from http:/www.ruralfinance.org

*Rural Urban Distribution of Population*. (n.d.). Retrieved December 26, 2013, from http://censusindia.gov.in/2011-prov-results/paper2/data_files/india/Rural_Urban_2011.pdf

Ryan, V. (2009). *World Association of Technology Teachers. How can we reduce our carbon footprint?* Retrieved from http://www.lbm.co.uk/Public/content/about/LBM%20Carbon%20Footprint%20report.pdf

Salas, E., Wildman, J. L., & Piccolo, R. F. (2009). Using Simulation-Based Training to Enhance Management Education. *Academy of Management Learning & Education. University of Central Florida*, *8*(4), 559–573.

Satyanarayana, J. (2004). *E-Government. The Science of the Possible*. New Delhi: Prentice Hall of India Pvt. Ltd.

Savitri, D. (2008). An approach of Sustainable development: Rural Revitalization as the Pioneer of OVOP movement. *Journal of OVOP Policy*, *1*(7), 21–30.

SELCO. (2014). *Rural financial infrastructure*. Retrieved from http:/www.selco-india.com

Serva UP Gramin Bank. (2013, October 7). *Serva UP Gramin Bank*. Retrieved October 7, 2013 from UPGB.com: http://www.upgb.com/keyfigures.htm

Seth, A. (n.d.). *The community radio movement in India*. Retrieved December 23, 2013, from http://www.gramvaani.org/wp-content/uploads/2013/05/community-radio-indian-history.pdf

Sethi, J. (2013). Urban slums data reinforces India's consumption story. *Mint and the Wall Street Journal*. Retrieved September, 16, 2013 from http://www.livemint.com/Politics/jMYppv9iGGknRWep7H0yrI/Urban-slum-dwellers-own-assets-permanent-houses-Census-201.html

Shaftesbury. (1711). Inquiry concerning Virtue and Merit. In *Characteristics of Men, Manners, Opinions, Times*. Oxford, UK: Oxford UP.

Shakya, G. (2011). Understanding One Village One Product in Japan, Thailand and Nepal. Agro Enterprise Centre/Japan International Cooperation Agency (JICA) Nepal Office.

Shanmugam, T. R., Chandrasekaran, M., & Vijayasarathy, K. (2011). *Economic Analysis of Farm and Market Risk*. Saarbrücken: LAP Lambert Academic Publishing.

Sharma, A., Gupta, S., & Yadav, S. (2011). *Identifying various Factors that Affect Quality of Agri-business Management Software*. Paper presented at International Conference on Issues and Challenges in Networking, Intelligence and Computing Technologies.

Sharma, B. R., Singh, P., & Sharma, A. (2011). *Role of Kisan Call Centers in Hill Agriculture*. Indian Society of Agricultural Economics. Retrieved October 11, 2013, from http://search.proquest.com/docview/912670948?accountid=50136

Sharma, K. D. (2013). *Impact Of Information Technology On Management Education Through Distance Mode*. Academic Press.

*Smart Grid for India*. (n.d.). Retrieved August 22, 2013, from http://smartgrid-for-india.blogspot.in/2012/05/mera-gao-microgrid-power-among-10.html

Smart, P., Maddern, H., & Maull, R. (2009). Understanding Business Process Management: Implications for Theory and Practice. *Ritish Journal of Management*, *20*(4), 491–507.

Smith, H., & Fingar, P. (2002). *Business Process Management: The Third Wave*. Meghan-Kiffer.

Smith, M., & Kollock, P. (Eds.). (1998). *Communities in cyberspace*. London: Routledge.

*Solar energy startups out to power rural India with cost-effective and less toxic solutions*. (n.d.). Retrieved September 25, 2013, from http://articles.economictimes.indiatimes.com/2013-10-02/news/42617599_1_azure-power-helion-venture-partners-power-company

Spennemann, D. H. R., Artkinson, J., & Cornworth, D. (2007). Sessional, weekly and diurual patterns of computer lab usage by students attending a regional university in Australia. *Computers & Education*, *49*(3), 726–739. doi:10.1016/j.compedu.2005.11.006

*SRM Community Radio | Home*. (n.d.). Retrieved October 7, 2013, from http://www.srmuniv.ac.in/muthucharam/

Stahl, G., Björkman, I., Farndale, E., Morris, S. S., Paauwe, J., Stiles, P., & Wright, P. et al. (2012). Six principles of effective global talent management. *Sloan Management Review*, *53*(2), 25–42.

*Status Paper on Rice in Uttar Pradesh*. (2012). Retrieved December 10, 2013, from http://www.rkmp.co.in/status-paper-on-rice-in-uttar-pradesh

Steiner, J., & Steiner, G. (2012). Business, Government and Society: A Managerial Perspective. New Delhi: Mcgraw Hill Education (India Pvt Ltd.).

Steiny, D., & Oinas-Kukkonen, H. (2007). Network awareness: Social network search, innovation and productivity in organizations. *International Journal of Networking and Virtual Organisations*, *4*(4), 413–430. doi:10.1504/IJNVO.2007.015723

Sternberg, R. J., & Lubart, T. I. (1999). The concept of creativity: prospects and paradigms, 3. In R. J. Sternberg (Ed.), *Handbook of Creativity*. New York, NY: Cambridge University Press.

Subotnik, R.; Duschl, R. & Selmon, E. (1993). Retention and attrition of science talent: a longitudinal study of Westinghouse Science Talent Search winners. *International Journal of Science Education*, 15(1), 61-72.

Successfactors. (n.d.). *Talent Management Strategy to Create a Higher-Performing Workforce*. Retrieved March15, 2015 from http://www.successfactors.com/en_us/lp/articles/strategic-talent-management-training.html

Successfactors. (n.d.). *Talent Management*. Retrieved March 15, 2015 from http://www.successfactors.com/en_us/lp/ppc/talent-management.html?Campaign_ID=21941&TAG=Q114_APJ_Google_PPC_India&CmpLeadSource=Search%20Engine&source=Google_ppc&kw=Talent%20Management&ad--id=35149490117&adgroup=Google&gclid=CNaA3q32rL4CFUwpjgodCHUAVwhttp://en.wikipedia.org/wiki/Talent_management

Suhotra Swami Ṣad-darśanam. (1997). *The Six Systems of Vedic Philosophies*. Mayapur: Bhaktivedanta Academy.

Sunley, J. (2006). New ideas on talent retention. *Hospitality*, *1*, 26-28.

Sure Start Services. Govt. of UK. (2014). *Sure Start Services*. Retrieved September 23, 2014 from http://www.nidirect.gov.uk/sure-start-services

Suresh, R. B. (2005). *Organic Farming: Status, Issues & Prospects – A Review*. Agricultural Economics Research Paper.

Surry, D. W., Ensminger, D. C., & Haab, M. (2005). A model for integrating instructional technology into higher education. *British Journal of Educational Technology*, *36*(2), 327–329. doi:10.1111/j.1467-8535.2005.00461.x

*Sustainable Access in Rural India*. (2014) Retrieved from http://www.tenet.res.in/rural/sari.html

*Sustainable Bioenergy Development in UEMOA Member Countries*. (2008). Retrieved December 10, 2013, from http://www.globalproblems-globalsolutions-files.org/gpgs_files/pdf/UNF_Bioenergy/UNF_Bioenergy_full_report.pdf

Tanaka, N., Kjorven, O., & Yumkella, K. K. (2010). *Energy Poverty: How to make modern energy access universal*. UNIDO.

Tarique, I., & Schuler, R. S. (2009). Global talent management: Literature review, integrative framework, and suggestions for further research. *Journal of World Business*, *45*(2), 122–133. doi:10.1016/j.jwb.2009.09.019

Tata & Bhada, P. (2012). *The Potential for Waste to Energy in India*. Retrieved October 5, 2013, from website: http://www.waste-management-world.com/

Taylor Fredrich Winslow. (1911).The Principles of Scientific Management. New York: Harper & Brothers.

Tempest, S. (2009). Learning from the alien: Knowledge relationships with temporary workers in network contexts. *The International Journal of Human Resource Management*, *20*(4), 912–927-912–927.

The Climate Group. (2013, August 16). *As India revives US$8.7 billion clean energy grid upgrade, off-grid projects also on rise*. Retrieved Dec 2013, from The Climate Group: http://www.theclimategroup.org/what-we-do/news-and-blogs/as-india-revives-us87-billion-clean-energy-grid-upgrade-off-grid-projects-also-on-rise

The Ecologist. (2013, October). *Carbon Footprint*. Retrieved from http://files.theecologist.org/resources/carbonfootprints.html

The Hindu. (2010, July 26). *Rice husk power to light up villages*. Retrieved from The Hindu: http://www.thehindu.com/news/national/article533665.ece

The Organic Institute. (n.d.). *History of the Organic Movement*. Retrieved from http://theorganicsinstitute.com/organic/history-of-the-organic-movement/

*The World Bank*. (n.d.). Retrieved 2 July 2014 from http:/www.worldbank.org

Thomson, W. (1965). *A Preface to Urban Economics*. Baltimore, MD: John Hopkins Press.

Tiwari, R. (2012). Government ropes in IFFCO Kisan Sanchar Limited to improve Kisan Call Centers [Agriculture]. *The Economic Times* (Online). Retrieved October 7, 2013, from http://search.proquest.com/docview/1011117854?accountid=50136

Topp, N., Mortenson, R., & Grandgenett, N. (1995). Building a technology-using faculty to facilitate technology-using teachers. *Journal of Computing in Teacher Education*, *11*(3), 11–14.

Torri, M. C. (2009). Community entrepreneurship among lower castes in India: A grassroots contribution towards poverty alleviation and rural development under conditions of adversity and environmental uncertainty. *Journal of Developmental Entrepreneurship*, *14*(04), 413–432. doi:10.1142/S1084946709001338

Torri, M. C. (2010). Community-based enterprises: A promising basis towards an alternative entrepreneurial model for sustainability enhancing livelihoods and promoting socio-economic development in rural India. *Journal of Small Business and Entrepreneurship*, *23*(2), 237–248. doi:10.1080/08276331.2010.10593484

Towers, P. (2005). The Business case for workers age 50+: planning for tomorrow's talent needs in today's competitive environment. In *AARP Knowledge Management* (p. 96). Washington, DC: AARP.

*Transforming rural India*. (2014). Retrieved from http://blogs.hbr.org/2014/02/transforming-rural-india-through-agricultural-innovation/

TRIFED. (2014). *Introduction to TRIFED*. Retrieved 10 October, 2014, from www.trifed.in/trifed/.../about_trifed.aspx

Tulder, R., & Zwart, A. (2006). *International Business-Society Management: Linking Corporate responsibility and Globalization*. London: Routledge.

Turner, J. W., Grube, J. A., & Meyers, J. (2001). Developing an optimal match within Online Communities: An exploration of CMC support communities and traditional support. *Journal of Communication*, *51*(1), 231–251. doi:10.1111/j.1460-2466.2001.tb02879.x

UNICEF. (2013) *India: Statistics*. Retrieved October 11,2013, from http://www.unicef.org/infobycountry/india_statistics.html

*United Nationals Conference on Trade and Development*. (n.d.). Retrieved 2 JULY 2014 from http:/www.unctad.org

United States Environmental Protection Agency. (2008). *Optional Emissions from Commuting, Business Travel & Product Transport (Publication No.EPA430-R-08-006)*. Washington, DC: Office of Air and Radiation.

Unnithan, C. (2013, August 10). MICA students launch new season of community radio. *The Times of India*. Retrieved October 7, 2013, from http://articles.timesofindia.indiatimes.com/2013-08-10/news/41265647_1_community-radio-listeners-mudra-institute

US Department of Health and Human Services. (2014). *Administration for Children and Families, ACF Programs for Children and Youth*. Retrieved September 23, 2014 from http://www.acf.hhs.gov/program-topics/children-youth

*User Manual Version 1.0 for Kisaan SMS Portal*. (n.d.). Retrieved September 8, 2013 from http://farmer.gov.in/advs/User%20Manual%20for%20Kisaan%20SMS%20Portal_Ver1%200.pdf

Vaani, M. (n.d.). *A voice-based communication platform for the BoP*. Retrieved December 23, 2013, from http://www.gramvaani.org/wp-content/uploads/2014/04/mobile-vaani-mar-2014.pdf

Vasishth, N., & Rajput, N. (2012). *Business Ethics and Values*. New Delhi: Taxman's Publications Pvt. Ltd.

Vet Helpline India (P) Ltd. (n.d.). *Starting a Dairy Farm in India*. Retrieved December 8, 2014 from http://www.vethelplineindia.co.in/starting-a-dairy-farm-india/

*Village, R., Tehsil, H., &District, G.* (n.d.). Retrieved December 24, 2013, from http://www.onefivenine.com/india/villages/Ghaziabad/Hapur/Raghunathpur

Walther, J. B., & Boyd, S. (2002). Attraction to computer-mediated social support. In Communication Technology and Society: Audience Adoption and Uses (pp. 153–188). Cresskill, NJ: Hampton Press.

Wang, K. S. (1998). *A process development for gasification of rice husk*. Retrieved October 8, 2013, from http://myweb.ncku.edu.tw/~wanghp/A%20process%20development%20for%20gasification%20of%20rice%20husk.pdf

Ward, C. (1996). Acculturation. D. Landis & R. Bhadat (Eds.), Handbook of Intercultural Training (pp. 124–147). Thousand Oaks, CA: Sage.

*Waste to Energy* . (2007). Retrieved October 8, 2013, from http://www.devalt.org/knowledgebase/pdf/Case%20Study-3.pdf

Water and Sanitation Program. (2012). *Handbook on Scaling up Solid and Liquid Waste Management in Rural Areas*. New Delhi: Lodhi Estate.

Wellman, B., Salaff, J., Dimitrova, D., Garton, L., Gulia, M., & Haythornthwaite, C. (1996). Computer Networks as Social Networks: Collaborative Work, Telework, and Virtual Community. *Annual Review of Sociology*, *22*(1), 213–238. doi:10.1146/annurev.soc.22.1.213

Wheelen, T. L., Hunger, D. J., & Rangarajan, K. (2010). Strategic Management and Business Policy. Noida, New Delhi: Dorling Kindersley (India) Pvt. Ltd, licensees of Pearson Education in South Asia.

*White paper*. (n.d.). Retrieved from http://edevelopment.media.mit.edu/SARI/papers/uncrd_report.pdf

*WWOOFindia*. (n.d.). Retrieved from http://www.wwoof-india.org/history.htm

Y, K. G. (2012). Rural Electrification in the Changing Paradigm of Power Sector Reforms in India. *International Journal of Electrical and Computer Engineering (IJECE)*, *2*(2).

Yadav, A. (2011). *Organic Agriculture in India*. Retrieved from National Centre of Organic Farming: http://ncof.dacnet.nic.in/Training_manuals/Training_manuals_in_English/Organic_Agriculture_in_India.pdf

Yadav, A., Gupta, R., & Garg, V. K. (2013, October). Organic manure production from cow dung and biogas plant slurry by vermicomposting under field conditions. *International Journal of Recycling of Organic Waste in Agriculture*. Retrieved August 10, 2014, from http://www.ijrowa.com/content/2/1/21

Ye, J. (2006). Traditional and Online Support Networks in the Cross-Cultural Adaptation of Chinese International Students in the United States. *Journal of Computer-Mediated Communication*, *11*(3), 863–876. doi:10.1111/j.1083-6101.2006.00039.x

Yoo, Y., Lyytinen, K., & Boland, R. J. (2008), Distributed Innovation in Classes of Networks. In *Proceedings of the 41st Hawaii International Conference on System Sciences*. Waikoloa: HI: IEEE.

Zafar, S. (2013, August 21). *BIO Energy Consultant*. Retrieved from http://www.bioenergyconsult.com/tag/energy-potential-of-rice-husk/

Zelin, R., & Baird, J. (2007). Training faculty to use technology in the classroom. *College Teaching Methods & Styles Journal*, *3*(3), 41–48.

Zhao, F. (2005). Exploring the synergy between entrepreneurship and innovation. *InternationalJournal of Entrepreneurial Behaviour and Research*, *11*(1), 25–41. doi:10.1108/13552550510580825

# About the Contributors

**Shalini Kalia**, PhD in English, has more than 12 years of teaching experience with management institutes of repute and is currently working as Associate Professor and Area Chairperson-Business Communication with Institute of Management Technology, Ghaziabad. Her teaching, training, research and consulting interests include business communication, cross cultural communication, soft skills, personality development, corporate etiquette etc. She has been actively involved in Executive Learning and Development (ELD) and has conducted workshops in various domains of business communication. She is trained to administer 'Thomas Personal Profile Analysis and its related instruments'; and was associated with British Council, New Delhi as BEC Examiner for speaking tests. Dr Kalia has coauthored a text book on Business Communication and has adapted three book titles by developing content for South Asian market. She has also written research papers, case studies and articles on various topics in different mainstream publications; and has presented papers in several seminars and conferences at national and international level.

**Bhavna Bhalla**, Assistant Professor, Business Communication at the Institute of Management Technology Ghaziabad, holds PhD from the Indian Institute of Technology Kanpur. She has 5 years of experience in teaching Communication courses to MBA/PGDM participants at IMT Ghaziabad. She has been a trainer to public and private sector organizations. She has conducted training sessions for executives from organisations such as Apollo Tyres, Reckitt Benckiser, EXL Services and BSNL. She has presented research papers at a number of international conferences including Harvard University, USA, Universiti Utara, Malaysia, and Cordoba University, Spain. She has co-authored two Indian Adaptations, reviewed book chapters, research papers and solution manuals for international editions by reputed publishers. Her journal articles appear in journals of repute and her cases are registered with The Case Centre (previously ECCH).

**Lipi Das** is Assistant Professor–Business Communication at (IMT) Ghaziabad, India .She has 18+years of experience in Academics, Trainings & Industry. Currently pursuing Doctoral Program in Business Administration from Grenoble Ecole de Management, she is Masters (History) from University of Delhi, Post-graduate in Business Management from AIMA-CME, and PG.ATHM (HON)-ITFT. Currently she is Faculty-In-Charge Alumni Relations Committee at IMT-Ghaziabad, Program Director-ECPM-01 and member of Committee's on Doctoral Program (DBA) and Industry Interface. Her wide ranging experience in Soft-Skill Consulting and Training has been for organizations like Jubilant FoodWorks (Global Master Franchise for Dominos & Dunkin Donut), Indian Institute of Public Administration (IIPA), Ashok Minda Group, CBSE-Centum Learning, Indian Postal Service Probationers, NHPC, BSNL, Vatika Ltd, IOCL, EXL, Mafoi Management Consultants, CSIR-HRDC, Her research interests are in the areas of

Mentorship, Leadership Communication, Case Development and Sectoral Study. Her Corporate domain expertise comes from handling Customer Relationship Management Leadership in organizations like Blue Dart Express, Thomas Nationwide Transportation Global Express Logistics and Head-Academics –ITFT Chandigarh. Some of her notable achievements include being awarded "SILVER STAR" –Trainer of the Month at Air Hostess Academy, New Delhi. As Customer Service Manager - Thomas Nationwide Transportation -Chennai, her team was awarded with "Regional High Flyer Award". She is also a recipient of "Bravo Blue Darter" award for outstanding performance in 1995.

**Neeraj Awasthy**, Manager Academic Programs at Institute of Management Technology, Ghaziabad. An FDP from IIM Ahmadabad, and PhD in Banking Management from Himachal Pradesh University, Shimla. Dr. Awasthy has a rich experience in the field of rural finance, rural development, education sector and NGO management. Dr. Awasthy Managed Centre for Rural Innovation, Capacity Building, Knowledge Management, Social Entrepreneurship and Technology (CRICKET) wherein he mentored various national and international students in the area of action research in Rural Upliftment and Development. In his research led to the production and development of a documentary about the livelihood of Birhor Tribes. Dr. Awasthy has authored and reviewed many research papers and books for national, International conferences and journals.

* * *

**Grandhi Venkata Abhinav** is pursuing PGDM (Marketing) from IMT Ghaziabad. He graduated with a Bachelors of Technology in Mechanical engineering and also holds a Dual Degree in Information Technology from VIT University, Vellore in 2011. Prior to joining IMT, he has worked in Hyundai Motor India Limited as an Area Manager for entire costal Andhra Pradesh for a period of 2 years.

**Aditya Vikram Agrawal** is currently pursuing his Post Graduate Diploma in Management from Institute of Management Technology, Ghaziabad with Finance as his core specialisation. Mr Agrawal is an engineer, having completed his Bachelor in Technology from Heritage Institute of Technology, with Computer Science & Engineering as his specialisation. Mr Agrawal is a member of FinNiche, the student run finance club of IMT. He is an avid reader, and keeps himself updated around the latest happenings in the financial community, and subsequently contributes regularly to the weekly finance magazine of IMT Ghaziabad. His current study pursuit has enabled him to portray and grow his creativity and knowledge, coupled with his innate sense of responsibility.

**Parag Agarwal** is a student of Marketing from IMT Ghaziabad. He has a B.Tech degree in Electronics & Communication from IET Lucknow. He served as a Quality Analyst in Tech Mahindra. He is passionate about helping and giving back to society. In IMT, he was a part of C.R.I.C.K.E.T. and Enactus. In CRICKET, he was involved in a project for "*Sustainable development for Sabar Tribe of Jharkhand*". He proposed the market based solutions for the tribes, constituted a brand "Palash" and also organized various exhibitions for studying the market. He also completed a project in collaboration with Copenhagen Business School to help a company called Tara Machines to achieve its target. During his stint at Enactus, he was involved in a project called "*Umeed ki Udaan*" for the sustainable development of underprivileged people of an NGO. He is an optimistic person and believes that, every individual should contribute back to society in his or her way. He is a regular blood donor and volunteer for *HelpAge India*. His hobbies include pencil sketching, writing poetry etc.

**Pragun Aggarwal** is currently in his 1st year of study in the Post Graduate Diploma Management Program at Institute of Management Technology (IMT), Ghaziabad. In March 2015, he will graduate with a Master of Business Administration degree, with specialization in finance. Mr Aggarwal is a member of FinNiche, the student run finance club of IMT. Mr Aggarwal has worked with India Yamaha Motor Pvt Ltd., a 100% subsidiary of Yamaha Motor Co., Ltd., Japan (YMC). He was assistant manager in Manufacturing Engineering division and responsible for development activities of new model – Project ‘Ray’. He successfully carried out product development tasks pertaining to Fuel Tank of scooter before its international launch. Mr Aggarwal earned his Bachelor of Engineering degree in Mechanical Engineering from Delhi College of Engineering (Presently Delhi Technological University), a nationally recognized and one of the best technological universities in India, in 2011. He also interned with Honda Cars India Ltd. in the PO (Plastic Objects) division while pursuing his engineering degree. Outside of academics, Mr Aggarwal is an avid fiction reader. He enjoys outdoor sports including badminton in which he represented his state at the national level badminton championship.

**Ranjana Agarwal** is currently working as Associate Professor, Economics at IMT Ghaziabad. A social scientist, she did her Doctoral studies from Jawaharlal Nehru University. Her specialization has been Economics of Education. She has worked extensively in the social sector. Some of her work include an investigate inquiry on PURA, Provision of Urban amenities in Rural areas in Bahraich in U.P. She is currently working on Sustainable Livelihood Options for Tribals in Jharkhand. Her work included a documentary AAROHAN, which was filmed on the lives and livelihood of particularly vulnerable Tribal Groups. She is working on the issues of finding livelihood solutions by finding marketing solutions for products made by tribal products. Apart from Managerial Economics, she is teaching a course, *Business, Government and Society* which sensitizes students on social issues.

**Rohit Agarwal** is pursuing Post Graduate Diploma in Management with majors in Marketing and Sales from Institute of Management Technology Ghaziabad. He has more than 2 years of experience working with Infosys Ltd. in the field of Cloud Computing and E-Commerce after completing his graduation in the field of Information Technology. His interest areas of research include strategic management, brand management and social media marketing.

**Shagun Agarwal** is currently pursuing Post Graduate Diploma in Management from IMT Ghaziabad was born and bought up in a business class family in Agra, city of Uttar Pradesh. He has done mechanical engineering after which he started his professional career as a stress analyst in Infosys Ltd. He worked around 18 months in Infosys after which he started his own venture by the name ‘R*RFoods’ which is a fruit ripening cold storage which has a capacity of ripening 100 metric tons of fruit load in a day. He is the Secretary and Founder of U.P Fruit Ripening Member’s Association. He went on to pursue PGDM as his business had gained sufficient market in Agra.

**Shailja Agarwal**, an Associate Professor with IMT Ghaziabad, brings with her a rich experience of 14 years of teaching and research. Prior to joining IMT Ghaziabad in October 2013, she was a faculty member with IIM Rohtak where she taught courses on communication and chaired the executive education programme. She has organized and conducted management training programs for more than 50 organizations till date, apart from getting published with some highly reputed publishers like Ivey, Emerald & Sage. Her current research and training areas include interpersonal communication, persuasive communication, cross cultural communication, and social media communication.

**Ronit Anand** is currently in his 1st year of study in the Post Graduate Diploma Management Program at Institute of Management Technology (IMT), Ghaziabad. In March 2015, he will graduate with a Master of Business Administration degree, with specialization in marketing. Mr. Anand has recently interned with VF corporation and Accenture in 2014. Mr Anand has worked with Adani Power Limited. He was Senior Engineer in Operation/Maintenance department and was responsible for development activities, resource handling and project management. He successfully shouldered the responsibility of setting up a new power plant facility in Mundra. Mr Anand earned his Bachelor of Engineering degree in Mechanical Engineering from Kalinga Institute of Industrial technology, a nationally recognized and one of the best technological universities in India, in 2010. He also interned with NTPC kahalgaon, Rungta Mines, ACC Cements while pursuing his engineering degree. Outside of academics, Mr Anand is an avid fiction reader. He enjoys outdoor and indoor sports too.

**Aparajita** is currently pursuing Post Graduate Diploma in Management with majors in finance and banking from Institute of Management Technology, Ghaziabad. She completed her engineering from SHIATS, Allahabad in the year 2012. She worked as a research scholar while pursuing her M.Tech. From National Institute of Technology, Rourkela in the field of Distributed Networks. Her interest areas of research include Distributed Networks, Wireless Sensor Networks, Investment Banking, Financial inclusion & Banking Innovation.

**Ayush Asthana** has completed his engineering degree from Manipal Institute of Technology in Electrical and Electronics (2009). He has worked in Tata Consultancy Services for three years and is currently pursuing an MBA degree in Marketing from the Institute of Management Technology, Ghaziabad.

**Sarthak Awasthi** is pursuing PGDM in Marketing at the Institute of Management Technology, Ghaziabad. He has a rich work experience prior to this in HCL Infosystems Ltd. As a Business Development Executive, he had overachieved his targets in BFSI and Central Government verticals. His interests include Business Development, Relationship management, and Business Prediction and Marketing management. He is an avid football fan and fairly competitive in spirit. He is seeking challenging assignments in the FMCG sector to learn and expand his knowledge base even more.

**Mayank Bapna** has Bachelors in Electronics and Telecommunication Engineering from Mumbai University and Masters of Business Administration (Distinction) from University of Wales. Currently, he has his own business in marketing and distribution of pharmaceuticals, food, cosmetic and veterinary ingredients. He is based in Jakarta, Indonesia since 2009 and often travels to India and Europe for his business. Reading and searching information are his hobbies with a keen interest in poetry. An extrovert by nature, he enjoys meeting people and learning from their experiences. With a quest for learning and acquiring knowledge, he shows profound interest in any field that interests him.

**Ashish Bhadauria** is a full time student of Business Management at the Institute of Management Technology, Ghaziabad. He has previously worked as a Senior Systems Engineer in Infosys, Bangalore. His interests include Marketing Research, Sales and Marketing Management and Business Analytics. He wants to be associated with an organization which will help him in expanding his horizons and developing a broader and a more international outlook. He is looking forward to a challenging career in the aviation sector and wants to polish his self-management, critical thinking, problem solving and interpretive skills in today's business world.

**Jitender Bhandari** is PhD (Economics) and also a UGC-NET. His area of expertise is in Microeconomics, Macroeconomics, Managerial Economics and International business. He takes classes at Graduate, Post Graduate and PhD level and is a Member of Academic Council and also Member-Board of Studies, Ansal University. He is also Editor of Ansal University Business Review, a half yearly management Journal.

**Neha Bhardwaj** was born and brought up in Delhi. She has completed her schooling from DAV Public School, Brij VIhar, U.P. and GGSSS, Vivek Vihar, Delhi. During her schooling, she has presented a research paper at State level in National Science Congress. She has pursued Computer Science Engineering from Guru Gobind Singh Indraprastha University, Delhi. She graduated with distinction. She has few accolades in Chess at Inter University level. She has 35 months of work experience in Infosys Technologies Limited, one of the biggest IT companies in India, at various locations - Mysore, Pune and Hyderabad. She was awarded 'Spot Award' during her stint In Infosys. Currently, she is pursuing PGDM in Marketing from IMT Ghaziabad. She is doing a live project with Tata Steel's Tribal Cultural Society. She likes playing Chess, travelling and cooking.

**Subhadeep Bhattacharyya** is pursuing his post-graduation in Management from IMT Ghaziabad. He has graduated in Computer Science from West Bengal University of Technology. He has worked in Infosys for 3 years as a Senior Systems Engineer in the Banking Domain. In his pastime he likes quizzing, reading novels and playing table-tennis.

**Kartik Chachra** is studying his PGDM Marketing from Institute of Management Technology, Ghaziabad. Prior to this, he was working with Headstrong (now Genpact Headstrong Capital Markets) as a Consultant in the IT Managed Services division. An engineer, born and brought up in Delhi, he involves himself with calligraphy.

**Shampa Chakraberty,** First Class First in B.A. (Honours) from Calcutta University, MBA from Indian Institute of Social Welfare & Business Management (IISW & BM) with specialization in Personnel Management. She has 22 years of experience in the jute industry; conducted training sessions in Air-India, Eastern Spinning Mills, Nicco Telelinks, IBP Co. etc; training programs of Central Board of Workers Education at various factories. She also has 10 years of experience in academics (ICFAI Business School, Kolkata from April, 2004 then NSHM Knowledge Campus, Kolkata from 1.08.07). Chakraberty is a member of the Editorial Committee of NSHM Journal of Management Research & Applications and a Life member of National Institute of Personnel Management (NIPM), Indian Society of Training and Development (ISTD), Calcutta Management Association and National HRD Network (NHRD). She is currently pursuing a Ph.D under Netaji Subhas Open University and has submitted her final thesis in 2012 and is awaiting defense of her thesis. Her publications include articles, case studies, book reviews etc. with publishers such as Sage Publications, Nova Science Publishers, USA, Excel Books, MacMillan Publishers etc.

**Indrani Chakraverty** is a human resource professional currently working with a start up into employability assessments. She completed her MBA from IMT Ghaziabad in 2014 and her Bachelors in Business Economics in 2008. She has been involved in teaching as a social cause and has also worked in the career counseling domain. She is passionate about causes concerning education and strongly believes that the reach of quality education defines our development as a society.

**Prashant Chandrashekar** is a student at Institute if Management Technology, Ghaziabad doing Masters of Business Administration in Marketing. In 2007 he graduated with a Bachelor of Engineering degree in Electronics and Communication from New Horizon College of Engineering, Bangalore affiliated to Visveshvaraya Technological University, Belgaum. From 2011 to 2012 he worked in Tata Consultancy Services in the Banking and Financial Sector. His research interests include studying, analysing and developing marketing strategies for companies in various sectors. His others research interests are sports analytics and its implications in Soccer.

**Pavan Dev Singh Charak** is a Finance student at Institute of management technology Ghaziabad, India with interest in corporate finance and social entrepreneurship. Prior to joining IMT Ghaziabad, he earned his Bachelors in Electronics and communication engineering from National institute of technology. In 2009 he joined TATA Consultancy services Ltd as a system engineer and worked for a banking client for 3 years. Being from an army background, Pavan spent most of his time in dealing with people from all walks of life. After he graduates in March 2015, Pavan, with his techno management experience is planning to start a social enterprise to generate employment opportunities for socioeconomically disadvantaged people.

**Somtirth Chaudhuri** was born and brought up in the sleepy little town of Bankura in West Bengal. He did the first ten years of his schooling there. In 2006 he moved to Kolkata where he finished his High School and earned an engineering degree in computer Science & Engineering from Techno India College of Technology. He is currently pursuing Post Graduate Diploma in Management from Institute of Management Technology (IMT), Ghaziabad. He has received numerous awards and scholarship for academic excellence. He was one of the top 100 students in the 7th National Science Olympiad. He also received a prestigious scholarship from Indian Institute of chemical Biology and Central Glass and Ceramic Research Institute, Kolkata. Apart from academic achievements, he also has a strong passion for sports. He represented his school in U-19 State Cricket Championship and won the trophy in 2006 as the captain. He is also a member of the Sports Committee at IMT Ghaziabad which recently conducted Chakravyuh 2014, the flagship event at IMT. He is also an amateur archer and an avid reader.

**Jaya Chitranshi** taught in the Department of Business Administration, Lucknow University for about eight years. She has been a member of the faculty at Jaipuria Institute of Management for about seven years. She did her Ph.D. in Psychology from Lucknow University. She is an MBA from the same University. She was a UGC Fellow and received Kali Prasad Memorial Award for her research work at the University. Her areas of teaching interest are Organizational Behaviour, Creativity and Cross-cultural management. Her areas of research interest are mentorship, people empowerment and diversity issues.

**Amit Choudhary** is currently in his first year, Post Graduate Diploma Management Program at Institute of Management Technology (IMT), Ghaziabad. In March 2015, he will graduate with a Master of Business Administration degree, with specialization in Marketing. He is currently an internee at Wacom India ltd. He has previously worked with Atotech India Ltd. as a Product Engineer in the General Metal finishing vertical. He was responsible for product sales and support to major OEM's located in south and west India. Other responsibilities included new project commissioning and customer development. Mr Choudhary earned his Bachelor of Engineering degree in Chemical Engineering from M.S Ramaiah Institute of Technology, Bangalore. He has been an active member of the IIChe for two consecutive years during his graduation and a member of Centre for Rural Innovation and Capacity Building though Knowledge Management, Entrepreneurship and Technology at IMT Ghaziabad .

**Gandharvika Choudhary** is currently doing Post Graduate Diploma in Management in International Business from IMT Ghaziabad (Batch of 2013-15) and is a Bachelor in Technology in Civil Engineering, 2013 from Jawaharlal Nehru Technological University, Kakinada. She has exhibited the project Nano Concrete in International Conference & Exhibition on Implementation Challenges on Precast Construction for Buildings and Infrastructure Projects, ICICPC 2013. She has organized The Hindu Education Plus- Inter Collegiate E-Plus Club Challenge 2012 and participated in Youth for Rural Development Camp-2012 under NSS, Ministry of Youth Affairs and Sports, Government of India. She won the 1st prize in the event Master Builder in Civil Engineering Association fest 2011, IIT Madras and has also presented a technical paper in Samyak'11 International Conference on Advances in Civil Engineering.

**Roma Mitra Debnath** is currently faculty at Indian Institute of Public Administration (IIPA) in the area of Applied Statistics. She is having more than 10 years of experience in management teaching in reputed management schools. She has published a large number of national and international research paper in various fields like service sector, hospitality and public policy. Apart from teaching, she is also a trainer and trains government officials and corporate employees on Quality management, Six Sigma, Project Management, Business analytics etc. She is also involved into policy research related to GoI policies. She has also conducted training programme for various ministries.

**Ambadipudi V Sai Dhiraj** is an Electronics and Communications engineer from Sri Venkateswara University, Tirupati. He has work experience in Business Intelligence domain where he worked for the buildup of a commercial data warehouse for a U.S Aviation company. Apart from reading books and honing his culinary skills during free time he is also an avid follower of sports ranging from F1 to Baseball. He likes travelling and absorbing different cultures and was a part of an exchange program at Tooulouse, France. He is currently pursuing PGDM from IMT Ghaziabad with a specialization in marketing.

**Mohan Krishna Gade** is currently pursuing Post Graduate Diploma in Management in Finance from Institute of Management Technology, Ghaziabad. He completed his Electronics and Communications Engineering from Hyderabad in the year 2010. He worked for couple of years as a Test Engineer in Infosys Limited before joining IMT. His interest areas of research include Corporate Finance, Financial Risk Management and Rural Entrepreneurship.

**Jaideep Garg** is right now pursuing MBA from IMT Ghaziabad. He is Bachelor of Technology from National Institute of Technology, Tiruchirappalli. He studied subjects on manufacturing technologies, operation management and artificial intelligence during his Bachelors. He had worked in Grail Research as quantitative research analyst. In this role, he was part of teams that were helping fortune 500 companies to develop strategies for new product launches and marketing campaigns. Before joining Grail Research, he was working as sales engineer in Larsen and Toubro, where he was responsible key accounts in National Capital Region for sales of industrial goods particularly pertaining to oil and gas sector.

**Riju Antony George** is pursuing Post Graduate Diploma in Management, majoring in Finance from Institute of Management Technology, Ghaziabad, India. He is a member of Make a difference Foundation, popularly known as MADF, which is the student initiated social wing of IMT Ghaziabad, aiming to make a difference in others lives, touching their lives in a beautiful way. He worked as Quality Assurance Engineer in Healthcare sector for a US client for more than 3 years in TATA Consultancy Services Ltd. He has done bachelors in Electronics and Communication Engineering from Kerala. His hobbies include cooking, travelling, solving Sudoku and playing various outdoor games.

**Astha Gupta** has completed Bcom (Hons) from Shri Ram College of Commerce, 2011 and PGDM (Marketing) from Institute of Management Technology, Ghaziabad, 2014. She has prior experience with PricewaterhouseCoopers Kuwait, and Ernst & Young GSS India. Some of her contributions are in projects like Benchmarking IM practices of retail segment with Akzo Nobel, Assessing the Effectiveness of Investor's Grievance Mechanism of Ministry of Corporate Affairs with Indian Institute of Public Administration, and other similar projects with Remorphing Consultants, Airtel, and PwC. After completing her masters, she has worked on the project Independent Evaluation of Technopreneur Promotion Programme TePP under IIPA for a short period.

**Mansi Gupta** is currently a first year student pursuing PGDM in Finance at Institute of Management Technology (IMT), Ghaziabad. She will complete her PGDM in Finance in 2015. She was previously working with Tata Consultancy Services Limited as a Microsoft SharePoint and Workflows developer for close to three years. Working with Life sciences and Healthcare giant she has successfully completed Pharma domain certification as well. She has completed her Bachelors in Electronics and Communication Engineering from I.E.T. Lucknow, one of the top 50 engineering colleges in India in the year 2010. She has also interned with BSNL and CEL India as a part of industrial training during B.Tech. Other interest includes reading fiction, exploring and travelling to new and diverse places, and outdoor sports.

**Parul Gupta** is pursuing Post Graduate Diploma in Management with majors in Marketing from Institute of Management Technology Ghaziabad. She completed her graduation in Economics (Honours) from Lady Shri Ram College for Women, Delhi University in 2012.

**Pulkit A Gupta** is currently pursuing Post Graduate Diploma in Management in Marketing from Institute of Management Technology, Ghaziabad. He completed his Mechanical Engineering from Malaviya National Institute of Technology Jaipur in the year 2012. He worked as a Territory Manager - Service at Vadodara Regional Office Hero MotoCorp Limited, before joining IMT. His interest areas of research include Sales Management, Marketing Channel and Distribution and Operation Management.

**Samarth Gupta** is currently pursuing a two-year Post Graduate Diploma in Management (PGDM) from Institute of Management Technology (IMT), Ghaziabad. IMT Ghaziabad is one of the top B-Schools in India with a huge legacy of more than 30 years and an Alumni base consisting of CEO's and CXO's. Samarth also studied as International Business Student at Reims Management School, France. Samarth earlier worked with Sopra Group, a French IT Giant, as an SAP ABAP Consultant to its biggest client, Airbus. He worked in the Airbus-CBO SAP-ERP development team which was responsible for developing Tech-Data Manuals of Aircrafts in the Product and Process Engineering Phase.

**Subhankar Halder** has earned his bachelor degrees in Mathematics and Physics from the University of Kansas. He is currently pursuing a management degree in Finance from the Institute of Management Technology, Ghaziabad. One of his key interests is listening to Hindustani Classical Music. At the University of Kansas, he was the president of the SPICMACAY KANSAS chapter, which organized Indian music concerts for free.

**Jeremiah Jacob**, a first year student of PGDM (Finance) at Institute of Management Technology (IMT) Ghaziabad, previously worked at Infosys Ltd as a Test Engineer. His areas of interest include Corporate Finance, Mergers and Acquisitions, Social Justice, Empowerment and Inclusive growth.

**Ankush Jain** has worked with HCL Technologies as a Specialist in Windows Server Administration for almost three years. He then joined Institute of Management Technology, Ghaziabad under PGDM Marketing. An Instrumentation and Control Engineer, he is from Delhi, the capital state of India.

**Anshul Jain** has a professional experience of around forty three months in the manufacturing and management consulting industry. He is currently a student at Institute of Management Technology, Ghaziabad and is associated with some Non-Government Organizations as well.

**Siddharth Jindal** is currently pursuing Post Graduate Diploma in Management from Institute of Management Technology, Ghaziabad in Sales, Marketing and Business Development as the core specialization. PGDM provided him a platform to show enthusiasm and creativity. Siddharth completed his Bachelor in Engineering from Institute of Technology and Management, Gurgaon in Electronics and Communication. Post B.E, Siddharth worked in Telecom industry for 3 years with Ericsson. He was a network integration engineer for AT&T and T-Mobile. While the professional experience helped him to expand horizon and hone team-skills, it also helped him to exhibit his innovation skills via various automations done for efficient process handling and delivery.

**Neha Joshi** is a PGDM (Marketing) student at IMT, Ghaziabad. She is originally from Uttarakhand but has completed her education in Lucknow. She did her Engineering, in Information Technology, from Uttar Pradesh Technical University, Lucknow. Thereafter, she worked in Tata Consultancy Services as an Assistant Systems Engineer. She worked for the Tata Ion project while in TCS. Neha is currently based in Ghaziabad, pursuing PGDM in Marketing Management form IMT Ghaziabad.

**Vaibhav Kango** is a PGDM student of Sales and Marketing in International Business at Institute of Management Technology, Ghaziabad. He studied his engineering from Shri G. S. Institute of technology, Indore in Computer Science. With professional work experience in IT industry under Insurance division of software development, Vaibhav has worked for Infosys Limited, Mangalore for close to 3 years. He played a role of Senior Systems Engineer at Infosys and worked on several projects on Business Intelligence and reporting tools. His key assignments included gathering system requirement specification from clients and participate in design and implementation of the software project.

**Amanpreet Kaur** is currently in her first year of study in the Post Graduate Diploma Management Program at Institute of Management Technology (IMT), Ghaziabad. In March 2015, she will graduate with a Master of Business Administration degree, with specialization in Finance. She has recently interned with Genpact in 2014. She has previously worked with Bharti Airtel Ltd. as a finance executive in the cost assurance vertical. She was responsible for looking into the expenses incurred by Airtel on tower infrastructure and was responsible for provisioning and actualization of the tower infrastructure expenses. Ms. Kaur earned her Bachelor of Commerce (honors) degree from Indraprastha College for Women affiliated to University of Delhi. She has been a member of the student union for two consecutive years during her graduation and a member of Centre for Rural Innovation and Capacity Building though Knowledge Management, Entrepreneurship and Technology at IMT Ghaziabad.

**Krishan Kumar** is a student at Institute of Management Technology, Ghaziabad pursuing Masters of Business Administration in Finance. In 2005 he graduated with a Bachelor of Engineering degree in Mechanical Engineering from DECT, affiliated to Punjab University. He has worked with Vedanta Resources as an assistant manager and has worked with Wintech Ferrites as a manager. His research interests include studying, analysing and developing financial strategies for companies in various sectors.

**Rishi Kumar** is a first year student of PGDM Marketing at IMT Ghaziabad. Prior to this he has worked with ARICENT GROUP as an Associate Network Engineer. His Areas of Interests include Marketing Research, Consumer Behavior, Ecological Social Justice and Rural welfare and empowerment.

**Somansh Kumar** is a 25 young student of Business Administration, majoring in Operations Management at the Institute of Management Technology, Ghaziabad, India. He is set to graduate in 2015. He received his Bachelor of Technology in Computer Science Engineering from VIT University, Vellore, India and eventually earned a spot at McAfee, Inc. Bangalore, India. After his 2 year stint at McAfee had taught him the nuances of Security Risks and Quality Management, Mr. Kumar decided to pursue his Master's in Business Administration. He is an avid football fan, and pledges his allegiance to Manchester United Football Club. He is a voracious reader, and an ardent fan of Jeffrey Archer. He is set to intern at Dr. Reddy's Laboratories, India, and wishes to gain a foothold in the pharmaceutical industry. Mr. Kumar is a foodie by heart, and has a reputation for discovering excellent local produces.

**Vijayshree M** is currently pursuing Post Graduate Diploma in Management at IMT-Ghaziabad, after a three year strenuous tint at Infosys as a SAP programmer. She hails from Chennai and is a Toastmaster. Her interests include diverse subjects from Carnatic music to the latest automotive machines. When she isn't working out the answer to the question of the chicken and the egg, she indulges in her hobbies of origami, singing and throw ball, of which she's a player of Olympic standards, till the time they include throw ball in Olympics.

**Akshay Maggu** is currently pursuing his masters in Marketing from Institute of Management Technology, Ghaziabad. In his under graduation, he studied Electronics and Tele Communication engineering from KIIT University, Bhubaneswar (2007-11). His interest lied in microprocessors and databases and that landed him in Tata Consultancy Services where he worked for 18 months on managing client side databases of a multinational pharmaceutical company based out of the US. After joining PGDM-Marketing in IMT, his interest lies in Marketing Research and analytics. Also, he has a keen interest in topics which deal with social development of India.

**Priyangshu Mahanta** is a student of Human Resources at Institute of Management Technology Ghaziabad and a member of IRC, the International Relations Committee at the institute. An electronics and instrumentation engineer from Guwahati, he acquired key skills in the banking domain during his tenure in State Bank of Mysore. Besides being an avid reader, Mr. Mahanta takes keen interest in researching emerging trends in the field of Business Management, Employee Engagement, and Knowledge Management and writes for journals of premier B schools. A blogger and a guitarist Priyangshu is also a member of a spiritual community and contributes in social welfare programmes and community development.

**Kapil Mendiratta** is currently/presently pursuing his Post-Graduation in Management with specialization in Marketing from IMT Ghaziabad. He is an engineer from IIT Kharagpur with majors in Biotechnology and Biochemical Sciences. He has prior experience of working with Evalueserve, India in the field of Data Analytics and Customer Insights. He has been awarded a Certificate of Excellence in Data Visualization at Evalueserve. He has also worked on the development of Edge Detection Algorithms for Image processing, used for the treatment of Retinal Prosthesis in the blind.

**Appasaheb Naikal** is an Information and knowledge Management professional from India and presently working as Librarian at S P Jain School of Global Management, Singapore. He received his Master of Science in Knowledge Management from Nanyang Technological University, Singapore in 2009 and Master of Library & Information Science from Karnatak Univeriesty Dharwad, India in 1999. He has more than 15 years' experience in managing both academic and corporate libraries at national and international level. His research interests include knowledge management, digital libraries, social media and ICT application to LIS education. Author is presently pursuing his Ph.D. from Tata Institute of Social Science (TISS), Mumbai.

**Neelendra Nath** was born and brought up in Patna, Bihar. He has completed his schooling from Loyola High School, Patna and Delhi Public School, Mathura Road (New Delhi). He has pursued Petroleum Engineering from Maharashtra Institute of Technology, Pune for which he was awarded Scholarship by Society of Petroleum Engineers (International) and Outstanding Student Award by Oil & Gas major Shell Technology. He has also founded and led Youth Mission, a social initiative under UNESCO chair at MIT, Pune and National Entrepreneurship Network - MIT Entrepreneurship Cell. After completing his engineering with distinction from Pune University in 2010, he worked with Halliburton, one of the biggest Oil & Gas Service Company. He quit Halliburton in 2012 to work with his own start-up, Petro-First Energy TechnoSolutions Private Limited. He is currently pursuing his Post Graduate Diploma in Management at Institute of Management, Ghaziabad. He also consults for start – up in area of brand positioning and revenue stream expansion. He is an amateur photographer, off beat traveller, avid reader and occasional writer.

**Pravin Patil** is pursuing Post Graduate Diploma in Management with majors in Sales and Marketing from Institute of Management Technology, Ghaziabad. He completed his engineering from Pune University in the year 2010. He has 1.5 years of work experience in software solutions for Communications with Cognizant Technology Solutions. His interest areas of research include Market Research, Strategic Marketing, Supply chain Management, & Rural Marketing.

**Nishant Puri** is currently working with Deloitte Consulting (US) as a Consultant. He did his Masters (MBA) in Finance from IMT Ghaziabad (2013) and brings with him experience in domains such as - Business requirements gathering and documentation; Business process mapping – improvements in processes and controls; Project Management etc. Prior to his MBA, he did his BE in Computer Science (2008) and worked in the IT industry for 3 years. He is an ardent follower of most of the English TV Series and true Foodie at heart.

**V. Raghavendra** is a Mechanical Engineer and a student of PGDM (Finance). He is originally from Hyderabad, India where he studied till under graduation. Raghavendra studied at National Institute of Technology Karnataka Surathkal as a Mechanical Engineer where he received the Graduation Degree. Previously Raghavendra worked at JSW Steels on Maintenance and operations of Belt conveyors including a Track Hopper project in Raw material handling systems department for a year before joining a start-up in Mumbai, India wherein he was devoting his work towards the design and execution of exhibition stalls as well as the backend infrastructure of the events. Raghavendra is now based in Ghaziabad, India where he is pursuing first year in Finance specialization from Institute of Management Technology.

**Manmohan Rahul** is a doctorate in Applied Economics area, M.Sc (statistics) and FDP from Indian Institute of Management, Ahmedabad and his area of Expertise is in Production and Operation Management, International Business and General Management. His research interests are in SCM and International business issues. He teaches Research Methodology to PhD Scholars and is currently guiding seven PhD scholars. He is a Member of Academic Council, Ansal University and is currently Professor of Management and Dean Student Welfare, Ansal University.

**Kaustubh Singh Rana** is from Agra, Uttar Pradesh. He has 3.6 years of experience at Infosys Ltd. Bangalore where he was working as a Quality Assurance Engineer for the critical features of Cisco Application Call Manager. He was also part of the Corporate Social Responsibility Group at Infosys. At IMT, he has done a project with Cafe Coffee Day to increase footfalls in their East Delhi outlets. He was amongst 200 delegates worldwide selected and invited for Harvard Annual Conference on emerging issues of concern in Asia. He likes to write and recently one of his articles was published on a social media website "BrandAppz".

**Roopesh Rao** is Assistant Professor at Shri Ramdeobaba College of Engineering and Mangement. He has also developed Video Cases and Documentary on Dr.APJ Abdul Kalam (Former President of India), Mandar Tulankar (Innovator), Etc. He has published Papers in many International journals like Asia pacific Journal of Business, ZIMJ, etc. He has been Session Chair in various conferences and Presented Research papers at Indian Institute of Management (IIMs), Great Lakes Institute of Management - Chennai, IBS – Business schools Hyderabad, Institute of Management and technology (IMT). He is an MBA (Marketing and Human Resources) from ICFAI BUSINESS SCHOOL. He is a Doctoral Research Scholar in Management. His research interests Include Innovations, Brand Management, Online Branding, Sales and Distribution Management, Retail Management, Trust and Behavioral sciences.

**Siraj Raja** is a Mechanical Engineer and has worked in automobile sector before taking up course in management in IMT. His interests lie in the field of marketing, information technology and research methods.

**Mayank Rawat** is a full time student of Business Management at the Institute of Management Technology, Ghaziabad. He is an Electronic and Telecommunication engineer with 3 year of experience in telecommunication. He had worked on 2G, 3G, CDMA and 4G projects of leading telecommunication companies in India. His interests include industrial analysis, market research and developments, strategy formulation, politics and cricket. He was the winner of Nielson ISB Consumer Insights Challenge organized by ISB. His area of study also includes innovative practices across the industries and geographies. He is a foodie.

**Allu Reshma** is currently doing Post Graduate Diploma in Management in International Business from IMT Ghaziabad (Batch of 2013-15) and is a Bachelor in Technology in Civil Engineering, 2013 from Jawaharlal Nehru Technological University, Kakinada. She has exhibited the project Nano Concrete in International Conference & Exhibition on Implementation Challenges on Precast Construction for Buildings and Infrastructure Projects, ICICPC 2013. She has organized The Hindu Education Plus- Inter Collegiate E-Plus Club Challenge 2012 and participated in Youth for Rural Development Camp-2012 under NSS, Ministry of Youth Affairs and Sports, Government of India. She won the 1st prize in the event Master Builder in Civil Engineering Association fest 2011, IIT Madras and has also presented a technical paper in Samyak'11 International Conference on Advances in Civil Engineering.

**Sayantan Saha** was born in Siliguri, a small town in the northern part of West Bengal, India. He did his schooling from Don Bosco School, Siliguri. He earned his Bachelor of Technology degree from Manipal Institute of Technology (Sikkim) in the field of Electronics and Communication in the year 2010. He has an experience of working in the IT industry for 2 years and 6 months. Currently he is pursuing PGDM (Marketing) from Institute of Management Technology, Ghaziabad. He is the recipient of numerous awards in both school and college. His notable achievements include a district and state level first prize in the Science project competition. He has also represented his school at the National level in the same. He has held many posts of responsibility in school and college and was always outstanding in both academics and extra-curricular activities especially sports, where he has represented his school and college in many sporting tournaments. His hobbies include Travelling and Philately. He takes active interest in pursuing social and environmental causes, especially wildlife conservation. He is a keen supporter of the development of renewable sources of energy and reducing our carbon footprint.

**Mayukh Sarkar** is a power engineer from Durgapur who joined Institute of Management Technology, Ghaziabad for his management studies as under PGDM Finance.

**Parikshit Sarkar** was born on 17th October, 1989 in a small town in Jharkhand, he consequently moved to West Bengal where he completed his schooling and then went onto attain a degree in Electrical Engineering from the West Bengal University of Technology. Following that he was associated with Jindal Power Ltd. for a period of around two years during which he worked on an upcoming hydroelectric project in the state of Arunachal Pradesh. Currently he is undergoing his MBA program in Finance from Institute of Management Technology, Ghaziabad. He has a keen interest in robotics and has been actively involved in many science projects during his graduation days. His other interests include cricket and travelling.

**Gowtham Seelam**, working as an electronics engineer for almost two years with Infosys, decided to do his PGDM Marketing from Institute of Management Technology, Ghaziabad.

**Sanya Sehgal** a Mathematics graduate, has worked as an online marketing analyst before taking course in management in IMT. Her interests lie in the field of finance, mathematics and sustainable management practices. In this chapter the authors try to give an insight of dairy practices in rural areas and how improvement in these practices can help in development of rural India.

**Anirban Sharma** is student of Post graduate diploma in management from Institute of Management and Technology, Ghaziabad. He attended Jadavpur University for doing his Bachelor in Engineering in Mechanical. Before pursuing management at IMT, He held positions as Senior Engineer at Dastur Co, India, an engineering consultancy Firm. He has done various projects with public and private international organizations. He has experience in project finance, market study and project management. Anirban has interested in Photography and he is a member of governing body of the non-profitable society Guiding Star. He worked in various part of rural West Bengal and involved in various projects. He has interest in Finance and operation.

**Charu Sharma** is currently pursuing PGDM at Institute of Management Technology, Ghaziabad with majors as Sales, Marketing and Business Development. She has graduated from YMCA University of Science and Technology as an electronics instrumentation and control engineer. She has served as a trainee at ST Microelectronics and Indian Oil Corporation Limited. She currently runs an event management start up while working in close association with media, advertising firm Magnon Solutions, New Delhi.

**Vedant Sharma** is currently pursuing Post Graduate Diploma in Management in Marketing from Institute of Management Technology, Ghaziabad. He completed his Chemical Engineering from NIT Durgapur in the year 2011. He worked for couple of years as a Process Engineer in Bharat Oman Refinery Limited before joining IMT. His interest areas of research include Marketing Channel and Distribution, Operation Management, Rural Entrepreneurship.

**Bineydeep Singh** was born and brought up in Chandigarh which is a Union Territory and capital of Panjab and Haryana. Biney did his schooling in Vivek High School, Chandigarh and engineering in Computer Science and Technology from Panjab University, Chandigarh. He is currently pursuing Post Graduate Diploma in Management and Technology from Institute of Management Technology (IMT), Ghaziabad. He has been a brilliant student all through his school time and has held scholar blazer and scholar badges. He has done various projects during his study time. He has participated in NASA space settlement project (Asia Level) where his team stood runners up. His is an active member of Enactus which is a worldwide famous social entrepreneurship organization. Binay has also done a project on rural marketing with Tata Steel (Tribal Cultural Society), where he went to Jamshedpur to do a research work in rural area and help the Tribal Cultural Society (TCS) to come up with a marketing plan for the rural products. Being an all-rounder he is also an outstanding basketball player, a consummate dancer and an avid reader.

**Harshit Singh** is a student of PGDM Finance from Institute of Management Technology, Ghaziabad and believes in the continuous process of learning. His interest lies in emerging technologies and numbers.

**Rahul Singh** is a 1st year management student of Marketing at Institute of Management Technology, Ghaziabad. Presently he is interning at Ogilvy and Mather, Chennai and has previously worked in short term projects with Procter and Gamble, Dr. Reddy's Lab, and MySTP. Rahul is an engineer in Bio-Technology from West Bengal University of Technology. During his engineering he was the president of the Film and Photography club of his college and also a student volunteer for Rotaract Club and many Non-Governmental organizations. He takes a keen interest in photography and graphic designing and has even piloted an online art and photography magazine, Digital Krafts, in the year 2013. Taking about future Rahul wants to apply his management knowledge and experience in helping and giving back to the society in every way he can.

**Shyamli Singh** is working as an Assistant Professor in the Centre for Environment and Climate Change, Indian Institute of Public Administration, I.P Estate, and New Delhi since 2012. Dr. Singh has obtained doctorate degree from DR. B.R Ambedkar University Agra. She has qualified NET examination for Assistant Professorship in Environmental Sciences in 2001.She has been awarded Gold Medal (199-2001) in M.SC (Environmental Management) from Guru Gobind Singh Indraprastha University, Delhi. She is a topper (1996-1999) of Delhi University in B.Sc Grp .B. She has been associated with high esteem organisations such as Teri, NISTADS in various capacities. She has authored a textbook entitled "Environmental Studies" published in 2012 and IIPA Discussion Paper Series No.7 Climate Change: Back to Basics Dr. Singh has more than nineteen research papers to her credit in various journals and conferences. Dr. Singh is an active member of various professional societies and has a life membership of The International Society of Botanists and Indian Society for Technical Education. She has participated in several conferences and workshops and has conducted capacity building programmes.

**Manjusha Subramanian** is a full time student of Business Management at the Institute of Management Technology, Ghaziabad. She has previously worked as a Lead Technical Consultant in the SAP/ERP domain in Deloitte Consulting India Pvt. Ltd. Her interests include Marketing Management, Sales Management and Marketing Strategy. As a part of the international exchange programme, she has spent three months in IPADE Business School, Mexico and was the winner of the regional round of the Novartis Global Case Competition. She is looking forward to a challenging career in the consumer goods sector and uses time effectively to manage her extra-curricular activities in the areas of music and social service.

**Shalini R. Tiwari** is an FPM (PhD) from MDI Gurgaon; FDPM (IIM Ahmedabad), M.Sc. and MBA. She has an experience of more than 16 years in academia and industry. Currently, she is working as Assistant Professor at IMT, Ghaziabad. She does research on knowledge networks, competitiveness of firms, entrepreneurship and management education. She has written and published cases, books, and scholarly articles. She teaches courses and MDP's under the discipline of strategic management and entrepreneurship across various management institutions and organizations. She likes to read variety, watch movies, travel to country sides and think.

**Kannan TS** graduated from Kerala University in Automobile Engineering. He started his career with Indian Auto OEM, Mahindra and Mahindra, in their research and development wing. While at Mahindra and Mahindra, he was responsible for commissioning a Pilot Production line which would enable the company to make vehicle prototypes in a proper assembly line environment. This project helped to reduce the time to develop prototypes and also helped to identify design limitations at an initial stage of product development. Later on he pursued his interest in teaching by joining Rajadhani Institute of Engineering and Technology, Kerala, as a lecturer. He is currently pursuing Post graduation in management from Institute of Management Technology, Ghaziabad. He has a deep interest in Operations Management and is passionate about automotive technology.

**Aditya Vashisth** is pursuing Post Graduate Diploma in Management with majors in finance and banking from Institute of Management Technology, Ghaziabad. He completed his engineering from Guru Gobind Singh Indraprastha University, Delhi in the year 2011. He has 2 years of work experience in software engineering solutions for financial analysis and risk technology with Birlasoft India limited. His interest areas of research include financial risk management, Investment Banking, Financial inclusion & banking innovation.

**Garima Yadav** is currently pursuing Post Graduate Diploma Management Program at Institute of Management Technology (IMT), Ghaziabad. In March 2015, she will be completing her degree in Master of Business Administration with specialization in HR. She is currently interning in Jubilant Foodworks Limited. She has completed her Bachelor of Commerce (Honours) degree from Shri Ram College of Commerce, Delhi University in 2013. She has been actively participating in various programs and was an active member of Fine Arts society and Commerce society of Shri Ram College of Commerce. She had also interned at Connaught Plaza Restaurants Pvt. Ltd., Mcdonaldsindia in 2012. She is also a member of Centre for Rural Innovation and Capacity Building though Knowledge Management, Entrepreneurship and Technology at IMT Ghaziabad.

# Index

## P



## R



## S



## T



## U



## V



## Y

CPSIA information can be obtained at www.ICGtesting.com
Printed in the USA
BVOW10*1335280615

406406BV00008B/60/P

9 781466 682597